**WITHDRAWN
UTSA LIBRARIES**

SOCIAL
AND POLITICAL
MOVEMENTS

GARY B. RUSH AND R. SERGE DENISOFF
Simon Fraser University   *Bowling Green State University*

SOCIAL AND POLITICAL MOVEMENTS

APPLETON-CENTURY-CROFTS
EDUCATIONAL DIVISION
MEREDITH CORPORATION NEW YORK

Copyright © 1971 by
MEREDITH CORPORATION
All rights reserved

This book, or parts thereof, must not be used or reproduced in any manner without written permission. For information address the publisher, Appleton-Century-Crofts, Educational Division, Meredith Corporation, 440 Park Avenue South, New York, N.Y. 10016.

731-1

Library of Congress Card Number: 72–146365

PRINTED IN THE UNITED STATES OF AMERICA

390–76519–8

*To my mother
and all the gang
at the "Foster Home"*

G. B. R.

To Carol

R. S. D.

CONTENTS

Preface	xi
Acknowledgments	xiii

1. VALUES IN THE STUDY OF SOCIAL MOVEMENTS — 1

THREE FOCUSES: SOCIOLOGY, PSYCHOLOGY, AND HISTORY	2
J. Stewart Burgess, "The Study of Modern Social Movements as a Means of Clarifying the Process of Social Action"	4
VALUE ORIENTATIONS IN THE STUDY OF SOCIAL MOVEMENTS	12
Nikolai Bukharin, *Historical Materialism*	16
Joseph R. Gusfield, "Field Work Reciprocities in Studying a Social Movement"	21
R. Serge Denisoff, "Folk Music and the American Communist Movement: A Case of Historical Confusion"	28
CONCLUSION	34

2. THEORETICAL AND CONCEPTUAL APPROACHES TO SOCIAL MOVEMENTS — 37

SOCIAL DISORGANIZATION	37
Joseph R. Gusfield, "Mass Society and Extremist Politics"	40
John Horton, "The Dehumanization of Anomie and Alienation: A Problem in the Ideology of Sociology"	54
CLASS AND SOCIAL MOVEMENTS	63
Nikolai Bukharin, *Historical Materialism*	64
Frances Bennett Becker, "Lenin's Application of Marx's Theory of Revolutionary Tactics"	72
STATUS AND SOCIAL MOVEMENTS	75
Bo Anderson and Morris Zelditch, Jr., "Rank Equilibration and Political Behavior"	80

Gerard Brandmeyer and R. Serge Denisoff, "Status Politics: An Appraisal of the Application of a Concept"   90
CONCLUSION   99

3. ANALYTICAL APPROACHES TO SOCIAL MOVEMENTS: HISTORY AND PSYCHOLOGY   103

   THE HISTORICAL CASE STUDY   103
      Jerold S. Auerbach, "Southern Tenant Farmers: Socialist Critics of the New Deal"   105
   SOCIAL PSYCHOLOGY AND SOCIAL MOVEMENTS   121
      Ira S. Rohter, "The Righteous Rightists"   124
      Christian Bay, "Political and Apolitical Students: Facts in Search of Theory"   141
   WHERE WE STAND   160

4. SOCIAL MOVEMENTS AS EMERGENT REALITIES   163

   THE PROBLEM OF DEFINITION   163
      Gary B. Rush, "Toward a Definition of the Extreme Right"   163
      Eugene D. Genovese, "Genovese Looks at American Left—New and Old"   172
   CONSCIOUSNESS OF DYSFUNCTION   185
      "The Women's Food Revolt—A Year Later"   191
   REFERENTS FOR MOBILIZATION   192
      Che Guevara, "Guerilla Strategy," "Guerilla Tactics," "The Guerilla Fighter: Social Reformer"   195
      Warren Hinckle, "The Social History of the Hippies"   205
      Irving Louis Horowitz, "Cuban Communism"   214
      Mary-Alice Styron, "A Hidden Chapter in the Fight Against War"   237

5. MODE OF EMERGENCE OF SOCIAL MOVEMENTS   255

      Maurice Jackson et al., "The Failure of an Incipient Social Movement"   255
      Talcott Parsons, "The Role of Ideas in Social Action"   271
      Theodore Abel, "The Pattern of a Successful Political Movement"   279
      Egon Bittner, "Radicalism and the Organization of Radical Movements"   286
      William Kornhauser, "Social Bases of Political Commitment: A Study of Liberals and Radicals"   299
      "Seven Kentucky Miners Join Party and Tell Reason Why"   313

6. TYPES OF SOCIAL MOVEMENTS   319

   REVOLUTIONARY MOVEMENTS   325
      G. William Domhoff, "How to Commit Revolution in Corporate America"   327

REGRESSIVE MOVEMENTS 339
    Robert Welch, *The Blue Book of The John Birch Society* 340
    Winston White, *Beyond Conformity* 351
REFORM MOVEMENTS 353
    Alan P. Grimes, *The Puritan Ethic and Woman Suffrage* 354
EXPRESSIVE MOVEMENTS 359
    Peter Worsley, *The Trumpet Shall Sound: A Study of "Cargo" Cults in Melanesia* 360
SUMMARY 365

7. THE TRUNCATION OF SOCIAL MOVEMENTS 367

MODES OF TRUNCATION 370
    John P. Roche and Stephen Sachs, "The Bureaucrat and the Enthusiast: An Exploration of the Leadership of Social Movements" 373
    Seymour Martin Lipset, *Agrarian Socialism: The Cooperative Commonwealth Federation in Saskatchewan* 381
    Robert C. Myers, "Anti-Communist Mob Action: A Case Study" 391
    Sheldon L. Messinger, "Organizational Transformation: A Case Study of a Declining Social Movement" 403
DISSENSION 414
    Robert J. Alexander, "Splinter Groups in American Radical Politics" 415

8. THE "END OF IDEOLOGY" AND CONTEMPORARY SOCIAL MOVEMENTS 421

    Daniel Bell, *The End of Ideology: On the Exhaustion of Political Ideas in the Fifties* 422
    Stephen W. Rousseas and James Farganis, "American Politics and the End of Ideology" 438
THE END OF PROGRESS 455
    R. Alan Haber, "The End of Ideology as Ideology" 458
THE IDEOLOGY OF THE EXTREME RIGHT 475
THE IDEOLOGY OF THE NEW LEFT 480
    R. Peter Lewis, "The New Left: A Political Movement?" 486
CONCLUSION 492

A Selected Bibliography of Political and Radical Social Movements 497
Index 515

PREFACE

The Communists disdain to conceal their views and aims. They openly declare that their ends can be attained only by the forcible overthrow of all existing social conditions. Let the ruling classes tremble at a Communist revolution. The proletarians have nothing to lose but their chains. They have a world to win.[1]

After having received only sporadic interest for nearly a century, the study of social movements has today become a legitimate concern for sociologists. In an age when tensions and conflicts within world societies are becoming greater and when the potential for social change is rapidly increasing, little justification is required for such study. Nevertheless, much of what is written on social movements today, particularly in the popular press, cloaks these phenomena in an aura of "conventional wisdom" and political value judgments. While it is not our intention to present a "value free" analysis of social movements—indeed, we specify at the outset that the study of social movements is particularly prone to coloration by the researcher's values—neither will this work serve as an apologia for any particular political inclination. However, one major premise which guides our analysis is that social movements are a normal and rational response to the human condition. This premise colors a good deal of the text and readings presented and places the authors in opposition to those students who view social movements as deviant phenomena which attract the psychologically and socially abnormal. Our major purpose is to critically assess the contemporary state of social movements research and to suggest alternative modes of theory and analysis.

In line with our objective of analyzing the current state of social movements research, the first three chapters provide not only a general introduc-

[1] Karl Marx and Friedrich Engels, *Manifesto of the Communist Party* (New York, International Publishers, 1948), p. 44.

tion to our investigation but also a summary and critical assessment of the existing literature. Chapter 1 contains a review of sociological, psychological, and historical perspectives on social movements as well as a discussion of the problem of values in research on this subject. The second chapter covers classical and contemporary theories of social movements, focusing on the social disorganization, class, and status approaches. The third chapter deals with the methodologies prevalent in social movement research, specifically the historical, case study, and social-psychological treatments.

Having thus introduced the field of this research, the authors develop, in the next four chapters, a general theory of social movements. In chapter 4, after discussing the problem of definition as it is approached in the literature, the authors present a definition of movements which emphasizes their emergent nature, their ideological content, a consciousness of dysfunction, and referents for mobilization. In chapter 5, the historical and social factors surrounding the emergence of movements as ideological organizations are discussed. This is followed, in chapter 6, by the development of a typology of social movements: revolutionary, regressive, and reform. In chapter 7 the social processes involved in the decline and failure of movements are assessed: co-optation, institutionalization, repression, discreditation, and dissension. Finally, chapter 8 is addressed to an evaluation of the "end of ideology" controversy—the meaning of this conception and its relevance for emerging ideological movements at this point in history.

The authors hope that those adopting this text will use it more as a framework for analysis than as a definitive work. The viability of the approach to social movements presented herein must be continually tested against emergent realities. If our concluding observations are correct, there should be ample opportunity for students to apply this analysis to ongoing movements. With this purpose in mind, we have been less concerned with treating individual movements per se than with developing generalizations about ideological organizations. This approach is reflected in the illustrative readings used, which were selected on the basis of the exposition of universal rather than specific processes. With this criterion in mind, the authors singled out classical readings, coupled wherever possible with other relevant material which has not been widely circulated. A wide range of additional readings and sources are cited in footnotes and the bibliography.

This book is concerned with social movements as ideological organizations which present more or less total solutions to perceived social problems. At this juncture in history, the bastions of liberal democracy throughout the world are under siege, both from the left and from the right. In this, an age of anxiety, the ideological forces of all extremes—left, right, and middle—are becoming increasingly convinced that their respective solutions are the only true ones; that they indeed have a "world to win."

G. B. R.
R. S. D.

ACKNOWLEDGMENTS

The authors wish to thank Professor Arthur J. Vidich for his valuable editorial advice and assistance.

We are indebted to our typist, Donna Watt, and to our students, for their patience, endurance, and criticism.

We also wish to acknowledge the assistance given, in the form of a President's Research Grant, by Simon Fraser University, for the preparation of the manuscript.

Finally, we wish to thank the authors and publishers of the material used for their permission to reprint. Specific acknowledgments are given throughout.

SOCIAL AND POLITICAL MOVEMENTS

VALUES IN THE STUDY OF SOCIAL MOVEMENTS

Two years before the outbreak of World War II, Theodore Abel lamented, "only a few attempts have been made at typological analysis of social movements. They constitute a neglected field of sociological inquiry, and in most textbooks of sociology . . . we look in vain for any reference to them."[1] The global impact of Hitler, his ideas, and his armies altered this pattern. Social scientists, not unlike the austere judges at Nuremberg, asked the question, "How could a Hitler come to power?" What, they asked, were the social conditions which made a Third Reich possible? A deluge of studies addressed to these questions heralded a new era of research into social movements.

Since the fall of German National Socialism, scholarly interest in social movements has increased greatly. Mass movements, which so fascinated and repulsed social philosophers in the nineteenth century, once again became the subject of serious inquiry. The spread of the Communist movement throughout the world, the civil rights struggle, and the emergence of the American right wing provided fruitful subjects for sociological monographs, theses, and other published investigations. More recently, the rise of student radicalism and black power has directed the attention of numerous social scientists to the nature and character of political protestors. What factors lead to the development of public protest? What is the relationship between such protests and social movements? How do such movements grow and decline? In this book, the authors will attempt to answer these and related questions as they present a historical and sociological view of the phenomena labeled social movements.

---

[1] Theodore Abel, "The Pattern of a Successful Political Movement," *American Sociological Review*, 2 (April 1937), 347.

THREE FOCUSES:
SOCIOLOGY, PSYCHOLOGY, AND HISTORY

Social movement research began during the mid-nineteenth century, when European intellectuals and revolutionaries placed their hopes for social change upon the masses. Since then, social scientists have tended to discuss social movements not only as vehicles of change but also (and consequently) as disruptive social forces, manifestations of abnormal psychology, and threats to the status quo. Although the normative implications of the latter approaches are apparent, we would contend that placing social movements within a framework of social change implicitly evokes the theoretical biases of the researcher.

The social change aspect is a central assumption for the study of social movements, whether such study is undertaken from a sociological, psychological, or historical point of view. Eric Hoffer, the philosopher-longshoreman, points to this area of concern in his oft-quoted work The True Believer: "It is a truism that many who join a rising revolutionary movement are attracted by the prospect of sudden and spectacular change in their conditions of life. A revolutionary movement is a conspicuous instrument of change." [2] To one extent or another this theme is also characteristic of most basic sociology texts. For example, Wilson and Kolb observe: "Many changes are effected . . . as a result of social movements, which have been described as collective enterprises attempting to establish some new order of life." [3] Broom and Selznick also suggest: "For the most part, social change occurs gradually and without design. However, new perspectives and aspirations have often generated collective action to combat presumed evils and to institute new ways of life. . . . When collective action is more unified and lasting and has certain characteristic features, we call it a 'social movement.' " [4] For sociological theorists, social movements are generally regarded as reactions to structural changes in the society. In this context, social movements are closely correlated with such variables as technology, economics, and population shifts. In this framework, social movements, whether defined as good or bad, whether studied from a functional or a conflict perspective, are viewed as inevitable consequences of structural strains within a system.

Other social scientists see social movements as expressions of the psychological processes of their adherents. At this level of analysis, social movements are viewed as manifestations of individual needs or discon-

---

[2] Eric Hoffer, The True Believer (New York: Mentor Books, 1960), p. 13.
[3] Logan Wilson and William Kolb, Sociological Analysis (New York: Harcourt Brace and Co., 1949), p. 801.
[4] Leonard Broom and Philip Selznick, Sociology, 2d ed. (Evanston: Row, Peterson and Co., 1958), p. 305.

tents. For example, Hans Toch has stated: "For the psychologist, these kinds of efforts [social movements] must be motivated. They must stem from specific discontents of specific people with specific situations in which they find themselves." [5] The basic premise of social psychological studies of social movements is, in Coleman's words, that ". . . the needs of individuals are the basis for the formation of groups." [6] The nature of these needs is suggested by Jung in The Undiscovered Self: ". . . separation from his instinctual nature inevitably plunges civilized man into the conflict between conscious and unconscious, spirit and nature, knowledge and faith, a split that becomes pathological the moment his consciousness is no longer able to neglect or suppress his instinctual side. The accumulation of individuals who have got into this critical state starts off a mass movement purporting to be the champion of the suppressed." [7] Another illustration of this emphasis is provided by Edwards: "The supporters of any social movement, it is true, tend to come from those groups which are already frustrated or anticipate frustration in some respect and which see this particular movement as a means of restoring equilibrium or obtaining relief for their anxiety." [8] Some of the more prevalent concerns of the psychological approach to movements are the individual problems which lead to participation in movements, the interactions found in the ranks of a social movement, and the personality types attracted to movements. The "psychological inadequacy" approach to participation reflects the Freudian model of human behavior. Terms such as authoritarian personality and true believer are commonly used to describe the personalities of people who are attracted to movements. Similarly, the ways individuals act and respond in social movements are usually discussed in terms of susceptibility to various appeals, often irrational. In short, a major emphasis of the psychological approach to social movements is on the needs and inadequacies of their adherents.

The historian is primarily concerned with the career of a social movement. One aspect of this approach is to trace how movements become institutionalized as commonly accepted features of our daily lives. For example, political parties, trade unions, churches, and many interest groups have at one time in their history been social movements. Another concern of the historian is the relationship between a social movement and other events and trends. For example, the Progressive and Populist movements are deemed historically significant in terms of their impact

[5] Hans Toch, *The Social Psychology of Social Movements* (New York: Bobbs-Merrill, 1965), p. 5.
[6] James C. Coleman, *Personality Dynamics and Effective Behavior* (Chicago: Scott, Foresman and Co., 1960), p. 250.
[7] Carl G. Jung, *The Undiscovered Self* (New York: Mentor Books, 1957), p. 93.
[8] Allen L. Edwards, "Signs of Incipient Fascism," *Journal of Abnormal and Social Psychology*, 39 (July 1944), 310.

upon the American polity. Moreover, these movements can also be considered as responses to the social and economic conditions of the early twentieth century.

Of these three approaches—the sociological, the psychological, and the historical—the psychological tended to dominate social movements research until the mid-1950s. An early assessment of the sociology of social movements has been provided by J. Stewart Burgess, who regarded social movements as sociopsychological laboratories. The following excerpts from an article published in 1944 not only illustrate the predominance of the psychological vis-à-vis the sociological and historical frames of reference but also serve as an introduction to our next problem, that of specifying the value orientation which researchers bring to the study of social movements.

Excerpts from J. Stewart Burgess, "The Study of Modern Social Movements as a Means of Clarifying the Process of Social Action," Social Forces, Vol. 22 (December 1944), pp. 270, 271–275. Reprinted by permission of the University of North Carolina Press.

Postponing the question of goals of action which are closely related to the fields of philosophy, ethics, and religion, has sociology something to offer to those who in groups seek to achieve certain—to them—desirable ends? Does the scientific study of social phenomena enable the specialist in that field to be a counsellor as to the means that might be effectively used?

One fruitful method of answering that question is to inquire how groups of persons who have desired to achieve certain changes in attitudes, institutions or social procedures have organized and worked together for such ends. The study of modern social movements is a living record of such processes of social action. . . . A study of the activities of a religious cult, of the groups promoting anti-semitic activities, or of the promotion of birth control clinics or of the cooperative movement is live and interesting material—certainly as valuable for the student of sociology as a visit to the poor-house or to a social settlement.

During the last four years, classes at Temple University studying "Modern Social Movements," have investigated in the following areas: in the educational field, Progressive Education, Workers Education, Parent Education; in the economic field, The Cooperative Movement, the C.I.O., Dr. Townsend's movement for old age security, Social Insurance, The National Association of Manufacturers; in the area of health and Social

Welfare, Socialized Medicine, Birth Control, Housing; in the field of conflict, Anti-Semitism, The Ku Klux Klan; in the political sphere, The Communist Movement in America, The American Socialist Party, Gandhi's Pacifist Movement in India, The Peace Movement in America; in the field of religion, The Bahai Cult, The Great I Am Sect, The Mormons, the Oxford group, The Quaker Movement, Zionism, Father Divine and his cult.

It is clear that several of these captions include much more than a movement as above defined. The students, however, concentrated upon the dynamic aspects in each area and endeavored to find the processes involved in the forms of action used to achieve the particular goals desired.

For purposes of analysis the following general categories were used in the study of these movements:

THE CATEGORIES USED TO ANALYZE MODERN SOCIAL MOVEMENTS

Definition of a Social Movement: A social movement is viewed as a joint organized endeavor of a considerable group of persons in some way to change or alter the course of events by their joint activities.

Origin, History, and Development

1. The extent to which they appear to have been the outgrowth of events, the result of unplanned circumstances, the direct result of outer conditions.

2. The extent to which they appear to have been the result of long or short time planning, of the conscious and definite activity of a small group of protagonists.

3. The description of the historical setting and background of the movement.

4. The description of the beginnings, early organization, growth and expansion of the movement.

5. The conditions in the cultural pattern that either blocked or facilitated the spread of the movement when once started.

The Organization of the Movement

1. *Membership*. How does one join the movement? The economic, intellectual, educational and general social status of membership. The participation of members in the activities of the movement.

2. *Leadership.* Does the movement appear to be dominated and originated by a few outstanding personalities or does it appear to have arisen spontaneously from the demands of the members and to be controlled by the members? How are the leaders chosen and what is their tenure of office? What are duties and obligations of the leaders? Do the purposes and plans of the leaders correspond to the ostensible aims of the movement or are the leaders seeking other ends than the members? How clearly are the objectives of the movement formulated in the minds of the leaders and in the rank and file?

Techniques of Spreading the Movement

1. *Propaganda.* What types of propaganda through public meetings, radio, the printed page, symbolization, dramas, etc., are used to further the interests of the movement?

2. *Scientific Research.* To what extent does careful analysis based on the social sciences enter into the planning and promotion of the movement and to what extent is its spread dependent primarily on emotional factors unrelated to carefully considered procedure?

Satisfactions Derived

1. What economic needs are met by those associated with the movement?

2. What satisfactions in terms of wishes, drives, sense of security, etc., result from joining the movement? What frustrations, blighted hopes, insecurities in the lives of those joining constitute the reason for their acceptance of the movement?

Evaluation of the Objectives and Results of the Movement

1. Just what does the given movement expect to accomplish in terms of economic advantages, psychological satisfactions, political power, etc.?

2. Does the history of the movement show changing objectives and consequently changing programs of action? What are the causes of these changes?

3. How do you estimate the effects of the movement: (a) on its members, (b) on the general social situation?

Under the first set of categories these movements show a great variety of patterns. While all of them point back to a particular situation that can be shown in a greater or less degree to explain why they arose and spread at the time they did, others seem more to depend upon the conscious planning of a group of protagonists that pioneered, often against strong opposition, new ways of behavior, new types of activity. Father Divine's movement and its rapid success can be seen to be related to an economic situation in which thousands of Harlem Negroes found themselves in the thirties. Townsend's rapid increase of adherents, similarly, is related to the changing economic and familial situation that left millions of older people without economic security. On the other hand, the birth control movement attained a degree of acceptance and an increasing number of followers in spite of the mores of our culture and in spite of constant opposition from the Roman Catholic Church. Lenin and the early communist protagonists made their plans and worked out their strategy long before the disorganized state of Russia made it possible for a small group to gain political power.

There is, of course, always a combination of the efforts of a group of protagonists and the particular setting which evokes and facilitates a movement. A study of socialized medicine shows certain conditions that are conducive to change in medical practice. Increased specialization, the growing cost of what is considered adequate equipment for medical practice were trends that helped focus attention on the need of some sort of change. Michael Davis' study of the cost of medical care with its discovery of the great number of persons who have no adequate care brought to the attention of the American public the need of some sort of change in medical practice. Experiments by physicians in the organization and practice of group medicine accompanied by opposition on the part of the A.M.A. gave publicity to the incipient movement and drew increased numbers of its adherents. The depression of the thirties made many a young doctor with a struggling practice think in terms of the possibility of stabilizing income by group effort. A loosely defined social movement, with its experimental groups, its growing number of advocates, is a result of all the factors above outlined.

That there are elements in any given culture that block the spread of a given movement as well as those that facilitate its spread is evident. For example, the attitudes of the average American towards the value of competitive effort and the spread of the chain store with its low prices, are two factors which have made the rapid spread of the cooperative movement difficult. Among minority groups in the Northwest, notably the Finns, the cultural heritage of the group made a very rapid spread of cooperative activities. The Bahai movement, a mystical neo-Mohammedan sect, with a belief in absolute pacifism, has grown very slowly in America. Our religious background has made us antagonistic to Mohammedanism. Americans are not in large numbers either pacifist or mystical.

The types of people drawn to different movements is itself a study of importance. The educational and economic status of Father Divine's followers is low while the followers of Dr. Buchman in the Oxford Group movement are usually well-educated and financially secure. The main strength of the Nazi movement was originally among the economically insecure lower middle classes and the students.

The degree of participation in the activities of the movements varies. In the communist party, members are required to take active part in the program of the party. So also the followers of Father Divine, who are of the angel grade, give all their property to the Father and actively work in his Heavens. The Oxford Grouper is supposed to be an energetic soul saver. An ardent Zionist, day and night, is proclaiming the great cause and persuading others to join it. In the cooperative movement a member of a local cooperative may spend all his spare time promoting the movement or he may merely draw his quarterly dividends.

The leadership of these movements also shows a wide variation. Some of them have at the center an outstanding personality. Father Divine, Hitler, Dr. Townsend, Margaret Sanger, Frank Buchman, Daniel DeLeon, Marx and Lenin, George Fox and William Penn, Gandhi, Bahai, Engineer Scott, Father Coughlin, John Dewey—each name is associated with a movement as its outstanding leader. In some cases the leader dominates and almost completely embodies the movement. In other cases the leader merely expounded or promoted an idea or a plan which is taken over by a large number of persons, elaborated and extended. Other movements are not so closely linked with an outstanding leader. The Ku Klux Klan, founded by a small group, represents the struggle of a class of people to maintain status. The cooperative movement has had many distinguished advocates and experimenters but no great personality dominates their program. The general movement for social insurance developed in many groups—members of labor unions, intellectuals, government officials, but has no clear-cut outstanding leader. There are great numbers of people interested in and actively advocating the extension of this form of social security.

Methods of promotion and propaganda vary from appeals dramatically made and based on what appear on analysis to be demonstrably false hypotheses, as for example the Nazis use of pseudo-scientific racial theory, Father Divine's claims as to his supernatural person, the Mormons' belief in their divine revelation written in an extinct language, to reasoned and experimentally verified arguments, such as those used by the birth control group, or evidences of effective learning gained from experiments in progressive education. The amount of research embodied in the material used for propaganda by these movements varies from none at all to careful studies. Davis' work on *The Cost of Medical Care*, Dr. R. L. Dickinson's studies of effective contraceptives, many monographs showing the effects of poor housing on health and crime, are effectively used in spreading the propaganda for socialized medicine, birth control, and good housing. The theories and hypotheses of Dr. Townsend will not stand up under the light of rigorous economic analysis, while the Technocrats appear to have a mixture of verified facts and tenuous hypotheses as material for propaganda. Religious insights and so-called facts of experience are used in the propaganda for certain religious cults. This material is, in the nature of the case, less demonstrable. The personal testimonies regarding the effectiveness of "hunches" gained at the morning quiet hour in the Oxford Group; the colorful testimonies at the healings and the joy that Father Divine brings are not likely to carry conviction to critically minded who do not share certain pre-suppositions. Negative testimony is also a weapon of propaganda. For example, the horrible acts of the Jews and the harmful results of race crossing, the decrying of the corruption of plutocratic democracy and the exalting of the efficiency of the Hitler regime by the Bundists are used to stimulate men to join the Bund.

That the aims of the leaders of some of these movements have a different emphasis from those held by the rank and file is clear in the case of the Great I Am cult. This appears to have been a fraudulent money raising plan promoted by clever leaders. The tactics of the American Communist Party, with its infiltration into other organizations in order to influence public policy in a direction that was ostensibly for America's good but actually for the good of Soviet Russia, is well known. Within the party membership the aims are probably known to all.

Of particular interest in the study of these movements is the analysis of the satisfactions derived from them. A good many of them, for example the Ku Klux Klan, the Townsend movement, and to a large extent the National Socialist movement, may be interpreted as drawing membership because it is believed that through them status can be maintained, frustrations overcome, a secure place in the community attained. There is a nostalgic desire on the part of members of many of these movements to return to a former place of security and dignity. Behind the Zionist movement is the desire for a glory and a nationhood that has gone. Father Coughlin loudly condemns the large financial interests, the bankers, the big business men. He would like to return to a former era of independent self-respecting individualistic enterprise. Other movements are directed not to a return to the past but to an adventure ahead. The old system is not good enough. A new way of living is sought. Socialized medicine seeks a new pattern. Contraception is a new cultural invention and promises a new era of planned parenthood. The Socialist and the Communist groups in America seek to change the system and branch out in new social and economic patterns. The Quaker movement originated in a revolt against the ritualistic, formal, creed-believing, war-making patterns of the age and resulted in the setting up of a pacifist religious body without a formal theology, creed or ritual. Gandhi sought to create a new political weapon of non-violent resistance and at the same time advocated a return to very ancient methods of economic production. Some of the groups that compose the Zionist movement have no interest in a mere return to ancient patterns but are experimenting in new methods of communal living.

The analysis of Cantril in his *The Psychology of Social Movements* might lead the reader to believe that all social movements afford a sort of psychological and economic refuge for distracted and thwarted people. In a crisis situation when the props under the value systems of groups are removed and frustration follows, a solution is offered by a movement. Promises and programs for meeting frustrated desires and maintaining status are eagerly adopted. Probably there is this element in all the movements studied. But in some of them, the factors of careful planning, long-sighted vision, persuasion to leave old ways and seek a potentially more satisfactory pattern were far more apparent than in others. The movement for socialized medicine in America is not merely a formula for meeting a crisis. The protagonists of the newer methods, by propaganda and demonstration, are creating a hitherto unfelt desire for a new method of organization in medical treatment. So, also, the advocates of progressive education are doing much to create dissatisfaction with old methods. They are meeting an actual need in the educational world, from their point of view. But it is not a felt-need on the part of many educators and of the general public. These ardent educators are attempting to make this need felt.

While it is true that the study of almost any of these movements will uncover techniques of influencing opinion and of promoting change, those few that are focused not on re-establishing a former order but on achieving a new one are more valuable. It is the study of those few movements that may be fruitful in affording insights that may be useful in furthering desired social changes.

Study of this latter type of movement is, in the years of war, especially timely. No one can read J. B. Priestley's *Out of the People* without realizing that the war crisis is leading many in Britain to disregard their former status and, rich or poor, to seek another and a more satisfying and equalitarian form of human relationship. In fact, the present world situation presents a great many problems that seem insoluble unless great numbers of people fundamentally change their attitudes and unitedly seek new types of social, political, and economic organization. Hundreds of organizations are being formed by thousands of protagonists of change in the field of international organization and world government. Other groups push their propaganda for new types of race relationship while still others stress a planned economy. Religious leaders call for a revolution in moral values. How may these movements be based on a careful and factual analysis of our present culture and also bring about an alteration in opinion so that practicable steps towards desirable social change may be achieved? It is possible that the careful analysis of certain of these movements may give some light on how movements of this kind may be effective.

The last division of questions in the above outline is the most intangible in the area of subjective valuation. The results achieved by the cooperative movement can be measured in economic terms but hardly with accuracy in terms of the furthering of the democratic concept of life and the strengthening of cooperative activities in the field of education and recreation. There are measurable results in terms of members gained, income received, material property acquired. Some information on such points can be gotten in studying such a movement as the Father Divine or the Zionist movement. The intangible results in terms of the attitudes and hopes of the Negroes or the Jews are even more important but difficult to measure. Elaborate tests of attitudes might be constructed and some measure of the achievement of the movements attained.

The last question regarding the student's estimate of the effect of the movement on its members and on the general social situation almost inevitably forces the investigator to appraise and justify his own scale of values. He must measure the results not only quantitatively but qualitatively. He is forced to bring in the words "social welfare," "social improvement," and to arrive at some philosophy of desirable social change. It is possible, of course, to omit this last general appraisal. Classroom experience indicates, however, that the questions raised in this section are the most interesting, at any rate, to the students. They usually have a practical interest in desirable change and want to appraise the value of this or that movement in terms of their own social objectives.

After a study of this heterogeneous group of movements, certain general conclusions may be summarized.

A study of these movements will show clearly how with differing groups, crisis situations have been used by a small number of protagonists to build large and powerful movements. Those who wish to lead in influencing large numbers to change attitudes, to adopt policies, to further programs, should be sensitive to crisis situations, to unfulfilled needs, and thwarted human cravings, and present their programs in terms of the nature of these demands.

It is possible to combine careful research and wide experimentation with the building of a movement for social change. Magnetic leadership, emotional appeal will draw certain types of people if and when they are in critical situations, but substantial movements may be built in the absence of such situations.

In starting an effort to achieve a needed social reform, the resistances and the favorable aspects of the given culture must be considered. Mere logically demonstrated need of change is no guarantee that large groups will accept it. In this connection the use, by the educated person, of the language and symbols of the people whom he wishes to win is needed.

Few of these movements illustrate the way in which a group may cooperatively further a desired objective, working together towards agreed-on ends, enlarging their influence by successful experiment and educational propaganda and modifying their objectives in view of their experience. The cooperative movement comes nearer to this ideally democratic process of social action than most of those studied. Some others approach such a procedure.

VALUE ORIENTATIONS IN THE STUDY OF SOCIAL MOVEMENTS

Of all those phenomena amenable to sociological analysis, the import of the researcher's values for the study of social movements is perhaps most crucial. Relevant values are not only those concerning the methodology of analysis but also those involving the researcher's theoretical conception of society and his personal beliefs about the desirability of certain kinds of social change. What are the values that social scientists bring to the study of social movements?

The positivistic social scientists of the nineteenth century were creative theory builders who attempted to solve significant social problems in a manner they considered scientific. Count Henri de Saint-Simon is a key theorist of this tradition, since his approach to social theory has structured much of the polemic concerning the role of social science. Saint-Simon postulated a science politique predicated on ". . . the solid inductions of history and observations . . . [which] . . . must be animated by the conception of development and progress."[9] Upon observing his society—France in the 1820s—Saint-Simon wanted a fundamental social change from capitalism to socialism. Explicitly, for Saint-Simon progress was the organization of a new social and political structure based on a new division of labor—socialism—and the establishment of a new fraternity of man, i.e., nouveau christianisme. One school of social scientists—the positivists as represented by Comte—argued against this form of change; however, the "Saint-Simonian school," symbolized by Bazard, Enfantin, and Buchez and followed later by Proudhon and Marx, supported the contention that this type of change was needed. Marx, in developing the theory of historical materialism, viewed science as a tool for bringing about social reorganization. For him, the role of the scientist was to define, clarify, and posit the contradictions in society and to create a class consciousness.[10] On the other hand, Comte and his successors, in part influenced by the same social disorganization in French society which Saint-Simon recognized, used the "scientific technique" as they understood it in an attempt to promote social cohesion and integration in society.[11]

---

[9] Harry Elmer Barnes, *An Introduction to the History of Sociology* (Chicago: University of Chicago Press, 1948), p. 74.
[10] Karl Marx, quoted in Erich Fromm, *Marx's Concept of Man* (New York: Ungar, 1963), pp. 197–219; V. I. Lenin, "What Is to Be Done?" in *Collected Works*, vol. 4 (New York: International Publishers, 1929), pp. 149–154, 201–207.
[11] Cf. Emile Durkheim, *Professional Ethics and Civic Morals* (London: Routledge and Kegan Paul, 1958), pp. 90–97; and *Suicide* (Glencoe: Free Press, 1951).

An example is Durkheim's classic study, Suicide, where his basic conclusion is that a lack of social cohesiveness (anomie) may lead to personal disorientation (e.g., suicide). In other writings, Durkheim suggested means of establishing social integration, for example, through intermediate organizations based on the division of labor.[12]

The social philosophical debate over the question of change which preoccupied sociologists, political scientists, and economists during the nineteenth century culminated in two divergent theories of society. One, which may be termed historical materialism or conflict theory, stresses social change and the building of an ideal society.[13] Some of the major contemporary advocates of this school are C. Wright Mills, Herbert Marcuse, Ralf Dahrendorf, and T. B. Bottomore. The other, generally described as social systems or structural-functional theory, emphasizes the study of societies as though they were inherently integrated and equilibrated systems, and advocates the maintenance of such societies. Proponents of this approach include Talcott Parsons, Robert K. Merton, Kingsley Davis, Wilbert Moore, and S. M. Lipset.

American social science, while occasionally flirting with the former model, has generally reflected the latter position. In keeping with this posture, one of the tenets of American sociologists has been the "value free" conception of social science derived from Max Weber.[14] Several decades ago, Gunnar Myrdal summarized this dominant ideology as follows:

When perhaps a majority of the foremost social scientists in America have an ambition toward, and take pride in, keeping entirely free from attempting to reach practical and political conclusions from their research, part of the explanation is their high professional standards. The quest for scientific objectivity is, I believe, more lively, and kept more explicit, in America than elsewhere. . . . The reaction against reformism and philosophical system-building has been particularly violent in American sociology where a concerted drive to build a social science on the model of the natural sciences is clearly apparent.[15]

Prior to the Depression years, most North American students of society conformed to Myrdal's description. In the late thirties, however, Robert Lynd issued an indictment of the "neo-positivist" approach and the notion of value free social science. Lynd's major thesis was that social scientists, too involved in methodologies and theories, were, as W. H. Auden would

[12] *Professional Ethics, op. cit.*, pp. 90–97; and *The Division of Labor in Society* (Glencoe: Free Press, 1947).
[13] Cf. N. Bukharin, *Historical Materialism* (New York: Russell and Russell, 1965).
[14] Max Weber, *From Max Weber: Essays in Sociology* (New York: Oxford University Press, 1946), pp. 129–156.
[15] Gunnar Myrdal, *An American Dilemma*, vol. 2 (New York: McGraw-Hill, 1964), pp. 1041–1042.

have it, "lecturing on navigation while the ship is going down." [16] Moreover, he argued that their only concern in the applied field was in collaboration with the interests of the status quo. According to Lynd, social scientists must be aware of the aspirations of people, but they tend to avoid this and their concomitant role as social innovators. He discounted the argument that social science is objective and has ". . . no criteria by which to allot priorities in importance." [17] Social scientists, argues Lynd, must address significant social problems: the values of human beings living together in the pursuit of their deeper and more persistent purposes ". . . are the questions to be investigated." [18] By doing this the social scientists can bring about structural change and improve the human condition.

The admonitions of Myrdal and Lynd were not, however, equal in impact to those of C. Wright Mills, the "gadfly" of sociology, who for over a decade conducted a vigorous assault upon contemporary American social science.[19] As one analyst of Mills' work, Herbert Aptheker, expresses it, the two essential themes of this assault were that "major social problems—which may appear to each individual in the form of a personal problem—are not resolvable except by alterations which affect the sources and the structural forms of such problems; . . . dominant American sociological inquiry has failed to provide the analysis required for significant solutions, but rather has taken directions which serve to sustain the status quo and to foster a sense of impotence in the face of these problems." [20] The reasons for this failure, according to Mills, are to be found within the paradigm, theory, methodology, and middle class orientation of American social scientists. Although Mills' polemical style made him an "outsider" to the mainstream of American social science, his work has had a considerable, if as yet unassessable, impact on younger social scientists.

Alvin Gouldner has also criticized the value free conception as a myth and has argued that value judgments are a part of the practice of social science.[21] According to Gouldner, this myth of ethical neutrality "resolves

[16] W. H. Auden, quoted in Robert Lynd, *Knowledge for What?* (Princeton: Princeton University Press, 1939), pp. 2–3.
[17] Lynd, *ibid.*, p. 181.
[18] Lynd, *ibid.*, p. 189.
[19] For a complete bibliography of C. Wright Mills' voluminous writings see Irving Louis Horowitz, ed., *Power, Politics, and People: The Collected Essays of C. Wright Mills* (New York: Ballantine Books, 1964). See also Mills' "The Professional Ideology of Social Pathologists," *American Journal of Sociology*, 49 (September 1943), 165–181; and *White Collar* (New York: Oxford University Press, 1951), pp. 112–160.
[20] Herbert Aptheker, *The World of C. Wright Mills* (New York: Marzani and Munsell, 1960), p. 98.
[21] Alvin Gouldner, "Explorations in Applied Social Science," *Social Problems*, 3 (January 1956), 169–180; Alvin Gouldner, "Anti-Minotaur: The Myth of a Value Free Sociology," *Social Problems*, 9 (Winter 1962), 199–213. Also see W. H. Werkmeister, "Theory Construction and Objectivity," in Llewellyn Gross, ed., *Symposium in Sociological Theory* (New York: Harper and Row, 1959), pp. 483–507; and Paul Furfey, "Sociological Science and the Problem of Values," in Gross, *op. cit.*, pp. 509–528.

... conflicts by making it seem that those who refrain from social criticism are acting solely on behalf of a higher professional good rather than their private interests." [22] This ethos, as a consequence, guaranteed the autonomy of and support for the social sciences, an environment necessary for the growth of science. As to the applied aspects of the social sciences, Gouldner argues that if sociologists adhere to any values these will be biased in support of the value free ethic.

Although few social scientists have explicitly stated their assumptions about the role of sociology in society, George Lundberg has done so in the following succinct statement concerning the value free ethic:

Social scientists, unfortunately, have failed as yet to convince any considerable number of persons that they are engaged in a pursuit of knowledge of a kind which is demonstrably true, regardless of the private preferences, hopes, and likes of the scientist himself. All sciences have gone through this stage. Physical scientists are, as a class, less likely to be disturbed than social scientists when a political upheaval comes along, because the work of the former is recognized as of equal consequence under any regime. Social science should strive for a similar position. Individual physicists may suffer persecution, but their successors carry on their work in much the same way. If social scientists possessed an equally demonstrable relevant body of knowledge and technique of finding answers, that knowledge would be equally above the reach of political upheaval. The services of real social scientists would be as indispensable to Fascists as to Communists and Democrats, just as are the services of physicists and physicians. The findings of physical scientists at times also have been ignored by political regimes, but when that has occurred, it has been the regime and not the science that yielded in the end.[23]

Lundberg goes on to derive the consequent implication of this position for the relationship between social scientists and the state as follows:

I have emphasized that physical scientists are indispensable to any political regime. Social scientists might well work toward a corresponding status. Already some of them have achieved it to a degree. Qualified social statisticians have not been and will not be disturbed greatly in their function by any political party as long as they confine themselves to their specialty. Their skill consists in the ability to draw relatively valid, unbiased, and demonstrable conclusions from observed data of social behavior. That technique is the same, regardless of social objectives. No regime can get along without this technol-

[22] Gouldner, "Anti-Minotaur," *ibid.*, p. 206. Goode and Hatt adopt a similar position in *Methods in Social Research* (New York: McGraw-Hill, 1952), pp. 21–22. Also see Leopold Labenz, "How Free Is Soviet Science," in Barber and Hirsch, eds., *The Sociology of Science* (Glencoe: Free Press, 1962), pp. 129–141. Labenz cites the lack of autonomy as resulting in the lack of development of social science. He writes: "As a rule the closer the subject is to sensitive ideological points, the smaller its chance of unfettered development" (p. 141).
[23] George A. Lundberg, *Can Science Save Us?* (New York: David McKay Co., Inc., 1961), pp. 56–57.

ogy. It is the possession and exercise of such skills alone that justifies the claim of academic immunity. To claim it for those who insist on taking for granted that which needs to be demonstrated can only result in the repudiation for everybody of the whole principle of academic freedom. For the same reason, we had better not become so devoted to blatant crusaders for academic freedom that we forget to bolster the only foundation upon which academic freedom can ever be maintained in the long run, namely, the demonstrated capacity of its possessors to make valid and impersonal analyses and predictions of social events.[24]

In contrast to this position, consider the following excerpts from Nikolai Bukharin's introduction to his Historical Materialism. Here, the author clearly defines the opposing value orientations in sociology and argues for the viability of what he calls "proletarian social science" for the promotion of change.

Excerpts from Nikolai Bukharin, Historical Materialism *(New York, Russell and Russell, 1965), pp. ix–xii. Reprinted by permission of Russell and Russell.*

THE PRACTICAL IMPORTANCE OF THE SOCIAL SCIENCES

The Social Sciences and the Demands of the Struggle of the Working Class

Bourgeois scholars speak of any branch of learning with mysterious awe, as if it were a thing produced in heaven, not on earth. But as a matter of fact any science, whatever it be, grows out of the demands of society or its classes. No one takes the trouble to count the number of flies on a window-pane, or the number of sparrows in the street, but one does count the number of horned cattle. The former figures are useful to no one; it is very useful to know the latter. But it is not only useful to have a knowledge of nature, from whose various parts we obtain all our substances, instruments, raw materials, etc.; it is just as necessary, in practice, to have information concerning society. The working class, at each step in its struggle, is brought face to face with the necessity of possessing such information. In order to be able to conduct its struggle with other classes properly, it is necessary for the working class to foresee how these classes will behave. For this it must know on what circumstances the conduct of the various classes, under varying conditions, depends. . . .

[24] *Ibid.*, pp. 57–58.

The Bourgeoisie and the Social Sciences

The bourgeoisie also has created its own social sciences, based on its own practical requirements.

When the bourgeoisie is the ruling class, it must solve a great number of questions: how to maintain the capitalist order of things; how to secure the so-called "normal development" of capitalist society, which means a regular influx of profits; how to organize for this purpose its economic institutions; how to conduct its policy with regard to other countries; how to maintain its rule over the working class; how to eliminate disagreements in its own ranks; how to train its staffs of officials: priests, police, scholars; how to carry on the business of instruction so that the working class may not become savage and destroy the machinery, but may continue to be obedient to its oppressors, etc.

For this purpose the bourgeoisie needs the social sciences; these sciences aid it in its adaptation to the complicated social life and in choosing a proper course in the solution of the practical problems of life. It is interesting, for example, to note that the first bourgeois economists were great practical merchants and government leaders, while the greatest theoretician of the bourgeoisie, Ricardo, was a very able banker.

The Class Character of the Social Sciences

Bourgeois scholars always maintain that they are the representatives of so called "pure science," that all earthly sufferings, all conflicting interests, all the ups and downs of life, the hunt for profit, and other earthly and vulgar things have no relation whatever with their science. Their conception of the matter is approximately the following: the scholar is a god, seated on a sublime eminence, observing dispassionately the life of society in all its varying forms; they think (and yet more loudly proclaim) that vile "practice" has no relation whatever with pure "theory." This conception is of course a false one; quite the contrary is true: all learning arises from practice. This being the case, it is perfectly clear that the social sciences have a *class* character. Each class has its own practice, its special tasks, its interests and therefore its view of things. The bourgeoisie is concerned chiefly with safeguarding, perpetuating, solidifying, extending the rule of capital. The working class is concerned in the first place with the task of overthrowing the capitalist system and safeguarding the rule of the working class in order to reconstruct life. It is not difficult to see that bourgeois practice will demand one thing, and proletarian practice another; that the bourgeoisie will have one view of things and the working class another; that the social science of the bourgeoisie will be of one type, and that of the proletariat unquestionably of a different type.

Why Is Proletarian Science Superior to Bourgeois Science?

This is the question we have now to answer. If the social sciences have a class character, in what way is proletarian science superior to bourgeois science, for the working class also has its interests, its aspirations, its practice, while the bourgeoisie has a practice of its own. Both classes must be considered as interested parties. It is not sufficient to say that one class is good, high-minded, concerned with the welfare of humanity, while the other is greedy, eager for profits, etc. One of these two classes has one kind of eye-glasses, red ones, the other class has a different kind, white ones. Why are red glasses better than white ones? Why is it better to look at reality through red ones? Why is there superior visibility through red ones?

We must approach the answer to this question rather carefully.

We have seen that the bourgeoisie is interested in preserving the capitalist system. Yet it is a well-known fact that there is nothing permanent under the sun. There was a slavery system; there was a feudal system; there was, and still is, the capitalist system; there also have been other forms of human society. It is evident—and incontrovertibly so—that we must infer the following: he who would understand social life on its present basis must also understand, at the outset, that all is changing, that one form of society follows upon another. Let us picture to ourselves, for example, the feudal serf-owner, who lived in the period before the liberation of the peasants from serfdom. Such a man in many cases could not even imagine that there might exist an order of society in which it would be impossible to sell peasants or exchange them for grey-hounds. Could such a serf-owner really understand the evolution of society correctly? Of course not. Why not? For the reason that his eyes were covered not by glasses, but with blinders. He could not see further than his nose, and therefore was unable to understand even the things going on right under his nose.

The bourgeoisie also wears such blinders. The bourgeoisie is interested in the preservation of capitalism and believes in its permanence and indestructibility. It is therefore blind to such phenomena and such traits in the evolution of capitalist society as point to its temporary nature, to its approaching ruin (even to the possibility of its destruction), to its being succeeded by any other organization of life. This is made most clear by the example of the World War and the revolution. Did any one of the more or less prominent bourgeois scholars foresee the consequences of the world slaughter? Not one! Did any one of them foresee the outbreak of revolution? Not one! They were all busily occupied in supporting their bourgeois governments and predicting victory for the capitalists of their own country. And yet, these phenomena, namely, the general destruction by warfare, and the unprecedented revolution of the proletariat, are deciding the destinies of mankind, are changing the face of the entire earth. But of all this, bourgeois science had not a single premonition. But the communists—the representatives of proletarian science—did foresee all this. The difference is due to the fact that the proletariat is not interested in the preservation of the old and is therefore more farsighted. . . .

Unlike the purged Russian revolutionary Bukharin, few American sociologists have totally questioned the validity of the "democratic" political system or of "state capitalism." As a consequence, movements oriented toward changing these institutions have received comparatively little professional attention until they intruded into the world views of academicians and researchers. As we noted earlier, American social scientists tend to view these institutions as part of the natural order of society, subject perhaps to evolutionary changes but certainly not productive of revolution. Therefore, they tend to regard challenges to these institutions as deviant manifestations subject to analysis in terms of social-psychological variables. For example, in his preface to his study *The Authoritarian Personality*, Adorno writes: ". . . no politico-social trend imposes a graver threat to our traditional values and institutions than does fascism, and . . . knowledge of the personality forces that favor its acceptance may ultimately prove useful in combating it." [25] Similarly, Ernst and Loth preface their study of the American Communist movement as follows: "The thesis of this book is that the people of the United States cannot wisely and successfully combat Communism unless they understand Communists. If we know . . . [why people join and leave the party] . . . we will be in a better position to prevent the rank and file, which is the backbone of any party, from joining in the first place." [26] The essentially negativistic value orientations of American social scientists toward social movements is also reflected in the frames of reference they use to analyze them. For example, Robert Merton analyzes rebellion as one of several possible "deviant" adaptations to social and cultural discrepancies.[27] Howard Becker, in a collection of articles on deviant behavior, devotes a chapter entitled "The Moral Entrepreneurs" to social movements.[28] Robert E. L. Faris discusses one category of social movements, which is viewed as "crack pot," in a volume entitled Social Dis-

[25] T. W. Adorno, et al., *The Authoritarian Personality* (New York: Harper & Row, 1950), p. i.
[26] Morris L. Ernst and David Loth, *Report on the American Communist* (New York: Henry Holt and Co., 1952), p. 1.
[27] Robert K. Merton, ed., *Social Theory and Social Structure*, rev. ed. (Glencoe: Free Press, 1957), pp. 131–160.
[28] Howard Becker, *The Outsiders* (Glencoe: Free Press, 1963), pp. 147–164.

organization.[29] Elliot and Merrill, in their book of the same title, treat social movements under the headings "revolution" and "totalitarianism." [30]

On the other hand, an equally evaluative position may be discerned on the part of students of social movements who favor change. Since to these students movements are either indices of discontent, "vanguards" of change, or the "movement of the masses," much of their research has idealized the movements under examination. As Selig Perlman suggests:

> . . . it has always been the main characteristic of the intellectual to think of labor as an abstract "mass" in the grip of an abstract "force." Labor then ceases to be an aggregation of individuals seeking as a group to control their common economic opportunity. . . . Instead, labor takes on the aspect of a "mass" driven by a "force" towards a glorious "ultimate social goal." . . . At bottom the intellectual's conviction rests . . . on a deeply rooted faith that labor is somehow the "chosen vessel" of whatever may be the power which shapes the destiny of society.[31]

Marxian scholars have not infrequently viewed specific social movements —such as labor and civil rights—as idealized "chosen vessels" or "sleeping giants" in the class struggle.[32] Thus, in addition to a theoretical or scholarly significance, social movements also have considerable political import for these analysts. These dual considerations, for example, led both Marx and Engels to devote considerable time to analyses of class-based phenomena; Marx's The Civil War in France, The Eighteenth Brumaire of Louis Bonaparte, Critique of the Gotha Programme, and Class Struggle in France; Engels' German Revolution and Counter Revolution and The British Labour Movement are such analyses.

When assessing the works of scholars who favor social change, few critics can avoid the observation that the political and ideological positions

---

[29] Robert E. L. Faris, *Social Disorganization*, 2d ed. (New York: Ronald Press, 1955), p. 573.
[30] Mabel Elliot and Francisco Merrill, *Social Disorganization* (New York: Harper & Brothers, 1950), pp. 667–706. Given the title, it is difficult to understand their use of the word totalitarianism, which generally refers to "total" organization.
[31] Selig Perlman, *A Theory of the Labor Movement* (New York: Macmillan Co., 1928), pp. 280–281. Also see Joseph A. Schumpeter, *Capitalism, Socialism, and Democracy* (New York: Harper & Brothers, 1942), pp. 145–155.
[32] See for example Wilson Record, *The Negro and the Communist Party* (Chapel Hill: University of North Carolina Press, 1947); Philip Selznick's cold war interpretation of this phenomenon in *The Organizational Weapon: A Study of Bolshevik Strategy and Tactics* (Glencoe: Free Press, 1960). For a sample of Marxist analyses see Herbert Aptheker's *American Negro Slave Revolts* (New York: International Publishers, 1963); Anna Rochester, *The Populist Movement in the United States* (New York: International Publishers, 1943). Also see the biographies of American radicals published by the Left: Ella Reeve Bloor, *We Are Many* (New York: International Publishers, 1940); and Bill Haywood, *Bill Haywood's Book* (New York: International Publishers, 1929).

of the analyst influence not only his theoretical framework but also his choice of movements for study.³³ While not denying this, we suggest that the same influences hold true for those scholars who adopt a more conservative view about the desirability of social change.

The dilemma of values in studying social movements is not confined entirely to the ideological or theoretical positions of their observers. While, as Bukharin tells us, shadings of eyeglasses do in fact color the end research product, other sources of bias must be considered. One consideration, pointed to by Mills in The Sociological Imagination, is that of the methodology by which a study is conducted.³⁴ For example, the historian relies essentially on existing records, documents, and accounts. To this extent, his analysis is subject to the original purpose for which such accounts were prepared and to the biases of those who prepared them. Moreover, the historian has little opportunity to capture or experience the dynamic spirit (Geist) of a movement, which is important for interpreting the data one has access to. On the other hand, the astute participant-observer or field interviewer has an opportunity to assess the biases of his informants and is in a good position to observe the inner workings of a movement. However, this very capability may limit his overall view and cause his perspectives to become increasingly narrow. Another, more cogent, value dilemma faced by the field worker is that of becoming less and less an observer and more and more a participant. As he interacts with members of an organization and begins to identify with them, he is also prone to identify with their values and aims. Joseph R. Gusfield, in describing his experiences in studying the Temperance movement, provides an insight into the effects of using a field study technique on the values of the researcher.

Excerpts from Joseph R. Gusfield, "Field Work Reciprocities in Studying a Social Movement," Human Organization, Vol. 14, (Fall, 1955), pp. 29–33. Reprinted by permission of Joseph R. Gusfield and the Society for Applied Anthropology.

This paper is a report of some experiences in interviewing members of a social movement—the Woman's Christian Temperance Union. The interviews were part of the data used in a study of the WCTU which

---

[33] S. M. Lipset, "Political Sociology," in Merton, Broom, and Cottrell, eds., Sociology Today (New York: Basic Books, 1959), pp. 86–87. Also see Lipset's introduction to his Political Man (Garden City: Anchor Books, 1963), pp. xix–xxxvi.
[34] C. Wright Mills, The Sociological Imagination (New York: Oxford University Press, 1959).

formed the author's Ph.D. dissertation.[35] These experiences will shed some light on the nature of the interaction between interviewer and interviewee. The point made here is that the interview conferred certain rewards on both parties involved. A definite social relationship was formed and governed by virtue of functions useful to both members. Several such functions will be discussed in this article. . . .

THE INTERVIEWER AS A SOCIAL ROLE

The relationship of interviewer to interviewee is an unusual one, for the former has no part in any other relationship of the latter. He demands a detached statement of views and ideas, outside any situational context, and this is not a form of behavior in which people characteristically engage. It is our conclusion, however, that this very detachment presents a role that facilitates research.

In organizing their behavior towards us, we found the respondents using two images of us—as members of the public and as informed strangers.

The Interviewer's Role as Member of the Public

The current public stereotype of the WCTU member is not at all favorable. The WCTU member is quite aware of the image of the "fanatic" and the "bluenose" with which people often identify her. Two kinds of attitudes were found among WCTU members towards the existence of this image. One is the "I'd rather be right than popular" attitude, and those who hold this attitude are proud of the strength of their convictions and the opprobrium with which many view the WCTU. Those who hold the second are deeply resentful of this image and want to change it. Insofar as the interviewer is a person capable of an attitude towards the WCTU, this kind of member may want to win him as a friend of the organization. My own status as a college professor increased this, since I may have been in a position to shape the attitudes of others.

This reasoning suggests that the interviewee may build a context in which his answers are purposeful *vis-à-vis* the interviewer. The behavior of the former towards the latter is, thus, a sample of the public relations attitude of the member.

Consider the interviewee who tried to convince me of her steadfast-

---

[35] For the complete study, see Joseph Gusfield, "Organizational Change: A Study of the Woman's Christian Temperance Union," unpublished Ph.D. dissertation, University of Chicago Libraries, 1954. For some aspects of the study, see the author's "Social Structure and Moral Reform: A Study of the WCTU," *Amer. Jour. of Sociology*, 61 (November 1955), 221–232.

ness in the face of the stereotype. My second interview was a listless affair; the respondent was passive and hostile. I asked her what she thought about the value of a return to Prohibition, and she turned the question on me: "What do you think of it?" I said that I was sympathetic but not certain. She was furious:

"What do you mean you don't know! You're just like all the rest. How can you not take a stand? There are too many people like that. Oh, I see them in the church every day. They are for whatever you're for. If you are for temperance so are they. But you can't depend upon them, you can't depend upon them. But I'm not afraid. I'll stand up and tell everybody, even Harry Truman. I'll live and die a temperance woman."

This type is not concerned about changing my impression of the stereotyped WCTU woman; she approximates it. Her characteristic response to the interview is an attack on the public that refuses to adhere to WCTU doctrine. She paints the WCTU as a militant temperance organization.

The other type is much more public relations oriented. She attempts to correct the stereotype and to change what she feels may be my image as a member of the general public. Several such women said that the WCTU is quite different from what it is commonly thought to be. For example, one woman concluded the interview by saying, on the doorstep: "We're not just a temperance organization. We're for everything human. We knit for the soldiers and send them things for overseas." The following is even more explicit in contrasting the public image with the interviewee's picture: "There was an age when people thought that you should wear black and preach all the time with a long face. We're getting over that now. We have a great many departments in the WCTU. We have one for every interest for which women have clubs. There are many different kinds of activities."

Women of the first type, with little concern for public relations, were more common in the Chicago group; they would fail to keep appointments or would confuse the day or time of the appointment. In upstate New York and in Evanston this was not true; the upstate group was more apt to be public relations oriented.

This poses a difficult problem for scientific verification. Was the public relations orientation of the New York and Evanston group a reflection of the importance of my status to them? Was I more important to them than I was to the Chicago group because they were more anxious to "sell" the organization, to accommodate public opinion, than the Chicago group? The number of total cases (46) was small, but the problem exists nevertheless. Whether, and in what ways, the interviewer is participating in a social relationship is a crucial question.

The Interviewer as Informed Stranger

In dealing with the interview process as a social process, we must ask what functions the interview plays for the respondent. Why should he tell anything? We have seen the public relations function as one possible gift the interviewer brings. We also found that the very anonymity and pose of objective detachment gives the respondent an opportunity for a rewarding experience. Simmel has noted this quality of the relationship of the stranger to a social group. In his famous essay he wrote: ". . . he often receives the most surprising openness-confidences which have the character sometimes of a confessional and which would be carefully withheld from a more closely related person. Objectivity is by no means nonparticipation . . . but a positive and specific kind of participation." [36]

This quality of the interview process enables the field worker to serve as a source of justification for the respondent's actions. To do this, you must be able to demonstrate to the respondent that you will understand, as well as keep the secrets revealed. Often, an interview will be a listless and dull affair until that moment when you ask some question that touches a deeply-felt issue and shows the respondent that he can trust your understanding. It is at this moment that the interview changes its tone and the interviewee seems to say: "That's it. Now you've got it."

An example of this relationship is seen in an interview we had with the Director of Scientific Temperance Instruction for the WCTU. This branch of activity has as its aim the education of children, via public schools, in temperance sentiment. We had been talking about the attitude of public school officials toward the WCTU, and we asked her: "What kind of background do most of the state directors have for this kind of work?" She replied:

"There you have the problem. Most WCTU directors have no background for the work at all. Many have no tact or policy. I know one place—a department of education—where when she comes everybody hides for the whole day. . . . In lots of places she's picked because, as somebody said, she's a good woman, a sweet woman, and *so* interested in the work. But she doesn't know anything about the work nor does she have any salesmanship ability."

It's plain that I had touched on the cross that this respondent had to bear. What she had told me is not the sort of thing one admits publicly, nor even to those other than intimates in the organization. Why should she tell me these things?

One answer to this question is that she can talk safely to me. I am at her mercy, and I have no relation to the WCTU which would give consequence to her answers. Because of this she can "let off steam" in a

[36] Georg Simmel, "Sociology of the Stranger," in Kurt Wolff, ed., *The Sociology of Georg Simmel* (Glencoe, Ill.: Free Press, 1950).

harmless manner. But the interviewer has another therapeutic function. He becomes the bearer of the justification and sympathy of the respondent. By presenting her grievances, the respondent may seek to gain the sympathetic alliance of the impartial person. The particular interviewee discussed above indicated that others in WCTU did not agree with her policies: ". . . essay writing is primitive as the ox cart. Why use the ox cart when you can use the airplane. But we still have state presidents who are using essay contests."

Was she conveying information to me in discussing these differences of policy? It later came to light that she was involved in a conflict with state executives over the very policy described, a conflict so deep that her job was threatened. She didn't tell these things, but apparently used the interview to seek sympathetic alliance and justification.

It is not simply the role of the stranger that is important in the interview, but the role of the *informed* stranger. It is by demonstrating that you know the "score" that you can best convince the respondent that he or she can secure understanding. This may involve the technique of challenging the respondent's initial answers. In one case, after getting a "formal" answer to a question: "What do most people think of the WCTU?" I switched my tone. I challenged her by asking: "But isn't it true that some members, and even some who aren't members, give the WCTU the reputation of being 'queer?'" Here was a very real problem to her. She then told the story of a Chicago member who is a big "problem to the WCTU because she reinforces the public image of the 'fanatic.'"

Earlier in the same interview I had told the respondent some things about Carry Nation that she had not known. On several occasions I was able to establish myself to members as an expert on the WCTU because of my knowledge of matters unknown to them. In one upstate group a good discussion of WCTU policy towards temperance groups resulted because a respondent knew little about the issues behind the national position, with which I was familiar. In telling her about it I was able to get her reaction to that policy.

The interviewee has to get something out of the interview otherwise there will be little reason for him to "open up." The interviewer must be able to create that social relationship which rewards the respondent for "good rapport."

THE INTERVIEWER AS PARTICIPANT

One of the central facts about social research is that it creates rewards for the researcher. We have examined some of the rewards of the interview for the respondent. We must also point out how the rewards to the interviewer influence the process of research.

At a late point in the study, I interviewed the president of a local Chicago WCTU unit. We had good rapport and I asked her if I could attend the next meeting. She was agreeable and, several days before the meeting, I received a letter from her asking me to join the WCTU as an honorary member. A pledge card was included. I didn't reply and hoped that nothing more would come of it. At the meeting, the president asked me if I would sign the pledge; I told her that, in all conscience, I could not. Following this incident I found that the Chicago WCTU had been ordered not to talk to me, as I was not a total abstainer. This meant the loss of several interviews that I had wanted to have.

Why didn't I sign the pledge and lie about my drinking habits? An understanding of my attitude may shed some light on the way the research worker becomes a part of the social movement he studies.

One thing was clear. The WCTU was my "bread and butter." Although I was not being paid to do the study, it was the basis of my Ph.D. thesis. I had no established relation to the WCTU and, probably, my study would not be to their liking. Indeed, they didn't seem to see how much I was discovering about them. Their conception of a sociological study was rather naive and at a highly formal level. They had been pretty helpful to me in many ways, and I was using them. This kind of situation is bound to fill the field worker with ethical misgivings, and I had a sincere feeling that they deserved some kind of repayment. Isn't our culture one that demands this kind of repayment? Little wonder that the field worker should feel the same when he deals with an organized group rather than an anonymous sample of people, as in a public opinion survey.

The feeling of obligation towards the WCTU was enhanced by the elements which served to develop an identification between myself and the WCTU. I had begun the study with the stereotyped image of the WCTU member as being "queer," but concrete experience illustrated the immense over-simplification of this. I came to see the WCTU in a different fashion, and, in a sense, I even became a partisan.

An illustration of the "interviewer conversion" process is seen in my experiences at a party about a year after I began the study. A group of old college friends were invited to a mutual friend's home. Among other things, we discussed my thesis, and this led to a general discussion of alcoholism as an industrial problem. I seriously suggested that one solution to the problem was the reintroduction of Prohibition. It was hard for my friends to believe that any rational person could seriously consider Prohibition. I had never thought very much about the problem of alcohol. I shared, and still share, the views of my own social group, which are anti-temperance. What, then, had happened to me?

I had, in studying the WCTU, become immersed in a new world and it had changed my perspectives, although not my opinions. Since I dealt with temperance arguments so much of the time, there was nothing unusual about them any longer. I had to look at their position apart from satirical motives. The ready discussions of their position, which I and my group held, were long ago dealt with by temperance writers. I began to see temperance views as intellectually defensible.

The stereotype of the WCTU is something against which the organization fights. Often the attitudes of my friends struck me as cruel. Almost any time that I told other academic people about my study someone would ask about the personality characteristics of WCTU members. The assumption was clear that there must be something eccentric about these ladies. But to me, being deeply immersed in the WCTU, they weren't unusual at all. They were sensitive to the public image of the WCTU, and so was I.

The WCTU became "my baby," and I became protective towards it. When *Time* Magazine reported a temperance event in what seemed to me to be an unfair way, I was indignant. It wasn't ethical. I may have been unconverted, but I had become a "friendly enemy."

I came to like the women in the WCTU. They had convictions that they held firmly, despite the ostracism entailed. They were interesting women and they had my admiration.

The foregoing background material is an attempt to explain my refusal to take the pledge. My statements concerning my own beliefs were the repayment to the WCTU at a point central to their views. Perhaps I might have acted otherwise had the study not been in its last stages. Perhaps my own personality led me to act differently than some other field worker. But the ethical problem still remains, regardless of how it was solved. The interviewer cannot avoid being a participant in a social process, if for no other reason than that he is getting something out of the interview.

Organized groups, such as social movements, involve the field worker in a much more complex pattern of possible roles and rewards than is true of less structured groups, such as are found in public opinion surveys. This fact makes it very necessary that we be increasingly sensitive to the context in which data is collected. That context is essential if we are to understand the results of our studies.

In addition to theory and methodology, the historical period in which a study is undertaken also reflects, and has an effect on, the values of the researcher. Consider, for example, the plight of the social scientist who wished to study the Communist movement during the McCarthy era or the German-American Bund after the bombing of Pearl Harbor. Unless the researcher was willing to adopt the prevailing social attitudes of the time toward these movements he would find it difficult to have his work published or accepted. Moreover, unbiased data upon which an adequate study of such movements could be based was hard to come by at the time. Therefore, the studies that did become part of the academic output, and hence influenced not only the thought of the time but also that of the future, reflect the dominant Geist of that historical period. This effect is most marked during periods of grave social crisis, such as World War II and the Cold War of the late 1940s and early 1950s.

One of the most striking examples of how the interactions between time and ideology color the perception of social facts is found in studies of the relationship of folk music to the American Communist Party. The pioneer work on this subject was undertaken at the time of McCarthy's investigations of Communists and the media blacklist of alleged left wing artists.[37] With the folk music revival of the late 1950s, interest in folk material and protest songs became legitimated. However, the major assumption of researchers in this area remained tied to the political events and analyses of the early years of the Cold War. One of the authors illustrates the impact of this aspect of values upon social movement research by examining the contemporary literature dealing with the American Communist movement and protest songs.

R. Serge Denisoff, "Folk Music and the American Communist Movement: A Case of Historical Confusion." Sections of this paper originally appeared in Folk Consciousness: People's Music and American Communism (unpublished Ph.D. thesis), Simon Fraser University, 1968. Reprinted by permission of R. Serge Denisoff.

The genesis of the urban folk music "movement" was closely linked with the left wing movements of the 1930s and 1940s.[38] Students began to investigate this topic after a change in the political climate of the United States in the early 1950s. At that time any association with the Communist movement was considered subversive. A person identified with the Communist movement was frequently penalized socially by loss of employment and other sanctions. The pioneer work on the political use of folk music appeared at the zenith of the McCarthy period in 1953. An exam-

[37] John Greenway, *American Folksongs of Protest* (Philadelphia: University of Pennsylvania Press, 1953).
[38] Cf. R. Serge Denisoff, "Protest Movements: Class Consciousness and the Propaganda Song," *Sociological Quarterly*, 9 (Spring 1968), 228–247; "The Proletarian Rei. 'scence: The Folkness of the Ideological Folk," *Journal of American Folklore*, 82 (January–March 1969), 51–65.

ination of the existing literature on this movement reflects the value difficulties involved in treating social movements in a given political climate.

Most students of urban folk music usage have ignored the Communist influence. Some have avoided any mention of the historical connection between various singers and social movements. Others have preferred to obscure the character and intent of social movements utilizing songs of persuasion by using such euphemisms as "liberal-labor movements." Ironically, extreme Rightists, relying upon Congressional citations, have missed most of the objective associations of protest singers and have pointed to folk singing in general as a Communist plot, which, of course, it is not.

Treatments of the relationship of folk music to social movements can be categorized in four major types, which reflect the evaluative assumptions of their authors: (1) segmental analysis, (2) selective avoidance, (3) sacrilege, and (4) conspiracy.[39]

The segmental analysis approach stresses one variable as opposed to alternative factors. Dunson's *Freedom in the Air* and Greenway's *American Folksongs of Protest* are two examples of this form of analysis. Dunson points out that "broad Left movements" helped bring folk music into the urban environment. He cites the influence of the Trade Union Unity League (TUUL), the Commonwealth Labor College, the Kentucky Workers Alliance, and the Highlander Folk School upon Northern social movements.[40] He further argues that the rejection of the "organization man" ethos by college students created a new generation of songmakers. Although Dunson's major contribution to the revival literature is his acknowledgment of the role of the Communists, this is done on a highly selective basis. For example, in comparison to the labor colleges the very important Almanac Singers receive little attention. Nor does Dunson answer such significant questions as: How did the TUUL color the musical migration of the early thirties? What was the role of the Socialist labor colleges such as Brookwood? Did Communist ideology play a significant role in the sectarian folk renaissance of the "red decade"?

In part, Greenway's controversial pioneer work on protest songs exhibits parallel trends.[41] While Dunson can be charged with journalistic overstatement in some areas, Greenway errs in the opposite direction. Greenway correctly associates songs with social movements, citing the Populists, the Industrial Workers of the World, and segments of the

---

[39] This typology is not exclusive since some of the works reviewed occasionally fall into more than one category.
[40] Josh Dunson, *Freedom in the Air* (New York: International Publishers, 1965), pp. 22–30.
[41] John Greenway, *American Folksongs of Protest* (Philadelphia: University of Pennsylvania Press, 1953), pp. 243–309.

CIO. At this point, however, this line of analysis ceases to exist. Instead, the author presents the lyrical and biographical portraits of four songmakers of protest material. Three of these performers are significant owing to their membership and participation in social movements, yet this relationship is never made explicit.[42] The affiliations of historical figures are obscured. Fred Beal, a Communist organizer in Gastonia, becomes a "union leader."[43] In the case of Molly Jackson, a TUUL organizer, Greenway suggests that she composed "The Murder of Harry Simms," which was later altered by a "foreign source" to include references to the Young Communist League (YCL). Other students, however, contend that Mrs. Jackson was not the composer of this piece and that the original lyric did in fact refer to the affiliations of a martyred YCL worker.[44] Woody Guthrie's politics and personality also receive a historical transformation. Woody's Communist associations are generally omitted: his tenure as a *People's World* and *Daily Worker* columnist are not mentioned, and his association with the Almanac Singers is almost entirely overlooked.[45] The political origins of "Union Maid," "The Rainbow Room Incident," and Guthrie's relationship to the Peoples' Songs, Inc., are equally misrepresented.[46] The importance of Ella May Wiggins, Molly Jackson, and Woody Guthrie, in the proletarian revival of the late 1930s is not to be underestimated, but Greenway's analysis of their abilities as singers does little to suggest this significance.[47] Pete Seeger offers a possible explanation of why an otherwise forceful book contains these errors: "I don't trust political analyses when they're made at the height of the Cold War and you can't speak the truth without getting someone in serious trouble."[48]

The second error of omission found in the literature is that of selective avoidance of key variables, usually reflected in the authors' use of esoteric meaning or innuendo. For example, terms such as radical, progressive, worker, anti-Fascist, partisan, or one big union, while they may suggest a specific meaning to students of left-wing lexicon, say little to the general reader. In the 1930s and 1940s the terms worker, working folks,

[42] Aunt Molly Jackson was an organizer for the National Miners Union, the Communist-led Trade Union Unity League, and the Trade Union Educational League. The latter organization also included Ella May Wiggins in its membership. In the forties, Woody Guthrie applied for party membership on several occasions, but was refused admittance.
[43] Greenway, *op. cit.*, pp. 134, 250.
[44] Jim Garland, "Murder of Harry Simms," *Sing Out*, 16 (1966), 12.
[45] Cf. Woody Guthrie, *American Folksong* (New York: Oak Publications, 1961), pp. 1–14.
[46] Cf. Gordon Friesen, "The Almanac Singers: End of the Road," *Broadside*, 16 (1962), n.p.; "People's Songs," *The Worker* (March 13, 1946), 7.
[47] Compare Greenway's account with Ellen Stekert's, "Cents and Nonsense in the Urban Folksong Movement: 1930–1966," in Bruce Jackson, ed., *Folklore and Society* (Hatsboro, Pennsylvania: Folklore Associates, 1966), pp. 153–168.
[48] Pete Seeger, "Remembering Woody," *Mainstream*, 16 (August 1963), 31.

and progressive movement referred to the Communist Party. Yet even the Communists would be confused by contemporary usage of these terms.[49]

Many examples of selective avoidance could be cited. Ellen Stekert, in characterizing Guthrie, writes: "He, like most of these people (Seeger, Lomax, etc.) was caught in the union and socialist movements of the time. . . ."[50] According to Brand, "the record shows an uncommon number of folk singers peopling activities of the left wing."[51] Silber characterizes the Stalinists as "the liberal-labor movement of the 1930s."[52] Dunson, the most explicit of these writers, notes that ". . . the Almanacs were part of the progressive and left movements of the time"[53] and says that "Not only the Almanacs, but many traditional singers in those years identified themselves, intellectually as well as musically, with broad Left movements."[54] Jargon phrases such as socialist-oriented or left wing, when not used by those involved in Marxian movements, are of little value since they are applicable to a myriad of organizations ranging from Social Democrats to Trotskyists. When Guthrie speaks of anti-Fascists or trade unionists or working folks, a specific meaning can be derived. Logically, when the terms progressive movement or the Left are used in the context of the thirties, they ought to indicate the Communist Party, the dominant movement of the period. However, the contemporary use of this terminology tends to obscure the variable of affiliation with the American Communist movement. Given these characterizations, many other observers have identified Guthrie, Seeger, and others as primarily labor or union singers.[55] Seeger, in a recent interview, outlined his relationship to the labor movement as follows: "Woody and I, when we went to sing for the labor unions . . . we didn't think of the union as a little protective association, we thought of it as one step to try to bring the world together."[56]

Avoidance also assumes the form of total omission of significant data. For example, except for the Friedland-Glazer album, no mention is ever made of Trotskyist material, however limited.[57] Lawless' biographies of folk performers also exclude all mention of social movements despite the

---

[49] R. Serge Denisoff, "Songs of Persuasion: A Sociological Analysis of Urban Propaganda Songs," *Journal of American Folklore*, 79 (October–December 1966), 585–586.
[50] Stekert, *op. cit.*, p. 161.
[51] Oscar Brand, *The Ballad Mongers* (New York: Funk & Wagnalls, 1962), p. 124.
[52] Irwin Silber, "Folk Music and the Success Syndrome," *Sing Out*, 14 (1964), 2–4.
[53] Dunson, *op. cit.*, p. 17.
[54] *Ibid.*, p. 17.
[55] Cf. Pete Seeger, "Whatever Happened to Singing in the Unions," *Sing Out*, 15 (May 1965), 29–31; and Page Stegner, "Labor History in Fact and Song," *Caravan* (June–July 1960), 8–16.
[56] "Pete Seeger–Profile," (Seattle, KING–TV, November 3, 1968).
[57] Bill Friedland and Joe Glazer, "Ballads for Sectarians" (notes), (Detroit: Labor Arts, 1952).

fact that a large number of the performers included in this book were politically active.[58]

Another trend found in the analyses of the "city-billy" phenomenon is that of sacrilege. This orientation assumes that traditional folk material has been tarnished by Communist association and usage. As one folklorist commented, "folklorists and musicologists have looked askance at the movement and regarded the new material as unworthy of their scholarly academic consideration."[59] This attitude is quite understandable since most aspects of the relationship of social movements to folk material are outside the definitional and conceptualized criteria of folklore. This, however, has not inhibited folklorists such as Wilgus, Dorson, and James from taking open issue with the urban-political use of folk material.[60] Wilgus has said of "peoples' song":

> The inconsistencies and sophistries of the "democratic" interpretation, and substitution of politics for scholarship and well-meant sympathies for facts, should not lead one to conclude that folksong is *undemocratic*; but one must recognize that it is *non-political* (in the sense that political considerations cannot rightly influence its definition or interpretation). . . .[61]

The most powerful statement encompassing the sacrilegious orientation is Ellen Stekert's "Cents and Nonsense in the Urban Folksong Movement: 1930–1966." Stekert begins by noting that folk songs were imported into the urban milieu by "conscientious and adamant left-wing political groups." At the same time, "unskilled performers" such as Woody Guthrie and Molly Jackson appeared on the scene to further the "politically oriented folksong movement of the 1930's."[62] In examining the work of Guthrie, the ideal type of the "red decade," she indicates that the Dustbowl singer "produced reams of abominable prose and ditties . . . only the smallest fraction of which is aesthetically worth anything either in the folk culture from which he came or in the urban culture to which he wanted at times to belong."[63] This psychologically and artistically based evaluation does little to add to the understanding of Guthrie's relationship to social movements or the "red decade."[64]

[58] See Ray M. Lawless, *Folksingers and Folksongs in America* (New York: Duell and Sloan, 1960).
[59] Willard Rhodes, "Folk Music, Old and New," in Jackson, *op. cit.*, p. 11.
[60] D. K. Wilgus, *Anglo-American Folksong Scholarship Since 1898* (Rutgers: Rutgers University Press, 1959), pp. 220–228. Richard Dorson, "Folklore and the NDEA," *Journal of American Folklore*, 75 (April–June 1962), 162–163; and Thelma James, "Folklore and Propaganda," *Journal of American Folklore*, 61 (October–December 1948), 311.
[61] D. K. Wilgus, "Folksong and Democracy," *Gifthorse* (1949), 19.
[62] Stekert, *op. cit.*, pp. 154–155.
[63] *Ibid.*, p. 162.
[64] Richard A. Reuss, *Woody Guthrie: Bibliography 1912–1967* (New York: Guthrie Children's Trust Fund, 1968), pp. i–v.

The final approach, that of conspiracy, is the argument that folk singers were conscious tools of a domestic or foreign conspiracy.[65] While the major contemporary advocates of this position are to be found in the ranks of the extreme Right, several of the articles and books discussed above have toyed with this theme. The demonological hypothesis is best summarized by Fred Schwartz of the Christian Anti-Communist Crusade, who argued that the Communists have been and still are using folk singing for subversive purposes.[66] Several government publications have stated a similar theme.[67] The most widely circulated and sophisticated exposition of this view is in David Noebel's *Rhythm, Riots, and Revolutions*. Noebel, relying upon government sources and very few Communist publications, argues that the Proletarian Musicians Association in Moscow ordered the use of folk music in the United States, a command carried out by Peoples' Songs, Inc.—some fifteen years later. The author continues his hypothesis, indicting performers and musical outlets of folk material, both traditional and political, as subversives attempting to indoctrinate American youth. The inaccuracy of many conclusions in this volume is best illustrated by the author's identification of the Weavers as members of the Communist Party, despite the fact that Noebel's own source, Harvey Matusow, disclaimed this accusation in his book *False Witness* (1955).[68] A number of "superpatriots," such as the Fire and Police Research Association of Los Angeles and the John Birch Society, have accused all folk singers of being Communists.

Another interpretation can be subsumed under the conspiratorial view. This position assumes the "innocent dupe" position advanced by Lyons in *The Red Decade*; according to this argument, Communists did play a part in the development of folk music to further their revolutionary aims, and "took in" performers in the process.[69] Josh White, in "I Was a Sucker for the Communists," employs this theme. Others, like Burl Ives and Oscar Brand, also present cases against Communist Party policy.[70] These singers argue that their talents were used and that they were not able to function freely in left wing circles such as Peoples' Songs, Inc.[71]

[65] Stekert, *op. cit.*, p. 169; Jere Real, "Folk Music and Red Tubthumpers," *American Opinion*, 7 (1964), 19–24; Fire and Police Research Association, "When Is Folk Not Folk Music?" (Los Angeles, 1963); David A. Noebel, *Rhythm, Riots, and Revolution* (Tulsa: Christian Crusade Press, 1966).
[66] "Be Careful,' *New Republic* (January 23, 1965), 8; and "A New and Effective Anti-Communist Weapon," n.d.
[67] See the Appendix to Noebel, *op. cit.*, pp. 280–320.
[68] *Ibid.*, p. 128; Harvey Matusow, *False Witness* (New York: Cameron and Kahn, 1955), p. 51.
[69] Eugene Lyons, *The Red Decade* (New York: Bobbs-Merrill, 1941).
[70] Josh White, "I Was a Sucker for the Communists," *Negro Digest* (December 1950), 26–31; Brand, *op. cit.*, p. 136; "Testimony of Burl Ives," *Subversive Infiltration of Radio, Television, and the Entertainment Industry* (Washington, D.C.: U.S. Senate, 1952), pp. 205–228.
[71] Cf. Brand, *op. cit.*, p. 136.

Since most of these statements were made during the McCarthy period, it is difficult to avoid giving credence to *Sing Out!* magazine's editorial statement that these disclaimers were in part politically inspired.[72]

Karl Mannheim, in developing his thesis of the sociology of knowledge, suggested that the societal conditions of a particular era give rise to ideology and thought. Consequently, several of the above treatments can be placed within a context of ideological and opportunistic anti-Communism based on the precepts of radical rightism and overt fear of media blacklists. Other students, plagued by the nightmare of "red-baiting" charges, have shied away from the political and ideological aspects of urban folk music growth. To label folk music as intrinsically Communist is to ignore history; to deny the relationship between the CPUSA and urban folk singing is to falsify history. Considering the state of urban folk music research, one is led to concur with Archie Green that little objectivity has been present in assessments of "the role of Communists in unions before and after World War II. Woody Guthrie, Leadbelly, Pete Seeger (and their fellow Peoples' Artists partisans) were important figures in the development of CIO lore. To date, students have shied away from this trio's politics in favor of accounts of charisma or conquest." [73]

In sum, the historical context of social movement research and the political attitudes of researchers can lead to a distortion of history and the presentation of a partial or false picture of what actually took place. As we have seen, these distortions are frequently carried on by other researchers who do not go beyond the original data.

CONCLUSION

Social movements research is a relatively new phenomenon, stemming in part from the nineteenth-century polemic between the "restorers" and "preservers" of the social order on the one hand, and the "reconstructionist," change-oriented social philosophers on the other. For both factions, the political and social implications of social movements justified their study of them. One of the first historical events that received attention as a social movement was the Bolshevik Revolution of 1917. Although this revolution motivated many accounts, generally journalistic and partisan, in the United States and Europe, the main attention of American social scientists was directed toward the fledgling labor movement, esoteric religious cults, and lynch mobs. All these topics, however, were over-

---

[72] "Oscar Brand Joins Witch Hunt Hysteria," *Sing Out*, 2 (1951), 16.
[73] Archie Green, "American Labor Lore: Its Meanings and Uses," *Industrial Relations*, 4 (February 1965), 66–67.

shadowed by the rise of the Nazi movement, which stimulated a vast amount of research and commentary. More recently, peace movements, the civil rights movement, and student radicalism have prompted numerous studies. By their very nature, then, the kinds of phenomena amenable to social movements research are those around which value controversies will rage. Consequently, it is this area of study in which the social scientist will find it most difficult to be ethically neutral.

Max Weber, in his classic essay "Science as a Vocation," was the first to expound the value free notion in the social sciences. In its most simplistic sense, this concept maintains that the values and opinions of the individual should not color his work as a social scientist. While many observers, among them Gouldner, Mills, and Myrdal, have correctly noted that this dictum is frequently vitiated by theoretical stances and methodological techniques, the fact remains that the value free notion is generally accepted by most social scientists. The authors contend, however, that ethical neutrality is a rare commodity in the social sciences.

In the area of social movements research, value judgments are particularly problematical. Social movements are, as most observers indicate, oriented to some form of social change which can influence the social scientist as a citizen. Consequently, the social scientist's perception of the desirability of the type of change advocated by a movement frequently colors his research. The theoretical perspective of the researcher also injects values into social movement research. For example, a Marxist analyst will often idealize a reformist movement as an indicator of the inevitable "movement of the masses." On the other hand, a functionalist is apt to view a movement as a product of some structural strain which requires correction rather than total change. For some psychologists, social movements are collectivities of the maladjusted or the frustrated. Even the particular methodology employed by the social scientist and the historical period in which a study is undertaken can influence the objectivity of studies of social movements. Neutrality in the study of social movements is therefore difficult, if not impossible, to achieve.

THEORETICAL AND CONCEPTUAL APPROACHES TO SOCIAL MOVEMENTS

When sociologists look at social movements, they do so in terms of certain implicit conceptual frameworks. These are part of the conventional wisdom of the discipline and may be traced to the sociological trinity—Durkheim, Marx, and Weber. Consequently, most views of social movements revolve around three concepts: social disorganization, class, and status.[1] In this chapter, we propose to describe and analyze the use of these frameworks by sociologists in their approaches to social movements.

SOCIAL DISORGANIZATION

The social and political upheavals which rocked Europe during the eighteenth and nineteenth centuries spawned both the metaphysical tenets of sociology and the notion of social movements. In the wake of the French Revolution, scholars and partisans alike debated the question of power and order in society and discussed the efficacy and necessity of socialist revolution. The social changes taking place on the European continent crystallized the political ideologies of both the Right and the Left and suggested to radicals and intellectuals that the actions or movements of either great men or the masses would determine social evolution. Ideas of movement and dynamism therefore permeated the social philosophy and sociology of the nineteenth century. Hegel and his intellectual successors pointed to the "man on a white horse" as leading history. For contemporary social scientists this Napoleonic horseman has become the

---

[1] In recent years a fourth variant, based on the social action model, has come into vogue. See Neil J. Smelser, *The Theory of Collective Behavior* (Glencoe: Free Press, 1963). Here, Smelser suggests a "normative" model of social movements within the broader context of "collective behavior."

charismatic leader. Others, however, suggested social rather than individual approaches to change. Another German, Lorenz von Stein, stated that movements of the proletariat—"the Social Movement"—were the crux of any explanation about society. Rudolf Heberle saw Stein's contribution as twofold:

> . . . he makes a clear conceptual distinction between the theoretical systems or doctrines . . . and the actual social movement . . . , and . . . he ascribes to the study of the social movement a central place in his system of sociology. Not only is the emergence of the social movement given as the reason why a science of society is needed, but Stein's entire system is really built around the analysis of the origin and movements of the social classes and their influence upon the forms of government.[2]

Revolutionary theorists perceived classes as the bearers of the seeds of change. Marx, Goodwin, Proudhon, Saint-Simon, and their followers could not conceive of armies of industrial workers living unquestioningly in the Dickensian misery of the overcrowded slums of England and the continent. On the other hand, many did not see fruitful change stemming from the "unwashed" mob. The English statesman and political theorist Edmund Burke, repulsed by the Reign of Terror, decried the liberation of the rabble. Theorists like Comte and Durkheim tried to find the answer to social order and change in man's religious beliefs, and addressed Ivan Karamazov's problem, "If God does not exist then everything is permitted," in an attempt to find a new morality based on science. The Hegelian nominalists, typified by Simmel, Tonnies, and Weber, desired change but, given their authoritarian conceptualizations of the social structure, could find little hope of success.

Thus, we find that most of the concepts now used, and misused, in the analysis of social movements have their roots in the social, political, and moral conditions of eighteenth- and nineteenth-century Europe. As Isabella laments in Wuthering Heights, "I can't go on living in all this disorder." For sociologists and other students of change and movements, the idea of social disorganization has become an integral part of their conceptual toolbox. Much of the blame for this disorganization has been laid at the feet of industrialization and its attendant specialization of labor. In his classic thesis, The Division of Labor in Society, Emile Durkheim postulated that in the "organic" form of society cohesion or integration is dependent upon a division of labor which, owing to increasing specialization, may in the long run create dissensus or lack of

---

[2] Lorenz von Stein, quoted and discussed in Rudolf Heberle, Social Movements: An Introduction to Political Sociology (New York: Appleton-Century-Crofts, 1951), pp. 4–5.

cohesion. He suggested that a highly specialized division of labor could lead to the individual being hemmed in by his task—isolated by the nature of his specialty. When this happens, "Collective sentiments become more and more impotent in holding together the centrifugal tendencies that the division of labor is said to engender, for these tendencies increase as labor is more divided, and at the same time collective sentiments are weakened."[3] The division of labor does not necessarily produce interdependence and solidarity in all instances. Indeed, it can produce anomie (normlessness). For Durkheim, anomie is a state of isolation from society which leads to individual pathologies such as crime and suicide.

Although Durkheim's concept of anomie was not originally addressed to the topic of social change, it appears to have suggested at least three explanations for the formation of social movements, although other theoretical forebears can be claimed. These explanations are: the politics of mass society, alienation, and the politics of isolation.

Mass Society

In the late eighteenth and early nineteenth centuries several political theories emerged in reaction to the social changes occurring in France. Edmund Burke advanced his notion of a mobocracy (mob-controlled society). Burke and other conservative writers postulated three major trends in society: (1) growing egalitarianism resulting from loss of traditional authority; (2) widespread readiness to support antiaristocratic forms of rule, that is, quest for popular authority; (3) rule of the masses or domination by pseudo-authority. The premise originally contained in the concept of mass society was, therefore, the incapacity of the mass to rule itself. This argument may be traced, of course, to the earlier writings of Hobbes, who saw a commonwealth of subjects unified by sovereign power as the only hope for social and political order. In contrast, John Stuart Mill held that every man was created equal and therefore had a stake in society and should be permitted access to the decision making process. Proudhon, Bakunin, Marx, and other theorists of the nineteenth century, while disagreeing with the Millsian view of economics, concurred with his social theories and suggested that elites were exploiting mass man and should be curtailed or done away with.

The basic dichotomy in these early theories was that of the individual in opposition to an elite—a democratic versus an aristocratic view of political man. Over half a century later, this political-theoretical polemic was to be resumed in the guise of the theory of mass society, or, more specifically, mass politics, advocated by Arendt, Fromm, Kornhauser,

[3] Emile Durkheim, *The Division of Labor in Society*, trans. George Simpson (Glencoe: Free Press, 1964), p. 361.

Mannheim, and Selznick. The basic premise of this conceptualization is that society has evolved from gemeinschaft to gesellschaft, from folk to urban, from mechanical to organic. Owing to this process, the masses, lacking social cohesion and integration, have become politically alienated. The individual, however, still requires a sense of identification and is therefore susceptible to the appeals of mass movements and extremist politics. Joseph R. Gusfield, in a dissenting article, outlines this mass society argument and suggests that although forces leading to political extremism are evident as a consequence of "massification," greater political integration is also possible. He argues that the conditions of mass society operate against the emergence of strong ideological attachments, promote an acceptance of innovation and a tolerance of dissent, and hence are consistent with balanced, pluralistic politics.

Excerpts from Joseph R. Gusfield, "Mass Society and Extremist Politics," American Sociological Review, *Vol. 27 (February 1962), pp. 19–27. Reprinted by permission of the American Sociological Association.*

A dominant stream of thought in current political sociology explains many contemporary anti-democratic movements as products of a distinctive social organization—Mass Society. Writers who utilize this approach have maintained that modern, Western societies increasingly show characteristics of mass organization which sharply differ from the features of such societies in the nineteenth and earlier centuries. Mass societies, in this view, demonstrate a form of politics in which traditional sociological concepts, such as class or culture, are not relevant to an understanding of the sources, genesis, or careers of extremist, anti-democratic political movements. Mass politics is the form of political action unique to mass societies. As modern democratic societies become mass societies, we may then anticipate that political crises are likely to generate extremist, anti-democratic responses. Leading advocates of this theory of "mass politics," in whole or part, are Hannah Arendt, Erich Fromm, Karl Mannheim, William Kornhauser, Robert Nisbet, and Philip Selznick.[4] This paper

[4] The following relevant writings embody the theory of mass politics: Hannah Arendt, *The Origins of Totalitarianism* (New York: Harcourt, Brace and Co., 1954); Erich Fromm, *Escape From Freedom* (New York: Rinehart, 1945); Karl Mannheim, *Man and Society in an Age of Reconstruction* (London: Routledge and Kegan Paul, 1940); William Kornhauser, *The Politics of Mass Society* (Glencoe, Ill.: Free Press, 1959); Robert Nisbet, *The Quest for Community* (New York: Oxford University Press, 1953); Philip Selznick, *The Organizational Weapon* (New York: McGraw-Hill, 1952).

is a critical analysis of this approach and a reformulation of some of the relations between mass societies and political action.

There are two major contentions in this paper. The first is a criticism of the assumptions about democratic politics underlying the theory of mass politics. The second is a reformulated theory of the relation between mass society and political extremism in contemporary, democratic societies.

It is our first contention that implicit in the theory of mass politics is an idealized conception of the pluralistic social and political system held necessary for the maintenance of democratic institutions. This conception is idealized in that it fails to give adequate weight to barriers which conflicts of interest offer to political harmony and compromise under any political structure.

Our second contention is that the elements of mass societies viewed with alarm by mass politics theorists in actuality contain positive connotations for the maintenance of democratic political institutions. Mass communications, bureaucratic institutions, and equalitarianism have implications which strengthen pluralistic political structure. Extremist politics may be expected in modern societies as a response of those adversely affected by the changes towards a mass society and most insulated from mass institutions. Contrary to the theory of mass politics traditional concepts of political sociology *are* adequate to the analysis of extremism.

It must be made clear that our major interest in this paper is in the explanation of anti-democratic movements as they develop within historically democratic societies. This excludes consideration of authoritarian regimes in traditional societies or the development of anti-democratic movements in developing economies under the impact of intensive social and economic change.[5] Our interest is confined to those writers who explain such modern extremist movements as Fascism, Communism, or McCarthyism by reference to the characteristics of mass society. These represent one variant of mass society theory, but an influential one.[6]

---

[5] See the discussion of the political effects of social and economic change in Western and non-Western societies in Kornhauser, *op. cit.*, Chs. 7, 8.

[6] We have confined our analysis here to theorists who find mass societies an explanatory tool in analyzing the rise of contemporary anti-democratic movements. Other writers have also described modern society as mass-like and have evaluated it in negative terms. This latter group, however, has not viewed political extremism as a likely consequence of mass conditions. Writers such as David Riesman, in *The Lonely Crowd*, and C. Wright Mills, in *The Power Elite*, have emphasized developing trends toward conformity and passivity rather than toward militance and activism. Still another stream in mass society writings is represented by E. A. Shils. He agrees that modern society is, by reason of mass conditions, best described as qualitatively different from earlier Western societies. This stream of writings, however, denies the disorganizing and overconforming consequences stressed by the other views. See the positive acceptance of mass society in Edward A. Shils, "Mass Society and Its Culture," *Daedalus*, 89, (Spring 1960), 288–314.

MASS SOCIETY AND THE THEORY OF MASS POLITICS

Mass Society analysts view modern social systems as significantly different from non-industrial and earlier societies. Whatever the differences among individual writers, there is a common core of description in the term "mass society" which suggests the attenuation of primary and local associations and groups. Impersonal, bureaucratized relationships in large-scale organizations have replaced the informal systems of loyalty in small groups and local affiliations. Equalitarian conditions and ideologies have weakened systems of political and social authority characteristic of stratified communities. Technological innovations have made possible a high degree of standardization, both of products and ideas. The elongation of the chain of organizational command has enhanced the possibilities of oligarchic control as local groups are less viable, hence less resistant to control. The emphasis is upon the breakdown of immediate relationships and differentiations so that the population is now more homogeneous but also less sharply identified and affiliated with distinctive social groups. It is in this sense that the theorist of mass society views the traditional categories of sociological analysis—family, class, community, ethnic identity, etc.—as having lost significance in mass societies. The mass is masslike: shapeless, structureless, undifferentiated. Mass politics theory traces the implication of this loss of differentiation for the bonds of loyalty to democratic political institutions.

Exponents of mass politics viewpoints have described modern Western, industrial societies as ones in which persons lack attachment to primary and secondary associations. "The chief characteristic of the mass-man," Hannah Arendt has written, "is not brutality and backwardness, but his isolation and lack of normal social relationships." [7] Political extremism, manifested in anti-democratic movements, is seen as a result of the *structural* and *psychological* consequences for political loyalty or disattachment to democratic procedures and aims.

Supporters of this view hold that structural characteristics of bureaucratization and equality undermine the functions of secondary and primary associations in inculcating values and in transmitting political norms. In mass society, such theories maintain, secondary associations of school, church, community or union, operate in a large-scale fashion. Rank-and-file identification with the organizational elite is diminished as the member's associational life is peripheral and tangential. The high mobility rates and standardized life styles destroy economic class as an important source of motivation and interest in political events. Institutions functioning under conditions of mass society do not touch the character and the personal values of those exposed to them. Being solely instrumental

[7] Hannah Arendt, *op. cit.*, p. 310.

means, the major associations and institutions of the society cannot act as agencies through which values are inculcated. Because of this, the political elites of the society cannot mediate political decisions to the acceptance of the rank-and-file. Such political "untouchables" are described by Selznick when he writes, "He has lost the meaning provided by the articulated social structure to which he belonged." [8]

In previous centuries the lack of integration of rank-and-file members of the society into political institutions was a matter of little political consequence. Mass societies, however, are politically equalitarian. The development of large aggregates of persons unattached to democratic political structures and norms is significant because such groups are capable of spontaneous development unguided by the norms of democratic society. The diminished role of intermediate structure—both institutions and specific political associations—leaves the person unattached and capable of being reunited into a new group. "A strong intermediate structure consists of stable and independent groups which represent diverse and frequently conflicting interests." [9] In mass society, however, the representative nature of these groups (classes, ethnic groups, regions, etc.) is undermined. Both because participation is peripheral and because political elites are limited in authority, mass societies are less able to control the values and political aspirations of citizens.

To the structural disintegration of society there is added the personal disorganization of the individual. The psychological consequences of mass society are described in terms of the feeling of detachment. The key word here is alienation, "a mode of experience in which the person experiences himself as an alien." [10] Whether the emphasis of the writer is on estrangement from work, the normlessness of contemporary culture or the powerless feeling of the individual in large-scale organizations, mass conditions are described as producing feelings of *malaise* and insecurity.

The alienation of the individual in modern societies is the psychological statement of detachment. It describes a condition in which the person is not involved in or committed to primary or secondary groups. It adds to this the description of the person as someone with positive, unfulfilled needs for identity, affection, and assurance.

In both its structural and psychological elements the theory of mass politics states that political alienation—the detachment of the person from political institutions—is a function of the disintegrating influences of mass society on the ties of sentiment and loyalty to specific groups which characterized the social structure of democracies in an earlier historical period. Without attachment to primary or to intermediate structures, the individual has no bond to national political institutions which command his loyalty to its political norms.

[8] Philip Selznick, *op. cit.*, p. 283.
[9] William Kornhauser, *op. cit.*, p. 78.
[10] Erich Fromm, *The Sane Society* (New York: Rinehart, 1955), p. 120.

PLURALISTIC AND EXTREMIST POLITICS

In the emphasis on a transition from an earlier historical period to a modern, mass society the theories here considered have suggested that political democracy functioned relatively unimpeded under non-mass conditions. It is imperative then that we examine the type of political structure from which mass politics is seen as differing. Political extremism is so defined in contradistinction to pluralistic politics. The mass theorist sees pluralist politics as impaired under current social conditions. As a corollary pluralistic structure is implicitly posited as an essential condition for democratic politics.

The theory of a balance of power among a plurality of groups has been the dominant analytical tool of American political scientists. Its classic defense has been presented in Hamilton's and Madison's *The Federalist Papers*.[11] The theory presupposes a society of many and diverse social groups. The political institutions force each group to moderate and compromise their interests in the interplay of party, secondary association, and locality. In the pluralist conception of the citizen, each person is integrated into politics in his capacity as member of some segment of the society—worker or manager, city or country dweller, Southerner or Northerner, immigrant or native, white or black. The units of politics are thus organized groups built upon the sentiments and interests of persons in their affiliations with specific primary associations which occupy positions and perform specific functions within the major institutions.

Pluralistic politics involves certain "rules of the game" by which political conflict is carried on. These "rules of the game," part of the definition of politics as an institution, are adhered to by the participants. Chief among tenets of democratic politics is acceptance of opposing forces into the political process on the same terms as those binding on one's own group. This acceptance supplies the necessity for political compromise and conciliation. If all groups possess some political power and are admitted into the political process, bargaining and negotiation are the chief modes of political conflict. Violence is ruled out as a possible way of solving social or economic conflicts.

It is essential to this process that each group be willing to accept the total or partial defeat of its aims and accept the total or partial achievement of the aims of its opponents. Compromise includes the ability to settle for less than full victory. This "realistic" orientation is achieved in an atmosphere governed by rational calculation of interests. It is most

[11] Roy P. Fairfield, ed., *The Federalist Papers* (Garden City, N.Y.: Anchor Books, 1961). For what are probably the best descriptions of this process in contemporary political science, see also David Truman, *The Governmental Process* (New York: Alfred A. Knopf, 1951), and V. O. Key, *Parties, Politics and Pressure Groups* (New York: Thomas Y. Crowell, 1947).

negated when objectives have become correlated with considerations of honor and when compromise, negotiation, and defeat are suffused with connotations of dishonor.

Political extremism occurs when movements advocate violation of the democratic, pluralist "rules of the game." Shils suggests a distinction between pluralistic and ideological politics which emphasizes the disattachment of the extremist from self-limiting and rationally calculative aspects of pluralism:

> Extremism consists in going to an extreme in zealous attachment to a particular value, e.g., private property, ethnic homogeneity, or status equality. . . . The extremist must be deeply alienated from the complex of rules which keep the strivings for various values in restraint and balance. An extremist group is an alienated group. . . . Its hostility is incompatible with that freedom from intense emotion which pluralistic politics needs for its prosperity. . . . The focus of the extremists' attention on one or a few completely fulfilled values and his impatience with compromise when a plurality of values, never internally consistent, have to be reconciled with each other makes the extremist feel that he is worlds apart from the compromising moderates.[12]

This distinction between pluralist and extremist politics differs, as others have pointed out,[13] from traditional distinctions between Right and Left, Conservative, Liberal and Radical, and reform and revolution. It is a distinction between styles and not between contents. It is in this sense that extremism is alienated from the institutions of democratic politics. It denies the legitimacy of democratic political institutions as devices for mediating conflict. Extremist style refuses to accept the possible or probable outcomes of whole or partial defeat. Total victory is too important in the hierarchy of values to permit of compromise.

In several ways, then, the extremist breaks with the normative patterns of pluralist political behavior: (1) *He attempts to close the political process to opposing forces:* Politics is held to be the legitimate area of conflict for some, but not for all groups. Both Fascism and Communism have made this a cornerstone of the political structure as well as a tenet of their movements.

---

[12] Edward A. Shils, *The Torment of Secrecy* (Glencoe, Ill.: Free Press, 1955), p. 231. In similar vein, Nathan Leites introduces his study of French politics by a statement exempting the Communists and the "extreme right" from his discussion. He reasons that their style in politics is distinctly different from the "national" groups of the Center. In the period of post-war politics which he studies, "the extremes entered but little in 'the game' so that the patterns of political calculation used in parliament had little reference to their behavior." Nathan Leites, *On the Game of Politics in France* (Stanford, Calif.: Stanford University Press, 1959), p. 1.

[13] Milton Rokeach, *The Open and Closed Mind* (New York: Basic Books, 1960), Ch. 3; Edward A. Shils, "Authoritarianism—Right and Left," in R. Christie and M. Jahoda, eds., *Studies in the Scope and Method of 'The Authoritarian Personality'* (Glencoe, Ill.: Free Press, 1954).

(2) *He attempts to carry on social and economic conflicts outside of political institutions:* The confinement of conflict to politics marks a cardinal principle of democratic politics. Violence, intimidation and fraud are excluded as a means of achieving group ends.

(3) *He impairs the culture of democratic discussion:* An emphasis is placed on the value of uniform opinions and behavior. The criteria of rational calculation of interests is replaced by intensive appeals to sentiment and symbolism. This strain in McCarthyism captured the attention of those concerned with extremism in politics. It is only in this sense that membership and participation in extremist movements seems authoritarian. The extremist style has little appreciation of dissent and schism in the total society.

The extremist movement is marked by the low degree of commitment to the values of procedure in democratic institutions. Pluralist norms enforce tolerance, barter, and the inclusion of opponents as joint members of the same social system. Extremist resentment against democratic politics is not that of indifference but that of intensive conviction. It is the thoroughly moralistic attitude which marks the extremist and distinguishes him from the slightly cynical pluralist.

As we have sketched it so far, political extremism is found in one or both forms: an increased attachment to a single, over-riding value or a weakened attachment to the norms of pluralist politics. In either case, the extremist is alienated from the *existing* democratic order.[14]

The theorists of mass politics visualize extremist movements as consequences of weakened attachments to political institutions and persons resulting from the breakdown in functioning of primary and secondary associations in mass societies. Without a sense of affiliation to specific interest groups, the citizen has no way to develop a frame of reference for political events. Intermediate secondary associations cannot touch him sufficiently to act as forces limiting intensity of opposition and resentment of rival political claims. Political figures become distrusted and democratic institutions no longer legitimate sources of social control. In Kornhauser's words: ". . . intermediate groups help to protect elites by functioning as channels through which popular participation in the

---

[14] It should be emphasized that the degree of commitment of democratic populations to its political institutions is a relative matter. Many studies of attitudes toward civil liberties show a great gap between the acceptance of civil liberties among a minority of educated and participating citizens and the rank and file, especially among the lower-income and lesser educated. In this case, political extremism represents less an alienation *from* political institutions than it does the advent of increased political democracy. For studies of civil liberties see Samuel Stouffer, *Communism, Conformity and Civil Liberties* (Garden City, N.Y.: Doubleday, 1955); Seymour Lipset, "Democracy and Working-Class Authoritarianism," in *Political Man* (Garden City, N.Y.: Doubleday, 1960), pp. 97–130, and Raymond Mack, "Do We Really Believe in the Bill of Rights?", *Social Problems*, 3 (April 1956), 264–269.

large society (especially in the national elites) may be directed and restrained." [15]

The mass theorist goes a step further and suggests that such detachment from democratic political institutions leaves the individual susceptible to political participation in extremist channels. The socially alienated individual is not only politically alienated; he is also more likely to become the extremist activist than is the member of a structured interest group. He is no longer limited in his attack on rivals by the controls of a structured pluralistic society. His resentments against opposing groups and against the existing institutions themselves need not be confined to the calculative, instrumental style of democratic politics. The mass man is a passionate supporter of ideology.

Lack of control mechanisms regulating the political attitudes and behavior of mass citizenry furthers the extremist character of participation in politics. It enables the person to project destructive impulses into the political arena. Mannheim, for example, maintained that in traditional societies collective impulses and wishes are absorbed by smaller groups and directed toward group aims. The social disintegration of modern society, he felt, set such impulses free to seek integration around some new object, often a symbol or a leader.[16]

The attenuation of local and primary associations and mediating secondary interest groups and associations is, in the theory of mass politics, the source of the extremism frequent in contemporary mass societies. As a system of analysis this view finds that traditional concepts of class and status aims are limited ways of characterizing political movements. As a philosophy of politics, the theory adds up to a defense of the virtues of a pluralistic political system. The transition from a pluralistic society to a mass society is implicitly and explicitly bemoaned. For this reason, the analysis of pluralist assumptions is central to our discussion.

PLURALISTIC SOURCES OF POLITICAL EXTREMISM

The theory of mass politics assumes that a pluralistic social structure diminishes the possibilities that political action will take extremist directions. Conflicts and demands for change will occur but will be moderated by adherence to the style of democratic institutions. An analysis of this assumption, however, shows that extremism both *can* and often *does* occur within pluralistic structures. There are at least four situations in which pluralism either invites or fails to forestall behavior outside the range of democratic norms for the mediation of conflict:

(1) *Disenfranchised classes*: Change often brings new groups into

[15] Kornhauser, *op. cit.*, p. 77.
[16] Mannheim, *op. cit.*, p. 62.

formation or increases the demands of old ones. In any case, at any given time, some groups are excluded from the political process. Often it is not in the interest of some or most of the included groups to accept new political forces. Excluded groups must either function outside of the political "game" or force their way into it. The militancy of the American Negro in the South today is of this nature. Compromise and legality are not relevant political alternatives unless a group is within the political structures in the first place.

(2) *Doomed and defeated classes:* The theory of democratic politics has never developed a satisfactory answer to the problem: When is compromise to be rejected? When is political defeat not an acceptable alternative to violence and other breaks with pluralist procedure? The facts of the American Civil War and of the Algerian crisis in contemporary France illustrate the thesis that well-structured groups, with channels of representation in parliamentary bodies, are far from willing to accept defeat of important aims through parliamentary procedures. Robert Dahl sees this as a serious impediment in democratic theory. Referring to the election of Abraham Lincoln in 1860, Dahl writes:

Thus any election interpreted as a clear-cut victory for one side was almost certain to be so intolerable to the other that it would refuse to accept the outcome. . . . Where each side is large and regards the victory of the other as a fundamental threat to some very highly ranked values, it is reasonable to expect serious difficulties in the continued operation of a (pluralistic) system.[17]

This is apt to be the case under conditions of social or economic change which gravely threaten a previous position of power and supremacy. To such "doomed classes,"[18] the future looks far less inviting than the past. A radical reorganization of society might be a solution to their problem but such a reorganization against politically ascendent forces is precisely what the moderating elements in the structure of political balance operate against. Recent discussions of the plight of the "old middle classes" in American life have stressed the indignation of these groups at their loss of power and status.[19] It is not a failure to "belong" that lies at the source of their alienation and possible "right-wing radicalism." Their response is touched off by the contents of the social changes to which they react.

(3) *Public opinion and the imbalance of competing interests:* The theory of democratic politics as a balance between competing interests often ignores the important role played by the neutral, non-competing

[17] Robert Dahl, *A Preface to Democratic Theory* (Chicago: University of Chicago Press, 1956), pp. 97–98.
[18] The term used by Franz Neumann in "Notes on the Theory of Dictatorship," in *The Democratic and the Authoritarian State* (Glencoe, Ill.: Free Press, 1957), p. 251.
[19] See the articles by Richard Hofstadter and by Seymour Lipset in Daniel Bell, ed., *The New American Right* (New York: Criterion Books, 1955). For a fuller treatment of this theme see Seymour M. Lipset, "Social Stratification and Right-Wing Extremism," *British Journal of Sociology*, 10 (December 1959), 1–32.

elements in the political process. A great many groups without specific interests in a particular issue nevertheless have power to effect governmental decisions. Such decisions are made with a concern for the general climate of opinion toward an issue. Whether the "public" is friendly or hostile is an important element in an interest group's decision to pursue its aims within or without the political process. As Murray Edelman has pointed out, labor will pursue its goals through economic processes (strikes, bargaining, etc.) when the political climate is hostile.[20] Recourse to non-political means is not ruled out by the existence of pluralistic machinery.

(4) *Development of periodic crisis:* Mass politics theory generally recognizes economic and military crisis as an essential "trigger" to extremist movements. Because pluralistic politics is oriented toward compromises between groups, it is less open to long run considerations. This is especially the case in issues of foreign policy. Unless there is some consensual basis other than group interest, elites must "sell" policy in terms communicable to specific classes and interests. Even assuming a diffusion of power in the form of what Riesman calls "veto groups,"[21] a hiatus develops between the long-run perspectives of government leaders and the short-run perspectives of intermediate associations and their constituencies. The result is often a stalemate and an immobilism which enables problems to develop into major crises. One instance of this is contained in LaPalombara's analysis of French and Italian politics in the post-war years.[22] He explains greater cohesion and agreement within the Italian moderate parties than among the French as a consequence of differences in the power of the Communist Party in each of the countries. Italian moderates were forced into agreement by fear. "While there has not been any serious fear in France that PCF could come peacefully to power, this reassuring assessment has been denied the democratic party leaders in Italy. . . . They have not been able to permit themselves the capricious inaction in which the French Center Party Leaders have indulged over the last decade."[23]

Inability of political elites to deal with crisis is itself one strong source of mass alienation from a political institution. Third parties have fared better at the polls in the United States during periods of economic depression than during periods of prosperity.[24] As Lipset has pointed out,

[20] Murray Edelman, "Government's Balance of Power in Labor–Management Relations," *Labor Law Journal,* 2 (January 1951), 31–35. This point is also discussed in C. Wright Mills, *The Power Elite* (New York: Oxford University Press, 1957), pp. 246–248.
[21] David Riesman, *The Lonely Crowd* (New Haven: Yale University Press, 1950), pp. 242–255.
[22] Joseph LaPalombara, "Political Party Systems and Crisis Government: French and Italian Contrasts," *Midwest Journal of Political Science,* 11 (May 1958), 117–139.
[23] *Ibid.,* p. 133.
[24] Murray and Susan Stedman, *Discontent at the Polls* (New York: Columbia University Press, 1950), Ch. 8.

there is a direct correlation between levels of economic well-being and the existence of democratic political systems.[25] Prosperous countries may avoid problems which threaten political stability in less affluent nations.

In each of these four situations, extremist politics is developed and conducted by well-structured groups, representing discrete and organized parts of the social structure, acting to secure goals related to group needs. While such groups are alienated from the existing political institutions they are not socially disintegrated or unrelated to the society and its political framework in which their values receive short shrift. Failure to recognize that pluralist assumptions cannot alone sustain political institutions is at the root of the implicit ideology of the theorist of mass politics.

THE PLURALIST IDEOLOGY

The sanguine view of political balance at the base of mass politics theory reveals a repetition of the ideological bias of nineteenth century liberalism —the assumption that there is a natural harmony of interests which sustains the social and political system. Occurrences of sharp conflict are therefore indicative of disruptions in the *form* of social arrangements. There is nothing in the *content* of interests and beliefs which makes compromise improbable. Mannheim reflects this ideology in a passage in *Man and Society* in which he suggests that experience in trade unions and in other associations trains participants for planning on a societal basis: "He is gradually realizing that by resigning partial advantages he helps to save the social and economic system and thereby also his own interest." [26]

The belief that participation in the primary and secondary associations of the society will moderate conflict arises from this ideological commitment to pluralist politics. It leads the mass politics theorist to identify political defeat with social alienation, to view extremist movements as actions of disattached persons, unrelated to specific social bases or pursuing interests of a discrete social base. Because of this tendency, the mass politics approach has felt traditional political analysis to be deficient.

It is *not* true that attachment to intermediate structures insures attachment to the larger national institutions and structures. As a society

---

[25] Seymour M. Lipset, "Economic Development and Democracy," in *Political Man, op. cit.*, pp. 45–76.
[26] Mannheim, *op. cit.*, p. 70. For discussions of the assumption of a natural harmony of interests see the analysis of sociological thought in C. Wright Mills, *op. cit.*, Ch. 11; Werner Stark, "Christian Thought in Social Theory" in *Social Theory and Christian Thought* (London: Routledge and Kegan Paul, 1959); Ralf Dahrendorf, *Class and Class Conflict in Industrial Society* (Stanford, Calif.: Stanford University Press, 1958).

undergoes change, it is likely that specific groups will be adversely affected by economic or social change. Similarly, some groups may develop new aspirations and objectives. In both cases they may come to feel that the existent political order is insufficient to command their allegiance. A shifting balance of forces is, however, not the same phenomenon as the breakup of an associational structure, the shattering of a class, or the decline of primary group support. It is even reasonable to maintain that an external threat to a group promotes its sense of solidarity and aids in the development of group identity and organization.[27] Attachment to intermediate structures may indeed promote a shared sense of alienation of the group from the total political order. The more informal organization the group possesses the more likely it is that politically extremist sentiments can be communicated and legitimated. In playing the game of politics, it is not only important whether or not one is permitted to play, but also whether one is winning or not. This problem is not solved by the degree of access which the group has to political association.

The point can be made through an analysis of a frequently used study of McCarthyist attitudes, which mass politics theorists have used as support for their position. Trow's study of Bennington, Vermont found a disproportionate amount of people for Senator McCarthy among small businessmen, especially those holding the nineteenth century liberal hostility to both big business and labor unions.[28] In explaining his findings, Trow maintains that not only are small businessmen "resentful of a world that continually offends their deepest values" but equally important is the fact that they have little voice or representation in political institutions, such as the major parties. Granting the rather dubious assumption that small business has little place in the current constellation of political and ideological forces in the United States, the picture of disaffection portrayed in Trow's study is a classic picture of a well-organized economic group losing out in the process of social and economic change. This type of disaffection is readily analyzed in terms of class and status conflict. If mass movements are not to be understood in traditional forms of political analysis, they must be shown to be unrelated to analysis in terms of group interests and discrete social bases. This would involve more than the traditional view that social change produces disaffection among groups adversely exposed to it.

The assumption of a natural harmony of interests gives rise to another failing of the mass politics approach. This is the lack of concern for the development of consensus around the norms of democratic politics. If it is assumed that representation of interests assures harmony, then the

[27] See the discussion of this factor in the history of labor movements in Sidney and Beatrice Webb, *History of Trade Unionism* (New York: Longmans, Green and Co., 1920), Ch. 1, and in Selig Perlman, *Theory of the Labour Movement* (New York: Augustus M. Kelly, 1928), Ch. 5.
[28] Martin Trow, "Small Business, Political Tolerance, and Support For McCarthy," *American Journal of Sociology*, 64 (November 1958), 270–281.

problem of achieving moral sentiments supportive of the political institution becomes meaningless. However, such moral sentiments *are* essential; otherwise, the source of moderate politics, of commitment to the political process *per se* is missing. When the values at stake are intensely held and the constellation of political forces is adverse to a group, there is nothing in pluralistic theory which suggests a source of loyalty to moderateness. Oscar Gass has expressed this in excellent fashion:

> I know that Democracy is a technique for reaching agreement, but it in turn rests upon a measure of agreement. It is, of course, formally true that, if only you agree on the techniques of getting decision, you don't have to agree on the outcome. But that is merely like saying that people can ride on the same bus even if they wish to get off at different places. The places must not be *too* different—or else they have to set a value on riding beyond that of getting to their destinations.[29]

A pluralistic system can be maintained only if the conflict of interest groups is balanced to some extent by cohesive elements in the cultural and social system which moderate the intensity of conflicts and which provide loyalties to maintenance of a defined area in which politics is conducted under pluralistic rules.[30] The ideology of pluralism has become a defense of moderateness, and an attack on political activism. Yet pluralist structure enhances activist sentiments. . . .

Alienation

In the Economic and Philosophic Manuscripts of 1844, *Marx employed the Hegelian term alienation to depict the essence of the capitalistic civil society. The alienated man "experienced himself not as an agent but as patient, not as creator but creature, not as self-determined but other-determined."* [31] *For Marx, the capitalistic mode of production alienates a man from the things he creates, from himself, and from his fellow men. As a consequence, man becomes a commodity. Many contemporary writers including Seeman, Nettler, Glazer, and Fromm, have attempted to specify this concept more precisely.*[32] *Although the analytical use of the*

---

[29] Oscar Gass, "Socialism and Democracy," *Commentary*, 29 (June 1960), 574.
[30] For an especially illuminating statement of this view, see Adolf Lowe, *The Price of Liberty*, Day-to-Day Pamphlets, No. 36 (London: Hogarth Press, 1937). Also see Edward A. Shils and M. Young, "The Meaning of the Coronation," *Sociological Review*, series 1 (1953), 63–81. Political consensus as a focus of sociological study is a central theme in Seymour M. Lipset, "Political Sociology" in Robert K. Merton, Leonard Broom, and Leonard S. Cottrell, Jr., eds., *Sociology Today* (New York: Basic Books, 1959).
[31] Lewis Feuer, "What is Alienation? The Career of a Concept," in Maurice Stein and Arthur Vidich, eds., *Sociology on Trial* (Englewood Cliffs, N.J.: Prentice-Hall, 1963), p. 129.
[32] Melvin Seeman, "On the Meaning of Alienation," *American Sociological Review*, 24 (December 1959) 783–791; Gwynn Nettler, "A Measure of Alienation," *American*

concept of alienation has been addressed most generally to investigations of institutional settings such as hospitals, reformatories, and industrial settings, it has also been applied to political analysis. Morton Grodzins' work provides one example. He discusses alienation as follows: "Disloyalty is . . . achieved under more generalized conditions of dissatisfaction, when the weakness rather than the strength of small loyalties is controlling. Marx called this illness of modern life alienation; others have described the same social facts as anomie and as the quality of social madness." [33] He then applies this "social illness" mode of analysis to conscientious objectors and members of the American Communist Party. Levin, another student of political alienation, defines alienation as a ". . . psychological state of an individual characterized by feelings of estrangement." [34] Thus, political alienation becomes ". . . the feeling of an individual that he is not a part of the political process." [35] Levin accounts for the rise of social movements by linking political alienation with projection, identification with a charismatic leader, and rational activism.

In recent years, the concept of alienation has been applied increasingly to student protest groups. David Horowitz, in The Student, was among the first to equate the university with the factory and the student with a product—the Marxian commodity. Although specifying these conditions, Horowitz does not use the term alienation. Other observers, however, have not been so restrained. Mario Savio, a leader of the Free Speech Movement (FSM) at the Berkeley campus of the University of California in 1964, also uses the Marxian theme: "There comes a time when the operation of the machine becomes so odious, makes you so sick at heart . . . that you've got to say to the people who run it, to the people who own it, that unless you're free, the machine will be prevented from working at all." [36] More explicitly, ". . . the students are frustrated; they can find no place in society where alienation doesn't exist." [37] The literature of the FSM also suggests a similar theme:

In our practical, fragmented society too many of us have been alone.[38]

The awareness of and concern for alienation . . . [opens up another approach

---

Sociological Review, 22 (December 1957) 670–677; Erich Fromm, ed., Marx's Concept of Man (New York: Ungar, 1963), pp. 43–69.
[33] Morton Grodzins, The Loyal and the Disloyal: Social Boundaries of Patriotism and Treason (Chicago: University of Chicago Press, 1956), p. 133.
[34] Murray B. Levin, The Alienated Voter: Politics in Boston (New York: Holt, Rinehart and Winston, 1960), p. 59.
[35] Levin, ibid., p. 61.
[36] Adam Hochschild, "The New UC Campus: A Year After FSM," San Francisco Chronicle (December 2, 1965), 6.
[37] S. M. Lipset and Paul Seabury, "The Lesson of Berkeley," The Reporter (January 28, 1965), 39.
[38] See "FSM: Moral Impetus, the Factory, and the Society," in "We Want a University" (Berkeley: FSM, 1965), p. 3.

to future activity because] . . . alienation is manifested as a state of mind.
. . . [It is caused by] the knowledge factory and its corporate domination.[39]
The nature of this deepest motivation is superficially summed up in the word
alienation, the object of hostility and cause of alienation is summed up in the
symbol of the IBM card. . . .[40]

Turning from this radical and normative use of the term alienation,
we find S. M. Lipset using it analytically as a causal variable in his discussion of the student revolt.[41] When applied to social movements in
this way, alienation has come to signify social isolation—a meaningless,
normless, powerless state in which individuals feel no sense of belonging.[42]
However useful these analytic concepts may be to social scientists, they do
not, as real states of consciousness, appear to be endemic to campus
radicals or advocates of student power. On the contrary, we may suggest
that they occupy the more classical role, that of ideological reference
points around which student opposition to the dehumanizing aspects of
the multiversity is organized.

In the following excerpt from John Horton's critical analysis of
contemporary sociology, we are reminded of the sociological and philosophical foundations of the concepts of alienation and anomie. According
to Horton, the original use of these terms was normative rather than
analytical.

*Excerpts from John Horton, "The Dehumanization of Anomie
and Alienation: A Problem in the Ideology of Sociology," The
British Journal of Sociology, Vol. 15 (December, 1964), pp.
285–291. Reprinted by permission of John Horton, Routledge
and Kegan Paul Ltd., and London School of Economics.*

ALIENATION AND ANOMIE AS RADICAL CONCEPTS: THE TRADITION OF MARX AND DURKHEIM

A first step in the ideological analysis of anomie and alienation is an
examination of their classical meanings in the works of Marx and Durkheim. The discussion will be organized around several contentions:

---

[39] Robert Kaufman and Michael Folson, "FSM: An Interpretative Essay," in *FSM*
(San Francisco, W. E. B. Du Bois Clubs of America, 1965), p. 50.
[40] *Ibid.*, p. 29.
[41] Lipset and Seabury, *op. cit.*, pp. 36–40.
[42] Grodzins, *ibid.*, p. 133.

(1) Classical definitions of anomie and alienation contain radical ethical and political directives. The concepts are ethically grounded metaphors for an attack on the economic and political organization of the European industrial middle classes. Paradoxically, alienation and anomie are used today by the successors of the very classes which the classical concepts attacked.

(2) Classical definitions of anomie and alienation contain different ideologies; they are counter-concepts with different directives for action; they describe essentially the same behaviour and discontents, but from polar opposite perspectives, which look for different causes and call for different remedies.

(3) These opposed perspectives follow from different interests in the social process, values, and assumptions about the relation between man and society.

Considered outside of any particular historical context, anomie refers to the problems of social control in a social system. Cultural constraints are ineffective: values are conflicting or absent, goals are not adjusted to opportunity structures or *vice versa*, or individuals are not adequately socialized to cultural directives. Whatever the particular meanings, anomie is a social state of normlessness or anarchy; the concept always focuses on the relationship between individuals and the constraining forces of social control. Durkheim used rates of deviation and the state of law and punishment as behavioural indices of anomie. Although he avoids psychological definitions, he implies that egotism, insatiable striving, meaninglessness, and aimlessness would be the probable reactions to living in an anomic society.

Alienation represents less a problem of the adequacy of social control than the legitimacy of social control; it is a problem of power defined as domination, a concept conspicuously absent from the anomie perspective. Anomie concentrates on culture or culture transmitted in social organization; alienation on the hierarchy of control in the organization itself. The critical focus of alienation is on whatever social conditions separate the individual from society as an extension of self through self activity, rather than as an abstract entity independent of individual selves. For Marx, alienation from society is *a priori* alienation from self. Anomie concentrates on barriers to the orderly functioning of society; alienation on barriers to the productive growth of individuals, and by extension, barriers to the adaptive change of the social system. The non-alienated condition is not necessarily social harmony as social control, but social harmony as the spontaneous result of individuals being free to realize their historical potentialities. Free means autonomous and self-determining, not controlled by external forces. Alienated persons are powerless and estranged from the reified creations of their own self (social) activity.

In the works of Marx and Durkheim, there are no simple operational definitions of alienation or anomie on either a purely psychological or sociological level. The concepts imply complete social theories explaining relationships between a social condition and behaviour. Critical concepts, they also imply the judgment of society in terms of ideal, or at least future and unrealized standards.

When alienation and anomie are returned to the concrete historical conditions which gave them their significance for social action, it becomes apparent that they represent radical criticism of specific historical situations. Neither Durkheim nor Marx was interested in abstract historical and psychological definitions of anomie and alienation. This observation cannot be over-emphasized because it is precisely the original radical, historical, and sociological content which has been removed or altered by contemporary definitions.

The classical definitions have in common their condemnation of economic individualism and its rationalization in the middle-class doctrines of economic and political liberalism. These were interpreted as expressions of thinking under anomic and alienating conditions. Marx and Durkheim critically describe societies in which economic self-interest has been reified and raised to the level of a collective end. The consequences, they agreed, were that economic activities and values had become separated from and commanding over all other spheres of collective life. The most intense social activity in modern industrial societies, economic activity, was the least social.

In *Suicide*, Durkheim writes that anomie is endemic in modern economic life. By this he means that the economy, traditionally restrained by the moral codes of church, state, or guild, now dominates as the realm of unrestrained self-interest, or even class interest. Formerly a means to, and a means limited by other ends, economic activity had become an end in itself. In other words, anomie has become institutionalized.

These dispositions (self-interested striving toward indefinite goals) are so inbred that society has grown to accept them and is accustomed to think them normal. It is everlastingly repeated that it is man's nature to be eternally dissatisfied, constantly to advance, without relief or rest, toward an indefinite goal. The longing for infinity is daily represented as a mark of moral distinction, whereas it can only appear within unregulated consciences which elevate to a rule the lack of rule from which they suffer.[43]

From a different perspective, Marx makes a similar observation in his *Economic and Philosophical Manuscripts*. Here he argues that self-in-

[43] Emile Durkheim, *Suicide* (Glencoe: Free Press, 1951), p. 257.

terest appears to be the motivating force of society because man has been alienated from his human and social activity, labour. The doctrine of self-interest is an example of alienated thinking.

Since alienated labor: (1) alienates nature from man; and (2) alienates man from himself, from his own active function, his life activity; so it alienates him from the species. It makes *species-life* into a means of individual life. In the first place it alienates species-life and individual life, and secondly, it turns the latter, as an abstraction, into the purpose of the former, also in its abstract and alienated forms.[44]

THE SOCIOLOGICAL FOUNDATIONS OF RADICALISM

A radical criticism cannot be derived from description of facts alone; it rests on standards which transcend them. In nineteenth-century Europe, where the middle-class ethic of self-interest was justified by an essentially psychological and atomistic interpretation of man and society, one source of radicalism was sociology itself. Marx and Durkheim made their criticism of the self-interest ethic and the contractual interpretation of society in the name of history and sociology. The radicalism of their concepts comes in part from a sociological and collectivistic definition of man. This is their counter to the psychological and individualistic images of man and society, which they saw as expressions of alienated and anomic life conditions. By definition their respective social images of man mean that history could not be explained with reference to what individuals think and that events are not necessarily, and certainly not ideally, the result of a universal self-interest drive. Even Durkheim has acknowledged his agreement with Marxists on this point.

We believe fruitful this idea that social life should be explained not by the conception which the participants have of it, but by the fundamental causes which escape their consciousness; and we think also that these causes ought to be sought principally in the way in which associated individuals are grouped. It is only on this condition that history can become a science and sociology, consequently, exist.[45]

Durkheim never tired of telling his reader that sociological facts must be explained sociologically. As Parsons suggests, his argument is

[44] Karl Marx, "Economic and Philosophical Manuscripts," in Erich Fromm, *Marx's Concept of Man* (New York: Ungar, 1961), p. 101.
[45] Emile Durkheim, book review of Antonio Labriola's *Essais sur la conception matérialiste de l'histoire*, in *Revue Philosophique*, 44 (1897), 648.

both formal and empirical.⁴⁶ The formal, logical argument rests on the assumption that society, being qualitatively different from its parts, cannot be explained only with reference to the characteristics of its parts. The empirical and sociological argument emerges in Durkheim's explanation of order and anomie, and in his attack on all who would explain and reform society with a psychological and atomistic definition of man.

In *The Division of Labor*, Durkheim questions Spencer's psychological concept of man and society when he asks essentially how can we explain order and co-operation, if man, whose dispositions are not universally the same, acted only out of their different and opposing definitions of self-interest.⁴⁷ He also makes a sociological and collectivistic criticism of what he understood to be socialism. Socialism, he argued, was basically as anarchistic in result as classical liberalism. Both fail to recognize the need for social control over individual and economic activities. "Because riches will not be transmitted any longer as they are today does not mean that the state of anarchy will disappear, for it is not a question as to the regulations of activity to which these riches give rise. It will not regulate itself by magic, as soon as it is useful, if the necessary forces for the constitution of this regulation have not been aroused and organized." ⁴⁸

Thus, Durkheim believed that the reification of self-interest was a contradiction of man's social nature, which required constraint through social control. Marx, on the other hand, contended that any reification of man's activity and products contradicted human nature, which developed fully only in the absence of reification and constraint. Far from being the natural disposition of man, whose dispositions are historically relative, the doctrine of the pursuit of self-interest was the propaganda of the capitalist ruling class, the ideological expression of class society and the alienating division of labour.

The critical content of alienation and anomie is sociological in the sense that Marx and Durkheim examined relationships between individuals and the collectivities which are products of their activity rather than psychological characteristics of individuals. Neither sociologist studied man outside of the subject-object (man-society) relationship; both condemned any attempt to do so. As sociologists they agreed that any doctrine which conceives of society as a congeries of contractual relationships between self-seeking individuals is false in its denial of the social nature of man. At the very most, such doctrines universalize the particular and transitory conditions of nineteenth-century industrial society.

---

[46] Talcott Parsons, *The Structure of Social Action* (Glencoe: Free Press, 1949), pp. 308–24.
[47] Emile Durkheim, *The Division of Labor in Society* (Glencoe: Free Press, 1960), pp. 200–6.
[48] *Ibid.*, p. 30. For an elaboration of this argument see Emile Durkheim, *Socialism* (New York: Collier Books, 1962).

THE PHILOSOPHICAL SOURCES OF RADICALISM: ANOMIE AND ALIENATION AS TRANSCENDENT AND IMMANENT INTERPRETATIONS OF THE RELATIONSHIP BETWEEN MAN AND SOCIETY

If Marx and Durkheim distinguish themselves as sociologists by interpreting man as a social relationship, they nevertheless are in complete disagreement on the precise nature of this relationship. Indeed, alienation and anomie are founded on opposite conceptions of man and society. The opposed conceptions parallel those used in theology to describe the relationship between man and God. God is transcendent if he is exalted above man and the world by his moral perfection. God is immanent when he dwells in the world, when he is the essence of the world and the world the essence of him. Similarly, society can be interpreted transcendentally and extrinsically as an entity different from and morally superior to individual men; or it can be interpreted immanently as the extension of men, the indwelling of men. Alienation assumes an immanent interpretation of man and society; anomie a transcendent one. Both interpretations provide an ethical basis for a radical criticism of society.

Anomie is basically a utopian concept of the political right; it criticizes traditional economic liberalism of the middle classes from a philosophical position which could be called naturalistic transcendentalism. It carries radical rightist implications as it derives from the philosophical positivism of Comte who founded his critique of the social organization of the rising middle classes on an analysis of the form of social control in the *ancien régime*.[49]

Alienation is a utopian concept of the radical left; it attacks economic liberalism from the futuristic perspective of the deprived classes and not from the backward glances of a declining class. The concept is formulated within a tradition of naturalistic and historical immanence; it represents an attempt to put the ideas of German idealism and the Enlightenment within a tradition of scientific and historical research.

---

[49] For a discussion of the relationship between Comte and Durkheim, see Alvin W. Gouldner, "Introduction," Emile Durkheim, *Socialism*, pp. 7–36. Gouldner argues that Durkheim was in fact a critic of Comte; much less conservative than Comte, he envisaged not a return to a Comtean mechanical solidarity. However, I believe that Gouldner goes too far in stressing Durkheim's reformism. Durkheim, like other utopian conservatives, wanted the re-establishment of social control and constraining moral forces. He held to a fixed and a historical conception of social control and a historical and relativistic conception of its expression. Whether the division of labour was simple or complex, social control still rested on supra-individual standards. Durkheim is essentially conservative in his Hobbesian conception of man and his transcendent conception of society.

Marx stressed the human and the active side of the man-society relationship and ultimately denied the dualism of man-society. Man's human and social activity is labour, and the products of labour, including society, are the extensions of man's own nature. Thus, man is his activity, his objects, man is society. Any reification of men's objects, any transcendence of men's products over men so that they do not see their interests, powers, and abilities affirmed and expressed therein, is evidence of the alienation of man from his self-activity, his objects, and himself. The whole notion of social alienation presupposes this immanent conception of human nature. Alienation is an historical state which will ultimately be overcome as man approaches freedom. Freedom for Marx, as well as for Hegel, meant autonomous and self-contained existence. Men will be free when the world has become so humanized and free of exploitation that man and society are one in theory and in practice. Marx's work could be interpreted as an empirical analysis of the historical process wherein man becomes separated from and reunited with society as self.

Preoccupied with the nature of order rather than change, Durkheim emphasized the passive side of the man-society relationship, how society makes and constrains men. His definition of anomie with its focus on the problems of social control and morality presupposes an absolute and eternal distinction between man and society and a dualistic conception of human nature. Marx's man is *homo laborans,* an historical variable developing through his own self-activity. But Durkheim's man is *homo duplex,* part egoistic, anarchistic and self seeking, part moral in so far as he is regulated and constrained by society, which is the source of all logic and morality.[50] The object of men's orientation, society, being collective and outliving the life of individual men, is transcendent, qualitatively different from the parts which compose it. Durkheim's transcendence is in part a logical extension of his sociological and relativistic interpretation of man. If man's nature is plastic and therefore without a system of inner direction and control, then the needed control system must be external. Society is the source of order and control since it is analytically, and, Durkheim apparently believed, actually independent of individual man. The transcendence like the immanence argument with its value of freedom as a condition of growth, is also an ethical argument. Influenced by Kant, Durkheim contended that morality is motivated not

---

[50] Durkheim clearly annunciated his doctrine of the dualism of man and the transcendence of society. This he contrasted with what he called monistic (immanent?) definitions of man and society. He argued that socialism and utilitarianism as monistic doctrines were false because they could not explain altruistic behaviour or the existence of general concepts. They failed to explain social phenomena which do not have their origin in self-interested and utilitarian motives of individuals. See Emile Durkheim, "The Dualism of Human Nature and its Social Conditions," in Kurt A. Wolff, ed., *Emile Durkheim, 1858–1917* (Columbus: Ohio State University Press, 1960), pp. 325–39.

by self-interest, but by *dis*-interest; men conform to rule out of feeling of obligation and duty in the face of a superior entity. Anomie is thus a state of amorality and anarchy which can be overcome only by establishing societal rules. Freedom for Durkheim does not end with constraint; freedom begins with constraint over the conflicting passions of man. Alienation, as the transcendence of society over particular men, is the condition of morality.

The immanence ideology of alienation and the transcendence ideology of anomie reveal themselves also in Marx's and Durkheim's respective criticisms of the self-interest ethic and in their programmes for social change. The concepts describe similar historical phenomena, but in sharply contrasting ways with radically different implications for action. For Marx, the doctrine of self-interest is one indication of alienation, self-estrangement and powerlessness in a class society. For the transcendentalist Durkheim, the same thing indicates anomie, a problem of inadequate rather than illegitimate social control. An immanent and materialist reform requires that alienation be overcome through revolutionary practice to end class society and to establish the material base for freedom in productive activities. But: "It is above all necessary to avoid postulating 'society' once more as an abstraction confronting man." [51]

Marx wanted to humanize society, to organize the actual world so that man could experience himself as man (free and autonomous in his human or productive activity). Durkheim proposed to humanize Hobbesian man through the extension of social control. He called for the re-establishment of morality in a way which would take into account, not abolish, the specialized division of labour in society. Durkheim's specific proposal was the establishment of occupational communities which would be the modern carriers of moral discipline and social control. "For anomie to end, there must exist, or be formed a group which can constitute the system of rules actually needed.[52] The problem must be put this way: to discover through science the moral restraint which can regulate economic life, and by its regulation control selfishness and thus gratify need. . . ." [53]

The Politics of Isolation

S. M. Lipset et al. have observed that certain groups in society are isolated from the values generally held by the majority.[54] Social and political isola-

[51] Karl Marx, "Economic and Philosophical Manuscripts," *op. cit.*, p. 77.
[52] Emile Durkheim, *The Division of Labor in Society*, p. 5.
[53] Emile Durkheim, *Socialism*, p. 285.
[54] S. M. Lipset, Paul F. Lazarsfeld, Allen H. Barton, and Juan Linz, "The Psychology of Voting: An Analysis of Political Behavior," in Gardner Lindzey, ed., *Handbook of Social Psychology*, Vol. II (Reading, Mass.: Addison-Wesley Publishing Co., 1954), pp. 1137–1138. Also see S. M. Lipset, *Political Man* (Garden City, N.Y.: Anchor Books, 1963), pp. 104–105, 135–137.

tion may be determined by a number of factors—ethnic, religious, geographical, and occupational. Of these, the latter two are most frequently stressed. For example, much of the work in the lumber and mining industries is carried out in remote areas. Individuals employed in these industries are separated from the outside society and its values for prolonged periods of time, allowing for the emergence of new values and attitudes which may conflict with those of the main society. Individuals in such socially isolated positions may interact with few persons from the outside and often find it difficult to move into other social milieus. With regard to the possible formation of social movements, Kornhauser has suggested that owing to this ". . . density of internal contacts, combined with the paucity of external relation, common grievances readily emerge and become shared rather than dispersed." [55] Lipset has argued that individuals who are socially isolated develop certain values that predispose them to become extremist in their political orientations. To support this thesis, he turns to voting records for the states of California and Michigan and concludes that, for these states, lumber areas provide more support for left wing movements than do other areas.[56]

The concept of political isolation, when used as an explanation for the rise of social movements, would seem to present several operational and empirical problems. A primary difficulty stems from a misplaced emphasis on the effects of isolation. As we have already pointed out, Durkheim maintained that isolation led to individual pathological behavior, not to collective political behavior. Thus, it may be expected that logging camps and other similar isolated and male-dominated societies are more likely to produce individual behavior such as gambling and drinking than collective political movements. Second, while labor movements such as the Communist-led National Miner's Union and the Industrial Workers of the World have received considerable support from geographically isolated communities, variables other than isolation would appear to have causal primacy. These include the effects of company town situations and the economic and social relationships between the community and its environs. Finally, investigations of isolated regions have shown their inhabitants to be characterized by apolitical behavior rather than by political activism.[57] In view of these considerations, we must conclude that the presumed political consequences of isolation remain little more than tenuous and largely unsupported hypotheses. In later chapters we shall argue

---

[55] William Kornhauser, *The Politics of Mass Society* (Glencoe: Free Press, 1959), p. 216.
[56] Lipset, *op. cit.*, pp. 242–243.
[57] See Harvey Swados, "The Miners: Men Without Work," in Philip Olson, ed., *America As A Mass Society* (Glencoe: Free Press, 1963), pp. 232–243; and Benjamin Ringer and David Sills, "Political Extremists in Iran: A Secondary Analysis of Communications Data," *Public Opinion Quarterly*, 16 (Winter 1952–1953), 689–701.

that contact and communication are essential elements in the development of radical political movements and ideologies.

CLASS AND SOCIAL MOVEMENTS

Karl Marx's theory of social class has been utilized both theoretically and empirically to point to the conditions necessary for the formation of social movements. One of the more crucial aspects of Marxian theory in this regard is his conceptualization of class consciousness. For Marx, consciousness was determined by material conditions: ". . . consciousness must be explained from the contradictions of material life, from the existing conflict between social productive forces and productive relationships." [58] Marx postulated that workers brought together in a capitalist mode of production would develop an awareness of common interests: "The great industry masses together in a single place a crowd of people unknown to each other. . . . But the maintenance of their wages, this common interest which they have against their employer, unites them in the same idea of resistance . . . [which] has a double end, that of eliminating competition among themselves [and enabling] competition against the capitalist." [59] Therefore, it would seem that one of the prime requisites for the emergence of class consciousness is a "common interest." C. Wright Mills has elaborated on this idea, as follows: "Thus for class consciousness, there must be (1) a rational awareness and identification with one's own class interests; (2) an awareness of and rejection of other class interests as illegitimate; and (3) an awareness of and a readiness to use collective political means to the collective political end of realizing one's interests." [60]

For the student of social movements, this aspect of Marxian theory contains two basic elements. First, the undifferentiated mass becomes a class when common economic interests are recognized. Second, there must be an impetus to engage in activity directed toward social change intended to ameliorate economic antagonisms. Regarding this second point, Marx never really explains how a revolutionary class consciousness is transformed into a social movement, although he does allude to the role of the Communist Party in bringing about such consciousness.[61]

For an elaboration of the conditions necessary for the emergence of class consciousness, consider the following excerpt from Bukharin's His-

[58] Karl Marx, "Preface to a Contribution to the Critique of Political Economy," in Fromm, *op. cit.*, p. 218.
[59] Karl Marx, *The Poverty of Philosophy* (New York: International Publishers, 1963), pp. 145–146.
[60] C. Wright Mills, *White Collar* (New York: Oxford University Press, 1951), p. 325.
[61] Karl Marx and Friedrich Engels, *Manifesto of the Communist Party*, Engels, ed. (New York: International Publishers, 1948), p. 22.

torical Materialism. *After a brief discussion of types of social classes, Bukharin turns to an analysis of class interest and the conditions necessary for a class to develop a revolutionary ideology.*

Excerpts from Nikolai Bukharin, Historical Materialism *(New York, Russell and Russell, 1965), pp. 276–293. Reprinted by permission of Russell and Russell.*

A social class—we have seen—is the aggregate of persons *playing the same part in production, standing in the same relation toward other persons in the production process, these relations being also expressed in things* (instruments of labor). It follows that in the process of distribution the common element of each class is its uniform source of income, for the conditions in the distribution of products are determined by the conditions in *production*. Textile workers and metal workers are not two separate classes, but a single class, since they bear the *same relation* to certain other *persons* (engineers, capitalists). Similarly, the proprietors of a mine, a brick-field, a corset-factory, are all of one class, for regardless of the physical differences between the things they manufacture, they occupy a common ("commanding") position with regard to the *persons* engaged in the process of production, which position is also expressed in things ("capital"). . . .

We are now prepared to take up a description of the most important *classes.*

1. *The basic classes of a given social form* (classes in the proper sense of the word) are two in number: on the one hand, the class which commands, monopolizing the instruments of production; on the other hand, the executing class, with no means of production, which works for the former. The specific form of this relation of economic exploitation and servitude determines the form of the given class society. For example: if the relation between the commanding and executing class is reproduced by the purchase of labor power in the market, we have capitalism. If it is reproduced by the purchase of persons, by plunder, or otherwise, but not by the purchase of labor power alone, and if the commanding class gains control of not only the labor power but also of body and soul of the exploited persons, we have a slaveholding system, etc. . . .

The basic classes may be subdivided into their various elements. In capitalist society, the commanding bourgeoisie was partly industrial, partly commercial, partly banking, etc. The working class includes skilled and unskilled workers.

2. *Intermediate classes:* these include such social-economic groups as constitute a necessity for the society in which they live, *without being a*

remnant of the old order. They occupy a middle position between the commanding and exploiting classes. Such are, for instance, the technical mental workers in capitalist society.

3. *Transition classes*: these include such groups as have emerged from the preceding form of society, and as are now disintegrating in their present form, giving rise to various classes with opposite roles in production. Such are, for example, the artisans and peasants in capitalist society, who constitute a heritage from the feudal system, and from whom both the bourgeoisie and the proletariat are recruited.

Thus, the peasantry is constantly falling to pieces under capitalism, economically speaking, it is differentiated; the rich peasant grows out of the medium peasantry, becoming a trader and, one step further up, a true bourgeois. On the other hand, the proletariat is also growing out of the peasantry, by some such process as this: the peasant has no horse; he becomes a farm laborer or seasonal worker; he becomes a true proletarian.

4. *Mixed class types*: these include such groups as belong to one class in one respect and to another class in another respect, for example, the railroad worker who runs a farm of his own, for which he hires a laborer; he is a worker from the standpoint of the railroad company, but an "employer" from the standpoint of his hired man.

5. *Finally* there are the so called *déclassé* groups, *i.e.*, categories of persons outside the outlines of social labor: the *lumpenproletariat*, beggars, vagrants, etc.

In an analysis of the "abstract type" of society, *i.e.*, any social form in its purest state, we are dealing almost exclusively with its basic classes; but when we take up the concrete reality, we of course find ourselves faced with the motley picture with all its social-economic types and relations.

The general cause of the existence of classes is defined by Engels in his *Anti-Duhring* as follows: ". . . that all previous historical contradictions between exploiting and exploited, ruling and oppressed classes are explained by the same comparatively undeveloped productivity of human labor. As long as the truly working population is so completely occupied by its necessary labor as to leave it no time for conducting the common affairs of society—division of labor, business of the state, legal matters, art, science, etc.—so long did we necessarily have a special class which, freed from actual labor, looked after these matters; in which connection, it never failed to place more and more work upon the shoulders of the working masses, for its own advantage" (Friedrich Engels: *Herrn Eugen Duhrings Unwalzung der Wissenschaft*, Stuttgart, 1901, pp. 190, 191). In another passage (p. 190), practically the same remark is repeated, with the added statement that society is divided into two classes. A recapitulation of the whole matter is this: "The law of the division of labor is therefore *the basic factor in the division into classes.*" . . .

Class Interest

We have seen that classes are specific groups of persons, "real aggregates," distinguished by their role in production, which role is expressed in the *property relations*. But these two phases in the production process also are accompanied by a third phase—the process of the distribution of products in one way or another. Production is paralleled by distribution.

The forms of distribution correspond to the forms of production. The position of the classes in production determines their position in distribution. The antagonism between administrators and the administered, between the class monopolizing the instruments of production and the class possessing no means of production, is expressed in an antagonism in income, in a contradiction between the shares held by each class in the product turned out. This different "being" of the classes also determines their "consciousness." The contradictions of the "being," of the conditions of existence, are directly reflected in the growth of *class interests*. The most primitive and general expression of class interest is the *effort of the classes to increase their share in the distribution of the total mass of products*.

In the system of class society, the process of production is at the same time a process of the economic exploitation of those who work physically.

They produce more than they receive, not only because a portion of the product turned out (*of values*, in capitalist society) goes for extending production ("accumulation," in capitalist society), but also because the working class is supporting the owners of the instruments of production, is working for them. The most general interest of the dominant minority may therefore be formulated as the effort *to maintain and extend the opportunities for economic exploitation;* while the interest of the exploited majority is *to liberate itself from this exploitation*. The first of these two efforts has an eye only to society as it exists at present; the second is a challenge to the existence of this society.

But the economic structure of society—as we have seen—is fortified in its state organization and supported by countless super-structural forms. It is therefore not surprising to find the economic class interest clothed also in the garment of political, religious, scientific interests, etc. The class interests thus develop into an entire system, *embracing the most varied domains of social life*. These coordinated interests, maintained in place by the general interest of the class, condition the construction of the so called "social ideal," which is always the quintessence of the class interests.

A few additional points require our attention in a discussion of class interests.

First: permanent, general interests must be distinguished from temporary, momentary interests. The "momentary" interests may even constitute an objective contradiction to the permanent interests. The English workers, for instance, were acting in accordance with their temporary interests when they accepted a class harmony with the English bourgeoisie, supporting them in the imperialist war; they acted in the interest of their wages, which were increased at the expense of the colonial workers. But because they thus destroyed the solidarity of *all* the workers, and made a compact with their employers, they were opposing the general and permanent interests of their class.

Second: the professional *interests of a group* must not be confused with the general *interests of the class*. Thus, the dominant bourgeoisie may, in capitalist society, win over the aristocracy of labor (skilled labor), whose special interests then do not coincide with those of the entire working class; they are group interests, not class interests. Another example: during any war, the commercial bourgeoisie violates the commercial laws with all its might, although the bourgeois state itself established these laws, and is waging war in the interest of the bourgeoisie as a *class*. In other words, the group interests of the commercial section of the bourgeoisie is in this case at variance with the interests of the bourgeoisie as a *class*.

Third: alterations in *principle and tendency* in the momentary interests of the class, proceeding simultaneously with the alterations in principle of its social situation, must not be left out of account. The example of the proletariat will serve to illustrate this point. In capitalist society, its most permanent and general interest is the destruction of the capitalist system. Its partial demands always have this general tendency: the conquest of strategic positions, the undermining of bourgeois society, the improving of the proletariat's material position, enhance its social strength, preparing its forces for the attack on the entire capitalist order. Now, let us assume that the proletariat has discharged its historical task. It has destroyed the old state machinery, built up a new machinery, produced a new social equilibrium; temporarily, the proletariat assumes the place of the commanding class. Obviously, the *direction* of its interests has radically changed: all its partial interests, taken from the point of view of the general interests, are now subordinate to the idea of *fortifying and developing* the new conditions, organizing them, offering resistance to every attempt at destruction. This dialectic transformation is an outgrowth of the dialectic evolution of the proletariat itself, once it has become a state power.

The common element behind both these opposed directions of interest is the construction of a new form of society, whose bearer is the proletariat, a construction which presupposes the destruction of the old envelope, which had become an obstacle to the evolution of the productive forces.

A new class, to be capable not only of destroying the old system of social relations, but of building up a new one, must necessarily turn its interests in the direction of *production*, *i.e.*, it must not approach social questions from the standpoint of division and mere distribution, but from that of a destruction of old forms for the purpose of a *construction* of forms with more perfect *production*, with more powerful *productive forces*. . . .

Class Psychology and Class Ideology

It is important to learn what are the traits that must be present in a class in order to enable it to accomplish a transformation of society, to shunt society from the capitalist track to the socialist track.

1. Such a class must be one that has been *economically exploited and politically oppressed* under capitalist society; otherwise, the class will have no reason for resisting the capitalist order; it will not rebel under any circumstances.

2. It follows—to put the matter crudely—that it must be a *poor class*; for otherwise it will have no opportunity to feel its poverty as compared with the wealth of other classes.

3. It must be a *producing* class; for, if it is not, *i.e.*, if it has no immediate share in the production of values, it may at best destroy, being unable to produce, create, organize.

4. It must be a class that is *not bound by private property*, for a class whose material existence is based on private property will naturally be inclined to increase its property, not to abolish private property, as is demanded by communism.

5. This class must be one which has been *welded together* by the conditions of its existence and its common labor, its members working side by side. Otherwise, it will be incapable of desiring—not to mention constructing—a society that is the embodiment of the social labor of comrades. Furthermore, such a class could not wage an *organized* struggle or create a new state power.

In the following table, the presence or absence of these characteristics in the various classes and groups is indicated by a + or − sign.

Class Properties	Peasantry	Lumpen-proletariat	Proletariat
1. Economic exploitation	+	−	+
2. Political oppression	+	+	+
3. Poverty	+	+	+
4. Productivity	+	−	+
5. Freedom from private property	−	+	+
6. Condition of union in production, and common labor	−	−	+

In other words, the peasantry—for instance—lack several elements necessary to make them a communist class: they are bound down by *property*, and it will take many years to train them to a new view, which can only be done by having the state power in the hands of the proletariat; also, the peasantry are not held together in production, in *social* labor and common action; on the contrary, the peasant's entire joy is his own bit of land; he is accustomed to *individual* management, not to cooperation with others. The *lumpenproletariat*, however, is barred chiefly by the circumstance that it performs no productive work; it can tear down, but has no habit of building up. Its ideology is often represented by the anarchists, concerning whom a wag once said that their whole program consists of two paragraphs. *Par.* I. There shall be no order at all; *Par.* 2. No one shall be obliged to comply with the preceding paragraph. . . . In each of the above classes, we find the ideology that corresponds to its psychology: in the proletariat, revolutionary communism; in the peasantry, a property ideology; in the *lumpenproletariat*, a vacillating and hysterical anarchism. Obviously, once such a psychological and theological nucleus is present, it will set the fundamental note for the entire psychology and ideology of the class or group concerned.

The "Class in Itself," and the "Class for Itself"

Class psychology and class ideology, the consciousness of the class not only as to its momentary interests, but also as to permanent and universal interests, are a result of the position of the class in production, which by no means signifies that this position of the class will *at once* produce in it a consciousness of its general and basic interests. On the contrary, it may be said that this is rarely the case. For, in the first place, the process of production itself, in actual life, goes through a number of stages of evolution, and the contradictions in the economic structure do not become apparent until a later period of evolution; in the second place, a class does not descend full-grown from heaven, but grows in a crude elemental manner from a number of other social groups (transition classes, intermediate and other classes, strata, social combinations); in the third place, a certain time usually passes before a class becomes conscious of itself through experience in battle, of its special and peculiar interests, aspirations, social "ideals" and desires, which emphatically distinguish it from all the other classes in the given society; in the fourth place, we must not forget the systematic psychological and ideological manipulation conducted by the ruling class with the aid of its state machinery for the purpose of destroying the incipient class consciousness of the oppressed classes, and to imbue them with the ideology of the ruling class, or at least to influence them somewhat with this ideology. The result is that a class discharging a definite function in the process of production may already exist as an aggregate of persons before it exists as a self-conscious class; we have a class, but no class consciousness. It exists as a factor in production, as a specific aggregate of production relations; it does not yet exist as a social, independent *force* that knows what it wants, that feels a mission, that is *conscious* of its peculiar position, of the hostility of its interests to those of the other classes. As designations for these different stages in the process of class evolution, Marx makes use of two expressions: he calls *class "an sich"* (*in itself*), a class not yet conscious of itself as such; he calls *class "für sich"* (*for itself*), a class already conscious of its social role.

This has been splendidly explained by Marx in *The Poverty of Philosophy*, in the case of working class evolution:

> It is under the form of these combinations that the first attempts at association among themselves have always been made by the workers. The great industry masses together in a single place a crowd of people unknown to each other. Competition divides their interests. But the maintenance of their wages, the common interest which they have against their employer, unites them in the same idea of resistance—*combination*. (*Combination* here means workers' combination, N. Bukharin.) Thus combination has always a double end, that of eliminating competition among themselves while enabling them to make a general competition against the capitalist. If the first object of resistance has been merely to maintain wages, in proportion as the capitalists in their turn have combined with the idea of repression, the combinations, at first isolated, have formed in groups, and, in the face of constantly united capital, the maintenance of the association became more important and necessary for them than the maintenance of wages. This is so true that the English economists are all astonished at seeing the workers sacrifice a good part of their wages on behalf of the associations which, in the eyes of these economists, were only established in support of wages. In this struggle—a veritable civil war—are united and established all the elements necessary for a future battle. Once arrived at that point, association takes on a political character.
>
> The economic conditions have in the first place transformed the mass of the people of the country into wage workers. The domination of capital has created for this mass of people a common situation with common interests. Thus this mass is already a class, as opposed to *capital*, but *not yet for itself*. In the struggle, of which we have only noted some phases, this mass unites, it is constituted *as a class for itself*. The interests which it defends are the *interests of its class*. (*The Poverty of Philosophy*, Chicago, 1920, pp. 188, 189, my italics, N. Bukharin.)

Class consciousness, as Marx perceived it, is not in itself a sufficient condition for the development of a social movement. A successful movement must be broadly based, and, as Bukharin has argued, only the condi-

tions of the proletariat can generate an indigenous class consciousness. Pragmatic revolutionaries saw the necessity to expand the idea of consciousness to accommodate a diversity of potentially revolutionary groups. This undertaking revolved around the notion of political consciousness. That is, it is necessary to translate an awareness of economic disadvantage (class consciousness) into an awareness of political disadvantage (political consciousness) before revolutionary change will occur.

Foremost among those concerned with this undertaking was V. I. Lenin. Lenin began his theoretical discussion by pointing to conditions which modified Marx's analysis of the trends in capitalism, e.g., imperialism.[62] In What Is To Be Done? he outlines the different forces which either inhibit or can lead to political consciousness. Lenin begins by describing the nature of class consciousness at the opening of the twentieth century. He claims that "workers were not and could not be conscious of the irreconcilable antagonism of their interests to the whole of the modern political system. . . ."[63] Thus, workers were only capable of what he termed "trade-union consciousness," i.e., an awareness of interests. Lenin viewed "trade-union consciousness" as being both functional and dysfunctional for the achievement of social change. It was functional in the sense that it provided political experience and could achieve short-range goals. On the other hand, it was dysfunctional in that this type of consciousness was not capable of fostering a revolutionary movement but led rather to reformism and opportunism on the part of the leadership. Lenin further argued against the trade union mentality by suggesting that minor economic reforms were not enough. He writes: "We must actively take up the political education of the working class, and the development of political consciousness. . . . The consciousness of the masses of the workers cannot be genuine class consciousness unless the workers learn. . . ."[64] According to Lenin, what the workers were to learn was the necessity for revolution and the means whereby it would be carried out. In the following excerpt, Frances Becker suggests how Lenin envisioned the transformation of the Marxian dialectic into a revolutionary political consciousness.

---

[62] V. I. Lenin, *Imperialism: The Highest Stage of Capitalism* (New York: International Publishers, 1939).
[63] V. I. Lenin, "What Is To Be Done?" in *Collected Works*, Vol. IV (New York: International Publishers, 1929), p. 114.
[64] *Ibid.*, pp. 139, 150.

Excerpts from Frances Bennett Becker, "Lenin's Application of Marx's Theory of Revolutionary Tactics," American Sociological Review, Vol. 2 (April, 1937), pp. 353–355. *Reprinted by permission of the American Sociological Association.*

So perfectly did Lenin carry through his lifetime task of realizing the potentialities of Marxian doctrine that his most original contributions have the air of being only organic outgrowths of the parent stock.

Marx held that revolutions are inevitable *once their prerequisites have materialized,* but he also held that the latter proviso must be given full weight. A cycle of "want" → "outworn institution" → unrest → "forcible repression" → violent revolution has been going on, said Marx, ever since "the original classless tribal organization" was disrupted, and the cycle will perpetually recur until the workers become the controllers of society and all exploitation and class struggle forever cease.[65]

In the present era of capitalism, first among the prerequisites of revolution is that the capitalist system must have reached a high state of development; the capitalist class must fully have established itself as the thesis of which the proletariat is the antithesis. The factor that effects the inevitable dialectic synthesis of these polar opposites is the revolutionary process ultimately issuing in a classless society. Second, intense class consciousness is essential, and capitalism itself engenders the conditions which make this possible.[66]

And here we come to a point often overlooked by both friends and foes of Marxian theory. "Inevitable" and "dialectic synthesis" have hypnotized many persons into the belief that human volition plays no part in the rise of class consciousness and the revolutionary mood. But note: "Man makes his own history, but he does not make it out of whole cloth; he does not make it out of conditions chosen by himself but out of such as he finds close at hand." [67]

This indicates that Marx recognized human volition as an indispensable link in the revolutionary chain. As he strikingly put it: "Circumstances may be altered by men." [68]

When "inevitable" and "alterable" are contrasted, a "pseudo-

[65] Marx, *Revolution and Counter-Revolution in France,* p. 14.
[66] Note that it does not create class consciousness automatically; it merely affords it opportunity for growth.
[67] Marx, *The Eighteenth Brumaire,* p. 9.
[68] Marx, "On Feuerbach," in Engels, *Feuerbach: The Roots of the Socialist Philosophy,* p. 133.

dilemma" arises, but it vanishes when ultimate and proximate causes are distinguished. Human desires undeniably play a vital role in history by availing themselves of the right moment for their realization, but the productive forces provide both the opportunities for and the limiting conditions of such realization.[69]

So said Marx. Following him, Lenin's belief in the inevitability of revolution when the times are ripe was so firmly ingrained [70] that it was the fundamental pattern of all his actions. Moreover, what Marx said about the dialectic function of capitalism in promoting the revolutionary process Lenin echoes in no uncertain terms: ". . . Socialism rises directly and *practically* from each great step in advance within Capitalism." [71] He was convinced that violent revolution under conditions prevailing in Russia would be ultimately inevitable, and was just as firmly persuaded that the Russian workers had to be *taught* immediately that their eventual revolutionary action would be inevitable.[72]

His conception of the preliminary phases absolutely indispensable to the revolutionary process in Russia shows how he dealt with the "pseudo-dilemma" mentioned above:

> Without the revolution of . . . 1905–1907, without the counter-revolution of 1907–1914, it would have been impossible to secure a . . . "self-determination" of all classes of the Russian people. . . . In addition to an unusual acceleration of world history, there were also needed particularly sharp historic turns so that during one of them . . . tsarism might be overturned in a trice. This . . . mighty accelerator of events was the imperialist World War.[73]

Here is a clear statement of the role of chance in *accelerating* what in due time would be occasioned by some other set of equally "fortuitous" events. Moreover, Lenin was keenly aware of the anomaly presented by the "vanguard role" thrust upon backward Russia through historical coincidence.[74]

At this point we should note that for Lenin men of ideas fell into two camps: those contemplative spirits to whom ideas are ends in themselves

---

[69] In a letter of Kugelmann dated April 17, 1871, translated in the *Communist Monthly*, March, 1927, p. 52, Marx says: "[World history] would be of a very mystical nature if 'accidents' played no role. . . . Hastening and retarding are very much dependent upon . . . 'accidents,' among which the 'accidents' of the character of the people who stand foremost at the head of the movement also figure."
[70] Lenin, *The State and the Revolution*, p. 25; *Complete Works*, Vol. XVIII, p. 304.
[71] Lenin, *Preparing for Revolt*, p. 153. In *ibid.*, p. 194, he says, "the proletariat, as in all its historical creative work, takes its implements from capitalism, and does not 'think out' and 'create things from nothing.'"
[72] Lenin, *The State and Revolution*, p. 25.
[73] Lenin, *The Revolution of 1917*, Vol. I, pp. 27–28.
[74] *Ibid.*, pp. 85–86.

and those "vanguard leaders" to whom they mean action. He relentlessly expelled from the party every ideologist of the former variety, for he knew that their aim was not to change the world but to interpret it.[75] His conception of the "party line" and all his organizing efforts were bound up with this conviction of the necessity of active intervention.[76] Furthermore, in *What Is To Be Done?*, Lenin insisted on the importance of a theoretical frame of reference for the guidance of the "active element." . . .[77]

One contemporary elaboration upon the idea of social class which should be discussed here is that of the psychology of social class. Unfortunately, attempts at a subjective analysis of social class have resulted in psychological reductionism. For example, Richard Centers perceives classes as comprised fundamentally of like-minded people who have defined themselves as being members of groups. These groups are ". . . essentially subjective in character, dependent upon class consciousness." [78] For Centers, therefore, class consciousness becomes the raison d'être of groups which create classes rather than being, as Marx would argue, an awareness that arises from the existence of a given class under certain conditions. Centers further reverses Marx's idea of class by suggesting that the individual's relationship to the means of production is not a determinant of class but rather a function of his perceived membership in a "stratum." [79] Moreover, his criterion of class is based on the question, "Which class do you belong to?"—an operational definition which totally ignores the Marxian notion of false class consciousness created by ideological and other elements in the superstructure of a given social system. The danger inherent in psychological analyses of class consciousness, therefore, hinges on a fallacy of misplaced concreteness. Although semantically analogous, psychological treatments of class consciousness do not address the same problem stated by Marx in the Poverty of Philosophy.

[75] Eastman, *Marx and Lenin*, p. 151.
[76] "A revolution . . . is produced when, in addition to the objective changes enumerated above (a weak ruling class and intense suffering and activity of the masses) certain subjective changes take place, viz., *when a revolutionary class shows ability to take revolutionary mass action sufficiently forceful to break, or at least to damage, the existing government. Even in times of crises governments do not 'tumble down of their own accord,' but require a force to 'overthrow' them.*" —Lenin, *The Collapse of the Second International* (Glasgow: 1915), p. 17. Cf. also *Complete Works*, Vol. II, p. 174.
[77] "Without a revolutionary theory there can be no revolutionary movement. . . . *the role of vanguard can be fulfilled only by a party that is guided by an advanced theory.*" —Lenin, *Complete Works*, Vol. II, p. 110.
[78] Richard Centers, *The Psychology of Social Class: A Study of Class Consciousness* (Princeton: Princeton University Press, 1949), p. 27.
[79] *Ibid.*, p. 27.

STATUS AND SOCIAL MOVEMENTS

While the theoretical successors of Marx have utilized class conflict and the concepts of political and class consciousness to deal with social movements, an increasing number of social scientists have challenged the unidimensional approach to social stratification which these concepts reflect. They have instead turned to the writings of Max Weber and the concept of status to deal with participation in social movements. Weber originally criticized Marx by pointing out that the economic concept of class was only one of at least three ways in which groups could be stratified. In his essay, "Class, Status, Party," [80] Weber distinguishes between these three dimensions as follows:

1. *Class:* this is the traditional economic dimension, stratification according to the relationship of groups to the production and acquisition of goods.

2. *Status:* this concept is within the "social" order in that status groups are stratified according to the principles of their consumption of goods as represented by a certain honor or prestige in following special styles of life. Weber subsumes occupation under the heading of status since social honor is claimed by virtue of the special style of life which may be determined by an occupation.

3. *Party:* this is stratification according to the acquisition of social power.

In recent years, these aspects of stratification have been applied, both objectively and subjectively, to the analysis of social and political movements. These two uses are manifested, respectively, in the notions of status consistency and status politics.

Status Consistency

Since Weber's initial specification of the three dimensions of social class, a number of sociologists have contributed to the development and implementation of a multidimensional model of social stratification variously called status equilibration,[81] status congruency,[82] status crystallization,[83]

---

[80] H. H. Gerth and C. Wright Mills, trans. and eds., *From Max Weber: Essays in Sociology* (New York: Oxford University Press, 1958), ch. VII, "Class, Status, Party," pp. 180–195.
[81] Emile Benoit-Smullyan, "Status, Status Types, and Status Interrelations," *American Sociological Review*, 9 (April 1944), 151–161.
[82] Stuart Adams, "Status Congruency as a Variable in Small Group Performance," *Social Forces*, 32 (October 1953), 16–22.
[83] Gerhard E. Lenski, "Status Crystallization: A Non-Vertical Dimension of Social Status," *American Sociological Review*, 19 (August 1954), 405–413.

and status consistency.⁸⁴ *The theoretical development of this model may be traced through the writings of Emile Benoit-Smullyan and Pitirim Sorokin.*

*In 1944, Benoit-Smullyan drew Weber's three concepts together under a more general concept of status, which he defined as location on a superiority-inferiority scale with respect to possession of common social characteristics.*⁸⁵ *According to Benoit-Smullyan, status may be operationalized in terms of three hierarchical scales upon which people could be stratified. These scales yield economic, political, and prestige statuses, which are respectively equatable with Weber's class, party, and status. Benoit-Smullyan then turns to a description of the interrelations between these various types of status, and it is here that the "status equilibrium" hypothesis is first stated. He notes that a person's positions on these three statuses may often be out of line. That is, the wealthiest are not always the highest in power or prestige (e.g., the nouveaux riches), nor are the most prestigeful always highest in wealth or power (e.g., the shabby genteel). He goes on to say, however, that when such dissimilarity does exist there is a tendency over time for a person's rankings of these various hierarchies to reach a common level, that is,*

. . . for a man's position in the economic hierarchy to match his position in the political hierarchy and for the latter to accord with his position in the hierarchy of prestige, etc. This tendency may conveniently be called "status equilibration" and a social situation in which a high degree of correlation obtains between the different forms of status, an "equilibrium status structure." ⁸⁶

*In 1947, Sorokin dealt with the same idea when he discussed various stratification schemas.*⁸⁷ *A state of equilibrium would obtain in what Sorokin terms the "innerly solidary or affine multi-bonded stratum." This would be a stratificational cross-section in which the stratifying bonds were mutually congenial. He raises the point of status disequilibration when he states that:*

. . . the correlation of the affine strata is never perfect. . . . The stratified pyramids of the uni-bonded groups never consolidate in such a way that all their strata coincide and create one integral consolidated social pyramid in which all the tops of the uni-bonded pyramids make one integral top, and all

---

⁸⁴ Irwin W. Goffman, "Status Consistency and Preference for Change in Power Distribution," *American Sociological Review*, 22 (June 1957), 275–281; Elton F. Jackson, "Status Consistency and Symptoms of Stress," *American Sociological Review*, 27 (August 1962), 469–480.
⁸⁵ Benoit-Smullyan, *op. cit.*
⁸⁶ *Ibid.*, p. 160.
⁸⁷ Pitirim A. Sorokin, *Society, Culture and Personality: Their Structure and Dynamics* (New York: Harper & Brothers, 1947).

the middle and lower strata consolidate into one integral middle or lower stratum.[88]

Thus, theoretically at least, both consistent and inconsistent status patterns should be investigated for dependent effects. Empirically, however, the effects of status inconsistency have been singled out as etiological in most studies applying the consistency model to research in social and political movements. For example, Benoit-Smullyan suggests that the blocking of a tendency toward equilibrium created social tensions of "revolutionary magnitude" among the eighteenth-century French bourgeoisie and the impoverished German middle classes of the 1930s.[89] Lenski concluded that certain types of status inconsistency lead to political liberalism, and predicted that the occurrence of acute status inconsistencies within a population would lead a proportionally large portion of that population to support programs of social change.[90] In testing this hypothesis Goffman found that preferences for change in the distribution of power in society were a solution to status inconsistency at high strata levels, where the opportunities for upward mobility (an alternative solution to inconsistency) are low.[91] Regarding participation in revolutionary movements, Lenski has stated:

Building on the present foundation, it also becomes possible to predict one of the sources of leadership of successful revolutionary movements. Years ago Marx and Engels noted that successful revolutionary movements are usually characterized by the combination of broad support from the masses or lower strata, and leadership recruited from the higher strata in the old order. The present study suggests that persons of poorly crystallized status may be an important source from which such leadership is recruited.[92]

In a later article, Lenski suggested that political extremism of both the Left and the Right would be associated with status discrepancies.[93] Ringer and Sills, in their study of political extremists in Iran, found that both left and right extremists shared common social characteristics, among which were the discrepant statuses of modest income and high education.[94] Other observations have linked right wing extremism to status inconsistency. Lipset and Bendix have observed that class discrepancies seem to predispose groups or individuals to accept extremist views,[95] and Rush

[88] *Ibid.*, p. 292 (italics in the original).
[89] Benoit-Smullyan, *op. cit.*, p. 160.
[90] Lenski, *op. cit.*, p. 411.
[91] Goffman, *op. cit.*
[92] Lenski, *op. cit.*, pp. 412–413.
[93] Gerhard Lenski, "Social Participation and Status Crystallization," *American Sociological Review*, 21 (August 1956), 458–464.
[94] Ringer and Sills, *op. cit.*
[95] Lipset and Bendix, "The Consequences of Social Mobility," in *Social Mobility in Industrial Society* (Berkeley: University of California Press, 1960), pp. 64ff.

has found right wing extremism to be associated with inconsistent status.⁹⁶

Research findings regarding the relationship between status inconsistency and political attitudes have been contradictory. William Kenkel, in a replication of Lenski's 1954 study, found no relationship between status inconsistency and political liberalism.⁹⁷ In a more recent article, Kelly and Chambliss support Kenkel's findings and further conclude that: (1) political liberalism is not a unidimensional phenomenon—persons may be liberal on some issues and conservative on others; (2) status inconsistent persons tend to be slightly more conservative than status consistent persons; (3) results tend to be the same whether consistency is objectively or subjectively (perceptually) defined; (4) social class membership and minority group status appear to be superior to status crystallization as explanatory concepts.⁹⁸ Brandmeyer, in his replication of Lenski's research, concluded that there is no relationship between status inconsistency and political liberalism.⁹⁹ Instead he found that status alone accounted for conservative and liberal orientations—the former being related to high scores for occupation, education, and ethnicity, the latter being related to low scores on these variables. Hyman found no general pattern of association between status inconsistency and liberal-conservative ideology.¹⁰⁰ He did, however, find evidence to suggest that inconsistency predisposes political responses that are either emotional reactions to the strains inherent in inconsistency or responses that are instrumental in the re-equilibration of inconsistency. Sokol, using the same status variables and the same measure of crystallization as Lenski, found no relationship between inconsistency and party preference, welfare liberalism, McCarthyism, desire for change in the national power structure, sociability, or mobility orientation.¹⁰¹ Finally, there is also an apparent contradiction between findings linking both political liberalism and right wing extremism to status inconsistency.¹⁰² However, it may be that both liberalism and conservatism are related to inconsistency. For example, one of the authors has found that, irrespective of income status, a combination of high occupation and low education statuses seems to predispose

---

⁹⁶ Gary B. Rush, "Status Consistency and Right-Wing Extremism," *American Sociological Review*, 32 (February 1967), 86–92.
⁹⁷ William F. Kenkel, "The Relationship Between Status Consistency and Politico-Economic Attitudes," *American Sociological Review*, 21 (June 1956), 365–368.
⁹⁸ K. Dennis Kelly and William J. Chambliss, "Status Consistency and Political Attitudes," *American Sociological Review*, 31 (June 1966), 375–382.
⁹⁹ Gerard A. Brandmeyer, "Status Consistency and Political Behavior: A Replication and Extension of Research," *Public Opinion Quarterly*, 6 (Summer 1965), 241–256.
¹⁰⁰ Martin D. Hyman, "Some Attitudinal and Behavioral Consequences of Certain Forms of Rank Inconsistency" (unpublished Ph.D. dissertation, Columbia University, 1964).
¹⁰¹ Robert Sokol, "Status Inconsistency: Specification of a Theory" (unpublished Ph.D. dissertation, Columbia University, 1961).
¹⁰² See Gerhard E. Lenski, "Status Crystallization," *op. cit.*, and Gary B. Rush, *op. cit.*, esp. p. 92.

to conservative attitudes, whereas low occupation and high education statuses result in a liberal response.

In addition to these empirical difficulties, certain theoretical problems associated with the status crystallization model should not be overlooked. Most salient among these are its biases toward a psychologistic explanation of human behavior and a consensus or equilibrium view of society. The majority of literature on status crystallization deals with motivated behavior as a consequence of subjective psychological states (e.g., stress, ambiguity, unstable self-image) created by status inconsistencies. A direct relationship between inconsistency, stress, and social behavior has yet to be established, however, and the proof for the intervening stress variable in this causal sequence remains tautological (that is, inferred from the presence of the dependent, behavioral variable). Moreover, many as yet untested factors can operate to determine responses to inconsistency under different conditions. For instance, we would expect different responses according to whether or not an individual perceives himself as status discrepant, according to his reference group orientations, and according to which status or statuses he focuses on. Aside from these objections, emphasis on subjective states of individual actors tends to obscure the possibility that motivated behavior is a consequence of objective social factors (e.g., economic, political) in characteristically social settings (e.g., class, interest group).

An apparent assumption in most of the empirical studies using status crystallization theory is that only inconsistent status is pertinent to social behavior. This would seem to imply that the "natural" state of affairs is one of status consistency, the absence of which generates activity. Moreover, much of this activity (e.g., upward mobility, motivation to action, desire for change) would appear to be oriented to achieving consistency between status variables. This assumption has been made explicit by a number of theorists.[103] Thus, the status crystallization hypothesis seems to imply a normative state of equilibrium toward which people strive either consciously or unconsciously. In contrast to this "equilibrium" point of view, is it not equally reasonable to envision a lack of status consistency as the prevailing condition of a society? This would be particularly applicable to dynamic societies characterized by rapid social change. This is essentially the position taken by Bloombaum, who suggests that a high degree of vertical mobility offers opportunities for status consistent individuals to become inconsistent with respect to income, educational, and occupational levels.[104]

---

[103] See, for example, Benoit-Smullyan, *op. cit.*, and Frederick L. Bates and Roland J. Pellegrin, "Congruity and Incongruity of Status Attributes," *Social Forces*, 38 (October 1959), 23–28.
[104] Milton Bloombaum, "The Mobility Dimension in Status Consistency," *Sociology and Social Research*, 48 (April 1964), 340–347.

The problem of the relationship between status inconsistency and political behavior is taken up in the following article by Anderson and Zelditch. Specifically, the authors argue that status inconsistencies can lead to responses other than political behavior and that, where a political response is chosen, its direction can be dependent upon a number of social circumstances.

Excerpts from Bo Anderson and Morris Zelditch, Jr., "Rank Equilibration and Political Behavior," Archives Européennes de Sociologie, Vol. V (1964), pp. 112–125. Reprinted by permission of Bo Anderson, Morris Zelditch and the European Journal of Sociology.

INTRODUCTION

The term "status politics" refers to a way of conceptualizing some aspects of political behavior, which at present enjoys a certain vogue among sociologists and political scientists. Briefly stated, this theory says that people vote the way they do, support certain organizations or political figures or express beliefs about and attitudes toward other groups or people because they are trying either to improve home rank(s) or defend some rank advantage(s) they see themselves as having over groups or people. "Rank" in this context refers to positively evaluated characteristics (achieved *or* ascribed) which people can possess to a greater or less extent. Education, Income, Authority (relative to some group), Seniority (in some work group for instance), Ethnicity (in some societies) are examples of ranks. . . .

The basic idea in this theory [rank equilibration] can be briefly sketched as follows. We assumed that $r_1, r_2 \ldots r_n$ are ranks in a given social system which includes two people A and B. A is *consistently* high on all his ranks, while B is high on some and low on others. Now, under some conditions, if B compares himself with A, a state of imbalance occurs. B may, for instance, notice that although he has the same education as A, his income is considerably lower. He then feels relatively deprived. A comparing himself with B may feel guilty about the same situation. *It is assumed that people, when confronted in comparison situations with states of imbalance occurring will often try, if possible, to act in such a way as to eliminate the imbalance.*[105]

The theory, then, has to specify the conditions under which dis-

---

[105] An important illustration is George C. Homans's study of clerical workers. His ledger clerks feel relatively deprived when they compare themselves with the cash posters. The ledger clerks point out that they actually have more responsibility and

covered inconsistencies actually will lead to imbalance and also with what the individuals concerned will try to do about it under varying conditions. . . .

Consider first a situation in which Ego has Low Education but a High Income and Alter has both High Education and High Income. No effects are going to result unless some comparison process between Ego and Alter occurs. Assume that Ego compares his ranks with those of Alter. Ego may feel that given the investment in education he has made he is doing well, since he makes as much money as Alter who has invested more in education. This situation may, then, lead to a feeling of *relative satisfaction* on Ego's part. Therefore, Ego may feel satisfied with the social order and will not attempt to change it. It is conceivable, however, that Ego will feel sorry for Alter if he thinks that Alter by no fault of his own has not gotten the rewards that his education would normally entitle him to. It is not easy to predict if this compassion will affect Ego's feelings about the social order, though.

Let us now assume that Ego and Alter have the same income, but that Ego has lower Ethnic rank than Alter.

	Rank 1 Ethnicity	Rank 2 Income
Ego	Low	Same
Alter	High	Same

We first consider the situation from Ego's point of view. We make the following assumption as part of what it means that Ego's Ethnic rank is lower than that of Alter:

Assumption (Partial definition of "Ego has lower Ethnic rank than Alter"): If Ego tries to engage in diffuse social interaction with Alter then Alter will rebuff Ego with probability p, $p > .50$.

If Ego compares himself with Alter he will focus attention on either the first or second of his ranks. Focusing on the first, he may reason that "for a (Jew, Negro . . .) I'm doing quite well, since I make as much as Alter." But focusing on his second rank he might say: "I make as much money as Alter but Alter still won't accept me socially because I'm a (Jew, Negro . . .)." The first choice is likely to lead to a feeling of rela-

---

seniority but get the same pay as the cash posters. The conditions under which imbalance does not occur include role differentiation. A welder in a plant, for instance, does not normally expect a manager to get less pay than himself although the manager is usually less competent at welding. This and other conditions are discussed in the theory paper. Cf. G. C. Homans, "La congruence du status," *J. psych.*, LIV (1957), 22–34, and "Status among Clerical Workers," *Human Organization*, XII (1953), 5–10.

tive *satisfaction*. The second, on the other hand, will lead to a feeling of relative *deprivation* (provided that Ego feels that his Ethnic group should be treated as equal to that of Alter).

What consequences does relative deprivation have in such a case?

A. Ego can cease comparing himself with Alter and people like Alter and instead interact solely with other members of his own Ethnic group. This response we term "insulation." In this way ethnicity eventually ceases to be a differentiating characteristic since everybody Ego compares himself with has the same Ethnic rank.

B. Ego can persist trying to interact diffusely with Alter and comparing himself with Alter, and in the course of this "atrophy" his Ethnic status. This is a form of individual mobility called "passing."

C. Ego can engage in activities designed to change the social evaluation given his Ethnic Group. This may lead him to participation in organized groups with such goals, such as the Antidefamation League or the NAACP. In the course of this, he may persist trying to interact with Alter to some extent in order to try to change Alter's behavior toward lower ethnic groups.

Responses A and C can, of course, occur in conjunction, but both appear to be incompatible with B. There may be some question about how appropriate it is to speak of the situation as one involving a *choice* between A, B and C. Instead of saying that "Ego chooses between A, B and C we might say that "one and only one of A, B and C will occur." We speak of a choice because we believe that *at least sometimes* the individual makes a *conscious and deliberate* decision about which alternative to select.

All three responses *may or may not* lead to political manifestations. A person who chooses to insulate may acquire power within his ethnic group, and may be able to influence the voting power of that group to further certain group interests. This, no doubt, presupposes that the ethnic group is an organized community, to some degree capable of united political action, and not merely a statistical aggregate of individuals scattered all over the social system. Some American Jewish communities seem to have this characteristic.[106] The "passer" may decide to embrace the traditionally conservative Republican's political views of the higher ranking group he is trying to pass into, in order to appear "respectable" or he may withdraw entirely from political commitment. The civil rights combatant is likely to engage in political action to attain his goals. He may become concerned with the rights of other ethnic and non-ethnic

[106] See, for instance, Herbert J. Gans, "The Origin and Growth of a Jewish Community in the Suburbs: A Study of the Jews of Park Forest," in M. Sklare, ed., *The Jews, Social Patterns of an American Group* (Glencoe: Free Press, 1958), 205–248. See also Judith R. Kramer and Seymour Levetman, *Children of the Gilded Ghetto: Conflict Resolutions of Three Generations of American Jews* (New Haven: Yale University Press, 1961).

underdogs as well, but the conditions for this generalization of attitudes to take place are not well understood.

Let us now look at the situation from Alter's point of view. Alter may reason either that (a) "I don't make any more money than he does but at least I'm . . . (high status Ethnic group) . . . ," or (b) "How comes that . . . (low Ethnic group) makes as much money as I do?" The first choice leads to relative satisfaction, and the second choice to relative deprivation. Regardless of which choice he makes, there is a possibility he will react to the comparison by reasserting his Ethnic rank. If, for instance, *general community rank* contains the weighted components Income, Ethnicity . . . , then Alter will try to increase the weight with which Ethnic rank enters into community rank. In politics this may create sentiments of "nativism," and antisemitism and xenophobia may be manifestations of this. If the second choice is made initially in the comparison, then reassertion of Ethnic rank may lead to hostility toward Ego in order to show him "his place." (Hostility directed toward Ego leads to social rebuff of Ego, and we have just seen that this may have affected how Ego responds after comparing himself with Alter).

Involved in this case is the "structural" fact that Alter cannot let Ego improve his ethnic rank without Ego losing some of his. A person of mainly Anglo-Saxon descent in the U.S., for instance, has high ethnic rank *only* because Negroes, Jews and others have low. So if ethnic rank matters much to Alter (and it will matter a lot for some persons whose *only* high rank is the ethnic one), then attempts by Ego to raise his may become a serious threat to Alter. This results in resentment and "rank saving" behavior, including prejudice and hostility. The only way in which Ego can change his ethnic rank without conflict with Alter is if ethnicity ceases to be a differentially evaluated characteristic. People may of course still be proud of their ethnic identity, but they no longer use it as a basis for invidious comparisons. This seems to considerable extent to be happening in America at present. Empirical findings showing that lower class people are more in favor of discrimination against Negroes than higher class people is certainly *consistent* with the rank saving hypothesis. However, it is hard to tell whether reported prejudice is due to attempts to save rank rather than some other factor, for instance lack of education. A well educated person is more likely than a less educated one to know that some of the beliefs underlying racial prejudice are *in fact* unfounded and may therefore find it impossible to hold some prejudiced opinions even though such opinions would be convenient as rank saving devices. A careful motivational analysis is required before we can impute rank saving as a motive behind bigoted opinions and behavior.

There are some data bearing on rank reassertion: Robert Sokol has studied the combination *High* Ethnicity/*Low* Income or Occupation and found that such people tend to support McCarthyism and to be more

Conservative in their politics than lower income and occupation people in general are. The historian Richard Hofstadter has used similar arguments to explain the rise of the Ku Klux Klan as a reassertion of rural Anglo-Saxon Protestants of their Ethnic rank in opposition to the more recently arrived Ethnic Groups.[107] A number of papers in a volume on "The New American Right" made the same point about McCarthyism.[108] Consider now a situation in which Ego and Alter compare themselves with one another. Assume that Ego has a white collar job, and makes $6,000 a year. Alter, we assume, has a blue collar job and makes the same amount of money.

	Income	Occupational Group
Ego	$6,000	White Collar
Alter	$6,000	Working Class

Again, when Ego compares himself with Alter he may focus attention on either of his two ranks. He may say that (a) "Alter may make as much money as I make, but I have a better job" or (b) "Why if I have a better job (with more prestige) don't I make more money than he does?" The second choice is clearly more likely to make him feel relatively deprived than the first choice.

Assume now that Ego has in fact chosen the second response. Whether or not he in fact gets seriously upset depends on at least one factor; namely, what he expects his future earnings to be. If Ego is 21 years old and just out of college and expects to rise gradually into higher income brackets he may not feel very deprived, especially if Alter is middle-aged and not likely to change *his* income upward in the future. On the other hand, if both Ego and Alter are middle-aged and if the relation between their earnings is not likely to change in the future, then Ego may come to feel that he makes unjustly less than he ought to in comparison with Alter. We can capture his difference in outcome in the proposition that if *Ego finds his rank inconsistent in comparison with Alter he will get upset to the extent that he perceives that upward mobility in his lower rank(s) is blocked.* If the situation is perceived to be transient then Ego is not likely to get upset.

Let us now assume that Ego does in fact get upset when he compares his ranks with those of Alter. Then there are in fact several possible reactions that can occur. (a) Ego may blame the unfavorable comparison in income on "monopolistic practices of the unions," and conclude that

---

[107] Richard Hofstadter, "The Pseudo-Conservative Revolt," in D. Bell, *The New American Right* (New York: Criterion Books, 1955), pp. 33–55.
[108] D. Bell, *op. cit.*

right-to-work legislation is called for. In pursuing this line of thought he may also expose himself to other political views propagated by advocates of right-to-work laws and he may again through some generalization process, come to take a more or less general radical rightist view of political questions.[109] (b) Ego may decide that the workman is better off economically because of his union, and conclude that a strong white collar union is called for to look after the interests of Ego's own group. He may thus develop a very pro-union attitude and may also expose himself to other "radical" influences as well.

Which factors will influence Ego's reactions in this situation? We know very little about this question, but one "structural factor" seems certain to influence Ego's choice: Response (b) can occur only if a substantial proportion of the people who are in the same occupational class as Ego are willing to join a union. The conditions for this to happen are not very well understood (when identified they will form the basis for a theory of the emergence of social movements) but according to our theory individual mobility expectations play an important role. *If a person experiences deprivation associated with his present status then the more strong his expectation is that he himself will be able to move to a higher status with less deprivation, the less likely he is to combine with others to remove the causes of deprivation in his present status.*

So if it is the case that the bulk of American white collar workers, especially those in the younger groups, expect to be potentially mobile into higher statuses (or for women to expect their jobs to be temporary) then there is little basis for a vigorous union movement. A consequence of this is that a rank inconsistent middle-aged person who no longer expects to be mobile will find it hard to choose response (b).

Among European white collar workers, on the other hand, individual mobility expectations are said to be less widespread and accentuated. Unions have consequently caught hold among white collar workers in England, the Scandinavian countries and France to a larger extent than in the U.S. This line of thought has been put forth by Lipset

[109] Lockwood reports some British data on the attitudes of the clerks to the working class organization. "In a Gallup Poll (1956) roughly one out of every three clerks who were interviewed on the causes of recent strikes and on the policy the government should take in this situation gave answers which clearly demonstrated their conception of the working class and trade unionism as a threatening and dangerous force which should be repressed." *The Blackcoated Worker* (London: Allen and Unwin, 1958), p. 104, footnote 2. Lockwood's entire chapter on the status problems of the British white collar workers contains many useful insights into status politics of the lower middle class in England. In his autobiography Ernst Wigforss, a Swedish socialist politician, gives excerpts from a letter containing a vivid eyewitness account of a meeting at which the Rev. Stocker, a prominent leader in the pre–World War I antisemitic movement in Germany, spoke. Stocker's speech blaming the Jews and the labor movement for all evils had a strong appeal among some lower middle class elements. See Ernst Wigforss, *Minnen, 1914–1932*, Vol. II (Stockholm: Tidens Forlag, 1951), pp. 27ff.

and Bendix in their discussion of social mobility.[110] They make a great deal of differences in values and beliefs about social mobility said to exist between European countries and the U.S. although the actual differences in mobility rates between European countries and the U.S. are quite small.

Thus, where, as in the United States, social mobility receives positive encouragement, the existing opportunities for upward mobility probably help to sustain the acceptance of the social and political order, by the lower classes. But such opportunities probably cannot shake the distrust of the prevailing order that exists among lower class persons in such countries as France, where the dominant historical image is one of an unfair distribution of opportunities, in which little mobility occurs.[111]

Lipset and Bendix point to several factors which in their view contribute to the maintenance of widespread mobility expectations among Americans: the absence of a feudal past, educational opportunities, the presence of successive waves of immigrant minorities who have taken over much of the manual labor from those that arrived at an earlier time and who are not assimilating into American society. A substantial increase in the standard of living has also benefited those immigrants who remain low class and their children, especially compared to the conditions they used to live under in the countries of origin.

Also, whether a rightist or a leftist response will occur in a rank-inconsistent situation will depend on the cultural modes of thinking available in the milieu of the actor. If, as seems to be the case with parts of the American middle class, rightist modes of thinking, expressed in suspicion of the central government, vague fears of Socialism, admiration for the tough self-made man and so on, permeate the milieu of an individual, he will be more likely to select a rightist than a leftist response. Also, if a strong external "enemy" like the Soviet Union in a way is identified with some of the symbols of leftism, such as socialism, state control and so on, then these symbols will take on an even more odious quality. It goes without saying that it is hard to get information about some of the individual's perception of these factors using conventional survey research methods.

Let us now summarize the main arguments presented so far.

1. From the three examples discussed it should be clear that (a) rank inconsistency does not invariably produce a political response and (b) that if a political response occurs it can be rightist or leftist or take

---

[110] Seymour M. Lipset and Reinhard Bendix, *Social Mobility in Industrial Society* (Berkeley: University of California Press, 1960).
[111] This is Lipset's and Bendix' main thesis, but the data advanced to support it are far from satisfactory.

the form of political apathy depending on certain not very well understood conditions.

2. We know little, if anything, about the factors governing which rank people will focus attention on. Also, we have assumed that Ego's choice of which rank he will focus attention on takes place in a situation where the alternatives are mutually exclusive. That is, if Ego focuses attention on Rank 1 then it follows that he does not focus on Rank 2 at *that particular time*. However, it may well be that Ego at one time focuses on Rank 1 and at some later time focuses on Rank 2. Oscillations between different ranks over time are definitely possible, and this will possibly have interesting psychological consequences. Does it lead to sentiments of ambivalence toward, let us say, Ego's Ethnic group if he alternately tells himself that "for a (Jew, Negro . . .) I'm doing quite well" and "why, if I make as much money as Alter, does he rebuff me?"

3. The theory remains rather indeterminate with respect to the response process following the occurrence of relative deprivation. For instance in case 2 above we list three possible results of feelings of relative deprivation on the part of Ego with low Ethnic rank, but we know little about the determinants of the choice between these alternatives. . . .

In using the concept of relative deprivation, Anderson and Zelditch subsume status politics as a special aspect of a more general theory of status equilibration. Although the theoretical and empirical rationales for this are considerable, the notion of status politics has been so widely used in the literature that we feel it merits consideration here as if it were an analytically distinct concept.

Status Politics

The notions of class and status consistency are objective criteria of social position; that is, a person has a defined location in the economic order and has achieved a certain educational level. However, beginning with Warner's concept of evaluated participation,[112] sociologists have also utilized subjective yardsticks of status, those of deference and prestige. The deference and prestige afforded to the incumbent of a social position in any given historical period are ascribed by the values of that society. Nevertheless, these values are not static. Over time, societal definitions of the relative worth of various strata fluctuate, possibly resulting in conflicts between the individual incumbent's perceptions of the worth of his position vis-à-vis the perceptions of others in his society. It should be

[112] W. Lloyd Warner et al., *Social Class in America: The Evaluation of Status* (New York: Harper & Brothers, 1949).

noted that the decline of a value held by a person is not necessarily related to the role he carries out in his social position. For example, the objective role of the small entrepreneur has essentially remained unchanged in the life of the small town or suburban community in the past two decades. However, the advent of the chain department store has placed him in a disadvantaged economic position. Since his margin of profit on one-of-a-kind sales is considerably lower than the gains enjoyed by the chain store on multiple sales, he must charge more for comparable goods. Therefore, his trade becomes dependent on "convenience" sales and he no longer enjoys the same "businessman" prestige he once relished, even though his role as a merchant remains the same. As a result, he feels disadvantaged as a member of the community. In the literature on social movements, these fluctuations in deference and prestige, and the attitudes and behaviors resulting from them, have been subsumed under the conceptual heading of status politics.

The application of the status politics concept in operational form began with the analysis of the right wing movements of the thirties.[113] At that time, the major focus of attention was the Nazi movement in Germany. Following the defeat of the Axis powers and the revelations of human and political abuses in Europe, other researchers attempted to document the nature and methods of totalitarianism. A mass of literature appeared dealing with the social variables leading to the rise and maintenance of the Nazis and the nature of political agitation. One of the more influential works was Hannah Arendt's The Origins of Totalitarianism. She indicated that one of the foundations of a stable society was a static and secure middle class. The decline of this stratum, she argued, contributed heavily to the rise of Nazism.[114] Other students of German Fascism have expounded similar themes. Seymour Martin Lipset observed that "The ideal-typical Nazi voter in 1932 was a middle-class self-employed Protestant. . . ."[115] Erich Fromm attributed support for Fascism to the status anxieties of the middle class in Germany, noting that "The increasing social frustration [of the middle class] led to a projection which became an important source for National Socialism."[116] Hadley Cantril added: "There was every reason for the white-collar worker, the member of the lower middle class, to feel that his status was threatened, that he would soon be indistinguishable from a member of the proletariat."[117] For these students of German nationalism, status factors contributed

---

[113] See Erich Fromm, *Escape From Freedom* (New York: Holt, Rinehart and Winston, 1941); Lewis Corey, *The Crisis of the Middle Class* (New York: Covici and Friede, 1935); Hadley Cantril, *The Psychology of Social Movements* (New York: John Wiley & Sons, 1941); Hannah Arendt, *The Origins of Totalitarianism* (New York: World Publishing Co., 1964).
[114] Arendt, *op. cit.*, pp. 314–317.
[115] Lipset, *op. cit.*, p. 148.
[116] Fromm, *Escape From Freedom, op. cit.*, p. 216.
[117] Cantril, *op. cit.*, p. 227.

heavily to the social bases of support for Fascist social movements. Lewis Corey, a Marxist, concurred in this view. Corey suggested that independent small entrepreneurs and other members of the middle class rallied to Fascism for security, did not find it, but continued to oppose social change because of their social position and false class consciousness.[118] In sum, the decline of given status groups leads to the formation and support of social movements. Recently this approach has been transferred from the study of the Third Reich to the analysis of other social movements by both historians and sociologists.

Richard Hofstadter introduced the notion of status conflict into the historical analysis of social movements in his treatment of the Populist and Progressive movements in The Age of Reform.[119] His general thesis was that social movements which emerged in times of prosperity were: ". . . to a very considerable extent led by men who suffered from the events of their time not through shrinkage in their means but through the changed pattern in the distribution of deference and power."[120] According to Hofstadter, two classes—the parvenu class and the older, "established" middle class—experienced an imbalance in social honor and prestige, the former because its members did not possess the social honor commensurate with their occupational role, the latter because its members perceived their status ranking being assaulted by the social and economic changes occurring in society. The rise of the extreme Right in a time of relative economic prosperity in America brought Hofstadter's thesis into vogue.

Observers of the extreme Right such as Trow, Hyman, Bell, Riesman, Hofstadter, and others have suggested hypotheses derived from Weber's notion of status groups—hypotheses embodying phrases such as nineteenth-century liberals, the threat oriented, the dispossessed, the discontented classes, and status politics—to account for the supporters of McCarthyism and the John Birch Society.[121] These scholars have sug-

[118] Corey, op. cit., pp. 278–309.
[119] Richard Hofstadter, The Age of Reform (New York: Vintage Books, 1955).
[120] Ibid., p. 135.
[121] See Roger Hagan, "American Response to Change," Contact, 3 (September 1961), 7–17; John R. Bunzel, The American Small Businessman (New York: Alfred A. Knopf, 1962), pp. 255–259, and "The General Ideology of American Small Business," Political Science Quarterly, LXX (March 1955), 87–102; Martin Trow, "Small Businessmen, Political Tolerance, and Support for McCarthy," American Journal of Sociology, 64 (November 1958), 270–281; Daniel Bell, "The Dispossessed," in Daniel Bell, ed., The Radical Right (Garden City, N.Y.: Anchor Books, 1964), pp. 1–46; Richard Hofstadter, "The Pseudo-Conservative Revolt," in ibid., pp. 75–96; David Riesman and Nathan Glazer, "The Intellectuals and the Discontented Classes," in ibid., pp. 105–136; S. M. Lipset, "The Sources of the 'Radical Right,'" and "Three Decades of the Radical Right: Coughlinites, McCarthyites and Birchers," in ibid., pp. 307–446; Richard Hofstadter, Anti-Intellectualism in American Life (New York: Alfred Knopf, 1963), pp. 117–141; William Kornhauser, op. cit., pp. 194–207. For criticisms of this approach see Margaret Mead, "The New Isolationism," The American Scholar (Summer 1955), 378–382.

gested that persons in declining religious, ethnic, class, occupational, age, family, and geographic groups are victims of status strains, and hence are prone to membership in extremist movements.

Empirically, however, the extreme Right has not been peopled exclusively by those subject to declining values or status positions. Rich and politically powerful oilmen, for example, are found in the ranks of the right, one notable example being H. L. Hunt. As a consequence of this empirical fact, several sociologists have added ascending ethnic and economic groups to the status politics conceptualization. These observers argue that while the new rich have economic power, they do not enjoy social honor. The use of the status politics argument in this dual manner has prompted one observer to write:

This kind of analysis, which explains every possible or supposed appearance of the phenomenon, is of course in part a function of the paucity of data on the issue. But, while such an analysis precludes surprises, it also explains a good deal too much. Unless we can account for the actual distribution of support for a given issue or for a leader or spokesman of this political tendency, without finessing the crucial question of "more or less," then our analysis loses much of its power and cogency.[122]

In the following paper, Brandmeyer and Denisoff expand upon Trow's remark. They argue that class politics and status politics are not mutually exclusive concepts and that they are frequently confused. The practices of viewing status politics as either irrational or as an example of scapegoating are examined. Finally, they contend that an overemphasis on Nazism as the social movement par excellence has had an unwarranted influence on the analysts of status politics.

Gerard Brandmeyer and R. Serge Denisoff, "Status Politics: An Appraisal of the Application of a Concept," enlarged version of a paper read at the Annual Meeting of the Pacific Sociological Association in Vancouver, British Columbia, April 8, 1966. Reprinted by permission of Gerard Brandmeyer and R. Serge Denisoff.

The term "status politics" represents a current effort to apply Weber's concept of status group to the analysis of political behavior. Weber's observation [123] that "class" interests based on the sharing of similar claims

---
[122] Trow, *op. cit.*, p. 271.
[123] Hans Gerth and C. Wright Mills, *From Max Weber: Essays in Sociology* (New York: Oxford University Press, 1946), pp. 180–95.

THEORETICAL AND CONCEPTUAL APPROACHES 91

to honor and prestige, are to be treated as distinct for analytical purposes has been shared by this generation of sociologists. Several social scientists, among them Gusfield, Hofstadter, and Lipset, have adapted Weber's class-status dichotomy in their work on political behavior. Weber is recognized as the source of the class-status division, though, with the exception of Gusfield,[124] these writers devote little attention to Weber's account of what he meant by the class-status group distinction. Perhaps it is fair to assume that Weber's ideas are second nature to us now and therefore do not require thorough discussion with each usage. Yet it may be, particularly with his writing on status groups, that Weber has not left us with a sufficiently precise legacy to justify a presumed adequacy.

First we shall examine Hofstadter's conception [125] of how the class-status dichotomy applies to political behavior. He views class (or interest) politics as "the clash of material aims and needs among various groups and blocs." Status politics represents the "clash of various projective rationalizations arising from status aspirations and other personal motives."

For Lipset,[126] class politics is a type of political division which flows from "the discord between the traditional left and the right." In class politics those who advocate redistributing national income engage apologists for the economic status quo. Status politics is defined as "political movements whose appeal is to the not uncommon resentments of individuals or groups who desire to maintain or improve their social status."

It is contended here that these definitions and distinctions are vague and do not provide a sound foundation upon which to base the sweeping analyses which they have prompted.

In Lipset's analysis [127] of support for the radical right, the class-status distinction dissolves when applied to specific groups. Lipset finds that status aspirations and status insecurities are particularly frustrating during periods of prosperity because those who have been upwardly mobile due to general prosperity appear as "a visible threat to the established status groups." And what of those from the established status groups who do not share in this general prosperity? They form the rentier *class*, consisting of those living on "fixed incomes" and "old businesses," both of which Lipset characterizes as *sources of income* "which are prone to decline in their relative position." Thus this rentier *class* has responded to its status problem by supporting the radical right in disproportionately large numbers. Here Lipset demonstrates the futility of attempting to maintain a conceptual distinction between class and status concerns when there are both

[124] Joseph Gusfield, *Symbolic Crusade* (Urbana: University of Illinois Press, 1963), Ch. 1.
[125] Richard Hofstadter, "The Pseudo-Conservative Revolt," in Bell, ed., *The Radical Right*, pp. 84–85.
[126] Seymour Martin Lipset, "The Sources of the 'Radical Right,'" in Bell, ed., *The Radical Right*, pp. 308–309.
[127] *Ibid.*, pp. 339–340.

economic and prestige implications in the situations being examined. This confusion is again illustrated in Trow's study [128] of McCarthy supporters. Status anxieties are seen as "arising especially out of the discrepancy between precarious and deteriorating economic positions and their status claims and aspirations." Here the two concepts are defined in terms of each other. Perhaps it is impossible to separate status and class factors for purposes of inquiry.[129]

Weber's observation that class conflicts abound during periods of economic turmoil, whereas status conflicts intensify during periods of economic stability, has been both misinterpreted and treated as fact rather than as hypothesis.[130] Weber held that focus on status matters intensifies with "every slowing down of the shifting of economic stratification." [131] Shifts in economic interest occur in periods of prosperity as well as in periods of depression. Those groups which do not share proportionately in prosperity are likely to be restive about the state of their economic interests. The fact that they are not as absolutely deprived during generally prosperous times as they might be during a period of general depression does not obviate the fact that there are class as well as status ramifications in any shifting of "economic stratification."

Lipset's work has left the impression that class and status issues operate more independently of each other than they actually do. Perhaps his most glaring confusion of the class and status notions appears in his comparison of the followers of Senator Joseph McCarthy and Father Coughlin. Here he redefines class in terms of socio-economic status by which he means "a measure of the style of life of the respondent, largely reflecting income." [132] In distinguishing between class and status, was not Weber concerned primarily to demonstrate that income does not necessarily indicate style of life?

The same tendency exists in Hofstadter's work. In *The Age of Reform* [133] he interprets the rise of the Progressives at the turn of the century as a response to a "status revolution." Hofstadter pictured the leaders as Progressives because they were victimized by an "upheaval in status" and not because of "economic deprivation." These leaders suffered "not through a shrinkage in their means but through the changed pattern in

---

[128] Martin Trow, "Small Businessmen, Political Tolerance, and Support for McCarthy," *American Journal of Sociology*, LXIV (November 1958), 278.
[129] Hofstadter's work provides still another instance in which the status resentments of Protestant fundamentalists are analyzed in terms of economic issues, i.e., support for business interests. See Richard Hofstadter, *Paranoid Style in American Politics* (New York: Alfred A. Knopf, 1966), pp. 81–82.
[130] See Hofstadter, "The Pseudo-Conservative Revolt," in *op. cit.*, pp. 84–85, and Lipset, *op. cit.*, p. 309.
[131] Garth and Mills, *op. cit.*, p. 194.
[132] Seymour Martin Lipset, "Three Decades of the Radical Right," in Bell, ed., *The Radical Right*, p. 401.
[133] Richard Hofstadter, *The Age of Reform*, pp. 135–137.

the distribution of deference and power." As Hofstadter noted, this was the period when America was being transformed rapidly from its small town and entrepreneurial traditions into a society dominated by large cities and power concentrated in the hands of big business, government, and labor leaders. While the independent businessmen and professionals were not "growing poorer as a class," they were becoming less important.

Yet Hofstadter was unable to explain this status revolution without invoking class considerations.[134] He found that the status revolution was accompanied by price increases which "continued to go up steadily throughout the Progressive era." The result was that the middle class person felt an economic pinch. The mushrooming trusts seemed responsible and so did the working class which was gaining economic power by "organizing to protect itself" and thereby intensifying the inflationary spiral. Thus he was reduced to being just one "of a vast but unorganized and therefore helpless consuming public." Clearly Hofstadter is no better able in his analysis of the Progressives than was Lipset in his treatment of the rentier class to maintain the promised distinction between class and status issues.

Many writers have noted one or another of the misapplications of the status group idea. For example, Gusfield [135] points to a confusion resulting from Hofstadter's conception of status politics. Hofstadter [136] has acknowledged the looseness of his initial conceptualization of status politics. By way of supplementing the original term, he has added cultural politics which involves questions "of faith and morals, tone and style, freedom and coercion, which become fighting issues." [137] As an example of such cultural politics, Hofstadter points to the prohibition campaign which Gusfield [138] has discussed as a prime example of status politics. Finally, Hofstadter introduces projective politics which "involves the projection of interests and concerns, not only largely private but essentially pathological, into the public scene." [139] Here he means the kinds of conspiratorial fantasies and suspicions conjured by the John Birch Society in spelling-out the so-called Communist conspiracy. It would seem that these refinements serve to confuse more than to enlighten.

A further unfortunate development in the unrestrained usage of psychological themes has been the tendency to label radical right politics as "irrational." Hofstadter has confessed disappointment at his own "excessive emphasis on what might be called the clinical side of the prob-

---

[134] *Ibid.*, pp. 168–170.
[135] Gusfield, *op. cit.*, Ch. 7.
[136] Richard Hofstadter, "Pseudo-Conservatism Revisited," in Bell, ed., *The Radical Right*, pp. 97–103.
[137] *Ibid.*, p. 99.
[138] Gusfield, *op. cit.*
[139] Hofstadter, "Pseudo-Conservatism Revisited," *op. cit.*, p. 100.

lem."[140] Too often the bizarre apocalyptic fantasies of the radical right have become central to the definition of status politics. Lipset suggests that "the political movements which have successfully appealed to status resentments have been irrational in character."[141] Hofstadter conceives of status politics as involving basic aspirations which are only "partially conscious."[142] Gusfield summarizes this "psychological expressivism" as reflecting "a view of politics as an arena into which 'irrational' impulses are projected."[143]

A parallel misapplication has occurred through the usage of the term scapegoat in the discussion of status politics. Lipset finds that the political movements of those suffering status resentments have "sought scapegoats which conveniently serve to symbolize the status threat."[144] Hofstadter observes "the tendency of status politics to be expressed more . . . in the search for scapegoats. . . ."[145] For Hofstadter the typical prejudiced person and the typical pseudo-conservative are ordinarily the same individual. Those groups which have been noted for racially discriminatory behavior in the past seek "other scapegoats" today due to "the expediencies and the strategies of the situation."[146] Undeniably much anti-minority group feeling is deliberately masqueraded under the pretext of fighting Communism. However, to accept the inference that right-wing political behavior merely consists of scapegoating is to permit opinion to supplant evidence. It is well to recall Gordon Allport's reminder that the scapegoat theory should not be "misapplied to cases of realistic social conflict."[147] It is generally agreed that many of those who become militant right-wingers face a loss of social prestige and are threatened by social currents which they do not comprehend. The stewards of change, for example, the intellectuals, the government officials, the civil rights leaders, these are often real adversaries of the right-wingers. Therefore, to oppose these changes and to vilify their

[140] *Ibid.* Yet in his book, *The Paranoid Style in American Politics*, Hofstadter has elaborated the psychological thematic approach as evidenced by his suggestion that it "is the use of paranoid modes of expression by more or less normal people" that interests him (Hofstadter, *The Paranoid Style, op. cit.*, p. 4).
[141] Lipset, "Sources of the 'Radical Right,'" *op. cit.*, p. 309.
[142] Hofstadter, "Pseudo-Conservative Revolt," *op. cit.*, p. 85.
[143] Gusfield, *op. cit.*, p. 177. It is puzzling that in their search for characterological explanations, these authors are disinclined to suggest the reciprocal possibility that the strength of one's commitments to a particular ideology may suggest the degree of likelihood that one will view all efforts to prevent the implementation of that ideology as due to a diabolical conspiracy. Perhaps as a consequence of the generally liberal sentiments of most social scientists, our work is impaired by a kind of perceptual myopia which prevents our recognizing the similarities in style among those deeply devoted to any ideology.
[144] Lipset, "Sources of the 'Radical Right,'" *op. cit.*, p. 309.
[145] Hofstadter, "Pseudo-Conservative Revolt," *op. cit.*, p. 85.
[146] *Ibid.*, p. 91.
[147] Gordon W. Allport, *The Nature of Prejudice* (Cambridge, Mass.: Addison-Wesley, 1956), p. 352.

THEORETICAL AND CONCEPTUAL APPROACHES

advocates is not to scapegoat. It should be noted that Hofstadter did not employ this scapegoat analysis in describing the responses of the Progressives to their status resentments, but then the Progressives were not the "typical pseudo-conservatives."

Perhaps the misuse of scapegoating resulted from the impact which the Nazi experience had on social scientists. There has been a tendency to attribute the more salient characteristics of the Nazis to all extremists, and especially right-wing groups. Many easy parallels have been drawn between Nazi Germany and the American political scene. A major source for these analogies has been Lowenthal and Guterman's *Prophets of Deceit* in which "the agitator" is portrayed as "guided by his professed sympathy for European totalitarianism or avowed anti-Semitism."[148] The subjects in this study are of the familiar depression-bred type, such as Gerald L. K. Smith, Gerald Winrod, and Father Coughlin. Hofstadter refers to this study of "the right-wing agitator" in documenting his assertion that status politics is expressed "in vindictiveness, in sour memories, in the search for scapegoats."[149]

The rise of the Nazi movement and the subsequent fate of the European Jews no doubt contributed to the belief among scholars that post-war right-wing political behavior is exclusively symptomatic of status resentments. Since status resentments had been linked conceptually to periods of prosperity, it became necessary to declare, as Lipset has, that it is especially during periods of prosperity "that status anxieties are most pressing."[150] Here Lipset is overlooking the fact that the status resentments of the German middle classes did not overwhelm Germany or threaten Europe until after a severe depression had crippled the German economy. It was only then that the Nazis could capitalize fully on latent anti-Semitism.

This tendency to overdraw in presenting the politics of prosperous times as status politics and the politics of depressions as examples of class politics can be found repeatedly in Lipset's analyses.[151] He pictures the Know Nothings, the A.P.A., the Progressives, the Ku Klux Klan, and the McCarthyites as scapegoating protestors peculiar to periods of prosperity as evidenced by their attacks upon those who threaten their values and their coincident inability to attract large followings during periods of economic distress. Lipset is correct in stating that "no mass social movement based on bigotry" was successful during the Depression. Yet Lipset later

[148] Leo Lowenthal and Norbert Guterman, *Prophets of Deceit* (New York: Harper & Brothers, 1949), p. 143.
[149] Hofstadter, "Pseudo-Conservative Revolt," *op. cit.*, p. 85.
[150] Lipset, "Sources of the 'Radical Right,'" *op. cit.*, p. 309. Trow has interpreted German middle class support for Hitler as resulting from fear which involved "concern with both material and status security." Trow, *op. cit.*, p. 277.
[151] Lipset, "Sources of the 'Radical Right,'" *op. cit.*, pp. 314–315.

wrote that feeling against the Jews was "much stronger in the 1930's than it has been since." [152] This would suggest that ethnic scapegoating has been more intense during periods of depression.

Here once again is a distortion of the class-status distinction. The Klan is widely held to have been a response to post-Civil War Reconstruction—a period of both social and economic dislocation throughout the South. When the Klan was revived in the 1920's, just as with its current restoration, concern for economic security was very much intermingled with status concerns. In the present instance, the reality of Negro demands for more equal access to scarce job opportunities undermines white working class perceptions of life chances both in the South and in the North where George Wallace's electoral strength in white working class neighborhoods in the Wisconsin, Indiana, and Maryland presidential primaries in 1964 has been construed as a reaction to fear over job security in a period of rapid technological displacement. It is apparent that general prosperity may not insulate the entire population from anxiety over economic security.

The view that depressions point economic classes toward specific targets in their quest for reform while prosperity accentuates status resentments which result in scapegoating might account for the observation made by both Hofstadter [153] and Lipset [154] that status conflicts do not suggest solutions. In this connection, Gusfield [155] has challenged Lipset's assertion that when "there are status anxieties, there is little or nothing a government can do." [156] The role performed by the federal government in the civil rights struggle refutes Lipset's claim. Yet Lipset's conclusion seems plausible when considered from the premise that status groups are preoccupied with reassurances involving their prestige aspirations while interest groups pursue instrumental goals such as higher wages or lower taxes. Gusfield [157] grasps the significance of this difference when he suggests that status groups pursue symbolic rather than instrumental goals. Symbolic goals are achieved in the performance of whatever behavior they inspire rather than in any state which they create.[158]

Accordingly, Gusfield views the struggles over school integration as

[152] Lipset, "Three Decades of the Radical Right," *op. cit.*, p. 441.
[153] Hofstadter, "Pseudo-Conservative Revolt," *op. cit.*, p. 85.
[154] Lipset, "Sources of the 'Radical Right,'" *op. cit.*, p. 309.
[155] Gusfield, *op. cit.*, p. 176.
[156] Lipset, "Sources of the 'Radical Right,'" *op. cit.*, p. 309.
[157] Gusfield, *op. cit.*, Chs. 1 and 7.
[158] In developing his "dramatistic theory" of status politics, Gusfield suggests that "status politics is a form of interest-oriented politics" when it involves the "enhancement or defense of a position in the status order," such as prevailing upon churches, schools, or the mass media to respect a given group's "tastes, morals, and other aspects of life styles." This would seem to be an important but confusing qualification of Gusfield's aforestated position on the symbolic nature of the goals of status groups. Gusfield, *op. cit.*, pp. 175–176.

symbolic rather than instrumental.[159] This issue is not whether "most Negroes will actually be attending integrated schools in the near future" or even whether "better educational conditions for Negroes will result." The issue is the symbolic one of equal rights represented by "acceptance of the principle of integration, expressed in token integration" which represents a symbolic "act of deference which raises the prestige of the Negro."

The symbolic value of the initial token achievements is not to be denied. However, soon after these token gains are secured, they are followed by pressure for more wide-spread and comprehensive accomplishments in each institutional area where discrimination persists. Hence while the initial success may appear more symbolic than instrumental, it rarely satisfied the appetite of those whose prestige claims have traditionally been ignored. The career of Martin Luther King demonstrates that his early successes with bus boycotts, marches, and lunch counter sit-ins have now stimulated challenges to his leadership. He must deliver tangible, instrumental gains in terms of open occupancy and equal employment opportunities for the black masses, if he is to escape the condemnation of the militants for whom his leadership was once charismatic.

Gusfield's [160] analysis of the 1960 presidential election contains the same flaw. He feels that "only the naive and the stupid" would accept the suggestion that, in voting against Kennedy, Protestants were "protecting the White House from papal domination." Gusfield viewed those Protestants as trying symbolically to protect their prestige vis-à-vis Catholics by maintaining their hold on the White House. Yet it is generally acknowledged that many fundamentalist Christians view Catholic political power as a threat to American Freedom,[161] so that to them a vote for Kennedy was a threat to religious liberty. Kennedy's election was construed as more than a symbolic defeat by these people.[162]

---

[159] *Ibid.*, p. 22.
[160] *Ibid.*
[161] While there may have been some decline in the degree of abhorrence which most fundamentalist Christians feel toward Catholicism, there is no evidence that many would welcome a union with Catholics to resist Communism with "grand ecumenical zeal" as Hofstadter suggests (Hofstadter, *Paranoid Style in American Politics, op. cit.*, pp. 74-80).

Also, the conservatism of many leading right wing Catholic spokesmen, especially the intellectuals, is founded on a desire to reinstate the world order of the pre-Reformation Holy Roman Empire. They might be willing to cooperate with fundamentalists for the achievement of short-range, limited goals. However, there is little reason to anticipate that William Buckley, for example, would be able to work in permanent harmony with Billy James Hargis.

[162] The senior author is familiar with one fundamentalist congregation several of the members of which felt betrayed when their pastor did not speak out against the vice-presidential candidacy of another Roman Catholic, Representative William Miller, on the Republican ticket in 1964. It was felt that the politically conservative minister had been manipulative in openly opposing the candidacy of the liberal Kennedy while tacitly accepting the conservative Miller.

Another important criticism of these and similar investigations of the sources of the radical right is that they lead to gross and self-defeating categorizations. Trow [163] has noted this practice "which explains every possible or supposed appearance of [the radical right] phenomenon," thus explaining "a good deal too much." Polsby [164] finds that the status politics hypothesis "neither differentiates successfully among groups, nor provides criteria by which some groups can be excluded from its purview." Gusfield [165] considers these studies which portray highly diverse and often conflicting groups as sources of right-wing support as testimony to the essentially "loose" character of status constituencies which respond to symbolic issues. Perhaps these investigations might best be characterized as unduly speculative and therefore easily confounded by contrary interpretations which offer competing claims to plausibility.[166] Occasionally these authors even contradict themselves. In his review of the data on support for McCarthy, Lipset [167] found little empirical evidence for the hypothesis that McCarthy appealed to traditional Populist sentiments.[168] Yet later in the very same essay Lipset [169] wrote that McCarthy attracted those outside the centers of power who were "opposed to the social and big-business elite and to the organized liberal and trade-union forces."

Finally, in working with impressionistic data, researchers tend to indulge the temptation to project their personal sentiments upon the group in question. Gusfield [170] reminds us that social scientists are not immune from this practice. The following statement was based upon his experience in studying the Women's Christian Temperance Union.

The stereotype of the WCTU is something against which the organization fights. Often the attitudes of my friends struck me as cruel. Almost any time that I told other academic people about my study someone would ask about the personality characteristics of WCTU members. The assumption was clear that there must be something eccentric about these ladies. But to me, being deeply immersed in the WCTU, they weren't unusual at all.

---

[163] Trow, *op. cit.*, p. 271.
[164] Nelson W. Polsby, "Toward an Explanation of McCarthyism," in Nelson W. Polsby, Robert A. Dentler, and Paul A. Smith, eds., *Politics and Social Life* (Boston: Houghton Mifflin Co., 1963), p. 812.
[165] Gusfield, *op. cit.*, pp. 186–187.
[166] For example, in contrast to the image of the *nouveaux riches* presented by Hofstadter who pictures them as obsessed and insecure about the prospects for keeping their new wealth (Hofstadter, "Pseudo-Conservatism Revisited," *op. cit.*, p. 109). Bensman and Vidich see the new tycoons as self-assuredly optimistic about future prospects for success. See Joseph Bensman and Arthur Vidich, "Business Cycles, Class, and Personality," in Philip Olson, ed., *America As a Mass Society* (Glencoe, Ill.: Free Press, 1963), pp. 445–446.
[167] Lipset, "Three Decades of the Radical Right," *op. cit.*, pp. 391–421.
[168] *Ibid.*, p. 420.
[169] *Ibid.*, p. 440.
[170] Joseph Gusfield, "Field Work Reciprocities in Studying a Social Movement," *Human Organization*, XIV (Fall 1955), 32–33.

CONCLUSION

Although the concept of social disorganization enjoys a certain vogue among social critics, few serious sociologists would employ it as a variable to explain the rise of social movements. "The times are out of joint" may be a sufficient rallying cry for social reformers, but it does little toward explicating the structural sources of social movements. Disorganization, and its attendant processes of anomie, alienation, and isolation, are best applied as Durkheim originally intended—to describe individual responses to social change. In fact, students such as Davies and Brinton would contend that improving social conditions generates revolutionary movements and social rebellion.[171] Although we intend, in time, to discuss the question of individual recruitment into social movements, the answer to such a question cannot explain the origins of a movement itself.

In addition to the foregoing argument, we have already discussed the conflicting theoretical and empirical evidence concerning the ideas of mass society, alienation, and isolation. Another cogent reason for avoiding these concepts is the very considerable difficulty in operationalizing them. In particular, alienation virtually defies operational measurement because it is such a multifaceted concept. The Josephsons, in discussing alienation, suggest that it is nearly impossible to distinguish the alienated from the nonalienated.[172] As we have suggested, these concepts should best remain as normative expressions of the feelings of individuals in response to certain structural conditions in society. Thus, it appears that either class or status would form the best basis for any discussion of the causes of social movements.

In the final analysis, class is an economic concept applicable to interest-oriented movements. Historically, economically related movements have been left of center, seeking to adjust or reorder the distribution of wealth in society. Ideologically, movements seeking these goals have included Communism, socialism, and industrial unionism. The main supporters of these movements have been workers and proletarians. Consequently, class analyses have been most successfully applied to highly stratified societies where class distinctions are clear. In Europe, for example, individuals possessing wealth are frequently identifiable by title or other symbols of social position. In the underdeveloped countries similar differentiations are observable. As these examples suggest, the concept of class is primarily addressed to working class and agrarian movements in relatively rigid social systems.[173]

[171] James C. Davies, "Toward a Theory of Revolution," *American Sociological Review*, 27 (February 1962), 5–19; Crane Brinton, *The Anatomy of Revolution* (New York: Vintage Books, 1957).
[172] Eric and Mary Josephson, eds., *Man Alone: Alienation in Modern Society* (New York: Dell Publishing Co., 1962), pp. 13–17.
[173] See also Richard Hoggart, *The Uses of Literacy* (London: Chatto and Windus, 1957).

Status, on the other hand, is a multidimensional concept stressing power and social honor. Therefore, noneconomic movements are more frequently analyzed in terms of status-oriented theories. These movements, centered around power and value considerations, have customarily been middle class in composition. As several observers have noted, conservatism and Fascism are manifestations of middle class radicalism (for example, Schiff's "obedient rebels" [174] and the supporters of Hitler identified by Arendt, Lipset, and Cantril). In contemporary writings, status analyses have been most frequently applied to North America, where class differences are less distinct than in Europe. As Mills, Harrington, and others suggest, stratification in the United States tends to be covert. Here, consumer credit and cheap imitations of symbols of rank are available to all but the most wretchedly, and largely invisible, poor. As a consequence, most Americans subjectively consider themselves part of the nebulous middle class. Except for a handful of Marxian observers, few sociologists have pointed to any evidence of class consciousness in the United States. Status, therefore, has popularly received more attention in examinations of social movements on this continent. Furthermore, economic movements in North America have been rare in the last three decades; radicalism has been more closely associated with the extreme Right and the metaphysically oriented New Left.

Another factor to explain the supremacy of the concept of status has been the apparent failure of Marxist doctrine and movements in America. The inability of Communists, socialists, and Trotskyists to activate the masses created a political vacuum in the late 1940s and early 1950s, leaving the political sphere open to the extreme Right and suburban reformism.

Social trends in North America have also directed attention to status problems. The increasing dominance of the megalopolis, the decline of religious fundamentalism, the diminution of the role of the small businessman, prosperity, and a decline in deference to social rank are all factors which have favored Weberian over Marxian analyses among students of social movements.

Nevertheless, the use of status as a variable in social movement research presents certain problems. Although the evidence for an association between right wing movements and the middle classes is considerable, no reasonable argument can be made for a status explanation of left wing movements. Nor are the middle classes involved exclusively in right wing movements. For example, it should be noted that middle class intellectuals, not proletarians, have peopled most contemporary left of center movements. The civil rights movement, at this writing, is particularly amenable to an explanation in terms of class. Indeed, a strong argument

[174] Lawrence Schiff, "The Obedient Rebels: A Study of College Conversions to Conservatism," *Journal of Social Issues*, 20 (October 1964), 74–95.

can be made for "black power" as a form of class consciousness.[175] Moreover, we have presented arguments to the effect that the notions of class and status are not as separable as some analysts would have them.

Finally, we would maintain that social disorganization, class, and status are not sufficient causes of social movements. Indeed, historical and social evidence seems to point to the need for a certain reformulation of accepted explanations for social movements. In later chapters we shall examine other factors, such as history, propinquity, and social significance. First, however, we shall look, in chapter 3, at the ways in which historians and social psychologists have analyzed social movements.

[175] See Martin Nicolaus, "The Contradiction of Advanced Capitalist Society and Its Resolution" (unpublished paper, Simon Fraser University, 1967), pp. 18–20.

ANALYTICAL APPROACHES TO SOCIAL MOVEMENTS: HISTORY AND PSYCHOLOGY

Traditionally, the study of social movements has focused either on the historical context and implications of a movement or on the characteristics of its personnel. These two approaches lend themselves, respectively, to inductive and deductive methodologies. The inductive approach is typified by the case study. Here the researcher examines and analyzes a given movement and from his observations extrapolates certain generalized conclusions. For example, Abel's analysis of the Nazi movement led him to posit that certain conditions are necessary for the growth and maintenance of a social movement.[1] The inductive approach is most commonly employed by historians, political scientists, and sociologists. The deductive approach, most characteristic of social psychology, is one in which a movement is studied as a means of testing a particular theory or model. For example, Marxists studied the labor movement in the 1930s as a manifestation of class consciousness; Hofstadter, Lipset, and Gusfield have studied the extreme Right and the Temperance movement to test hypotheses dealing with status groups.[2] In this chapter, we shall examine the inductive method, as found in the case study, and the deductive approach, as utilized by social psychologists.

THE HISTORICAL CASE STUDY

The essence of the historical case study is the accumulation of descriptive facts, ostensibly to point to the causes and consequences of specific phe-

[1] Theodore Abel, "The Pattern of a Successful Political Movement," *American Sociological Review*, 2 (April 1937): 347–357.
[2] Cf. the Hofstadter and Lipset contributions to Daniel Bell, ed., *The Radical Right* (*The New American Right* expanded and updated), (Garden City, N.Y.: Doubleday and Co., 1963), pp. 63–86 and 260–312; and Joseph R. Gusfield, *Symbolic Crusade* (Urbana, Ill.: University of Illinois Press, 1963).

nomena. More precisely, the historian is primarily concerned with interpreting the present in the light of the past. As Edward Carr puts it: "The past is intelligible to us only in the light of the present; and we can fully understand the present only in the light of the past. To enable man to understand the society of the past and to increase his mastery over the society of the present is the dual function of history." [3] Ideally, the historian is concerned with the cumulative effects of events over time. The consequences of these events are those aspects which have a bearing on the interpretation of the present and, although perhaps to a lesser extent, the prediction of the future. Carr illustrates this concern in his statement that history ". . . seeks to link the past with the future in a continuous line along which the historian himself is constantly moving." [4] However, the case for historical prediction, which was based on the Enlightenment philosophy of progress, is logically and empirically unsound. The belief that knowledge of the past enables prediction of, and control over, the future must be held on faith alone. In his appraisal of the idea of progress, Georg Iggers states:

The position that "history has no meaning" is shared today by thinkers coming from very different intellectual positions. It is a key concept in the existentialism of Jean-Paul Sartre, in the Protestant crisis theology of Karl Barth and of Reinhold Niebuhr, and in the positivism of Karl Popper. . . . In conclusion, we must frankly admit that the idea of progress is untenable as a scientific explanation of historical movement.[5]

As a consequence of the objectification of history, broad analyses of historical causes and consequences are being replaced today by detailed investigations of specific historical phenomena. As Hoselitz notes: "Whereas the main efforts of earlier historians had been devoted to painting a large canvas, writers on historical subjects now concern themselves with minute and accurate miniatures." [6] According to another account, this growing specialization has led to a concern with ". . . particular facts regarding the past [which do not serve] an instrumental role as data for laws. Indeed . . . the historian is not a producer of general laws, but a consumer of them." [7]

When the historian looks at a social movement, he is primarily concerned with its personnel, documents, and internal dynamics. As in other areas of contemporary historical research, the case study method deals

[3] Edward H. Carr, *What Is History* (London: Macmillan and Co., Ltd., 1962), p. 49.
[4] Edward H. Carr, *The New Society* (Boston: Beacon Press, 1961), p. 14.
[5] Georg G. Iggers, "The Idea of Progress: A Critical Assessment," *American Historical Review*, 71 (October 1965): 9, 16–17.
[6] Bert F. Hoselitz, "To History," in *A Reader's Guide To The Social Sciences* edited by Bert F. Hoselitz (Glencoe, Ill.: The Free Press, 1959), p. 57.
[7] Carey B. Joynt and Nicholas Rescher, "The Problem of Uniqueness in History," in George Nadel, ed., *Studies in the Philosophy of History* (New York: Harper Torchbooks, 1965), p. 7.

primarily with descriptive facts, which may or may not relate to the present. The case study is most frequently treated by historians as slices of time in which actors shape the future of man. David Shannon, for example, describes his study of the Communist Party of the United States as ". . . a complete story, for it has a beginning, a middle, and an end." [8]

The following selection from a prominent historical journal clearly illustrates the case study approach. Of note here is the author's emphasis upon people and events rather than upon theoretical or predictive questions.

Jerold S. Auerbach, "Southern Tenant Farmers: Socialist Critics of the New Deal," Labor History, Vol. 7 (Winter 1966), pp. 3–18. In slightly altered form this paper was presented at the Thirtieth Convention of the Southern Historical Association, Little Rock, 1964. Reprinted by permission of J. S. Auerbach and the Tamiment Institute.

In 1927 Harry L. Mitchell, the son of a Tennessee tenant farmer, moved to Tyronza, a tiny Arkansas town thirty-five miles west of Memphis. Mitchell hoped to make a crop there, as he had done earlier in Tennessee and in Mississippi. Local sharecroppers fared so poorly, however, that he decided to purchase a small dry-cleaning establishment instead. The Depression left Mitchell with unexpected leisure; he used it to read Upton Sinclair and to follow the progress of Huey Long's Share Our Wealth program. One day he wandered into the gas station operated by his neighbor, Henry Clay East. After listening to East expound his political theories Mitchell told him that he sounded like a socialist. Before long, both men were exploring socialist solutions to capitalism's mounting ills. During the 1932 presidential campaign they drove to Memphis for inspiration from Norman Thomas, the Socalist Party's nominee. Thomas' speech struck a responsive chord; Mitchell and East returned to Tyronza and decided, "We should organize." [9]

Mitchell became state secretary of the Socialist Party. He and East organized Socialist locals and led vigorous protests against planter control over administration of New Deal relief and public works programs. In-

[8] David Shannon, *The Decline of American Communism* (New York: Harcourt, Brace, and Co., 1959), p. ix.
[9] Harry L. Mitchell, "Biographical Sketch," Southern Tenant Farmers Union Papers (cited below as STFU), Box 80, Southern Historical Collection, University of North Carolina, Chapel Hill; Harry L. Mitchell Memoir, Columbia Oral History Collection (cited below as COHC), pp. 2–9; Donald H. Grubbs, "The Southern Tenant Farmers Union and the New Deal" (unpublished Ph.D. dissertation, University of Florida, 1963), 81–83.

creasingly, however, their attention turned to the desperate plight of thousands of sharecroppers and tenant farmers, who constituted a "kingdom of neglect and want. . . ."[10]

The rich Delta bottom lands of northeastern Arkansas, which thirty years earlier had supported a prosperous lumbering industry, no longer seemed capable of sustaining their human inhabitants. Sharecroppers tilled the cotton fields "from can to can't," but entire families rarely received as much as two hundred dollars for a year's work. Their diet consisted of cornbread, molasses, and fatback, and their decrepit hovels could hardly be called homes. Many tenants, it was said, "could study astronomy through the openings in the roof and geology through holes in the floor. . . ."[11] Scantily clothed children attended school primarily to keep warm; malaria and pellagra took a constant toll. Sharecroppers owned nothing but their own labor. An archaic credit system, which left them without cash and at their planters' mercy, also contributed to an impoverished and degrading rural society.[12]

The Agricultural Adjustment Act of 1933, the New Deal's initial response to the rural ravages of the Depression, only exacerbated the sharecroppers' distress. Congress paid scant attention to the croppers when it considered this legislation. They were not parties to AAA contracts between landlords and the Secretary of Agriculture. Nor did sharecroppers participate in local administration of the act; county committees were invariably dominated by the planters. AAA provisions for acreage reduction often meant tenant displacement. From the sharecroppers' perspective, however, the act's most deplorable feature was the disproportionate allocation of benefit payment to landlords, because of their greater equity in the crops produced. Initially, when payments went directly to landlords, croppers complained that they rarely received their share. Subsequently, when payments to croppers were required, landlords altered their status to wage hands to disqualify them. AAA policy thus tended to drive sharecroppers and tenant farmers from the land, to lower their status still

---

[10] Mitchell, COHC, pp. 9–10; Grubbs, "Southern Tenant Farmers Union," p. 84; Arthur F. Raper and Ira De A. Reid, *Sharecroppers All* (Chapel Hill, University of North Carolina Press, 1941), p. 20.
[11] Charles S. Johnson, Edwin R. Embree, Will W. Alexander, *The Collapse of Cotton Tenancy* (Chapel Hill: University of North Carolina Press, 1935), p. 12; Howard Kester, *Revolt Among the Sharecroppers* (New York: Covici, Friede, 1936), pp. 39–41; Herman C. Nixon, *Forty Acres and Steel Mules* (Chapel Hill, University of North Carolina Press, 1938), p. 23.
[12] Kester, *op. cit.*, pp. 42–43; Johnson, Embree, Alexander, *Collapse of Cotton Tenancy*, p. 8; Rupert P. Vance, *Farmers Without Land* (New York: Public Affairs Committee, 1938), p. 1; Gunnar Myrdal, *An American Dilemma* (Twentieth Anniversary Edition; New York: Harper and Row, 1962), pp. 246–251; for Arkansas tenancy see H. W. Blalock, *Plantation Operations of Landlords and Tenants in Arkansas*, Bulletin No. 339 (Fayetteville: Agricultural Experiment Station, 1938), and J. A. Baker and J. G. McNeely, *Land Tenure in Arkansas I. The Farm Tenancy Situation* (Fayetteville: Agricultural Experiment Station, 1940).

further, or to reinforce their subservience to their landlords. The purpose of the act, AAA director Chester Davis reminded his district agents, was to meet the agricultural emergency, not to solve a "deep-seated social problem."[13] However justifiable New Deal policy appeared to officials in Washington, it enraged the sharecroppers, who hoped for so much and, as always, received so little.

Friction between landlords and tenants in the Arkansas Delta, fanned by AAA, threatened to ignite a social conflagration. Delta plantations— new, large, and highly commercialized—attracted thousands of tenants, whose distress absentee planters rarely gauged. Displacement resulting from government policies, which coincided with rapidly increasing mechanization, confronted the sharecroppers with a dismal future.[14] Disenchanted with the New Deal, and disgruntled over their squalid existence, they grew receptive to alternatives. The Socialist Party, which spawned vigorous locals in the Delta, eagerly became the catalyst for their discontent.

In northeast Arkansas, a Party organizer told Norman Thomas late in 1933, "you will find the true proletariat . . . moving irresistibly toward revolution and no less." Communists, Thomas was warned, might "sweep these bottom-lands like wildfire"; therefore, "We *must* have a socialist program for sharecroppers."[15] Heartened by the news that H. L. Mitchell had "pepped up things" in the Delta, Thomas decided to personally encourage his southern disciples.[16]

In mid-February 1934, Thomas visited Tyronza and addressed gatherings of socialists and sharecroppers. During lunch at Clay East's house, Mitchell and East related their recent futile attempt to run for local office on the Socialist Party ticket. Thomas conceded that political activity was a risky venture for Arkansas socialists but, he suggested, why not organize a sharecroppers' union.[17] The idea appealed to Mitchell and East, both of whom pledged their cooperation.[18] Within six weeks Mitchell was

---

[13] Edwin G. Nourse, Joseph S. Davis, John D. Black, *Three Years of the Agricultural Adjustment Administration* (Washington, D.C.: Brookings Institution, 1937), pp. 255–256, 342–348; Henry I. Richards, *Cotton Under the Agricultural Adjustment Act* (Washington, D.C.: Brookings Institution, 1934), pp. 17–19, 135–146; Myrdal, *op. cit.*, pp. 255–256; Harold Hoffsommer, "The AAA and the Cropper," *Social Forces*, Vol. XIII (May 1935), pp. 495–502; David E. Conrar, "The Forgotten Farmers: The AAA and the Southern Tenants, 1933–36" (unpublished Ph.D. dissertation, University of Oklahoma, 1962), pp. 56, 78–80, 101.
[14] Stuart Jamieson, *Labor Unionism in American Agriculture*, U.S. Department of Labor, Bureau of Labor Statistics, Bulletin No. 836 (Washington, D.C.: Government Printing Office, 1945), pp. 303–306.
[15] Martha B. Johnson to Norman Thomas, November 7, 1933, Norman Thomas Papers, Box 6, New York Public Library.
[16] Clarence Senior to Thomas, November 22, 23, 1933, *ibid.*
[17] Mitchell, COHC, pp. 19–20B; Norman Thomas, COCH, pp. 92–93; Mitchell to Thomas, March 11, 1934, Thomas Papers, Box 9.
[18] Mitchell to Thomas, February 21, 1934, *ibid.*, Box 8.

predicting that nearly every sharecropper would join; in fact, he told Thomas, with ample time and sufficient funds all the croppers might be brought into the Socialist Party as well. "No other organization or persons," Mitchell observed, "have dared to challenge the landlords' supremacy." [19]

While Mitchell and East extended their network of Socialist locals, Thomas launched a vigorous verbal assault against the New Deal's agricultural program. "Never in America," he told Secretary of Agriculture Henry Wallace, "have I seen more hopeless poverty" than among the Arkansas sharecroppers. "My criticism is not of a section," he insisted, "but of a nation and of an economic program." [20] The political overtones of Thomas' and Mitchell's activities did not escape notice. Tyronza's town council passed a resolution deploring the Socialist Party's "frenzied efforts to organize and send forth propaganda intended to discredit the Democratic party. . . ." And the chief of AAA's cotton section noted the development of "a well-defined and very widespread political attack upon our entire agricultural adjustment program. . . ." [21]

Mitchell's tireless efforts soon registered impressive results. By July he could count on three full-time organizers and more than a dozen communities with Party locals. Mitchell even hoped to swallow up Huey Long's Share Our Wealth clubs. "We can fix things," he promised Thomas, "so that it won't look as tho' these things are direct party activities." [22] Mitchell was particularly successful in the Tyronza area where, two years earlier, absentee landlord Hiram Norcross had earned the sharecroppers' enmity by evicting fifty of them from his plantation. Subsequently Norcross, his sharecroppers alleged, cheated them out of their AAA benefit payments. During the spring of 1934 Mitchell organized Norcross' croppers into a branch of Tyronza's Social Party local. When Norcross insisted that they sign a contract which they considered highly unjust, they verged on rebellion.[23] Mitchell parlayed their discontent into the sharecroppers union suggested by Thomas.

On a sultry July evening a small group of white and Negro croppers, encouraged by Mitchell and East, gathered in a rickety schoolhouse on

[19] Mitchell to Thomas, March 25, 1934, *ibid.*, Box 9.
[20] Thomas to Henry Wallace, February 22, 1934, *ibid.*, Box 8; Thomas to Editor, Memphis *Commercial Appeal*, March 3, 1934, *ibid.*, Box 9.
[21] Resolution, Town Council of Tyronza, March 17, 1934; Cully Cobb to Paul Appleby, March 28, 1934, both in Agricultural Adjustment Administration Papers, RG 145, National Archives, Washington, D.C. During March, Mitchell and East flooded AAA with allegations of sharecropper evictions. For their charges, and AAA's response, see letters in *ibid.*, RG 145 and RG 16; also Chester Davis to Franklin D. Roosevelt, March 19, 1935, Franklin D. Roosevelt Papers, OF 1-K, Hyde Park.
[22] Mitchell to Thomas, June 18, 1934, Thomas Papers, Box 11; Mitchell to Thomas, July 4, 1934, *ibid.*, Box 12.
[23] Mitchell, COHC, p. 13; Mitchell to Thomas, April 12, 1934, Thomas Papers, Box 10; Mitchell to Thomas, July 28, 1934, Workers Defense League Papers, New York City.

the Norcross plantation to organize the first local of the Southern Tenant Farmers Union. Several had been members of a Negro union wiped out in the Elaine massacre fifteen years earlier; some of the whites were former Ku Klux Klan members. For the moment, however, they put racial animosities aside and elected a white sharecropper as chairman and a Negro minister as vice-chairman. Mitchell and East arrived during a heated debate on the merits of the union becoming a legal organization; they supported the proposition. On July 26 the union was incorporated. Its declaration of principles spoke of two agricultural classes: exploiters, and "actual tillers of the soil who have been ground down to dire poverty. . . ." The union dedicated itself to the abolition of tenancy. "We seek," it stated, "to establish a co-operative order of society by legal and peaceable methods." [24]

The very existence of the union posed a direct and radical challenge to the established order in Arkansas. Militantly class conscious and avowedly interracial, it ran roughshod over local prejudices. Borrowing some of the tactics of trade unions and the fervor of religious revivals, it quickly became the sharecroppers' advocate, teacher, preacher, and lobbyist. But the salient characteristic of the Southern Tenant Farmers Union was its role as Socialist critic of New Deal agricultural policy. Its organizing drive illustrated its agitational character; the attendant nationwide publicity never ceased to be a Socialist thorn in the New Deal's side. Perhaps in no other area did Socialists mount such an effective counterthrust to the Roosevelt Administration.[25]

The union took its radical cues from H. L. Mitchell, its indefatigable leader and spokesman. Mitchell's primary interest was to build a strong radical movement; the union, he thought, could lay the foundation for such a movement in the South. "I felt that it was necessary to have some support," he explained, and "we had none whatever until we aligned ourselves with Thomas and his crew." [26] Mitchell tried to camouflage the union's Socialist ties. "We have got to be as wise as owls," he said, "and appear as gentle as lambs." [27] In private, however, Mitchell showed less restraint. "If we can build the Union," he told a close friend, "we will take over all the damn plantations. . . ." He anticipated the time when, as he expressed it, "the whole South can come under the Collectivist Farm system." [28]

[24] Mitchell, COHC, pp. 22–25; documents in STFU, Box 80; Kester, *op. cit.*, pp. 55–57; STFU Constitution, copy in Workers Defense League Papers.
[25] For a contrary view, see Grubbs, *op. cit.*, pp. 89–91. Grubbs states, despite evidence that indicates the opposite, that the union "never was and never became an adjunct of the [Socialist] Party. Never did the Socialists or any other outside organization formulate policy or choose personnel."
[26] Mitchell to Gardner Jackson, September 3, 1936, STFU, Box 4.
[27] [Mitchell] to J. R. Butler, February 2, 1936, *ibid.*, Box 1.
[28] Mitchell to Howard Kester, March 22, 1936; Mitchell to Clyde Johnson, April 20, 1936, both in *ibid.*, Box 2. See also Mitchell to Edward Johnson, February 22, 1934,

Mitchell may have looked to the future but he never ignored the present. He and Clay East became the union's best organizers; every night they drove to an outlying church or schoolhouse to rally the croppers. East, who was Tyronza's sheriff, showed a fine grasp of local *Realpolitik*; he prominently displayed his star and pistol on these nightly ventures. Mitchell instructed his organizers: "Never promise the workers that the Union is going to do something for them. Let them join the Union and do something themselves." [29] He won pledges of support from county preachers, Negro and white, and from local businessmen who faced financial ruin from competition with the planters' commissaries. Early in August he assured Norman Thomas that "the share-croppers black and white are going to go down the line with us. . . . The union is growing." [30]

As it spread to adjacent counties the Southern Tenant Farmers Union attracted fervent supporters. Howard Kester, an ordained Methodist minister and member of the Socialist Party's executive council, learned of union activities through Party contacts and offered his services. Kester, who described AAA as the "bastard child of a decadent capitalism and a youthful Fascism," became Mitchell's devoted assistant. Other young and radical ministers flocked to Arkansas to enlist for the duration. The Socialist Party's Workers Defense League sent a representative to handle publicity and the League for Industrial Democracy made financial contributions. Protestant denominations lent spiritual support and the American Civil Liberties Union furnished legal aid. Students from Commonwealth College in Mena journeyed across the state to help with assorted tasks; the president of their Student Association was an Arkansas youngster named Orval E. Faubus. H. L. Mitchell admitted: "If it had not been for outside support . . . we never would have been able to continue. . . ." [31]

Sharecroppers responded to their union—which they occasionally confused with a religion—with boundless devotion and courage. Gathering in abandoned warehouses or in the cotton fields, always late in the evening after a full day of backbreaking toil, they sang "We Shall Not Be Moved" and recited the Lord's Prayer before attending to union business. "I do not mind giving my life for the union," one of them told Mitchell. "We ant goner quit it for eneything," promised the president of the Rand Pond

---

Thomas Papers, Box 9; Mitchell to A. S. Bayne, April 7, 1936, STFU, Box 3; Mitchell to W. E. Boone, February 8, 1936, *ibid.*, Box 1.
[29] Kester, *op. cit.*, p. 58; Mitchell, COCH, p. 24; "Instructions to Organizers," Number I, STFU, Box 1.
[30] Mitchell to Thomas, August 2, 1934; Mitchell to Thomas, August 9, 1934, both in Workers Defense League Papers.
[31] Kester, *op. cit.*, p. 26; Oren Stephens, "Revolt on the Delta," *Harper's Magazine*, CLXXXIII (November 1941), pp. 656–664; Grubbs, *op. cit.*, pp. 268, 304–308; Mitchell, COHC, pp. 68–69; Arthur M. Schlesinger, Jr., *The Coming of the New Deal* (Boston: Houghton Mifflin Co., 1959), p. 377.

local, "for We are in the Union to live or Die." Another sharecropper wanted "to help in The Fight for Rightiousness" because he had been "ignored and rejected. . . ." The planters, Mitchell was told, "are far worse than Fairrow was in his day." [32]

Planters translated their political and economic power into persistent anti-union violence. They padlocked church doors and packed schoolhouses with bales of hay to deter union rallies. Their riding bosses flogged sympathetic croppers and drove them from their plantations. The Harahan bridge, spanning the Mississippi at Memphis, became the gateway to safety for union organizers.[33] Two days after the formation of a Crittenden County local, its organizer, a Negro minister, was beaten and jailed. His arrest posed a grave challenge to the union: failure to defend a Negro member might split it asunder. Mitchell and East approached a Memphis attorney but he told them: "I'm one Jew who isn't going over to Crittenden County to get a Negro out of jail because he is charged with organizing a union." The lawyer claimed to have left his courage in the Argonne Forest and ushered them out of his office with a copy of *Progress and Poverty* as a gift. But an attorney from Marked Tree, accompanied by fifty white sharecroppers, marched to the local jail and secured the organizer's release.[34]

During the winter of 1934–35 the union, confronted by unremitting violence, sought redress from Washington. When the Department of Agriculture failed to respond with sufficient vigor, union demands upon the Roosevelt Administration grew more strident and union criticisms of the New Deal became increasingly vitriolic. The union despaired of government action, yet it never tired of seeking federal assistance. Alleged federal indifference served as a perpetual union rallying cry; union leaders vented their local frustrations in attacks against a remote target which, unlike the planters, could not retaliate.[35] Furthermore, union publicity was grist for the Socialist Party's mill. As one Party official wrote, during a well-publicized union fracas: "This is our chance to make a real splash in the country, because we are right there in the heart of the business." [36]

The Socialist Party and the Southern Tenant Farmers Union maintained a filial relationship throughout the union's early years. Norman Thomas' suggestion was the seed from which the union sprouted. A socialist editor in Oklahoma sent the union the model for its constitution. An

---

[32] Thomas, COHC, pp. 96–97; Naomi Mitchison, "White House and Marked Tree," *New Statesman and Nation*, Vol. IX (April 1935), p. 586; Workers Defense League, *The Disinherited Speak* (New York, 1937), pp. 16, 17, 19, 27, 29.
[33] Kester, *op. cit.*, pp. 61–62, 78.
[34] *Ibid.*, pp. 60–61; Mitchell, COHC, pp. 29–30; Mitchell to A. L. Wirin, August 13, 1934, American Civil Liberties Union Papers, Vol. 733, Princeton University.
[35] For AAA's confusion over the union's attacks and entreaties, see Paul A. Porter to William R. Amberson, April 2, 1935, Thomas Papers, Box 17.
[36] Clarence Senior to Edward Levinson, February 6, 1935, Socialist Party Papers, Duke University.

Arkansas socialist proposed the union's name. The Socialist Party gave H. L. Mitchell a monthly check for forty dollars; this was virtually his sole source of income. Whenever the union encountered difficulty, the Party dispatched friends or funds to assist it. Mitchell accepted aid from any source, "as long as there are no strings attached." Although the union never behaved as a Socialist Party puppet, its rhetoric and personnel revealed its Socialist lineage.[37]

Early in 1935 two incidents focused national attention on the union, winning it many new converts and underscoring the New Deal's failure to alleviate sharecropper distress. At a union rally in Marked Tree, called to celebrate the return of a delegation from Washington, Methodist preacher Ward Rodgers told the assembled sharecroppers that if necessary, in the absence of relief, he "would lead a group that would lynch every planter in Poinsett County. . . ." Rodgers was arrested as he left the speakers' platform and charged with anarchy, blasphemy, and attempted overthrow of the government. A jury of planters, meeting in an impromptu court session held in a local store, convicted him of anarchy. Shortly thereafter, Marked Tree adopted an ordinance prohibiting public speeches without the prior consent of town officials.[38]

The Rodgers incident had predictable consequences. It enraged the planters, some of whom had heard Rodgers' remarks; it attracted hundreds of new union members, who responded to Rodgers' foolhardy courage; and it made the union a pawn in efforts by Socialists and Communists to capitalize upon the incident. Socialists in New York worked diligently to thwart attempts by the International Labor Defense, legal arm of the Communist Party, to assume responsibility for Rodgers' defense. A trusted Socialist was sent to work with the union and Norman Thomas decided to return to Arkansas.[39]

In mid-March Thomas arrived in the Delta. Union leaders hoped that his visit would expedite the transfer of their following to the Socialist Party. Rodgers expected Thomas' appearance to spur "a terrific organizational campaign for the Socialist Party of Arkansas. . . ." Mitchell told

[37] Mitchell, COHC, pp. 25–26; Clarence Senior to Mitchell, February 18, 1935; Mitchell to Senior, February 1, 1935, both in Socialist Party Papers. One of the union's founders, who subsequently broke with Mitchell, wrote: "The purpose of the union was fine, and would have been a great help to the sharecropper if it had been carried on for the interest of the sharecropper and not used for political, Socialist, and Communist activities." Memphis *Commercial Appeal*, September 26, 1936, clipping in STFU, Box 85.
[38] Ward Rodgers to Thomas, January 24, 1935, Thomas Papers, Box 16; Mitchell, COHC, pp. 34–36; *The New York Times*, April 16, 1935.
[39] On union gains, see Amberson to Lucille B. Milner, January 25, 1935, ACLU Papers, Vol. 827; Amberson to Thomas, January 26, 1935, Thomas Papers, Box 16. On Socialist-Communist rivalry, see Thomas to Mitchell, January 26, 1935; Senior to Mitchell, January 29, 1935; Senior to Thomas, February 5, 1935, all in Socialist Party Papers.

the Party's executive secretary that Thomas' trip "would mean that the entire section would go for us."[40] Thomas' visit was, however, abruptly interrupted. Speaking in Birdsong, he was surrounded by a crowd of angry planters and deputies. Thomas, demanding to know by whose authority he was being restrained from speaking, was told that "no Gawd-Damn Yankee Bastard" was welcome in Arkansas.[41] Thomas was driven from the platform and pursued to the county line; he returned to New York and described a "reign of terror" to a nationwide radio audience. Eastern Arkansas, he told a friend, "is more cruel and barbarous than any place I've ever seen."[42]

The Rodgers and Thomas debacles marked the onset of a critical period for the Southern Tenant Farmers Union. Arkansas planters and officals, observed a *New York Times* correspondent, had become firmly convinced that only drastic steps would forestall the overthrow of "white supremacy, Christianity, the American flag and the sanctity of home and family ties. . . ."[43] They banned union meetings and arrested members on the slightest pretext. Sharecroppers were evicted, their churches were burned, and vigilantes patrolled the highways. Mitchell and other union officers fled to Memphis to establish new headquarters. Night riders tried to assassinate the union attorney and vice-president; Clay East was escorted from Mississippi County; and the body of a union member was found floating down the Coldwater River. Planters in Marked Tree sponsored a company union, placed a loyal minister in charge, and tried to lure union members with promises of immediate employment. "We are on the edge of bloodshed," Mitchell told the Department of Agriculture. "When that blood flows it will drip down over your Department, from the Secretary at the top to [the] Cotton section at the bottom."[44]

The union was virtually defenseless against these tactics. It could neither recruit new members nor hold meetings to sustain the morale of old ones. Racial discrimination and the poll tax deprived union members of political power. Union leaders, in Memphis, were cut off from the rank-and-file and seriously considered recasting the union as an undercover organization.[45] In desperation a delegation of croppers drove to Washing-

[40] Rodgers to Senior, March 10, 1935; Mitchell to Senior, February 10, 1935, *ibid*.
[41] H. L. Mitchell, "Norman Thomas Visits the Cotton Fields," copy in Thomas Papers.
[42] Thomas, COHC, 82–84; Kester, *op. cit.*, pp. 80–85; Thomas to Brooks Hays, March 30, 1935, Thomas Papers, Box 16.
[43] *The New York Times*, April 15, 1935.
[44] Kester, *op. cit.*, pp. 82–84; Mitchell to Jack Herling, March 22, 1935; Mitchell to Thomas, March 26, 27, 1935, all in Thomas Papers, Box 16; Harold E. Fey, "Sharecroppers Organize," *Fellowship* (April 1935), clipping in ACLU Papers, Vol. 786; Mitchell to Paul A. Porter, March 27, 1935, AAA Papers, RF 145.
[45] Mitchell to Herling, April 1, 1935; Thomas to C. T. Carpenter, April 2, 1935, both in Thomas Papers, Box 17.

ton and picketed the Department of Agriculture. But Cotton Division chief Cully Cobb, commenting on their presence, declared that few of them knew a cotton stalk from a jimson weed.[46]

Internal dissension augmented union woes. The president, acting in concert with two other members, accused Mitchell of malfeasance and took legal action to secure the union seal and papers. Mitchell, assisted by Howard Kester, repulsed the challenge, which had its roots in politics and in personalities.[47] This rebellion, which further sapped the union's strength, hinted at the resentment felt by some union members at Mitchell's Socialist ties. Because the sharecroppers could not articulate their grievances or develop effective leadership from within their own ranks, the Socialist Party had filled the vacuum. Norman Thomas once asked a friend whether he believed that the croppers "will ever organize themselves without such help as I have given them?" The sharecroppers, Thomas noted, "were forgotten men until comparatively few of us brought them to public attention." [48] Mitchell himself displayed occasional traces of paternalism. "Our people," he once said, "are just like children. . . ." [49] Mitchell acted accordingly: he gave valiant service to the union but the price he exacted for it was virtually absolute power.

Seeking ways to strengthen the union and unify the sharecroppers, Mitchell proposed a strike. Union members enthusiastically endorsed his suggestion; in September nearly five thousand cotton pickers struck for higher wages. After ten days the union claimed a resounding victory, though it doubtlessly exaggerated its success in securing wage increases. As a tactic to solidify the union and to expand membership, however, the strike was indisputably successful. Throughout the Delta it boosted the morale of union members. Union headquarters were flooded with applications for new charters. Even the American Federation of Labor offered assistance. Early in October Mitchell told Norman Thomas: "We are in a strong position that will not be easy for the planters to overcome." [50]

By the time of its second annual convention, three months later, the union boasted 25,000 members in two hundred locals scattered through six states.[51] Its strategy was now clear: to combine relentless pressure on

---

[46] *The New York Times*, May 19, 1935.
[47] For a discussion of this internal squabble, see Grubbs, *op. cit.*, pp. 318–320; letters in Thomas Papers, Box 17; Mitchell, COHC, pp. 47–48.
[48] Norman Thomas to Paul [Porter], April 2, 1935, Thomas Papers, Box 17.
[49] Mitchell to Donald Henderson, October 6, 1937, STFU, Box 9. The previous year Mitchell had told Thomas, "We ought to have some sharecropper as President but there is a great danger that he might go haywire. . . ." Mitchell to Thomas, April 29, 1936, *ibid.*, Box 2.
[50] Mitchell to Will Hale, Jr., September 17, 1935, *ibid.*, Box 1; Mitchell, COHC, pp. 49–51; *Sharecroppers Voice*, October 1935; Jamieson, *op. cit.*, pp. 309–310; Mitchell to Thomas, October 4, 1935; Mitchell to Frank Morrison, October 4, 1935, both in Thomas Papers, Box 18; Mitchell to Herling, October 22, 1935, Workers Defense League Papers.
[51] Southern Tenant Farmers Union, Convention Proceedings (Little Rock, 1936), p. 1.

the New Deal with trade union tactics. During its first eighteen months both had served the union well, although neither weakened the foundations of the plantation system. Political pressure made the Roosevelt Administration, and the nation, sharecropper conscious. The purge of liberals from AAA early in 1935 had marked a defeat for the sharecroppers but establishment of the Resettlement Administration and numerous government investigations testified to the union's impact. New cotton contracts also reflected union pressure; payments to sharecroppers increased by 10 percent over their 1935 levels. Trade union tactics brought fewer successes as landlords displayed far more stubbornness than did New Dealers. Yet union leaders did not relinquish the strike as a weapon and they never minimized its impact upon the sharecroppers. As the union newspaper advised, "Raise plenty of Hell and you will get somewhere." [52]

In many respects 1935 had tested the union's capacity for survival. Nineteen thirty-six began with a test of durability and ended with the union apparently a permanent southern institution. A wave of evictions during the worst weeks of the winter ushered in the new year. More than one hundred sharecroppers camped in snow drifts in below freezing weather, without food, adequate clothing, shelter, or firewood. To publicize their distress, and hopefully to alleviate it, union officials pressed for a congressional investigation. A signal consequence of their efforts was Senate authorization for a civil liberties inquiry. In the spring of 1936 the La Follette Civil Liberties Committee launched the most extensive investigation of infractions of the Bill of Rights in American history.[53]

The union could not, however, afford to wait for congressional action. Throughout the winter and spring its fortunes ebbed. Arkansas Governor J. Marion Furtell, called "old Futile" by the union, dismissed its protests as "much ado about something which amounts to very little." [54] H. L. Mitchell complained bitterly: "We need men and money and we don't have either." [55] Once again a strike call seemed the only alternative to disaster.

In May, after planters had refused to meet union wage demands, cotton choppers in Cross, Crittenden, and St. Francis counties refused to work. Union members marched hundreds abreast across the cotton fields to gather additional recruits. Instead, they incensed planters and politicians. Memphis police broke picket lines at the Harahan bridge; striking croppers were arrested and leased to planters to work off their

[52] *Sharecroppers Voice*, January 1, 1936.
[53] On the Amlie Resolution, H. R. 270, see ACLU Papers, Vols. 779, 781; Kester to Thomas, January 18, 1936; Gardner Jackson to Mary Fox, January 20, 1936; Mitchell to Thomas [January, 1936]; Herling to Thomas, February 9, 1936, all in Thomas Papers, Box 20. On the work of the La Follette Committee, see Jerold S. Auerbach, "The La Follette Committee: Labor and Civil Liberties in the New Deal," *Journal of American History*, Vol. LI (December, 1964), pp. 435–459.
[54] Memphis *Press-Scimitar*, February 28, 1936.
[55] Mitchell to Kester, March 18, 1936, STFU, Box 2.

fines and court costs; and a Crittenden County landlord built and filled a small concentration camp. On the fourth day of the strike Governor Futrell sent in National Guardsmen and State Rangers and the union quietly surrendered. "We didn't make one dent," Mitchell conceded.[56]

During these troubled months Mitchell found many New Dealers "very sympathetic" to the union, but he concluded that "their hands are tied by the southern bourbon politicians. . . ."[57] The union's nemesis, Arkansas Senator Joe Robinson, had dismissed the union organizing drive as the work of "professional agitators, representatives of communistic and socialistic organizations. . . ."[58] Roosevelt's disinclination to embarrass Robinson, who faced a campaign for re-election in 1936, deterred a federal investigation of Arkansas terror.[59]

Roosevelt aroused the union's wrath when he spoke in Little Rock shortly after the cotton choppers' strike, without mentioning the sharecroppers. Norman Thomas had admonished him in advance for participating in the centenary celebration of a state "which has not yet abolished slavery in [its] cotton fields," but to no avail. A delegation of union members tried to present a petition to the President or to his secretary, but without success.[60] This rebuke marked the high-water mark of official indifference to the sharecroppers. As the union persisted, and as the 1936 election grew near, its actions brought party, state, and federal reactions.

At the Democratic convention Mitchell won Robinson's consent to platform planks protecting the sharecroppers' civil liberties and their right to organize.[61] Before the summer ended Governor Futrell announced that he would appoint a farm-tenancy commission; Futrell also called a conference of southern governors to discuss the problem.[62] At the federal level the Department of Justice indicted Paul Peacher, town marshal of Earle, for peonage; during the cotton choppers' strike Peacher had arrested thirteen croppers on vagrancy charges, secured their convictions, and forced them to work out their sentences on his farm.[63]

[56] STFU Strike Bulletins, Nos. 2, 3; Jamieson, *op. cit.*, pp. 311–312; Mitchell, COHC, pp. 55–59; STFU Press Release, June 2, 1936; Mitchell to Clarence Senior, June 4, 1936, both in STFU, Box 3; Amberson to Thomas, June 8, 1936, Thomas Papers, Box 21; James Myeters, "Brief Digest of Trip to Arkansas . . . , June 2–10," in ACLU Papers, Vol. 925; Workers Defense League, *To Establish Justice* (New York, 1940), pp. 10–11.
[57] Mitchell to Daniel O'Connor, March 30, 1936, STFU, Box 2.
[58] *Congressional Record*, 74th Cong., 1 Sess., Vol. 79 (April 18, 1935), p. 5928.
[59] Grubbs, *op. cit.*, pp. 372–373; Rexford G. Tugwell to FDR, March 10, 1936, Roosevelt Papers, OF 1650.
[60] Frances Perkins to Marvin McIntyre, June 8, 1936; Thomas to FDR, June 9, 1936, both in *ibid.*, OF 407-B; *Sharecroppers Voice*, July 1936.
[61] Grubbs, *op. cit.*, pp. 514–515; Mitchell, COHC, pp. 72–73.
[62] *Sharecroppers Voice*, October–November, 1936; STFU release, November 9, 1936; STFU, Box 4.
[63] *Sharecroppers Voice*, October–November, 1936. The union charged that Peacher was not the only person to have practiced peonage, but the United States attorney in Arkansas maintained that the Peacher case was "the only case that could be discovered after a thorough investigation. . . ." Fred A. Isgrig to N. J. Whitney, November 13, 1936, Workers Defense League Papers.

President Roosevelt also responded. During the campaign he urged Senator Hollis Bankhead (D.-Ala.) and Representative Marvin Jones (D.-Tex.) to formulate plans for a federal program to reduce tenancy. Soon after his re-election Roosevelt appointed the President's Committee on Farm Tenancy; its efforts laid the groundwork for the Bankhead-Jones Farm Tenancy Act of 1937 and for establishment of the Farm Security Administration.[64]

The appointment of a union representative to the President's Committee, the union claimed, "is a recognition that the union is a power in the movement to end the condition of tenancy and that its point of view must be heard by the Government."[65] The New Deal's cautious responses to the problems of tenancy hardly detracted from the magnitude of union achievements. By the end of 1936 it had enrolled nearly 31,000 members in seven states.[66] Anti-union violence had subsided and Democratic administrations in Little Rock and in Washington were committed to redressing the sharecroppers' grievances. New crises awaited the union, but its right to exist and its ability to be heard were no longer in doubt.

Viewed from the perspective of traditional trade unionism, the organizing drive of the Southern Tenant Farmers Union seemed an anomaly. Its most effective weapons were agitation and publicity, not strikes or collective bargaining. The union's Socialist antecedents, leadership, and sources of support dictated a strategy based on jeremiads against the New Deal. During these early years the union's organizing drive always had twin objectives: recruitment of new members and propagation of radical alternatives to New Deal agricultural policy. The Southern Tenant Farmers Union sought to organize a protest movement no less than to organize the sharecroppers.

Shrill pronouncements from the union, which served both of these ends, often made it seem more unique than it really was. It probably encountered no more violent resistance to its organizing drive than did new and militant unions elsewhere in the country during the 1930's. Norman Thomas' laments to the contrary, the Southern Tenant Farmers Union did not suffer disproportionately.[67] Furthermore, although the union unfurled the banner of interracial justice, it was not integrated at the local level. Socialist ideology, and the previous failures of segregated

---

[64] M. S. Venkataramani, "Norman Thomas, Arkansas Sharecroppers, and the Roosevelt Agricultural Policies, 1933–1937," *Mississippi Valley Historical Review*, Vol. XLVII (September 1960), pp. 241–244.
[65] *Sharecroppers Voice*, January 1937.
[66] Jamieson, *op. cit.*, p. 314. The seven states with union locals were Arkansas, Tennessee, Mississippi, Texas, Oklahoma, Missouri, and North Carolina.
[67] James Myers, Industrial Secretary of the Federal Council of Churches and a veteran labor observer, noted that "the general problem is the same as in other states. . . . Reaction against organization takes place regardless of whether the inside leadership of the union is Socialist (as in this case), or Communist, or A. F. of L." Myers to McNeill Poteat, May 2, 1935, Federal Council Industrial Department Papers, New York City; see clipping from Memphis *Press-Scimitar* [1936] in STFU, Box 85.

unions in the South, may have encouraged integration but local mores exerted a powerful pull in the opposite direction. While Negroes and whites were welcome, an overwhelming percentage of union locals contained members of one race only. "Separate but equal" governed race relations within the union.[68]

The distinctiveness of the Southern Tenant Farmers Union was a product of its hostility to capitalism and its vision of the future. A member once predicted that the union "will speed up the day when the rope spun by God will be used to hang the planters." [69] His prophecy proved to be inaccurate: plantations outlived the union, which barely survived a disastrous two-year affiliation with the CIO's United Cannery, Agricultural, Packing and Allied Workers of America and virtually ceased to function by 1941, when H. L. Mitchell declared that no basis existed for trade unionism in southern agriculture. The STFU seemed like a dismal union failure. Yet as an outspoken but effective critic of the New Deal the Southern Tenant Farmers Union was unsurpassed.

As Auerbach's stress on the role of H. L. Mitchell indicates, the historical case study approach tends to underline the actions of specific men. Another example of this emphasis is found in Harvey Goldberg's discussion of the role of radicals and revolutionaries: "American radicals have honored democracy by trying to make it better. With the courage and conviction to stand hard against the current they have contributed new ideas and helped to build better institutions." [70] Other students, such as Shannon and Hicks, have also stressed individual action. Shannon, in describing Socialist Party leader Norman Thomas, wrote: "Thanks to Thomas' vigor, the Socialist party was in a fairly good position to exploit the advantage that came to it in the economic crash of late 1929." [71] Hicks, in his discussion of the Populist movement, provides an equally illuminating

---

[68] Statements by Grubbs, historian of the union, that the STFU "solved" the problem of race relations and that union locals "almost always" included members of both races are contradicted by the available evidence. For Grubbs' views, see *op. cit.*, pp. 109–116. For evidence to the contrary, see "Local Questionnaire Returns," Preliminary Report—June 29, 1937, STFU, Box 11, indicating that of 103 locals, 73 were all-Negro or all-white; of the remaining 30, 7 had only one Negro or white member. See also Ward Rodgers to Thomas, August 6, 1934, Thomas Papers, Box 12. On the Socialist Party and the Negro worker, see Ernest Doerfler, "Socialism and the Negro Problem," *American Socialist Quarterly*, Vol. II (Summer 1933), pp. 23–36.
[69] Quoted in Lucien Koch, "The War in Arkansas," *New Republic*, Vol. LXXXII (March 27, 1935), p. 184.
[70] Harvey Goldberg, *American Radicals* (New York: Monthly Review Press, 1957), p. ix.
[71] David Shannon, *The Socialist Party of America* (New York: Macmillan Co., 1955), p. 189.

statement on the role of individual action: "Macune, with his tact and power of persuasion, proved to be the man of the hour." [72]

Although he may not accept this emphasis on individual actors, the sociologist is to a large extent indebted to the historian in his study of social movements. For example, Auerbach suggests in his work a continuity of movements of the Left, i.e., in the relationship of the Southern Tenant Farmers Union to the Northern-based Socialist Party of America headed by Norman Thomas. He also supplies insights into questions of organizational work and provides biographical material on radicals such as Mitchell. From studies such as Auerbach's, the sociologist may induce certain hypotheses which in turn can be applied to other situations and movements. For example, we can ask the question, "How did Socialist movements differ from their Stalinist or Communist counterparts in the sphere of labor organizing?" In this sense, the sociologist extrapolates from the case study general theories and hypotheses which can be used to study other movements. For example, Howe and Coser studied the history of the Communist Party in order to formulate a "theory of Stalinism." [73]

Despite the contributions of historians, there are several problems of case study methodology which the student of social movements must consider. First, a specific case under study is all too frequently viewed as an isolated phenomenon. Investigations limited to the consideration of a given movement tend to ignore other more important aspects of general theory. It is not enough to state, for instance, that the racism and hyper-ruralism voiced by Tom Watson led to the dissolution of Populism as a movement.[74] We must ask further questions, such as: How does this relate to other movements? Have other movements alienated possible converts by their statements? Is there something in the nature of radical movements which leads to their failure? A case study generally does not address these sociological questions, but remains content merely to describe its subjects.

A related difficulty of the case study is that the phenomenon being investigated may not be representative of the class of phenomena under which it is subsumed. For example, the protest analyzed by Jackson et al. in their discussions of the failure of an "incipient social movement" may not be isomorphic to other movements.[75] Consequently, to extrapolate from this work may create a false impression of the nature of social movements and the factors in their support. Although a property owners' revolt against higher tax assessments, George Wallace's American Independence

[72] John D. Hicks, *The Populist Revolt* (Lincoln, Nebraska: Bison Books, 1961), p. 107.
[73] Irving Howe and Lewis Coser, *The American Communist Party: A Critical History* (Boston: Beacon Press, 1957).
[74] Hicks, *op. cit.*
[75] Cf. Maurice Jackson, et al., "The Failure of an Incipient Social Movement," *Pacific Sociological Review*, 3 (Spring 1960): 35–40.

Party, and the Ku Klux Klan may all have a similar base of public support in southern California, they are not analogous. In structure and ideology, in terms of the problems they address, and in the eyes of the public, they are different phenomena. Therefore, in generalizing from a case study, one should bear in mind the degree of representativeness of such a study.

A more serious difficulty with the historical case study is "standardization of error." This refers to the tendency for a factual error to become accepted, over time, as an empirical and historical fact. A pioneer work frequently colors and influences those that follow it. For example, John Greenway, writing in the McCarthy period, chose to obscure the sectarian politics of folk singer Woody Guthrie by characterizing him as a "labor singer." Today, many writers still picture Guthrie as a songster for the CIO when in fact he was not directly connected with the industrial union movement.[76] In the realm of social movement research, similar instances have occurred. H. Wayne Morgan, in Eugene V. Debs: Socialist for President, utilized David Shannon's speculation that "perhaps" Allen Benson's stress on noninvolvement in Europe "played right into the hands of the advocates of preparedness." [77] Morgan, however, reported Shannon's speculation as fact. He wrote, "Benson played into the hands of the preparedness supporters, who now used him as a scapegoat." [78] According to Weinstein, both historians were incorrect. Weinstein argues that Benson's "antipreparedness" policy was popular enough to gain him the Socialist Party nomination.[79] It is not our intention to imply that historians consciously falsify history, but rather that original errors tend to be repetitive. Weinstein's analysis of nine historical evaluations of the Communist and Socialist Parties of America led him to observe: "While the form of these party histories leads to the fragmentation of the radical past, the myths and traditions of post-1920 radicalism (in which historians are hopelessly entangled) blur the distinction of the periods before and after." [80] Furthermore, after pointing to a number of instances of the standardization of error and other solecisms, Weinstein concludes: "Every generation of historians rewrites its history to fit its needs and the books under review here demonstrate that their authors are not exceptions." [81]

The pitfalls and problems of the historical case study notwithstanding, the sociologist must use the historical perspective to understand the nature of social movements. What conditions in a given slice of time give

---

[76] See R. Serge Denisoff, "The Proletarian Renascence: The Folkness of the Ideological Folk," *Journal of American Folklore*, 82 (January–March 1969): 51–65.
[77] See David Shannon, *op. cit.*, p. 91. Benson was the Socialist Party candidate for president in 1916.
[78] H. Wayne Morgan, *Eugene V. Debs: Socialist For President* (Syracuse, N.Y.: Syracuse University Press, 1962), p. 151.
[79] James Weinstein, "Socialism's Hidden Heritage: Scholarship Reinforces Political Mythology," *Studies On the Left*, 3 (Fall 1963): 99.
[80] *Ibid.*, p. 90.
[81] *Ibid.*, p. 108.

rise to given movements? Are periods of economic depression more conducive to left wing movements than those of the Right? Why did a political sect like the American Communist Party attract many intellectuals in the Red Decade? All these questions must be answered within the framework of history. Therefore, the sociologist must frequently rely, albeit with care, upon historical case studies to obtain his data.

SOCIAL PSYCHOLOGY AND SOCIAL MOVEMENTS

"Masses of men—as well as small conspiratorial groups, alienated from institutions, and living, for a while, outside stable and stabilizing institutional structure—have smashed whole societies and promptly built vast new domains." [82] As this quote from Gerth and Mills suggests, the major orientation of social psychologists to social movements has been in terms of their memberships, individually, or collectively as "masses of men." The social psychologist, it appears, is primarily concerned with the psychological characteristics of members and their collective impact rather than with the organizational structure of the movement, its ideology, or the structural problems generating revolutionary activity. This emphasis on the individual may be attributed, in large measure, to the influence of Sigmund Freud on American social psychology. His influence is reflected in the literature on social movements in terms of three basic themes: (1) the frustration of individual drives by social restraints, (2) collective behavior, and (3) the neurotic or psychotic personality.

Society, as Freud saw it, imposes controls upon the individual, both externally and internally (in the form of the super-ego). These controls can hamper the achievement of certain drives, which in turn create psychic discontents. The resulting conflict between man and society is expressed by Freud as follows: "A good part of the struggles of mankind centres round the single task of finding an expedient accommodation—one, that is, that will bring happiness—between this claim of the individual and the cultural claims of the group; and one of the problems that touches the fate of humanity is whether such an accommodation can be reached by means of some particular form of civilization or whether this conflict is irreconcilable." [83] If this conflict cannot be successfully resolved, the individual is prone to respond in ways detrimental to his social integration: "The neurotic creates substitutive satisfactions for himself in his

---

[82] Hans Gerth and C. Wright Mills, *Character and Social Structure: The Psychology of Social Institutions* (New York: Harcourt, Brace and World, Inc., 1953), p. 427.
[83] Sigmund Freud, *Civilization and Its Discontents* (trans. J. Strachey), (New York: W. W. Norton and Co., 1962), p. 43.

symptoms, and these either cause him suffering in themselves or become sources of suffering for him by raising difficulties in his relations with his environment and the society he belongs to." [84] For Freud, the restraints of society versus the drives and biological needs of the individual lead to two basic responses: frustration and aggression. This theoretical point has become the focus for a number of social scientists concerned with the rise and maintenance of social movements. Heberle summarizes this application of Freud's concept as follows:

Individuals who are prevented—by conditions which may be beyond their control—from attaining their goals may react to this situation in two different ways: they may face the facts squarely and adjust themselves in rational ways to their misfortune and, perhaps, try to find practicable remedies for goal blocking conditions, or they may become frustrated, that is, develop attitudes of aggression, without having opportunity to commit aggressive actions. In the latter case, ensuing tensions may find release by participation in a social movement which may direct aggressive tendencies at conditions or groups which are not responsible for the initial causes of frustration. The leaders of such movements may themselves be frustrated individuals or they may artfully exploit their followers' frustrations in pursuit of their own rationally perceived goals.[85]

Specifically, the idea of social frustration has been applied to several studies of the rise of the Third Reich. Edwards, for example, states the case as follows: "The supporters of any social movement, it is true, tend to come from those groups which are already frustrated or anticipate frustration in some respect and which see in this particular movement a means of restoring equilibrium or obtaining relief for their anxiety." [86] Fromm cites frustration as an essential element in the support for National Socialism: "The increasing social frustration led to a projection which became an important source for National Socialism: . . . Those psychological conditions were not the 'cause' of Nazism. They constituted its human basis without which it could not have developed. . . ." [87]
Maier, in studying the rise of National Socialism, states that: "The German people experienced a long period of frustration which was heightened by the depression. . . . This mass frustration in Germany had no immediate outlet." [88] Other studies, such as those by Rinaldo and Lasswell,

---

[84] Ibid., p. 55.
[85] Rudolf Heberle, *Social Movements* (New York: Appleton-Century-Crofts, 1951), p. 107.
[86] Allen L. Edwards, "The Signs of Incipient Fascism," *Journal of Abnormal and Social Psychology*, 39 (July 1944): 310.
[87] Erich Fromm, *Escape From Freedom* (New York: Farrar and Rinehart, 1941), pp. 216, 217–218.
[88] Norman R. Maier, "The Role of Frustration in Social Movements," *Psychological Review*, 49 (November 1942): 591–592.

have employed similar ideas to explain the etiology of social movements.[89]

In recent years, the "social frustration" theme has been extrapolated from the individual level to that of social groups and applied particularly to those possessing certain occupational or status characteristics. Here the source of frustration is located in inconsistencies of status or prestige rather than in the individual psyche. This modification of Freud is reflected in Lofland and Stark's study of conversion to a religious cult.[90] In this work, the authors utilize the idea of frustration (operationalized as "tension") within the framework of Smelser's "value-added" model (wherein collective behavior is the outcome of a cumulation of determinants which, in their combination, eliminate alternative patterns of behavior).[91] According to Lofland and Stark: ". . . tension is best characterized as felt discrepancy between some imaginary, ideal state of affairs and circumstances in which these people saw themselves caught up. We suggest that acutely felt tension is a necessary, but far from sufficient, condition for conversion." [92]

Although somewhat removed from its psychoanalytic antecedents, the "status frustration" or "status politics" theme has been popularized in several studies of the extreme right. Richard Hofstadter, for example, in discussing the extreme Right as "pseudo-conservatism," states: ". . . pseudo-conservatism is in good part a product of the rootlessness and heterogeneity of American life, and above all, of its peculiar scramble for status and its peculiar search for secure identity. . . . Such status strivings may help us to understand some of the otherwise unintelligible figments of the pseudo-conservative ideology. . . ." [93] Daniel Bell defines the extreme Right as an example of protest movements of ". . . new divisions [within the society] created by the status anxieties of new middle class groups. . . ." [94] In his analysis of right wing extremism S. M. Lipset defines status politics as follows: "Status politics . . . refers to political movements whose appeal is to the not uncommon resentments of individuals or groups who desire to maintain or improve their social status." [95] The status frustration theme has been clearly enunciated by Ira S. Rohter in "The Righteous Rightists." An interesting aspect of Rohter's discussion is

---

[89] Joel Rinaldo, *Psychoanalysis of the Reformer* (New York: Lee Publishing Co., 1921); Harold D. Lasswell, *Psychopathology and Politics* (Chicago: University of Chicago Press, 1930).
[90] John Lofland and Rodney Stark, "Becoming a World Saver: A Theory of Conversion to a Deviant Perspective," *American Sociological Review*, 30 (December 1965): 862–874.
[91] Neil J. Smelser, *The Theory of Collective Behavior* (Glencoe, Ill.: The Free Press, 1963), pp. 13–22.
[92] Lofland and Stark, *op. cit.*, p. 864.
[93] Richard Hofstadter, "The Pseudo-Conservative Revolt," in Daniel Bell (ed.), *The Radical Right, op. cit.*, pp. 69, 76.
[94] Daniel Bell, "Interpretation of American Politics," in Bell, *ibid.*, p. 59.
[95] S. M. Lipset, "The Sources of the 'Radical Right,' " in Bell, *ibid.*, p. 260.

his attempt to support the status politics theme by offering an analysis of the "rightist personality."

Ira S. Rohter, "The Righteous Rightists," TRANS-action, Vol. 4 (May, 1967), pp. 27–35. Copyright © May, 1967 by TRANS-action, Inc., New Brunswick, New Jersey.

The Watts riots have been traced directly to plans laid down by Lenin in Moscow. (The Los Angeles Communists, who organized the riots, cleverly blew up their own headquarters in order to appear as innocent martyrs.)

Progressive education (a term including most modern educational methods) was inaugurated by a Columbia University professor on his return from Moscow; it is a deliberate design to expedite the Red take-over by turning our children into un-Christian, un-American, mindless, and will-less robots. For proof of success, we have only to look at Berkeley.

The two stories above—much more heavily elaborated and "documented" —are typical of the items that appear in radical right publications. They illustrate well the characteristic that distinguishes radical rightists from other Americans.

Radical rightists are not merely conservatives or even arch-conservatives. What occupies them full time, what gives them their unique voltage and drive, is not their reverence for oldfashioned fiscal policies and morals, but what Richard Hofstadter calls their "paranoid style"—the overriding and galvanizing belief in a gigantic, insidious Communist conspiracy that has infiltrated and infected all levels of American government and most of its social institutions. The calm conservative who would merely like to see a balanced budget and less welfare is not really a rightist, and they both know it.

Another distinct characteristic by which the rightist (I shall call him that for brevity) may be known is his dedication to *action*. When the enemy is already within the gates attacking all that we hold dear, the true patriot does not sit idly by discussing the income tax or civil rights —he mounts the counterattack.

For the purposes of this study, therefore (and because membership lists and other identifications are often secret) I have used these two characteristics—belief in Communist conspiracy and in direct action—to define and describe rightists, and I have drawn my samples accordingly.

WHO'S RIGHT?

How do people get to be rightists? A major thesis of this article is that rightists are the victims of *status frustration*. That is, for some reason they are dissatisfied or insecure about their places in society and feel that others do not esteem them sufficiently; further, they express their frustration, and compensate for it, by political and social acts which give them emotional identity and support as well as real influence.

Many psychologists regard the striving for self-regard as an essential social and psychological need. To a large extent self-regard must depend on how others regard us. Nobody can really tolerate feeling downgraded or ignored; he must make some defense. The rightist chooses the path of radical right ideology and action, which pinpoints and personifies his enemy as a horrendous evil (and the rightist, therefore, as a kind of St. George) and gives him a means to combat it—not merely for himself but as a champion for all decent mankind.

The rightist becomes loudly superpatriotic—which makes anyone disagreeing suspect of un-Americanism. Those who are higher or richer than he (as the Communist-infiltrated world sees them) or who possesses different values can be pulled down to their true levels—below the rightist on the scale of virtue—by being exposed as "Communist."

DUEL WITH THE DEVIL

Of course, such an orientation—and such action—depend heavily on a highly charged emotionalism and a closed system of paranoid-like logic that is impervious to objective facts that happen to differ. For instance, Communism cannot be considered primarily a political, social, and economic movement and system of thought capable of objective study. Such an idea horrifies the rightist. Communism is Satan personified; it can be faced only in a fight to the death, and only by those properly armed and inoculated.

People who undergo status frustration generally fall into three categories: the *decliners*, the *new arrivals*, and the *value keepers*.

The Decliners. These are the people in our modern, changing society who are going down in the social scale—undeservedly, as they see it.

Modern technology and modern organizations increasingly require new skills, new orientations, more education. Those trained under different and outmoded disciplines (small farmers, for instance) and those with insufficient or outdated educations must feel their positions becoming more and more insecure.

Also threatened are the old professional and entrepreneur classes, especially from the smaller communities: the smalltown general practitioner in medicine, the small home builder, gas station owner, neighborhood grocer—in fact most independent operators trying to survive in the shadows of the great corporations, large labor unions, and big government agencies. The well-educated professionals and corporate executives are taking over the small businessman's role in the community. He is being shoved aside; the hard work and independence on which he had built his self-esteem and his concept of the good and righteous life become increasingly worthless and irrelevant. He begins to ask *why?* Who is doing this to me?

A similar process affects workers, both white and blue collar, displaced by new methods and machinery. They find themselves useless, and their self-regard wavers. The elderly without funds are in an even worse situation—our society no longer respects age, especially when it pulls no economic weight.

As these groups decline, their consciousness of rejection is made even more acute by the rise of those formerly considered low-class or rejected. An Irish Catholic, grandson of an immigrant, is elected President; a Negro "agitator" receives many honors and confers frequently at the White House. Jews are everywhere in prominent places. Again the decliner—often of old white stock—asks *why?*

The New Arrivals. Status frustration occurs not only on the way down, but on the way up. There is almost always a lag between the time the gauche new arrival achieves success and the time those who got there first accept him as an equal. Like the decliner he can easily feel that he has come into a closed and unfriendly society that will not recognize virtue. He is especially upset since he earned it himself in the good old American way instead of being handed prestige on a silver platter.

To the newly arrived, radical rightism can be a potent weapon to destroy their mighty enemies—those who had the opportunity to be better educated, better mannered, more cosmopolitan, and, obviously, more prone to liberal ideas and "bohemian" behavior and immoralities. The charge of "Communism" is a great leveler, and the newly rich can often be counted upon to be twice as narrowly patriotic as anybody.

The Value Keepers. Those moving up or down the ladder of success are bound to find themselves, temporarily at least, among aliens who know not the Lord, but so should those who merely stand still long enough in a society that changes as fast as ours.

A person of any conviction or integrity has social and moral values and beliefs that help determine his behavior, his self-definition, and his place in the community. But let the community begin to re-examine those values critically or displace them with others, and the foundation of his whole universe begins to turn to sand.

For the great majority of us, many of the traditional rural or small town ways or virtues are no longer useful or true. Modern society needs education and expertise more than hard work and self-denial; an expanding economy rather than thrift; organized community welfare programs rather than primary reliance on savings, personal charity, relatives, and contemplation of the sufferings of Job.

Moreover, the preponderance of political and economic power, for good or ill, has definitely shifted from the country with its white settlers to the metropolis with its combinations of minority populations. Those whose beliefs and behavior were shaped by older traditions—who, as they see it, settled and built this country—now find themselves, in effect, increasingly disinherited.

Even more important than the objective loss of power and prestige are the *subjective* feelings of loss, of being displaced and discredited. God and the devil, good and evil, are absolutes and do not change; therefore, the change that discredits and displaces the old morality must be evil triumphing over good. Only by such rationalization can true believers retain their orientation and self-regard.

The values defended include hard work, saving, prudent investment, and self-discipline—the Protestant ethic. As the name implies, these values are not only economic but moral, with deep psychological meaning. They are supposed to result in independence and individualism, as the rightist sees them. An apparent attack on them—such as increased government control or taxes—becomes not only an economic change but an immorality and must be answered.

Therefore, as experience demonstrates daily, those most closely identified with older traditional values reduce and discuss almost all social problems to moralistic terms: If the wayward society or individual would only cease transgression and return to the old tried-and-true paths of religion, decency, and family virtue, all would in time be well.

This accounts for much of the intense and emotional opposition to social change by rightists—the counterattack, often blind, to government controls, integration, religious secularism, welfare, the United Nations, foreign aid, Supreme Court decisions, modern education, and even such apparently non-controversial scientific and health advances as fluoridation and mental health programs.

Fundamentalism is an important source of rightist fervor. In fact, from their titles and rhetoric, it is hard to distinguish between a rightist political rally and an evangelistic campaign—note the Rev. Carl McIntire's "Twentieth Century Reformation" and Dr. Fred Schwartz's "Christian Anti-Communist Crusade." Communism, a twentieth century abomination, becomes the catch-all for everything that seems evil and unacceptable in the easygoing, affluent, sophisticated, urban twentieth century.

These then are the theses advanced about the rightist which I tested in this study:

•Rightists are people undergoing status frustration. They feel they do not have the prestige and power they should have if the world were just—and their enemies have too much. They are on the move as far as status is concerned—either they are going down in a changing world (which should be true of most of them), they are standing still as the world passes them by, or they are rising more rapidly in economic position than in social recognition.

•They identify themselves with the older, traditional (Protestant ethic) values of work, religion, and morality, so that their fight for status recognition also becomes a crusade for truth, justice, decency, God, and America.

•They believe that their troubles—and therefore also the attack against Christianity and America—are caused by an all-pervasive conspiracy, wholly evil and implacable, called Communism.

•They relieve their anxieties and feelings of resentment and inadequacy by radical right belief and activity. This gives them an effective explanation and compensation for their difficulties, a means of bringing their enemies down, and a method of gaining power, prestige, and mutual support.

Do these hypotheses survive empirical examination?

To start with objective findings first: Are the rightists of our sample actually undergoing status mobility and frustration?

The data show that there are only 10 percent of rightists in the highest occupations, such as executives and professionals, compared to 24 percent of non-rightists; and that rightists are over-represented among the lower-middle class (such as clerical and salesworkers)—15 to 4 percent. Further, nearly twice as many rightists as others are retired—removed, for most practical purposes, from economic importance to society altogether. Rightists also tend to be older (median age 54 compared to 45) and are more often self-employed (although at lower levels)—if businessmen, they tend to run smaller businesses; if professionals, their standing is low.

In profile, therefore, the radical rightist is older, less secure financially, and less often an important part of a major modern industrial enterprise; he more often has a low prestige white collar job or is thrown on his own resources—retired or operator of a marginal "independent" business. Such a picture is quite consistent with the status frustration hypothesis; such a person, especially if he identifies with an older tradition that was once dominant, could hardly help feeling frustrated.

Occupation alone, however, is not enough to measure social standing. What of education? In our increasingly sophisticated society, education is not only a necessity but a mark of prestige, especially in the middle and upper classes. But even in these occupational strata the rightists have less education than their non-rightist equivalents. In the highest levels (high executives, proprietors, major professionals, etc.) almost twice as many non-rightists as rightists have graduate degrees (64 percent to 33 percent), while three times as many rightists (12 percent to 4 percent) never went beyond high school. In the middle levels over twice as many nonrightists got college degrees (27 percent to 12 percent) while over twice as many rightists (54 percent to 24 percent) never went beyond high school.

DOWN AND TO THE RIGHT

What about mobility? Comparing a male rightist's (or a female rightist's husband's) occupation and education with those of his father (this is called "inter-generational status mobility"), we found, as hypothesized, that the rightist did undergo much more status mobility than nonrightists, most often downward.

In the *lowest* occupation (typically, unskilled blue collar) the rightists had fallen farther and more consistently than non-rightists had done anywhere. Thirty-eight percent of rightist men compared to 6 percent non-rightist had declined sharply. Rightist laborers were quite apt to have had middle class or farm-owning fathers.

In the *middle* groups (white collar, small business) rightists were more mobile, both up and down, than non-rightists. Relatively few had stayed at the same occupational and educational level as their father (14 to 29 percent). There tended to be a few more losers than winners.

In the *highest* status, however, rightists on the way up surpass not only those on the way down but even the relatively static non-rightists. This fits in very well with the thesis that the "newly arrived" undergo status frustration.

As predicted, therefore, the rightists had significantly greater mobility, especially downward, and less education where it counted most.

Another way to measure mobility should be by length of residence in a neighborhood. The old fundamentalist morality is closely associated with a rural and small town past; many people from that background, who cling to the old standards, have moved to a faceless Babylon of a city where they have few skills they can use. Those on the way down—or in from the farm—must move into poorer neighborhoods; those on the way up, though they take their values and their accents with them, are most likely, as soon as possible, to move to higher status suburbs or neighborhoods. Those who stay the shortest time should therefore be the most mobile.

Studying the length of residence of people under 50, we found two basic groups of rightists. One seems to be primarily composed of people new to the community who seem unable to accept or be accepted by the community; also, they are declining in status more rapidly than a similar group of equally mobile non-rightists.

The other rightist cluster is composed of oldtimers who have lived in their communities most of their adult lives; they are considerably older than their neighbors, and many more turn up in the 50 and 60 age brackets. Their neighborhoods have gone down, and they have declined in status with them. Here too, therefore, there seems a clear association between decline (whether in new or old residency) and radical rightism.

THAT OLD TIME RELIGION

Are rightists to any significant extent fundamentalists? Belief in traditional values, along with many rightist attitudes, was earlier related to religious fundamentalism. Empirically, this is true. Rightists very much subscribe to fundamentalist tenets and belong to these churches; nearly half the rightists (44 percent compared to 17 percent of the non-rightists) are affiliated with fundamentalist denominations. Rightists were also more often raised in rural areas or small towns, environments most likely to produce traditionalism and hostility toward modernity.

So much for the objective factors. How do the people themselves view their plights?

Fewer rightists than non-rightists actually belong to the upper class; but more of them *rated themselves* "upper class." When asked, "How hard do you think it is for people today to move upward from one social class to another?" their answers revealed a view of society as essentially closed, dominated by personalities, controlled by the wrong kind of people: "Not much opportunity anymore; it's getting harder; depends on having money, knowing the right people." The views of the non-rightists were much more objective and impersonal: "Depends on education; must work hard and have abilities to get it; special skills; hard to change direction of early life. . . ."

We asked, "Do you think that people . . . influential in this community are, in *general*, friendly . . . or cliquish?" Rightists answered "cliquish and unfriendly" more often than non-rightists. When those answering "cliquish" were asked to give reasons, rightists more often indicated belief in a closed structure run by a small group: "Old residents tend to look on new people as outsiders; certain families run things here; segregated groups want their own way; all have common political views."

The rightist, then, more often sees himself as the outsider, discriminated against in a closed society run by an elite.

What about the predicted concern with the Protestant ethic? We asked, "Are there any differences between what you believe should be the American way of life and the way things are done in the country nowadays?" "In what ways are things different?" Typically, from the rightists:

"Morality and standards are going bad; the American way of life is deteriorating because of a suppression of morality; we need a moral and spiritual revival among our leaders; we need to follow the Ten Commandments more."

RUGGED INDIVIDUALISTS

What about individual initiative, self-reliance, respect for authority? "I am worried about the drift of the country; the amount of crime and disrespect for authority shows things are going the other way; we must instill more emphasis on respect, integrity, and individual responsibility; parents aren't teaching their children the right things anymore."

Traditional morality and values dominate many rightists' perception of everything. No matter what the topic—what things they worried about, what community concerns they had, what qualities they admired, what things Communists actually believed in, whatever—sooner or later they indicated that if we would only return to the old morality every problem would be solved.

Our findings are clear: The rightists are more dissatisfied with the values of contemporary American society; they adhere to the "old truths" and believe everyone else should "return" to them. They suffer severe frustration because of this, a frustration heavily reinforced by religious righteousness expressed in absolute and positive terms.

"In your own case . . . do you think that *everyone* gives you as much respect as *you feel you* deserve?" This question was deliberately worded to emphasize extremes—yet rightists answered "no" more frequently than non-rightists. This is true both of rightists who are on the way up and those on the way down; but the decliners say "no" *twice* as often as those on the rise—emphasizing that it is the losers who are most impelled to seek radical rightism. (Presumably, once those on the rise secure recognition, they will cease attacking high-status people and changing times.)

Rightists felt more unaccepted than non-rightists, and rightists on the decline more unaccepted than anybody.

Does joining radical right organizations and causes help the rightist combat his anxieties successfully? By being more patriotic and anti-Communist than anybody else, the rightist seems to wrap himself in greatness and goodness, in importance, righteousness, and self-satisfaction. He is a savior carrying out a holy crusade. As the John Birch Society Bulletin (November 1964) points out, if you join their society ". . . you feel a tremendous satisfaction . . . to save for our children and their children the glorious country and humane civilization which we ourselves inherited."

We asked them to select "two great Americans" and describe what is admirable about them. Later, we asked them to describe "the typical member of an anti-Communist group"—that is, in effect, an idealized version of themselves. Their great people, they said, were "true" Americans and "very" patriotic; 75 percent found the same things true of themselves (compared to 22 percent of non-rightists, who tended to use less extravagant terms). Courage, strength, and "guts" were likewise qualities they shared with the great, as was deep Christian faith and high moral standards. And 50 percent further saw the great to be honest, truthful, and sincere—like themselves.

Non-rightists, however, viewed rightists very differently—"dishonest," "hypocrites," "no integrity," "use character assassination."

This tactic of rightists to acquire status and importance by associating themselves closely with the great and the good is perhaps best illustrated by their emphasis on "self-education." They are, in fact, less well-educated than the non-rightists. But the world of radical rightism is full of parades of quasi-experts, study groups, monographs, footnotes, and bibliographies—almost all with no standing among scholars. But the rightists study them avidly, mention intelligence and education highly among those things they admire in the great, and give themselves strong ratings as "intellectuals, very brilliant," "well informed," "people with sound judgment, good reasoning," and "lots of sense." Needless to add, non-rightists hold almost precisely the opposite view of them.

THE RIGHTIST PERSONALITY

The need to relieve status anxiety and to attack values that do not conform to their beliefs are not enough to explain why some people become radical rightists and others, in like circumstances, do not. The rightist tends also to have certain personality characteristics—to be, in effect, a particular kind of human being.

Simplism. Psychologists say that a basic need of man is his desire for meaning, to understand what is happening to him. In an important sense the rightist, a traditionalist in changing times, is adrift in frightening darkness—he needs landmarks, he needs simple guidelines, before he loses direction altogether. Radical rightism gives him this "understanding"— and this security. All becomes clear and very simple. It is all a conspiracy. Nothing is really changed—God is still in His heaven; but He needs help.

Extremely simple explanations have great attractions for the confused. They are a necessity for those personalities who have what psychologists call "simplistic cognitive structure"—who have a strong need for simple, firm, stereotyped views of people and events, with no place for ambivalence or ambiguity. Such persons reject unbelievers, need external authorities, and, for emotional reasons, hold their beliefs so rigidly that compromise is intolerable.

Testing for this rigidity of belief, using statements on Communism and Russia ("Communism is a total evil." "The Soviet Union is 'mellowing'."), on intolerance of ambiguity ("There is usually only one right way to do anything."), on anti-compromise and close-minded stance ("The compromise of principles leads to nothing but destruction." "A group which tolerates too much difference of opinion cannot exist for long."), we found the rightist to fit this description. He is intolerant of ambiguity, opposed to compromise, and close-minded.

Extra-Punitiveness. It is difficult not to be struck by the strident negativism and combativeness of rightist writings, thought, and speech. Terrible things exist all about, the future is steeped in gloom; everything is in strong blacks and whites—the forces of light are locked in mortal combat with the forces of darkness. It is not only necessary, therefore, but moral and virtuous to be resentful, discontented, belligerent and full of hate. While the rightist justifies his behavior in the name of Americanism and anti-Communism, the actual thrusts of his attacks are against the political, social, and intellectual leaders of the community—those who have the respect and influence he does not.

This vehement scapegoating is characteristic of a psychological defense mechanism called "extra-punitiveness." The extra-punitive have a great deal of free-floating hate and aggression they project outward, blaming others or the world for their personal or social failures. Their view of the world is paranoid.

We tested for extra-punitiveness by asking what measures they would take against "Communists" and, in later questions, against other "safe" scapegoats (those with few defenders, such as delinquents, sex deviants, homosexuals, and "disrespectful persons"). Rightists were more in favor of strong measures against Communists (sample statement with high response: "Take them out and hang them"); but their *generalized* hostility showed up even more clearly in their attitudes toward nonpolitical deviants. (Sample statements: "There is hardly anything lower than a person who does not feel a great love, gratitude, and respect for his parents." "Homosexuals are hardly better than criminals and ought to be severely punished.")

Rightists not only condemn Communists but define them so differently that it is sometimes hard to believe they are talking about real people. There is a heavy emphasis on religion and black-or-white morality: To believe that we can live with Communism is to be a dupe or worse. Communism is the anti-Christ, it is evil incarnate. This allows for convenient projection of personal hatreds. Rightists often find the highly educated—including professors—to be Communists. "From what racial or religious groups are Communists most likely to come?" Rightists frequently mentioned "atheists," "Jews," "Methodists," "Unitarians," and "modernistic religious groups." (Non-rightists denied more frequently and more vigorously that race or religion was involved.)

Powerlessness. It is a basic tenet of rightism that individual freedom —as they define it—is being lost and that the ordinary citizen (meaning themselves) is being ignored. Is "the federal government . . . extending too much . . . power into . . . everyday life?" Nearly 70 percent of the rightists "agreed very much." "Are there any groups . . . that you think have too much power or influence?" "Yes," the rightists said, significantly more often than non-rightists, and listed labor (and its leaders), Communists, big government, and such groups as the ADA, ACLU, and Council on Foreign Relations. Who has *too little* power? They mentioned twice as many groups as the non-rightists, most often the two surrogates for themselves: the individual "common man" and "conservative" organizations.

Do rightists, as hypothesized, feel maligned and persecuted? They pointed out with considerable heat that their idealized "great men," with whom they identify, were mistreated: "Got a raw deal; treated badly by others, his country; a victim of injustice."

Alienation. We found our rightists to be significantly more politically alienated than the non-rightists, to feel that their elected public officials do not actually represent them, that local officials avoid or ignore them, responding only to special interests. On referenda on community issues— such as bond issues or taxes—they more consistently than others vote "no."

Do they trust other people? (A person who feels lost, who has little sense of personal competence, often lives in a jungle of suspicion and distrust.) We found significant association between radical rightism and low trust in others. Generally, the rightists in our sample were less often involved in social and community organizations.

Finally, the rightist *feels* that by joining other rightists he can overcome his own powerlessness and estrangement.

Extra-punitiveness, a paranoid view of society, a great deal of free-floating hostility and aggression, desire for direct action, a rigid devotion to absolutes in religion and morality and to black-or-white standards— all these characteristics describe particular kinds of closed-minded, insecure, authoritarian persons undergoing particular kinds of status crises. And that is who the rightists are.

A NOTE ON THE STUDY

Radical rightists generally keep their membership lists secret. Therefore, for the purposes of this study they were defined in terms of their characteristic activities and beliefs.

Radical rightists were defined as those people who believed, to a large degree, in the existence of an internal Communist conspiracy infiltrating all levels of government and most social institutions in the United States and who are deeply involved in action to counter this Communist threat.

The sample was selected from lists of people who, through such activity and through their expressions, had made their rightist orientations matters of public record. Specifically, names were taken from a newspaper article listing members of the John Birch Society and the Liberty Amendment Committee in a Northwestern city; others were found through published "letters to the editor." Fifty-six came from a list of contributors and subscribers to a radical right organization and publication. Similarly, the sample of non-rightists was selected through content analysis of other "letters to the editor" and from referenda petitions. The final sample from which the analysis was made contained 169 rightists and 167 non-rightists.

One of the main difficulties with Rohter's analysis is that he extends "status frustration" to such an extent that it can cover literally any status group in the society. That is, in Rohter's view, status frustration is a consequence of upward mobility ("new arrivals"), nonmobility ("value-keepers . . . those who merely stand still long enough in a society that changes as fast as ours"), and downward mobility ("decliners"). If this is the case, how is the status-frustrated Rightist to be distinguished from the unfrustrated non-Rightist in terms of the mobility dimension? It is altogether likely that Rohter is really discussing, in his three aspects of mobility, only two types—upward and downward—for, after all, is not standing still in a changing world a form of downward mobility? If, as a consequence of social mobility, an individual occupies out-of-line social statuses and thus experiences status frustration, then it should be theoretically important to consider whether he arrived at this state of affairs through upward or downward mobility. Certainly his world view may be expected to differ according to the direction of his mobility. Another important factor in any analysis of responses to status inconsistency should be the particular pattern of inconsistency which is manifest. Differences between ascribed and achieved statuses (e.g., ethnicity and occupation) may be important: i.e., will the political behavior of the Negro banker differ from that of the white porter? Differential rank on achieved statuses may also be an important factor: high education, low income inconsistency may well lead to different political orientations than those resulting from the reverse pattern.

A further aspect of Rohter's analysis which must be considered concerns the data which he presents to support his description of the extreme

Rightists, particularly data pertaining to the "rightist personality." For the most part, these cannot be considered exclusively characteristic of the extreme Right. Those who are "dissatisfied with the values of contemporary American society" include not only extreme Rightists but also members of civil rights groups, "hippies," advocates of "black power," the "New Left," and antiwar demonstrators. Rightists may advocate a return to old truths and values, but so do most conservatives. A simplistic world view and extrapunitiveness are not exclusive to the extreme Right; these elements may be found in vulgar Marxism, Trotskyism, or Maoism. Finally, powerlessness and alienation are experienced by all those who are disadvantaged by the contemporary political and economic structures of society. There are many more possible responses to these feelings than extreme rightism.[96]

All in all, it is questionable whether "frustration" can be considered an adequate explanation for the etiology of social movements. Turner and Killian, in discussing the topic of frustration, state: ". . . frustration by itself is never a guarantee of receptivity to movements. Long-continued frustration characteristically leads to hopelessness which mitigates against participation in the promotion of any reform. Frustration from recent losses in the experience of improving conditions is more likely to make receptive individuals than long-continued frustration.[97] Moreover, frustration per se will not necessarily eventuate in participation in protest movements. Krout and Stagner's study of the members of the Young People's Socialist League and the Young Communist League suggests that symptoms of frustration and maladjustment were as prevalent among their control groups as among the radicals studied:

Finally, we should like to emphasize two points: one, that these results do not indicate that radicals are neurotic; and two, that they are not an evaluation of radical ideologies as such. With regard to the first point our data show as many symptoms of maladjustment among controls as among radicals. It is with the specific form of these symptoms that we have been concerned. Radicalism is an aspect of social change directly related to the functioning of social institutions. We see no justification in our data for considering radicalism less closely related to mental health than is conservatism.

As regards the second point this study has no particular contribution to offer. The validity of socio-economic philosophies must be determined by facts outside the realm of individual psychology. The acceptance of radical doctrines is the only point with which we have been concerned. It may be worth while to point out that, since the fathers of our republic espoused radical ideas, it ill behooves us to put an unfair interpretation on the attitudes of those

[96] For a further discussion, see G. B. Rush, "The Righteous Rightists," *TRANS-action*, 4 (July–August 1967): 78.
[97] Ralph Turner and Lewis Killian (eds.), *Collective Behavior* (Englewood Cliffs, N.J.: Prentice-Hall, Inc., 1957), p. 432.

accepting radicalism (especially since our data do not justify it). The facts rather indicate that avowed radicals display certain forms of inferior adjustment, and that they display some forms generally considered superior.[98]

The most popular non-Freudian psychological analysis of social movements has been Hadley Cantril's The Psychology of Social Movements.[99] In brief, Cantril's thesis is as follows: An individual is socialized into specific norms and frames of reference, which constitute his feelings of being and self-regard. However, these norms may be at variance with the normative order of the "social values" in existence at any given time. As a result of this "dissensus," discontent may arise from four major sources: (1) from discrepancies between an individual's aspirations and his achievements; (2) from a lack of status recognition or deference; (3) from a lack of means by which individuals may satisfy their innate or acquired needs; (4) from the failure of society to provide recognition for values that individuals cherish.[100] As a result of experiencing these discontents, individuals are susceptible to participation in social movements because these movements provide satisfactions not available in the external world. As Turner and Killian describe Cantril's position: ". . . the movement is a small world in itself commanding the total allegiance of its members and providing a totality of values and gratifications requiring renunciation of the large world outside." [101]

Several decades after Cantril's work, one of his former students, Hans Toch, attempted, in The Social Psychology of Social Movements, to expand upon the original conceptualization.[102] The first factor in Toch's analysis is the existence of a "problem situation," reflecting either a "personal or social deficit." This problem situation must therefore have an "impact on individual people." As such, "social movements draw their members from the ranks of persons who have encountered problems," that is, individuals who suffer from a lack of "personal dignity and self-respect." If these individuals feel that change of the problem situation is possible, and if they feel a desire to become involved in bringing about this change, then they will be "predisposed to join a social movement . . . designed to remedy their difficulties."

For both Cantril and Toch, the existence of "discontents" and "problem situations" leads the individual experiencing these conditions into the ranks of a social movement. Aside from the fact that merely

[98] Maurice Krout and Ross Stagner, "Personality Development in Radicals: A Comparative Study," *Sociometry*, 2 (January 1939): 44–45.
[99] Hadley Cantril, *The Psychology of Social Movements* (New York: John Wiley and Sons, 1941).
[100] *Ibid.*, pp. 48–51.
[101] Turner and Killian, *op. cit.*, p. 421. See also Cantril, *op. cit.*, pp. 137, 184.
[102] Hans Toch, *The Social Psychology of Social Movements* (Indianapolis: Bobbs-Merrill, 1965). The discussion is excerpted from pp. 9–10.

suffering the effects of personal or structural strains does not in itself place people in the ranks of a social movement, the theoretical point remains that explaining or identifying the orientations and perceptions of individuals does not explain the formation and maintenance of social movements. Separate research undertaken to analyze the psychological variables underlying membership in extremist movements have found similar variables and processes operating in both left and right extremes.

Solomon and Fishman, in their analysis of Turn Toward Peace demonstrators, found that activists were characterized by: (1) moralistic idealism; (2) sudden political interest during the later years of high school or early years of college; and (3) having initiated their political activity outside the family.[103] Peace activists were most likely to be first-born children in their families and to have had some previous political experience.[104] Their reasons for participating were, in part, a defense against anxiety and a "desire for political action."

Lawrence Schiff, in a study of the Young Americans for Freedom (YAF), identified parallel characteristics among these campus-based conservatives.[105] For example, student conservatives were converted either as high school seniors or during the first two years of college, when they made "shocking" discoveries about the new universe. They, like their pacifist counterparts, were likely to be eldest children who began their political activities outside the family environment. Schiff also describes his youthful Rightists as "obedient rebels" characterized by a desire to appear as dutiful sons.[106] As for the peace activists, Solomon and Fishman report that seventy-five percent of the parents of antiwar protestors were liberal. Therefore, it may be speculated that the youthful peace advocates also identified with their elders' political attitudes. In sum, individuals with similar psychological attributes are found in both spheres of political radicalism. Thus, focusing on the psychological characteristics of the members of diverse social movements can tell us little about how these movements are formed in the first place.

If Toch and others using a similar approach do not treat either the origin of movements or the factors determining which movement an individual seeking a solution to problems will join, then we must make two related theoretical assumptions before their analysis has any credibility. First, we must assume that social movements exist a priori to the individual's experiencing strain. Second, we must assume that certain intervening

[103] Fredric Solomon and Jacob R. Fishman, "Youth and Peace: A Psychological Study of Student Peace Demonstrators in Washington, D.C.," *Journal of Social Issues*, 20 (October 1964): 54–73.
[104] *Ibid.*, pp. 54–55.
[105] Lawrence F. Schiff, "The Obedient Rebels: A Study of College Conversions to Conservatism," *Journal of Social Issues*, 20 (October 1964): 74–95.
[106] *Ibid.*, p. 88.

variables operate to determine the individual's selection of one movement over another. Whether these assumptions are tenable, and how they fit into the analysis of social movements, will be taken up in chapters 4 and 5.

Another contribution of Freudian thought to the analysis of social movements lies in the conception of certain kinds of social participation as being irrational and contagious. This theme is most prevalent in the "collective behavior" approach to social movements. In this framework, a movement is treated as a "sort of extended crowd made up of people acting under a delusion fostered by the mechanisms of crowd behavior." [107] In this sense, collective behavior is viewed as having a biological basis (e.g., note the use of concepts such as "emotional contagion" and "collective mind"), rather than a social one.

One of the best illustrations of the collective behavior approach is that of Robert Lindner, who, in Prescription for Rebellion, argues that industrial societies have "sex-regulated economics." As a result: ". . . the dispossessed of a society become legion, as the ranks of the disinherited grow, the collective ego of the mass discovers itself." [108] Consequently: ". . . unrestrained by repression, the psychopathy of the proletarianized mass is loosed. . . . Mass Man, no longer the docile, 'adjusted,' passive cipher his creators hoped he would remain and thought him to be is revealed. . . ." [109] This "mob pathology" argument has frequently been used to explain Negro riots.[110]

In our view, the crowd psychology approach to social movements is completely untenable. Crowd behavior is, as its analysts point out, basically irrational and spontaneous. On the other hand, movements oriented to social change are not irrational, and involvement in them is, on the whole, a conscious act on the part of the participants. Nevertheless, several scholars have taken the position that social movements and their members are fundamentally irrational and unreasonable.[111] A number of conditions have contributed to this bias. In the first place, the moral indignation of civilized men toward the practices of the Nazi movement, which has been overemphasized in social movement research, has contributed greatly to the "irrational" conception. In fact, many of the techniques for studying

---

[107] Turner and Killian, *op. cit.*, pp. 307–308. See also Gustav LeBon, *The Crowd: A Study of the Popular Mind* (London: Ernest Bonn, Ltd., 1947).
[108] Robert Lindner, *Prescription for Rebellion* (New York: Holt, Rinehart and Winston, Inc., 1952), pp. 99–144, quoted at p. 180.
[109] *Ibid.*, p. 180.
[110] See, for example, The Chicago Commission on Race Relations, *The Negro in Chicago* (Chicago: The University of Chicago Press, 1922).
[111] See, for example, William Bruce Cameron, *Modern Social Movements: A Sociological Outline* (New York, Random House, 1965), p. 11; Thelma McCormack, "The Motivation of Radicals," *American Journal of Sociology*, 56 (July 1950): 17–24.

social movements have been derived from studies of Nazism.[112] Another factor, suggested by McCormack, is that pioneer research into social movements was conducted during the twenties and thirties by abnormal psychologists, for whom radicalism was motivated by nonrational factors.[113] Finally, as Mills has suggested, American sociologists who study activity antithetical to their own value structure frequently label it as abnormal or deviant.[114] As Heberle puts it: "A common reaction towards people who propose fundamental changes in the social order of society is to declare them scoundrels, egoists, morally bad people, or crackpots. [However, namecalling] . . . is a rather unsophisticated weapon. In our age more crushing effects can be achieved by labelling one's adversaries as neurotics, as psychopathetic cases." [115] As an alternative to the irrational approach, Heberle suggests that: ". . . an aggressive attitude and militant behavior may be a perfectly sound and normal response to a challenge—for example, the violent reaction of striking workers against strike breakers or plant police." [116] One Soviet sociologist, in criticizing the Freudian approach, argues as follows: "[Freud] . . . fails to understand that the irreconcilability of the masses during revolutionary action springs from social and class causes, not biological ones, that fury is a fully justified expression when used in connection with the struggle of revolutionary classes for their own interests." [117]

In support of the hypothesis, both Becker, in The Outsiders, and Hofstadter, in "The Pseudo-Conservative Revolt," maintain that the members of social movements are in large part motivated by perceived rational interests concerning economics, power, and prestige.[118] In the following article, Christian Bay concludes, from his survey of a number of studies on personality and political attitudes, that radicalism is generally associated with emotional security, rationality, and independence.

[112] See Abel, op. cit.; Heberle, op. cit., pp. 104–109.
[113] McCormack, op. cit., pp. 19–21.
[114] C. Wright Mills, "The Professional Ideology of Social Pathologists," American Journal of Sociology, 49 (September 1943): 165–181.
[115] Heberle, op. cit., p. 105.
[116] Ibid., p. 109.
[117] Ervand Pogosyan, "Social and Cultural Problems in Contemporary Neo-Freudianism," Soviet Review, 3 (Spring 1962): 27.
[118] Howard Becker, The Outsiders (Glencoe, Ill.: The Free Press, 1962), chap. 8, pp. 147–163; Richard Hofstadter, "The Pseudo-Conservative Revolt," in Bell, op. cit., pp. 84–85.

Christian Bay, "Political and Apolitical Students: Facts in Search of Theory," Journal of Social Issues, Vol. 23 (July 1967), 76–91. *This is a revised version of a paper prepared for a symposium on "protest on the American Campus" presented on September 2, 1966, during the Annual Meeting of the Society for the Psychological Study of Social Issues in New York City. I am most grateful to Joseph Katz and Edward E. Sampson for their constructive criticism of an earlier draft; also to my colleagues at the Institute for the Study of Human Problems at Stanford University, for helpful discussions prior to the first draft. Reprinted by permission of Christian Bay and The Society for Psychological Study of Social Issues.*

Why do students active in protest movements tend to do better academically, and be more intelligent and intellectually disposed, compared to more apolitical students? There is a wealth of data to show that this is so, but an astounding absence of efforts to make theoretical sense of it. Moreover, for decades we have known that more liberal or radical students have, statistically speaking, been more intelligent or academically able than more conservative students; and similar relationships have been found with a corresponding regularity in studies, though fewer in number, of adult populations. How can we account for this apparent preponderance of intelligence and intellectual resources on the left side of the political spectrum?

In this paper I hope to contribute toward such a theoretical accounting. My main task is to try to make theoretical sense of three categories of data, to be briefly discussed or summarized in the following sections: (a) traditional attitude measurement studies, from the 1920's on, mainly administered to students but at other times to adults, which almost invariably have found those who are more liberal doing better on intelligence, educational achievement, etc. compared to those who are more conservative; (b) work on authoritarianism and related neurotic tendencies, which again has demonstrated a clear affinity between these tendencies and rightwing views, compared to a much less clear, or more tenuous, affinity with leftwing orientations; and (c) recent work on student political activists, which abundantly shows liberal and leftist militancy to correlate with high academic or intellectual achievement.

The attempted theoretical explanation is based on fairly recent work by social psychologists, whose theory of the functions of attitudes will be extended toward a theory of individual political rationality as an aspect of human development.

TRADITIONAL STUDIES OF RADICAL VERSUS CONSERVATIVE ATTITUDES

The invention and subsequently the continued improvement of techniques for the measurement of attitudes, together with increasingly sophisticated techniques of correlational analysis and the related knacks of applied statistics, have stimulated an enormous number of studies of attitudes and relationships between attitudes, beginning around 1920. A large category of attitude studies dealt with political orientations. Among the latter studies there must have been hundreds reported in the journals of the twenties and thirties which either focussed on or paid attention to characteristics of *radical* versus *conservative* attitudes and their respective correlates.

There is one difference in particular between students (the major population studied) with more radical or liberal and students with more conservative views that shows up in study after study: more radical students kept scoring higher either on intelligence tests or by way of academic grades, compared to more conservative students. There were exceptions, but there is no gainsaying the general tendency. Speaking of the literature reporting research on conservative attitudes on American campuses, Newcomb reports an almost unanimous finding: "Whatever the context of the term 'conservatism,' those who show it least on any given campus tend to make higher scores on intelligence tests, or to make better scholastic records, or both, than those who show it most" (Newcomb, 1943, 171).

Beginning around 1930, there also have been a good number of studies of attitude change, especially during the college years, and more are being published today. In Newcomb's classic study of Bennington students during the late thirties, published in 1943, the fact that most students left college considerably more liberal or radical than they had been as entering freshmen is accounted for mainly in terms of peer group influence: ". . . nonconservative attitudes are developed at Bennington primarily by those who are both capable and desirous of cordial relations with their fellow community members" (Newcomb, 1943, 148–149).

But why was Bennington a breeding ground for radicals and liberals in the 1930's? Newcomb's explanation is plausible but somewhat atheoretical: Bennington College was founded in 1932, the year FDR took office, and many faculty members were interested in and sympathetic to the New Deal, as were many other American intellectuals at the time. But is there nothing about the educational process itself that should lead us to expect, in the best colleges, a liberal rather than a conservative climate? To this question, Newcomb's otherwise excellent study does not address itself.

Samuel A. Stouffer, in his valuable 1955 volume, *Communism, Conformity, and Civil Liberties,* finds that community leaders invariably are more tolerant of the freedom of dissent, compared to the bulk of the population. For example, 84% of the leaders would allow a socialist to speak compared to 58% of the general population. For the atheist's right to speak, the corresponding figures are 64 compared to 37; for the communist's, 51 compared to 27. And so on.

Based on composites of replies to all his tolerance questions, Stouffer constructed a scale of tolerance of nonconformists. Stouffer's "more tolerant" respondents, as of May–July, 1954, are younger: 47% of those in their twenties, compared to 18% in their sixties, are "more tolerant"— and there is a linear relationship for the in-between age groups. Secondly, the more liberal respondents are better educated: 66% of the college graduates, compared to 16% of those with grade schools only, and again a clear linear relationship. Further breakdowns indicated, too, that the better educated are more liberal also for matching age levels, while the younger are more liberal also at matching levels of education. Stouffer also found that optimism concerning one's personal future—generally higher for younger than for older people—correlates highly with liberalism (or, in his terms, tolerance).

In addition, Stouffer found a clear relationship between urbanization and liberalism, both nationally and for each region of the United States: West, East, Middle West, South. The degree of liberalism is also related to the region, with descending degrees from West to South in the order listed.

By way of explanation of these and related findings, Stouffer suggests that a factor essential to tolerance may be "contact with people with disturbing and unpopular ideas . . . [schooling] *puts a person in touch with people whose ideas and values are different from one's own*" (1955, 125–128). Urban living does this and so, probably, does living in the West, where a higher proportion of the population has lived in other regions. The cities of the Far West "which have grown at such an astonishing rate by recruiting from all parts of this country, are the highest of all in our scale of tolerance," Stouffer has found (1955, 127–128).

But why is it that the younger people, regardless of levels of education, tend to be more liberal than the older people? The only hypothesis Stouffer suggests is that it is easier for the young to be optimistic about their personal future; and degrees of optimism ("my life will be better") are significantly related to youth and also to tolerance, as his data bear out. But why should optimists tend to be tolerant of nonconformists? Stouffer here merely states that "there is substantial psychological theory which would predict a relationship between optimism about personal affairs and tolerance toward nonconformists"; he elaborates only to the extent of suggesting the need for scapegoats for individuals who are very troubled and the availability of communists and other nonconformists as "obvious targets for blame, directly for the world's troubles and indirectly, if sometimes unconsciously, for one's personal troubles" (Stouffer, 1955, 100). Is this all there is to the relationship he demonstrated between youth and liberalism?

PERSONALITY AND POLITICAL ATTITUDES

In *The Authoritarian Personality* a number of factors were found to be related to neurotic authoritarianism as measured by the F-scale. Among these were political-economic conservatism, measured by the PEC scale in its several forms, all of which gave a high score to respondents indicating a high degree of "support of the *status quo* and particularly of business; support of conservative values; desire to maintain a balance of power in which business is dominant, labor subordinate and the economic functions of government minimized; and resistance to social change" (Adorno, *et al.*, 1950, 154–155).

Rokeach's Criticisms

There are serious methodological shortcomings in this work, as is often the case with pioneering ventures. While Edward Shils had charged the authors of *The Authoritarian Personality* with a kind of ideological blindness to the phenomenon of authoritarianism on the Left, a charge based on political assumptions of his own rather than substantive evidence (Bay, 1965, 209–210), Milton Rokeach, one of the work's major critics, has made a more specific charge. He has stated that there was something wrong with the F-scale; it was politically slanted and could tap only rightwing-dogmatism (Rokeach, 1956; 1960). To demonstrate that he could remedy this defect, Rokeach developed not only a Dogmatism scale which claimed to be politically neutral along major conventional right-left dimensions; he also proceeded to substantiate this claim by developing two Opinionation scales, one measuring vehement intolerance of leftist views and the other doing the same for rightist views. Having achieved a reasonably high reliability for both Opinionation scales in several samples, Rokeach proceeded to demonstrate that his Dogmatism scale, *unlike* the F scale, the E scale and the PEC scale, correlated positively not only with his Right Opinionation scale but with his Left Opinionation scale as well.

Strictly speaking there probably is no such thing as a politically neutral scale, unless it be devoid of all social content; what Rokeach showed is that the F scale does not, while his own Dogmatism scale does correlate with the degrees of vehemence (which presumably were symptomatic of the closemindedness) with which leftist as well as rightist opinions are held, at least in certain populations. As a matter of fact, Rokeach notes that both his Dogmatism scale and his combined Opinionation scale show a weak but consistently positive relationship to conservatism, and also that Dogmatism in all his samples shows somewhat closer affinity to Right than to Left Opinionation. He raises but dismisses perhaps too lightly the possibility that his scales are less neutral than intended; his principal explanation is that communism, unlike fascism, is humanitarian in its ideology (or *content*, as he puts it), at least; and that the same, to a more modest extent, may be true of liberal versus conservative ideology. In support of his belief that the psychological functions of communist beliefs may differ from those of fascist beliefs he cites the phenomenon of *disillusionment* which, he believes, occurs far more often among former communists than among former nazis or fascists, indicating a sudden awareness of contradictions within the communist creed which may not exist within fascist creeds, whose anti-humanism pertains to ends as well as means, or content as well as structure. He also refers to Robert Lindner's theory that communists more often have neurotic problems, often guilt-related, while fascists more often are psychopaths, or people with an underdeveloped conscience (Lindner, 1953).

McClosky's Findings

Another, more massive study comparing conservatives to liberals is reported by Herbert McClosky, whose more than 2000 respondents were drawn from Minnesota population samples. These are his principal findings of relevance here: (a) "By every measure available to us, conservative beliefs are found most frequently among the uninformed, the poorly educated and so far as we can determine, the less intelligent"; (b) "Conservatism, in our society at least, appears to be far more characteristic of social isolates, of people who think poorly of themselves . . . who are submissive, timid, and wanting in confidence"; and (c) "In the four liberal-conservative classifications, the extreme conservatives are easily the most hostile and suspicious, the most rigid and compulsive, the quickest to condemn others for their imperfections and weaknesses, the most intolerant, the most inflexible and unyielding in their perceptions and judgments. Although aggressively critical of the shortcomings of others, they are unusually defensive and armored in the protection of their own ego needs. Poorly integrated psychologically, anxious, often perceiving themselves as inadequate, and subject to excessive feelings of guilt, they seem inclined to project onto others the traits they most dislike in themselves" (McClosky, 1958, 35–38).

McClosky divided his respondents into four categories: "liberals," "moderate liberals," "moderate conservatives" and "extreme conservatives"; these labels suggest that he felt he had more "extreme conservatives" than liberals in his main samples. The three tables he presented are astoundingly consistent in yielding entirely linear correlations from "liberal" to "extreme conservative," without a single exception; "moderate liberals," for example, are found to be higher on hostility, lower on education and intellectuality, etc., than "liberals"; and McClosky claims that his data "could be buttressed by numerous other related findings" (1958, 38).

McClosky's analysis of these striking findings is couched more in descriptive than in developmental terms. For example: "From whatever direction we approach him, the prototypic conservative seems far more impelled to contain, to reject, and to take precautions against, his fellow creatures" (1958, 38). But why? McClosky is cautious indeed on this score. The closest thing to a suggestion of a causal relationship is his statement that "education is likely to lead to liberal rather than conservative tendencies" (1958, 41). Among his concluding cautionary remarks, he says that conservative doctrines "appear, in some measure, to arise from personality needs, but it is conceivable at least, that both are the product of some third set of factors." Conservatism and a host of undesirable personality traits clearly, in these Minnesota samples, "go together. *How* they go together, and which is antecedent to which, is a more difficult and more elusive problem" (1958, 44).

There has been a remarkable lack of follow-up of this striking demonstration of affinity between degrees of conservatism and widely disvalued personality and social characteristics. If *The Authoritarian Personality*'s findings of affinity between conservatism and neurotic authoritarianism can be questioned on methodological grounds, and if Rokeach's data only mildly suggested a similar affinity, McClosky's tables appear methodologically solid and of great theoretical import.

RECENT WORK ON STUDENT ACTIVISTS

I shall not attempt an exhaustive survey of all available data on student activism or student leftism generally. The reader is referred to several of the articles in this issue for a summary of these data; the articles by Trent and Craise and by Flacks are particularly relevant. Of especial importance to the line of argument which I have been developing are the following findings.

Berkeley, 1957—Selvin and Hagstrom Findings

Hanan C. Selvin and Warren O. Hagstrom in December, 1957, while things were still fairly quiet on the Berkeley campus, did a study of the views on civil liberties in a sample of 894 Berkeley students (Selvin and Hagstrom, 1965). Anticipating that abstract statements favoring the Bill of Rights would sooner indicate conformism than liberalism, these investigators elicited responses to specific civil liberties issues involving conflicts with other values. On the basis of these responses they constructed a Libertarianism Index. They divided their sample into three groups: highly libertarian (34%), moderately libertarian (46%), slightly libertarian (20%).

Of interest here are the data comparing the highly libertarian students with the Berkeley student body in general. In a linear relationship, again, the proportions of highly libertarian students on the Berkeley campus ascend from freshmen to senior and graduate level: 21%–29%–34%–40%–54%. The relationship between libertarianism and grades is inconclusive in the lower division, but clear in the upper division: among A to B+ students 54% are "highly-libertarian," compared to 37% among B to C+ students and 25% among students at C level or below.

Children of blue collar workers among Berkeley students are libertarians more often, by a wide margin, than are children of parents better able to support their offspring financially through college; this is true in spite of the fact that blue collar parents average lower educational attainments than other parents and are likely to be relatively non-libertarian themselves. "Greater economic independence, in the sense of self-support," conclude Selvin and Hagstrom, "is strongly associated with having more libertarian attitudes than one's parents" (Selvin and Hagstrom, 1965, 504).

Among male students the social science and humanities majors were by a wide margin found more libertarian than the rest, with engineering and education (a field that has recruited low achievers in Berkeley) and business administration at the bottom. Among female students, social welfare majors were most libertarian, while life science majors shared the next level of libertarianism with social science and humanities majors, and with education majors once again at the bottom. And, finally, fraternity and especially sorority students—who are least likely to get to know well people with unorthodox ideas—are least likely to be libertarians, compared to students with other living arrangements.

Berkeley, 1964—Somers' Data

In November, 1964, when the student rebellion at Berkeley was under way, Robert H. Somers interviewed a carefully drawn sample of 285 Berkeley students. He found 63% to favor the goals of the Free Speech Movement, while about 34% approved of the FSM's tactics; clearly favoring goals as well as tactics were 30%, and Somers calls this group the *militants*, while the *moderates*, again 30%, clearly supported FSM's goals but not the means used, and 22% *conservatives* were opposed to the ends sought as well as the tactics used (Somers, 1964).

For my purposes the crucial findings of this study are summarized as follows by Somers: "it is hard to overlook the fact that in our sample there is a strong relation between academic achievement and support for the demonstrators. Among those who reported to our interviewers a grade point average of B+ or better, nearly half (45 per cent) are militants, and only a tenth are conservatives. At the other end, over a third of those with an average of B— or less are conservatives, and only 15 per cent are militants." If the FSM represented a minority of students, Somers concluded, it would be "a minority vital to the excellence of this university" (1964, 544).

Berkeley, 1965—Heist's Findings

Early in 1965 Paul Heist did a study of a sample drawn from a list of more than 800 persons said to have been arrested in the Sproul Hall sit-in (Heist, 1965). On advice of their legal counsel, about 50% of the 33% sample refused to return the questionnaire but the rest cooperated, 128 in all; an additional 60 FSM activists were recruited subsequently as subjects for the study. In addition, a random sample of 92 seniors (class of 1964–1965) were given the same two questionnaires. Also, Heist had access to the same attitude inventory data from 340 seniors (class of 1962–1963) and from 2500+ entering freshmen, all at Berkeley. Further details of this study by Heist plus other related work are presented by Trent and Craise in this issue.

Heist developed an Intellectual Disposition Index on the basis of six of the twelve scales in his attitude inventory, and with this instrument divided his FSM sample and his three general student samples according to eight "degrees" from low to high Intellectual Disposition. Here is what he found:

For the total FSM group we find almost 70 per cent in the top three categories and none in the bottom three, and it is to be remembered that a large proportion, in fact, the majority, of the FSM persons were freshmen, sophomore and juniors. The number of persons in these upper categories in the senior sample amounts to 25 and 31 per cent. The Free Speech Movement drew extraordinarily larger proportions of students with strong intellectual orientations, at all levels (freshmen through graduate) (Heist, 1965, 21–22a).

Watts and Whittaker and FSM

William A. Watts and David N. E. Whittaker's study of FSM activists compared to Berkeley students generally started with this hypothesis:

"We expected that FSM members would be more flexible as defined and measured by personality tests of flexibility-rigidity . . . than their counterparts who were less committed, neutral, or even opposed to the Movement" (Watts and Whittaker, 1966, 43).

Their study was based on questionnaires administered to a chance sample of 172 participants among the 1000–1200 students who "sat in" at Sproul Hall in the afternoon of December 2nd, 1964 (and who were on this occasion not arrested, or not yet, except for the two-thirds who stayed on all night). In addition, the same questionnaire was given to a random sample of 182 Berkeley students at about the same time; 146 of these cooperated. The instrument included a 27-item rigidity-flexibility scale. The most important result of this study, for present purposes, is its indication of "strong support for the prediction of greater flexibility among the FSM members" (1966, 59). The authors conclude that this latter finding is of particular interest considering the purported rigidity of the FSM members in negotiations with the University administration, and suggests the necessity of distinguishing between a trait of rigidity as psychologically defined and commitment.

Two other findings of the study by Watts and Whittaker should be noted in passing. First, with an additional sample of 181 students drawn from the District Attorney's arrest list for December 3, and 174 names drawn at random from the Student Directory, they failed to establish greater academic achievement on the part of the FSM'ers compared to other students, and concluded that these activists were quite typical or average with respect to grade point averages (1966, 52). While Watts and Whittaker's objective check is more trustworthy than the data on grade point averages reported in the Somers study which were based on respondents' information, I am inclined to discount, until substantiated by further research, this particular finding by Watts and Whittaker, because it appears to run counter to so many other findings discussed in this article. It may well be valid for the 773 who were arrested, though I would have liked to see a replication of the study, which can easily be done; if it is valid for this group, I would still doubt that it is valid for FSM activists generally. It is possible, for example, that the most *academically* as distinct from *intellectually* oriented students among FSM activists felt greater anxiety than the rest about their academic credits, and were more likely to shrink from taking the most extreme risks.

Secondly, the FSM students were far more likely to have parents with advanced academic degrees, compared to the cross-section sample: "approximately 26 per cent of the fathers and 16 per cent of the mothers of the FSM sample possess either Ph.D. or M.A. degrees compared to 11 per cent and 4 per cent respectively in the cross-section" (Watts and Whittaker, 1966, 53 and Table 4). This finding does not contradict Somers' finding that student militants were more likely than the rest to have blue-collar fathers. Among several factors that could be taken into account here, I would emphasize the difference between having militant attitudes and being prepared to jeopardize academic achievements; the value of academic credits may well loom somewhat larger to the self-supporting student from a working class background, than they do to students from families in which academic proficiency or intellectual gifts or future financial safety tend to be taken for granted. The latter category among the militants may be more likely to risk jail and expulsion for their beliefs.

I have confined this brief inquiry to activists on the Left, who are far more significant than those on the Right, both by their numbers (at least in the better universities), and by their tendency to persist in political activities disturbing to the university "image" desired by most administrators and trustees. In so far as rightist student groups, the most important one among them at the moment being Young Americans for Freedom, have staged demonstrations, they have usually been *ad hoc* counter-demonstration, directed *against* issue-oriented protests by liberal or leftist student activists; there have been no protracted campaigning or even articulate political programs; and while student leftists have tended to be fiercely independent of older leftists, or of the "generation over thirty" generally, there has been no evidence of a corresponding intellectual independence among organized rightist students.

TOWARD A PSYCHOLOGICAL THEORY OF RADICAL VERSUS CONSERVATIVE ATTITUDES

The most promising approach to theorizing about the psychological nature of liberal and radical *versus* conservative political attitudes, I believe, is to consider what kind of functions political opinions may serve for those who hold them, in terms of their personality and social needs. It is quickly apparent that the function of serving a rational, realistic understanding of the political world is one but only one possible function of a person's politics.

Types of Motives Underlying Political Opinions

The over-all function of any political or other social opinion write M. Brewster Smith, Jerome S. Bruner and Robert W. White (1960, 275) is to strike a "compromise between reality demands, social demands, and inner psychological demands." Daniel Katz (1960) distinguishes between rationality (or reality-testing) motives, value-expressive motives, social acceptance motives, and ego defense motives. These are suggested analytical categories; specific opinions usually serve a mixture of needs or motives.

The relative weight of each type of motive varies from person to person, from attitude to attitude and from time to time; few of us, if any, are free of neurotic ego defensiveness, and none of us are free of social acceptance needs or desires for consistency and for realistic understanding of the world in which we live.

In their 1954 papers, Irving Sarnoff and Daniel Katz applied their three categories of motives in a discussion of a clearly *undesirable* type of attitude, namely anti-Negro prejudice; and one of their main concerns was to show how a better understanding of the motives of attitudes could facilitate processes of attitude change. Thus, to the extent that prejudice is rationally founded,—on the basis, say, of the limited knowledge available to many a Southern American white boy or girl, it presumably can be influenced by new knowledge. To the extent, however, that prejudice is based on social acceptance motives, it will take evidence of an entirely different kind of influence to do away with it,—namely evidence that such a change of opinion would not reduce a person's acceptance in whatever groups he wants to be or become part of. To the extent, finally, that ego defensive motives determine the prejudice, it may take psychotherapy to reduce it.

Ego Defensive Motives

There is evidence, wrote Gardner Murphy more than twenty years ago, "that functional intelligence can be enormously enhanced, first by the systematic study and removal of individual and socially shared autisms, second, by the cultivation of curiosity, and third, by the art of withdrawal from the pressures of immediate external tasks, to let the mind work at its own pace and in its own congenial way" (Murphy, 1945, 16).

The most fundamental obstacle, of course, to the "freeing of intelligence" is the active presence of ego defensive motives. Severely repressed anxieties about one's worth as a human being, which may well be the result of a childhood starved of affection, may predestine a person to become a "true believer" in Eric Hoffer's sense,—a person who seeks a new collective identity because he cannot live with his own self (Hoffer, 1951). Such anxieties, if unresolved, may predestine a person to become an authoritarian or an anti-authoritarian personality (cf. Bay, 1965, 207–217), a bigot, a right-winger, or, more rarely, a left-winger. This type of person is not psychologically free; his views may keep his anxieties and fears manageable but contributes no realistic understanding of the external political world.

Some of the data discussed previously can be understood in this light; Adorno *et al.*, Rokeach and McClosky all found right-wing views statistically associated with indices of neurosis of one kind or another. But what of McClosky's finding that, for example, "liberals" appeared less hostile than "moderate liberals," and what of the data on student activists?

Social Acceptance Motives

To account for such data we need to consider the prevalence of social acceptance motives, too, as obstacles to the freeing of political intelligence. To the extent that a person is deeply worried about his popularity, his career prospects, his financial future, his reputation, etc., he will utilize his political opinions not for achieving realistic insight but for impressing his reference groups and his reference persons favorably. These processes of obfuscation may be conscious or, more likely, subconscious, but they are above all pervasive in our society, and in every other society, too,—above all in highly competitive and socially mobile societies, in which the difference between "success" and lack of it may make for vast differences in prospects for the satisfaction of physical and self-esteem needs, and perhaps for many other kinds of needs as well. Social acceptance-motivated political beliefs serve the individual's desired image, status and career, etc., but contribute little toward a realistic understanding of his political world,—at least in so far as it extends beyond his immediate reference groups and persons.

Social acceptance-motivated opinions may well tend to be liberal in some university faculties, as charged by some conservative writers, including conservative students wishing to explain why liberalism increases with amount of education (cf. Naylor, 1966 for a discussion of this). But by and large, in every stable social order, they tend to be conservative, or at most mildly liberal, firmly within the established framework of constitutional objectives and processes. In every stable society there are rich and poor, strong and weak, privileged and underprivileged; and not only political power and influence but social status and respectability are associated with seeing political problems through the eyes of the former rather than the latter, in each paired category.

Statistically speaking, therefore, *more conservative views among students or adults generally, are likely to be less rationally, less independently motivated, compared to more radical-liberal views*.

I am by no means arguing, of course, that liberal and radical views cannot be neurotically motivated. The point is a more modest one: the frequency of neurotic motivations—now including not only deeply repressed anxieties about the individual's own worth but also milder ego deficiencies such as constant worry about popularity or career prospects—is probably higher the further away the politically active person is from the left side of the political spectrum (I did not say left *end*).

The statistical data surveyed make good sense if viewed in this perspective. With reference to the Berkeley data, surely one should expect ego defensiveness to be manifested by a fear of anarchy and equality, and lead the individual to detest both the style and the objectives of FSM-type movements. And the more intensely or neurotically one is preoccupied with career worries, the less one would be disposed to mingle with the student rebels; these students, more typically, appear to have decided that certain values are more dear to them than conventional career prospects. The articles by Keniston and Flacks make this same point. As rebels they are more likely to have made a choice and to have marshalled the intellectual and emotional resources, at some point, to stick to it, also in situations of severe stress. Obviously, some will for spurious or chance reasons pursue neurotic social acceptance needs with FSM-type groups as their reference systems; but this happens in almost every group, and is likely to occur with less frequency in a rebellious political action group than in less demanding and socially more homogeneous groups like, for example, fraternities and sororities.

"Only Rebellion Can Expand Consciousness"

As Albert Camus saw, only rebellion, on some level, can expand consciousness; "with rebellion, awareness is born." Awareness of being human,—of being more than an aspiring carpenter, merchant, lawyer, educator or military officer. Or dutiful son or daughter. "In our daily trials rebellion plays the same role as does the 'cogito' in the realm of thought: it is the first piece of evidence. But this evidence lures the individual from his solitude. It founds its first value on the whole human race. I rebel—therefore we exist" (Camus, 1958, 15 and 22).

Camus' portrait of the rebel presents a normative ideal in persuasive terms: to become fully human, a constant tendency to be revolted by and to rebel against oppression and injustice is required. While I admit to sharing this normative position, my present argument is empirical, though speculative: I submit that it will help make sense of all the data reviewed in this paper if we consider Camus' rebel a developmental model,—a *probable* type of person to develop *to the extent that* not only ego defensive but more mildly neurotic social acceptance anxieties are resolved or successfully faced up to.

This kind of theory is bound to be speculative if only because such social anxieties are so pervasive. Yet it is possible to argue that the various data associating leftism with academic competence, intelligence, psychological and socio-economic security, etc., may be seen as tending to support this theory. Further research in this area is desirable and feasible, and can be usefully focused by this kind of theory.[119]

---

[119] One Polish study by Hannah E. Malewska, for example, ought to be followed up: she found that children's notions of moral norms become more responsible (less formal and superficial) the less severely disciplinarian their parents and the more

The more secure and sheltered a person's infancy and childhood, and the more freedom that educational and other social processes have given him to develop according to his inner needs and potentialities, the more likely that a capacity for political rationality and independence will develop, simply because the likelihood of severe anxieties is relatively low. In addition, again converting Camus' ideal into empirical-theoretical currency, the better the individual has been able to resolve his own anxieties, the more likely that he will empathize with others less fortunate than himself. A sense of justice as well as a capacity for rationality is, according to this theory, a likely development in relatively secure individuals, whose politics, if any, will therefore tend toward the left,—toward supporting the champions of the underdog, not the defenders of established, always unjust, institutions. And young people, with the proverbial impetuousness of youth, are likely to seek extremes of social justice, or militant means, simply because their emotions, and more particularly their sense of elementary morality and justice, have not yet been dulled by daily compromises and defeats to the extent that most older persons' emotions have been.[120]

---

urbanized their surroundings (Malewska, 1961). Work on children's politics is on the increase, but often restricts itself unduly to cognitive aspects. An exception is the work of Fred J. Greenstein (1965).

Patricia Richmond and I a few years ago found that among liberals in a pacifistically oriented organization, the more "extreme" supporters of rights of specific unpopular minorities tended to be somewhat less dogmatic in Rokeach's sense, than the more moderate supporters of such rights (Bay and Richmond, 1960). More work is needed to improve on instruments like Rokeach's Dogmatism scale, and to develop additional instruments to measure neurotic obstacles to rationality in the general population, so that we might discover how widely and in what types of contexts it is true that resolution of anxieties and reduction of other psychological burdens stimulate tendencies toward rationality, political activism, leftism and related phenomena.

Let me in conclusion mention the valuable, still small but apparently growing literature that seeks in-depth understanding of the political views and their motivations in particular individuals, whether prominent or humble, and whether dead or still living. A masterly political biographical study in psychological terms is *Woodrow Wilson and Colonel House* by Alexander and Juliette George (1956). Justly famous is Erik H. Erikson's *Young Man Luther* (1958). Arnold A. Rogow's *James T. Forrestal* is particularly valuable for its searching analysis of the issues associated with possible mental disorder in high office (1964). Among psychological studies of the politics of humbler individuals, who are left anonymous, reference has been made to *Opinions and Personality* by M. Brewster Smith et al. (1960), a study limiting its scope to attitudes toward the Soviet Union. Three other very useful works are Robert E. Lane's *Political Ideology*, a study of fifteen "average" New Englanders, mostly working men; David Riesman's *Faces in the Crowd*, dealing with "average" Los Angelese; and an excellent Australian study of five more or less politically active individuals,—*Private Politics*, by Alan F. Davies (1966).

[120] Now there are some older persons, too, who for all the toll of many years of practical experience, seem to have remained able to share the basic moral and political outlook (if not necessarily the views on tactics) of militant student activists. As I read some of Erik H. Erikson's recent work, he appears to conclude that man's sense of social responsibility and his degree of social sensitivity depend on his maturation beyond the Freudian psychological stage of genitality; he calls this hypothetically

Let me sharpen my own position as follows: *Every new human being is potentially a liberal animal and a rebel; yet every social organization he will be up against, from the family to the state, is likely to seek to "socialize" him into a conveniently pliant conformist.*

Many parents and some schools are child-oriented to the extent of trying to give children the security and freedom to develop according to their own inner needs and potentialities. With a good start of this kind, the children may, when they approach adulthood, be able to resist the socializing of privilege-defending states, universities and other established institutional pillars of the *status quo*; if so, they become the student rebels, the civil rights workers, and the peace activists: a small minority, but a growing one in terms of influence among young people.

REFERENCES

1. Adorno, Theodore W., Frenkel-Brunswik, E., Levinson, D. J., and Sanford, R. N. *The authoritarian personality.* (New York: Harper, 1950).
2. Bay, Christian. *Structure of freedom.* (New York: Atheneum, 1965 [1968]).
3. Bay, Christian, and Richmond, Patricia. Some varieties of Liberal experience. Unpublished paper, 1960.
4. Camus, Albert. *The rebel.* (New York: Vintage, 1958).
5. Davies, Alan F. *Private politics.* (Melbourne: Melbourne University Press, 1966).
6. Erikson, Erik H. *Young man Luther.* (New York: Norton, 1958).
7. Erikson, Erik H. *Insight and responsibility.* (New York: Norton, 1964).
8. George, Alexander, and George, Juliette. *Woodrow Wilson and Colonel House.* (New York: John Day, 1956).
9. Greenstein, Fred J. *Children and politics.* (New Haven: Yale University Press, 1965).
10. Heist, Paul. Intellect and commitment: The faces of discontent. (Center for the Study of Higher Education, Berkeley, 1965). (mimeo.)
11. Hoffer, Eric. *The true believer.* (New York: Harper, 1951).
12. Katz, Daniel. "The functional approach to the study of attitudes." *Public Opinion Quarterly*, Vol. 24 (1960), 163–204.
13. Lane, Robert E. *Political ideology.* (New York: Free Press, 1962).

---

higher developmental stage *generativity*: "I refer to a man's *love for his works and ideas as well as for his children*, and the necessary self-verification which adult man's ego receives, and must receive, from his labor's challenge. As adult man needs to be needed, so—for the strength of his ego and for that of his community—he requires the challenge emanating from what he has generated and from what now must be 'brought up,' guarded, preserved—and eventually transcended" (Erikson, 1964, 130–132). Erikson describes parenthood as "the first, and for many, the prime generative encounter" but argues that those who approach or reach the generative stage of psychosocial development to that extent *need* to teach, to instruct and influence, and in other ways actively work for the good of not only their children but of their community and their society, or mankind, as well.

14. Lindner, Robert. "Political creed and character." *Psychoanalysis*, Vol. 2 (1953), 10–33.
15. Malewska, Hannah E. "Religious ritualism, rigid ethics, and severity in upbringing." *Polish Sociological Bulletin*, Vol. 1 (1961), 71–78.
16. McClosky, Herbert. "Conservatism and personality." *American Political Science Review*, Vol. 52 (1958), 27–45.
17. Murphy, Gardner. "The freeing of intelligence." *Psychological Bulletin*, Vol. 42 (1945), 1–19.
18. Naylor, Robert W. "Why intellectuals are liberal." *Western Politica*, Vol. 1 (1966), 33–37.
19. Newcomb, Theodore M. *Personality and social change.* (New York: Holt, Rinehart and Winston, 1943).
20. Riesman, David. *Faces in the crowd.* (New York: Free Press, 1952).
21. Rogow, Arnold A. *James T. Forrestal.* (New York: Macmillan, 1964).
22. Rokeach, Milton. "Political and religious dogmatism: An alternative to the authoritarian personality." *Psychological Monographs*, Vol. 70 (1956), 1–43.
23. Rokeach, Milton. *The open and closed mind.* (New York: Basic Books, 1960).
24. Sarnoff, Irving, and Katz Daniel. "The motivational bases of attitude change." *Journal of Abnormal and Social Psychology*, Vol. 49 (1954), 115–124.
25. Selvin, Hanan C., and Hagstrom, Warren O. "Determinants of support for civil liberties." In Seymour M. Lipset and Sheldon S. Wolin (eds.), *The Berkeley student revolt.* (New York: Anchor, 1965), 494–518.
26. Shils, Edward. "Authoritarianism: Right and Left." In Richard Christie and Marie Jahoda (eds.), *Studies in the scope and method of "The authoritarian personality."* (Glencoe: The Free Press, 1954).
27. Smith, M. Brewster, Bruner, Jerome S., and White, Robert W. *Opinions and personality.* (New York: Wiley, 1960).
28. Somers, Robert H. "The mainsprings of the rebellion: A survey of Berkeley students in November, 1964." In Seymour M. Lipset and Sheldon S. Wolin (eds.), *The Berkeley student revolt.* (New York: Anchor, 1965), 530–557.
29. Stouffer, Samuel A. *Communism, conformity, and civil liberties.* (New York: Wiley, 1955).
30. Watts, William A., and Whittaker, David. "Free Speech Advocates at Berkeley." *Journal of Applied Behavioral Science*, Vol. 2 (1966), 41–62.

The third approach to the analysis of social movements which manifests a Freudian influence is that of "personality." Basic to this approach is the idea that specific child-rearing practices determine personality structures which can eventuate in the support of certain kinds of social movements.[121]

In the past several decades two personality types have received much attention: Adorno's "authoritarian personality" and Hoffer's "true be-

[121] See Daniel Miller and Guy Swanson, *The Changing American Parent* (New York: John Wiley and Sons, Inc., 1958).

liever." The former conception is primarily rooted in the Freudian approach while the latter is intellectually most indebted to Cantril's notion of "individual satisfactions" gained from involvement in social movements.

A major catalyst for the "authoritarian personality" school of research was the Nazi movement in Germany. This movement was the stimulus for the extensive study, The Authoritarian Personality, published in 1950 by Adorno and his associates.[122] Ideologically, authoritarianism is thus generally equated with extreme right movements. Adorno's major concern was with the "potential fascistic individual, one whose structure is such as to render him particularly susceptible to antidemocratic propaganda." [123] Adorno identifies six types of personality structures which would make their holders vulnerable to fascism: (1) the surface resentment stereotype; (2) the conventionalist; (3) the authoritarian; (4) the rebel and the psychopath; (5) the crank; and (6) the manipulator.[124]

The "surface resentment" type refers to "people who accept stereotypes of prejudice from outside, as ready-made formulae, as it were, in order to rationalize and—psychologically or actually—overcome overt difficulties of their existence." [125] The "conventional" syndrome refers to persons "prejudiced in the specific sense of the term: taking over current judgements of others without having looked into the matter themselves." [126] The third type, the authoritarian, is primarily a "subject [who] achieves his own social adjustment only by taking pleasure in obedience and subordination." [127] The "rebel" and the "psychopath" are two types of tough guy. The rebel is characterized by "a penchant for tolerated excess" and the psychopath by being "a-social" and possessing "destructive urges [that] come to the fore in an overt, nonrationalized way." [128] The "crank" is pictured as being "isolated" and therefore removed from "reality principles." [129] Finally, the manipulative type is defined as an extreme type whose "rigid notions become ends rather than means and the whole world is divided into empty, schematic, administrative fields." [130] In the contemporary literature, these six types have been combined into one all-inclusive personality structure. Toch, for example, devotes several pages to an ideal type: "prejudice against persons other than Jews . . . [possessing] a strong sense of loyalty to their own kind, whom they hold in high

---

[122] T. W. Adorno, et al., The Authoritarian Personality (New York: Harper and Brothers, 1950).
[123] Ibid., p. 1.
[124] Ibid., pp. 753–778. See particularly the remarks on page 753 for the Freudian basis of this typology.
[125] Ibid., p. 754.
[126] Ibid., p. 756.
[127] Ibid., p. 759. This description is taken almost entirely from Fromm, op. cit., pp. 164–221.
[128] Ibid., p. 763.
[129] Ibid., p. 765.
[130] Ibid., p. 767.

esteem, . . . [viewing] all other people with suspicion and contempt." [131]

Eric Hoffer, in painting his portrait of the "true believer," views "mass movements" as primarily constituted by fanatics who fulfill a need by migrating from one social movement to another.[132] For Hoffer, such personality types are negatively motivated. That is, Hoffer maintains that mass movements do not appeal: ". . . to those intent on bolstering and advancing a cherished self, but to those who crave to be rid of an unwanted self. A mass movement attracts and holds a following not because it can satisfy the desire for self-advancement, but because it can satisfy the passion for self-renunciation." [133] Thus, for the true believers: "Their innermost craving is for a new life—a rebirth—or failing this, a chance to acquire new elements of pride, confidence, hope, a sense of purpose and worth by an identification with a holy cause. An active mass movement offers them opportunities for both." [134] A fanatic having these traits and lacking a cause "is a lost man, and must hitch a ride on the next passing movement, almost without regard for its actual content." [135]

The conceptualization of a "rebel without a cause" frenetically seeking his identity in one movement after another presents difficulties in the study of social movements, particularly for those embodying a radical or revolutionary ideology. Empirically, it appears that "transfer of personnel" is not infrequent in religious cults.[136] Moreover, "transferability" has also been cited as an element in current leftist movements.[137] However, shifting allegiances in radical movements may be attributed more to the external effects of history and to ideology than to psychological quirks. For example, the tactical and ideological cleavages within the ranks of the Industrial Workers of the World in the later 1920s led over 2,000 Wobblies to join the embryonic American Communist Party.[138] Conversely, the Soviet Nonaggression pact with Germany in 1939, the invasion of Poland, and the later Cold War era all contributed to the decline of American Communism. Although we would not deny that many individuals do exhibit the characteristics of Hoffer's "true believer," such factors are not adequate explanations for the formation and development of social movements.

---

[131] Toch, *op. cit.*, p. 57.
[132] Eric Hoffer, *The True Believer* (New York: Mentor Books, 1958).
[133] *Ibid.*, p. 21.
[134] *Ibid.*, p. 21.
[135] Cameron, *op. cit.*, p. 45.
[136] See H. T. Dohrman, *California Cult* (Boston: Beacon Press, 1958), p. 117; Arthur Orrmont, *Love Cults and Faith Healers* (New York: Ballantine Books, 1961).
[137] See Richard Armstrong, "The Explosive Revival of the Far Left," *Saturday Evening Post* (May 8, 1965), pp. 27–39; Gabriel Almond, *The Appeals of Communism* (Princeton, N.J.: Princeton University Press, 1954), pp. 150–162; and Paul Jacobs, *Is Curly Jewish?* (New York: Atheneum Press, 1965).
[138] John S. Gambs, *The Decline of the IWW* (New York: Columbia University Press, 1932), p. 89.

As noted earlier, the analysis of social movements in terms of personality is anchored in the notion of child-rearing practices. Theorists using this Freudian approach generally posit that if certain early socialization elements are present, a characteristic personality vulnerable to participating in and maintaining a social movement will emerge. However, for the student desiring to analyze class-based movements, little in the way of consistent findings about the consequences of child-rearing practices in different classes can be found. On the one hand, observers such as McKinnon and Centers, Christie and Cook, and Lipset view lower class socialization as conducive to authoritarianism.[139] On the other hand, similar observations about middle class socialization have been made by Bennet and Tumin, Davis and Havighurst, and Waller.[140] We are therefore led to concur with Reissman that: "The studies [on class and child-rearing practices] do not provide firm enough findings to point the way. It still seems plausible to assume that different class environments create important differences for the socialization of the child, even though none of the studies fully substantiated that assumption." [141]

Even if we accept Reissman's criterion of "plausibility" and assume that lower class socialization is conducive to authoritarianism, the empirical evidence linking the lower class with extremist movements is not forthcoming. Numerous studies of the National Socialist movement in Germany, American and foreign Communist parties, and the American Extreme Right indicate that the proletariat is least present in the membership lists of these movements.[142] In terms of social and political participation, the fact remains that the lower class, although labeled "authoritarian," is the most withdrawn, politically alienated, and apathetic class.[143]

Although psychology can contribute to an understanding of the behavior of both individuals and small groups within social movements, few social psychologists have been content to limit their efforts to studies of

[139] See William McKinnon and Richard Centers, "Authoritarianism and Urban Stratification," *American Journal of Sociology*, 61 (May 1956): 610–620; Richard Christie and Peggy Cook, "A Guide to Published Literature Relating to the Authoritarian Personality," *Journal of Psychology*, 45 (January 1958): 171–199; and S. M. Lipset, "Working Class Authoritarianism," in *Political Man: The Social Bases of Politics* (Garden City, N.Y.: Doubleday and Co., Inc., 1960), pp. 97–130.
[140] See John W. Bennett and Melvin Tumin, *Social Life* (New York: Alfred Knopf, 1948), pp. 669–671; Allison Davis and Robert J. Havighurst, *The Father of Man* (Boston: Houghton-Mifflin Co., 1947); and Willard Waller, *The Family* (New York: Henry Holt and Co., 1951), p. 405.
[141] Leonard Reissman, *Class in American Society* (Glencoe, Ill.: The Free Press, 1959), p. 243.
[142] William Kornhauser, *The Politics of Mass Society* (Glencoe, Ill.: The Free Press, 1959); Irving Howe and Lewis Coser, *op. cit.*; Gabriel Almond, *op. cit.*; and Daniel Bell, *op. cit.*
[143] See S. M. Lipset, "Working-Class Authoritarianism," *op. cit.*, pp. 126–130; Murray B. Levin, *The Alienated Voter: Politics in Boston* (New York: Holt, Rinehart and Winston, 1960).

this scope. For the most part, they have attempted to construct overall theories of social movement recruitment and participation. However, we must conclude that these attempts fall short of an adequate explanation of the etiology and careers of social movements sui generis. Concerning these social psychological studies, we would concur with Heberle that: ". . . we are skeptical about their value for the understanding of the causation of social movements. We maintain that the immediate and significant causes will be found in the conditions of society rather than in the condition of the leaders' minds or in the neuroses of their followers." [144]

WHERE WE STAND

As we have seen, most studies of social movements follow a similar empirical format. They focus either on the structure of the movement itself or on the psychological characteristics of its members. With the exception of Marxist theories, which attempt a predictive approach to social movements, most studies have been ex post facto. Finally, most studies utilize the historical "case study" approach to movements, the standard model of which is the history of the Nazi movement. In the following chapters, the authors will attempt to integrate a historical approach to movements with a sociological appreciation of the ideology of movements. Before turning to this task, it may be helpful to summarize our analysis to this point.

Of those definitional and conceptual problems plaguing social movement research, the most vexing concerns the source of movements. The majority of sociological treatments suggests that social movements are products of problem situations, discontent, deprivation, strain, frustration, anomie, isolation, hopelessness, or status reassertion. The primary motif of these conceptualizations is that a structural or individual dysfunction gives rise to the development of and participation in a social movement. Lasswell argues that dislodged workers joined the Communist-led Unemployed Councils because of the impact of the early years of the Depression.[145] Howe and Coser, and more recently Samuel Kaplan, have pointed to "relative deprivation" as an etiological factor in the American Communist Party and the Berkeley Free Speech Movement.[146] Others have posited that individualistic problems or crisis situations have mobilized members for organized action. Students of the extreme Right note that the "dispossessed middle class," unable to cope with status anxieties, is

---

[144] Heberle, op. cit., p. 111.
[145] Harold D. Lasswell and Dorothy Blumenstock, *World Revolutionary Propaganda: A Chicago Study* (New York: Alfred A. Knopf, 1939), p. 39.
[146] Howe and Coser, op. cit., p. 514; and Samuel Kaplan, "The Revolt of an Elite: Sources of the FSM Victory," *The Graduate Student Journal*, 4 (Spring 1965): 77–78.

the backbone of the John Birch Society and similar conservative organizations.

Seemingly inherent in these conceptualizations is a one-to-one causal connection between "X" problem (e.g., status anxiety, relative deprivation) and "Y" movement (e.g., right wing extremism, student protest movements). Empirically, however, we would argue that social strains or problem situations are neither necessary nor sufficient causes of social movements. More often than not, these etiological variables lead to forms of collective behavior or apolitical affiliation which cannot be considered social movements. Even if we grant that strains or problems are, at some point, etiological for participation in (as distinct from source of) social movements, we still cannot posit a direct causal relationship. For example, Lasswell's unemployed worker during the Depression could, and did, choose from a myriad of adaptations not involving membership in the Unemployed Councils. Similarly, in the 1930s a dissenter could choose among a wide spectrum of alternative social movements ranging from the Trotskyists to the Coughlinites. Therefore, even assuming that "X" leads to movement affiliation, the problem of why individuals choose a given organization still requires explanation.

The dilemma, it appears, is answered post factum. That is, the movement under consideration is correlated with a structural or psychological dysfunction, with the result that a characteristic dysfunction is viewed as the cause of a characteristic movement. Yet, as the study of Lasswell's worker suggests, the movement exists prior to a given individual's membership. Similarly, the dispossessed of today's suburbia must seek out an organization to join. Therefore, to say that a problem situation experienced by a collectivity leads to a social movement ignores both the fact that in most cases an organizational framework already exists and that other courses of action are open to the individual. Thus, one problem we must address is the source of participation in social movements.

These observations suggest that among the problems which must be met in our analysis of social movements, those concerning what constitutes a movement, the emergence of movements, recruitment to and participation in movements, and the careers of movements are of prime importance. In chapter 4, we shall turn to the first of these problems.

4
SOCIAL MOVEMENTS
AS EMERGENT REALITIES

THE PROBLEM OF DEFINITION

Among the difficulties related to the sociology of social movements, the problem of definition is paramount. Before attempting to study movements, one must first distinguish them from other collective phenomena such as political parties, institutions, associations, pressure groups, and mass migrations. Because of the definitional confusion frequently found in the literature, these distinctions are important.

Before elaborating on some of the general definitional problems in the analysis of social movements, we should, by way of introduction, consider two discussions of the specific shortcomings of definitions of two contemporary social movements—the "extreme Right" and the "New Left."

Excerpts from Gary B. Rush, "Toward a Definition of the Extreme Right," Pacific Sociological Review, *Vol. 6 (Fall, 1963), pp. 64–73. Reprinted by permission of G. B. Rush and the Pacific Sociological Association.*

A basic assumption of the present investigation is that the Extreme Right is essentially political in nature. The fact that this country has a two-party political system tends to obscure the possibility that a variety of political attitudes can and, in fact, do exist. In countries having a multi-party system, such as France, institutionalized channels of expression for various types of political attitudes are manifest. Consequently, a wide range of political attitude is laid open to investigation by an equally wide range of political behavior. In the American political system, on the other hand, splinter parties operating through alternative channels of political expression have not been successful in gaining direct political power, and are either short-lived or doomed to obscurity. The necessity for the two dominant political parties to compete for the support of a heterogeneous electorate tends to reduce the difference between them, and institutionalized channels of extremist political expression are forestalled from developing within the existing political framework since they would be antithetical to the necessary "middle of the road" posture of both parties.[1] The militancy and millenarianism of the Extreme Right reflect the "crises of legitimacy" to which this element in the American political system is exposed. Frustrated in gaining access to formal and institutionalized political power, the Extreme Right has pinned its hope on a policy of militant and unilateral action designed to bring about desired changes in the political system in a not-too-distant millenium.[2]

Further evidence of the political nature of the Extreme Right lies in the fact that most of the changes which extremist groups advocate are designed to be implemented primarily through the political framework of society. In addition, the Extreme Right seeks alignment with institutionalized conservative political forces. This is evidenced, for example, in Right-Wing support for Senators Goldwater, Tower, and Eastland.

In sum, then, the Extreme Right may be regarded as an as yet noninstitutionalized political ideology. The use of the term "ideology" here is in the sense in which it is defined earlier—an organization of attitudes, opinions, and values about society. In the literature on social movements, ideology is usually distinguished from the specific program of change that a group advocates, as, for example, in the following statement from Turner and Killian: "At the outset we may distinguish the particular program of change that a movement advocates from the conception of society through which it justifies that program. The latter we shall call the *ideology* of the movement. . . ."[3] This conception of ideology will thus permit a study of the attitudinal characteristics of the Extreme Right with-

---

[1] Daniel Bell, in "Interpretations of American Politics," in Bell (ed.), *The New American Right* (New York: Criterion Books, 1955), pp. 4–5, discusses this situation as follows: "Perhaps the most decisive fact about politics in the United States is the two-party system. Each party is like some huge bazaar, with hundreds of hucksters clamoring for attention. But while life within the bazaars flows freely and licenses are easy to obtain, all trading has to be conducted within the tents; the ones who hawk their wares outside are doomed to few sales. This fact gains meaning when we consider one of the striking facts about American life: America has thrown up countless social movements, but few political parties; in contradiction to European political life, few of the social movements have been able to transform themselves into political parties."
[2] This problem of inability to gain formal political power and recognition is discussed in S. M. Lipset, *Political Man* (Garden City, N.Y.: Doubleday and Company, Inc., 1960), chapter III, "Social Conflict, Legitimacy, and Democracy," pp. 77–96.
[3] Ralph M. Turner and Lewis M. Killian, *Collective Behavior* (Englewood Cliffs, New Jersey: Prentice-Hall, Inc., 1957), p. 331.

out going into a detailed analysis of the content of the *programs* of Right-Wing groups. The utility of this approach has been referred to earlier in this paper.

The next phase of this investigation will be to establish, by the process of "intuitive induction," [4] a definition capable of being operationalized which will delimit the Extreme Right from other phenomena. To this end, we shall attempt to discern a number of the outstanding characteristics of the Extreme Right. The most extensive survey of such characteristics published to date is that of Ellsworth and Harris.[5] To those which they have identified, I have added a number drawn from my own surveys of available literature.[6] The initial investigation took the form of a content analysis of this material to determine what the Extreme Right advocated or supported and what they opposed or rejected. As might be expected, a considerable overlapping of the attitudes expressed by different groups and individuals occurred. However, some twenty-eight relatively distinct attitudes, mostly negativistic, appeared manifest. A preliminary inspection of these attitudes suggested that they fell under four general headings.[7] These hypothesized categories and the attitudes constituting them are as follows:

I. *Attitudes regarding government:*
Opposition to strong central government.[8]

[4] Basically, this process consists of making empirical observations of a phenomenon in order to arrive at a basic knowledge of it. For a discussion of this form of reasoning, see Morris R. Cohen and Ernest Nagel, *An Introduction to Logic and Scientific Method* (New York: Harcourt, Brace and Company, 1934), pp. 273–275.
[5] Ralph E. Ellsworth and Sarah M. Harris, *The American Right Wing: A Report to the Fund for the Republic* (Washington, D.C.: Public Affairs Press, 1962).
[6] A comprehensive list of more than 1800 Right-Wing Groups is given in *The First National Directory of "Rightist" Groups, Publications and Some Individuals in the United States*, fourth edition (Los Angeles: Alert Americans Association, 1961). The major sources investigated in the present survey are speeches made by acknowledged Extreme Right spokesmen; pamphlets published by *America's Future, Inc.* (New Rochelle, New York); pamphlets published by *Bible Recordings, Inc.* (Baltimore, Maryland); transcripts of testimony given before the *House Committee on Un-American Activities*; radio broadcasts and newsletters of *The 20th Century Reformation Hour*, Rev. Carl McIntire, Director (Collingswood, New Jersey); "Dawn" a monthly newspaper published by *Independence Foundation, Inc.* (Portland, Indiana); the "Blue Book" and monthly bulletins published by *The John Birch Society, Inc.* (Belmont, Mass.); Frank J. Donner, *The Un-Americans* (New York: Ballantine Books, 1961); Gene Grove, *Inside the John Birch Society* (Greenwich, Conn.: Fawcett Publications, 1961); Telford Taylor, *Grand Inquest* (New York: Ballantine Books, 1961); Richard Vahan, *The Truth About The John Birch Society* (New York: McFadden Books, 1962); Donald Janson and Bernard Eismann, *The Far Right* (New York: McGraw-Hill Book Company, Inc., 1963).
[7] A subsequent cluster analysis of attitudinal indicators, too extensive to report in the present paper, substantiated the division of Extreme Right into these four categories.
[8] It must be borne in mind that this opposition is selective. The Right-Wing Extremist's conception of the function of the state is not unlike that of the classical liberal who saw the state as a protector of property and a preserver of order, much like a night watchman, rather than as an entity which imposed positive obligations upon

Belief in strong government and leaders, but at the local level.
Dissatisfaction with the United States Supreme Court.
Opposition to the Federal Reserve System.
Conviction that there is corruption in government.
General distrust of the federal government.
Opposition to increased government spending, higher taxes.
Opposition to metropolitan government.
Opposition to urban renewal.

II. *Attitudes regarding international relations:*
Opposition to foreign entanglements.
Dedication to an "America First" approach.
Opposition to the United Nations.
Opposition to foreign aid, Point Four Programs, NATO, etc.

III. *Attitudes regarding modern social principles:*
Opposition to modern education.
Opposition to racial integration.
Suspicion of international collectivism (e.g., the Common Market).
Militant anti-Communism.
Political cynicism.[9]
Opposition to "social gospel" Protestantism.

IV. *Attitudes regarding modern social structure and operation:* [10]
Opposition to socialized medicine.
Opposition to collective bargaining.
Support of "right to work" proposals.
Support of "free enterprise."
Opposition to "full employment."
Opposition to the "welfare state."
Opposition to federal aid to health and education.
Suspicion of modern "progressive" innovations.[11]

---

individuals. Thus, the extremist's major opposition to the federal government is in those areas where he is told what he *should do* (e.g., desegregation). On the other hand, Right-Wing support is given to strong government in matters pertaining to security (e.g., congressional investigating committees). For an interesting discussion of this conception of the state, see Harry K. Girvetz, *From Wealth to Welfare: The Evolution of Liberalism* (Stanford, California: Stanford University Press, 1950), pp. 68–78.

[9] This attitude refers primarily to the attitudes and motivations of politicians and to the operation of the political system in general rather than to any specific political issue.

[10] A distinction should be drawn between this category and the preceding one regarding "modern social principles." The latter refers primarily to a generalized attitudinal framework through which the Right-Wing Extremist regards his society. "Modern social structure and operation," on the other hand, refers more to specific programmatic policies, particularly those of the contemporary liberal state.

[11] E.g., fluoridation, psychiatry, pastoral counseling, mental health programs, mental hospitals, etc.

The main theme running through these attitudes appears to be a general opposition to certain forms of "collectivism." This view is strengthened by a review of statements made by some of the leaders of Extreme Right groups. Robert Welch, for example, devotes all of section two of his *Blue Book* to the "cancer of collectivism." [12] Leslie Fleming, President of the Oregon John Birch Society, states that the program of the Society is ". . . individuality opposing collectivism," [13] and R. K. Scott, President of America's Future, Incorporated, writes of his organization's ". . . unbending opposition to all forms of collectivism including the communist conspiracy." [14] The kinds of collectivism opposed by the Extreme Right are primarily Communism and the type of contemporary liberalism practiced in the United States. With a few notable exceptions (such as the Tennessee Valley Authority and the Bonneville Power Administration), contemporary American liberalism does not tend toward governmental ownership and management of the means for the production and distribution of goods. Rather, the governmental role in the economy tends more toward increasing control and regulation while relying, for the most part, on a market system economy and its corollaries of private property and private profit.

In addition to this control or regulatory aspect, Extreme Right opposition also extends to an underlying philosophy of contemporary American liberalism—one which may be called the "ameliorative" or welfare function of the state. This function refers not only to an acceptance of responsibility on the part of the state for the basic well-being of its members, but also to systematic planning aimed at providing fuller lives for *all* members of the state. Extreme Right antagonism to this kind of welfare function, or "quasi-paternalism," reflects not only a practical opposition to taxation—a requisite for the financing of welfare and aid programs—but also a belief that man will not be motivated to work unless he suffers deprivation. This belief has its roots in the *classical* liberal view of the psychological nature of man.[15] According to this view, man is motivated by self-interest ("egoism") or pleasure ("hedonism").

---

[12] Robert Welch, *The Blue Book of the John Birch Society*, sixth printing, 1961, Section Two, "But Let's Look Deeper . . . ," pp. 41–55.
[13] Excerpted from the transcript of a speech delivered by Leslie Fleming, President of the Oregon John Birch Society, at Clark College, Vancouver, Washington, February 26, 1962. Published in *Pace: The Emerald Features Supplement*, University of Oregon, Thursday, May 17, 1962, under the following affirmation: "This is the views (sic) of myself and the John Birch Society, LESLIE FLEMING (signed), Box 3174, Eugene, Oregon, May 5, 1962."
[14] Quoted from a personal communication received from R. K. Scott, President of *America's Future, Incorporated*, 542 Main Street, New Rochelle, New York, March 12, 1963.
[15] For a full discussion of the nature of this view and its consequences for classical liberal thought, see Harry K. Girvetz, *op. cit.*, esp. pp. 7–27 and 28–42.

From this, it follows that purposive activity must somehow be induced and that unless some enticement is offered by way of pleasure or advantage man will remain apathetic and inert ("quietism"). However, man is also basically rational ("intellectualism"). Given a choice of alternatives, reason will balance the quality of pleasure or pain involved, and conduct will follow that course of action which carries the greatest pleasure or the least pain. In order to motivate man to purposive activity, the pains of deprivation must therefore exceed those of work. If, on the other hand, public welfare and assistance programs permit man to consume without toiling, the pleasure derived will be so great as to encourage perpetual indolence.

It is against the collectivistic or socialistic principles of contemporary American liberalism that the main force of Extreme Right expression is directed. Since a great deal of the policy of the present liberal government is based on these principles, it is understandable that the federal government should be a primary target of the Extreme Right. However, tendencies toward socialism at *any* governmental level are decried. At the state level, public (*i.e.*, governmental) management of state supported institutions (particularly educational institutions) is closely scrutinized. At this level, however, extremists must walk a very thin line since "States' Rights" is a battle cry against the extension of federal government power. Socialistic tendencies at the local government level (such as urban renewal—a joint federal-local project—and metropolitan government) are also opposed by the Extreme Right, primarily for tactical reasons. This is understandable in light of the extremist conviction, articulated by spokesmen such as Carl McIntire, Billy Hargis, Fred Schwartz and W. Cleon Skousen, that the fight against collectivism must begin at the local or "grass roots" level.

At the international level, the greatest source of concern to the Extreme Right is the United Nations and America's participation in it. In the eyes of the extremist, that body is collectivism incarnate, and practically every group in the Extreme Right has expressed vehement opposition to it. American aid to foreign countries is also protested, being regarded in the same light as social welfare on the domestic scene.

The militant anti-Communism of the Extreme Right can also be understood under this frame of reference, since the Right Wing considers that Communism is either the polar extension of socialism, or, what is worse, that socialism is merely Communism by another name. This approach to the anti-Communism of the Extreme Right also explains the bias against intellectuals, liberals, modernists, and progressives. Since these are the main groups advocating socialism, it is understandable that they be labelled as "Communist" and treated as such.

By the same token, it is natural that most of the modern philosophies and programs advocated by these liberal groups be suspect in the eyes of the Extreme Right. Thus, "progressive education," a modern innovation, is regarded by the extremists as a means through which the scholastic, liberal elements in the society are attempting to indoctrinate the younger generation with their insidious beliefs. Higher education, primarily in the liberal arts and the social sciences, is also a target of the Extreme Right. Similarly, modern innovations such as pastoral counseling, mental health programs, psychiatry, mental hospitals, and even fluoridation are all regarded as part of a modern collectivistic conspiracy.

What the extremist proposed as an alternative to this collectivism is a political state in which the individual is the final arbiter of truth. A consistent and militant theme in the agitation of the Extreme Right is for the individual to awake, to arouse himself from the apathy to which he has been led, to be aware of the dangers which surround him, and to take action against those dangers, as well as against the leaders who have brought him to this pass. The notion of an enslaved people dominated by corrupt leaders is a recurrent one in Extreme Right expression. The Right-Wing Extremist views his world in terms of a simplistic, black-and-white dichotomy. In his eyes, an impersonal, rationalized, complex, technical, bureaucratic "society" is destroying the simple virtue of man as an "individual." [16]

Given this picture of the extremist "world view," the philosophy underlying the Extreme Right may be discerned. The essence of this philosophy lies in the Right-Wing Extremist's *atomistic*, as opposed to *organicist*, view of the relationship between man and society. "Atomism" refers to the conception that the whole is nothing more than the sum of its parts. "Organicism," on the other hand, refers to the conception of the whole as something more than the sum of its constituent parts—a reality *sui generis*. Applied to society, "atomism" is the view that individuals make society; "organicism" is the view that society makes individuals.[17]

---

[16] This extremist "world view" has been recognized by several of the contributors, in their 1962 articles, to Daniel Bell (ed.), *The Radical Right* (*The New American Right* expanded and updated), (Garden City, New York: Doubleday and Company, Inc., 1963). See for example, Daniel Bell, "The Dispossessed," pp. 1–38; David Riesman, "The Intellectuals and the Discontented Classes: Some Further Reflections," pp. 115–134; Talcott Parsons, "Social Strains in America: A Postscript," pp. 193–199.

[17] Theories of society based on these polarities have characterized almost the entire history of social thought. Although their roots go back into classical philosophy, the development of atomism and organicism may be conveniently traced from their Eighteenth Century formulations. The former is evidenced in the writings of men such as Hobbes (1588–1679), Rousseau (1712–1778), Burke (1729–1797), Bentham (1748–1832) and, in its Nineteenth Century specification, Spencer (1820–1903). Organicism may be traced through the writings of Locke (1632–1704), Hume (1711–1776), Blackstone (1723–1780), DeMaistre (1754–1821), DeBonald (1754–1840), Comte (1798–1857) and Durkheim (1855–1917). The empirical validity of such polarities is an academic problem, and one which need not concern us here. What is essential is the fact that the Right-Wing Extremist *does view his society in*

Girvetz has summarized the atomistic philosophy as follows:

> The classical liberals, in accord with their atomistic outlook, regarded social institutions as the handiwork of pre-existing individuals whose characteristic mental and emotional endowments antedate the social arrangements into which these individuals enter. Even rights are often regarded as natural, that is to say, as antedating the state. Social arrangements affect individual human nature only superficially. They are additative and artificial, and their importance is largely negative, an importance which consists mostly of removing obstacles which might prevent individuals from achieving complete self-expression. The relationship between individuals and society is an external one; the individual with his various propensities and faculties is given, and society is an arrangement of convenience, whereby faculties operate more effectively and propensities are more likely to find fruition. To repeat, social institutions are created by the fiat of self-contained individuals; they are instruments, even expedients, which the individual can employ or discard without fundamentally altering his own nature.[18]

This quotation, although somewhat extensive, is included in its entirety because of its central importance to the thesis which is being developed in these pages. This atomistic philosophy, together with the classical psychological view of the nature of man discussed earlier, constitute the basic identifying characteristic of the Extreme Right—a characteristic which will be referred to herein as "individualism." Individualism is defined by Webster as: "A theory or policy having primary regard for individual rights, specifically one maintaining the independence of initiative, action and interests. . . ."[19]

This individualism is not unlike that discussed by Max Weber in his essay on the Protestant Ethic.[20] Specifically, it is epitomized in the Ascetic Protestant attitude that the success or failure of every man, both in this world and in the next, rests on his own individual initiative. This is the attitude which finds expression in the Right-Wing Extremist's opposition to "assistance" programs and his abhorrence of the maxim, "from each according to his ability, to each according to his need." It is from the expression of this attitude by Right-Wing Extremists that many writers deduce the notion of "regression" as a dominant characteristic of the Extreme Right—a desire to return to the nineteenth century. In maintaining this principle of individualism in opposition to what has earlier been

---

these terms. That he does so has important implications for the study of his attitudes and behavior, for, as W. I. Thomas has pointed out in his concept of "definition of the situation," what men believe to be true are true in their consequences.
[18] Harry K. Girvetz, *op. cit.*, p. 23.
[19] *Webster's New International Dictionary of the English Language*, second edition, unabridged (Springfield, Massachusetts: G. and C. Merriam Company, 1935), p. 1268.
[20] Max Weber, *The Protestant Ethic and the Spirit of Capitalism*, translated by Talcott Parsons (New York: Charles Scribner's Sons, 1958).

described under the heading of "collectivism," the Right-Wing Extremist is opposing a system which would not only take away the fruits of one's labors (through taxation) to distribute it to those who did nothing to earn it (through social welfare), but would also restrict (through government control) one's prerogative to act in his own best interest in all matters.

The form of individualism which is advocated by the Extreme Right is selective in nature. First, independence of initiative, action and interest would not be extended to all individuals or groups. Minority groups would be excluded, as would those individuals who did not share the Extreme Right's opposition to collectivism (such as modernists and liberals). Second, the infringement of individualism would be tolerated in those situations where intervention and/or control may be regarded as furthering the aims and interests of the Extreme Right. This explains the Extreme Right's Janus approach to the federal government. For example, while federal intervention in school desegregation is regarded as an infringement of States' Rights and is thus vigorously opposed, the granting of federal defense contracts is seen as a benefit to the economic situation of the state, and the federal control accompanying such a form of intervention is overlooked. Moreover, strong government control is advocated by the Extreme Right in matters pertaining to the "police function" of the state for the protection of property, the preservation of order, and the maintenance of security, both internal and external. Thus, as indicated earlier, the Extreme Right supports the F.B.I. and congressional investigating committees. Toleration of collectivism is also extended to corporate "big business," which the Extreme Right courts as a source of economic support. It may be said that the Extreme Right opposes collectivism by proposing individualism, except in those areas where collectivism can be rationalized as furthering extremist interests.

The foregoing discussion of the nature of the Extreme Right may now be summarized, preparatory to establishing a definition of this phenomenon. Throughout this discussion, the concepts of "collectivism" and "individualism" have been used extensively. Unfortunately, no one word can completely express the complexities of a phenomenon such as the Extreme Right. However, it is hoped that the particular contextual meaning of these terms, as they are applied to this study of the Extreme Right, has been made clear in the preceding pages. By "collectivism" we mean primarily the "quasi-paternalistic" welfare functions of twentieth century American socialism, and, on the international scene, Communism. Thus, Right-Wing opposition is directed primarily against government, whose function it is to administer aid and welfare programs. This opposition to government is not universal, however, since the Extreme Right tolerates and even supports certain functions of the state (such as the "police function" and the maintenance of the "market-place economy"). Corporate business which, in the classical "laissez-faire" sense, may be regarded as detrimental to the individualism of entrepreneurial business, is also spared extensive Right-Wing attack primarily because it is a potential source of economic support for Extreme Right groups. It has been proposed that the Extreme Right opposes this form of collectivism by advocating "individualism." This latter term, as it is used in this investigation, also has a certain restricted meaning. This principle of individualism has its basis in the classical "atomistic" view of society—the view that social institutions are subordinate to the individual. Thus, the Extreme Right tolerates those functions of the state that protect the interests and conditions of the individual. The individualism advocated by the Extreme Right is limited, however, since the right to act in one's own best interests would not be extended to all individuals. Those who would subvert what the Right-Wing Extremist regards as "the greatest good" (e.g., liberals and leftists), as well as the non-productive and shiftless members of the society (e.g., most minority group members), would not be afforded the privileges of individualism.

In conclusion, it is proposed that the Extreme Right be defined as follows:

The Extreme Right is a militant and millenarian political ideology, espoused by numerous Right-Wing groups and individuals, which maintains as an ideal the principle of "limited individualsm"; this principle being articulated as opposition to "collectivism" in government, in international relations, to modern social principles, and modern social structure and operation.

By focusing thus on the ideological aspects of the Extreme Right, rather than on individual groups of this persuasion, it should be possible to delineate more sharply the attitudinal indicators of this phenomenon, thus facilitating the scientific study of it.

Excerpts from Eugene D. Genovese, "Genovese Looks at American Left—New and Old," National Guardian *(February 19, 1966), pp. 6–7. Reprinted by permission of Eugene D. Genovese and the* National Guardian.

The New Left has been, in part, a response to . . . previous defeats and current game of charades. SNCC, in the field of civil rights; SDS in domestic affairs; and May 2 in foreign affairs—as well as other groups— have arisen to introduce a critical and combative element into American political life. The increasing interest by all of them in the Vietnam war alone demonstrates their radical potential and sense of principle.

The New Left has sought to avoid many errors of the Old. It has repudiated Stalinism and refused to use a double standard in judging socialist and capitalist countries. It has refused to sanction the suppression of civil liberties in the Soviet Union, or the infringements on intellectual freedom in Yugoslavia, or the stringent demands for subordination of the individual in China. However naive the New Left may be in its inability to face the historical dimension of these manifestations of Stalinism and in its insistence on an absolute and moralistic view of society, there can be no doubt that its break with Stalinism has been a liberating factor and a necessary prelude to a new American radicalism.

The New Left has extended its repudiation of Stalinism to a repudiation of bureaucracy and organizational manipulation and has quite properly noted that democratic centralism usually means democratic forms to disguise a centralizing content. These young radicals insist on the widest freedom of individual participation and non-participation. They have replaced the demand for revolutionary discipline with the assertion of individual conscience. Like the Protestants of the 16th Century they have ruthlessly swept away all demands for submission to authority, however legitimate, with the cry of "follow the inner light." In place of a single disciplined church for all men, they have offered us appeals to the right of private judgment. It is no accident, in my opinion, that the New Left is so noticeably Anglo-Saxon in complexion, whereas the Old was so noticeably composed of Jews, Irish, Italians, and other more recent immigrant groups from eastern and southern Europe.

If we review the main characteristics of New Left politics in general, we may note certain striking, positive contributions:

1) A refusal to become involved with coalition politics—that is, a refusal to tie anti-war action to alliances with the Democratic Party or other Establishment groups.

2) The assertion that American foreign policy arises from a sick and unjust society, not merely from tactical errors or misunderstandings.

3) An extraordinary courage and militancy linked firmly to the principle of an individual's responsibility for his actions.

4) A profound and honest concern with the moral tenor of American life and an attempt to find the sources of our moral decay.

5) A struggle to build a movement open to all and immune to red-baiting.

6) A determination to reassert unambiguously the principles of individual freedom, and an attendant refusal to sacrifice those principles to promises of some future utopia.

These and other positive qualities have been largely responsible for the revitalization of American radicalism in the 1960's, and they must become a permanent part of any new radical movement in America, if it is to have the slightest chance for success. . . .

Unfortunately, the New Left has carried over a great many weaknesses from the Old Left and, what is worse, has invented a few of its own. I do not think it extreme to assert that unless these weaknesses are overcome, the New Left has no future; but the greatest difficulty lies in the curious identification of strength and weakness. Some of the most serious weaknesses seem inseparable from the greatest strengths. It is precisely this contradiction that defines the New Left and even much of the wider peace and civil rights movements.

Much of the New Left has refused to become involved in coalition politics and has rejected the dreary calls of the Communist Party for a people's front with allegedly progressive sections of imperialism. This rejection has the virtue of being in accordance with historical experience, for this kind of popular-frontism has been a failure in every advanced country in which it has been tried. However, the fear of being compromised has led many sections of the New Left into a sectarian course and threatens to remove them from all possibilities of political effectiveness. Certainly, the Freedom Democratic Party in Mississippi, SNCC in Georgia, or the parallel efforts of the struggling movement in New Jersey are worthy experiments, which offer hope of new solutions to old problems. But the fact remains that much of the New Left, like much of the Old, is basically frightened by the prospect of participation in major party politics. . . .

The Communist party, the Progressive Labor Movements, the Trotskyists, and other Leninists have a theory of imperialism. It is no longer an adequate, comprehensive theory, but it is a coherent and satisfactory first approximation to a complex reality. The difficulty is that little has been done to develop that theory in relation to contemporary world capitalism and especially in relation to the structure of American society.

As a result, few useful analyses of present trends and future prospects have emerged from any of these groups. They have, nevertheless, a body of Marxian thought on which to build. Their failure to build on it has been due primarily to their contempt for theoretical work, which has expressed itself in practices designed to force dogmas and policies down the throats of party intellectuals. Naturally, the best minds and most principled men have deserted, leaving the field to an incredible collection of windbags, hacks, hangers-on, and a small band of good men trying desperately to save a lost situation.

Now, what has the New Left done about this estrangement of intellectuals and political cadres? The truth is that it has widened, not narrowed, the breach. Most of the New Left prides itself on its pragmatism, which in this case means mindlessness, and its freedom from Marxian dogma. Actually, it has no theory at all; nor an understanding respect for history; nor even a knowledge of what it does not know. The New Left, notwithstanding the efforts of *Studies on the Left* and a number of individuals, is more violently and stupidly anti-intellectual than the Old Left ever was.

Consequently, the New Left may know that American society is unjust and sick, but it hardly knows why. It has no theory of society, no theory of social change, and no understanding of the nature and promise of socialism, which it is incapable of discussing apart from the experience of the present-day socialist countries. Its concern with the deterioration of moral values lacks focus, either historical or theoretical. Here as elsewhere, it comes up against the limits of its romantic commitment to individual freedom.

If the Old Left constantly trampled on individuality in the sacred name of the collective good, the New Left constantly tramples on the collective good in the sacred name of individuality. I am not certain that anything has been gained by this swing of the pendulum, for neither is much good without the other. The Old Left understood organization, discipline, the prerogatives and the legitimacy of leadership and authority. If it pushed these things too far, it at least understood that the world cannot be run without them in a manner fit for civilized men and women. . . . The point is not that the organizations of the New Left consist primarily of slobs and beatniks, as their enemies charge, but that they are so committed to an anarchist view as to be unwilling to force conformity to those practices on which ultimate success depends. . . .

If we look at the movement today, we find it facing dilemmas. The peace movement has found that it cannot bring peace without changing society. The civil rights movement is finding that capitalism can and probably will grant legal equality but cannot solve the deeper problems of racial adjustment and the abolition of a racially colored poverty. More and more dissenters, young and old, are beginning to recognize the need for an all-inclusive radical movement capable of offering a total alternative to American capitalism. Yet, the stuff out of which the most courageous and promising sections of the component movements have been formed offers little hope or leadership for that major breakthrough.

Perhaps the most pathetic manifestation of New Left illusion has been the notion of building communities outside the Establishment, where people may participate democratically in running their own lives. For example, we are called upon to leave the universities in order to found "free universities" in which we shall be able to express ourselves. I would criticize this view in detail, if I were not so embarrassed for my friends who put it forward. Was ever a more hopeless and self-defeating program projected for American radicalism? Our problem remains what it has always been—only it gets harder—to transform our universities, trade unions, community organizations, and even business organizations into socially responsible forces determined to defend their autonomy and integrity, capable of providing our people with more fruitful lives, and prepared to serve as vehicles for socialist transformation. I have no simple formulas for how to do it. I am quite certain that running away to the alleged purity of the ghetto is no answer.

We are rapidly reaching the end of the New Left phase. With luck, we could come out of it with a united socialist organization that can give stability and direction to other movements while preparing for a long slow climb in American politics. At worst, the New Left will end in the ashes of the Old, a victim of its own illusions and incapacities as well as of the blows of the Establishment. . . .

Some months ago the editors of *Studies on the Left* analyzed the peace and civil rights movements and warned that they were approaching a dead end. Today we are seeing the truth of that prediction. Civil rights legislation cannot prevent more Harlem and Watts riots; peace marches cannot provide a decent foreign policy. These movements have accomplished much, but their future depends on their ability to avoid frustration and piecemeal, energy-wasting activities. The way out remains a viable political movement and a broad-based radical party capable of giving ideological leadership so that each local rights or peace worker sees his efforts as part of a long-term struggle for national reconstruction.

The New Left has given us a new chance to build such a movement, but it also threatens us with disaster by its infantile anarchism, its beatnik posturing, its ideological innocence, and above all, its contempt for sustained, disciplined organizational effort. No matter how effective or promising or romantically appealing work in the ghettos may be, the main task remains to win the American masses, which are increasingly "middle class" in their outlook and character. Their new prosperity remains insecure and tied to a war machine that threatens their lives. They are terrified of nuclear war. They are frightened by the decline of the solid old virtues, no matter how great their personal sins. They want to recapture some sense of a stable family life. Their political passions are for federal support for everything but also for local autonomy and freedom from big brother. They want an orderly life without racial strife, slum populations, and social unrest.

It is time we realized that these are not such bad aspirations, even if they do not exhaust everything worthwhile in life. We may then find that the areas which are today breeding grounds for the extreme right will be ours, and with them the traditional working class areas as well. If after all, the trouble with capitalism is that it breeds war, racism, and poverty, and suffocates individuality, then the cause of socialism represents not merely the cause of peace and plenty but the restoration of social order.

That lesson has, I think, been burned into the consciousness of our so-called tired old radicals. It is essential that they stop looking at their children with awe and stop flattering them into persistence in their worst faults. The future of the peace movement is bound up inextricably with the future of a movement for socialist reconstruction. The Good Book may say a child shall lead us, but with due respect, I should suggest that we shall have to lead ourselves and that we shall never do so until we can draw on the experience, judgment, and maturity that even the most brilliant and courageous of our young people cannot be expected to give us.

"Social movements are not institutions . . . ," write Horton and Hunt, since "social institutions are relatively permanent and stable elements of a culture, whereas social movements are highly dynamic and have an uncertain life span." [21] Social institutions consist of the established, prescribed, and normative practices surrounding basic human activity, whereas social movements, more often than not, are addressed to changing the institutional order. For example, in the contemporary industrial system of North America, a labor union is not a movement, in spite of George Meany's use of the phrase "labor movement," which by now is part of the rhetoric of the militant thirties. In the thirties, the union movement challenged existing industrial relations, whereas today's unions are an integral part of the industrial status quo: they have become institutionalized. Similarly, a political party, through its efforts to elect its candidates to office, is integrated into the existing institutions of government. In contrast, a political movement usually challenges the legitimacy of these institutions and seeks to provide an alternative to the existing party structure. Social movements are also distinguishable from associations in that members of the latter reinforce the normative order of the social system. Thus, the Parent-Teacher Association, the National Association of Manufacturers, and the American Medical Association cannot be classed as social movements, unless, of course, they were to challenge the existing normative and structural order. Even the present-day civil rights associations, such as the National Association for the Advancement of Colored People or the Congress of Racial Equality, cannot be regarded as social movements, because they are accepted by the majority of society as legitimate organizations. The changes they urge are generally acceptable to the public, although the specific means of implementing them may be a matter of debate.

In the context of political pluralism, interest and pressure groups may also be distinguished from social movements, although they all share similar goals. Political scientists generally define interest and pressure groups as: "Groups which seek to advance the interest of their members in the

[21] Paul B. Horton and Chester L. Hunt, *Sociology* (New York: McGraw-Hill Book Co., 1964), p. 512.

political arena." [22] Their methods lie within institutionalized channels: "An interest group forms to further or to realize some goal. If the group decides to bring its case in whole or in part to government, it is a pressure or political interest group." [23] Sociologists provide a similar picture of interest and pressure groups. Heberle states: "[A pressure group is] . . . an organized group formed for the pursuit of a particular limited political goal, usually a special interest; it attempts to create a favorable public opinion and to impose its policy upon one or more of the political parties." [24] According to Horton and Hunt: "pressure groups merely want the existing norms and values to be interpreted to their benefit." [25] However, as Hofstadter, Gusfield, and others have indicated, social movements, when viewed as interest groups, may conform to the above specifications.[26] Reform movements, for example, may adhere to existing norms and values by petitioning the government for redress of grievances. Examples of this orientation include the Anti-Saloon League, the Populists, and the Suffragettes. In resolving this apparent contradiction regarding social movements as operative either within or outside established social structures, we would concur with Horton and Hunt's analysis: "Social movements sometimes act as pressure groups, . . . but social movements are primarily and consciously concerned with promoting or resisting actual changes in these social norms and values. Occasionally, but only occasionally, do social movements function as pressure groups." [27]

In dealing with the distinction between political parties and social movements, we would also rely on the legitimate versus nonlegitimate criterion. However, the possible interactive relation between a party and a movement should also be noted. That is, a political party may emerge from a social movement, or a movement may, in acting as a pressure group, influence a party. In this context, pressure group activity may be a tactic of a social movement, but it would not constitute the movement's raison d'être.

The greatest difficulties in distinguishing movements from other phenomena arise in connection with what Turner and Killian term "quasi-movements"—entities which possess "some but not all of the characteristics of a movement." [28] Among these phenomena is the "mass movement," which Kornhauser describes as follows: "their objectives are remote

[22] William H. Young, *American Government*, 11th ed. (New York: Appleton-Century-Crofts, 1956), p. 141.
[23] Hugh Bone and Austin Ranney, *Politics and Voters* (New York: McGraw-Hill, 1963), p. 61.
[24] Rudolf Heberle, *Social Movements: An Introduction to Political Sociology* (New York: Appleton-Century-Crofts, 1951), p. 9.
[25] Horton and Hunt, *op. cit.*, p. 512.
[26] Cf. Joseph R. Gusfield, *The Symbolic Crusade* (Urbana, Ill.: University of Illinois Press, 1963).
[27] Horton and Hunt, *op. cit.*, p. 512.
[28] Ralph Turner and Lewis Killian, *Collective Behavior* (Englewood Cliffs, N.J.: Prentice-Hall, Inc., 1957), pp. 308–309.

and extreme; they favor activist modes of intervention in the social order; they mobilize uprooted and atomized sections of the population; they lack an internal structure of independent groups." [29] In his discussion of mass movements, Hoffer includes religious movements, social revolutions, and nationalistic movements.[30] As utilized by these authors, the term "movement" loses its meaning in that it is used to encompass fairly broad epochs of general social unrest and change. In this framework, one would have to include such all-inclusive events as the Calvinist Reformation, the French Revolution, and contemporary right wing extremism. These phenomena, although embodying some of the characteristics of social movements, cover too broad a period of time and space to be properly analyzed as social movements. Moreover, as we shall later argue, social movements, by their very nature, cannot be mass or all-inclusive.

The term "mass movement" has also been equated with "mass migration" in the literature on social movements.[31] However, migrations are not movements, although they may contribute to their formation. For example, the migration of Negroes from the rural South to the urban North was a factor in the characteristic development of the civil rights movement, and the mass migrations from Ireland during the "potato famine" contributed to the founding of the "Molly McGuires" in the United States. Nevertheless, several authors do confuse migration with movement. For example, Horton and Hunt state: "whenever a significant fraction of the people move and their shift is accompanied by considerable public discussion and comment, the migration surely forms a social movement." [32]

Similarly, Hoffer asserts that "mass migrations become mass movements." [33] In spite of these assertions, demographic movements are not synonymous with social movements. They do not involve attempts to change society; they are responses to external "pushes" or "pulls" and do not have an internal dynamic of ideology; they are legitimate responses to specific social, economic, or political conditions.

The question of what a social movement is has also been obscured by the concepts of "latent" and "ostensible" social movements, which were introduced into the literature by Hans Toch in The Social Psychology of Social Movements. According to Toch: "Latent social movements . . . are business enterprises with latent appeals. The relationship between such a business and its clients includes all the elements of a transaction between a social movement and its members." [34] For Toch, such enter-

---

[29] William Kornhauser, Politics of Mass Society (Glencoe, Ill.: Free Press, 1959), p. 47.
[30] Eric Hoffer, The True Believer (New York: Mentor Books, 1958), n.p.
[31] Turner and Killian, op. cit., p. 309.
[32] Horton and Hunt, op. cit., p. 521.
[33] Hoffer, op. cit., p. 18.
[34] Hans Toch, The Social Psychology of Social Movements (New York: Bobbs-Merrill, 1965), pp. 90–91.

prises are social movements because: "persons join [them] in an effort to solve a problem created for them by a recurrent social deficit. The situation here is social isolation, the problem is loneliness, and the solution is companionship in a framework that carries respectability and meaning." [35] Thus, dance studios, lonely hearts clubs, and similar enterprises come to be considered social movements.

An "ostensible social movement" is defined by Toch as one that: "enlists support for a collective cause [related to a social problem], but really functions for the purpose of making a profit." [36] In this context, Toch discusses fan clubs and health food cults as social movements.

These conceptualizations suggest some of the considerable difficulties inherent in the social psychological approach to social movements. First, Toch assumes the a priori existence of social movements, thus ignoring the social processes of movement formation. Second, to define problem situations perceived by individuals as etiological for social movements implies that all organizations dealing with individual problems are social movements. Finally, factors such as isolation, loneliness, need for personal attention, or concern over aging are not sufficient to explain the type of organization an individual will join in his search for companionship, involvement, or health. A lonely person, for example, may join a church group or an occupational fraternity instead of a lonely hearts club. Teenagers, in their search for identity, may turn to a variety of peer groups or adult-sponsored organizations rather than to the fan clubs of their idols. Toch's analysis, however, does not deal with the intervening factors predisposing an individual to choose one mode of adaptation over another.

In sum, we do not consider associations, pressure groups, political parties, mass migrations, clubs, cults, crazes, and fads to be social movements. Social movements may evolve into some of these organizations or may exhibit certain of their characteristic modes of behavior, but these aspects are not sufficient to warrant defining these phenomena as social movements. Having thus delineated what social movements are not, we must now specify what they are. As a first step, we shall examine some contemporary definitions of social movements.

The concept of social movement has been defined in a number of contexts stressing several general themes. The following are some of the more prevalent definitions.

(1) When collective action is . . . unified and lasting and has certain characteristic features [perspective and ideology, solidarity, idealism, and action], we call it a "social movement." [37]

---

[35] *Ibid.*, p. 93.
[36] *Ibid.*, p. 99.
[37] Leonard Broom and Philip Selznick, *Sociology: A Text with Adapted Readings*, 3d ed. (New York: Harper and Row, 1963), p. 302.

(2) . . . represent conscious and intentional collective effort to repair a social structure which appears to be disintegrating.[38]
(3) . . . can be viewed as collective enterprises to establish a new order of life.[39]
(4) . . . a collectivity acting with some continuity to promote a change or resist a change in the society or group of which it is a part.[40]
(5) . . . aims to bring about fundamental changes in the social order, especially in the basic institutions of property and labour relations.[41]
(6) . . . represents an effort by a large number of people to solve collectively a problem that they feel they have in common.[42]
(7) . . . a joint endeavor of a considerable group of persons to alter or change the course of events by their joint activities.[43]
(8) . . . a group venture extending beyond a local community or a single event and involving a systematic effort to inaugurate changes in thought, behavior, and social relationships.[44]
(9) . . . occurs when a fairly large number of people band together in order to alter or supplant some portion of the existing culture or social order.[45]
(10) . . . distinguished . . . by their "subversive character." They are imperfectly assimilated to the larger society and more or less in revolt against society.[46]
(11) A social movement may be said to exist wherever a group of individuals, operating within a community, aims to win the support of that community for establishment of some innovation in the ways and means of promoting a common interest.[47]

Two central features emerge from these statements: (1) social movements are collective organizational phenomena; (2) social movements function in relation to some form of social change. While these definitions present the general sociological view of what constitutes a social movement, they evidence several shortcomings. One of the most significant of these is the exclusion of ideology as an essential element in the formation of a movement. That is, although most authors do concede that

---

[38] Robert Faris, *Social Disorganization* (New York: Ronald Press, 1955), p. 572.
[39] Herbert Blumer, "Social Movements," in Alfred M. Lee, ed., *Principles of Sociology* (New York: Barnes and Noble, 1946), p. 199.
[40] Turner and Killian, *op. cit.*, p. 308.
[41] Heberle, *op. cit.*, p. 6.
[42] Toch, *op. cit.*, p. 5.
[43] J. Stewart Burgess, "The Study of Modern Social Movements," *Social Forces*, 22 (December 1944): 270.
[44] C. Wendell King, *Social Movements in the United States* (New York: Random House, 1956), p. 27.
[45] William Bruce Cameron, *Modern Social Movements* (New York: Random House, 1966), p. 7.
[46] Roger W. Brown, "Mass Phenomena," in Gardiner Lindzey, ed., *Handbook of Social Psychology*, vol. II (Cambridge, Mass.: Addison-Wesley, 1954), p. 871.
[47] Theodore Abel, "The Pattern of a Successful Political Movement," *American Sociological Review*, 2 (April 1937): 348.

ideology is tactically important for recruitment into a movement, we would argue further that ideology also sets the goals and defines the characteristic nature of a movement. These aspects of ideology are supported in much of the literature. Smelser, for one, sees social movements as existing "in the name of a generalized belief." [48] King regards ideology as "the justification for the movement's existence." [49] Jackson et al. argue that ideology is essential for a movement in that it provides a rallying point for members as well as for potential adherents.[50] Blumer states: "ideology plays a significant role in the life of a movement, it is a mechanism essential to the persistence and development of a movement." [51] Toch also sees ideology as an important element in the makeup of a movement: "The ideology of a social movement is a statement of what the members of the movement are trying to achieve together, and what they wish to affirm jointly." [52]

In a word, the ideology of a movement is interwoven with the type of social change its members desire. In this sense, ideology serves as a guidepost to the future. But ideology is also grounded in the past. Ideology, as we shall use it here, means a coherent set of beliefs arising from man's past which he uses to interpret and rationalize the present and to provide him with a conception of an idealized future. In this sense, we would incorporate certain ideas presented by Adorno and Lane into our definition:

The term ideology is used . . . to stand for an organization of opinions, attitudes, and values—a way of thinking about man and society. . . . Ideologies have an existence independent of any single individual; and those which exist at a particular time are results of both historical processes and of contemporay social events.[53]

[Ideology embraces] . . . a set of emotionally charged political beliefs, a critique of alternative proposals, and some modest programs of reform. These beliefs embrace central values and institutions; they are rationalizations of interests (sometimes not his own); and they serve as moral justifications for daily acts and beliefs.[54]

Thus, "ideology" subsumes both Mannheim's notion of "utopia" and Weber's "elective affinity." [55] As a guide to the future, its achievement

---

[48] Neil J. Smelser, *Theory of Collective Behavior* (New York: The Free Press, 1963), pp. 270, 313.
[49] King, *op. cit.*, p. 32.
[50] Maurice Jackson, et al., "The Failure of an Incipient Social Movement," *Pacific Sociological Review*, 3 (Spring 1960): 35–39. See also Regis Debray, *Revolution In the Revolution?* (New York: Grove Press, 1967); and Abel, *op. cit.*
[51] Blumer, *op. cit.*, p. 210.
[52] Toch, *op. cit.*, p. 21.
[53] T. W. Adorno, et al., *The Authoritarian Personality* (New York: Harper and Row, 1950), p. 2.
[54] Robert Lane, *Political Ideology* (Glencoe, Ill.: Free Press, 1962), p. 15.
[55] Karl Mannheim, *Ideology and Utopia: An Introduction to the Sociology of Knowl-*

becomes the goal toward which human effort should be directed. In this sense, there is a connotation that man's beliefs precede his objective state; that is, by acting in terms of utopian ideals, man can change his material circumstances. To the extent that they have a plan for the future, all movements contain a utopian element. This applies not only to left wing movements but also to movements of the right. To argue that right wing extremists desire to go back in time does not refute the fact that their idealized conceptions of the past become incorporated into their utopian plan for the future. Nor is this truism any less applicable to the radical Left: concepts such as freedom, justice, and democracy are, after all, very much a heritage of our past. In this sense, ideology provides a link between the past and the future.

However, ideology is also a set of beliefs about what is. This is basically the meaning of Weber's concept of "elective affinity"—man "elects," from a wide range of ideological conceptions, those ideas which have an affinity with his interests or objective circumstances. These ideas act as a justification or rationalization of his material existence. Essential to this conception of ideology is the assumption that ideology follows, and does not precede, objective material conditions. In this analysis, we do not wish to imply that the age-old question of whether material conditions precede ideology or vice-versa is a viable one. In point of fact, there is a constant and inseparable relationship between these two elements. At any given point in time, there exist numerous bodies of ideological beliefs from which men, from their various vantage points, can select (and in doing so, modify) a rationalized interpretation of the past, present, and future. Thus, ideology is a logically consistent system of ideas which exists independent of any single individual, which offers an interpretation of human history (of which it is a product), which provides a theory of the existing social system, and which points to a better future. This latter aspect can be the basis for recruiting adherents to programs of social action. At this juncture, we are concerned with drawing attention to the fact that ideology plays a significant role in defining the nature of a social movement. Subsequently, we shall discuss social movements as ideological organizations (see chapter 5).

Another problem inherent in a number of the definitions under consideration is that they do not distinguish social movements from pressure groups, lobbies, political parties, and other interest groups which attempt to manipulate the social system for collective or group benefit (i.e., numbers 1, 3, 4, 6, 7, and 11). The necessity of making such distinctions has already been discussed in this chapter and we will not repeat the rea-

---

edge (New York: Harcourt, Brace, and World, 1936), pp. 59–64; and Max Weber, "The Social Psychology of the World Religions," in H. Gerth and C. W. Mills, trans. and eds., *From Max Weber: Essays in Sociology* (New York: Oxford University Press, 1958), pp. 267–301.

sons here. However, the important point to be borne in mind is that the latter groups are perceived as legitimate in the eyes of the public, whereas social movements, because of their advocacy of basic or radical change in society, are not. In fact, as we shall later argue, this is the dilemma of social movements—once they have achieved public respectability, they are no longer social movements but part of the status quo.

This socially nonlegitimate role of a social movement is related to the fact that movements have a problem orientation. Their membership constitutes a vanguard of those who perceive dysfunction in the accepted institutions of society. Although most authors agree that social movements have a problem orientation and some incorporate this into their definitions (e.g., numbers 2, 6, and 10), none equate a specific consciousness of dysfunction with the social role of a movement. In fact, several of the definitions under consideration suggest a static or integrative interpretation of social movements inasmuch as they assume an equilibrium model approach (e.g., definitions 2, 4, and 11). That is, the role of a movement in these analyses seems to be that of repairing the effects of a dysfunction rather than ameliorating those elements of the social structure responsible for the dysfunction in the first place.

Very closely related to this element of consciousness of dysfunction is the perceived role of a given social movement as a viable means of confronting the social structure which brought about the given problems. This is what we mean by the emergent nature of social movements: they do not exist full-blown in limbo, waiting to be called forth, but rather emerge as characteristic of a specific time and place, to fulfill a specific social role. Perhaps the greatest weakness of current analyses of social movements is that they fail to concentrate on the emergent social role of these collective organizations. The part which a viable and acceptable (at least to a portion of the public) social role plays in the emergence of a social movement cannot be overlooked. To illustrate, the American Communist Party (CPUSA), with a current roll of 7,000 members, is a collective organization seeking social change. So was the Communist Party of the 1930s, with a membership of 80,000 and the legal status of a legitimate political party. However, the CPUSA of the 1960s cannot be considered as having the same social significance or prestige it possessed in the Red Decade. At this time, the Communist Party presented a program of "bread and roses" which promised to ameliorate the contradictions of capitalism. Similarly, the Anti-Saloon League and other "dry" organizations of the 1910s offered programs of social change which were perceived by a segment of the population as valid alternatives to the social problems of the time. In the United States today, however, neither Communism nor Temperance is widely regarded as being within the realm of reason or the "common-sense world." Therefore, it would seem that the temporal and perceived social role of an organization must be incorporated into any definition and analysis of a social movement.

To summarize to this point, the concept of social movement suggests the following elements: a socially defined "problem," an ideology, collective action, and ameliorative change. Before presenting our definition of social movements as emergent realities in response to specific problems, we must elaborate on two features of the social role of a movement: the consciousness of dysfunction which leads to the development of and participation in a movement, and the referents for mobilization which provide the ideology and models for the movement and direct the attention of its members toward exorcising the existing social structure.

CONSCIOUSNESS OF DYSFUNCTION

Existing social institutions are reified, in the process of interaction, by individuals. The result of this reification is a "common-sense" view of society, or what Durkheim referred to as the conscience collective. That is, people generally accept the existing social order and its organization— they do not question the institutional status quo. Individuals who experience personalized strain in this context commonly react through idiosyncratic behavior. This pattern of response is limited to unrelated individuals and does not infer collective action. The thief steals from economic institutions. He does not attempt to change them in a Robin Hood fashion. Consequently, individual deviation does not affect the main portion of society which is "hooked up to" and adheres to societal norms and perceptions.[56] These commitments, as Parsons observes in his theory of general action, maintain the existing order. The problem-solving and system maintenance function of social institutions such as the family, the polity, and the economy reaffirms the conscience collective. In this context, social problems such as crime and riots are defined as being outside the sphere of institutional etiology or responsibility. Therefore, the fundamental public opinion is that the social order remains sacred and that most problems are attributable to individual "misfits."

Inherent in the social system, however, are structural contradictions and conflicts arising from the division of labor and other differentiating factors such as race. By and large, these areas of conflict are treated in a similar manner to that of criminal behavior. Ideally, major social problems such as corporate conflict, poverty, and medical care are seen as stemming from the callousness of political parties or from individual greed or mis-

[56] Peter L. Berger, *Invitation to Sociology: A Humanistic Perspective* (Garden City, N.Y.: Doubleday and Co., Inc. [Anchor Books], 1963), pp. 129–131.

behavior. The notion that Herbert Hoover and his Republican cronies caused the Depression is illustrative. Furthermore, the advent of programs such as the "New Deal," the "Fair Deal," and the "Great Society" imply melioristic political action to rectify these social problems. That is, the Roosevelt administration was dedicated to curing the effects of the Great Depression and the loss of face suffered by the titans of American industry. Truman's "Fair Deal," following the close of the Second World War, promised to continue Roosevelt's policies and to institute new programs in such areas as medical care and education. The "Great Society" envisioned by Lyndon Johnson was designed to end social and economic inequality, especially in the sphere of race relations. In each case, however, these programs did not succeed in eliminating the social ills they addressed. By their failure, they reinforced the consciousness of dysfunction held by certain segments of the population.

An application of Durkheim's notion of consensus to the problem of economic depression will further illustrate the nature of structural contradictions. To overcome an economic depression, new institutional norms must be formulated to cope with this dilemma or strain. However, given a collective consciousness that the existing social order is viable, innovative norms cannot be found. Consequently, economic deprivation will continue and change must await public agreement upon action. This inactivity may generate further structural strain, which in turn weakens the consensus of the conscience collective.

What are the structural sources of dissensus? Both Marx and Durkheim attributed it to the division of labor. That is, dissensus is generated by the accelerating specialization of labor: as the division of labor increases, groups and classes are driven further apart. This in turn may lead one group to formulate a set of rules (institutional practices, laws, economic and governmental policies) which they attempt to impose on another group. For example, employers formulate norms that block the aspirations of the workers. Workers view these rules as undesirable. The assumption of a dominant role by one group or class may conflict with the goals of the subservient class, leading the latter to view the former as negativistic or problem-generating. The subordinates therefore undergo a negative homogeneity of experience.

This notion of the dissentual aspect of the division of labor is made explicit by Marx, who suggests:

. . . the division of labor implies the contradiction between the interest of the separate individual or the individual family and the communal interest of all individuals who have intercourse with one another . . . as long as a cleavage exists between the particular and the common interest, as long therefore as activity is not voluntarily, but naturally, divided, man's own deed becomes an alien power opposed to him, which enslaves him instead of being controlled by him.[57]

Under these circumstances, the structural institutions and practices previously considered sacred begin to break down. This erosion begins to occur when those in power overestimate their position. The factory owner or capitalist, for instance, believes that his profit contributes to the common good, a notion shared by his peers. Believing their own propaganda, they continue to act in a profit-seeking manner. Workers, on the other hand, may not concur in this perception, and may feel that they are unjustly exploited by this profit motive. This imposition of power can result in the unification of workers previously divided by individual interests. Marx states: "Competition drives their interest. But the maintenance of wages, this common interest which they have against the boss, united them in common thought of resistance—combination [which] has a double aim, that of stopping the competition among themselves in order to bring about general competition with the capitalist." [58]

Edmund Wilson's account of the organizing of miners in the company town of Ward, West Virginia, in 1931 illustrates the development of a consciousness of dysfunction. By paying in company scrip, holding back two weeks' pay, and forcing residents to trade at the company store, the coal company virtually held the miners in a state of indentured servitude. Periodic layoffs had brought many of the people in Ward to the edge of starvation. At one point, 150 miners and their families marched to Charleston to appeal to the Governor. He commended the marchers, told them there was nothing he could do, and informed them that the company would open the mines the following week. When the mines did reopen, not all miners were taken back, however, and the leaders of the march were soon being evicted from their homes and having their furniture removed. Wilson recounts how these sanctions escalated the miner's consciousness of dysfunction:

Yesterday some of the younger men got sore and stopped the truck and brought a load of furniture back. It belonged to a young married man who had been one of the leaders of the hunger march and who had been laid off and turned out on that account.

This resistance frightened the constable: he was afraid something worse might happen. So he had a warrant served the next morning and arrested five of the miners, on the charge of interfering with an officer in the performance of his duty. They were sent to the Charleston jail, and their people are now angrier than before. Many of them have lived here all their lives, and they are

[57] Karl Marx, *The Poverty of Philosophy* (New York: International Publishers, n.d.), pp. 145–146.
[58] *Ibid.*, p. 145.

dismayed at being treated like poultry to be casually dumped out of their coops. They know they are human beings.[59]

Wilson also points out the important role of organizers in promoting, among the traditionally independent miners, a sense of their position vis-à-vis that of the power structure:

As for the [miners], they seem easygoing, good-humored and straightforward Southerners, so much in the old tradition of American backwoods independence that it is almost impossible to realize that they have actually been reduced to the condition of serfs. They themselves, in spite of much harsh experience, seem surprised at their position today. Some of them were Knights of Labor in the eighties of the last century, when labor had some reverberating victories. "I've lived in this hollow forty-two years," says one man, with wide serious eyes. "This country's gittin' corrupt! Under conditions, the President's agin' us and everybody." "If it wasn't for conditions," says another —the young man who has been put out of his house—"Ward would be a right good place to live."
But they are not without leadership. Recently men who came originally from their own hollows and were trained in their strikes of ten years ago, have again become active among them. . . .
The coal miners have hailed these organizers as wrecked sailors would a ship. They are men, and the organizers are men. And the operators—who are they? They are corporations, holding companies, interests; vice-presidents, stock-holders, boards of directors, a controversy with Pittsburgh, in the newspapers, over rates for freight to the Great Lakes, a franchise guaranteeing a monopoly of the Minneapolis docks: an office staff in a Charlestown office building.[60]

Finally, Wilson predicts how a coalition of self-interest between two elements of the power structure—the mine operators and the American Federation of Labor—will have the effect of uniting the workers in a common cause of opposition:

Last of all, prodded into activity, the John L. Lewis organization has come to life and has been sending representatives to West Virginia to try to sign the miners up. By a characteristic stroke, it has made with some of the operators in the northern part of the state an agreement which calls for a wage rate six cents lower than the wage of thirty-six cents a ton which is the average in the Kanawha field. This agreement means that the operators everywhere in West Virginia will have to lower their rates, and this means that the Kanawha miners will have to strike.[61]

[59] Edmund Wilson, "Frank Kenney's Coal Diggers," in *The American Earthquake* (Garden City, N.Y.: Doubleday and Co., Inc. [Anchor Books], 1964), p. 314.
[60] *Ibid.*, pp. 314–315.
[61] *Ibid.*, p. 321.

For both Durkheim and Marx, the excessive exercise of power in a given situation creates a common experience for members of the subordinate class—that of having an "illegitimate" set of norms imposed upon them. This experience may redefine the collective consciousness in a community or society. John Dewey noted that thinking occurs "when there has been some kind of blockage." [62] When activity is proceeding smoothly, he reasoned, there was no occasion or motivation to think. Karl Mannheim also observed that only in unstable situations can old conceptualizations be destroyed and replaced by new ones.[63] Under these circumstances —when the individual becomes aware that he shares a disadvantaged condition with others and begins to seek alternatives to this condition—we may say that a consciousness of dysfunction has occurred.

Thomas Kuhn, in his insightful analysis of the scientific enterprise, The Structure of Scientific Revolution, illustrates how the emergence of alternative modes of thought is correlated with a failure of "conventional wisdom." [64] Kuhn argues that in each science there exists a paradigm consisting of laws, models, and theories. This paradigm is the conscience collective that prepares a neophyte student for membership in the academic and scientific community. It is within the framework of this mode of thinking that empirical and theoretical research is undertaken. The paradigm of a specific period is the locus of scientific inquiry: in Kuhn's terminology, after a paradigm is established, "mopping up operations are what engage most scientists throughout their careers." [65] Thus, science becomes a puzzle-solving activity in that the articulation of a paradigm does not aim at the unexpected novelty. Scientific research, as such, is metaphorically a jigsaw puzzle in which, although the pieces are scattered, the existence of a solution is assured. The puzzle, as defined by the paradigm, is the phenomenon to be studied; theory is the box in which the puzzle is contained; method is the manner in which the puzzle is fitted together.

For Kuhn, paradigms are self-perpetuating until they can no longer solve significant problems. Each paradigm, once established, provides the framework for scientific research and pedagogical activity to the exclusion of other possible world views, thus creating a group of scientific adherents to that specific paradigm. To return to our metaphor of the jigsaw puzzle, the loss of a piece of the puzzle or the inclusion of a foreign element by the manufacturer can create new and unacceptable results. "Discovery

---

[62] John Dewey, quoted in Tamotsu Shibutani, *Society and Personality: On Interactionist Approach to Social Psychology* (Englewood Cliffs, N.J.: Prentice-Hall, Inc., 1961), p. 76.
[63] Karl Mannheim, *Ideology and Utopia: An Introduction to the Sociology of Knowledge* (London: Routledge and Kegan Paul Ltd., 1960), p. 64.
[64] Thomas S. Kuhn, *The Structure of Scientific Revolutions* (Chicago: University of Chicago Press, 1962).
[65] *Ibid.*, p. 24.

commences with the awareness of anomaly," writes Kuhn, "with the recognition that nature has somehow violated the paradigm-induced expectations that govern normal science." [66] Scientists may begin to lose faith and to consider alternatives, but rarely do they renounce the paradigm which led them into the crisis. Many modifications and searches will be initiated within the framework of the old paradigm. It is during this time that innovators come to the fore, each with his own assumptions and "claims to truth." Eventually, a new or complementary paradigm will redefine and create a new systematic world view.

The above process is equally true of any social system. The conscience collective can be viewed as a paradigm accepted by the populace. Only when faced with new crisis which the old paradigm cannot solve does a consciousness of dysfunction take place. Chalmers Johnson, employing the functionalist model, presents the following argument:

. . . society can best be understood as a functionally integrated system. In such a system, if one of the various component structures does not function in the way that it must in order to maintain equilibrium, then first the affected substructure and then, if no remedial action occurs, the entire system will move out of equilibrium. The condition that causes the disequilibrium, and that demands remedial action in order to restore or create a new equilibrium, we call dysfunction.[67]

Johnson further argues that the existence of this dysfunction, in combination with an inability of the elite to cope with necessary sociopolitical changes through nonviolent means and the presence of an "accelerator of dysfunction" can lead to a revolution or social change.[68]

Consciousness of dysfunction is similar to the notion of a "class in itself," that is, awareness of others possessing like interests in a common situation. This perception of the problem situation does not necessarily suggest a course of action. Response at the individual level may be varied, ranging from withdrawal to aggression. Collectively, the mode of adaptation to this awareness can result in emotional contagion and lead to riots, mob action, and other forms of spontaneous outbursts such as the Luddites' destruction of machines. On another plane, an aggregate may attempt legitimate manipulation of sanctioned institutions using conventional means. Jurisdictional disputes, interpretation of existing law, and individual participation in established political parties are evidences of this phenomenon. The following news item about a "women's food revolt" in Phoenix illustrates such a legitimate, and hence nonrevolutionary, response to a consciousness of dysfunction.

[66] *Ibid.*, pp. 52–53.
[67] Chalmers Johnson, *Revolution and the Social System* (Stanford, Calif.: Stanford University, Hoover Institute, 1964), p. 5.
[68] *Ibid.*, p. 12.

San Francisco Chronicle, (*October 14, 1967*), *p. 40. Associated Press, Phoenix, Arizona.* © *1967 by the Associated Press.*

"THE WOMEN'S FOOD REVOLT—A YEAR LATER"

It has been a year since Phoenix housewives launched an attack on food prices that mushroomed into nationwide consumer protests.

The only thing left today is a frozen loaf of bread, newspaper clippings, higher food bills and a hundred memories.

The movement started when two sisters, Mrs. Earl Friedman, 28, and Mrs. George Donaldson, 25, decided that it was time to do something about spiraling food prices.

They organized, and copyrighted the Housewives' Voice for Lower Prices.

The group's chief spokesman was an attractive mother of two, Mrs. Robert Weleba, who says today she won't try it again.

Starting with a "speak now or forever pay the price" motto, the women first launched a bread boycott.

"It was tremendously successful," Mrs. Weleba said. "We got the price down to 25 cents a loaf by boycotting the grocers' 29-cent loaves."

The group held rallies, passed out flour and bread recipes and generally gave grocers headaches.

The program grew and grew. Mrs. Weleba said she received hundreds of phone calls a day and night, a landslide of mail and she organized 13 out-of-state chapters by phone.

But the action slowed down, the group raised its sights to protest the games, stamps and gimmicks offered by supermarkets.

"We found these always meant a 2-3 per cent rise in the price of food," Mrs. Weleba said.

But the women gave it all up when splinter groups formed, politics entered, and the founders' families suffered.

"It was really a matter of conscience," Mrs. Weleba said. "We just exhausted ourselves and had to end the battle."

"Our husbands were happier, and despite the notoriety, we all became women of the house again," she said.

Another group took over the crusade under the name Homemakers Organized for Economy.

Led by Mrs. Bobby Griffith, it tried to change the scope of the protest.

"We felt we had to enter the political arena to get anything done about prices," she said. "But women aren't as comfortable reasoning with politicians. It was easier fighting a grocer with a breadpan in their hands."

But, she said it was definitely worth the time.

"We were just sorry our efforts went down the drain," she added.

A year later the group's original spokesman, Mrs. Weleba, said it did achieve one thing.

"If nothing else, it achieved awareness. It showed intelligent women could make a consumer protest known and heard," she said.

But she feels the nation-wide protest got out of hand at times.

"We felt the Denver pickets were undignified and unladylike. Picketing is not the way to protest," she said.

Mrs. Weleba said she guessed that was what made a Michigan psychology professor send her a questionnaire about the movement to help him find the "social phenomena" behind the protests.

Mrs. Weleba keeps only a few momentos of the hectic 6-week period.

She has a boxful of newspaper clippings and a rather flat loaf of bread in her freezer, the first of two loaves she baked when the ban-the-bread movement started.

Today she's working as director of personnel and public relations for the Phoenix General Hospital.

"I decided if you can't lick them, join them. I'm working to pay the higher food prices," she said.

In sum, the following sequence of factors leading to a consciousness of dysfunction is suggested: Individuals reify institutions and accept the status quo; blockage of interests at the individual level may lead to individual "pathology," such as crime. Acceleration of the division of labor creates increasing dissensus and social strain, leading those in power to formulate arbitrary norms which they attempt to impose on the subordinate class. This results in a negative set of experiences for this group, breaking down the conscience collective and leading to a redefinition of the situation. Awareness of dysfunction can in turn lead to several modes of individual or collective adaptation. At the individual level innovation or retreatism are observable. Collectively, riots, mobs, and other responses are evidenced. However, for a social movement to emerge a reference for mobilization must be added to this consciousness of dysfunction.

REFERENTS FOR MOBILIZATION

In order for a temporarily organized public to develop into a social movement, a referent for mobilization is essential. Without this element, prob-

lem-oriented collective behavior will not be directed at existing political relationships (a condition which we have discussed as essential to the organization of an ideology). To accomplish the goal of remedying a social problem, some referent for mobilization must be present to provide guidance and to channel the activities designed to alter the power relationships of the social system. Although riots, mobs, and spontaneous protests may be emergent collective phenomena, they generally lack direction and political purpose. For example, the Luddites' destruction of factory machines did little to alter the basic distribution of power in the primitive industrialism of the early nineteenth century. Similarly, race riots, in themselves, have little impact upon the power held by the ruling elite of any society.

Referents for mobilization are abstract or concrete models for emulation which are significant to the members of an emerging movement and which thus provide direction and leadership for it. Such referents may include significant individuals as well as existing or ideal (utopian) models of social organization. In terms of the former, our definition encompasses Max Weber's notion of "charisma" and Carlyle's view of "men of history." This form of leadership is most frequently found in cults and nationalistic movements where the individual leader becomes the symbol of the movement. Father Divine, Elijah Muhammad, and Mohandas Gandhi are but a few examples. Politically, both the Right and the Left have had their "charismatic" referents: Hitler, McCarthy, John Birch; Mao, Castro, Che Guevara.

The "significant individual" aspect of our definition, however, is not limited to charismatic leaders but also includes the past experiences of individual members of a given movement. These persons, trained and grounded in revolutionary philosophy, strategy, and tactics, serve to clarify the goals of the movement and to guide the activities of its members. In The Communist Manifesto, Marx and Engels suggest this role of the individual referent when they state that "they [members of the First International] have over the great mass of the proletariat the advantage of clearly understanding the line of march, the conditions, and the ultimate results of the proletarian movement." [69]

One form of individual referent may consist of political agitators and organizers coming from outside the immediate milieu of as yet undirected conflict. A classic statement of the external organizer and his role is found in Lenin's What Is To Be Done. For this Russian revolutionary, the proletariat was not and could not be "conscious" of the irreconcilable antagonisms of their interests. As such, workers were singularly engaged in "outbursts of desperation" and "trade union consciousness." What was needed was a "cry for justice." To rectify this, an organization of dedicated men had to be formed to "take up the political education of the

[69] Karl Marx and Frederick Engels, *The Communist Manifesto* (New York: International Publishers, 1948), p. 22.

working class and the development of political consciousness. . . ."[70] What was needed, then, were propagandists and agitators to create and furnish direction for "political consciousness."

The literature is replete with examples of the attempts of agitators and propagandists to enter given communities and mobilize individuals into some form of social action or social movement. For example, the Mississippi Summer Project of 1964 sent northern college student organizers into a specific subcultural milieu and attempted to motivate the residents to make their claims to political participation.[71] During the industrial conflicts of the 1930s, organizations such as the Commonwealth Labor College, Rand School, Brookwood Labor College, and various Marxist groups were militantly engaged in injecting their personnel into situations where labor strife was in progress. Tom Tippett, for example, of Brookwood Labor College—a socialist-oriented institution—took part in the Gastonia textile strike and many other conflicts in the coal and textile industries in the Southern states. Mother Bloor of the Communist Party similarly appeared anywhere "class struggle" was imminent. The Almanac Singers, a pro-Stalinist folk singing group, extolled the workers of unions from coast to coast to "take it easy, but take it." Howe and Coser, in their critical history of the Communist Party of the United States (CPUSA), suggest the importance of external referents for the Congress of Industrial Organizations (CIO) in the thirties: "At this time, it might be remembered, there was precious little glory and still less comfort in organizing for the CIO, and as a rule, only men moved by a conviction that unionization of mass-production industries was a step toward a larger social end were willing to take the risks that come with the job. Not many other people cared enough. . . ."[72] The caring or concerned persons were, of course, Communists and radicals of other persuasions. Sidney Lens describes the role of these radicals during the Red Decade as follows:

Standing on improvised soapboxes at factory gates or on platforms in meeting halls, they [Communists] made thousands of impassioned speeches condemning the moguls of industry. In urging a worker to join a union to end speed up or win a nickel an hour raise, they also reminded him how evil was the capitalist system. . . . They passed out leaflets, held organizing meetings, led strikes with a zeal that no one else could muster. . . . It is doubtful whether American labor would have experienced so forceful a resurgence without them or other radicals.[73]

[70] V. I. Lenin, *What Is To Be Done?* in *Collected Works*, vol. IV (New York: International Publishers, 1929), p. 139.
[71] Cf. "The New Radicals," *Johns Hopkins Magazine*, XVII (October 1965): 39–40.
[72] Irving Howe and Lewis Coser, *The American Communist Party: A Critical History* (Boston: Beacon Press, 1957), p. 371.
[73] Sidney Lens, *Radicalism in America* (New York: Thomas Y. Crowell and Co., 1967), p. 318.

It may be argued that the introduction of external organizers is merely a phase in an a priori social movement and that they do not constitute the referents for mobilization of an incipient social movement. This would be correct if, in fact, the ideology of a social movement had already been crystallized. However, we are discussing the role of outside organizers in injecting an ideology into a problem situation where some form of collective action is immanent. Selznick refers to this phenomenon as the "strategy of access," which entails the use of "techniques which transform organizationally skeletal operations into mass operations [movements]." [74] Recalling John L. Lewis' "ideological birddogs," Selznick suggests that they operated as: ". . . devices for establishing access to and control over unorganized sections of the population. In creating such weapons, the Communists seek to generate a useful 'mass' by transforming an unstructured segment . . . into one which has an established leadership and effective channels of communication and mobilization." [75]

Since the writing of The Communist Manifesto, revolutionaries ranging from Lenin and Sorel to Mao and Guevara have stressed the importance of access to the masses and have put forth universal revolutionary programs. Che Guevara, the Cuba guerrilla fighter killed in Bolivia, has outlined, in the following extracts from his handbook on revolutionary activity, a model for the strategy, tactics, and role of the revolutionary advocate of social change.

Che Guevara, "Guerrilla Strategy," "Guerrilla Tactics," and "The Guerrilla Fighter: Social Reformer," from Guerrilla Warfare (New York, Monthly Review Press, 1961), pp. 20–23, 23–29, 43–45. © 1961 by Monthly Review Press. Reprinted by permission of Monthly Review Press.

GUERRILLA STRATEGY

In guerrilla terminology, strategy is understood as the analysis of the objectives to be achieved in the light of the total military situation and the overall ways of reaching these objectives.

To have a correct strategic appreciation from the point of view of the guerrilla band, it is necessary to analyze fundamentally what will be the enemy's mode of action. If the final objective is always the complete destruction of the opposite force, the enemy is confronted in the case of

---

[74] Philip Selznick, The Organizational Weapon: A Study of Bolshevik Strategy and Tactics (New York: The Free Press, 1960), p. 101.
[75] Ibid., p. 171.

a civil war of this kind with the standard task: he will have to achieve the total destruction of each one of the components of the guerrilla band. The guerrilla fighter, on the other hand, must analyze the resources which the enemy has for trying to achieve that outcome: the means in men, in mobility, in popular support, in armaments, in capacity of leadership on which he can count. We must make our own strategy adequate on the basis of these studies, keeping in mind always the final objective of defeating the enemy army.

There are fundamental aspects to be studied: the armament, for example, and the manner of using this armament. The value of a tank, of an airplane in a fight of this type must be weighed. The arms of the enemy, his ammunition, his habits must be considered; because the principal source of provision for the guerrilla force is precisely in enemy armaments. If there is a possibility of choice, we should prefer the same type as that used by the enemy, since the greatest problem of the guerrilla band is the lack of ammunition, which the opponent must provide.

After the objectives have been fixed and analyzed, it is necessary to study the order of the steps leading to the achievement of the final objective. This should be planned in advance, even though it will be modified and adjusted as the fighting develops and unforeseen circumstances arise.

At the outset, the essential task of the guerrilla fighter is to keep himself from being destroyed. Little by little it will be easier for the members of the guerrilla band or bands to adapt themselves to their form of life and to make flight and escape from the forces that are on the offensive an easy task, because it is performed daily. When this condition is reached, the guerrilla, having taken up inaccessible positions out of reach of the enemy, or having assembled forces that deter the enemy from attacking, ought to proceed to the gradual weakening of the enemy. This will be carried out at first at those points nearest to the points of active warfare against the guerrilla band and later will be taken deeper into enemy territory, attacking his communications, later attacking or harassing his bases of operation and his central bases, tormenting him on all sides to the full extent of the capabilities of the guerrilla forces.

The blows should be continuous. The enemy soldier in a zone of operations ought not to be allowed to sleep; his outposts ought to be attacked and liquidated systematically. At every moment the impression ought to be created that he is surrounded by a complete circle. In wooded and broken areas this effort should be maintained both day and night; in open zones that are easily penetrated by enemy patrols, at night only. In order to do all this the absolute cooperation of the people and a perfect knowledge of the ground is necessary. These two necessities affect every minute of the life of the guerrilla fighter. Therefore, along with centers for study of present and future zones of operations, intensive popular work must be undertaken to explain the motives of the revolution, its ends, and to spread the incontrovertible truth that victory of the enemy against the people is finally possible. *Whoever does not feel this undoubted truth cannot be a guerrilla fighter.*

This popular work should at first be aimed at securing secrecy; that is, each peasant, each member of the society in which action is taking place, will be asked not to mention what he sees and hears; later, help will be sought from inhabitants whose loyalty to the revolution offers greater guarantees; still later, use will be made of these persons in missions of contact, for transporting goods or arms, as guides in the zones familiar to them; still later, it is possible to arrive at organized mass action in the centers of work, of which the final result will be the general strike.

The strike is a most important factor in civil war, but in order to reach it a series of complementary conditions are necessary which do not always exist and which very rarely come to exist spontaneously. It is necessary to create these essential conditions, basically by explaining the purposes of the revolution and by demonstrating the forces of the people and their possibilities.

It is also possible to have recourse to certain very homogeneous groups, which must have shown their efficacy previously in less dangerous tasks, in order to make use of another of the terrible arms of the guerrilla band, sabotage. It is possible to paralyze entire armies, to suspend the industrial life of a zone, leaving the inhabitants of a city without factories, without light, without water, without communications of any kind, without being able to risk travel by highway except at certain hours. If all this is achieved, the morale of the enemy falls, the morale of his combatant units weakens and the fruit ripens for plucking at a precise moment.

All this presupposes an increase in the territory included within the guerrilla action, but an excessive increase of this territory is to be avoided. It is essential always to preserve a strong base of operations and to continue strengthening it during the course of the war. Within this territory, measures of indoctrination of the inhabitants of the zone should be utilized; measures of quarantine should be taken against the irreconcilable enemies of the revolution; all the purely defensive measures, such as trenches, mines, and communications, should be perfected.

When the guerrilla band has reached a respectable power in arms and in number of combatants, it ought to proceed to the formation of new columns. This is an act similar to that of the beehive when at a given moment it releases a new queen, who goes to another region with a part of the swarm. The mother hive with the most notable guerrilla chief, will stay in the less dangerous places, while the new columns will penetrate other enemy territories following the cycle already described.

A moment will arrive in which the territory occupied by the columns is too small for them; and in the advance toward regions solidly defended by the enemy, it will be necessary to confront powerful forces. At that instant the columns join, they offer a compact fighting front, and a war of positions is reached, a war carried on by regular armies. However, the former guerrilla army cannot cut itself off from its base, and it should create new guerrilla bands behind the enemy acting in the same way as the original bands operated earlier, proceeding thus to penetrate enemy territory until it is dominated.

It is thus that guerrillas reach the stage of attack, of the encirclement of fortified bases, of the defeat of reinforcements, of mass action, ever more ardent, in the whole national territory, arriving finally at the objective of the war: victory.

GUERRILLA TACTICS

In military language, tactics are the practical methods of achieving the grand strategic objectives.

In one sense they complement strategy and in another they are more specific rules within it. As means, tactics are much more variable, much more flexible than the final objectives, and they should be adjusted continually during the struggle. There are tactical objectives that remain constant throughout a war and others that vary. The first thing to be considered is the adjusting of guerrilla action to the action of the enemy.

The fundamental characteristic of a guerrilla band is mobility. This permits it in a few minutes to move far from a specific theatre and in a few hours far even from the region, if that becomes necessary; permits it constantly to change front and avoid any type of encirclement. As the circumstances of the war require, the guerrilla band can dedicate itself exclusively to fleeing from an encirclement which is the enemy's only way of forcing the band into a decisive fight that could be unfavorable, it can also change the battle into a counter-encirclement (small bands of men are presumably surrounded by the enemy when suddenly the enemy is surrounded by stronger contingents of men located in a safe place serve as a lure, leading to the encirclement and annihilation of the entire troops and supply of an attacking force). Characteristic of this war of mobility is the so-called minuet, named from the analogy with the dance: the guerrilla bands encircle an enemy position, an advancing column for example; they encircle it completely from the four points of the compass, with five or six men in each place, far enough away to avoid being encircled themselves; the fight is started at any one of the points, and the army moves toward it; the guerrilla band then retreats, always maintaining visual contact, and initiates its attack from another point. The army will repeat its action and the guerrilla band the same. Thus, successively, it is possible to keep an enemy column immobilized, forcing it to expend large quantities of ammunition and weakening the morale of its troops without incurring great dangers.

This same tactic can be applied at night time, closing in more and showing greater aggressiveness, because in these conditions counter-encirclement is much more difficult. Movement by night is another important characteristic of the guerrilla band, enabling it to advance into position for an attack and, where the danger of betrayal exists, to mobilize in new territory. The numerical inferiority of the guerrilla makes it necessary that attacks always be carried out by surprise; this great advantage is what permits the guerrilla fighter to inflict losses on the enemy without suffering losses. In a fight between a hundred men on one side and ten on the other, losses are not equal where there is one casualty on each side. The enemy loss is always reparable; it amounts to only one percent of his effectives. The loss of the guerrilla band requires more time to be repaired because it involves a soldier of high specialization and is ten percent of the operating forces.

A dead soldier of the guerrillas ought never to be left with his arms and ammunition. The duty of every guerrilla soldier whenever a companion falls is to recover immediately these extremely precious elements of the fight. In fact, the care which must be taken of ammunition and the method of using it are further characteristics of guerrilla warfare. In any combat between a regular force and a guerrilla band it is always possible to know one from the other by their different manner of fire: a great amount of firing on the part of the regular army, sporadic and accurate shots on the part of the guerrillas.

Once one of our heroes, now dead, had to employ his machine guns for nearly five minutes, burst after burst, in order to slow up the advance of enemy soldiers. This fact caused considerable confusion in our forces, because they assumed from the rhythm of fire that this key position must have been taken by the enemy, since this was one of the rare occasions where departure from the rule of saving fire had been called for because of the importance of the point being defended.

Another fundamental characteristic of the guerrilla soldier is his flexibility, his ability to adapt himself to all circumstances, and to convert to his service all of the accidents of the action. Against the rigidity of classical methods of fighting, the guerrilla fighter invests his own tactics at every minute of the fight and constantly surprises the enemy.

In the first place, there are only elastic positions, specific places that the enemy cannot pass, and places of diverting him. Frequently the enemy, after easily overcoming difficulties in a gradual advance, is surprised to find himself suddenly and solidly detained without possibilities of moving forward. This is due to the fact that the guerrilla-defended positions, when they have been selected on the basis of a careful study of the ground, are invulnerable. It is not the number of attacking soldiers.

Once that number has been placed there, it can nearly always hold off a battalion with success. It is a major task of the chiefs to choose well the moment and the place for defending a position without retreat.

The form of attack of a guerrilla army is also different; starting with surprise and fury, irresistible, it suddenly converts itself into total passivity.

The surviving enemy, resting, believes that the attacker has departed; he begins to relax, to return to the routine life of the camp or of the fortress, when suddenly a new attack bursts forth in another place, with the same characteristics, while the main body of the guerrilla band lies in wait to intercept reinforcements. At other times an outpost defending the camp will be suddenly attacked by the guerrilla, dominated, and captured. The fundamental thing is surprise and rapidity of attack.

Acts of sabotage are very important. It is necessary to distinguish clearly between sabotage, a revolutionary and highly effective method of warfare, and terrorism, a measure that is generally ineffective and indiscriminate in its results, since it often makes victims of innocent people and destroys a large number of lives that would be valuable to the revolution. Terrorism should be considered a valuable tactic when it is used to put to death some noted leader of the oppressing forces well known for his cruelty, his efficiency in repression, or other quality that makes his elimination useful. But the killing of persons of small importance is never advisable, since it brings on an increase of reprisals, including deaths.

There is one point very much in controversy in opinions about terrorism. Many consider that its use, by provoking police oppression, hinders all more or less legal or semi-clandestine contact with the masses and makes impossible unification for actions that will be necessary at a critical moment. This is correct; but it also happens that in a civil war the repression by the governmental power in certain towns is already so great that, in fact, every type of legal action is suppressed already, and any action of the masses that is not supported by arms is impossible. It is therefore necessary to be circumspect in adopting methods of this type and to consider the consequences that they may bring for the revolution. At any rate, well-managed sabotage is always a very effective arm, though it should not be employed to put means of production out of action, leaving a sector of the population paralyzed (and thus without work) unless this paralysis affects the normal life of the society. It is ridiculous to carry out sabotage against a soft drink factory, but it is absolutely correct and advisable to carry out sabotage against a power plant. In the first case, a certain number of workers are put out of a job but nothing is done to modify the rhythm of industrial life; in the second case, there will again be displaced workers, but this is entirely justified by the paralysis of the life of the region. We will return to the technique of sabotage later.

One of the favorite arms of the enemy army, supposed to be decisive in modern times, is aviation. Nevertheless, this has no use whatsoever during the period that guerrilla warfare is in its first stages, with small concentrations of men in rugged places. The utility of aviation lies in the systematic destruction of visible and organized defenses; and for this there must be large concentrations of men who construct these defenses, something that does not exist in this type of warfare. Planes are also potent against marches by columns through level places or places without cover; however, this latter danger is easily avoided by carrying out the marches at night.

One of the weakest points of the enemy is transportation by road and railroad. It is virtually impossible to maintain a vigil yard by yard over a transport line, a road, or a railroad. At any point a considerable amount of explosive charge can be planted that will make the road impassable; or by exploding it at the moment that a vehicle passes, a considerable loss in lives and material to the enemy is caused at the same time that the road is cut.

The sources of explosives are varied. They can be brought from other zones; or use can be made of bombs seized from the dictatorship, though these do not always work; or they can be manufactured in secret laboratories within the guerrilla zone. The technique of setting them off is quite varied; their manufacture also depends upon the conditions of the guerrilla band.

In our laboratory we made powder which we used as a cap, and we invented various devices for exploding the mines at the desired moment. The ones that gave the best results were electric. The first mine that we exploded was a bomb dropped from an aircraft of the dictatorship. We adapted it by inserting various caps and adding a gun with the trigger pulled by a cord. At the moment that an enemy truck passed the weapon was fired to set off the explosion.

These techniques can be developed to a high degree. We have information in Algeria, for example, tele-explosive mines, that is, mines exploded by radio at great distances from the point where they are located, are being used today against the French colonial power.

The technique of lying in ambush along roads in order to explode mines and annihilate survivors is one of the most remunerative in point of ammunition and arms. The surprised enemy does not use his ammunition and has no time to flee; so with a small expenditure of ammunition large results are achieved.

As blows are dealt the enemy, he also changes his tactics, and in place of isolated trucks, veritable motorized columns move. However, by choosing the ground well, the same result can be produced by breaking the column and concentrating forces on one vehicle. In these cases the essential elements of guerrilla tactics must always be kept in mind. These are: perfect knowledge of the ground; surveillance and foresight as to the lines of escape; vigilance over all the secondary roads that can bring support to the point of attack; intimacy with people in the zone so as to have sure help from them in respect to supplies, transport, and temporary or permanent hiding places if it becomes necessary to leave wounded companions behind; numerical superiority at a chosen point of action; total mobility; and the possibility of counting on reserves.

If all these tactical requisites are fulfilled, surprise attack along the lines of communication of the enemy yields notable dividends.

A fundamental part of guerrilla tactics is the treatment accorded the people of the zone. Even the treatment accorded the enemy is important; the norm to be followed should be an absolute inflexibility at the time of attack, and absolute inflexibility toward all the despicable elements that resort to informing and assassination, and clemency as absolute as possible toward the enemy soldiers who go into the fight performing or believing that they perform a military duty. It is a good policy, so long as there are no considerable bases of operations and invulnerable places, to take no prisoners. Survivors ought to be set free. The wounded should be cared for with all possible resources at the time of the action. Conduct toward the civil population ought to be regulated by a large respect for all the rules and traditions of the people of the zone, in order to demonstrate effectively, with deeds, the moral superiority of the guerrilla fighter over the oppressing soldier. Except in special situations, there ought to be no execution of justice without giving the criminal an opportunity to clear himself.

THE GUERRILLA FIGHTER: SOCIAL REFORMER

We have already described the guerrilla fighter as one who shares the longing of the people for liberation and who, once peaceful means are exhausted, initiates the fight and converts himself into an armed vanguard of the fighting people. From the very beginning of the struggle he has the intention of destroying an unjust order and therefore an intention, more or less hidden, to replace the old with something new.

We have also already said that in the conditions that prevail, at least in America and in almost all countries with deficient economic development, it is the countryside that offers ideal conditions for the fight. Therefore the foundation of the social structure that the guerrilla fighter will build begins with changes in the ownership of agrarian property.

The banner of the fight throughout this period will be agrarian reform. At first this goal may or may not be completely delineated in its extent and limits; it may simply refer to the age-old hunger of the peasant for the land on which he works or wishes to work.

The conditions in which the agrarian reform will be realized depend upon the conditions which existed before the struggle began, and on the social depth of the struggle. But the guerrilla fighter, as a person conscious of a role in the vanguard of the people, must have a moral conduct that shows him to be a true priest of the reform to which he aspires. To the stoicism imposed by the difficult conditions of warfare should be added an austerity born of rigid self-control that will prevent a single excess, a single slip, whatever the circumstances. The guerrilla soldier should be an ascetic.

As for social relations, these will vary with the developments of the war. At the beginning it will not be possible to attempt any changes in the social order.

Merchandise that cannot be paid for in cash will be paid for with bonds; and these should be redeemed at the first opportunity.

The peasant must always be helped technically, economically, morally, and culturally. The guerrilla fighter will be a sort of guiding angel who has fallen into the zone, helping the poor always and bothering the rich as little as possible in the first phases of the war. But this war will continue on its course; contradictions will continuously become sharper; the moment will arrive when many of those who regarded the revolution with a certain sympathy at the outset will place themselves in a position diametrically opposed; and they will take the first step into battle against the popular forces. At that moment the guerrilla fighter should act to make himself into the standard bearer of the cause of the people, punishing every betrayal with justice. Private property should acquire in the war zones its social function. For example, excess land and livestock not essential for the maintenance of a wealthy family should pass into the hands of the people and be distributed equitably and justly.

The right of the owners to receive payment for possessions used for the social good ought always to be respected: but this payment will be made in bonds ("bonds of hope," as they were called by our teacher, General Bayo,[76] referring to the common interest that is thereby established between debtor and creditor).

The land and property of notorious and active enemies of the revolution should pass immediately into the hands of the revolutionary forces. Furthermore, taking advantage of the heat of the war—those moments in which human fraternity reaches its highest intensity—all kinds of cooperative work, as much as the mentality of the inhabitants will permit, ought to be stimulated.

[76] Colonel Alberto Bayo, a Cuban veteran of guerrilla warfare in Spain, served as instructor of the forces assembled by Fidel Castro in Mexico for training prior to the invasion of Cuba in December 1956.

The guerrilla fighter as a social reformer should not only provide an example in his own life but he ought also constantly to give orientation in ideological problems, explaining what he knows and what he wishes to do at the right time. He will also make use of what he learns as the months or years of the war strengthen his revolutionary convictions, making him more radical as the potency of arms is demonstrated, as the outlook of the inhabitants becomes a part of his spirit and of his own life, and as he understands the justice and the vital necessity of a series of changes, of which the theoretical importance appeared to him before, but devoid of practical urgency.

This development occurs very often, because the initiators of guerrilla warfare, or rather the directors of guerrilla warfare, are not men who have bent their backs day after day over the furrow. They are men who understand the necessity for changes in the social treatment accorded peasants, without having suffered in the usual case this bitter treatment in their own persons. It happens then (I am drawing on the Cuban experience and enlarging it) that a genuine interaction is produced between these leaders, who with their acts teach the people the fundamental importance of the armed fight, and the people themselves who rise in rebellion and teach the leaders these practical necessities of which we speak. Thus, as a product of this interaction between the guerrilla fighter and his people, a progressive radicalization appears which further accentuates the revolutionary characteristics of the movement and gives it a national scope.

Another referent for mobilization is the external ideal model (either abstract or concrete). As an illustration of an abstract model, one of the principles of utopian socialism (as typified by Fourier and Owen) suggested that the creation of a model society would motivate others to emulate it. As Harbison indicates: "Fourier hoped that the principle of 'association' would build communities, then federate them in larger groups which would pyramid up to a world confederation." [77] Similar abstract (utopian) ideals are Stalin's "one socialist state" and Lenin's "victory of revolution in one country." The important element in Stalin's concept is that the rise of the U.S.S.R. would illustrate to the international proletariat of the nonsocialist countries the superiority of a system based on the tenets of Marxist-Leninism. For Lenin, the successful revolution would spread: "In the country where it is victorious, the revolution must regard itself not as a self-sufficient quantity, but as a support, a

[77] E. Harris Harbison, "Socialism in European History to 1848," in Donald Egbert and Stow Persons, eds., *Socialism in American Life*, vol. I (Princeton, N.J.: Princeton University Press, 1952), p. 46.

means for hastening the victory of the proletariat in all countries." [78] In terms of the American Communist movement, James P. Cannon took up Lenin's model: "Soviet Russia is not a 'country.' [It] is a part of the world labor movement. Soviet Russia is a strike—the greatest strike in all history. When the working class of Europe and America join that strike it will be the end of capitalism." [79]

Several illustrations of "concrete" models as referents for mobilization may also be given. Noyes, in the History of American Socialism, views "phalanxes"—model socialist communities—as providing referents for those conscious of dysfunction.[80] The October Revolution of 1917 had a similar impact, as Draper observes: "The impact of the Bolshevik Revolution on the American Left Wing was stunning. It was as if some Left Wing Socialists had gone to sleep and had awakened as Communists." [81] The advent of the so-called hippie movement provides an excellent example of how an idealized style of life can act as a model for nonadherents. The hippie phenomenon began in the Haight-Ashbury district of San Francisco. The hippies did not desire an explicit change in society; but rather, they were engaged in establishing a life style they considered superior to that of the "organization men" or the "straights." In part, their style of life, clothing, and musical tastes have been emulated by college students and many others in American society, including the wealthy dowagers of Park Avenue. In the following article, Warren Hinckle describes the genesis of the hippie movement and its impact upon the social order.

Excerpts from Warren Hinckle, "The Social History of the Hippies," Ramparts, 5 (March 1967), 9–11, 17–20, 26. Reprinted by permission of Ramparts.

Where was Allen Ginsberg, father goddam to two generations of the underground? In New York, reading his poetry to freshmen. And where was Timothy Leary, self-styled guru to tens or is it hundreds of thousands of turned-on people? Off to some nowhere place like Stockton, to preach

---

[78] V. I. Lenin, *The Theory of the Proletarian Revolution* (New York: International Publishers, 1936), p. 85.
[79] James P. Cannon, *The Fifth Year of the Russian Revolution* (New York: Workers Party of America, 1923), p. 21.
[80] John H. Noyes, *History of American Socialism* (New York: Hilary House Publishers, Ltd., 1961), p. 91. In discussing Owen, Noyes states, "His business was to seed the world, and especially this country, with unquenchable desire and hope of Communism. . . ." Cf. p. 33.
[81] Theodore Draper, *The Roots of American Communism* (New York: Viking Press, 1957), p. 101.

the gospel of Lysergic Acid Diethylamide to nice ladies in drip dry dresses.

The absence of the elder statesmen of America's synthetic gypsy movement meant something. It meant that the leaders of the booming psychedelic bohemia in the seminal city of San Francisco were their own men—and strangely serious men, indeed, for hippies. Ginsberg and Leary may be Pied Pipers, but they are largely playing old tunes. The young men who make the new scene accept Ginsberg as a revered observer from the elder generation; Leary they abide as an Elmer Gantry on their side, to be used for proselytizing squares, only.

The mountain symposium had been called for the extraordinary purpose of discussing the political future of the hippies. Hippies are many things, but most prominently the bearded and beaded inhabitants of the Haight-Ashbury, a little psychedelic city-state edging Golden Gate Park. There, in a daily street-fair atmosphere, upwards of 15,000 unbonded girls and boys interact in a tribal, love-seeking, free-swinging, acid-based type of society where, if you are a hippie and you have a dime, you can put it in a parking meter and lie down in the street for an hour's suntan (30 minutes for a nickel) and most drivers will be careful not to run you over.

Speaking, sometimes all at once, inside the Sierra cabin were many voices of conscience and vision of the Haight-Ashbury—belonging to men who, except for their Raggedy Andy hair, paisley shirts and pre-mod western levi jackets, sounded for all the world like Young Republicans.

They talked about reducing governmental controls, the sanctity of the individual, the need for equality among men. They talked, very seriously, about the kind of society they wanted to live in, and the fact that if they wanted an ideal world they would have to go out and make it for themselves, because nobody, least of all the government was going to do it for them.

The utopian sentiments of these hippies were not to be put down lightly. Hippies have a clear vision of the ideal community—a psychedelic community, to be sure—where everyone is turned on and beautiful and loving and happy and floating free. But it is a vision that, despite the Alice in Wonderland phraseology hippies usually breathlessly employ to describe it, necessarily embodies a radical political philosophy: communal life, drastic restriction of private property, rejection of violence, creativity before consumption, freedom before authority, de-emphasis of government and traditional forms of leadership.

Despite a disturbing tendency to quietism, all hippies *ipso facto* have a political posture—one of unremitting opposition to the Establishment which insists on branding them criminals because they take LSD and marijuana, and hating them, anyway, because they enjoy sleeping nine in a room and three to a bed, seem to have free sex and guiltless minds, and can raise healthy children in dirty clothes.

The hippie choice of weapons is to love the Establishment to death rather than protest it or blow it up (hippies possess a confounding disconcern about traditional political methods or issues). But they are decidedly and forever outside the Consensus on which this society places such a premium, and since the hippie scene is so much the scene of those people under 25 that Time magazine warns will soon constitute half our population, this is a significant political fact.

This is all very solemn talk about people who like to skip rope and wear bright colors, but after spending some time with these fun and fey individuals you realize that, in a very unexpected way, they are as serious about what they're doing as the John Birch Society or the Junior League. It is not improbable, after a few more mountain seminars by those purposeful young men wearing beads, that the Haight-Ashbury may spawn the first utopian collectivist community since Brook Farm.

That this society finds it so difficult to take such rascally looking types seriously is no doubt the indication of a deep-rooted hang-up. But to comprehend the psychosis of America in the computer age, you have to know what's with the hippies.

[KEN KESEY—I]

Games people play, Merry Prankster Division

Let Us Go, then, on a trip.

You can't miss the Tripmaster: the thick-necked lad in the blue and white striped pants with the red belt and the golden eagle buckle, and watershed of wasted promise in his pale blue eyes, one front tooth capped in patriotic red, white and blue, his hair downy, flaxen, straddling the incredibly wide divide of his high forehead like two small toupees pasted on side-ways. Ken Kesey, Heir Apparent Number One to the grand American tradition of blowing one's artistic talent to do some other thing, was sitting in a surprisingly comfortable chair inside the bus with the psychedelic crust, puffing absentedmindedly on a harmonica.

The bus itself was ambulatory at about 50 miles an hour, jogging along a back road in sylvan Marin County, four loudspeakers turned all the way up, broadcasting both inside and outside Carl Orff's Carmina Burana and filled with two dozen people simultaneously smoking marijuana and looking for an open ice cream store. It was the Thursday night before the Summit Meeting weekend and Kesey, along with some 15 members of the turned-on yes men and women who call him "Chief" and whom he calls the "Merry Pranksters" in return, was demonstrating a "game" to a delegation of visiting hippie firemen.

Crossing north over the Golden Gate Bridge from San Francisco to Marin County to pay Kesey a state visit were seven members of The

Diggers, a radical organization even by Haight-Ashbury standards, which exists to give things away, free. The Diggers started out giving out free food, free clothes, free lodging and free legal advice, and hope eventually to create a totally free cooperative community. They had come to ask Kesey to get serious and attend the weekend meeting on the state of the nation of the hippies.

The dialogue had hardly begun, however, before Kesey loaded all comers into the bus and pushed off into the dark to search for a nocturnal ice-cream store. The bus, which may be the closest modern man has yet come to aping the self-sufficiency of Captain Nemo's submarine, has its own power supply and is equipped with instruments for a full rock band, microphones, loudspeakers, spotlights and comfortable seats all around. The Pranksters are presently installing microphones every three feet on the bus walls so everybody can broadcast to everybody else at once.

At the helm was the Intrepid Traveler, Ken Babbs, who is auxiliary chief of the Merry Pranksters when Kesey is out of town or incommunicado or in jail, all three of which he has recently been. Babbs, who is said to be the model for the heroes of both Kesey novels, *One Flew Over the Cuckoo's Nest* and *Sometimes a Great Notion*, picked up a microphone to address the guests in the rear of the bus, like the driver of a Grayline tour: "We are being followed by a police car. Will someone watch and tell me when he turns on his red light."

The law was not unexpected, of course, because any cop who sees Kesey's bus just about *has* to follow it, would probably end up with some form of professional D.T.'s if he didn't. It is part of the game: the cop was now playing on their terms, and Kesey and his Pranksters were delighted. In fact, a discernible wave of disappointment swept across the bus when the cop finally gave up chasing this particular U.F.O. and turned onto another road.

The games he plays are very important to Kesey. In many ways his intellectual rebellion has come full circle; he has long ago rejected the structured nature of society—the foolscap rings of success, conformity and acceptance "normal" people must regularly jump through. To the liberated intellect, no doubt, these requirements constitute the most sordid type of game. But, once rejecting all the norms of society, the artist is free to create his own structures—and along with any new set of rules, however personal, there is necessarily, the shell to the tortoise, a new set of games. In Kesey's case, at least, the games are usually fun. Running around the outside of an insane society, the healthiest thing you can do is laugh.

It helps to look at this sort of complicated if not confused intellectual proposition in bas relief, as if you were looking at the simple pictures on Wedgwood china. Stand Successful Author Ken Kesey off against, say, Successful Author Truman Capote. Capote, as long as his game is accepted by the system, is free to be as mad as he can. So he tosses the biggest, most vulgar ball in a long history of vulgar balls, and achieves the perfect idiot synthesis of the upper middle and lower royal classes. Kesey, who cares as much about the system as he does about the Eddie Cantor Memorial Forest, invents his own game. He purchases a pre-40's International Harvester school bus, paints it psychedelic, fills it with undistinguished though lovable individuals in varying stages of eccentricity, and drives brazenly down the nation's highways, high on LSD, watching and waiting for the cops to blow their minds.

At the least, Kesey's posture has the advantage of being intellectually consistent with the point of view of his novels. In *One Flew Over the Cuckoo's Nest*, he uses the setting of an insane asylum as a metaphor for what he considers to be the basic insanity, or at least the fundamentally bizarre illogic, of American society. Since the world forces you into a game that is both mad and unfair, you are better off inventing your own game. Then, at least, you have a chance of winning. At least that's what Kesey thinks. . . .

Meanwhile, in San Francisco, Allen Ginsberg remembers an evening in 1955 which could stand as well as any for the starting point of what was to become the most thorough repudiation of America's middlebrow culture since the expatriates walked out on the country in the 1930's. The vanguard of what was to be the Beat Generation had gathered at the 6 Gallery on Fillmore Street for a poetry reading moderated by Kenneth Rexroth, a respectable leftish intellectual who was later to become the Public Defender of the Beats. Lawrence Ferlinghetti was in the audience, and so were Kerouac and his then sidekick, Neal Cassady, listening to Michael McClure, Phil Lamantia, Gary Snyder and Philip Whalen read their poetry. Ginsberg was there too, and delighted everyone with a section of the still unfinished "Howl," better known to Beats as the Declaration of Independence.

Two distinct strains in the underground movement of the '50s were represented at this salient gathering. One was a distinctly fascist trend, embodied in Kerouac, which can be recognized by a totalitarian insistence on action and nihilism, and usually accompanied by a Superman concept. This strain runs, deeper and less silent, through the hippie scene today. It is into this fascist bag that you can put Kesey and his friends, the Hell's Angels, and, in a more subtle way, Dr. Timothy Leary.

The other, majority, side of the Beats was a cultural reaction to the existential brinkmanship forced on them by the Cold War, and a lively attack on the concurrent rhetoric of complacency and self-satisfaction that pervaded the literary establishment all the way from the Atlantic Monthly to Lionel Trilling. Led by men like Ginsberg and Ferlinghetti, the early Beats weighed America by its words and deeds, and found it pennyweight. They took upon themselves the role of conscience for the machine. They rejected all values and when, in attempting to carve a new creative force, they told America to "go fuck itself," America reacted, predictably, with an obscenity trial.

The early distant warnings of the drug-based culture that would dominate the Haight-Ashbury a decade later were there in the early days of North Beach. Marijuana was as popular as Coke at a Baptist wedding, and the available hallucinogens—peyote and mescaline—were part of the Beat rebellion. Gary Snyder, poet, mountain climber, formal Yamabushi Buddhist, and a highly respected leader of the hippie scene today, first experimented with peyote while living with the Indian tribe of the same name in 1948; Ginsberg first took it in New York in 1951; Lamantia, Kerouac and Cassady were turned on by Beat impresario Hymie D'Angolo at his Big Sur retreat in 1952. And Beat parties, whether they served peyote, marijuana or near beer, were rituals, community sacraments, setting the format for contemporary hippie rituals.

But the psychedelic community didn't really begin to flourish until late 1957 and 1958 in New York, and for that story we take you to Chester Anderson in the Village. . . .

According to Chester's files, LSD didn't arrive in any large, consumer-intended supply in the Village until the winter of 1961–62, and not in the Bay Area until the summer of 1964, but by that time something unusual had happened to America's psychedelic gypsies: they had become formal enemies of the State. Massive harassment by the cops in San Francisco, by the coffeehouse license inspectors in New York, had led the heads and the young middle class types who came in caravan proportions, to test the no-more-teachers, no-more-books way of bohemian life, to view the Establishment as the bad guy who would crush their individuality and spirituality in any way he could. This is the derivation of whatever political posture the hippies have today. It will be significant, of course, only if the Haight-Ashbury scene doesn't go the way of the Beat Generation—assimilated by a kick-hungry society. For the serious, literary Beats, it was all over but the shouting when the Co-existence Bagel Shop became a stop on sightseeing tours.

In 1962, the Village was pulsating with psychedelic evangelism. LSD was so cheap and so plentiful that it became a big thing among heads to turn on new people as fast as they could give LSD away.

Pot, also, was being used more widely than ever by middle class adults, and spread from the urban bohemias to the hinterlands by small folk music circles that were to be found everywhere from Jacksonville, Florida, to Wausau, Wisconsin. At the same time, almost the entire Village was treating LSD like it was a selection on a free lunch counter, and a scruffy folknik called Bobby Dylan was beginning to play charitable guest sets in the Washington Square coffeehouses. "Things," Chester said, "were happening more rapidly than we knew."

What was happening, Mr. Jones, was that folk music, under the influence of early acid culture, was giving way to rock and roll. Rock spread the hippie way of life like a psychedelic plague, and it metamorphosed in such rapid fashion from the popularity of folk music, that a very suspicious person might ask if seemingly safe groups like the Kingston Trio were not, in fact, the Red Guards of the hippie cultural revolution.

There was a rock and roll before, of course, but it was all bad seed. The likes of Frankie Avalon, Fabian and Elvis Presley sent good rock and roll musicians running to folk music. Then absolutely the world's greatest musical blitz fell and the Beatles landed, everywhere, all at once. The impact of their popular music was analogous to the Industrial Revolution of the 19th century. They brought music out of the juke box and into the street. The Beatles' ecstatic, alive, electric sound had a total sensory impact, and was inescapably participational. It was "psychedelic music." "The Beatles are a trip," Chester said. Whether the Beatles or Dylan or the Rolling Stones actually came to their style through psychedelic involvement (Kenneth Tynan says a recent Beatles song "Tomorrow Never Knows" is "the best musical evocation of LSD I've ever heard") is not as important as the fact that their songs reflect LSD values—love, life, getting along with other people, and that this type of involving, turn-on music galvanized the entire hippie underground into overt, brassy existence—particularly in San Francisco.

Drug song lyrics may, in fact, be the entire literary output of the hippie generation. The hippies' general disregard for anything as static as a book is a fact over which Chester Anderson and Marshall McLuhan can shake hands. For acid heads are, in McLuhan's phrase, "post-literate." Hippies do not share our written, linear society—they like textures better than surfaces, prefer the electronic to the mechanical, like group, tribal activities. Theirs is an ecstatic, do-it-now culture, and rock and roll is their art form. . . .

[THE MERCHANT PRINCES—II]

Where Dun & Bradstreet Fears to Tread

Allen Ginsberg asked 10,000 people to turn towards the sea and chant with him. They all did just that, and then picked up the papers and miscellaneous droppings on the turf of Golden Gate Park's Polo Field and went contentedly home. This was the end of the first Human Be-In, a gargantuan hippie happening held only for the joy of it in mid-January. The hippie tribes gathered under clear skies with rock bands, incense, chimes, flutes, feathers, candles, banners and drums. Even the Hell's Angels were on their good behaviour—announcing that they would guard the sound truck against unspecified evil forces. It was all so successful that the organizers are talking about another be-in this summer to be held at the bottom of the Grand Canyon with maybe 200,000 hippies being-in.

The local papers didn't quite know how to treat this one, except for the San Francisco Chronicle's ace society editor Frances Moffat, who ran through the crowd picking out local socialites and taking notes on the fashions.

Mrs. Moffat's intense interest reflects the very in, very marketable character of San Francisco Hippiedom. Relatively high-priced mod clothing and trinket stores are as common in the Haight-Ashbury as pissoirs used to be in Paris. They are run by hippie merchants mostly for square customers, but that doesn't mean that the hippies themselves aren't brand name conscious. Professing a distaste for competitive society, hippies are, contradictorily, frantic consumers. Unlike the Beats, they do not disdain money. Indeed, when they have it, which with many is often, they use it to buy something pretty or pleasureful. You will find only the best hi-fi sets in hippie flats.

In this commercial sense, the hippies have not only accepted assimilation (the Beats fought it, and lost), they have swallowed it whole. The hippie culture is in many ways a prototype of the most ephemeral aspects of the larger American society. If the people looking in from the suburbs want change, clothes, fun, and some lightheadedness from the new gypsies, the hippies are delivering—and some of them are becoming rich hippies because of it.

The biggest Robber Baron is dance promoter Bill Graham, a Jewish boy from New York who made it big in San Francisco by cornering the hippie bread and circuses concession. His weekend combination rock and roll dances and light shows at the cavernous, creaky old Fillmore Auditorium on the main street of San Francisco's Negro ghetto are jammed every night. Even Andy Warhol played the Fillmore. Although Graham is happy providing these weekend spiritual experiences, he's not trying to be a leader. "I don't want to make cadres, just money," he said. Graham's cross-town competitor is Chet Helms, a rimless-glasses variety hippie from Texas who has turned the pioneer, non-profit San Francisco rock group called The Family Dog, into a very profit-making enterprise at the Avalon Ballroom.

A side-product of the light show dances, and probably the only other permanent manifestation of hippie culture to date, is the revival in a gangbusters way of Art Nouveau poster art. Wes Wilson, who letters his poster in 18, 24 and 36 point Illegible, . . . originated the basic style in posters for the Fillmore dances. Graham found he could make as much money selling posters as dance tickets, so he is now in the poster business, too.

The posters, at $1 apiece, as common as window shades in the Haight-Ashbury, demand total involvement from the reader, and are thus considered psychedelic manifestations of the existential, non-verbal character of hippie culture. . . .

[EMMETT GROGAN—II]

A Psychedelic "Grapes of Wrath"

Every bohemian community has its inevitable coterie of visionaries who claim to know what it is all about. But The Diggers are, somehow, different. They are bent on creating a wholly cooperative subculture and, so far, they are not just hallucinating, they are doing it.

Free clothes (used) are there for whomever wants them. Free meals are served every day. Next, Grogan plans to open a smart mod clothing store on Haight Street and give the clothes away free, too (the hippie merchants accused him of "trying to undercut our prices"). He wants to start Digger farms where participants will raise their own produce. He wants to give away free acid, to eliminate junky stuff and profiteering. He wants cooperative living to forestall inevitable rent exploitation when the Haight-Ashbury becomes chic.

Not since Brook Farm, not since the Catholic Workers, has any group in this dreadfully co-optive, consumer society been so serious about a utopian community.

If Grogan succeeds or fails in the Haight-Ashbury will not be as important as the fact that he has tried. For he is, at least, providing the real possibility of what he calls "alternatives" in the down-the-rabbit-hole-culture of the hippies.

Grogan is very hung up on freedom. "Do your thing, be what you are, and nothing will ever bother you," he says. His heroes are the Mad Bomber of New York who blissfully blew up all kinds of things around Manhattan over 30 years because he just liked to blow things up, and poet Gary Snyder, whom he considers the "most important person in the Haight-Ashbury" because instead of sitting around sniffing incense and talking about it, he went off to Japan and became a Zen master. "He did it, man."

This is an interesting activist ethic, but it remains doubtful just what the hippies will do. Not that many, certainly, will join Grogan's utopia, because utopias, after all, have a size limit.

The New Left has been flirting with the hippies lately, even to the extent of singing "The Yellow Submarine" at a Berkeley protest rally, but it looks from here like a largely unrequited love.

The hip merchants will, of course, go on making money.

And the youngsters will continue to come to the Haight-Ashbury and do—what?

That was the question put to the hippie leaders at their Summit

Meeting. They resolved their goals, but not the means, and the loud noise you heard from outside was probably Emmett Grogan pounding the table with his shoe.

The crisis of the happy hippie ethic is precisely this: it is all right to turn on, but it is not enough to drop out. Grogan sees the issue in the gap "between the radical political philosophy of Jerry Rubin and Mario Savio and psychedelic love philosophy." He, himself, is not interested in the war in Vietnam, but on the other hand he does not want to spend his days like Ferdinand sniffing pretty flowers.

This is why he is so furious at the hip merchants. "They created the myth of this utopia: now they aren't going to do anything about it." Grogan takes the evils of society very personally, and he gets very angry, almost physically sick, when a pregnant 15-year-old hippie's baby starves in her stomach, a disaster which is not untypical in the Haight-Ashbury, and which Grogan sees being repeated ten-fold this summer when upwards of 200,000 migrant teenagers and college kids come, as a psychedelic "Grapes of Wrath," to utopia in search of the heralded turn-on.

The danger in the hippie movement is more than over-crowded streets and possible hunger riots this summer. If more and more youngsters begin to share the hippie political posture of unrelenting quietism, the future of activist, serious politics is bound to be affected. The hippies have shown that it can be pleasant to drop out of the arduous task of attempting to steer a difficult, unrewarding society. But when that is done, you leave the driving to the Hell's Angels.

Internationally, the Cuban experience, like the Bolshevik Revolution, provides a model for revolutionary change in Latin America. Professor Irving Horowitz discusses Cuba's role as a model in the Western hemisphere in the following paper.

Irving Louis Horowitz, "Cuban Communism," TRANS-action, 4 (October 1967), 7–15, 55–57. Reprinted by permission of I. L. Horowitz and the Washington University Press. © 1967 by TRANS-action magazine, St. Louis, Mo.

Cuba today is restless and righteous. Her restlessness derives from a universal heating up of the Cold War, over which she has seemingly little control; while her righteousness stems from a feeling that she has made the first socialist revolution for Third World countries to emulate. The idea of Cuba's being absent from current news, of her disappearance behind a wall of legality erected by the Organization of American States, is not indicative of the dynamics within Cuban society.

On July 26 of this year, the Organization of Latin American Solidarity (O.L.A.S.) convened in Havana. For Fidel Castro and his partisans, not merely in Latin America but throughout the world, July 26 is the founding day of the Cuban Revolution. This paramount anniversary commemorates Castro's assault on the Moncada Barracks in 1953. Despite his speedy capture and imprisonment then, he has continued to celebrate this first strike against the dictatorship of Fulgencio Batista. Castro came to power as leader of the 26th of July Movement, and every year since, the country has turned out for parades and speeches and has had a day off from work on July 26.

In his speech welcoming the O.L.A.S. delegates, Castro momentously echoed Karl Marx: "A specter is haunting the continent. It is the specter of the Organization of Latin American Solidarity, and this specter is causing insomnia among the reactionaries, imperialists, henchmen, *gorilas* [militarists], and exploiters." In fact, however, the Fidelista specter seems to be haunting the communists of the Western world. For Castro's remarks promptly elicited a stinging response from leading Chilean communist, Luis Corvalan, a response that appeared in *Pravda*, the leading newspaper of the Soviet Communist Party. Corvalan warned: "Any effort by communists to impose their views on other ranks of the anti-imperialist forces does not help the achievement of unity." He added, "Lenin warned against the danger of adventurism, which as a rule results in the loss of precious lives of revolutionaries and the retreat of the movement." What is more, the roster of those absent from the O.L.A.S. meeting is striking. Along with Corvalan, other old-guard Chilean communists boycotted the convention, as did veteran party leaders from Venezuela and Argentina. Even some old Cuban party-liners were conspicuously absent. Despite the meeting's name, then, solidarity was *not* its leitmotiv.

Less than a decade ago, Fidel Castro was the idol of Latin America's communist leaders. Why has he now become a focus of intra-party factional divisions? An even more urgent question deals with Cuban policy, which—like the Chinese—remained relatively prudent from 1962 to 1966. Just what has led to this immense tactical shift toward belligerency? Clearly, these two questions are related, for it is Cuba's shift toward belligerency that has, in large part, estranged her from other communist parties in other countries.

Some of the answers to both questions are suggested in the works of Regis Debray and those imputed to Che Guevara. Debray, a 26-year-old philosophy professor and authority on guerrilla warfare, was absent from the O.L.A.S. meeting, having been detained by the Bolivian military on a charge of practicing guerrilla warfare. Despite his arrest, U.S. readers learned from reviews in *The New York Times* (July 26) and elsewhere that Debray's analysis of the Cuban process, *Revolution in the Revolution?*, is now available in English. Guevara was also away from the meeting, and the officially, and unofficially, encouraged explanation was that Che was off spreading the revolution on other stages—although it should be noted that the style of Guevara's recent pamphlets is noticeably lacking in either the sophistication or humanism that characterized his earlier writings. At the conference, the O.L.A.S. delegates named him Honorary President *in absentia*.

The writings of Debray and Guevara are key documents in the history of the Cuban Revolution. Their writings follow the pattern established by the two previous major communist revolutions, for Stalin— once victory had been consolidated—proceeded to rewrite universal history in terms of the experience of Russia's Communist Party, and Mao did likewise for the Chinese party. Now Guevara, and more recently Debray, are reinterpreting traditional communist doctrine, and it is their "revisions" that have evoked the wrath of conventional communists. And because Debray and Guevara have revised traditional communist doctrine to conform with the actualities of Cuba's past and present, let us now examine these actualities.

THE MAKING OF A PARTY

Ever since Castro's movement started 14 years ago, the Communist Party has played an ancillary role. As an ideology, Castroism began with a charismatic leader and a band of dedicated nationalists. It moved from that point to a series of insurrectionary successes, which compelled the leader to form a movement—the 26th of July Movement. Then came victorious revolt, which ultimately compelled him to form a party, the Communist Party. The corresponding organizational stages were:

The prerevolutionary phase (1953–1959), during which Castro's politics operated outside the communist movement and its bureaucracy;

The united-front stage (1959–1962), when the communists from the urban centers and the revolutionaries from the rural sectors were fused into the *Organizaciones Revolutionarias Integradas*;

The popular-class stage (1962–1965), as Cuba came to be ruled by socialist-Marxist ideology; and

The communist stage (1965–   ), during which the name of the party was changed to "Partido Comunista de Cuba." Internal organizational strife, it is true, speeded the attainment of this most recent stage. Still, it is clear that the Partido Comunista de Cuba is a direct reflection of Castro's will and charismatic authority. Domestically, during this stage the old-line Cuban communist leaders were purged; internationally, this stage witnessed Cuba's ideological separation from old-line Latin American communist parties. And this separation constitutes the substance of the Cuba "revolution in the revolution," positing a commitment not merely to the Cuban Revolution, but to a revolution throughout Latin America.

The break with the old-line communist parties, as well as the commitment to a concept of permanent revolution, were demanded by the dynamics of Cuban society—and by the original ideals of the Cuban Revolution.

After the 26th of July Movement had crushed the forces of Batista, the new regime quickly became committed to Marxism-Leninism and to Soviet patronage. Next, Cuban politics took a nationalistic, inner turn: The Fidelistas would consolidate their power, while building their economy along industrial lines so as to free the nation from her dependence on commodity imports. This course had two grave weaknesses. The attempt at industrialization proved suicidal: Cubans, still dependent upon agriculture, badly needed income from their sugar and tobacco crops. Further, this program of autarchy made in the name of independence in fact threatened to result in Cuba's economic dependence upon the Soviet Union and Cuba's domination by a traditional communist party apparatus.

As early as 1963, when Castro denounced Anibal Escalante, an old-time Cuban communist and a symbol of old-time Cuban communism, Castro had begun to realize that the old Communist Party constituted an assault upon the ideals of his revolution, and for the following reasons:

The centralization of the Communist Party would elevate Havana to a supreme place in the bureaucratic hierarchy, thus depriving Castro of the *rural* mystique so vital to his outlook.

The party bureaucracy threatened the charismatic basis of Castro's leadership.

If orthodoxy were victorious, Castro would be saddled with not only material but ideological dependence upon the Soviet Union.

Orthodox communists threatened Cuba with isolation from other Latin American revolutionaries. Like Stalin, these old-time communists were afraid that every other revolution would be "premature," "lacking in basic historical conditions for change." Finally,

Castro felt that orthodoxy would be likely to smother the revolutionary "will," that human quality that had overcome so many hardships and had actually made the Cuban Revolution possible.

Consequently, Castro felt he had to reinvigorate the revolutionary will. This meant emphasizing the immediate creation of revolutionary situations in the Hemisphere. A new stress was laid on "exporting revolution"—the Cuban model. And the success of this campaign rested upon a rejection of all who challenged the Cuban experience—by treachery, advice, comparison, or any of the tricks played by intellect upon the act.

The recalcitrant, orthodox communist machinery was either to be captured by the *guerrilleros*, or—failing this—transcended, bypassed, and even reviled as a nonrevolutionary force.

This new militancy underscores the doctrinal independence of Castro's Communist Party: It is charismatic rather than bureaucratic. This is the ineradicable heritage of the days in the Sierra Maestra mountains. Guerrilla activity gave Castro faith in will rather than in doctrinal blueprints. "The school of war," Fidel told farm-machine workers on Feb. 20, 1967, "taught us how men can do many things, how they can accomplish many tasks when they apply themselves in a practical way. This was the school of war, where a small nucleus of combatants developed into an army without bureaucracy. Without bureaucracy! It went to war, waged war, and won the war without bureaucracy. . . . And war taught us what man can do when he dedicates himself to working with enthusiasm, interest, and common sense."

The revolution in the revolution is also meant to describe the revolutionizing of party organization, for in Cuba the traditional communist order of priorities has been transformed. As Regis Debray formulates it, there must first be the guerrilla group; second, the ripened social class; and only third will there be the authentic revolutionary party. The guerrilla movement is the party apparatus in gestation. In March of this year, Castro defined the party's prime goal: "To us the international communist movement is in the first place just that: a movement of communists, of revolutionary fighters. And those who are not revolutionary fighters cannot be called communists. We conceive of Marxism as revolutionary thinking and action." Castro has thus found a way to differentiate his brand of communism from European and Asian modes—without going outside the framework of Marxism. The Fidelistas have made it clear that Marxism is the *heuristic principle for making revolution*, rather than what lies at the end of the revolutionary rainbow.

But how does one build a new political party? Clearly the mass base, the popular front, the urban compromises, the bait dangled before representatives from all social sectors—the features common to the organizational base of the conventional communist party—all these are anathema to the Fidelistas. For them, the traditional bureaucratic communist party can be a downright liability, frustrating rather than fomenting revolutionary action. In this sense, the current stress on rural revolution abroad may turn out to be Castro's last hurrah—the final settlement of accounts and the ultimate nostalgic bow to the new generation. The question is, Can the revolution survive its own faith in its adolescence?

What this would require, in part at least, is the retention of the heroic image of the Cuban Revolution. That revolution and the Chinese are the two outstanding indigenous socialist revolutions in the post-World War II era. Each, by virtue of its autonomy, felt under few constraints to the Soviet model of 50 years ago. Consequently, Castro's revolution in the revolution goes beyond rebellion against the orthodox dominion of the communist party and the communist ideology as a springboard for recruiting activists. In this sense, the pained if sterile cries of the communists that the Cuban revolutionaries are urging the "liquidation" of the party are right. If the party is to become the refuse heap of the old and the infirm, if it is to give up its manliness, then Castro will indeed enforce its liquidation.

Castro's unconventional view of time and age has led him to other revisions farther and farther from the Marxist-Leninist doctrines. Lurking in the background is what Debray posits as a Manichaean struggle between "socialist guerrillas" (the good guys) and "political commissars" (the bad guys). Debray's juxtaposition is sharper than any made by either Castro or Guevara, but all three support this heresy.

As long as economic conditions in Latin America continue as they are now, or deteriorate relative to the United States and Western Europe, Castro's insurrectionary romanticism, his idealization of will over ideas, will displace the traditional communist long-range view that ultimate victory is expressed by history rather than action: a faith in the ultimate deterioration of the capitalist economy and in the long-range tendencies of capitalist nations to conflict with one another. The short range is thus an expression of discontent with and disbelief in the "historically determined" processes assumed to guide society. The long-range view, that history determines structural change, becomes suspect—as if history itself is a cloak for cowardice and inaction.

CAUDILLISMO AND CHARISMA

A counterpart of Castro's unorthodox position on determinism versus free will is found in the problem of the relationship between his person and the party. For although his rule is undoubtedly based on overwhelming popular support, he must still face the problem of succession—of the transfer of power from self to society. Sporadically during the past two years, Castro has announced that in the future the mass slogan will be transformed from "Everyone with Fidel" to "Everyone with the Party." This is one transformation that has not taken place. Because Castro is still relatively young (40), the matter is eased but not eliminated. The legitimacy of the revolution requires some demonstration of the capacity of the social system to survive the original revolutionary group. It requires that some decision-making machinery be set up. This has not yet been forthcoming; instead, the Fidelistas have launched sustained attacks on the rational decision-making machinery of conventional communist parties.

The specter of personalism, *caudillismo*, continues to haunt the Cuban Revolution, and in this sense Fidel's role is rooted in Latin American tradition. For the *caudillo*—the boss of a province who angles, often successfully, to become dictator of the nation—is the Latin American embodiment of personalism. This in itself is a form of the love-hate relationship of serfs in bondage to the chief (or *jefe*) who played an essential role in the transition from pre-industrial to modern societies. The Cuban Revolution was a military revolution and required the caudillo figure to offset the traditional role of the regular army. A good case can be made that this kind of leadership was indispensable in the context of Cuba, which is undergoing socioeconomic transformations not unlike those sponsored by the more "enlightened" *caudillos* of past times, such as Obregon in Mexico or Quiroga in Argentina. But if the 19th century *caudillo* had contempt for the masses he served and remained responsive to the machinations of the middle-class parties, the new-style *caudillo* has only love for the masses and seeks to eradicate the apparatus of electoral politics merely because it is cumbersome.

A symptom, if not a consequence, of *caudillismo* is the rather widespread existence of nepotism throughout the governing ranks. This is especially characteristic of Castro. In picking political leaders, he leans heavily toward long-time cronies and familial contacts. Because of his brother Raul's steady rise to power (following his appointment in 1959 as heir to the leadership) and the influence of other members of Fidel's extended family, he is surrounded with non-threatening figures.

The *caudillo* spirit in Latin America has traditionally served to enhance the leader's direct link to the people. In Fidel's case it enables him to bypass, when necessary, the only stable "bureaucratic" apparatus remaining in the country—the Communist Party. Castro even has his alter ego in the post of President—Osvaldo Dorticos—much as Stalin could boast of his in the person of Kliment Voroshilov. The trusted political lieutenant serves to legitimize the remarks of the *caudillo*.

Castro's tendency to nepotism reveals itself most decisively in his humiliation of old-line associates and in his replacing them either with himself or with nonentities. The family power held by Fidel Castro, Raul Castro, and Vilma Espin (Raul's wife) cannot be underestimated. Raul and Vilma, along with Dorticos and Juan Almeida (an old Sierra Maestra companion, now Minister of Labor), are about the most visible leaders in the new Cuba. This is the politics of the purge, the dismemberment of any possible opposition. The purging of a score of veteran Cuban Communist Party leaders—including Anibal Escalante, Joaquin Ordoqui, Edith Garcia Buchaca, Juan Marinello, Manuel Luzardo, and Lazaro Pena—had nothing to do with their competence, but simply with their politics. One of the inner-directed aspects of the revolution in the revolution is the elimination of the old party cadre. The ouster of Carlos

Rafael Rodriquex as head of the National Institute of Agrarian Reform (I.N.R.A.) in 1965 is the best example of the nexus between personal style and potential ideology. The fact that Castro himself assumed this post is a sign of his increasing concentration of power in himself.

Further, the appointment of a guerrilla cohort—Major Raul Curbelo, Chief of the Air Force—as Vice President of I.N.R.A. is only one instance of the continued militarization of Cuban society. Only Brazil has a larger army, and only the combined strength of the Argentine armed forces equals the regular armed force size of Cuba. The fusion of personal and political aspects of behavior has served to justify an increased politicization of the military and, no less, of the diplomatic corps. The replacement of the Army Chief of Staff, Armed Forces Vice Minister, Commander of the Navy, and leading officials in the Foreign Ministry represents not simply a tightening of the political net but an increased penetration by the *Lider Maximo* (Maximum Leader) into middle echelons of power. With each series of dismissals, the actual power lodged in civilian agencies seems to become correspondingly weaker; the replacements are less able (or willing) to make decisions independently. Thus, the general militarization of the Hemisphere has had its Left-wing reflex in Cuba.

For the Hemisphere, in turn, these transformations evoke their own terrors. Since it is the impression of most foreign observers that Cuba today is being placed on a wartime footing and is in a state of permanent mobilization, the external ramifications of the revolution in the revolution cannot be dismissed casually.

POLICY FOR THE HEMISPHERE

Restlessness and righteousness have undoubtedly combined to produce the new look in Cuba's foreign policy: the abandonment, to a large extent, of the prudence or caution Castro practiced in the 1962–66 period. This transformation represents responses on three distinct levels:

Castro's realization of the dangers attendant on conservatism and bureaucracy, which could obstruct efforts to consolidate the Cuban Revolution.

The frustration stemming from Cuba's Hemispheric isolation. Indeed, the list of military-sponsored, Right-wing *golpes de estado* (*coups d'etat*) since 1959 is awesome. And third,

The international crisis created by the Vietnam conflict.

The first problem is largely a domestic concern, and it has been dealt with above in terms of Cuba's internal contradictions. It remains only to add that, when Castro threw out prudent foreign policy, he also threw out the baby. The nation-building phase in Cuba came to an end in 1966, and with it ended a certain belief in the viability of a strictly Cuban solution.

In the first years after the Cuban Revolution, its leadership went through the euphoric phase of thinking that Latin American social revolution was on the march. In a sense, the Fidelistas behaved much like the Leninists following their victory after the conclusion of World War I. So certain were the Leninists that the revolution would spread at least to Germany that they made no contingency plans for problems that might emerge from a frustration of communist ambitions. The collapse of international communism in the 1920's helps explain Stalin's single-minded foreign policy. The similar collapse of Latin American communism in the 1960's helps to explain Castroism. For up to 1966, Castro seemed bound by a similar belief that the Cuban revolutionary model projected a unique radiant energy that would power other Hemispheric revolutions.

Yet during this time, the Cuban revolutionaries helplessly watched the utter disarray of Latin America's Leftists. In 1964, Goulart's Brazil went down to crashing counterrevolutionary defeat, and in 1965 Cuba could not mount even a token effort to prevent the Dominican Republic from being restored to a former Trujillo henchman. Throughout Latin America, the image of a mighty torrent of 200 million oppressed peons crushing all obstacles flickered and faded.

Nevertheless, Guevara and his disciples continued to press for total revolution in the Hemisphere. In 1964, Guevara made his "Colonialism Is Doomed" speech before the United Nations. He warned of a "wave of heightened fury, of just demands, of rights that have been flouted, which is rising throughout Latin America." Even after Che left Castro's side, in 1965, the assault on nation-building continued, and by 1966 any strict tendencies toward internal economic development had been repudiated.

In some measure the new turn in Cuban ideology, away from nation-building to continental communism, represents the politics of desperation. For while there are hundreds of thousands of students and workers who share the Cuban perspective, the guerrillas throughout Latin America cannot be numbered even in the thousands. *The New York Times* places the figure at about 750 men. Further, no governments have fallen as a result of the guerrilla activities. In fact, in Colombia, Bolivia, and Venezuela, the guerrilla menace has boomeranged, producing a united front from above—an opposition fusion of military and civilian sectors otherwise often at odds. If this lack of revolutionary victories has stirred the Cubans and their followers to new heights of forensics, it has also, and more substantially, permitted the old-line communists to announce the "bankruptcy" of the new turn.

Castro's retort to these frustrations throughout the Hemisphere constitutes the second level of the transformation of his foreign policy. Its organizational expression is the Organization of Latin American Solidarity, an obvious response to the Organization of American States, from which

Cuba was expelled three years after the revolution. This expulsion, taken enthusiastically by the foreign ministers of the United States and reluctantly by those of Latin American states, isolated Cuba solely from the *governments* of other Hemispheric nations—and did that only partially. The governments of Canada and Mexico continued to maintain diplomatic and trade relations with Cuba, and all sorts of private organizations and institutions elsewhere in the Hemisphere continued to provide Cuba with Hemispheric links. Indeed, special tours from Montevideo to Havana are constantly arranged despite the absence of formal diplomatic ties. There is, in fact, a dramaturgical conflict between government and people, with the Castro forces in the vanguard of the latter.

What cannot be lost sight of is that the very existence of the O.A.S. serves to legitimize the O.L.A.S. If an organization can be used for the sole effective purpose of preventing "communist penetration" of the Hemisphere, as is indicated by the Declaration of Caracas, then on a *quid pro quo* basis there is no reason why a parallel organization to rid the Hemisphere of "imperialism" should not also be set up. The O.L.A.S.'s ambiguous situation arises from the fact that the United States is the acknowledged leader of the O.A.S., though whether this leadership function is welcomed by the Latin Americans or imposed upon them is a moot point. But Cuba has not even been accepted as the leader of the Latin American revolutionary forces. And given Cuba's dependent economic status and diminutive size, it is hard to imagine that Castro can impose the same sort of authority on the "communists" of the Hemisphere as the United States can on its "capitalists." This is a clear example of the price paid for having the first socialist revolution in the Hemisphere conducted by one of its smallest nations.

A NON-EUROPEAN REVOLUTION

But Castro still holds a few trump cards—one of them, the simple fact that he has made a socialist revolution in an underdeveloped nation. What characterizes revolutions in underdeveloped areas is their discontinuities with the European experience, and even more with the North American experience. The prevailing political framework in Latin America is a juridical delight, a world of laws and orders that employs the forms of constitutionalism without realizing the substance of democratic politics. From the days of the Spanish viceroys, leaders were men who made rules, not those who abided by them. Despite their access to power, the Latin American middle classes have failed to convert their political compassion into affluence for all. Therefore, Castro attacks all sectors of society—including the communists—that affirm their devotion to European political traditions without a corresponding reformation of the social structure.

Regis Debray flatly admits that the bourgeoisie cannot be challenged on the electoral terrain with any hope of victory—at least not in the majority of Latin American countries. In such circumstances, armed struggle must replace parliamentary cretinism. This is the "new dialectic" to which the revolution in the revolution has given rise. "It is possible," Debray declares, "to move from a military *foco* ["center of operations," or focus] to a political *foco*, but to move in the opposite direction is virtually impossible." Debray points out that, expressed schematically, the fundamental lesson of the Cuban Revolution is that it represents the progression "from the military *foco* to the political movement." Thus, at the ideological level the revolution in the revolution represents the transformation of guerrillas into *gorilas*, into advocates of the total militarization of Latin America. This seems to incorporate Rightist doctrine into a Leftist framework. Indeed, for Debray, the physical symbol of the new Left is the military tunic; his heroes, in addition to Fidel, are Ho Chi Minh, Mao Tse-tung, and Ernesto Guevara. But is not the physical representation of the old Right also the military tunic?

There is no plausible reason for equating fascism with Castroism. But the fusion of militarism with revolutionary minoritarianism has no more place in it for classical socialist politics than it has for classical bourgeois politics. Actually, the revolution in the revolution is not so much a call for sheer militancy or a reflection of new class alignments as it is a call for the primacy of the military.

Debray calls the primacy of the military *foco* a "class involution." However, what it more nearly represents is a return to the politics of radical irrationalism characteristic of French insurrectionary socialism from Babeuf to Sorel. The present stage of the Cuban Revolution represents an unparalleled romantic outburst, but this is very much in keeping with the Latin (French as well as Spanish) ethos. Its romanticism is certified by dead heroes—young soldiers who did not fade away, but died or were captured by the enemy (as Debray was). It is intellectually and emotionally underwritten by a Marxism of free will to replace the Marxism of historical determinism. Real men instead of impersonal man once again make history. This exaltation of flesh-and-blood heroes comes through most clearly in remarks published in the magazine *Tricontinental*, in April 1966, and attributed to Guevara: Tribute is paid to the "martyrs, who will figure in the history of Our America as having given their necessary quota of blood in this last stage of the fight for the total freedom of man."

The resurrection as well as the death is also certified by individuals. As Castro noted earlier this year:

The active mobilization of the people creates new leaders; Cesar Montes and Yon Sosa raise the flag of battle in Guatemala; Fabio Vazquez and Marulanda in Colombia; Douglas Bravo in the western half of the country and Americo Martin in El Bachiller direct their respective fronts in Venezuela. New uprisings will take place in these and other countries of Our America, as has already happened in Bolivia; they will continue to grow in the midst of all the hardships inherent in this dangerous profession of the modern revolutionary.

The case of Yon Sosa demonstrates how even the concept of romanticism has been transformed by Castro in line with his new turn in ideology. At his closing address to the January 1966 Tri-Continental Conference, Castro devoted considerable time to a critique of Yon Sosa's conduct in Guatemala. He charged that Yon Sosa was a romantic; he did not know revolutionary strategies; he did not know how to win the people. He had allowed himself to be captured by agents of imperialism, by Trotskyites. Ironically enough, Castro's attack was not much different from the attacks the official Communist Party of Cuba made against Castro himself when he was a guerrilla leader in the mountains.

The man Castro defended at the Tri-Continental meetings was Luis Augusto Turcios, who represented Guatemala. Turcios was upheld by Castro as the proper sort of guerrilla revolutionary, a believer in the national rather than in the socialist character of revolution. Since Turcios' death late in 1966, however, criticism of Yon Sosa has been muted, and (as we have seen) this year the Cuban regime restored him to leadership status—in the interests of a common Latin American revolutionary front. Nothing could better indicate the militant turn in Cuban foreign policy.

Cuban romanticism is partially a function of the scale of the revolution and of the nation. Castro today repeatedly harks back to the simpler, purer air of the Sierra Maestra, where an inspired handful of men came down from the mountains to defeat the Goliath in Havana. In assuming the spiritual leadership of the Hemisphere, Castro almost makes a nostalgic appeal for his adherents to go tell it on the mountains. Speaking to Lee Lockwood, a U.S. photographer and journalist, earlier this year, Castro said:

. . . Had we been men with little faith in the Revolution we would have given up the fight following our first setback at the Moncada Garrison [in July 1953], or when our little army landed from the Granma [the boat Castro used in December 1956 for his landing from Mexico] only to be dispersed three days later, and only seven of us were able to reunite. Thousands or rather millions of reasons could have been used as a pretext to say that we were wrong, and that those who said that it was impossible to fight that army, those great forces, were right. However, three weeks later, on January 17, we who at the end of December had barely reunited our forces carried out our first successful attack on an army post, killing its occupants.

In the same vein, Debray expresses the romantic revolutionary irrationale in claiming that "For a revolutionary, failure is a springboard. As a source of theory it is richer than victory. It accumulates experience and knowledge." The young French philosopher clearly learned his lessons well from such irrationalist radical predecessors as Sorel, Peguy, and Bergson. He is, in fact, more a product of *fin de siècle* France than postrevolutionary Cuba.

Of course, Castro has been forced to convert his liabilities into assets, and he has done so very shrewdly. An irreversible fact that he must contend with is Cuba's physical limitations. The major socialist revolutions in Europe and Asia were concluded within the largest land masses in the world (Russia and China). Each had the potential for economic independence, for sustained take-off, for inducing a restructuring of the economic balance of power within their respective spheres of influence. But what could Cuba, the first socialist revolutionary regime in Latin America, do on this score? She was a debtor nation; she could offer no viable economic assistance to revolutionary regimes in trouble.

Paradoxically enough, while Cuba's smallness may be a liability as far as her revolutionary potential is concerned, she has retained intact her function as an exemplary case of a nation breaking her links with the colonial past. But this is a two-edged weapon. The Cuban leadership tends to underestimate the fact that a model for revolutionaries can also serve as a warning for the established order. In fact, the United States has already stepped up its counterrevolutionary programs in the Hemisphere. And the absence of socialist victories since the Cuban Revolution can scarcely be dismissed as happenstance.

But the happenstance that the first socialist system in the Western Hemisphere has been organized in one of the smallest and least representative nations has clear consequences in political cost accounting. It has raised the cost of revolutions anywhere else. Revolution has become more "expensive" in every other country of the Americas at the very time that the impotence of the first socialist republic became manifest.

In this equation, the United States' intervention in the Dominican Republic in 1965 paid dividends. It unmistakably informed the Latin American nations that the North Americans were in Santo Domingo; the Cubans were not. Nor could they come. Through this action the United States succeeded in defining the Cuban Revolution as something less than a total Latin American revolution. That lesson was not lost. Quite the contrary. Schisms and splits erupted throughout the rest of Latin America, particularly within Cuba.

In Castro's reaction to the stinging taunts about his inaction during the Dominican crisis, righteousness was the keynote. In 1966 he attacked guerrilla insurgents throughout Latin America. In 1967 he generalized his attacks, challenging the right of major non-Hemispheric communist nations, as well as of communist parties in the Hemisphere, to dictate the character of resistance to the United States. In attacking other communist parties, Castro made it plain that their right of leadership had been abrogated. Here restlessness at his own impotence began to seep in. Cuba now proclaimed herself the unique model for guiding revolutionary destinies in resisting the United States. In this way Cuba laid the groundwork for a position as a Third Force within the communist world and within the Third World—a grandiose ideological presumption that again takes advantage of the very smallness of Cuba's base, geographically, demographically, and economically. For underlying this presumption is the profound conviction that Big Power communism is also Big Power chauvinism. The highhanded conduct of the Soviet Union during the missile crisis is a sore point in Cuba today. This is plain in Castro's statement to Lee Lockwood earlier this year:

Khrushchev had made great gestures of friendship toward our country. He had done things earlier that were extraordinarily helpful to us. But the way in which he conducted himself during the October crisis was to us a serious affront. . . . After the missile crisis, while the Soviet Union was pressing for the withdrawal of the remaining Soviet military personnel in Cuba, the subversive activities of the United States were growing increasingly frequent. In Central America a series of bases had been organized in order to promote aggressions against us. All of which, from our point of view, justified the position we had taken at the beginning of the crisis. . . . The subsequent climate of distrust [between Khrushchev and Castro] could never be completely overcome.

CUBA VS. CHINA

This "climate of distrust" is even more overt in Castro's attitude toward China, despite the many surface resemblances between the two countries. In its first phase, Castro's critique of the Chinese Communist Party could be viewed as a rejection of both foreign domination and also of any unnecessary foreign entanglements. Today, Cuba believes that China also represents Big Power chauvinism.

The basic dilemma of the Cuban revolution in the revolution is whether communism is a national movement or an international movement. Now, for the orthodox communist parties, China's ideological approach represents not Stalinism but Trotskyism. This schism has in fact plagued communism from the first days of its success. At the start of World War I, German and French socialists were faced with a choice between working-class solidarity and nationalism. Naturally, they chose nationalism. A decade later, the Russian Bolsheviks had to choose between "socialism in one country" (the nationalist focus on building and industrializing) and "permanent revolution" (based on the notion of the international solidarity of workers). The path chosen was the former—

Stalin's road. Leon Trotsky, the Gray Eagle of the Revolution, was sent into ignominious exile.

The Chinese Revolution has been facing much the same dilemma, but in this case the outcome remains unclear. The young and the old revolutionaries have forced a united front against the Soviet-trained, nation-building, middle-aged generation. Since the old and the young have the upper hand now, China supports the necessity of world revolution—not just of any revolution, but of socialist revolution.

From the orthodox ideological point of view, Castro's attack on China may seem yet another attack on Trotskyism, in its most "insidious" form—Chinese communism. But from the perspective of the recent internal transformation of Cuban ideology, it is an attack on Big Power chauvinism, its rationale and its revolutionary pretenses. From this, even the potential perpetual revolution of the Chinese is not exempt. Then too, one cannot forget that Cuba's bitter assaults on China date from the time it became clear that China could not fulfill her promises of lavish aid.

However severe Cuba's attacks on China are, of course, they are caresses compared with the attacks on "Yankee imperialists." Regis Debray has again made the official formulation: "No one can avoid seeing that in Latin America today the struggle against imperialism is decisive. If it is decisive, then all else is secondary." What is painfully absent from Debray's work, and from any Cuban pronouncements, is any operational analysis of what "imperialism" is all about. It is almost as if subtlety and sophistication would jeopardize the single-minded assault on the enemy.

Cuba has thus carved out for herself a peculiarly Hemispheric role—one in which both Russia and China are denied much of a voice. If the United States defined the Western Hemisphere as off-limits to the European and Asian powers in terms of the Monroe Doctrine, Castro—despite his sensitivity to confrontation—seems to have drawn the same geographic limitations, but in terms of a "Bolivar Doctrine."

In implementing his program for the Hemisphere, Castro faces three essential strategies of change that are now current in Latin America:

The United States's strategy—concentrating on developing a national politics of a multiclass variety.

The Soviet model—developing a politics of an industrial-class variety in a predominantly urban setting.

The Chinese model—developing politics on the basis of mass peasant movements.

REFORM OR REVOLUTION?

The difference between the first and the second and third is nothing short of a choice between reform and revolution. The second and the third differ in that they are two tactics for making revolution. And any knowledge of socialist history will make clear that, once reformist options have been dismissed, the tactical and strategic disputes between revolutionary factions become awesome and fierce. One need look no further to understand why Corvalan and many other Latin American communist leaders boycotted the O.L.A.S. meeting in the summer.

Castro openly supports the revolutionary guerrillas in Venezuela, Guatemala, and Colombia. At the same time, he makes scarcely veiled attacks on the communist leaderships in these countries. The revolution in the revolution, he notes, "acts within revolutionary forms and respects those forms," but this does not prevent "practice coming first and then theory." This practice demands support for the guerrillas as a prime form of foreign relations. Castro indicates that even diplomatic recognition of other Hemispheric nations will not be forthcoming "until there are revolutionary governments leading those countries."

Castro's relations with other, older communist parties in the Hemisphere reached a boiling point in March. With brimstone and vitriol, he lashed out at the Venezuelan party's rejection of the primacy of the guerrilla tactic as "defeatist." In unmistakable terms, he served notice that he would at no time be bound to a "Rightist, capitulationist current" simply because it is bureaucratically promoted "in the name of the international communist movement." At stake here is not merely the course of Venezuela's revolution. In time-honored communist technique, these words cloak a deeper design. Venezuela serves Castro as a surrogate for expressing not simply his frustration at the inaction of socialism elsewhere in the Hemisphere, but also for expressing his claim to ideological leadership in the Hemisphere.

The bitterness of the exchange reveals with terrible clarity the rapid disintegration of the party monolith in the Hemisphere. The current debate is only the latest episode in the long history of controversy within Latin American communism. In the 1940's and 1950's, the pro-Perón and anti-Perón Communist Party factions in Argentina disputed how the party could exploit the dictator's opportunistic swings between Moscow and Washington. During the Goulart epoch, there was the equally critical antagonism between the Chinese-oriented and the Soviet-oriented wings of the Brazilian party. But the Cuban-Venezuelan competition for loyal revolutionists has an especially acrimonious tone, since it involves the interference of a foreign communist party into the affairs of another communist party. Within the O.A.S., the doctrine of nonintervention has generally paralyzed action—despite fervent arguments by the United States for solidarity. Among communists, sovereignty is no less hotly contested. But once Castro adopts the view that his revolution is only the advanced phalanx of a Hemispheric army, no country is foreign to him, none of his revolutionary activities can be defined as "intervention."

MORALITY AND POLITY

In Castro's attack on the Venezuelans, the Righteous Revolutionary did not even entirely spare his Soviet benefactors: "You see how the Venezuelan puppets talk, with their demands that the U.S.S.R. withdraw from the Tri-Continental organization, that the U.S.S.R. do no less than virtually break with Cuba, the 'dead-end street,' to enter through the wide, expansive, and friendly door of the Venezuelan Government, the Government that has slaughtered more communists than any other on this continent." Castro then introduced a defiant note: "As for us, we are Marxist-Leninists. Let others do as they please. We will never re-establish relations with such a government." In an obvious challenge to Soviet leadership, Castro concluded with a barbed understatement: "All is not rose-colored in the revolutionary world. Complaints and more complaints are repeated because of contradictory attitudes. While one country [Rumania] is being condemned for reopening relations with Federal Germany, there is a rush to seek relations with oligarchies of the sort run by Leoni [President of Venezuela] and company. A principled position in everything, a principled position in Asia, but a principled position in Latin America, too."

The Venezuelan Communist Party responded with immediacy and savagery, which can in some measure be attributed to the Soviet Government's certain displeasure at Castro's open and unprecedented challenge to its Latin American policy. Curiously, the Venezuelan response was less a rejoinder than an exposure. Castro, too, was called an opportunist: The Cuban regime, while calling for a "principled" stand in the Hemisphere, traded and carried on diplomatic negotiations with the fascist Franco regime. And, to justify its own position, the Venezuelan Communist Party invoked the classical contest between polity and morality. In 1966 Castro took virtually the same moralistic tack in criticizing China's actions: "From the first moment, we understood the obvious opportunistic position taken by China in trade relationships. . . . A much more important and fundamental question than food is whether the world of tomorrow can assume the right to blackmail, extort, pressure, and strangle small peoples." This year, at Cuba's instigation, the O.L.A.S. meeting adopted an astoundingly harsh resolution condemning the U.S.S.R and other East European states for trading with the oligarchic regimes of Latin America. These are clearly idiosyncratic Latin American responses, for the accepted role of the sovereign state is to conduct foreign policy in the best interests of its own people. The substitution of moral absolutes for such a practical goal must seem as suicidal to communist politicians as to bourgeois politicians. In sum, the Cuba-Venezuela dispute has tangled somewhat the threads of national self-interest and international solidarity among communists. Ideological disputes are not unresponsive to nationalist sentiments, particularly in Latin America, where such sentiments are powerful among the Left as well as the Right. And if the Fidelistas have moved closer to "permanent" Hemispheric revolution since the Tri-Continental Conference, the Venezuelans, in the wake of their activist guerrilla wing's bitter defeats and the internal disaffiliation of their Armed Forces of National Liberation, have moved further toward intense nationalism and political accommodation.

The tone of the Venezuelan response to Castro makes clear the "classical" nature of the contest. In a sharp rebuke, the response noted that "the aberration in the Castro position is that it makes him unable to pronounce the word 'peace.' It does not constitute a renunciation of any principles to urge the formulation of a democratic peace for Venezuela—particularly at a time when the most rapacious sectors of the ruling class are interested in gathering excuses for a policy of violence, and when a policy of violence has been repudiated by the majority of the country." The Venezuelan party further reasserts the primacy of organization over will: "It is necessary to point out that we are not attempting to provoke communist insurrections or create pure communists. We are attempting to prepare and organize a national revolutionary movement capable of opening new pathways of independent development for our nation. In this sense, it is imperative that the C.P.V. organize a vast movement, with the workers and peasants in a mutually reenforced alliance, which also has the potential for including those sectors of the middle class and those national patriots able and willing to put an end to colonization and underdevelopment." Teodoro Petkoff and his fellow leaders of the C.P.V. put the matter of Cuban assistance bluntly: "We will never accept agents of Cuba in Venezuela—as if they are the only true communist party in the world. We are Venezuelan communists and we cannot accept tutelage under anybody." The declaration added tauntingly that "if there are small revolutionary groups that are eager to come under the tutelage of Fidel Castro, that is their business, not ours. The C.V.P. will never accept such subordination."

Underneath the rousing rhetoric emanating from Cuba and Venezuela is a sociological disagreement. The orthodox communist position holds that a genuine national politics can emerge only when industrial classes within the cities perceive themselves as linked to the peasant masses in the rural area. It follows that the forces that control the cities control the nation. The catch is that today the aspirations of the organized working classes are much more nearly those of the middle sectors than those of the peasant masses. Urbanization and modernization have cut the ground from under traditional communist prescriptions. In Castro's almost pathological disdain for big-city politics, there is more than a hint of the nostalgic yearning for an age of peasant innocence, untouched by the corruption of the monstrous secular city.

The alternative position presented by Castro is an adaptation from Mao Tse-tung: The peasant mass surrounds the cities and overwhelms the urban-based sectors. At least in the initial guerrilla phase, those who control the rural countryside control the nation. The supreme difficulty of this approach in Latin America is the heavy concentration of the population in the coastal regions—the result of the masses' reliance upon migration rather than insurgency to obtain their goals. Castro's emotional response, inconsistent with his long-run aim of industrialization, is to identify urbanism with bureaucratic corruption.

In many parts of Latin America, moreover, the peasant masses may be unwilling to play their assigned role; may remain so tied to a semifeudal culture that their primary allegiance is to the *latifundistas* (big landowners) rather than to the revolutionaries. The recognition of this social variable by Debray, Guevara, and others has led to a view of guerrilla insurgency as dependent less upon the rural peasant than on the mountain terrain. This shift from a class approach to an ecological approach contributes to making romanticism a far more profound ingredient of present-day guerrilla insurgency in Venezuela, Guatemala, and Colombia than it ever was in the actual forging of the Cuban Revolution. In this sense, the revolution in the revolution can be seen as an attempt to transcend the actual empirical situation and return to the very theorizing Castro shows such contempt for on other grounds.

A CALL FOR MANY VIETNAMS

One more cause of Castro's new boldness in foreign policy is his reaction to the war in Vietnam, a reaction that links his Hemispheric ambitions with his pretensions to Third World leadership. It also brings this small socialist state into a confrontation with the United States. Again it is Che Guevara who announces the theme. In the *Tricontinental* article presumably written by him, he defined Cuba's Third Force approach in relation to Vietnam. He pictured Vietnam as the primary ally of Cuba. As an outpost of socialism in Asia, Vietnam's position is parallel to Cuba's in the Western Hemisphere: "This is the sad reality: Vietnam—a nation representing the aspirations, the hopes of a whole world of forgotten peoples—is tragically alone. . . . The solidarity of all progressive forces of the world with the people of Vietnam today is similar to the bitter irony of the plebeians urging on the gladiators in the Roman arena." Guevara is quite precise on this point. "It is not a matter of wishing success to the victim of aggression, but of sharing his fate; one must accompany him to his death or to victory. When we analyze the lonely situation of the Vietnamese people, we are overcome by anguish at this illogical fix in which humanity finds itself. U.S. imperialism is guilty of aggression—its crimes are enormous and cover the whole world. We already know all that, gentlemen! But this guilt also applies to those who, when the time came for a definition, hesitated to make Vietnam an inviolable part of the socialist world; running, of course, the risks of a war on a global scale, but also forcing a decision upon imperialism. The guilt also applies to those who maintain a war of abuse and maneuvering—started quite some time ago by the representatives of the two greatest powers of the socialist camp."

Guevara then called for many Vietnams throughout Latin America. This exhortation, he asserted, is a consequence of the general impotence and shortcomings of China and the Soviet Union. Unsparingly he described the masculine, apocalyptic warfare and warriors these Vietnams would require: "Relentless hatred of the enemy impels us over and beyond the natural limitations of man and transforms us into effective, violent, selective, and cold killing-machines. Our soldiers must be thus; a people without hatred cannot vanquish a brutal enemy. We must carry the war as far as the enemy carries it: to his home, to his centers of entertainment, in a total war. It is necessary to prevent him from having a moment of peace, a quiet moment outside his barracks or even inside; we must attack him wherever he may be, make him feel like a cornered beast wherever he may move." Guevara concludes with a call to arms: "What a luminous, clear future would be visible to us if two, three, or many Vietnams flourished throughout the world."

Not to be overlooked is the belief shared by the Cuban political leadership that an end to the fighting in Vietnam would signal the beginning of a United States offensive to "rid the Hemisphere of communism." Cuba sees the opening of this crusade in the Venezuelan Government's complaint to the Organization of American States that Castro is supplying and providing men for the anti-Government guerrilla movement.

If the best defense is an offense, then the Cuban leadership is performing correctly. The regime refused to disclaim any knowledge of the three Cubans in a landing party of revolutionists caught by Venezuelan Government forces. Instead, Havana declared on May 18, 1967, that "Cuba is lending and will continue to lend aid to all those who fight against imperialism in whatever part of the world." This commitment, in turn, rests on a profound conviction that a more active insurrectionary role would not harm Cuba—and would probably yield heightened respect in those sectors of the Latin American Left most disillusioned and disheartened by Cuba's prudent response to the U.S. intervention in the Dominican Republic.

The question of morale remains an important constituent of Castro's thinking. Guevara has cautioned: "We must not underrate our adversary; the U.S. soldier has technical capacity and is backed by weapons and resources of such magnitude as to render him formidable. He lacks the essential ideological motivation which his bitterest enemies of today— the Vietnamese soldiers—have in the highest degree." Castro's newly radical foreign policy itself seems to rest on the belief that no matter what the United States-dominated O.A.S. orders, the people of Latin America will never willingly fight Cuba. Furthermore, there is a tacit belief that the Soviet Union will never willingly stop supporting Cuba, at least to the extent of underwriting her sugar crop, no matter how resentful orthodox Latin American communist parties may become—or for that matter, the Soviet Union itself. It is doubtful whether this will be enough to fuel Castro's ambitions, however. In defending his passivity during the Dominican civil war, Castro pointed out (perhaps inadvertently) the purely defensive nature of the Cuban armed forces: "Cuba has weapons to defend herself, but in relation to the imperialists, they are infinitely inferior. Cuba has defensive arms."

Nevertheless the new Cuban ideology downgrades the role of weaponry. In the romantic rationale, technology cannot halt the human agent of social change. On April 19, 1967, the sixth anniversary of the Bay of Pigs landing (now a Cuban national holiday), Castro reasserted his willingness to have Cuba serve as the Vietnam of the West, a kind of Second Front within the Third World. Plainly referring to the United States, he warned that "the fire-power and combat capacity they would find here is equivalent to more than three times the fire-power of the revolutionary combatants of South Vietnam. . . . As to the rest, let them find out for themselves should the time come. The imperialists must confront Vietnam, plus the several Vietnams that are developing on this continent, plus the Vietnams that they are going to find here if they attack us."

THE POSSIBILITY OF WAR

Even with the final proviso, "If they attack us," the unabashed and uninhibited defense of guerrilla combat, along with the clear willingness to flout existing diplomatic truces, could well be the opening gambit in a Cuban maneuver to provoke the United States to a line of action that would once and for all crystallize the polarization of the United States and Latin America.

Amazingly, this Cuban programming of U.S. foreign policy may succeed. Castro now seems to have the United States military programmed to adopt a form of precipitate behavior that might well induce a second Vietnam. While on the surface this appears to be a Cuban invitation to attend her own suicide, there are several factors operating for Castro in

Cuba that did not exist in any country where the United States previously intervened.

Cuba is fully mobilized and prepared, militarily and psychologically, for attack.

The Cuban population's support of the regime appears solid enough to rule out the possibility of any immediate collapse of the regime. Finally,

In any future invasion, the United States—unlike its hands-off posture in the Bay of Pigs expedition—would have to draw on its own heavily committed armed forces. It could not rely on exiles to perform Hessian services.

If this analysis is correct, then there has been a profound transformation in the Castro regime: not merely an abandonment of the prudent policy that characterized the first eight years of the regime's existence, but—more than that—the possibility of full-scale military operations "only ninety miles from home."

There is monumental tragedy in this prospect—for Castro, for the United States, for the Hemisphere. The revolution within the revolution proposes a transcendence of the party organization through a reassertion of personality. The *true* party, in contrast with the established party, would be manned by symbolic leaders of proved revolutionary capacity, organizing for the great push outward against Big Powers and Big Brothers. At the psychological level, the new turn in Cuban ideology calls for liberation from the dominance of the bureaucratic party and instead the exaltation of the individual. At the political level, the new turn calls for a redefinition of victory as a Hemispheric issue rather than a national issue. Marx observed that when history repeats itself, what was tragedy returns as comedy. In Hemispheric history, under Castro's impact, the class tragedy of the schism between organization and humanism, internationalism and nationalism, may return not as comedy, but as calamity.

COMMENT BY THE AUTHOR: THE GUERRILLA MYSTIQUE

In Cuba's renewed emphasis on guerrilla warfare, there is an extraordinary psychological component. Abundant evidence, though indirect, suggests that a premium is now placed upon the *deed*, the revolutionary will. These are the values of a masculine world. Even the Cuban Revolution's heroines are now cast in the military mold. Certain sedentary occupations, like banking, have even come to be known as "women's work."

Now, the guerrilla is the incarnation of *machismo*—the Latin American cult exalting virility in speech, action, and dress, virility expressed by bravado, courage, and ruthlessness. Elsewhere in Latin America, where the middle classes and the upper classes are dominant, the contemplative thinker (*pensador*), the overripe lawyer, and—above all—the man practiced in diplomatic respectability still prevail. In Cuba, the elevation of proletarian *machismo* has become official policy. (No doubt Castro's castigation of effeteness has a class dimension—his overaction against his middle-class origin.) In 1965, there was a concerted attack on alleged cases of homosexuality, an attack featured by a parade of deviants in Havana and reported by the radical poet Allen Ginsberg. Since guerrilla activity is conducted by young, physically powerful men, and—in general —by men with cunning and animal instincts of survival, it is this model that prevails in Cuba; the anti-intellectual type, the nondiplomatic, somewhat uncouth figure, the young man.

FURTHER READING
SUGGESTED BY THE AUTHOR

Studies on Cuba continue to grow, but their quality has declined markedly ever since the inundation of an apologetic and tendentious exile literature. Still, there are a number of recent works in English that deserve careful attention.

Revolution in the Revolution? by Regis Debray (New York: Monthly Review, 1967). The famed study by the French philosopher-guerrilla fighter who has sought to provide ideological backbone to the new turn in Cuban politics.

Castro's Cuba, Cuba's Fidel by Lee Lockwood (New York: The Macmillan Company, 1967). A remarkable set of interviews with Fidel Castro, providing the most up-to-date account of the Cuban Premier's beliefs and attitudes.

Revolutionary Politics and the Cuban Working Class by Maurice Zeitlin (Princeton, N.J.: Princeton University Press, 1967). The first significant sociological field-study of postrevolutionary Cuba. The attitudes of the masses expressed, though based on data obtained in 1962, remain unquestionably correct.

It has been argued that models frequently have little empirical significance for the individual.[82] *While this may be the case, the role of models as referents for mobilization is not precluded. That is, the model exists as a*

[82] Robert Bierstedt, "Nominal and Real Definitions in Sociological Theory," in Llewellyn Gross, ed., *Symposium on Sociological Theory* (New York: Harper and Row, 1959), pp. 121–144.

guide which may be interpreted in specific conflict situations by external or internal organizers.

A third type of referent for mobilization—the previous experience of individuals within a preconflict or conflict situation itself—may now be considered. During periods of general social unrest marked by strikes and other collective outbursts, individual ideologues are likely to find themselves in a number of successive conflict situations, to each of which they can generalize their previous experience. This phenomenon was previously illustrated with reference to the workers involved in industrial conflict in the coal town of Ward, West Virginia, many of whom had received prior training in the United Mine Workers Union strikes ten years earlier.

A more contemporary illustration of the previous experience of participants is found in the formation of the Free Speech Movement on the Berkeley campus of the University of California, where members of SNCC, CORE, and other civil rights groups were in the vanguard:

. . . despite all the complaints of isolation, the lack of cohesion, the excessive separateness forced on students by the impersonal immensity of the place, the militants in fact knew one another and were well organized. . . . About half of the eighteen groups which originally banded into the United Front were active in civil rights work the previous year and before . . . when the protest had spilled beyond the militants, the proportion of participants who belonged to SNCC and CORE was about 25 percent and the other 18 percent belonged to groups which formally took part in civil rights activity.[83]

An outstanding example of previous experience as a referent for mobilization is provided by the Okinawa "Bring the Troops Home" revolt of 1945, discussed by Styron in the following reading. Many of the soldiers participating in this revolt, such as Emil Mazey, had been active in the CIO organizing drives of the late 1930s.

Mary-Alice Styron, "A Hidden Chapter in the Fight Against War," Young Socialist, 9 (November-December 1965), 12–21. Reprinted by permission of Mary-Alice Styron and the Young Socialist magazine.

One of the major debates now going on in the growing national movement against the war in Vietnam centers on the problem of reaching

---

[83] Kaplan, op. cit. For corroborating material see S. M. Lipset and Sheldon S. Wolin, eds., *The Berkeley Student Revolt: Facts and Interpretations* (Garden City, N.Y.: Doubleday and Co., Inc. [Anchor Books], 1965).

out to the non-student layers of the American population. How can we enlist the active participation of the community at large? How should we approach the problem of the draft? How can we appeal to the draftees being sent to Vietnam? How can we increase public awareness of connections between foreign and domestic policy? These are all questions of vital importance, but they are not new questions. In the months immediately following the Second World War not only were these same issues raised, but they were settled by a mass movement which had profound significance for the entire post war era.

I have called this a "Hidden Chapter in the Fight Against War" because the vast majority of our generation is totally unaware of the fact that the end of 1945 and the beginning of 1946 saw the greatest troop revolt that has ever occurred in a victorious army. The central issue was whether the troops would be demobilized, or whether they would be kept in the Pacific to protect Western interests from the growing colonial revolution.

The typical American college textbook makes only a passing reference to the "Bring the Troops Home" movement. A good example is found in *The American Republic* by Hofstadter, Miller and Aaron (p. 641). "At the end of the war, strong pressure arose within the army and among civilians for the return of American soldiers from overseas. The government responded so quickly that for a time it seemed that we might be incapable of even occupying the countries we had defeated." The text then goes on to state that this "impaired the United States position in international affairs."

This is the officially endorsed interpretation of the troop revolts and their consequences. American military officials said the same thing in order to defend themselves against the angry demands of the troops and their supporters in the U.S. But the G.I.'s had another point of view on demobilization. A pamphlet issued by the Soldiers' Committee in Manila during the height of the demonstrations declared:

"According to a War Department spokesman, 'demobilization is proceeding with alarming rapidity.' Alarming from whose point of view? Alarming to generals and colonels who want to go on playing war and who do not want to go back to being captains and majors? Alarming to business men who stand to make money having their investments rebuilt at Army expense? Alarming to the State Department, which wants an army to back its imperialism in the Far East?"

The conflicting interests illustrated by these two statements generated a mass movement that changed the entire course of post war history.

RESENTMENT AMONG TROOPS EXPLODES

When V-J Day brought an end to the war in the Pacific, the American troops expected to be speedily returned to the U.S. Quite naturally, they felt that there was no longer any need for fifteen million men in arms and that they should be released.

Contrary to their expectations, however, the army command started transferring combat troops from Europe to the Pacific. The official explanation was that troops were needed for occupation duty. Congress was immediately flooded with petitions and letters from the G.I.'s protesting this action. Even the White House announced on August 21, 1945, that it had received a protest telegram from 580 members of the Ninety-fifth Division stationed at Camp Shelby, Mississippi.

The Ninety-seventh Infantry Division which had already spent five and one-half months in Europe was ordered to the Pacific. En route across the U.S. the soldiers displayed signs from the train windows saying "Shanghaied for the Pacific," "We're Being Sold Down the River While Congress Vacations," and "Why Do We Go From Here?" (*Saint Paul Dispatch*, September 6, 1945). Several reporters who tried to interview soldiers on the train were arrested by the Army Security Guard under the pretext that troop movements were still classified information. They were released several hours later after the military command reprimanded the Security Guard for exceeding their peace-time authority.

The New York newspaper, *PM*, carried a January 13, 1946 dispatch from Nuremberg, Germany saying: "The fact is the G.I.'s have strike fever. Almost every soldier you talk to is full of resentment, humiliation and anger. . . . The G.I.'s now feel they have a legitimate gripe against their employers. If the gripe does not include a wage scale, that is purely a minor consideration. They don't like their conditions of work, they don't like the length of their contract, they don't like their bosses."

On December 26, the day after the large demonstration in Manila, Col. Krieger, an army personnel officer in the Philippines, assured 15,000 men in the Replacement Depot that they would be swiftly returned to the U.S. on January 4. However, *Stars and Stripes*, the widely read army newspaper, carried an announcement by the War Department that Pacific demobilizations would be cut from 800,000 to 300,000 per month due to the difficulties in obtaining replacements. On the same day Lt. General Lawton Collins, Director of Army Information, admitted, contrary to earlier statements by the military, that shipping was available to bring back all eligible men overseas in three months.

The G.I.'s were infuriated. Their mood was well expressed by a soldier whose letter was read into the *Congressional Record* on January 23, 1946. He wrote, "First it is no ships, now no replacements; are we going to sit by and let them blackmail our families and hold us hostages to push through their compulsory military training program?"

On January 6, 1946, thousands of these "hostages" demonstrated at different points in Manila. One group was dispersed at Quezon Bridge and another "broken up" by Military Police as it approached Lt. General Styer's headquarters.

Demonstrations continued on the following day. Two thousand-five hundred marched four abreast to the General's headquarters carrying banners reading, "What does Eligible mean?", "Service yes, but Serfdom, Never."

That night between 12,000 and 20,000 (reports vary) soldiers jammed into the bombed out shelter of the Philippine Hall of Congress to continue the demonstration and listen to speakers angrily denounce U.S. aggression in North China and the Netherlands Indies, and demand that the Philippines be allowed to settle its own problems. A UPI dispatch from Manila on January 7 described the capital as "tense."

During the fall of 1945 the campaign to bring the men home increased as families and friends held mass meetings across the country, and as resentment among the troops grew stronger. Drew Pearson reported on September 15, that "General Harry Lewis Twaddle, Commander of the Ninety-fifth Division, Camp Shelby, Mississippi [the same group which had earlier protested to the White House] assembled his troops to explain occupation duty in Japan. The boos from the soldiers were so prolonged and frequent, it took him 40 minutes to deliver a 15 minute speech."

By December, the resentment among the troops had reached explosive proportions and on Christmas Day in Manila 4,000 troops marched on the Twenty-first Replacement Depot Headquarters carrying banners demanding: "We Want Ships." The demonstrations, touched off by the cancellation of a troop transport scheduled to return men to the U.S., lasted only 10 minutes. The high point of the day occurred when the enraged Col. J. C. Campbell, thundered, "You men forget you're not working for General Motors. You're still in the army." At that time there were 225,000 workers picketing General Motors plants across the United States. Since the G.I. demonstrations coincided with the greatest labor upsurge in American history, the obvious similarities between the actions of the soldiers and the actions of the striking workers in the U.S. drew comments from many quarters.

As news of these mass protests spread, the wave of G.I. protests began to sweep around the world. On January 7, the second day of demonstrating in Manila, 2,000 G.I.'s staged a mass meeting at Camp Boston, France, demanding a speed up in European demobilization. On

January 8, 6,000 soldiers on Saipan wired protests against the slow-down in demobilization and on Guam, 3,500 enlisted men of the 135 Bombing Wing of the Twentieth Air Force staged a hunger strike. The following day on Guam, 18,000 men took part in two giant protest meetings. From Honolulu, Alaska, and Japan, thousands of cablegrams flooded into the U.S. directed at friends, families, Congress, churches, veterans' groups, and unions, demanding that pressure be put on the War Department to bring the troops home.

On January 9 the protests continued to spread. At Andrews Field, Maryland, 1,000 soldiers and WACs booed down their commanding officer when he tried to explain the delay in discharging them. In Frankfort, a demonstration of 5,000 was met at bayonet point by a small group of guards and 20 were arrested. Five thousand soldiers demonstrated in Calcutta and 15,000 at Hickman Field in Honolulu while in Seoul, Korea, several thousand protested and a resolution was reportedly issued stating, "We cannot understand the War Department's insistence on keeping an oversized peacetime army over seas under present conditions."

At Batangas, Philippines, 4,000 soldiers voted funds for a full page ad in U.S. papers demanding the removal of Secretary of War Patterson, "whose incompetence had been shown by his own statement that he didn't know men overseas had stopped accumulating points." Simultaneously, a service paper issued in Hawaii bore the headline: "Patterson Public Enemy #1."

As the G.I. demonstrations developed greater organization and militancy, the protest within the United States deepened too. For months the troops had been rubber stamping the mail sent to the U.S. with slogans such as "Write your Congressman—Get Us Home" and "No Boats—No Votes." They had been carrying on a vigorous letter writing campaign themselves, writing Congress, families, friends, and newspapers demanding they be released and asking others to write letters too. In the midst of the G.I. revolt, Senator Elbert D. Thomas, head of the Military Affairs Committee complained to the press: "Constituents are on their (Congressmen's) necks day and night. The pressure is unbelievable. Mail from wives, mothers, sweethearts demanding that their men be brought home is running to almost 100,000 letters daily." That phenomenal figure did not include appeals direct from the servicemen!

As the first wave of mass protest subsided the issues became broader and the soldiers protested against other abuses. On January 13, 1946, 500 G.I.'s in Paris adopted a set of demands which a UPI release characterized as "a revolutionary program of Army reform."

The Enlisted Man's Magna Charta, as this program was called, demanded:

1) Abolition of officers messes with all rations to be served in a common mess on a first-come first-served basis.

2) Opening of all officers clubs, at all posts, camps, and stations to officers and men alike.

3) Abolition of all special officers quarters and requirement that all officers serve one year as enlisted men except in time of war.

4) Reform of army court martial boards to include enlisted men.

In addition, the soldiers demanded the removal of Secretary of War Patterson. They elected a committee to present the Magna Charta to a Senate investigating committee scheduled to come to Paris in two weeks. The final action of this important meeting was to establish the "G.I. Liberation Committee" and urge everyone to join its units and organize for further actions.

OFFICERS FAIL TO CURB REVOLT

The danger to the U.S. military system posed by this massive G.I. revolt was certainly not lost to the Truman Administration. The army of WW II was not designed to permit criticism from the ranks and G.I.'s who protested to their congressmen or participated in any similar actions left themselves open to severe reprisals. However, the massive character of the G.I. protests after WW II did not give the authorities much leeway. They could not victimize the leaders without stirring up even larger protests; and at the same time it was difficult to crack down on hundreds of thousands of men at once. Yet, from the military's point of view the situation was critical and the rapidly dissolving discipline had to be halted somehow. When privates and sergeants started requisitioning planes and jeeps to carry elected G.I. representatives to meetings with Congressional investigating committees to talk about arranging transportation home, the officers knew they were in trouble.

The military used a soft hand at first, merely "requesting" that all complaints go through normal channels, and imposing greater censorship on service newspapers. On January 11 the staff of *The Daily Pacifican*, an army newspaper in Manila printed a statement that, "new restrictions on freedom of expression imposed from above no longer enable us to bring full news and full truth to our G.I. readers."

However, demonstrations continued and broadened in scope, as indicated by the Paris meeting where the Magna Charta was proclaimed. Furthermore, the military had no intention of immediately living up to the promises it had made to pacify the soldiers. A UPI dispatch on January 16 announced that, "The USS Cecil, carrying veterans to the U.S. left Manila one third empty, the Navy disclosed today." The Manila Soldiers Committee on that same day, January 16, announced plans for another mass demonstration.

At this point the army decided things had gone too far and on January 17, Chief of Staff General Eisenhower issued an order banning any further soldier demonstrations. A similar order was issued by General McNarney, commander of U.S. forces in the European theater who stated that, "further meetings may prejudice the prestige of the occupation forces," and Lieut. General Richardson ordered court-martial for any soldier or officer in the mid-Pacific who continued to agitate for speedy demobilization.

On the same day, General Richardson also confined to quarters three leaders of the Honolulu protests while the army "investigated" their remarks about the demobilization policy. The three were later released. Other minor reprisals followed, primarily in the form of transfers and threats of disciplinary action. Two men were removed from the staff of *Stars and Stripes* and sent to Okinawa—considered the "Siberia of the American Army"—for signing a joint protest against official muzzling of the paper.

Leaders of the Manila Soldiers Committee were also transferred to Okinawa and one of these leaders was Sgt. Emil Mazey, former president of the militant Briggs Local 212 of the CIO United Auto Workers. Mazey had led the fight at the 1943 UAW convention to revoke the no-strike pledge and introduced a resolution to form a labor party. Although his recent history hasn't been so inspiring—Mazey is now Secretary-Treasurer of the UAW and Reuther's right hand man—the leading role he played in the "Bring the Troops Home" movement was extremely significant.

WORKERS IN ARMY AND UNIONS UNITE IN STRUGGLE

A conscript army of many hundreds of thousands depends on the working class for its human raw material, and many of the men who served in the U.S. forces during WW II had just participated in the greatest labor upsurge in American history. Thousands upon thousands of them had taken part in the CIO organizing drives of the late 1930's and had learned the methods and tactics of mass struggle from their experiences. They had gained organizational ability and knew the power of united action. These lessons and the abilities of men like Emil Mazey were used with great effectiveness by the revolting troops.

At almost every base where soldiers demonstrated they began organizing themselves immediately. One news item after another reported, that "the soldiers elected representatives to present their demands" or "the G.I.'s chose a committee to plan further action." The highest point of organization was reached by the Manila Soldiers Committee. On

January 10, 156 delegates, elected by each outfit in the Manila area, and representing 139,000 soldiers, held their first meeting. The delegates unanimously elected a chairman and adopted a program. The chairman appointed a central committee of eight, which according to the *New York Times* (January 11), included "two officers and (was) widely representative of creeds and backgrounds." In addition to Emil Mazey, the group was composed of a North Carolina Negro, an Alabama white, a Jew, an Italian, and regional representatives from different sections of the U.S.

The protesting soldiers were as conscious of their union allies as Col. Campbell had been when he reminded the soldiers that they were not working for General Motors. The outfit stationed at Batangas, Philippines, headed by Mazey, sent an appeal to the United Auto Workers asking for support. The cablegram was immediately made public by the union and UAW President R. J. Thomas issued a statement saying:

"I have the utmost sympathy for the outraged feelings of these G.I.'s. The War Department having made a public commitment on the rate of discharge, that commitment should be carried out in full at least in non-hostile countries. What soldiers and sailors do we need to occupy the Philippines? To ask the question is to expose how ridiculous it is." The CIO council of Los Angeles called a demonstration in front of the Chinese consulate on January 5, in order to show their support for the G.I.'s demands, and many unions passed resolutions similar to the one passed by the Akron CIO Council which stated, in part:

> WHEREAS: Committee members of soldiers in Manila and other fields of occupation have requested the aid of the labor movement in speeding their return to their homes and families.
> THEREFORE BE IT RESOLVED: That the Akron Industrial Union Council joins in the soldiers' protests against the slowdown in demobilization and gives support to the millions of workers in uniform who long for peace, for home, and for a return to normal life, and
> BE IT FURTHER RESOLVED: That the Akron Industrial Union Council is in full accord with the demonstrating soldiers who protest against being used to protect the wealth and foreign properties of such anti-labor corporations as Standard Oil and General Motors . . .

These would be surprising words to hear from the American labor movement today, but in 1946, while the troops were demonstrating abroad, the unions on the home front were engaged in a struggle for their very existence, and these two fights were really twin battles in the same war.

From 1941 to 1945 the American labor movement operated under tremendous restrictions imposed by the Roosevelt government with the assistance of the labor bureaucracy. A War Labor Board was established which settled all disputes by compulsory arbitration. Hours were lengthened, wages were frozen at the pre-war level and a war Manpower Commission was established with control over some 2,300,000 federal employees, including workers in many of the industries classified as "essential." Civil liberties were severely curtailed and outspoken opponents of the war, such as leaders of Teamster Local 544 in Minneapolis, members of the Socialist Workers Party, were jailed under the Smith Act. All the major political tendencies in the country united in support of the war drive and in denouncing any attempts by workers and Negroes to protect their rights. This left the field wide open for the right wing to launch an all out attack on the gains made by the unions during the thirties. They were not long in taking advantage of this opportunity. As Admiral Ben Moreell, Chief of the U.S. Bureau of Yards and Docks, told a meeting of the AFL Building and Construction Trades Department in October, 1942 in Toronto, "I will admit that no one can live without labor, but they certainly can live without labor unions. They are living without them in Germany, and in Italy and in Japan and they seem to be doing right well—at least for the moment—and in my opinion, they will damn well live without them here if all of us don't get in there and pitch."

As the war drew to a close, the bitterness of the workers toward the restrictions and toward right wing attempts to destroy their organizations reached explosive proportions. Within six months after V-J Day, there were more than 1,700,000 men and women on the picket lines in the U.S. demanding better hours and decent wages to compensate for the soaring cost of living.

The employers, remembering the post World War I era, hoped that the millions thrown out of jobs by the cut back in war production plus the millions of returning veterans could be used to break the unions. But the labor situation in 1945 was far different from that of 1919, because the struggles of the 1930's had developed a high degree of consciousness of the need for labor solidarity.

Also, during the war, the unions had guaranteed jobs, full seniority rights, and other benefits to their members in the armed forces. The union consciousness of the leaders of the troop demonstrations helped to assure that the vast majority of veterans would be sympathetic to organized labor. As a result, returning veterans joined the picket lines and fought with the unions for a decent standard of living. It was a common sight to see men marching under banners that read: "This Entire Group —Veterans of World War II," and "Veterans Demand 18½ cents an Hour."

AMERICAN TROOPS REFUSE
TO CRUSH COLONIAL REVOLTS

One of the most important results of the "Bring the Troops Home" movement was that it served notice to all that the American troops would not allow themselves to be used against their brothers, either at home or abroad. The resolutions, letters and telegrams written by the G.I.'s themselves give a clear indication of their mood. They protested being used to back what they themselves labeled American imperialism in the Far East and resented the role of protecting business interests abroad. What was behind these accusations, and what were the American troops being used for that created such bitter resentment?

The events in Indochina are an excellent example. At the Potsdam conference it was decided that northern Indochina would be awarded to Chiang Kai-shek's government as a sphere of influence, and that southern Indochina would be given to the British. Immediately following V-J Day, the anti-Japanese guerrilla forces led by the Viet Minh, rode to power on the wave of popular revolution and established the Democratic Republic of Vietnam. When the British occupation forces arrived, the Ho Chi Minh government welcomed them with open arms, only to find that the British had no intention of allowing Vietnam to become an independent nation. As the British were having their own troubles in India, Burma, and elsewhere, they returned the colony to France, and French troops, together with Japanese troops, launched a military campaign to wipe out the Vietnamese liberation army (See *War and Revolution in Vietnam*, Doug Jenness). American troops stationed in the Far East were well aware that the U.S. was aiding the effort to subjugate the Vietnamese people. In addition to other material aid, many U.S. troop ships, instead of bringing American soldiers home, were used to transport French reinforcements to Indochina. The New York newspaper, *PM*, carried the following story on November 12, 1945: "Victory ships Taos and Pauchog left Marseilles on October 31, each carrying more than 1,000 troops to Indochina. The crewmen of the Taos signed on in New York with the understanding that they were to proceed to India to bring American troops home. Upon their arrival (in Marseilles) they learned they were also to be used to carry French troops to the Orient.

"Prior to the sailing of the Taos and the Pauchog, three other [American] Victory ships left for French Indochina carrying French troops."

The Indochinese story was repeated in the Netherlands Indies (Indonesia). With the conclusion of the war against Japan, the Indonesian nationalist forces set up a government and proclaimed their independence. The Dutch launched a campaign of extermination against them which can easily be compared to the atrocities committed by the U.S. in Vietnam today. An AP dispatch on December 30, 1945, pointed out that American aid to the Dutch was considerable. "Two thousand American-trained and equipped Dutch marines arrived off Batavia [Indonesia] today. . . . Trained at Quantico, Va., Camp Lejeune, N.C., and Camp Pendleton, Calif., and fully supplied with American equipment, the marines are considered among the finest troops in the Netherlands armed forces."

An extremely bitter marine stationed in China described how the soldiers felt about American aid to the Dutch in a letter to his father read into the *Congressional Record* by Rep. Vursell of Illinois on December 3, 1945. He asked, "Is our Navy to be used for ferrying supplies to the Dutch in Java or for getting our troops homes? . . . We have a great fleet, but when a group of ships carrying United States troops are stopped at Hollandia, the troops ordered off, and supplies for Java put aboard, then it is time to call a halt. That little story we got from our First Marine Division news sheet."

Why was the U.S. government so concerned with the situation in the Netherlands Indies? The December 28, 1945 *United States News* explained it by saying, "If the Javanese people are successful in their challenge to Dutch rule, the effect may be felt through a large part of Asia. Already in Sumatra, Malaya, Siam, and French Indo-China, there are evidences of unrest. . . ." The outcome of the events in Java ". . . may determine what happens to the white man's position in neighboring areas inhabited by hundreds of millions of people."

The U.S. government was vitally concerned that these hundreds of millions of people and their countries rich in natural resources should not be lost to American economic domination. Several months before the war was over, Senator Tunnell, in a speech to Congress on February 15, 1945, spelled it out very clearly. "It would be an anomalous position for the United States to occupy, after putting up the men, the money and enduring all the sacrifices which these mean, to have our country precluded from the markets we liberated."

The most blatant use of American troops to suppress the colonial revolution occurred in China. At the end of the war Chinese communist forces were supported by the vast majority of the Chinese population, but Chiang Kai-shek's troops still controlled part of the south. The U.S. immediately moved in American soldiers to support Chiang and try to suppress the revolution. China was *the* great prize market of the Pacific, and men like Senator Tunnell did not want the U.S. to be excluded. According to the U.S. *Foreign Policy Bulletin* of November 30, 1945, the strength of Nationalist troops "was reinforced by the presence in North China of over 50,000 United States marines, who have made possible the entrance of Chunking divisions by holding certain cities for them until their arrival, jointly patrolling these centers with the Central troops thereafter and guarding stretches of railway in the Peiping-Tientsin area."

How did the American soldiers feel about being used this way? A pilot in the Army Air Force at Kunmig, China, wrote a bitter letter to the New York newspaper *PM* on December 2, 1945, saying, "We hear news reports daily over the radio about the Chinese war and the United States' intention of staying out. We know now that our country lies even as German Nazism lied to the German people." He then went on to explain how American pilots were ordered to paint over the insignias on their planes before they flew missions.

The marine who wrote the letter that was entered in the *Congressional Record* on December 3, by Rep. Vursell (quoted earlier), complained that, "Today General Wedemeyer stated that the marines would remain in North China until the 'unsettled affairs are settled.' . . . That means we are protecting the Chinese nationalists from the communists. That's the truth. We are preventing the communists from controlling this area until the Nationalists get here. In short we are deciding what government China should have. We are doing exactly what we told Russia not to do. No wonder they don't trust us in Russia." After asking why Wedemeyer and Truman are using repatriation of the Japanese forces as a pretext for settling Chiang's revolution for him, the marine goes on to say, "Dad, if I could only impress you with the bitter hatred that exists among the marines over this, perhaps you could understand how we feel."

WHY DID AMERICAN TROOPS REVOLT?

Today, American troops are again fighting in Asia. They are being used in a colonial war even more brutal and destructive than those which followed World War II. Their morale is low, and most do not like what they are doing, but their resentment has not yet reached the heights it did following the Second World War. Why did soldiers refuse to fight then?

First of all, they were just plain tired of fighting. They had had enough and wanted out. But this does not adequately explain their rebellion. Had they been convinced of the need to fight, and had they felt it was their duty to crush the growing colonial revolution they might have done so. However, five years of war-time anti-fascist propaganda could not be wiped out in a matter of months. World War II had been described as a war to liberate subjugated people from the yoke of fascism, as a war to destroy a system that practiced genocide, as a war against Nazi totalitarian oppression of the working class and its organizations. At the end of the war, when the allied powers tried to reconquer their former colonies, the American soldiers simply said, "No, this is not what we fought and died for." In an open letter to President Truman, reported in the December 22, 1945 issue of the *New York Times,* an Army psychiatrist warned of a "psychological breakdown" among the troops as a result of "being used to stifle the very democratic elements they hoped to liberate."

Another reason the soldiers refused to go on fighting was that a fear of communism that over-turned all other considerations had not been ingrained in them yet. The Soviet Union had been an ally in the fight against fascism, and the American troops were not psychologically prepared to fight their former friends.

A final and very significant aspect of the troop revolt was the racist character of the U.S. foreign policy. The role of the American Negro population during World War II is another hidden chapter in U.S. history, but the important point here is that the Jim Crow practices of the American military machine did not make the Negro troops very enthusiastic about subjugating Asia. They knew from long, bitter experience the racist attitudes that made wholesale slaughter of non-white people "acceptable" to the military command.

HISTORICAL CONSEQUENCES OF TROOP REVOLT

The mass demonstrations to "Bring the Troops Home," brief as they were, had far reaching consequences in the post World War II era. First of all, *they did force the U.S. government to demobilize the troops.* Fifteen million men and women served in the armed forces during the war, and by mid-summer 1946 the army had been reduced to one million five hundred thousand troops. The strength of the revolt, its size and depth, and the massive support it received within the United States brought about a near disintegration of the American military machine. The government had no choice but to disband the large draftee army.

Second, the revolt gave notice to the military that the entire concept of a permanent, disciplined, peacetime conscript army could not be easily foisted on the American population. It is hard for our generation to comprehend this fact, but a conscript army never existed, except in time of large-scale war, prior to our lifetimes. The charges made by the soldiers that they were being used as hostages in the military's campaign to force universal military training made it evident that the American people wanted no part of such a program, and it was two years before Congress could safely pass a law instituting universal military training. Madison Avenue advertising techniques had to swing into high gear before Americans "bought" the idea.

Third, the "Bring Us Home" demonstrations made it clear that a new propaganda campaign was needed and must begin immediately if Americans were to be convinced of the "communist menace" and the need to play a world-wide counterrevolutionary role. It was time for the Cold War to begin in earnest when American troops rebelled at fighting the Chinese Red Army and "communist" guerrillas. Anti-fascism propaganda, and the struggles of the colonial people for independence had to be transformed into "Communist conspiracies."

Fourth, the troop revolt postponed the entire post-war time schedule as proposed by Churchill and Truman for the war against the Soviet Union. Because the American army served notice that it would no longer fight, and because it became necessary to allow time to generate the Cold War atmosphere, the Soviet Union gained a breathing space to recoup from the war, to rebuild its economy, and to develop into a nuclear power. This breathing space gave the colonial revolution a chance to advance, and prevented the U.S. from crushing the Chinese Revolution. The victory of the Chinese Revolution and the possession of nuclear arms by the Soviet Union produced a stalemate during the Korean War and prevented the American government from reversing the North Korean revolution.

The inability of the U.S. to win in Korea, and the unpopularity of that war, in turn, made Americans very hostile to entering the Indochinese war on the side of the French in 1954. This, and the decision by France to turn down Eisenhower's offer, were the only factors that prevented him from asking Congress for permission to use nuclear weapons already en route to Vietnam at the time of Dien Bien Phu in 1954.

Fifth, the close ties that existed between the Come Home Movement and organized labor made it evident that returning soldiers would not be anti-union and could not be counted on to serve as strike breakers. This gave a tremendous boost to the labor struggles occurring simultaneously in the U.S. It meant that the CIO was not crushed in the post war period, but on the contrary made significant gains. Although the Cold War redbaiting campaign served to split and seriously weaken the unions, they were not physically destroyed as were the working class organizations of Germany, Italy, Spain, and Japan under fascism. Had such a defeat occurred in the post war era the working class would probably not yet have recovered. A case in point is Spain, where thirty years after the smashing of the Spanish workers, they are only now beginning to rise again.

Sixth, the struggle for the Negro emancipation was given impetus by the Come Home Movement. The inclusion of Negroes on the soldiers' committees and the inter-racial solidarity against the most blatant racist aspects of American foreign policy served only to encourage the freedom struggle within the U.S. as well as abroad.

And seventh, the "Bring Us Home" movement is graphic proof of the fact that the American working class is capable of mass action on noneconomic issues. The American community can be moved by something other than its stomach.

Finally, the post war troop revolt has tremendous significance for those of us involved in the anti-war movement today. One of the most important questions being debated on the west coast last summer at the time of the troop train demonstrations in Berkeley and Oakland was the problem of how to approach the troops, how to reach them and appeal to them to join our protest. The Come Home Movement provides an answer to those questions as it gives proof that ultimately, when the troop resentment is great enough, the American G.I.'s will unite in a protest that will shake the very foundations of American foreign policy and the American military machine.

Furthermore, "Bring the Troops Home" is the slogan they will raise and is the major slogan that will mobilize the hundreds of thousands of men and women we must mobilize in order to stop the war. A demand to negotiate, or to call a cease fire, or to send in the United Nations—which for the soldiers simply means exchanging a brown hat for a blue one— will be recognized by the troops as a subterfuge for continuing the war. When the troops and their supporters have had enough, they will want out and nothing less.

What are the prospects for such a mass movement against the war in Vietnam? There are two very promising indications. For the first time in American history an anti-war movement has emerged at the *beginning* of a war. Never before has an organized opposition to a war grown and gained momentum while the war was actually being fought. The significance of this cannot be underestimated.

Second, anti-communism as an almost religious justification for any act of American aggression abroad is on the defensive, not the offensive. We are moving away from the McCarthy period, not towards it, and more and more American people, especially the students and youth, are beginning to question the basic premises of the entire Cold War era.

As the number of conscript troops in Vietnam grows, their response to demands to "Bring the Troops Home" will increase. We should raise this demand continuously and settle for nothing less, as our uncompromising fight at home will let them know that they are not alone in their dissatisfaction with the war in Vietnam. This time we will not have to wait for the end of a six year war involving 15,000,000 troops. The process is beginning now.

To summarize, referents for mobilization may take the form of outside agitators and organizers, abstract or concrete models, and/or the experience of participants in a conflict situation; they are essential for sustained and politically oriented activity; and they provide not only goals but also tactics. It should also be noted that the three referents discussed above are not necessarily independent of one another. In any given conflict situation, all three may play a significant role in mobilizing activity.

The foregoing emphasis on the role of referents for mobilization in a social movement is not intended to lend support to the hypothesis, popular in the conventional wisdom, that social or political protest is caused by "outside agitators." Such agitators do, of course, fan the flames of discontent, but we should bear in mind that the conditions of discontent existed prior to the arrival of the external referent for mobilization. For example, Hitler was not the catalyst for the discontents of Germany in the early 1930s, nor did Lenin or Trotsky trigger the chaos of World War I czarist Russia. In America, the Musteites of Brookwood Labor College would have failed to organize the Ward coal miners had not the evicted and exploited miners sought guidance and assistance. Similarly, the Communist organizers in Harlan County and in the textile mills of Gastonia would not have been successful if it were not for the social and economic conditions of the workers. Despite the opinions of some public officials, the "long hot summers" of recent years are not products of individual agitators such as Stokely Carmichael or Rap Brown but of the socioeconomic status of Negroes in the urban ghettos. In short, while outside agitators are a factor in the gestalt of an organized ideology and do profit from the structural conditions leading to unrest, they are not causally responsible for protest activity or for the social conditions leading to social movements.

To summarize further, the concept of social movement suggests the following elements: a socially defined "problem" and ideology, collective action, and ameliorative change. Combining these elements, the authors propose that social movements are emergent ideological realities given social significance during periods of a consciousness of dysfunction, which provide referents for mobilization to bring about desired change within and/or of the social system. Social movements are emergent realities, sui generis, which evolve through a series of phases, climaxing as an organization of ideology or a collective unity of meaning for social change, and which can hold the attention of a community or segments of it. For example, should ghetto conditions lead to the concept of "black power" being accepted by significant sections of the Negro population (this refers to a number potentially adequate for social action affecting power relationships), and should they be mobilized by an external referent advocating this notion, we may say that an organization of ideology has emerged.

We have chosen to focus on social movements as organized ideologies in order to direct attention to the period in which they are politically and socially significant. Significance here refers to the period when the movement is receiving attention, recruiting members, and addressing power relations. In this sense, for example, the Communist Party can be regarded as an organized ideology during the period of the Front Populaire and during the World War II era. Organized ideology, then, emerges during the era of social significance when the movement is addressing the power relationships of a social order. Power is used here to mean the ability to direct other persons or groups toward one's aims (in the Weberian sense), and thus refers essentially to the power bonds characteristic of superordinate-subordinate relationships. Social movements emerge as organized ideologies when they dispute these power bonds. The mode of address to these bonds, however, differs from that of political parties and interest groups in that organized ideologies do not, in total, accept the existing distribution of power or its usage. For example, the union lobbyist, working through legitimate channels, may demand legal protection for his membership from the government. Unlike the labor revolutionary, he does not wish to usurp the power of government and give it to the workers. In his paper "The Termination of Conflict," Lewis Coser sketches the difference between the approach to power of a "legitimate" organization (business unionism) and an organized ideology (revolutionary syndicalism). He writes:

> Agreements as to goals and determination of outcome shorten the conflict. Once a goal has been reached by one of the parties and this accepted as a clue to the acceptance of defeat by the other, the conflict is ended. The more restricted the object of contention and the more visible for both parties the clues to victory, the higher the chances that the conflict be limited in time and extension. . . . The history of trade unionism provides interesting examples.
>
> Struggles engaged in by business unionism, given its limited goals, provide for the contending parties an opportunity for settlement, and furnish them at the same time with recognizable signals as to the opportune moment for ending a conflict. Revolutionary syndicalism, on the other hand, has always been plagued by the problem of ending strike action. Since its goal is the overthrow of the capitalist order rather than improvements within it, it cannot accept as the end of the conflict outcomes which would constitute victories from the point of view of business unionism. Revolutionary syndicalism is faced with the dilemma that no outcome of a strike short of the overthrow of capitalism, can be considered an acceptable form of conflict resolution, so that its strategy is fore-doomed to failure. Not sensitized to clues which allow them to conclude that a victory has been reached, unable to recognize peace overtures or concessions from the adversary, revolutionary syndicalists are not in a position to take advantage of partial gains.[84]

In this context, the advocacy on the part of the Industrial Workers of the World (IWW) and other populist movements of granting or

---

[84] Lewis A. Coser, "The Termination of Conflict," in Amitai and Eva Etzioni, eds., *Social Change: Sources, Patterns and Consequences* (New York: Basic Books, 1964), pp. 472–473.

restoring direct political power to segments of the public is characteristic of an organized ideology. New Left concepts such as participatory democracy and extraparliamentary action must also be viewed as ideological power alternatives to the dominant conscience collective of democratic rule through the electorate.

Organized ideology, therefore, is melioristic in that its purpose is to modify existing power or political relationships. However, organized ideologies qua social movements are unlike "temporary organized publics," which direct their attention toward specific ad hoc issues, often in a reformist frame of reference, and which do not wish to alter existing power relationships. Nevertheless, the continuance of a single ad hoc issue, coupled with an external referent for mobilization into a social movement, can transform a "protest public" into the framework of an organized ideology under specified conditions. The nature of and conditions for this transformation will be the subject of the next chapter.

MODE OF EMERGENCE
OF SOCIAL MOVEMENTS

Having specified the necessary conditions for the emergence of a social movement—a consciousness of dysfunction relative to a social problem and mobilization of action to ameliorate the problem—we must turn to a consideration of the circumstances under which this action takes on the characteristics of a social movement. Of primary importance here are the related elements of "nonlegitimacy" and a focus on the political (i.e., "power") sources of dysfunction. It is only when these conditions prevail that social movements, as we have been discussing them (i.e., as organizations of ideology), emerge.

Even though a consciousness of dysfunction may be mobilized for change, the emergence of a social movement is conditional on certain factors related to legitimacy. "Temporary organized publics" center around a desire for a specific change, that is, a limited reinterpretation of the conscience collective or a modification of the presumed causes of a dysfunction. This orientation to an issue, however, does not suggest a clearly developed ideology for continuing action, which is a necessary condition for a social movement. These protest publics are therefore highly vulnerable to social response and often do not become movements. Jackson et al., point to this susceptibility in the following analysis of a Los Angeles protest public concerned with property taxes.

Maurice Jackson et al., "The Failure of an Incipient Social Movement," Pacific Sociological Review, 3, No. 1 (Spring, 1960), 35–40. Reprinted by permission of Maurice Jackson and the Pacific Sociological Association.

A major goal of research and theory in collective behavior and in political sociology has been to specify the conditions which determine whether a social movement will be successful or unsuccessful. Conclusions from such investigations have generally been presented in one or two forms, either as a set of general conditions for success,[1] or as a characteristic life cycle incorporating different conditions at different stages of development.[2] The evidence for such generalizations has been drawn predominantly from case studies of conspicuously successful movements, emphasizing either the origin of the movement in socialized discontent or its characteristics as a fully developed movement. Two deficiencies in such data are notable, however. Without studies of unsuccessful movements there can be no assurance that the crucial conditions have been properly identified in the study of successful movements. And without sufficient study of movements in their earliest stages, life cycle generalizations must necessarily be based on uncertain historical reconstructions.

The objective of this report is to describe an incipient social movement which was (a) notably unsuccessful after an impressive beginning, and (b) could be observed almost contemporaneously at a very early stage. From the description an attempt will be made to specify the crucial circumstances which accounted for the failure of this movement to progress successfully beyond the stage of mass discontent and sporadic group protest. The generalizations are intended to apply to a movement which is value oriented and mass based. By *value oriented* is meant a movement which is "directed or limited in its activity and recruitment of adherents by its publicly understood program." By *mass based* is meant a movement that draws its support from a widespread public.[3]

If a movement is to constitute the basis for plausible generalizations of this type, two further conditions must be met. First, there must be sufficient evidence to suppose that the movement could have developed successfully under more favorable circumstances. Protest of many sorts is endemic and can be expected to subside in the normal course of events. Second, there must be sufficient evidence to judge that the movement has failed and is not merely passing through a stage of consolidation.

A movement which appears to meet all the essential conditions for this type of analysis is the Los Angeles County property tax protest which occurred during November and December of 1957. In the remainder of the paper, the term "tax" will refer to property tax. Inquiries concerning the tax protest were begun in the early spring of 1958. Metropolitan and

---

[1] Theodore Abel, "The Pattern of a Successful Political Movement," *American Sociological Review*, Vol. 2 (June 1937), pp. 347–52.
[2] Rex D. Hopper, "The Revolutionary Process: A Frame of Reference for the Study of Revolutionary Movements," *Social Forces*, Vol. 28 (March 1950), pp. 270–279.
[3] Ralph H. Turner and Lewis M. Killian, *Collective Behavior* (Englewood Cliffs, N.J.: Prentice-Hall, 1957), pp. 331–338.

suburban newspapers were examined for the entire relevant period. Interviews were secured with key figures in the movement and with officials in the local government and in interested private organizations. Periodic inquiries were made until December, 1958, to insure that the assessment of the movement's failure was correct. The history of this abortive movement will be briefly reviewed; evidence to indicate its potentiality for success will be given; and finally, the possible causes for its failure will be discussed.

CHARACTERISTICS OF THE TAX PROTEST

The receipt of county tax bills on November 5, 1957 marked the beginning of the tax protest movement. Taxes for 1957–58 were increased appreciably in Los Angeles County, particularly in the rapidly growing suburban areas. The office of the county tax assessor received many complaints by telephone during the days immediately following the receipt of the tax bills. Within weeks, a number of taxpayers' meetings, some of which were attended by councilmen and county supervisors, were held in various parts of the county. According to the report of one of the major newspapers, on November 8, "an angry 800 people jammed the Covina High School auditorium." [4] Another mass meeting which reportedly drew 1800 people was held at West Covina High School on November 13.[5] As a final example, on November 26, 8000 people were said to have met at Mt. San Antonio College stadium to protest the increased taxes.[6] Newspapers, radio, and television maintained a running commentary which kept the public informed of these events. The tax protest ended, in effect, with a mass meeting at the Los Angeles Coliseum on December 6, 1957.

A certain amount of protest normally occurs every year in which there is an increase in taxes. The complexity of the system of arriving at final tax bills is responsible for the sudden impact on taxpayers of an increased tax bill, since it is seldom possible to anticipate the amount of the bill. The final tax bill is a composite of the individual rates of many taxing authorities who may change local rates independently of one another from year to year. The tax bill also reflects the assessed valuation on property, which is changed periodically. However, a cursory review of newspapers from previous years and the testimony of tax officials revealed nothing like the continuous attention the increased bills received in 1957. In previous years there was no indication that either neighborhood meetings or mass meetings had occurred.

---

[4] *The Los Angeles Herald Express,* November 9, 1957.
[5] This was reported by the most publicized local leader in the tax protest.
[6] *The Los Angeles Mirror-News,* November 27, 1957.

A possible reason for the greater protest in 1957 is revealed by an examination of the distribution of the impact of the increased property taxes and the resulting popular protest. They tended to be concentrated in the following respects. The increased taxes were proportionately higher in suburban rather than metropolitan areas of the county and, more specifically, in newer suburbs rather than in older settled suburbs. The protest emanated largely from residential property owners. Apparently this greater protest was chiefly a result of the sudden rise in the value of property in new tract areas where persons were already burdened with maximum financing.

POTENTIALITY FOR SUCCESS

As a basis for judging whether the movement could have been successful, or whether it could have progressed successfully to the next stage, four essential characteristics for the birth of a movement have been assumed. In making a statement of these four conditions, we have drawn upon the works of Blumer, King and Hopper.[7] The stage in which we are interested corresponds approximately, but not perfectly, to the organizational stage as King uses it. It will be shown that the tax protest included these characteristics, thus indicating its potentiality for success.

First, there must be a precipitating event. In the case of the tax protest, the precipitating event was the recipient of the increased tax bills which are mailed to all property owners on the same date. The bills are based on assessments made eight months prior to mailing. They are to be paid in two installments, approximately one half due within a month and the remainder within four months. The bill combines into one lump sum school district, city, and county taxes, as well as those of a large number of smaller taxing districts such as smog control district, garbage control district, etc.

Secondly, for a social movement to develop, individual discontent has to become socialized into social unrest. Individual discontent was first manifested by numerous telephone calls of protest to the tax assessor's office. This discontent became socialized into social unrest as neighbors discussed their increased tax bills with each other. Newspapers, radio, and television played an important part in this socialization process by making taxpayers aware of the widespread discontent. The extent of this preoccupation is indicated by such events as the following: a large number of radio and television programs were devoted to the pros and cons of the

---

[7] Herbert Blumer, "The Field of Collective Behavior," in Alfred McClung Lee, *Principles of Sociology* (New York: Barnes and Noble, 1953), Chapter 20, pp. 174–177 and Chapter 22, p. 203; C. Wendell King, *Social Movements in the United States* (New York: Random House, 1956), pp. 39–49; R. D. Hopper, *op. cit.*

tax question; representatives of the tax assessor appeared several times to answer questions and to explain the procedures used in arriving at the tax bill; neighborhood newspapers featured the tax situation in news articles and editorial columns.

Next, there must be a focusing of the unrest on a specific object. In their search for a reason for higher taxes, taxpayers focused their unrest on the tax assessor. While the tax assessor does not set tax rates, his agents determine the assessed value of each taxpayer's property and thus in a direct way determine each property owner's share of the tax load. The extent to which attention was focused on the tax assessor was indicated by the number of occasions in which he was forced to defend himself in the public press and on radio and television.

Finally, there has to be spontaneous organization of the unrest. Many small neighborhood groups combined in a spontaneous organization of mass protest meetings. These meetings occurred throughout the county, but particularly in the areas where tax increases had been greatest. They were reported in such widely dispersed areas as Reseda and West Covina, in the extreme western and eastern portions of the county, respectively. Another manifestation of this phenomenon was the spontaneous inception of citizen tax committees initiated by city councilmen to study the tax structure.

There is ample evidence to justify regarding the tax protest movement as an unsuccessful social movement. While there were numerous spontaneous organizations, as mentioned above, these groups persisted as independent units, seldom cooperating and often working at cross purposes. As far as we know only one of these spontaneous organizations is still in existence. It is now a corporate body whose stated purpose is to study further the tax structure. The fact that the board of directors of this organization consists entirely of individuals from the same neighborhood is indicative of the diminished mass interest in the incipient movement.

The most striking evidence of failure was the overwhelming vote for re-election of the tax assessor in the June, 1958, primary elections. The incumbent received more votes (669,294) than the combined total (643,756) of the other three candidates for the office. A candidate sponsored by one of the protest organizations received approximately one-third of the number of votes accumulated by the tax assessor and only four-fifths of those received by a former employee with many years of experience in the tax assessor's office.

Furthermore, by midsummer of 1958 it became generally known that the county, city, and school taxes would be increased again in the following year. This knowledge appeared to have been accepted resignedly by the populace. Finally, the annual mailing of tax bills in November, 1958, brought no comparable protest and reactivated none of the earlier organizations, in spite of the fact that taxes were again higher than in the preceding year.

It is appropriate to ask whether any movement concerned with tax reform could have succeeded at this time, or whether such protest was not foredoomed to failure. Striking evidence in this connection is the aftermath of the movement in the suburb where the most active leaders of the movement lived. Several months after the movement ceased to be a power in the larger metropolitan community, it was announced that only this one school district in the entire county would have a reduced budget for the following year. Informed persons gave major credit for the reduction to the earlier public arousal over tax increases and the budget review by a vocal group in the area.[8]

DETERMINANTS OF FAILURE

Some protest may persist where the source of trouble is constantly present. But interest ordinarily cannot be maintained unless there is a welding of spontaneous groups into some stable organization which will supply effective communication, leadership, an ideology and plan of action, and a viable public image. Our objective is to explain why the tax protest movement failed to make a successful transition from the stage of scattered and sporadic groups to one of comprehensive organization embracing all the groups. There are four conditions which appear to be requisite for progression to this stage of organization. We shall take up these conditions in turn and examine the extent to which the tax protest met or failed to meet each of them.

Communication. First, there must be effective communication linking like-minded people over an extended area into one group whose images and actions can be effectively coordinated. Such communication would normally involve both the mass media, to which all are exposed, and special networks among those concerned in the movement. Such communication must supplement the person-to-person communication characterizing earlier stages.

The evidence suggests that the mass media provided adequate communication. Inadequate newspaper coverage can contribute to the failure of a movement to pass into the organizational stage. However, the newspaper coverage of the tax protest was extensive. With the exception of eight days during the period of thirty-one days covered by this study, one or more articles dealing with the tax protest appeared each day in the newspapers which were examined. In addition, our interviews disclosed

[8] This information was gathered from interviews with the assistant tax assessor and a well-known news commentator.

no important occurrence that was not included in the newspaper accounts following the first big protest meeting.

Furthermore, it appears that the newspapers did not contribute to alienation of potential supporters from the leaders. Many movements fail because they are discredited by a public image of leaders with ulterior motives. Examination of the tax protest yielded no evidence that such was the case, i.e., the image of the tax protest leaders did not appear to be distorted by the newspapers.

Mass communication alone is probably insufficient without a network of communication specifically linking those interested in the matter, permitting leaders to emerge and draw up plans, and keeping the leaders and followers in touch through trusted spokesmen. If a movement is to grow rapidly it cannot rely upon its own network of communication, but must capitalize on networks already in existence. Advocates of humanitarian reforms, for example, try to involve key religious groups so that their communications can be carried through the already well-established denominational and interdenominational channels. Similar use is sometimes made of veterans' organizations, labor organizations, and chambers of commerce, all of which have a hierarchy through which communication can be rapidly disseminated to many individuals and reactions quickly assessed at the central agency. No such pre-existing network was located or made use of by the various leaders in the tax protest, and it is altogether possible that none was available.

A consideration of the social organization of the metropolis suggests that the tax protest movement was foredoomed to failure so long as it remained a movement principally of suburban residential property owners, because the established lines of metropolitan communication do not link suburb to suburb.[9] The relevant established communication networks link suburbs through agencies in the central city. Suburban chambers of commerce, for example, join forces through the downtown chamber rather than directly. The powerful taxpayers' organization in downtown Los Angeles, which had ready lines of communication to influential local groups throughout the metropolitan area, failed to give its support to the protest. Their action stemmed partly from distrust of the emerging leadership of the protest. But more significantly, the central city organization represents principally the interest of business and industrial property owners, rather than residential owners. Interests of the two groups regarding taxation for schools, the proper distribution of taxes between residential and business property, and the relative assessment of property in outlying and central areas were at odds. No other central city organization with lines of communication to the suburbs filled the gap so as to trans-

[9] This hypothesis was suggested by Dr. Ralph H. Turner.

form the movement from parallel protest in several suburbs to a metropolis-wide movement.

Thus one of the contributing factors in the failure of the tax protest movement appears to have been deficient communication. While the agencies of mass communication alerted the entire community, there was no central organization with a pre-established network of communication which could be quickly employed to link the suburban residential property owners who constituted the principal base for the movement. It is further hypothesized that no movement reflecting primarily the interests of suburban-dwellers could achieve sudden success because the pre-existing communication networks of the metropolis do not link suburbs directly, but only indirectly by way of the central city where financial, business and industrial interests are dominant.

Leadership. Second, there must emerge leadership which will be followed by individuals from a variety of local areas, and which is able to operate primarily on a community-wide basis rather than a local one. At the earlier stage small protest demonstrations may be led by figures with special local identities and perspectives, but some of these local leaders must effectively identify themselves with the more inclusive group, or already recognized community leaders must espouse the movement, or, as is most often the case, both must occur in combination.

The tax protest leadership seems to have been deficient in several respects. No evidence was presented in the newspapers that any of the spontaneous organizations combined their efforts.[10] However, a leader from one of these local groups did emerge to be identified by the mass media as a community-wide leader. For reasons we could not ascertain fully, he refused to incorporate many local leaders into his group. His explanation was, "I wanted to keep my organization free of persons with political and selfish interests who would exploit the organization for their own purpose." We suggest that this kind of activity eliminated one of the most important means by which the various organizations could have been welded together. In addition, a number of recognized community leaders allowed themselves to be identified as "figure heads" with the

---

[10] The following list represents some of the protest organizations mentioned but does not include all the groups involved in the protest: November 9, 1957, the *Los Angeles Herald Express* reported that a taxpayers' association was formed in Covina to study the tax problem. November 13, 1957, the *Los Angeles Herald Express* reported an account of the creation of the East San Gabriel Valley Taxpayers' League. November 21, 1957, the *Valley News and Green Sheet* reported that the city council had formed a twenty-member citizens' committee to study ways of cutting property taxes. November 22, 1957, the *Los Angeles Mirror News* stated that the Covina Valley Board of Realtors was asking for the recall of the tax assessor. December 1, 1957, the *Valley News and Green Sheet* reported that the West Valley Property Owners Protective Association, Incorporated was meeting to discuss the recalling of the tax assessor or limiting his powers. December 5, 1957, the *Los Angeles Herald Express* announced the meeting of the Los Angeles City Council's Committee on Government Efficiency and Economy to discuss the tax structure.

movement. None, however, devoted himself to the movement in sustained enough fashion to be acceptable as the principal leader. As a result, a man inexperienced in such leadership, unwilling to make working compromises, and generally failing to transform his own popular image from that of a local agitator to a metropolitan statesman continued to direct the fortunes and to symbolize the character of the movement.

Program and Ideology. Third, an ideology and a program suitable for rallying the bulk of protestors must be developed and widely disseminated through the communication channels already indicated. The ideology must effectively reflect the character of the prevailing protest sentiments and the program must afford a promising line of action which can command relatively unqualified support from a wide group of people.

The tax protest movement cannot be disposed of as one which did not develop a program since there was a concentration of attention, although late in the movement, on removing the tax assessor. However, because of the contemporary situation the program and ideology which were chosen probably could not in fact command wholehearted support from the contestants.

There are two lines along which the program could have developed: (1) the general reduction of taxes, or (2) the equalization of tax assessments. The first alternative conflicted with the increasing emphasis on the value of education following the launching of Sputnik I early in October, 1957. Many of the taxpayers affected were small property owners with children, living in recently developed suburban areas, and therefore were likely to identify with educational needs. Consequently, they were willing to accept the higher taxes to the extent to which they felt that the increase in taxes was due to the cost of education.[11] Further, the repeated opposition of established taxpayers' organizations to school budgets in preceding years had tended to discredit all general tax-reduction proposals in the eyes of the Parent-Teacher Associations and others interested in public schools. Consequently, any program to lower property taxes met with initial suspicion from a large share of the potential supporters of the movement under investigation.[12]

Equalization of taxes was the other direction in which the program could have developed. Many people felt that their higher tax bills were due to inequitable tax assessments. Conflicts were also involved in pur-

[11] This point was made in interviews by a well-known news commentator, a leader of one of the spontaneous tax protest groups, and an officer of a local taxpayers' organization. The latter also declared in the *Mirror News,* November 28, 1957, that "the taxpayers' wrath should be directed to school boards." The *Los Angeles Times* and the *Mirror News* of December 10, 1957 carried a statement by one of the county supervisors that the school boards as well as city councils and the board of supervisors were responsible for the high tax.
[12] The school board's position on the tax issue as reported in the *Los Angeles Times,* December 6, 1957, was that taxes should be reduced if "necessary and desirable" services were not reduced.

suing this alternative since it was not made convincingly clear to taxpayers that cases of inequitability were general enough to account for their high taxes. Although a few alleged cases of unjust assessments were cited, there was no systematic study made by any of the organizations which appeared to demonstrate that the higher tax bills were due to inequitable assessments.[13] Also, the question was never answered as to who would benefit and who would lose in the equalization process, since lowering some taxes presumably meant raising others. We interpret this to mean that people were reluctant to follow a protest program stressing equalization of taxes because they might be the ones who would have to pay higher taxes following a revision of tax assessments. Without convincing demonstration of malfeasance or incompetence in tax assessments, many people may have feared that the movement might lead to less rather than more equitable assessment. Consequently, as in the case of the first alternative, taxpayers could not be given promise of a clear-cut remedy to the situation.

As previously stated, the tax protest movement did have a program—the removal of the tax assessor from office. However, several factors posed difficulties with this type of program. First, there was a substantially long period of time before the tax assessor was singled out. Next, the case against the assessor was not made convincingly clear. Although a few cases of inequitable assessments were recounted, there apparently was no further probe to determine malfeasance of office, such as hiring incompetent personnel, accepting money for a lower evaluation, etc. Furthermore, this program ran counter to one of tax reduction championed by established taxpayer associations. Consequently, the latter associations sought to redeem the tax assessor in the eyes of the public.

A further characteristic of any program which might contribute to failure is absence of both short and long range goals.[14] However, the tax protest could not be judged inadequate on this score since it had a range of goals. Short range goals were specific rallies and the necessary planning for succeeding rallies; an intermediate goal was recall of the tax assessor; and a long range goal was reorganization of the tax structure.

Public Image of the Movement. Fourth, the public image of a movement must be that of sustained and growing strength, promising tangible accomplishments in the near future as sufficient reward for the disruption of ordinary routines involved in supporting a protest movement. Unless the situation is one of desperation—nothing could be worse—the promise

---

[13] On November 25, 1957 the *Los Angeles Times* and the *Mirror News* reported some of the charges of inequitable assessments made by a local leader to 8,000 persons the preceding night.

[14] A discussion of the importance of a variety of goals will be found in Thomas H. Greer, *American Social Reform Movements* (New York: Prentice-Hall, 1949), pp. 280–281.

of fairly prompt successes is essential to sustained support on a mass basis.

The amount of attention given by the mass media to the tax protest gave an impression of considerable strength. But a single ill-conceived mass meeting served as the event which seriously damaged this impression. This meeting was held in the Los Angeles Coliseum, which has a seating capacity of approximately 100,000 persons. The organizer of the meeting stated in the *Los Angeles Times,* December 5, that "the swarm of letters they had received from sympathizers" was the reason they called a mass meeting in such a large structure. The mass meeting was to represent the culmination of efforts to arouse sufficient support for the recall of the tax assessor and subsequent revision of the tax structure. The program for the meeting was carefully planned to include leaders from various interested groups. A well-known TV news commentator was master of ceremonies. A popular TV and motion picture actor gave the keynote address, stating that he was present only as a protesting taxpayer. The list of speakers also included a State senator, the president of the State Board of Equalization, a County supervisor, the chief deputy tax collector, and a former mayor of West Covina. The public was made aware of this meeting by telephone calls from organizational members, by handbills, and by the usual mass media.[15]

The impression of failure was created by the presence of a relatively small number of people in relation to the capacity of so large a stadium. The event was reported by all the leading newspapers which estimated attendance figures ranging from 6,000 to 10,000 persons. In the Los Angeles Coliseum such a crowd appeared negligible. It is not altogether clear that this small attendance indicated a lack of interest in the protest. The Coliseum is located far from the interested areas, so that persons had to travel a long way through heavy traffic to attend. (December 6th was a Friday.) In addition, we suspect that many were young persons who either had to leave their wives at home or hire baby sitters. Furthermore, although it did not rain as forecasted, the weather was cool.

By the standards usually applied to such rallies, the meeting was a success in terms of attendance. If the rally had, for example, been held in the nearby Shrine Auditorium with its seating capacity of approximately 6400 persons, the rally would have been regarded as a tremendous success. Therefore, the choice of the Coliseum as a meeting place must be considered an error in strategy.

We could find no evidence that any of the established community leaders mentioned above took any interest in the movement after the

[15] The meeting was announced in the *Los Angeles Times,* November 27, and December 1 and 5, 1957; the *Herald Express* on December 5 and 6, 1957; the *Valley News and Green Sheet* on December 5, 1957; and the *Mirror News* on December 6, 1957.

mass meeting. Apparently they felt that they could not gain in stature from further association with such a movement.

It is likely that prospects of success operated even more immediately on the established community leaders than on mass support. That is, the small number was discouraging to all at the meeting, but if the community leaders had continued to support the movement they might have influenced others in this direction. The fact that the community leaders felt they had nothing to gain also affected the leadership structure since there was no longer leadership which could command mass following.

CONCLUSION

In the foregoing report we have examined a variety of factors which existing theory in social movements led us to believe should have something to do with the success or failure of a movement in reaching a stage of comprehensive organization. Our analysis has led us to conclude that any or all of four specific conditions could have accounted for failure in this instance. These conditions were the lack of a pre-existing network of communication linking those groups of citizens most likely to support the movement, the failure of the emergent leader to incorporate neighborhood and community leaders into his organization, the lack of a program to which a major section of the protestors could give wholehearted support, and a highly publicized conspicuous failure which weakened the public image. Confirmation of these suggested factors awaits research which circumvents the weaknesses contained in this exploratory study.

In the analysis of a single case there is no way to be sure of causal connections. Therefore, more studies of unsuccessful social movements are needed in order to compare them with successful ones so that the conditions essential for the success of social movements can be more rigorously specified. The special contribution of this study has been to supplement the usual reports on large-scale, highly successful movements with an examination of a smaller movement which was unsuccessful.

For the most part, approaches to social problems such as that taken by the Los Angeles tax protestors are acceptable under the rubric of "consensus politics." Here, the expression of protest and the organization of a protest public are quite within the accepted tolerances of pluralistic politics and a social movement does not develop. Thus, one of the essential elements in the emergence of a movement is the necessity for a temporary organized public to face a "crisis of legitimacy" concerning its approach to a social problem. Since the goal of such a public is to change an existing practice or belief, it and its tactics must become regarded as nonlegitimate vis-à-vis existing institutions and practices in order for the public to emerge into a social movement. The importance of nonlegitimacy for the transformation of a protest public into a social movement is recognized by the historian Asa Briggs in his analysis of the Chartist movement:

> During the last years of the [Chartist] agitation there was an unmistakable shift in emphasis from the demand for political reform within the framework of a parliamentary ideal . . . to the search for social democracy, a search which led some Chartists—notably Jones and Harney—into socialism. "Chartism in 1850," wrote "Howard Morton" in the first issue of Harney's Red Republican, "is a different thing from Chartism in 1840. The leaders of the English Proletarians have proved that they are true Democrats, and no shams, by going ahead so rapidly within the last few years. They have progressed from the idea of a simple political reform to the idea of a Social Revolution." [16]

The element of nonlegitimacy which ultimately led Chartism to become a national social movement (albeit short-lived) was its opposition to the middle class consciousness embodied in the Anti-Corn Law League. As Briggs states it: "It was irritation with and frustration engendered by the Anti-Corn Law League, itself a child of the business depression, which was set up after the Chartist movement had been inaugurated, that provoked the Chartists to their most violent class declarations. The Annual Register described Chartism in 1839 as 'an insurrection which is expressly directed against the middle classes'." [17]

Inescapably, the factor of nonlegitimacy directly affects the opportunities for the maturation and success of a social movement, yet nonlegitimacy is the "Catch 22" of protest: nonlegitimacy invites repression; but if protest becomes legitimate it ceases to be viable protest. The opposition to a segment of the conscience collective which nonlegitimacy entails creates a threat to the status quo. On the one hand, the ensuing sanctions which will be imposed on an emerging movement serve to further estrange the protest group from legitimate channels of protest and will further heighten the membership's collective perception of dysfunction in existing structures and procedures. On the other hand, these sanctions will operate to create both external and internal pressures upon the survival of a temporary organized public emerging into a social movement. Externally, the most common threats are co-optation and suppression. The result of co-optation is that the leaders of the protest public and their ideas are made legitimate and part of the social order. Plant agitators are made foremen, and their ideas for factory reform are "to be studied." Bertrand Russell once quipped that in some uncanny way British revolu-

[16] Asa Briggs, "National Bearings," in Briggs, ed., *Chartist Studies* (London: Macmillan and Co., Ltd., 1960), pp. 288–303, quoted at p. 290.
[17] *Ibid.*, p. 297.

tionaries who exhibit any potential for success are made members of the House of Lords and are rarely heard from again. The history of American third party movements abounds with examples of this process. Bryan's nomination as the Democratic presidential candidate in 1894 made the Populist movement impotent; Roosevelt's "New Deal" took the steam out of the American Socialist Party's program and resulted in the defection of many leading Socialists to the Democratic Party in the early 1930s. The effects of co-optation are aptly expressed by Guenther Roth in his discussion of the phenomenon he terms "negative integration": "A radical mass movement constitutes at least a potential source of instability, but if it can be legalized without sharing in governmental power it may contribute to the stability of the dominant system by leaving intact the latter's basic structure and developing vested interests in its own legal status." [18]

More frequently, however, suppression is the means used to control identified leaders of ad hoc protest groups. It has been accomplished through dismissal from a position, factory, or company town; through arrest and detention; and, in extreme cases, through physical violence and murder. The murders of civil rights workers Goodman, Schwerner, and Chaney in Mississippi and the assassinations of Medgar Evers and Martin Luther King document the perils of threatening the social order. The history of the American labor movement is amply punctuated with evidence of the subjugation of individuals who advocated industrial unionism and reform. Members of the Industrial Workers of the World were harassed, jailed, and not infrequently killed for their efforts to create "One Big Union." Legalized lynching and vigilante action marked the fate of Joe Hill in Utah and, several years later, his comrades in Centralia, Washington.[19] In the Appalachians, Harry Simms, Ella May Wiggins, and other organizers were felled for their attempts to unionize coal and textile workers.

Of these two external responses (co-optation and suppression), the latter is least effective in repressing an emerging social movement: the problem remains unresolved while the protest public's consciousness of dysfunction is heightened by the violent reaction to its dissent and the possibility of legitimate amelioration of the problem becomes precluded. This response to suppression is illustrated by the events surrounding the House Committee on Un-American Activities (HCUA) hearing in San Francisco in May 1960. The brutal police attack upon some two hundred demonstrators protesting the hearings on May 13 brought out more than four thousand pickets on the following day. As one analyst put it:

[18] Guenther Roth, *The Social Democrats in Imperial Germany* (New Jersey, The Bedminster Press, 1963), p. 6.
[19] See, for example, Sidney Lens, *Radicalism in America* (New York: Thomas Y. Crowell and Co., 1967). Numerous examples of violence directed at the labor movement are also documented in various issues of *Labor History*.

There was by no means uniform hostility toward the committee [HCUA], nor uniform sympathy for the witnesses [among those who had come to observe the hearings].

At the moment of the clash with police something changed. . . . All neutrality vanished, to be replaced with a hot, sustained anger still evident in those who witnessed the events. One of the merely curious who was hosed and arrested returned the next day to join the protest commented ruefully, "I was a political virgin, but I was raped on the steps of City Hall." [20]

Thus, although suppression may have short-run success in quelling dissent, it can in the long run create a widespread support for the protest it is directed against.

Temporary organized publics also undergo internal forces leading to disintegration. Since members of temporary organized publics are recruited from the existing society, they generally adhere to a considerable portion of the established conscience collective. Therefore, dissolution of a public can occur when individuals begin to realize that the achievement of their goal requires greater alterations in society or in the conscience collective than they are willing to undertake. For example, the MacDoo scheme to nationalize American railroads in the twenties was supported by railroaders until they were told it was the first step to socialism. Similarly, civil rights moderates were recently neutralized by being told that further aid to black ghettos may hamper the war effort in Vietnam. In other words, in the "big picture" viewpoint, the established conscience collective (never really having been forgotten) is reinforced. Frequently, after the dissidents have "been to the gates of Hell" and have seen the implications of the changes they seek, a process of moral reaffirmation of the existing social order occurs. Another internal threat to temporary organized publics is that of dissensus caused either by a haphazard approach to the problem or by a multidimensional definition of the situation. The present dissension between black and white student radicals over the goals of the student protest movement is illustrative. Even if individuals concur with the definition of the problem, another difficulty can arise because of divergent views about solutions. John Mitchell, the founder of the United Mine Workers of America, frequently found that although miners saw their conditions as deplorable, their diverse ethnic backgrounds precluded acceptable common solutions. More recently, the difficulties of Vietnam war protest publics in finding a common strategy to end this conflict have rendered united action almost ineffectual, and activity has become confined to marches and other forms of "public witness" activities.

In the event that a temporary organized public is not suppressed, made a part of the established order, or dissolved from within, certain

[20] Jessica Mitford Treuhaft, "The Indignant Generation," *The Nation*, 192, 21 (May 27, 1961): 453.

factors can strengthen ideology and reinforce a political approach to the problem at hand, thus providing the impetus for the emergence of a movement. As we have already pointed out, excessive external coercion or threat may serve to heighten a group's sense of dysfunction rather than eliminating it. The history of the Berkeley Free Speech Movement (FSM) provides an excellent example. During the 1964 Thanksgiving break at the University of California, the FSM was demoralized and internally split over tactics and goals. At the same time, the Chancellor decided to expel five leaders of the student protest group, including Mario Savio. As a result of this action, the FSM resumed its activities with renewed vigor the following week—activities which culminated in the Sproul Hall sit-in. Thus the administration, through its own actions, highlighted the issue of free speech and lowered its own legitimacy in the eyes of many students.

The deterioration of a problem situation can also transform a temporary organized public into a movement. Marx's "law of increasing misery," which postulates that the conditions of workers will increasingly deteriorate under the capitalist system, illustrates this phenomenon.[21] Similarly, the continuation of an aggressive military policy in Vietnam by succeeding United States administrations has widened the credibility gap and mobilized widespread domestic opposition to the war.

On the other hand, the legitimation of a problem and/or the individuals protesting it may increase discontent rather than placating the dissidents.[22] Although the problem may have been officially defined as legitimate, the reforms undertaken by the Establishment may not eradicate the problem, thus leading to a further breakdown of the conscience collective. For example, enfranchising the Negro was heralded as a significant step in ameliorating the segregation problem, yet most disadvantaged urban Negroes already had the vote. This attempt to solve the segregation problem did, however, legitimate the grievances of ghetto dwellers as well as suggest that solutions outside the legislative process might be more effective (e.g., black power). Other examples of this consequence of legitimation can be found in the urban renewal program and the so-called war on poverty.

In the final analysis, the effect of the various conditions we have been discussing will be to frustrate the achievement of the goals held by a temporary organized public. When such goals are not achieved, the attention of the public may shift to other means of amelioration (e.g., from the factory to the political arena, from the legislature to the streets). In a sense, what occurs is akin to Marx's notion of the development of class consciousness. That is, the processes in the development of class con-

[21] This is discussed in Theodore Keller, "A New Vocabulary for the New Left," *Journal of Contemporary Revolution*, 1 (Spring 1967): 18–31.
[22] See James C. Davies, "Toward a Theory of Revolution," *American Sociological Review*, 27 (February 1962): 5–18.

sciousness described by Marx pertain to the development of a social movement: identification of interests, rejection of other interests or solutions, and a readiness to engage in social action to enhance group interests.[23]

To summarize to this point, the position of a temporary organized public enroute to becoming a social movement is very tenuous. It must, of necessity, be defined as nonlegitimate (i.e., contrary to the established conscience collective), and is therefore subject to a variety of external and internal threats to its existence. The response of official agencies or "sincere people" frequently determines the fate of organized publics, not only with regard to repression but also in terms of the achievement of goals. Social movements come to the fore when a consciousness of dysfunction persists and becomes structured with a perception toward political and/or social action.

At this point, when the necessity of goal-oriented action becomes apparent, the crucial element in social movement formation enters in: the development of an ideology. As we pointed out in the preceding chapter, ideologies are basically rationalized, consistent interpretations of the past, present, and future. The impact of ideas on social action has been underscored by Talcott Parsons in "The Role of Ideas in Social Action." Of particular interest here is his analysis of the relationship between existential ideas (both empirical and nonempirical) and normative ideas in goal-oriented behavior.

Excerpts from Talcott Parsons, "The Role of Ideas in Social Action," American Sociological Review, 3 (October 1938), 652–664. Reprinted by permission of Talcott Parsons and the American Sociological Association.

The subject of this paper has given rise to much controversy which has on the whole, turned out to be strikingly inconclusive. It may be suggested that, in part at least, this is a result of two features of the discussion. On the one hand, sides have tended to be taken on the problem in too general terms. Ideas *in general* have been held either to have or not to have an important role in the determination of action. As opposed to this tendency, I shall attempt here to break the problem down into different parts, each of which fits differently into the analytical theory of action.

On the other hand, the discussion has, for the taste of the present

---

[23] Karl Marx, *The Poverty of Philosophy* (New York: International Publishers, n.d.), pp. 145–146. These processes are also discussed in C. Wright Mills, *The Power Elite* (New York: Oxford University Press, 1951), p. 325.

writer, been altogether too closely linked to philosophical problems and has seldom been brought fairly into the forum of factual observation and theoretical analysis on the empirical level. This paper is to be regarded as a theoretical introduction to attempts of the latter sort.

I am far from believing that social or any other science can live in a kind of philosophical vacuum, completely ignoring all philosophical problems, but even though, as I have stated elsewhere,[24] scientific and philosophical problems are closely interdependent, they are nevertheless at the same time independent and can be treated in relative abstraction from each other. Above all, from the fact that this paper will maintain that ideas do play an important part in the determination of action, it is not to be inferred that its author is committed to some kind of idealistic metaphysics of the sort from which it has so often been inferred that ideas must arise through some process of "immaculate conception" unsullied by social and economic forces or that they influence action by some automatic and mysterious process of self-realization or "emanation" without relation to the other elements of the social system.

The paper, then, will be devoted to the statement of a theoretical framework for the analysis of the role of ideas on an empirical, scientific basis. Without apologies, I shall start with an explicit definition of my subject matter. Ideas, for the purposes of this discussion, are "concepts and propositions, capable of intelligible interpretation in relation to human interests, values and experience." So far as *qua* ideas, they constitute systems, the relations between these concepts and propositions are capable of being tested in terms of a certain type of norm, that of logic.

The definition just given is so stated that it can serve as the definition of a variable in a system of interdependent variables. That is, it is a combination of logical universals to which many different particulars, the values of the variable, may be fitted. Since the present concern is wholly scientific, the sole important questions to be asked are three. 1. Do differences which are accurately ascertainable obtain between the specific content of the ideas held by different individuals or groups in social systems at different times? 2. Is it possible to establish important relations between these differences and other observable aspects of, or events within, the same social systems? 3. Are these relations such that the ideas cannot be treated as a dependent variable, that is, their specific content deduced from knowledge of the values of one or more other observable variables in the same system? If all three of these questions can be answered in the affirmative, it may be claimed that ideas play an important role in the determination of social action in the only sense in which such a claim has meaning in science. Ideas would be an essential variable in a system of theory which can be demonstrated to "work," to make intelligible a complex body of phenomena. Whether in an ultimate, onto-

[24] *The Structure of Social Action*, 20 ff., New York, 1937.

logical sense these ideas are real, or only manifestations of some deeper metaphysical reality is a question outside the scope of this paper.

Ideas obviously could not be treated as a variable in systems of social action unless their specific content varied from case to case. But besides the variations of specific content from case to case, it may be possible, as has been suggested, to divide them into certain broad classes which differ appreciably from one another in their relations to action. How these classes shall be defined, and how many there are, are pragmatic questions in the scientific sense; the justification of making a distinction between any two classes is that their members behave differently in their relations to action. Whether this is the case or not is a question of fact. I shall outline such a classification and then present an analysis of the role of each so as to demonstrate the importance of making the distinctions.

The first class may be termed "existential" ideas. The concepts which comprise such ideas are the framework for describing or analyzing entities, or aspects or properties of them, which pertain to the external world of the person who entertains the ideas, the actor. These entities either are or are thought to be existent at the time, to have existed, or to be likely to exist. The reference is to an external "reality" in some sense. The ideas involve existential propositions relative to some phase or phases of this reality, real or alleged. The most general type of norm governing existential ideas is that of "truth."

Of existential, as of other ideas, it is convenient to distinguish two subclasses, the distinction between which is of cardinal importance. The one are empirical ideas, the concepts and propositions of which are, or are held to be, capable of verification by the methods of empirical science. All other existential ideas, on the other hand, I shall class together as nonempirical, regardless of the reasons why they are not scientifically verifiable.[25]

The second main class are what may be called normative ideas. These refer to states of affairs which may or may not actually exist, but in either case the reference is not in the indicative but in the imperative mood. If the state of affairs exists, insofar as the idea is normative the actor assumes an obligation to attempt to keep it in existence; if not, he assumes an obligation to attempt its realization at some future time. An idea is normative insofar as the maintenance or attainment of the state of affairs it describes may be regarded as an end of the actor. The states of affairs referred to may also be classified as empirical and nonempirical according to the above criteria.[26]

[25] This residual category is formulated for the immediate purposes in hand and its use is not to be held to imply that no distinctions between subclasses of nonempirical ideas are important for any other purposes.

[26] There is a third class of ideas which may be called "imaginative." The content of these refers to entities which are neither thought to be existent nor does the actor feel any obligation to realize them. Examples would be a utopia which is not meant as defining a program of action, or the creation of an entirely fictitious series of

The first set of problems to be discussed concerns the role of empirical existential ideas. I think it fair to say that no branch of social science has been subjected to more thorough and rigorous analysis than this, so it forms an excellent starting point.[27] The context in which this analysis has taken place is the range of problems surrounding the concept of the rationality of action in the ordinary sense of the maximization of "efficiency" or "utility" by the adaptation of means to ends. It is the sense of rationality which underlies most current analysis of technological processes in science, industry, medicine, military strategy and many other fields, which lies at the basis of economic theory, and much analysis of political processes, regarded as processes of maintaining, exercising, and achieving power.

The common feature of all these modes of analysis of action is its conception as a process of attaining specific and definite ends by the selection of the "most efficient" means available in the situation of the actor. This, in turn, implies a standard according to which the selection among the many possible alternative means is made. There is almost universal agreement that the relevant basis of selection in this kind of case involves the actor's knowledge of his situation which includes knowledge of the probable effects of various possible alternative ways of altering it which are open to him. One of the necessary conditions of rationality of his action is that the knowledge should be scientifically valid.[28]

Valid empirical knowledge in this sense is certainly a system of ideas. It consists of concepts and propositions and their logical interrelations. Moreover, in all the above analyses of action, this knowledge is treated as a variable in the system of action; according to variations in its specific content, the action will be different. In explaining, above all, failure for the actual course of action to conform with a rational norm describing the "best" course, we continually refer to features of the store of knowledge of the actor. We say "He did not know . . ." with the implication that if he had, he would have acted differently, and "He supposed erroneously that . . . ," with the corresponding implication that if he had not been in error on the level of knowledge, he would also have acted differently. Thus, two of the coordinates of variation of knowledge which

---

situations in a novel. At least the most obvious significance of such ideas in relation to action is an indices of the sentiments and attitudes of the actors rather than as themselves playing a positive role. To inquire whether indirectly they do play a role would raise questions beyond the scope of this paper and they will be ignored in the subsequent discussion. They are mentioned here only to complete the classification.

[27] Much of this analysis is discussed in *The Structure of Social Action*. See esp. chap. 4, 161 ff.; chap. 5, 180 ff.; chap. 9, 344 ff.

[28] "Efficiency" involves choice among two or more alternative ways of attaining an end. The validity of knowledge alone is not a sufficient criterion to determine the relative efficiency of the different alternatives. Statement of the other necessary criteria would involve difficult questions far beyond the scope of this paper.

are relevant to its role in action are that in the direction of ignorance and of error. There is, for the attainment of any given end in any given situation, a certain minimum of valid knowledge which is adequate. If the knowledge actually falls short of this, if the actor is ignorant of any important features of the situation, or if his ideas are invalid, are in error, this is an adequate explanation of the failure of his action to be rational. . . .

But in addition to ideas which will stand the test of scientific validity, there are current in every society many ideas which in one respect or another diverge from this standard. So far as their reference is existential rather than normative or imaginative, the question arises as to what is the basis of this divergence. In answer to this question, a certain positivistic bias is very widely prevalent, and must be guarded against. It is the view, implicit, or explicit, that divergence from the standard of empirical shortcomings in the sense that the ideas in question are not only, negatively, not verifiable, but that they can be shown to be *positively* wrong, that is, that the basis of their unverifiability is ignorance or error, or both. This judgment clearly implies that there is available an adequate positive scientific standard by which to judge them.

At least in the field of empirically known systems of existential ideas, it can be stated with confidence that this class, which may be called *un*scientific ideas, does not exhaust the departures from empirical verifiability, but that, in addition, there is a class of concepts and propositions which are unverifiable, not because they are erroneous, but because, as Pareto put it, they "surpass experience." Such ideas as that the universe is divided between a good and an evil principle, that souls go through an unending series of reincarnations, that the only escape from sin is by divine grace, are in this category. They are *non*scientific rather than unscientific.[29]

What, then, can be said about the role of such nonscientific ideas? So far as they are existential rather than normative or imaginative in character, there are certain formal similarities with empirical, scientifically

[29] I do not wish to maintain that this distinction possesses ontological significance. To do so would be to alter the plan of the discussion of this paper, which has set out to adhere to the scientific level. Inevitably, the basis of the distinction must be found in current standards of scientific methodology. From this point of view, a nonempirical proposition is one, not only which cannot, because of practical difficulties, be verified with present techniques, but which involves, in the strict operational sense, "meaningless" questions, questions which cannot, in the present state of our scientific and methodological knowledge, be answered by a conceivable operation or combination of them. Whether, at some future time, a completely positivistic philosophy will be capable of demonstration is another question. But I should like to point out that objection to this distinction usually involves the positivistic philosophical position; it is arbitrarily laid down that all departures from the standard of empirical verifiability *must* be in terms of ignorance and error. The position taken here is such that the burden of proof is on him who would object to the distinction. It is his task to show empirically that what have here been called unscientific and nonscientific ideas in fact do not stand in different relations to action. This shifts the argument from the methodological to the factual plane.

valid ideas. The latter may, in one aspect, be considered as mechanisms of orientation of the actor to his situation. Insofar as man is treated as a purposive being, attempting rationally to attain ends, he cannot be considered as fully oriented to his situation until, among other things, he has adequate knowledge of the situation in the respects which are relevant to the attainment of the ends in question, or other functionally equivalent mechanisms.

But the role of existential ideas has so far been considered only in one context, that of the basis of choice of means to given ends. There is in addition the necessity of cognitive orientation of another sort, an answer to the problem of justification of ends which are in fact pursued.[30] If the justifications men give of why they should pursue their ultimate ends are systematically and inductively studied, one fact about them stands out. One very prominent component of all known comprehensive social systems of such justifications must be classed as nonempirical. The more the attempt is made to state the explicit or implicit major premises of such arguments clearly and sharply, the more evident it becomes that they are metaphysical rather than scientific propositions. This, I maintain, is true of all *known* social systems; whether it is ultimately possible to eliminate these nonempirical elements is not a relevant question in the present context.

But the mere demonstration that a certain class of phenomena exists does not prove that their description involves, for the purposes in hand, important variables. The question is not whether nonempirical existential ideas are always to be found in social systems, but whether important features of these social systems can be shown to be functions of variations in the content of these ideas. How is this problem to be attacked?

Most attempts in this field have been couched in terms of the historical or genetic method alone. Of course the only possible causal factors [31] in the genesis of any particular state of affairs are components of particular antecedent states of affairs in the same sequence. But even then causal relationship can be demonstrated only by the use of general concepts and generalized knowledge of uniformities. The question here at issue does not touch the explanation of particular facts, but the establishment of uniformities. The only possible procedure by which this can be done in our field is comparative method which permits the isolation of variables. It is the strict logical counterpart of experiment. One important reason for the unsatisfactory character of the discussion of these problems revolving about Marxism is the fact that it has been almost uniformly couched in genetic, historical terms, as the Marxian theory itself is, and

---

[30] On this problem, see *Structure of Social Action*, chap. 5, 202 ff.
[31] "Factors" in the sense of concrete events or states of affairs, or parts or aspects of them, not of *generalized*, analytical elements like "mass" or "ideas." The two are often confused. See *Structure of Social Action*, chap. 16, 610 ff.

analytical generalizations as to the role of ideas cannot in principle be either proved or disproved by such a method. Hence the indeterminate issue of the controversy.

By far the most significant empirical studies available in this particular field are those of Max Weber in the sociology of religion.[32] Weber was interested in a particular problem of historical imputation, that of the relative role of "material" factors and of the religious ideas of certain branches of Protestantism in the genesis of what he called rational bourgeois capitalism. But Weber's methodological insight showed him that, in the absence of well established general uniformities touching the role of ideas, it was hopeless to attack the problem by more and more elaborate genetic studies of the immediate historical background of modern capitalism. So he turned to the comparative method, the study of the influence of *variations* in the content of religious ideas. . . .

The result of this very comprehensive comparative study in all these phases was not only to build up a strong case for his original historical thesis, that the ideas of ascetic Protestantism actually did play an important causal role in the genesis of modern capitalism. It also resulted in the formulation of a generalized theory of the role of nonempirical existential ideas in relation to action. It is this which is of primary interest here.

It was not Weber's view that religious ideas constitute the principal driving force in the determination of the relevant kinds of action. This role is rather played by what he called religious interests. A typical example is the interest in salvation, an interest which has in turn a complex derivation from, among other things, certain stresses and strains to which individuals are sometimes subjected in social situations where frustration of their worldly ends seems inevitable and founded in the nature of things. But the mere interest in salvation alone is not enough. The question arises as to what kinds of specific action it will motivate. This, Weber's comparative analysis shows, will be very different according to the structure of the existential religious ideas according to which the individual achieves cognitive orientation to the principal nonempirical problems he faces in his situation. . . .

The function of religious ideas is, in relation to the interest in salvation, to "define the situation," to use W. I. Thomas' term. Only by reference to these ideas is it possible to understand, concretely, what specific forms of action are relevant to attainment of salvation, or certainty of it. Weber succeeded in showing that rational, systematic, workmanlike labor in a worldly calling has had this significance to ardent believers in Calvinism and related religious movements, whereas it would be totally meaningless to a believer in Karma and Transmigration on a pantheistic background

---

[32] *Gesammelte Aufsätze zur Religionssoziologie.* 3 vols. The most comprehensive secondary accounts in English are in L. L. Beenion, *Max Weber's Methodology,* and *Structure of Social Action,* chaps. 14 and 15.

no matter how strong his interest in salvation. In this sense, the content of the religious ideas is a significant variable in the determination of the concrete course of action.

So far discussion has been confined to the role of existential ideas. These have been dealt with in two quite different contexts. Empirical ideas have been analyzed in their relation to the problem of selection of means according to the norm of rationality. Nonempirical ideas, on the other hand, have been treated in relation to the teleological problem of orientation of the actor, the justification of selection of ends to pursue. There is a gap between these two treatments which must now be filled. Selection of means has no significance except in relation to ends, while what has been called teleological orientation is equally meaningless unless there is, facing actors, a problem of choice between alternative ends.

Indeed the whole analytical procedure which has here been followed implies that a fundamental role in action is played by normative elements.[33] In the first place, analysis of the underlying assumptions involved in treatment of empirical knowledge as an independent variable in the choice of means has shown that both a positive role of ends, and the existence of determinate relations of ends in a more or less well integrated system are essential to the attribution of causal importance to knowledge. Rational action, in the sense of action guided by valid knowledge, is at the same time action which is normatively oriented. Similarly, the definition of the situation with reference to religious interests could have no meaning apart from the contention that it made a difference to the course of action what ends, among the various alternatives, were chosen.

Not only is action normatively oriented in the sense of pursuing ends, it is also subject to certain normative conditions, to rules which guide it. For instance, in pursuing the end of closing a profitable deal, a business man may consider himself subject to the condition that it shall be done "honestly." From some points of view, such rules may be considered themselves as ends, but they are not the immediate ends of the course of action under analysis. They appear rather as considerations limiting the acceptable range of alternative means, choice among which is to be guided by considerations of rational efficiency.

Now both ends and guiding norms involve a cognitive element, an element of ideas, however little the normative pattern may be exhausted in these terms. That such an element is involved may be brought out by considering the implications of the questions which are inevitably asked when we try to understand action in terms of such normative elements. "What is the end . . ." of a given course of action; for instance, what is meant by making a profitable deal, or "what do you mean . . ." by the

[33] The problem of the significance of normative elements in action is extensively treated throughout the *Structure of Social Action*.

norm to which a course of action is subject, for instance, by honesty in making a deal? It is obvious that the answers to all questions must be in the form of propositions, that is, of ideas. But in this case, ideas are in some sense imputed, not only to the sociological observer of action, but to the actor himself. It is a question not of what honesty means to the observer, but to the actor. It means, for instance, among other things, that he should not attempt to get the other party's consent to the deal by making statements about his products as true which he knows to be false.

The essential point for present purposes is that, in so far as analysis of action in terms of orientation to ends and norms is scientifically useful at all, it implies two things. 1. That it is possible to impute to the actor with adequate precision for the purposes in hand, not only a "will" to attain certain ends or conform with certain norms, but a content of those ends and norms which is capable of formulation as a set of ideas. 2. That variations in this content stand in functional relations to the facts of the system of action other than the system of ideas of the actor. . . .

Turning from Parsons' theoretical treatment of the role of ideas, we can see the relationship between the perception of a problem and ameliorative action in Theodore Abel's "The Pattern of a Successful Political Movement." Although Abel makes a distinction between issue and ideology, which may be considered roughly coterminous with Parsons' existential and normative ideas, we prefer to see them linked. That is, ideology embodies not only a set of ideas about existing social relationships (issues) but also a plan for a better future.

Theodore Abel, "The Pattern of a Successful Political Movement," American Sociological Review, 2 (June 1937), 347–352. Reprinted by permission of Theodore Abel and the American Sociological Association.

"Is Fascism possible in America?," "Does Communism have a chance?," "How can the movement for Birth-control Legislation be made more effective?"

In current discussions of national affairs we frequently encounter questions like these. They demand predictions about social movements and ask for guidance in the execution of plans of change. "Social Movements," being modes of collective or pluralistic behavior, fall in the province of sociology, and the sociologist ought to be equipped to furnish a reply to questions about them.

However, prediction and guidance with regard to social movements, presuppose a generalized knowledge of the subject. We have to know the common and distinct features of social movements, and the factors or conditions significant in determining their development. We must be able to view a given situation, with its unique constellation of factors as the instance of a type; we must appraise it in terms of a general pattern, if we want to express any valid judgment about it. For the type or pattern, when constructed on the basis of intensive studies of individual cases by the method of analytical induction [34] gives us the clues to what is relevant and significant. It tells us what we have to look for in studying a particular situation, and in weighing it in relation to certain questions we may be asked about it.

In short, in order to make valid statements about a particular movement, an adequate *theory* of social movements is necessary.

As yet we have no such theory. In fact, only few attempts have been made at a typological analysis of social movements.[35] They constitute a neglected field of sociological inquiry, and in most text books of sociology, or social psychology we look in vain for any reference to them.

It is the aim of this paper to present a few preliminary considerations of a general nature about social movements. Our remarks on the pattern of social movements shall be limited to a discussion of the significant factors that account for the persistence, growth, and successful termination of a political movement. The propositions set forth here are derived from an intensive study of the Hitler Movement in Germany, made by the author on the basis of six hundred life stories of members of the National Socialist Party.[36]

What is a social movement? As a mode of pluralistic behavior, it belongs to the general class of social phenomena which includes mob actions, booms, crazes, panics, revolutions, and so forth. As a sub-class, a social movement is circumscribed by pluralistic behavior functioning as an organized mass-effort directed toward a change of established folkways or institutions. A social movement may be said to exist wherever a group of individuals, operating within a community, aims to win the support of that community for the establishment of some innovation in the ways and means of promoting a common interest. The innovation or change may be a new or untried mode of procedure, or the restoration of a mode applied in the past. In either case, the intention that underlies the attempted

---

[34] For a discussion of the method of analytical induction, cf. Znaniecki, *The Method of Sociology*, New York, 1934, chap. vi.
[35] Jerome Davis, *Contemporary Social Movements*, N.Y., 1930.
[36] The points discussed in this paper will be more fully developed in a forthcoming book by the author, entitled *The Hitler Movement, an interpretation based upon 600 autobiographies*.

change arises from the experience of the inadequacy of a given procedure, and the belief in the adequacy of the proposed change.

A collective effort may be properly called a social movement only if it operates within the medium of a community. An attempt, for example, to change the by-laws of some association is not a social movement, since such action, as a rule, does not bear upon a community interest. The most significant social movements are those which take place on a national scale, and affect political, religious and moral folkways and institutions.

From the definition of a social movement just given, it follows that a movement is, on the one hand, directed *against* something which it endeavors to combat and eliminate, and on the other hand, favors something, i.e., it is directed *toward* some goal which it is striving to realize. These two opposite but complementary intentions we call respectively the *Issue* and the *Ideology* of a movement.

What is the basis of an issue or an ideology? About behavior in general we know that the intention to act against or for something results from a problem-experience induced by some event impinging upon some value or values that the individual holds. An impinging event is always some action that brings about the modification of existing arrangements through the activities of human beings. The reaction of an individual to an event depends on how he feels or thinks it will affect his social position, possessions, intentions, relations with others—anything that is an integral part of his life organization, and thus is a value which he is set to protect, defend and promote. The event obtains its meaning, is named or defined by the individual according to the way in which he experiences it in terms of his values.

In view of this we may say that underlying the issue of movement is the experience of a *threat* to certain values, while at the basis of an ideology lies the experience of an opportunity to *promote* certain values.

We may now ask what are the significant aspects of an ideology or issue that determine the success of a social movement. Concerning the issue, the following special conditions, favorable to concerted action, must be present, in order that a movement may materialize and maintain itself.

1. The experience of events as a threat to values must be common to many individuals. This presupposes that events will be operative over a wide area, and the values affected will be prevalent in that area.

2. A strong emotional reaction of dissatisfaction and opposition is required to sustain a movement. Assuming a rank-order of values, the strength of the reaction may be said to be directly proportional to the place which the affected values occupy in the individual's hierarchy of values.

3. No movement can occur unless *personal* values are involved, such as social status, income, and so forth. This was the case in the Hitler movement, insofar as it grew out of the dissatisfaction and opposition

induced by such events as the revolution of 1918, the inflation, the economic insecurity of the white-collar class, unemployment,—all of which affected directly the personal welfare of many individuals. But for a movement to materialize, a threat or impairment of personal values must be linked to the experience of a threat or impairment of *social* values. These are values *shared* by members of the same group or community, such as traditions, group prestige, group symbols, and possessions. In terms of such values events in Germany, as for example the establishment of a republican regime, the Versailles treaty, the occupation of the Ruhr were experienced as threats. The linking of social with personal values is important not only because it enables the individual to rationalize his negative reaction, justifying a selfish reason by a group purpose, but also because it facilitates concerted action, and makes possible the fanaticism which in most cases is necessary to keep a movement alive.

4. When different events are experienced as affecting personal and social values the dissatisfaction and opposition resulting therefrom must be capable of being focussed upon some object that can be regarded as the *common source* of the disturbing events. For example, in the case of the Hitler movement, such object was the Republican regime (more specifically the groups and individuals that enacted and supported it), the "System," as it was called, which was made responsible for all the troubles that confronted the individuals and the nation.

An adequate issue is the groundwork upon which enterprising individuals may organize some collective action. But if such action is to become a genuine social movement, there must be not only concerted opposition, but also collective striving for the realization of some plan, or scheme of betterment. Without an ideology, as we called such plans, pluralistic behavior will at best be a revolt.

An adequate ideology is one which first of all appeals to some ideal. In the case of the Hitler Movement in Germany this ideal was the realization of a *Gemeinschaft*, i.e., a primary group relationship, uniting all Germans and in which everyone puts the common interest before self.[37]

Secondly, an adequate ideology expresses the ideal in terms of current glow words, i.e., ideas that carry a strong and prevalent emotional tone. In the Hitler Movement such words were: nationalism, socialism, racial superiority,[38] and so forth, all capable of being reinterpreted in terms of *Gemeinschaft* as the unifying concept.

Thirdly, an ideology, in order to function as the basis of a successful

---

[37] F. Tönnies classical treatise on *"Gemeinschaft und Gesellschaft,"* Berlin, 1887, and subsequent editions, has contributed to the receptivity of this ideal!

[38] Anti-Semitism was an important propaganda device of the Hitler Movement, which appealed to sentiments and beliefs that were inculcated during 1870–1890, when the first wave of organized anti-Semitism since the emancipation of the Jews swept Germany under the leadership of Stoeker, Ahlward, and others. In the ideology, however, anti-Semitism is incident to the idea of "community of blood," as the basis of the *Gemeinschaft* that was to be realized, and in consequence of which the exclusion of all "non-Germans" was advocated.

movement, must link up the goal with the issue. This can best be accomplished by setting forth a plan in which the items are the opposite of that which is regarded as the cause of the problem-experiences. For example, in Germany it was dictatorship vs. parliamentarianism, *Gleichschaltung* vs. liberalism, a policy of the strong hand in dealing with the Allies vs. a policy of concession and compromise, etc.

Fourthly, an ideology must be propounded by a *charismatic* leader—to use Max Weber's terminology [39]—one who can induce in his followers an identification with the ideology as a cause worth fighting and dying for.

In dealing with the issue and ideology of a movement, we are considering only one group of significant factors which have to be present in order to make a movement successful. However, issue and ideology are, in a sense, only *structural* elements of a movement. The *dynamic* elements are the activities of individuals who on the basis of an issue and an ideology engage in propaganda and organization for the purpose of winning the support of the community, and in the quest for power. These individuals are banded together into what we may call the *promotion group* of the movement. The National-Socialist-German-Workmen's Party was such a promotion group. From the point of view of the causal analysis of a movement, the issue and ideology may be regarded as the basic conditions, or the potential factors which might induce individuals to action in a certain direction. For the initiation, growth and successful termination of the action, however, the activities of a promotion group and its leaders are primarily responsible. Applied to the Hitler Movement, for example, this means that it is wrong to account for its success in terms of unemployment, Versailles treaty, and similar causes. On the basis of these factors many other promotion groups attempted to organize a movement and obtain control of the government, such as the *Stahlhelm*, the Communists, and others. Primarily responsible for the success of the Hitler Movement was the way in which the promotion group presented the issue, made the ideology attractive, and manipulated the technique of propaganda and organization.

It is necessary, therefore, to consider a second group of factors, those relating to the activities of the promotion group of a movement, if we want to complete a pattern of the significant and relevant elements of a social movement.

It is more difficult to generalize on the promotion aspect of a movement than on its issue and ideology. The difficulty is due in part to the scarcity of comparable data. To a large extent, it is due, however, to the fact that the activities of a promotion group involve matters of strategy and tactics, which are to a considerable degree dependent upon the *particular* situation in which the group operates. This question awaits further investigation.

For the time being, we can generalize with a certain degree of con-

[39] M. Weber, *Wirtschaft und Gemeinschaft*, 1922, p. 124.

fidence on the *tasks* which confront a promotion group, and which it must solve if a strong and successful movement is to materialize.

A promoting group must first of all hold the *attention* of the community. In the case of the Hitler Movement this task was accomplished by maintaining a persistent barrage of propaganda through meetings, the press, pamphlets and posters, displays of symbols, ostentatious demonstrations, like parades and party congresses and participation in affairs affecting the community, as in the case of the Young Plan.

Secondly, it must *justify* its claim for leadership. This task the Hitler group achieved by keeping the issue alive, continuously stirring up prevalent dissatisfaction and opposition, and skilfully linking dissatisfactions with its ideology. Acceptance of the ideology was sought for by appeal to traditions and prevailing sentiments, for example, to sentiments for "discipline and order," for unity, and for the abolition of classes.

Thirdly, a promotion group must win the *confidence* of the masses, by maneuvering itself into a position of ascendancy over competing groups, and by successfully combating its opponents. Thus, in the case of the Hitler Movement, the National Socialist Party succeeded in absorbing the members of most other groups with a nationalistic ideology, by pursuing a policy of "no compromise and no alliance." These members, as well as the large numbers of voters who supported the movement eventually, were won over in many cases by the shows of strength and successful defiance of the radical leftist groups, particularly the communists. This the promotion group accomplished by direct invasion of the "strongholds of the enemy," and readiness to "fight it out" if necessary.

A fourth task is the development of an adequate organization not merely for the carrying out of propaganda, and for the struggle with competing and opposing groups, but also in preparation for the taking over of power.

These tasks require adequate leadership. What determines adequate leadership is a question we cannot answer here. We can emphasize only this point: the success of a promotional group depends to a considerable extent on its having a charismatic leader, who functions as a glorified symbol of the movement and can command the unquestioned obedience and devotion of his followers. For allegiance to a leader, the inspiration of his charisma is primarily responsible for the winning and holding of active participants, who not only carry on the propaganda and struggle, which frequently requires neglect of personal interests, but who possess the peculiar fanaticism that enables an individual to be steadfast in the face of abuse and persecution. The fact that the Hitler Movement had a charismatic leader was, therefore, an important factor in its success.

The propositions advanced in this paper require further testing and elucidation. They indicate the direction in which a theory of social movements should be developed. As we advance our knowledge by further studies, and particularly, as we succeed in developing indices that will test the presence or absence of *significant* factors in *particular* situations, we shall be able as sociologists to perform the important function of predicting and guiding social movements, in a better fashion than we can at present.

The structuring of a new world view such as class consciousness or radical awareness—that is, the organizations of ideology—is what we term an "emergent reality." As we have seen, the organization of ideology involves a rejection of the generally accepted commonsense view of the world and the creation of another sense of reality. This newly significant world view becomes in itself an alternative conscience collective adhered to by the members of a social movement. For example, the middle class person who joined the Stalinist movement in the thirties adopted the world view of the "working class intellectual," taking on both the clothing style and the jargon of his idealized proletariat. Lemert notes: "a radical group bidding for the support of the working classes must necessarily mirror working class morality in rules of conduct for its members. . . . American Communists at one time discarded neckties and affected leather jackets in order to symbolize their working class identification." [40] Similarly, the insurance salesman who gives up his weekend golf in favor of guerrilla training with the Minutemen begins to see himself as an undercover freedom fighter. Insurance forms and Rotary Club activities become part of another, less significant, reality: they constitute his "Clark Kent" identity. His newly significant consciousness is embodied in his role as a preserver of freedom against an international conspiracy. Organized ideology, therefore, does not accept the generalized tenets of status quo values and norms; its adherents see the world through different eyes. In turn, this perception affects the movement's societal role and the internal interactions of its members. In the following article, Egon Bittner points out that radicals do not share the commonsense view of the world—the conscience collective. For this reason, they are disadvantaged vis-à-vis the established social system. As a result, their alternative unity of meaning or ideology becomes more and more important as a basis for action.

[40] Edwin E. Lemert, *Social Pathology* (New York: McGraw Hill Book Co., 1951), pp. 192–199.

Excerpts from Egon Bittner, "Radicalism and the Organization of Radical Movements," American Sociological Review, 28 (December 1963), 928–929, 932–940. *Revision of a paper read at the annual meetings of the Pacific Sociological Association, 1962. Reprinted by permission of Egon Bittner and the American Sociological Association.*

Sociological and psychological approaches to the study of radicalism tend to focus on one aspect of the problem and neglect another. Both take for granted, or find as an immediately given datum, the existence of a form of opinion or belief which they variously identify as radicalism, totalitarianism, extremism or authoritarianism and beyond that find that such beliefs motivate the activities of select collectivities. Having found such groups and persuasions, these scholars attempt to determine what kinds of persons are suitably motivated to hold radical beliefs and engage in radical action. Thus, for example, Adorno and co-workers have shown how to account for the supply of psychologically suitable persons.[41] Similarly, Lipset accounts for the supply of interested participants by using one of the most important schemas of manifest self-interest, social class.[42] But the discovery of discriminable types of classes of persons who are appropriately motivated to accept some pattern of belief as true and some pattern of conduct that accords with this belief as right, does not yet constitute an adequate explanation for the existence of these patterns in the first place.[43] This paper attempts to deal with this unsolved problem in the sociological study of radicalism.

It is important to emphasize that the following argument is not polemically opposed to, or even independent of, the fine researches cited in the foregoing remarks. We will seek to give an account of the rise of

[41] T. W. Adorno, E. Frenkel-Brunswick, D. J. Levinson & N. R. Sanford, *The Authoritarian Personality* (New York: Harper, 1950). See also Richard Christie and Marie Jahoda (eds.), *Studies in the Scope and Method of the 'Authoritarian Personality'* (Glencoe, Ill.: The Free Press, 1954).
[42] Two of Lipset's papers are of primary interest here: "Democracy and Working-Class Authoritarianism," *American Sociological Review,* Vol. 24 (August 1959), pp. 482–501; and "Social Stratification and Right Wing Extremism," *British Journal of Sociology,* Vol. 10 (December 1959), pp. 346–382. Both of these papers are reprinted in slightly modified form in his *Political Man* (Garden City, N.Y.: Doubleday, 1960).
[43] For a critique of all efforts to interpret normatively governed, socially structured action in terms of motivational states of actors, see Talcott Parsons, *The Structure of Social Action* (2nd ed.); (Glencoe, Ill.: The Free Press, 1949), especially Chapters II, III, and IV.

radicalism without regard for the question of motivation at the level of participating persons, but we insist that no pattern of belief or morality can effectively structure action unless there are persons who are disposed to accept it and comply with it.

RADICALISM AND THE COMMON SENSE OUTLOOK

In the following, radicalism will be discussed as a pure type of social event, with the aim of defining its constitutive property. What will be said will have to hold with equal force for beliefs and actions that find their primary expression in politics, religion, economics, philosophy or any other major domain of human concern, regardless of their content. We will not set out with a definition of radicalism, or even sets of features commonly associated with radicalism in order to relate them to known properties of social systems. Only in a sense of vaguely anticipating the results of our reasoning are we at the onset informed that radicalism refers to:

1. "a conspicuously stressed attitude or frame of mind . . . which may envisage the entire complex of a society or a culture . . . [or] tends to expand in scope until [its] field is coincident with the entire setup of a society."
2. "a distinct philosophy and program of social change looking toward systematic destruction of what is hated, and its replacement by an art, a faith, a science or a society logically demonstrated as true and good and beautiful and just. . . ."[44]

We take from this reference that a definitive feature of radicalism is that it differs from the normal, ordinary, traditionally sanctioned worldview prevalent in any society and that this is not a difference of degree but a juxtaposition of opposites. . . .

PROPHECY AND RATIONAL CONSISTENCY OF MEANING

Not all radical critiques are . . . shared off against the realm of common sense by the injunction of moral neutrality [as in the case of science] and it is to those that we now turn. These critiques share only one, but a critically important, feature with science, namely, *they seek a unified and internally consistent interpretation of the meaning of the world.* In a

---

[44] Horace M. Kallen, "Radicalism," in *Encyclopedia of the Social Sciences*, Vol. 13, pp. 51–52.

narrow reading of Max Weber such revisions are called prophecies.⁴⁵ Weber stated that

> prophecy always means, in the first place for the prophet himself, and then for his helpmates: a unitary view of life won by taking a deliberately *unified meaningful* position to it. Life and the world, the social and the cosmic events, have for the prophet a decidedly systematic unity of meaning, and the conduct of men must, in order to bring salvation, be oriented toward it and must be formed by this relationship to produce a sense of meaningful unity . . . [prophecy] always involves, only in various degrees and with various results, the synthesis of all practical conduct into a *way-of-life (Lebensfuehrung)*, no matter what the appearance of the individual case may be.⁴⁶

Weber discussed one other feature of prophecy with equal emphasis, namely the personal charisma of the prophet. Since we are at this point interested in the outlook rather than the person who promulgates it, we will disregard this feature now and return to it later. The crucial characteristic of prophecy which in our argument defines it as a radical outlook, is not to be found in its contents, nor in its emotionalism, nor in its intolerance, nor even in the fact that it presents a new rationalization of the past, present and future, but in the fact that it juxtaposes to a traditionally sanctioned, heterogeneous interpretation of meaning a rationally consistent interpretation.⁴⁷

Weber repeatedly insisted that although prophetic rationalizations have their focus of appeal at the level of the lower classes as doctrines of redemption from meaningless suffering, they are not indigenous to these strata. Long before Ortega y Gasset, he taught that the masses are, even when suffering, culturally inert.⁴⁸ Prophecy itself is the demand

---

⁴⁵ By narrow reading we mean that we will disregard the voluminous historical qualifications that Weber attaches to the defining characteristic of prophecy. Extensive discussions of this problem can be found in at least four places in Weber's work: *Wirtschaft und Gesellschaft* (4th ed. by Johannes Winckelmann) (Tubingen, J. C. B. Mohr, 1956), Zweiter Teil, Kapitel V; *Gesammelte Aufsaetze zur Religionssoziologie* (Tubingen, J. C. B. Mohr, 1923), Vol. 1, pp. 237–275, and 323–359; and *ibid.*, Vol. II, pp. 281–400. A superb summary of Weber's major points can be found in Parsons' *The Structure of Social Action*, pp. 563–575.

⁴⁶ *Wirtschaft und Gesellschaft*, p. 275 (p. 257 in 1st, 2nd and 3rd editions, emphases in original, translation by the author of this paper).

⁴⁷ Weber's argument on the principled character of prophecy has been confirmed in the researches of a scholar of an entirely different bent. Ronald A. Knox in his tart but illuminating history of enthusiastic heresy proposed that the heretic prophet selects one element of the creed and expands it into a universal principle. In his appraisal of Tertullian as the principal spokesman for Montanism he stated: "He was incurably a logician, his whole temper was impatient of compromises, of half-way houses . . . his intellectual bias impelled him towards the party of consistency." Concerning a heresy that occurred 1500 years later, he writes "It is the vice of Quietism, that it cannot leave these half-resolved antimonies alone; it must always be trying to tidy up the situation." *Enthusiasm: A Chapter in the History of Religion* (New York: Oxford University Press, 1961), pp. 46 and 270 respectively.

⁴⁸ "By themselves, the masses have everywhere remained engulfed in the massive and archaic growth of magic—unless a prophecy that holds out specific promises has swept

"that *the world order in its totality* is, could, and should somehow be a 'meaningful' cosmos. This quest, the core of *genuine religious rationalism*, has been borne precisely by the strata of intellectuals."[49] To be sure, a prophetically inspired *movement* requires the presence of persons who are systematically deprived of their share of good fortune, that is, groups that Lipset calls "displaced."[50] The presence of such groups is not in itself, however, a sufficient condition for the appearance of prophecy or prophetically inspired movements.

Weber's argument is in the context of his study of religion but there is no reason why it should not be extrapolated to the secular realm.[51] If the heterogeneous beliefs, judgments, maxims and pieties that characterize archaic forms of religion are recognized as cognate with the realm of every-day life, consisting largely of heterogeneous but traditionally stereotyped and sanctioned domains of meaning in empirical lore and in practical morality, then religious prophecy is cognate with radical secular doctrines.

In studies of radical, revisionist, totalitarian and extremist movements, the importance of underlying doctrines has been both affirmed and denied.[52] Some scholars, guided by the radical's strong concern with purity of belief, have proposed that radical movements cultivate the appearance of doctrinal consistency without necessarily being in fact restrained by the implied discipline.[53] This view suffers from a difficulty inherent in much current work concerning rationality. Failure to recognize rational consistency in radical doctrines and practices goes back to the work of Vilfredo Pareto. Pareto proposed that thought and conduct may be considered rational if, and only if, the means-end relations involved are construed in accordance with formal logic and science. This conception of rationality throws error, mistake, intuition, sentiment and visceral whim into the undifferentiated category of the irrational. Instead,

---

them into a religious movement of an ethical character." Hans H. Gerth and C. Wright Mills (eds.), *From Max Weber: Essays in Sociology* (New York: Oxford University Press, 1958), p. 277.
[49] *Ibid.*, p. 281 (emphases supplied).
[50] "Social Stratification and Right-Wing Extremism," *op. cit.*, p. 352.
[51] We cannot here go into Weber's discussion of the historical circumstances that gave rise to prophetic rationality nor the importance he attributes to the phenomenon for the development of the Western tradition. These points are fully recognized and lucidly discussed in Reinhard Bendix, *Max Weber: An Intellectual Portrait* (Garden City, N.Y.: Doubleday, 1960).
[52] Carl J. Friedrich and Zbigniew Brzezinski, *Totalitarian Dictatorship and Autocracy* (Cambridge: Harvard University Press, 1956), pp. 9, 118 ff., 130 ff.; similarly Joseph M. Bochenski and Gerhard Neumeye, *Handbuch des Weltkommunismus* (Freiburg-Munchen: Alber, 1958), p. 13; but cf. C. W. Cassinelli, "Totalitarianism, Ideology and Propaganda," *Journal of Politics* 22 (February 1960), pp. 68–95.
[53] Alex Inkeles, "The Totalitarian Mystique: Some Impressions of the Dynamics of Totalitarian Society," in Carl J. Friedrich (ed.), *Totalitarianism* (Cambridge: Harvard University Press, 1954), pp. 88–108; see also the discussion of Ketman in Czeslaw Milosz, *The Captive Mind* (New York: Vintage Books, 1959).

we use the term rational in accordance with the teachings of Max Weber, that is, as pertaining to the grasp of meaning, and with full recognition of the difference between formal and substantive rationality.[54]

By speaking of rational unity of meaning, we do not *ipso facto* submit it to the jurisdiction of standards that are relevant to the thought and work of the scientist. We merely propose that the radical gives *unity of meaning* evaluative primacy, that he tends to think, argue and act on grounds of an over-riding principle, even if the way in which he expands the relevance of the principle is utterly absurd in the light of formal logic. Thus, we propose that it is incorrect to deny unity of meaning to the expressions of Hitler because his writings and speeches contain elements that the political scientist recognizes as contradictory or obscure. The whole import of Hitler's thought and action denies the validity of *formalized* reasoning and derives from the non-logical presuppositions of *Rasse und Volksgeist*. Similarly, logically coherent rationalizations of the theological doctrine of Charity either impoverish it to the limit of oblivion or are imponderable, but this did not prevent the movement of Port Royal, because the coherence of its radical beliefs, rested on what its greatest exponent, Rascal, called a *logique de coeur*.

In short, by making the unity of meaning the defining characteristic of an outlook and way of life called radicalism, we indicate that an adherent adopts as morally binding an internally consistent schema of interpretation and that he is, therefore, obliged to reason from a rigidly supreme principle to all occasions of actual conduct. In practice this means that the relevance of a single principle can never be justifiably denied and that a principled justification of action can always be demanded and obtained under the threat of sanction. In the following we should like to demonstrate that all the other well known features of radical action groups can be derived from this single characteristic.[55]

RADICALISM AND THE ORGANIZATION OF ACTION

If we consider that we must so order our practical affairs as not to run afoul of a very considerable variety of standards of judgment that are not fully compatible with each other, do not have a clear-cut hierarchy of primacy and are regarded as binding and enforceable only in the light of

---

[54] Max Weber, *The Theory of Social and Economic Organization* (Glencoe, Ill.: The Free Press, 1947), pp. 89 ff., 184 ff.

[55] In a similar way, Martin Drath speaks about a "Primarphenomen des Totalitarismus, das seine Eigenart bestimmt und bis ins einzelne durchformt." "Einleitung," in Ernst Richard, *Macht ohne Mandat*. (Schriften des Instituts für Politische Wissenschaft, No. 11, Köln-Oplanden, 1958). He defines the "Primarphenomen," without much elaboration, "das dieser (Totalitarismus) gegenüber den in der Gesellschaft herrschenden Wertungen ein ganz anderes Wertungssystem durchsetzen will."

additional vaguely denied information; if we consider that for every maxim of conduct we can think of a situation to which it does not apply or in which it can be overruled by a superior maxim; if we consider that unmitigated adherence to principle is regarded as vice or at least folly; and if we finally consider that this knowledge orients our behavior in its course, then it is clear that all efforts to live by an internally consistent schema of interpretation are necessarily doomed to fail. This must be true for any doctrinally pure outlook, regardless of its superior virtue, empirical adequacy, economic efficiency, or logical coherence. As with so many other things, this was first seen by great poets who have provided us with many examples showing that uncompromising moral rectitude leads to tragedy in an "imperfect" world. The heroes of classical tragedy are victims not of villains but of reasonable men.

In only two ways could radical revisions of traditionally sanctioned heterogeneous interpretations of meaning effectively govern conduct in organized collectivities. The first way abandons the purity of the doctrine through a slow assimilation of casuistic interpretations, the development of dogma and bureaucratization. This process is best known in the transformation of cults into churches and has been described by Weber as the process of routinization of charisma.[56] There can be no doubt that, save for the rarest of exceptions, this is the course of development encountered in prophetically inspired movements that remain active for protracted periods of time.[57]

The alternative to this development is to impose upon the believers conditions that would make doctrinal impurity as difficult and unattractive as possible. This cannot be done by discouraging and penalizing the attitude of skepticism alone. Nor is it sufficient to continue to furnish proof of the merits of the doctrine because contradictory evidence will be unavoidable in practical experience. The task can only be accomplished by eliminating the possibility that believers will assign to any experience the significance of counterevidence discrediting the professed faith. Inasmuch as strict adherence to a fully integrated doctrine inevitably leads, in a rich and varied life, to reversals that will reflect unfavorably upon the creed, radical action groups must have some way to reduce the horizon

[56] Max Weber, *Theory of Social and Economic Organization*, pp. 367–373. About the world of secular politics he says, "the crusading leader and the faith itself fade away, or, what is even more effective, the faith becomes part of the conventional phraseology of political Philistines and banausic technicians." See "Politics as a Vocation," *From Max Weber: Essays in Sociology*, p. 125. Similarly, Lipset observed, "The history of most leftist parties has been largely an evolution from a conscious internationalist Marxist position to an 'opportunistic' appeal in which large segments of the population are wooed." *Agrarian Socialism* (Berkeley and Los Angeles: University of California Press, 1950), p. 156.
[57] Interestingly, however, the seed of radicalism remains viable in them, for such dogmatised creeds continue to produce radical prophetic apostasies, as Ronald Knox has demonstrated for Christianity.

of possible encounters and cause the remaining contingencies of potential embarrassment to be seen as either not pertaining or, when "correctly" seen, further boosting the doctrine.

One might say that the radical is in a position of peculiar polemic disadvantage with respect to the person using the socially sanctioned outlook of common sense. On the one hand, he has an initial advantage, in part because his opposition will tend to accept the validity of the premise from which the radical can argue cogently to conclusions that his opponent never envisioned and will not accept, and in part because the radical's deliberate concern with doctrine makes him a superior polemicist.[58] On the other hand, the radical can never win an argument in the long run if experience is defined as the relevant test of validity, as it must be if the creed pertains to existential and moral matters.

If radical movements can retain their purity only as long as they manage to discredit all possible counterevidence peremptorily, then coping with reversals cannot be left to the occasion of their actual occurrence, and life in radical movements must contain norms of conduct and belief that blanket a maximum of future contingencies. Of course it must not be thought that such norms have the deliberately intended effect of enhancing the loyalty of the believers and the integrity of the movement. From the member's point of view, they are usually seen as integral to the substantive content of the doctrine. Regardless, however, of how they are seen, these normative features of radicalism are at a different level of analysis than the rule of internal coherence and unity of the schema of interpretation. Whereas the latter defines an outlook as radical, the former occur only if the outlook is used as a principle governing a paramount way of life.

These normative features organize the loyalties of the members to generate the movement's impetus and power from within.[59]

We can, therefore, speak of the task of eliminating the possibility that derogatory significance will be attached to experience as the organizational task of the movement, and of various features of belief and actions often encountered in such movements as the preferred solutions of this task.

---

[58] The radical's opponent is here seen as a normal wide awake, generally competent adult using the outlook of common sense, who will tend to grant the validity of the premise *inter alia*, a restriction which the radical never intended to respect.

[59] Talcott Parsons recently defined the sociological analysis of power to consist of two problems. The first, traditionally recognized as the principal, concerns the allocation of power within the system, the second concerns the mobilization of existing facilities and resources to generate power for the system as a whole. See "The Distribution of Power in American Society," in *Structure and Process in Modern Societies* (Glencoe, Ill.: The Free Press, 1960), pp. 199–225. Elsewhere, in a more restricted framework, he speaks of the second problem of power as "organization in the technical sense of the term." See "A Sociological Approach to the Theory of Organization," *ibid.*, pp. 27–28.

Arguing from the standpoint of Parsons' theory of system analysis, three mechanisms are involved here.

1. The members' cathectic drives must be so directed as to make gratification instrumental in, or at least compatible with, promoting the system's movement toward its goals. Participation in the movement must contain some psychologically satisfying pay-offs in return for its very considerable claims on the members' energy and devotion.

2. There must exist a stable solution of internal system problems to minimize the amount of energy required to maintain internal harmony. This pertains particularly to allocation of authority and distribution of inequality. The solution must leave as little as possible to negotiation between potentially competent claims.

3. Relatively rigid boundaries against the system's environment must exist to prevent energy leaks. This is done primarily by reducing the members' contributions to outside causes and monopolizing his interests for the movement.[60]

It is important to emphasize that the functional focus of these mechanisms is to protect the validity of the doctrine as a code of conduct for its adherent, to enhance his disposition to comply with its tenets, and through this, to contribute to the viability, integrity and continuity of the movement. They must be retained and cultivated even if their implementation increases hostility and resistance to the movement and thus impedes its progress toward its goals.

ORGANIZATIONAL SOLUTIONS OF RADICAL MOVEMENTS

On the basis of these formal considerations, and on the basis of descriptions of existing movements that have been characterized as radical, totalitarian, authoritarian, extremist and the like,[61] the following list of substantive features of belief and conduct is proposed as an inventory of efficient solutions of a radical movement's organizational tasks. The inventory is encumbered with all the deficiencies and risks involved in ideal-type constructions;[62] it is admittedly incomplete, and it cannot be

[60] The *first* mechanism operates on the boundary of hierarchical control exerted from the social system to the personality as a system, and the *latter two* differentiate along the axis of internal-external significance of system function. Although these mechanisms operate in all social systems to some extent, they receive in radical movements a monotonous emphasis that justifies their characterization as extreme.
[61] The source to which the following presentation is most indebted, aside from the earlier cited book by Ronald A. Knox, is Philip Selznick, *The Organizational Weapon* (Santa Monica: The Rand Corporation, 1952).
[62] There is no need to consult the critics of Weber for the limitations of ideal-type constructions; see *The Theory of Social and Economic Organization*, pp. 89 ff., 108 ff., and *The Methodology of the Social Sciences* (Glencoe, Ill.: The Free Press, 1949), pp. 89 ff.

said that its component parts are necessary in the way in which they are outlined here. Because it would be unrealistic to attempt to relate the proposed solutions preferentially to the three organizational tasks outlined above, it is suggested that all of them overdetermine the outcome to which they seem to be functionally related, thus serving the three requirements more or less indiscriminately.

1. *A sense of charisma must attach to the movement and its creed.* According to Weber, this quality is invested in the person of the prophet and bestowed through him on his followers. But this is not the only way it can be perceived. Not all leaders say, "Verily, verily, I say unto you, he that believes in me has everlasting life. I am that bread of life." [63] Many great reformers were over-powering personalities, unhesitatingly followed as captains of policy and interpreters of the faith without claiming to be, or being seen as incumbents of special statuses in the divine cosmos. . . .

2. *The doctrine that inspires the movement should contain information from outside the realm of every-day life.* This condition is most obviously fulfilled in the hierophany of the religious prophet; he announces the mystical origin of his teachings. . . .

3. *On all rungs of membership, there must be an intensive concern for the purity of belief.* The value sought must be purity, not clarity, of belief. Soul-searching on the level of the individual believer and purges on the level of the collectivity continuously cleanse the doctrine of foreign elements. . . .

4. *No part of a member's life can be defined as lying outside the scope of the doctrine or the movement.* That is, nothing is so private as to be merely a matter of personal choice or preference. Members are obliged to carry the burden of their convictions into every nook and cranny of their personal lives, to eliminate as far as possible any source of distraction. . . .

5. Since disappointments, reversals and failure are commonplace in the lives of radicals, *suffering must be made an integral part of the conception of the progress of the movement* in order to minimize its effects on the morale of the members. . . .

6. *All traditional extra-group ties must be suspended;* the member owes nothing to the outside, regardless of the nature of the pre-existing bond. . . .

7. *The movement should exploit outside sentiment against it for its own organizational advantage.* We have already noted that the member must sacrifice his position in the outside world. Beyond that, he should be publicly compromised by his participation in the movement, so that his return to the world is unacceptable to his former associates and incompatible with his feelings of self-respect. The member can put himself and his resources at the disposal of the movement with much less hesitation if he knows that all alternatives are practically closed to him.

[63] St. John, 6:47, 48.

CONCLUSION

It goes without saying that the here-described features of life and belief in radical movements are no more likely to be found in complete and pure form in any concrete movements than the ideal-type features of bureaucracy are to be found in any functioning structure of authority, and no more than the real distance traveled by any actually falling object can be determined by using the formula $D = \frac{1}{2}gt^2$ alone. Obviously, situational factors, the substantive content of the doctrine, and the makeup of the group, will influence the choice of solutions of its organizational tasks. Unique exigencies must be met topically, and all movements must engage in contingently justified tactics. Further, all groups must develop symbolic expressions to emphasize their distinctiveness and to celebrate their cause, and they will tend to select them from the existing symbolism peculiar to the society within which they occur.

If, however, we postulate that the definitive characteristic of radical movements is that they are inspired by doctrines and beliefs that seek to impose a unified, internally consistent schema of interpretation upon a world of heterogeneous meanings, a schema necessarily disconfirmed in practical experience, and if we assume that the cited organizational solutions discredit the disconfirmation and thus protect the validity of the doctrine in the eyes of the believers as well as the unity and continuity of the movement, then we must consider the contingent problem of finding persons most suited to participate in it. The question arises necessarily because no socially structured order of interaction will remain stable over time unless the persons whose activities produce it find it compatible with their psychological needs and the pursuit of self-interest as they see it. Earlier we pointed out that previous researches on radicalism have gone a long way toward solving this problem.

A variety of characteristics commonly associated with participation in radical movements, such as origin in a socially displaced stratum of the society and the personality traits of dependence, rigidity, sado-masochism, and others, appear to fit the solution of organizational tasks of the movement. It may well be that such movements could never get started or gather momentum were it not for the presence of suitably disposed adherents in the larger society. In this sense only is radicalism in movements a function of personality traits and social position. Movements and their characteristics as such are not the product of the presence of these persons: to say that some social order benefits the perceived interests and cathectic drives of some persons is only half the explanation of its structure. Irrational moods and inclinations produce chaos, not order. It is necessary to show that personal attitudes are socially sanctioned and that these sanctions are social facts precisely in the sense Durkheim gave the term; that they are not felt by many is no reason to disregard their existence.[64] That we are not merely guessing at the existence of social restraints is evident in the many testimonials of apostate members of radical movements, for they show that wherever the right psychological disposition is absent the desired attitudes are enforced as a matter of bitter discipline.

When considered not as a person's way of relating to his environment, but as a group's organized response to its peculiar disadvantage, the features of radicalism appear as calculated and efficient mechanisms. That they must be compatible with or even feed on the emotional life of the persons who implement them is almost a foregone conclusion. It was Karl Mannheim who remarked about the revolutionary proletariat: "Here then we are confronted with the combination of the most extreme rationalism with some of the most extreme irrational elements; this shows that the 'irrational' proves on closer observation more complex than we are at first inclined to imagine." [65]

As we can see from the preceding examples, a movement's social role, vis-à-vis both the society in which it emerges and its own membership, is an important factor in its continuing viability. If it manages to avoid the hazards of external suppression and internal dissolution, it must continue to play a dual, and sometimes contradictory, role. On the one hand, it must remain nonlegitimate in terms of existing institutional goals and practices in order to provide relevant alternatives. Otherwise, it is merely part of the status quo. On the other hand, its members must be provided with a radically consistent world view—an historically based interpretation of the present and a plan of goals and tactics for the future—in order to hold their allegiance and mobilize their activities. Therefore, mere reaction to a problem or an issue is not enough. A social movement is inextricably involved with basic (i.e., radical) questions such as "How have things come to be as they are?" and "What is to be done?" For this reason, we have emphasized the ideological aspects of social movements: they are, in the final analysis, ideological organizations.

This emphasis helps to clarify the question of recruitment into social movements—a question which has been largely ignored in the literature, except from the viewpoint of social psychology. However, as we pointed out in chapter 3, recruitment into movements depends not upon the psychology of individuals but rather upon the differential social significance (rele-

---

[64] In an inimitable sentence, which I am unable to locate in his work again, Durkheim said, "If to a certain extent sensibility has the same end as reason, it cannot be humbled by submitting to the latter."
[65] Karl Mannheim, "Conservative Thought," in *Essays on Sociology and Social Psychology* (London: Routledge and Kegan Paul, 1953), p. 92.

vance vis-à-vis the problems of society) of movements during any historical period. Considering the element of social significance is a manifest consequence of focusing on social movements as organizations of ideology.

All the necessary structural conditions for a movement exist at any given point in time. These conditions exist in the fact, in the Durkheimian sense, of social problems. Social problems may be inherent in any number of real conditions and practices, such as racial discrimination, urban blight, slum lords, labor injunctions, the draft, and so on. These social facts are not, however, sufficient conditions for the emergence of a movement. This is because the conscience collective accepts these conditions and procedures as part of the status quo—they are the facts of life (evil, perhaps, but functionally necessary). For example, racial discrimination existed long before Rosa Parks sat in the "white only" section of a Montgomery bus in 1955 and triggered (according to many observers) the Southern civil rights movement. Similarly, massive draft protests are a relatively recent phenomenon despite the fact that a peacetime conscription has been in effect ever since the advent of the Cold War. What must be added to these social facts is a changed state of mind in those who are experiencing them (a consciousness of dysfunction). With this addition, the social fact of dysfunction becomes a salient prerequisite for the organization of an ideology. In other words, necessary conditions for a social movement become sufficient at the point when they attain social significance.

Social significance is bestowed on ideologies, directly and indirectly, by the conscience collective when the social problems they address are considered legitimate and affect a reasonable portion of the general population. For example, the Great Depression resurrected the fragmented Socialist Party and added significance to the American Stalinists. The Cold War revived the populist sentiments of an earlier period in the form of Senator Joseph McCarthy and later the John Birch Society. The 1954 Brown vs. the Board of Education decision by the United States Supreme Court provided a similar impetus for those concerned with the injustices of racial segregation. It is important, however, to bear in mind that social significance does not imply legitimation. The programs of the John Birch Society, while viewed by many as long-overdue solutions to the "menace of international Communism," are widely condemned by other segments of the society. Similarly, black power is a socially significant ideology, but it is not regarded as legitimate by the (white) public in which political power resides.

Thus, a key factor determining the significance of an ideology appears to be the historical relevance of a problem situation. In describing individual motivation for affiliation with given movements, a number of accounts have suggested this historical-situational factor. Paul Jacobs, in his discussion of the City College of New York (CCNY), suggests the historical confluence of the Depression, Fascism, and race and ethnic prejudice as contributing to a radical atmosphere during the thirties:

> So Hitler was everywhere and forced us to talk continually about politics.
> Arguing excitedly about politics, about the depression, about anti-Negro prejudice, about anti-Semitism, and how to fight against German and Italian fascism took up a lot of time at City College. . . . There, . . . I watched the other students eating their sandwiches from paper bags, studying and playing chess, and, among the politicals, always arguing. Each political group had its own alcove, and an informal understanding existed that no other group would attempt to dispossess it. Very often, though, the "members" of one alcove drifted over to another, either for a discussion if there was any common political bond between them or for a violent argument when the groups were as widely separated as, say, the Stalinists and the Trotskyists.
> As far as I was concerned, those alcove discussions were the most important part of life at City College. I knew there were classes, for I had to attend them, and I knew there were other student activities, for the posters advertising the clubs and lectures were everywhere; but for me there was only one world into which I wanted to be taken and accepted: the radical atmosphere which dominated City College in those years. . . .
> What I also sought and found as I wandered through the alcoves, listening intently to the talk, was an affirmation of my contempt for and impatience with business and with the making of money, pursuits I identified with my parents. The CCNY radicals regarded businessmen as a very low form of life. Because of the depression, the businessman and business generally had become objects of contempt and hatred. . . .[66]

An ex-Stalinist describes his political involvement as follows:

> I thought that these young people were fighting for things I wanted. I hated discrimination and I didn't like to see people pushed around. I saw in my new friends an organized way of fighting these injustices and having fun while doing it.
> I was invited to attend a meeting of my local American Youth for Democracy club, an invitation which I accepted. . . . There were fifteen or so people there. The wall was barren except for a few posters. I received a warm welcome. The subject of the meeting was the fight against universal military training. There was also a discussion on saving the Office of Price Administration.
> Before the evening was over I was a member of the American Youth for Democracy.[67]

These accounts suggest that when a person is ready to become a radical (i.e., has a consciousness of dysfunction), it is often the movement that

---

[66] Paul Jacobs, *Is Curly Jewish: A Political Self-Portrait* (New York: Atheneum Press, 1965), pp. 18–19.
[67] Harvey Matusow, *False Witness* (New York: Cameron and Kahn, 1955), p. 24.

gets to him first that will recruit him. This element of propinquity is illustrated in the following selection by William Kornhauser.

William Kornhauser, "Social Bases of Political Commitment: A Study of Liberals and Radicals," in Human Behavior and Social Processes, Arnold M. Rose, ed., (Boston: Houghton Mifflin Company, 1962), pp. 321–339. Reprinted by permission of William Kornhauser and Houghton Mifflin Company.

To incur a commitment is to become more or less unavailable for alternative lines of action. Commitment entails more than merely voicing a choice, although a pledge or promise certainly is a simple way of becoming committed. The additional element in commitment is the "force of circumstances" to which one becomes exposed by virtue of pursuing a course of action. A commitment consists in the various relations which are formed in the process of acting in a certain direction, so that to shift the line of action requires changing these relations.

The relations formed in the course of striving for a goal possess certain general characteristics. They include much more than was bargained for in the initial decision to seek the goal. The unanticipated relations result from the nature of the effort (or means) required by the goal. They are binding on the individual who would continue to seek the goal. Hence, commitments are *requirements* for seeking a goal.

One kind of circumstance surrounding any sustained effort to achieve a goal consists in other relations and goals. Thus a certain course of political action may enforce a wide range of non-political relations. The *interdependence of spheres of action* is responsible for many of the attributes of commitment. This circumstance creates tension and resistance, as commitments generated in the course of seeking one goal clash with requirements of other goals. The individual faces the problem of integrating the various relations which command his allegiance. To say that an individual seeks conflicting goals usually means that he cannot fulfill both sets of commitments engendered by them. Therefore, *the strength of a commitment can be measured by the number of social spheres for which it enforces lines of action.*

The idea of commitment, then, implies more than choice, and also more than what we initially believe to be our obligations as a result of the choice. We may *feel* committed and yet not *be* committed; and we may be committed without full cognizance of that fact. Appreciation of what is comprised in a commitment may come only when we try to break it; then the consequences of our involvement are revealed to us, often for the first time.

In order to explore the social bases of commitment, we studied a group of people whose goals engendered high commitment, and compared them with people whose goals summoned only limited commitment. We also studied people who broke off each kind of commitment. We selected radical political goals as ones which produce strong commitment, and liberal political goals as ones which invite only moderate commitment. Our sample was composed of leaders of radical political groups in Chicago, namely, Communist and Trotskyist organizations, and of the major liberal political organization in Chicago, the Independent Voters of Illinois (affiliated with Americans for Democratic Action). We found people who had terminated their commitments by asking these leaders for the names of persons they knew who had quit the organization after having held similar positions. Since we sought intensive interviews covering a wide range of topics, we had to impose severe limits on the number of people studied. We secured case histories of 20 presently active local leaders of radical organizations, and of 10 who quit these organizations and revolutionary politics altogether. We also secured the same number of cases of present and former leaders of the liberal organization. Our analysis of these 60 cases first treats the political commitment of the radical, and then the political commitment of the liberal.

SOCIAL BASES OF A RADICAL COMMITMENT

Radicals stand apart from society, living their lives primarily as "outsiders." Politics must be of unsurpassable importance for them to give of themselves thus. By the same token, the political future must hold great promise of success. High expectations on both counts are necessary for the radical's commitment. This confidence in the future clashes with the poverty of radical achievements in present-day America. Faced with innumerable disconfirming events on all sides, the radical party in America continuously must contend with what it is wont to call "defeatist tendencies."

A radical leader noted that, among new recruits, political expectations often are excessive, even by radical standards:

One of the toughest problems we [leaders] face is the great hopes new comrades bring into the party. They are expecting the revolution to be right around the corner. When it doesn't come, they get discouraged and may leave the revolutionary movement. We have to teach them that immediate victory is not in sight. That's tough to do. Revolutions are only made when the objective conditions are ripe. A professional revolutionary knows this and is braced for defeats.

A radical in the process of breaking from his party was able to reveal the strain between high expectations and low achievements as he first began to experience it:

The more optimistic among us expected revolutionary conditions to follow the war. The party would never admit this, but when you're in the revolutionary movement, you have to think the revolution is coming in five or ten years. Or, at least, you have to believe that the revolution is coming in your lifetime! You have to think that! You can't keep up the pace unless you have that hope.

Radicals, then, face the continuous problem of maintaining high expectations in the face of disconfirming events. Resolution of the problem cannot be made simply by lowering expectations, since revolutionary demands for change are of such scope and weight as to require sustained effort at the expense of other aspects of life, and this in turn requires overriding belief in the promise of political success. Instead, adaptation to the wide gap between expectations and achievements tends to be made by *enforced isolation* from people who do not hold revolutionary goals.

Our case histories show that persons currently holding revolutionary goals are isolated from the community, whereas persons who have terminated their ties to radical groups are not isolated. Specifically, radicals generally do not have close ties with persons who are not radicals, nor do they seek a professional career outside the political movement.

Revolutionary groups seek to place their members in jobs where they can make a political contribution. For example, members frequently are instructed by party leaders to take a job in a plant to help organize or penetrate a trade union. The hard core of the party consists of members on the party staff or members who are working in jobs through which they can be politically effective. One radical followed this party expectation in the selection of work for several years, but then he took a job with no political potential:

I can't do any union work where I am now. It's too small a shop. I could go into a bigger shop, but I don't want to. I'm glad to have a breather for awhile. There is nothing stirring nowadays. I figure it's better for the party [sic] as well as for me to do some other things during this quiet period. I want to do some writing and reading, work on my inventions, see new friends. . . . My job gives me a chance to get some more money.

Although it is of course possible to disengage oneself from politically relevant work for short periods of time without divorcing oneself from radical politics, once the individual begins to satisfy non-political gratifications in his work it will be more difficult for him to give them up for political action. In this case, the respondent's *private* interests in writing, reading, working on inventions, seeing friends, and making money portend a movement away from radical politics. As a matter of fact, this person quit radical politics a year or so after we first interviewed him.

The radical who is effectively insulated from influences outside the radical movement does not attach an important value to his work over and above its political significance. He does not change jobs simply to gain more money, nor does he expend major energies to gain promotions and to advance a career. Where the radical's job has political potential, the party demands that he use it to advance its interests. This means that a union official, for example, must be prepared to sacrifice his career in the labor movement if party leaders decide that this is the course required by the political needs of the party. The harshness of this commitment is indicated by the frequency with which union leaders have broken with radical groups.

Where a job does not have political potential, the committed radical will seek a job which consumes the minimum amount of time, leaving him with the most freedom to engage in political work. The radical commitment involves the full use of "spare time" for political purposes.[68]

A radical discussed the problem in these terms:

I would take a university job if the circumstances seemed right; at least, I would do it for a short time. I can't see myself working in business much longer. The crucial thing is that I get a job with the most freedom to do what I want—working for the party. For a well-educated Marxist, party work is fulfillment enough. You can get your prestige and you can use your skills there [in the party]. It has tremendous status to be a party staff member. That's my ultimate aim.

By virtue of his political goal, the radical activist is required to reject the pursuit of a career. His political relations enforce this commitment, for example, by not leaving him time to develop new interests. Party members are so busy with party activities that they are effectively insulated from outside influence.

A second major indication of the enforced isolation of the radical is his lack of personal ties to people who are not also radicals. None of the radicals we interviewed had close friends and members of his immediate family who did not also belong to the same political group. The radical's lack of personal ties outside his political group is not a matter of his choice alone. His political associates enforce it. The tendency for the community to ostracize the radical for his politics also plays a role in isolating the individual, as the following account of one individual's experiences shows:

[68] Almond's study based on interviews with former Communists reports findings similar to ours on this point.

Former friends and associates thought I was dead wrong in my politics, that I was a threat to the community, and did everything they could think of to cut me off and ruin me. Now they think I'm just eccentric—it's gone that far! I have faced the whole range of intimidations. But I haven't curtailed my actions. Once you are in, there is no going back, even if you wanted to.

The radical will seek to terminate personal ties outside the party, not merely because he is constrained to do so, but also because he feels uneasy with people who do not share his central mission in life. When asked to describe his closest friends, a radical replied:

When you are in the party for many years, as I have been, you develop warm bonds with your comrades. I have had a few friends outside the party, but they can never be as close friends. They can't be friends at all if they are hostile to the party. You never feel as comfortable with an outsider as you do with your comrades. But each of us has to work out these personal problems as best he can, always keeping in mind that personal considerations must be changed to fit the needs of the party.

In order to continue actively seeking radical goals, the individual needs to give up personal ties outside the radical group; he also must develop new personal relations within the radical group. Unless he terminates outside relations, the individual will be exposed to conflicting demands. Unless he forges new ties within the group, the individual will be exposed to disillusionment and discouragement. When the radical must maintain his political allegiance in order to maintain his personal relations and social status, then he will be less ready to entertain doubts about that allegiance. Too many non-political relations are at stake to judge the political relationship in purely political terms. If the political relationship does not find support in non-political attachments, then it can readily be disrupted by disconfirming events in the political world.

Festinger and his colleagues have shown how a small sect in Chicago was able to sustain itself in spite of the fact that its key expectation—that the world would come to an end on a certain date—was not fulfilled (2). One of the reasons why the sect did not disintegrate when its prophecy failed was that the participants were bound together in close personal relations and provided strong support for one another in the face of failure. So, too, with our radical groups: their prophecies have by and large also failed; yet they frequently have maintained their cohesion because they have not formed merely a special-purpose association of like-minded people but a closed *society* in which a variety of needs are fulfilled. To leave such a group is not merely to terminate a political relationship: it also entails the rupture of all kinds of non-political relations.

One of our respondents who is a leading radical illustrates to what extent a political relationship may come to involve a total commitment.

He joined a radical party when he was a young man. A short time later he was appointed to the staff of the party. At this point, he changed his name at the direction of the party. Shortly thereafter, he married a girl who also worked on the party staff. Now his name, his job, and his wife were all acting to support his political goals. During this period he terminated all personal relations with people who were not also in the party, and built up a completely new circle of friends. He also gave up any aspirations for a career outside the party.

At the same time, the radical's politicalization of his personal relations tends to attenuate them. Non-political relations become *restricted* by incorporation into the political relation. This is especially true of personal relations, for this kind of social bond involves mutual trust and spontaneity, something which cannot be given fully and easily where political tests are always being applied. Thus radicals insist that the movement comes before personal relations, which means that those who leave the movement cut themselves off from all personal as well as political consideration.

The social bases of the radical commitment are further revealed by the kinds of orientations and relations that characterize persons who defect from radical groups. The process of defection involves the loss of political hope, rather than an initial change in political values or in the assessment of the group's adherence to these values, and the growth in concern for personal interests, which are felt to be threatened by the radical commitment. Corresponding to this change in orientation, defection is associated with certain changes in personal relations: the loss of personal relations with political associates, which signifies the failure to fulfill the radical commitment, and the development of close ties to persons who are not political associates, which also violates the radical commitment. We shall first consider changes in orientation by persons who have quit radical politics, and then changes in personal relations.

One of our respondents expressed his changing political orientation in these terms: "The party's isolation made me feel that there was no point in being a Communist and sacrificing my whole life. The party was through, and I didn't feel like sticking around as a caretaker, even though I still believe the party is right."

We may view the sense of increasing hopelessness of the radical party as a rationalization for the desire to jump back into the mainstream of society; or it may be that the desire to return to the community results from the judgment that political life appears increasingly pointless. In all probability, the two grow together, indistinguishable from one another. Loss of political expectations is closely associated with a shift in orientation away from the group and toward the self. When this happens, as it did in the following case of a person who left the Communist party, the individual sees himself caught between a political commitment and the satisfaction of personal interests.

I still hold to the same position of Marxism. I just decided that I came first. It wasn't worth the sacrifices to stay in. Nothing can be done now, anyway. Yes, I've changed a lot in recent years. I've always been an egotist. I finally decided I didn't want to be a martyr. I want to get a good job, not too good, but sufficient so that I don't worry about money. And lead a normal life for a change.

As doubts about the possibilities of political effectiveness grow, concern over the impact of political relations on personal interest grows apace.

When I went to work at [a business firm], I didn't want to be known as a radical. I didn't want to be an outsider. I got to know a lot of people there who would have thrown me over if they knew. Not to mention the boss. I've seen too many lives wasted by those who have cut themselves off from everything to be a radical. They have made tremendous sacrifices to do it. They have never made a decent living, they have turned down good jobs, they have made their families suffer. Brilliant people who could have made a real success of their lives. Thrown away for a cause that can't ever be successful. Socialism will never come in this world!

Our interviews show a consistent pattern of inner conflict over leaving radical politics. One of our respondents made this conflict very clear.

I'm not doing anything political these days. I've lost contact for the most part. It's hard to be active along with a job and family. . . . I'm getting older. I have two kids. You start thinking about putting something away for them. Against all these things, when you've been in the movement for years, you feel a duty to go on, you feel like hell when you don't. So what do you do? When things become quiet, you let your wife pull you out. Maybe if things were really happening, then you would choose the movement and let the family go.

People leave radical politics when they come to define the situation as a choice between a hopeless political cause and a hopeful personal life. In order for the lines to be so drawn, the individual must have more or less fully divorced himself from significant personal relations *within* the political group, or failed to have developed such relations in the first place. Termination of a radical commitment tends to occur when several of the individual's closest personal associates have decided to break their radical commitment. They may not make such a decision consciously as a group; they may not leave together. But the fact is that most of the ex-radicals we interviewed reported that they talked over the question of leaving with intimates in the party, and that they left the party at about the same time.

It would be an over simplification to conclude that the individual quits a radical group when he decides to sacrifice his political relations in favor of his personal relations. In the first place, there must be a process of political disillusionment, usually born of pessimism over the party's future. In the second place, it is too neat to suppose that the individual's personal relations all function to keep him in the political group or to pull him away from the political group. Generally, the individual's personal relations pull him in both directions simultaneously. The evidence we have collected points to a net balance on the side of personal relations which pull the individual who quits radical politics away from his political commitment. But consider the case of one of our respondents who quit radical politics in spite of the influence of close friends: "I had friends in the party I wanted to keep. They were my closest friends, and I knew that it meant losing them [if I quit]. The party won't have anything to do with the fellow who breaks. He's a renegade, finished, dead. Once you have been in, you can't leave without this stigma." This respondent reports that when he quit, he made a strenuous effort to keep in touch with a few of his closest friends. Belying his own prediction, this effort met with some success, but only because he remained ideologically sympathetic to the party.

Once outside the radical movement, former members frequently associate with one another, at least during the early period of their alienation from radical politics. The tendency for ex-radicals to seek one another out helps bridge the great distance between the world of radical politics and the community. In effect, they are leaning on one another for support in their often painful return to the society from which they had withdrawn.

As people who have terminated their membership in a radical group reintegrate themselves into society, they slowly give up their radical ideas. Among our respondents there is no case of a dramatic shift to the opposite extreme, as in the much-celebrated cases of ex-Communists returning to the Catholic Church or joining the political right. It might be expected that a certain proportion of ex-radicals will overconform to the dominant political temper of the community in their anxiety to be accepted. But among our respondents this type of response does not appear.

A final word about the consequences of defection for radicalism itself. Defection from a radical group has much more serious consequences for radicalism as an organized movement and as an ideology than does defection from a liberal group. For when a radical drops out of a political organization, he cuts himself off from radical influences and becomes more open to influences which operate to change his ideas and values. But the liberal, adhering to ideas and values closer to widely held views, may sustain them without active membership in an organization. The liberal rarely becomes isolated from the community in the first place on account of his politics. On the contrary, the liberal's political action generally heightens his ties to the community.

SOCIAL BASES OF A LIBERAL COMMITMENT

Liberals lead only part of their lives as political men. Politics may be judged to be very important, but liberals can be politically active without great expectations. Politics may be hopeful, but liberals can commit a part of their lives to the pursuit of political goals without the conviction that success is imminent or certain. They have not invested that much of themselves in politics to feel basically threatened if political demands are not realized.

If the limited nature of liberal expectations and demands reduces the danger of political disillusionment, by the same token it poses the problem of maintaining political interest. The gap between the liberal's expectations and achievements tends to be so small as to provide little *incentive* for political action. This is the opposite of the problem facing the radical, who must suffer a very great disparity between expectations and achievements. The liberal's weak political motivation is illustrated by one of our respondents who quit liberal politics:

I resigned from IVI last year. I had too many other things to do. It was a question of where to put my time. And, frankly, I was bored! The meetings became awfully boring, just terribly dull. Instead of discussing issues, all the time was spent talking about how to raise funds. I tried to stir up discussions on issues, but didn't get anywhere.

An IVI leader observed that "with no major election for some time if there is no transfer of interest somewhere, interest will die." The modest goals of liberal groups fail to summon the intense energies available to radical groups. Nor is a liberal organization prepared to use the full energies of many of its members even if they were forthcoming. There is relatively little *work* to be done in a liberal organization, precisely because its goals are so limited. Many a liberal group seeks to make work for its members, but this merely serves to underscore the problem rather than to solve it. In short, liberal goals invite only moderate commitment to political activity.

At the same time, the liberal's commitments to non-political goals tend to be strong and demanding. This applies especially to his professional goals, and also to his family obligations. Running throughout our interviews with liberals are statements to the effect that "I can't put in so much time"; "IVI is taking up too much of my time"; "I'm neglecting my work"; "My family objects to my politics because I'm never home";

"Now that the children are out of the way [going to school], maybe I can give some more time to IVI"; "When my partner comes back from his vacation, then I can go to IVI meetings again"; "When you get older, you can't maintain the same pace in political action because you have so many more responsibilities."

Respondents were asked what kinds of political action they enjoyed and what kinds they disliked. In every interview with liberals, a ready and definite reply was forthcoming, specifying what was pleasurable and what was distasteful. Representative liberal responses referred to personal gratifications derived from backstage maneuverings in deciding whom to endorse for public office, the promotion of candidates, and the excitement of election night, and to the tedium of such routine work as door-bell ringing. Only two radicals expressed such preferences or dislikes. The other replied with such answers as: "I never really thought about that." "I don't like campaigning, but it is all necessary." "It is serious business." One radical said: "This [political action] is not a pleasurable matter. It is a difficult and serious matter. I don't enjoy any of the work. It's just something that has to be done."

Here is additional evidence that the characteristic motivational problem facing radicals is maintaining political expectations, and that of the liberals is sustaining political interest.

The liberal group cannot seek to generate or sustain political interest among its participants in ways analogous to those employed by the radical group. Given its basic acceptance of the political order, and its limited demands for change, the liberal group can neither claim from its members nor use "the whole of their lives." Furthermore, the wholly political man is an anti-liberal conception in and of itself. Liberalism implies pluralism in interests and relations. Liberal groups are thus debarred from seeking to absorb the whole of their members' lives, nor can they seek to insulate their members from the larger society. Quite the contrary. *A liberal group finds strength in the multiple ties its members establish to the community.*

Radicals are constrained to avoid deep involvement in a career outside of politics; liberals are valued for their successful business or professional careers. Membership in a radical group is an *exclusive* relationship; members of liberal groups characteristically have multiple group affiliations. Radicals are required to confine close personal relations to other members of the political group; liberals are expected to value a diversity of beliefs among their close associates. These three major differences between liberals and radicals in the social bases of the political commitment will be considered in order.

Two-thirds of the liberals we interviewed occupy high professional and business positions. Two-thirds of the radicals hold considerably lower occupational positions. This difference in occupational status is reinforced by the political commitment. We have already shown that radicals are discouraged from placing career interests ahead of political interests. In contrast, liberal leaders are sought among the members of certain major law firms, universities, and businesses in order to gain access to their skills, contacts, money, and prestige. Much of the power of the liberal group consists in the influence of individual members, rather than in the power of organization. The strength of the liberal group depends more on its *selective recruitment* of leaders, whereas the strength of the radical group depends more on its *intensive socialization* of leaders.

All of the liberals we studied who have remained active in IVI were also members of at least three civic or reform groups in addition to their political affiliation. In contrast, only two radicals maintained any organizational affiliations in addition to their membership in the political group. The groups to which liberals belong have memberships which overlap one another and that of the political group. A cross-tabulation of names appearing on the letterheads of six major liberal organizations in Chicago shows that a large number of persons appear on more than one letterhead. In fact, about one-half of the total list of names on six letterheads are accounted for by about one-fourth of the people. Half or more of the names on each letterhead also appear on one or more of the other five letterheads. Furthermore, the most active leaders of each group are more likely to appear on more than one letterhead than are the less active persons. One of our respondents analyzed this "community of liberal leaders" from his own experience:

My work in housing led me into conferences of the Mayor's Commission on Human Relations, because housing always leads to race relations. From this, I was invited on the board of the American Civil Liberties Union, and the Chicago Council Against Racial and Religious Discrimination. Then, I was working with an IVI leader, who asked me to serve on that board. And I've been on the board of the Chicago Council of Foreign Relations, Committee for the Nation's Health, Housing Conference of Chicago, and probably a dozen more I don't even remember. *Once you get involved in one of these groups, you meet people who are in other groups and they invite you to join the boards of these other groups.* They're all interlocking directorates. . . . What happens is you get to be something of a name in these circles, so you get invited to all these committees and boards, because each group figures your name will appeal to certain other people.

Thus, where the radical commitment enforces isolation from the community, the liberal commitment enforces participation in it.

The liberal's personal relations also testify to a broad community involvement. Whereas all the radicals we studied had most of their friends in the party, only one liberal did so. The other liberals report that their friends were often very different from them politically, that they "go across the board politically," that they run the "whole gamut of political views." These respondents refer to the diversity of political views among their friends with no regret. They would not have it any other way, because "one does not want to appear to be choosing his friends on a political basis," and "differences of opinion make for a more interesting life," and "everyone has a right to his own political views." Frequently, these liberals try to proselytize friends who are not IVI members. But politics rarely is a condition of friendship. By and large, *the liberal commitment does not involve a shift in the locus of the personal world.*

At the same time, those who have persisted in their liberal loyalties have *some* strong personal ties with other members of IVI. These ties typically were formed outside the political group and carried over into politics. Or, if they were formed in political contexts, they subsequently were integrated with associations outside of politics. Thus members of a liberal group are absorbed into the organization only to a limited extent. Even in a liberal group, however, some personal ties are needed to lend stability to the pursuit of liberal political goals through organized efforts. This is indicated by an examination of those who left the liberal group.

Those who quit IVI did not have close personal relations within the group; nor did they belong to other civic or reform associations. Thus, there were few social supports for the political relation, and few social obligations contingent upon it. Consequently, when pressures from professional or family roles increased, the fragile political ties readily collapsed.

Representative of our respondents who quit liberal politics was a man who had been very active in IVI for several years. At the same time he was just breaking into a large law firm. Then he received a sudden promotion in the firm, and shortly thereafter began to cut down on his political action. When he mentioned how much time he used to put into politics, he quickly added: "Please don't write that down! I would hate to have my firm know about this!"

This person seized upon a minor disagreement with IVI as an occasion to break off his commitment. The incident would have been quickly forgotten by this man unless he were looking for an excuse to quit. After that incident, he stated: "Now I'm through with politics. When I withdrew my political career came to an end. It's more comfortable looking in from the outside. I enjoyed it while it lasted, but I'm sure I'll never get involved again. I have a busy and growing law practice which I couldn't risk by being politically active."

In short, those who quit IVI had two major characteristics in common prior to their withdrawal: (1) few personal ties within IVI, and (2) few ties to the larger community of which IVI is a part. They left IVI under the following conditions: certain personal interests either conflicted with the political affiliation, or simply were not being satisfied by the political affiliation. In several cases, disturbances in their political relations within IVI facilitated the withdrawal, but in all cases the decisive factor appears to be the pull of outside family and professional commitments. In no case did a person arrive at a new ideological position, and leave the group on that basis. In several cases, there is evidence that IVI may be rejoined sometime in the future.

Involvement in a liberal political group generally is an *extension* of involvement in a wider community of professional, civic, and personal relations. Rather than weakening ties to the community, liberal politics tends to strengthen multiple attachments to the community. As a result of the integration of the liberal political group in the larger society, the individual who joins a liberal group does not become dependent primarily on political associates to satisfy primary-group needs. This difference from the radical is only a matter of degree, however. Liberals who do not find *any* gratifying personal relations in their political life are also likely to withdraw from politics.

When the individual does drop out of a liberal group, his political beliefs generally remain more stable than does the individual who quits a radical group. The liberal is closer to widely held views and therefore can sustain liberal values even after he gives up membership and participation in a liberal organization. This is to say that radical beliefs require much more *organizational support* than do liberal beliefs. Radical groups tend to become closed societies, set apart from the community, whereas liberal groups are open associations.

CONCLUSION

The radical suffers from a very wide disparity between what he has learned to expect about ultimate political victory and day-to-day political achievements. As a consequence, he is prey to doubts about the worth of sacrificing a life in the community. The radical group seeks to counter these tendencies among its members by separating them from the community and absorbing them into the movement. The community cooperates by ostracizing those in its midst who are believed to be radicals. Insofar as this isolation is enforced by the political group and the community, the individual avoids cross-pressures between his political and non-political relations. The radical incurs commitments far transcending his political obligations, especially pressures on him to terminate involvement with work associates, family, friends, neighbors, etc., who are not also radicals. In addition, he incurs commitments to fellow radicals which are not specific to the political enterprise, often including obligations of a highly personal nature. All of his relations support the political allegiance by being *fused* with the political role, which *dominates* the non-political roles. This is the only way the radical can integrate his political and non-political roles, precisely because the radical movement is isolated from and at war with the larger society. For under these conditions, a web of non-political involvements, by requiring the individual to maintain his political allegiance in order to sustain his personal relations, is a major source of support for radical goals. Movement away from radical politics is at the same time movement back into the community. Persons in the process of breaking their ties to a radical group, as well as those who have already defected, form multiple relations in the community. Persons securely attached to radical groups, on the other hand, have no such relations and therefore are not readily vulnerable to threatened deprivations at the hands of the community.

The liberal suffers from *too small* a disparity between his political expectations and achievements. The gap is so small that it provides little *incentive* to engage in political action. The liberal is vulnerable to loss of political interest. Unlike the radical group, the liberal group cannot seek to isolate its members from competing interests and loyalties, because it is part of the community. It also cannot seek to absorb its members into the group, since its goals and activities permit only the limited use of its members' energies. Instead, the liberal group constrains the individual to form and sustain multiple involvements in the community. The sustenance of political interest is facilitated when the liberal shares multiple ties with other members of his political group—as colleagues, as friends, in voluntary associations. In this case, political ties are supported by non-political relations centering in the community rather than in the political group. These independent *mediating* relations help to support the political goal by stimulating political interest in it. Furthermore, this is the only way the liberal can integrate his political and non-political relations just because the liberal group is part of the community. If he does not *differentiate* his political and non-political relations, he is more likely to face cross-pressures between them. If he *shares* non-political concerns with some of the people with whom he also shares political concerns, but does not confound them (as does the radical), he is less likely to face cross-pressures between them. Conflict may arise from increasing involvement in one role which requires decreasing involvement in other roles. An element of stability in the allocation of involvement among several roles is introduced by sharing different involvements with some of the *same* people. For then the expectations of each role include expectations that the other roles will be performed.

But this is not to say that the liberal's non-political relations are contingent on his fulfilling political obligations to the extent that this is true for the radical. Liberal goals enforce much less commitment than do radical goals. But then liberal goals entail much less sacrifice of personal interests outside of politics, and therefore do not need much strong support. Furthermore, liberal values are much more consistent with the culture of the larger society, whereas radicalism is a deviant subculture. In general, the more distinctive the subculture, the more precarious it is, and therefore the greater the commitment it requires.

REFERENCES

1. Almond, Gabriel A. *The Appeals of Communism*, Princeton, N.J.: Princeton University Press, 1954.
2. Festinger, Leon, et al. *When Prophecy Fails*. Minneapolis: University of Minnesota Press, 1954.
3. Selznick, Philip. *TVA and the Grass Roots*. Berkeley, Calif.: University of California Press, 1949.

Another situational factor in recruitment concerns the extent to which a given movement is an alternative to others. For example, a John Birch Society organizer told one researcher: "The current members of the Society were already conservatives and when the John Birch Society came along, it was as natural for many of them as it was for him [sic]." [69] In other words, people may "shop around" among alternative movements until they find one that suits their objectives and interests. This process is illustrated in the following column from the Daily Worker.

"Seven Kentucky Miners Join Party and Tell Reason Why,"
Daily Worker (*February 18, 1932*), *p. 2*.

The Communist Party added seven strong working class soldiers to its ranks today. Seven miners, two Negro and five white, most of them born and bred in Kentucky, joined the revolutionary fighting organization of the working class to become leaders in the struggle against the bosses and their system. All but one have families. Each has a story of constant struggling and suffering.

"We've been struggling as far back as I can remember," one said. In Kentucky the bosses try to keep the miners away from the Communist Party with the cry of "Russian Reds" and the hypocrisy about Communism destroying "home, religion and order." What will the coal oper-

[69] J. Allen Broyles, *The John Birch Society: Anatomy of a Protest* (Boston: Beacon Press, 1964), p. 96.

ators say now to the Kentucky miners in face of these seven who not only were themselves born on American soil, but can name generations of their ancestors born here.

Why did you join the Communist Party, the miners were asked? And each gave a ready answer. They know the party through struggle and were won to it through its fight for them and their fellow workers.

"I feel like this," said one miner—there was feeling in his voice, he spoke as if he would like to say more but found it hard getting the right words—, "I joined the Communist Party because I see that they are the only ones leading the workers to better conditions. I tried out everything else, I belonged to the United Mine Workers of America, the A.F.L., the Junior Mechanics and I found that none of them was for the workers, they were all failures except the National Miners Union and the Communist Party."

The working class solidarity he found everywhere he went in support of the Kentucky strife impressed one miner perhaps more than anything else and he wants to send this message back home to his fellow miners: "We seed in New York, we seed in Philadelphia, we seed in Baltimore, everywhere we seed the workers are backing the miners' fight in Kentucky."

He also asked his fellow workers in Kentucky "not to believe the lies going in the capitalist papers, the capitalists are against the working men," he said.

"I joined the Communist Party," another miner solemnly said, "because it stands for all races, color and nationality. I want to tell everybody that the Communist Party platform has been misrepresented to me or I would have been a member 27 years ago."

The lies used by the bosses in Kentucky are the same lies being used all over. "We was told," the miner said "that the Communist Party is the head of the Catholic Church and we was agin the Catholics, or else we was told that the Communist Party takes a man's wife away and breaks your home up. They said the Communists was awful people but I found the Communists to be the best people I met in my life, they'd take their shirt off their back for you. Through the learnin' in the National Miners Union I learnt the benefit of the Communist Party to the laborin' man and I want to say to all workers that want to change this system of capitalism for the laboring man's benefit to join the Communist Party."

A Negro miner told of his hard life, suffering, besides hunger, Jim Crowism and discrimination and found in the Party the unity of all colors against all of this.

Mathew Armstrong, a minor who went to the Soviet Union with a workers' delegation told how he started working in mines since eleven years old and contrasted conditions in the Soviet Union with Kentucky. In the Soviet Union a miner works six hours a day: in Kentucky a miner works 12 and 14 and starves."

Social movements, therefore, may become significant to the individual radical for historical-situational factors, such as propinquity and the availability of alternative organizations, rather than for reasons of psychological affinity. Similarly, movements themselves become significant as organized ideologies for the same historical reasons. An examination of the rise of the Communist Party (CPUSA) in the 1930s and the radical Right in the 1950s will illustrate this thesis.

During these two periods the significant social problems were, respectively, economic depression (structural) and "anti-Communism" (moral). In both of these decades presidents dedicated to ameliorating these problems were elected. Roosevelt and the New Deal addressed the breakdown of laissez-faire capitalism; Eisenhower and the Republican Party faced the "menace of Communism." The solutions offered by both presidents, however, did not even partially solve the problem situations. In 1940 unemployment was still above the acceptable level, and in 1960 Soviet Russia could predict the "victory of Communism in the Western hemisphere." For those concerned with these issues, and who felt that not enough had been done, the alternatives lay in the then socially significant organizations like the Communist Party of the 1930s and the John Birch Society of the 1950s. The attitude taken toward the New Deal by the CPUSA has been described as follows:

The Communist Party, while demanding many of Roosevelt's reforms, clearly pointed out that the New Deal was not a program of steps towards socialism, as Social-Democrats all over the world declared. There was nothing whatever socialistic about it. The capitalists were left in complete control of the banks, factories, and transportation systems, to exploit the workers as before. Nor was the New Deal a program of "progressive capitalism," as the labor leaders, liberals, and eventually Earl Browder called it. Economically, it was simply a plan to shore up broken-down capitalism in this country, to recondition American imperialism so as to help it survive in a world capitalist system enmeshed in its deepening general crisis.[70]

Two decades later, disaffection with the existing political structure gave impetus to the extreme Right. Robert Welch, in describing his reasons for founding the John Birch Society, stated:

In December, 1954, . . . I wrote a long letter to a friend, in which I expressed very severe opinions concerning some of the top men in Washington. The record of some of these men was already full of extremely questionable actions. But the final straw that prompted my letter was the visible betrayal of the Republican Party by this so-called Republican Administration. . . .[71]

[70] William Z. Foster, *History of the Communist Party of the United States* (New York: International Publishers, 1952), p. 294.
[71] Quoted in Gene Grove, *Inside the John Birch Society* (Greenwich, Conn.: Fawcett Publications, Inc. [Gold Medal Books], 1961), p. 20.

That the Left and the Right were ascendant during their respective historical periods is not to suggest that organizations of an opposing viewpoint did not exist during these times. The policies of Roosevelt evoked rightist opposition from such groups as the American Liberty League and the Silver Shirts (from the initials of Hitler's SS), led by spiritualist William Dudley Pelley. The Liberty League was doomed by its insistence on a return to the policies of Harding and Hoover, and the Silver Shirts did little to stir public imagination. Arthur M. Schlesinger has noted that American fascists at this time were "in the main a collection of crackpots working the back alleys." [72] During the McCarthy era the American Left occupied an even more isolated position than the Right during the thirties. Harassed by government agencies and Congressional committees, the Communist Party was forced underground, never to return again. During the fifties, all socialists, and even the liberal Americans for Democratic Action (ADA), were politically suspect.

Historically, then, neither the Right nor the Left has been socially significant when their ideological adversaries were ascendant. This has less to do with ideological conflict between political groups than with the fact that the solutions they offered for social problems were not historically relevant. Quite simply, social significance is bestowed on those ideologies (and the groups espousing them) which provide a viable solution to the problems about which publics are concerned. At the time of the advent of the Cold War and the ensuing McCarthy period, the CPUSA was not seen as providing a reasonable solution to social ills, and was therefore not socially significant. However, the solutions offered by the radical Right did become significant to those opposing the administration position on the Communist issue. On the other hand, the laissez-faire notions of the Right were discredited during the 1930s by the Depression and the rise of Hitler in Germany. The Stalinists, being opposed to Nazism and supporting a government where a depression had not occurred, were socially significant, especially to intellectuals familiar with the tenets of Marx and Lenin.[73]

In this chapter, we have focused on the historical gestalt of social movements in order to clarify the factors leading to their emergence. We have seen that, just as historical events lead to the existence of problem situations, they will also suggest alternative modes of ameliorative action. Social movements, embodied as ideological organizations, are inherent in the context of problem situations. Since these ideologies address the dis-

[72] Arthur M. Schlesinger, Jr., *The Politics of Upheaval* (London: William Heinemann Ltd., 1961), p. 82.
[73] See the discussions in Daniel Bell, "The Background of Marxian Socialism in the United States," in Donald Egbert and Stow Persons, eds., *Socialism in American Life*, vol. I (Princeton, N.J.: Princeton University Press, 1952), p. 305; and Irving Howe and Lewis Coser, *The American Communist Party* (Boston: Beacon Press, 1957), pp. 273–318.

tribution of power in society, they will be regarded as nonlegitimate. Nevertheless, they will attain social significance inasmuch as they address legitimate problems and to the extent that a public acquires a consciousness of dysfunction relative to such problems and that referents for mobilization are available. Provided that an emerging movement can avoid suppression, co-optation, or internal dissolution, social significance will play an important role in the recruitment of members and the viability of the movement. Paradoxically, the actions of the status quo power structure relative to an emerging movement or to the problem it addresses can contribute to the development of a radical ideology.

The import of social significance has been illustrated with examples from the history of the Left and Right in America during the thirties and fifties. This reference, although brief, has an important bearing on organized ideologies at the present point in history. As we shall see in chapter 8, the Left and Right in America have developed not entirely dissimilar ideologies about problems such as Vietnam and poverty. They differ primarily in those ideological aspects concerning the goals of social action and appropriate tactics. However, since the conscience collective contains strong elements of both left and right persuasion, neither ideology is, as yet, sufficiently nonlegitimate to evoke a concerted opposition from the status quo power structure. Hence, we should predict an increased tempo of dissension about these problems and an increased tempo of repression before either the Left or the Right can emerge as a viable social movement. The question of which ideology is likely to be ultimately ascendant will be considered in chapter 8. First, however, we will discuss types of movements in chapter 6 and the dissolution of movements in chapter 7.

TYPES OF SOCIAL MOVEMENTS

The method of constructing "ideal types" for the purposes of social analysis was pioneered by Max Weber in his studies of world religions.[1] For Weber, the intended function of the ideal type in empirical investigation was clear: "Its function is the comparison with empirical reality in order to establish its divergencies or similarities, to describe them with the most unambiguously intelligible concepts, and to understand and explain them causally." [2] The term "ideal" is not evaluative, but rather refers to typical recurrent patterns of structure, action, or attitudes. For Weber, the ideal type was a methodological tool to be used to isolate certain properties found in individual action patterns and ideological and value orientations, e.g., the Protestant ethic. Ideal types or pure classifications rarely reflect a total phenomenological trait but rather emphasize frequently occurring characteristics or action patterns. As Bendix suggests: "These models [ideal types] are artifacts of the researcher based on historical materials; Weber felt such artifacts were justified as long as the special purpose of such constructions was clearly stated." [3] Classification schemes, by their very nature, are highly arbitrary, depending upon the dominant variables of concern to the investigator and the major focus of attention in the research. In this context, Horton and Hunt indicate: "To classify social movements is not always easy, for sometimes a movement is intermediate or mixed in nature, or it is different at different stages of its career. As always [categories of social movements] are 'ideal types' into which actual movements more or less perfectly fall." [4]

---

[1] See Max Weber, *The Sociology of Religion*, trans. Ephraim Fischoff (London: Methuen and Co. Ltd., 1965).
[2] Max Weber, *The Methodology of the Social Sciences*, trans. and ed. Edward A. Shils and Henry A. Finch (New York: The Free Press, 1949), p. 43.
[3] Reinhard Bendix, *Max Weber: An Intellectual Portrait* (Garden City, N.Y.: Doubleday and Co., Inc., 1960), p. 281.
[4] Paul B. Horton and Chester L. Hunt, *Sociology* (New York: McGraw-Hill Book Co.,

A number of taxonomies and typologies of social movements have been devised by various analysts. These classification systems stress the tactics, goals, public definitions, political orientations, degrees of change advocated, and the types of leadership found in social movements. As has been indicated, the variables emphasized by the researcher have a determining effect on the nature of the classification derived. For example, Turner and Killian, in classifying movements in terms of public definitions, character of opposition, and access to legitimate means of action, find a revolutionary movement to be a movement receiving "violent suppression" and employing "chiefly illegitimate means of actions." [5] Blumer, on the other hand, distinguishes revolutionary movements in terms of the "scope of their objectives," which in turn suggest tactics, respectability, and "vantage point of attack" as essential typifying characteristics.[6] Yet another point of view sees revolutionary movements as seeking "to overthrow the existing social system and replace it with a greatly different one." [7] In these three classifications there are three distinct criteria for typologies of social movements: (1) public definition and response; (2) tactics; (3) type of social change advocated. As noted in previous chapters, one essential feature of a social movement is its nonlegitimacy vis-à-vis the conscience collective. Therefore, we would regard "public definition and response" as a nonvariable element of social movements: the majority public response will be negative. Similarly, focusing on tactics will not lead to a viable classification of social movements. Substantively, since a movement operates largely outside existing social structure and procedures, the range of tactics and action available to it is severely limited. Social movements are concerned primarily with radical interpretations of existing relationships. The activities stemming from such analyses, and undertaken by a movement to change these relationships, will be largely extralegal. For example, one of the most frequently invoked features of revolutionary movements is the tendency toward violence. As Smelser suggests, "because of the hostile component in the beliefs of all value-oriented movements, the potential for violence is always present. . . ." [8] However, it should be noted that so-called counterrevolutionary or resistance movements frequently utilize similar tactics. Moreover, Smelser's definition of a value-oriented movement places equal emphasis on nonviolent movements which operate in terms of some ideology or value orientation. Thus, al-

---

1964), p. 521. See also Ralph H. Turner and Lewis M. Killian, *Collective Behavior* (Englewood Cliffs, N.J.: Prentice-Hall, Inc., 1957), pp. 320–321.
[5] Turner and Killian, *ibid.*, p. 329.
[6] Herbert Blumer, "Social Movements," in Alfred M. Lee, ed., *College Outline Series: Principles of Sociology* (New York: Barnes and Noble, Inc., 1951), pp. 212–213.
[7] Horton and Hunt, *op. cit.*, p. 526.
[8] Neil J. Smelser, *The Theory of Collective Behavior* (Glencoe, Ill.: Free Press, 1963), p. 319.

though there does appear to be some relationship between degree of ideological rigidity and the use of violence as a tactic, we would argue that movements cannot be adequately distinguished on the basis of tactics. Therefore, it would appear most useful to examine "type of social change advocated" as the paramount variable around which social movements may be differentiated. Let us examine some of the existing classifications in this light.

In the literature, social movements have been viewed as ranging from revolutionary—to resistance or reactionary—to a less extreme specific or reform type. Included in the revolutionary category are Horton and Hunt's "revolutionary," [9] Smelser's "value oriented," [10] Blumer's "specific-revolutionary movement," [11] Wirth's "militant," [12] and Faris' "revolutionary" organization.[13]

These movements are generally conceptualized as "seeking to reconstruct the entire social order." [14] This view is based upon Tocqueville's model of "social revolution," where there is: "drastic declassification from membership in a society of certain categories of persons, the replacement in leadership of one class by another, or the substitution of one system of property for another." [15] Many of the standard definitions of revolution and movements engaged in this process rely heavily upon this model. Sigmund Neumann's popularly cited delineation, for example, characterizes revolution as: "a sweeping, fundamental change in political organization, social structure, economic property control and the predominant myth of a social order, thus indicating a major break in the continuity of development." [16] More simplistically, perhaps, Horton and Hunt define a revolutionary movement as one "seeking to overthrow the existing social system and replace it with a greatly different one." [17]

The nature of the revolutionary movement is best described by the French existentialist novelist and essayist Albert Camus in The Rebel, where he argues that revolt is incubated when people become aware of the existence of oppression.[18] This alteration of consciousness is brought about

---

[9] Horton and Hunt, *op. cit.*, p. 526.
[10] Smelser, *op. cit.*, pp. 313, 316.
[11] Blumer, *op. cit.*, p. 202.
[12] Louis Wirth, "Types of Minority Movements," in Turner and Killian, eds., *op. cit.*, p. 325.
[13] Robert E. L. Faris, *Social Disorganization*, 2d ed. (New York: Ronald Press Co., 1955), pp. 599–615.
[14] Blumer, *op. cit.*, p. 212.
[15] Melvin Richter, "Tocqueville's Contribution to the Theory of Revolution," in Carl J. Freidrich, ed., *Revolution* (New York: Atherton Press, 1966), p. 90.
[16] Sigmund Neumann, "The International Civil War," *World Politics*, 1 (April 1949): 333, fn. 1.
[17] Horton and Hunt, *op. cit.*, p. 526.
[18] Albert Camus, *The Rebel: An Essay on Man in Revolt* (New York: Alfred A. Knopf, 1956).

by the master, the holder of power, who has transgressed against human rights which the powerless feel intuitively are rightfully theirs. This view, the reader will remember from our discussion in chapter 4, is similar to Marx's attempt to define class consciousness. In translating this awareness of injustice into action, the slave, the submissive one, is affirming the existence of human rights and limiting the absolute freedom of the master: "Rebellion . . . is the very movement of life and it cannot be denied without renouncing life. Its purest outburst, on each occasion, gives birth to existence." [19] At this point the slave or oppressed class is no longer willing to continue under submission and demands the same freedom exercised by the holders of power; the slave, the oppressed, the proletarian, becomes a rebel.

Even though, by becoming a rebel, the individual is open to suppression and even death, Camus argues that the adoption of this stance affirms the legitimacy of human rights for the rebel and for all men: "I rebel—therefore we exist." [20] This stance of defiance and defense of the human dignity of all mankind is Camus' basic definition of rebellion. Indeed, one rarely finds revolutions not being carried out for the "benefit of man." However, Camus notes that the concept of common human dignity ideally places a check on or limits the act of rebellion. If the revolution transcends these limitations and the oppressed claim absolute freedom, then the slave becomes the master, and another power relationship has been established, in the Orwellian sense of Animal Farm.

In order to exist, man must rebel, but rebellion must respect the limit it discovers in itself—a limit where minds meet and, in meeting, begin to exist. Rebellious thought, therefore, cannot dispense with memory: it is a perpetual state of tension. In studying its action and its results, we shall have to say, each time, whether it remains faithful to its first noble promise or if, through indolence or folly, it forgets its original purpose and plunges into a mire of tyranny or servitude.[21]

In contrast, resistance movements are generally viewed as being reactionary phenomena brought about by some form of structural strain, e.g., the French Resistance to the Petain regime. To "resist" has a static implication: resisting change has a different goal orientation from bringing about change. However, conservative movements such as the Ku Klux Klan can desire reactive changes in the social system as drastic in scope as those of the so-called revolutionary movements. That is, conservative movements desire change from the present to another (past) point in

---

[19] Ibid., p. 304.
[20] Ibid., p. 22.
[21] Ibid. See also Crane Brinton, *Anatomy of Revolution* (New York: Vintage Books, 1959), pp. 185–250.

time and are not entirely limited to resistance per se. Movements of this type have been treated as revivalistic and nationalistic by Blumer.[22] Horton and Hunt employ the classic definition in this category, stating: "The resistance movement is an effort to block a proposed change or to uproot a change already achieved."[23] Louis Wirth sees resistance movements as focusing upon the factors of nationalistic and racial purity.[24] Smelser also notes that conservative movements, given their ideological nature and their concern with individual belief systems, are value-oriented movements.[25]

The essence of the resistance movement involves a reaction to social change. It stresses traditional values such as nationalism and, frequently, racial superiority. As one text observes:

> The Ku Klux Klan is perhaps our best-known resistance movement organized in the South after the Civil War, to keep Negroes "in their place" by terror and intimidation . . . and reborn in the North after World War I as a nativistic movement. The nativistic movement is an attempt to protect the purity of the group and its culture from new or foreign intrusions. . . .[26]

In sum, a resistance movement most frequently arises to maintain a given social position or to improve it, on the basis of some traditional appeal. Classic examples of this form of movement are the American Nazi Party and George Wallace's American Independence Party. As Lewis Corey wrote in one of the few Marxist analyses relevant to the United States: "Fascism, using radical phrases and middle class action, provides the ideological justification, the 'popular' sanctions and mass support to suppress violently all progressive forces and prevent the transformation of collectivism into socialism."[27]

The third general category of movements treated in the literature is the reformist-change type. Activity here is oriented to achieving some limited alteration in the social structure without a total transformation of the system. This type of movement has been labeled by various analysts as "reformistic,"[28] "normative,"[29] "specific,"[30] "secular or limited,"[31] "secessionalist,"[32] and "respectable-nonfactional" and "respectable-factional."[33]

[22] Blumer, op. cit., p. 219.
[23] Horton and Hunt, op. cit., p. 529.
[24] Wirth, op. cit., p. 324.
[25] Smelser, op. cit., p. 348.
[26] Horton and Hunt, op. cit., p. 529.
[27] Lewis Corey, Crisis of the Middle Class (New York: Covici, Friede, 1935), p. 235.
[28] Horton and Hunt, op. cit., p. 529.
[29] Smelser, op. cit., pp. 270–312.
[30] Blumer, op. cit., p. 202.
[31] Faris, op. cit., p. 529.
[32] Wirth, op. cit., p. 324.
[33] Turner and Killian, op. cit., p. 329.

Of the three ideal types of movements under discussion, the reformist is generally described as being necessary for the maintenance of a pluralistic society, since it attempts to redress grievances ignored by dominant political institutions. Most observers correlate reform movements as being endemic only to democratic states: "Reform movements are impossible in an authoritarian society whose rulers will tolerate no criticism."[34] Faris sees reform movements as fundamentally political and pragmatic. Reform movements accept the overall conscience collective and play the game according to the rules of pluralism. This form of movement is addressed to one specific or limited issue such as prohibition, women's rights, the single tax, and the like. Smelser defines the reformist movement as follows:

A norm-oriented movement is an attempt to restore, protect, modify, or create norms in the name of a generalized belief. Participants may be trying either to affect norms directly (e.g. efforts of a feminist group to establish a private education system for women) or induce some constituted authority to do so (e.g. pressures from the same group on a governmental agency to support or create a public co-educational system). Any kind of norm—economic, educational, political, religious—may become the subject of such movements.[35]

A labor union attempting to get better working conditions for its members can, under certain conditions such as a wildcat strike, be seen as a reform movement. Similarly, the NAACP is a reform movement since it is not concerned with total social revolution. Instead, the NAACP attempts to improve the status of a specific racial group in America. Because of this limitation in goals, reform movements are usually treated as quasi-legitimate vis-à-vis the conscience collective and the distribution of power in society.

Reform movements are the ones most frequently confused with political parties and pressure groups, since the goals of these three kinds of organizations are often coterminous. Nevertheless, we must reiterate that whereas political parties and pressure groups operate within the accepted framework of political pluralism and consensus politics, a reform movement will attempt to bring about its changes outside the political arena. Note, for example, the simultaneous activities surrounding the civil rights issue in the early sixties: sit-ins and freedom rides to confront segregation in public facilities (extralegitimate action); voter registration drives to realize political potential (legitimate action). However, since the goals of a reform movement are close to those of the legitimate power structure,

---

[34] Horton and Hunt, *op. cit.*, p. 525.
[35] Smelser, *op. cit.*, p. 270.

it is the type of movement most typically truncated by institutionalization, i.e., being made a part of the status quo.[36]

The above trichotimization of social movements suggests an ideal typology based on the nature of changes sought in the social system. As we have indicated in previous chapters, social movements basically address the power relationships of a society. Therefore, we propose to amplify this classification according to how social movements, as organized ideologies, seek to change an existing distribution of power. Concerning ideology, we must bear in mind that it offers not only a program of change but also an analysis of present dysfunctions and how they have come to pass. Since social movements are historically relative, those of a given historical period will tend to react to the same significant problems. Thus, variations in types of organized ideologies will not surround the present existential state, but rather will focus on how this has come to be and what is to be done.

Focusing on "what is to be done," our trichotomous scheme suggests three alternatives: (1) institute an idealized new state of power relationships; (2) reinstitute an idealized past state of power relationships; (3) modify the existing state of power relationships so as to make them more viable. Thus, the social goals available to movements suggest that they may be analyzed as "left," "right," and "reform." We shall now focus on the characteristics of these three ideal types.

REVOLUTIONARY MOVEMENTS

Movements of the left are characterized by the goal of altering power relations for the purpose of achieving social change defined in terms of total philosophical frameworks for "charter myths" (e.g., those proposed by the Saint-Simonians and the left-wing Hegelians: Marx, Proudhon, Bakunin, and Bazard). Revolutionary movements possess a metaphysical rationale for bringing about a new social order based upon a body of thought which defines the past and the present and interprets the future (e.g., anarchism, utopian socialism, and the various models of the ideal Communist state). According to Camus, contemporary "charter myths" —those conceptions defining the ideal allocation of power in society—may be traced back to Hegel. Hegel, it is argued, replaced the traditional concepts justifying the social order, such as God, justice, and truth, with the notion of "concrete universal reason." This reason, the constant striving of all things to attain their natural potential, was the force determining the structure and development of the universe. For the Hege-

---

[36] Note, for example, the institutionalization of the labor movement into the "house of labor." The process of institutionalization will be discussed at length in chap. 7.

lians, the dialectic process of history—thesis, antithesis, synthesis—was the manifestation of reason in social and cultural institutions. The Hegelian model was invoked by the instigators of the French Revolution to institute a united social system through government based upon reason. Instead, the revolution culminated in a reign of terror. As Camus puts it:

> . . . the philosophers who supported the doctrine of an incessant dialectic replaced the harmonious and strict constructors of reason. From this moment dates the idea (hostile to every concept of ancient thought . . .) that man has not been endowed with a definitive human nature, that he is not a finished creation, but an experiment of which he can be partly the creator.[37]

Thus it is that the future, the unfolding of the Geist or the "autobiography of God," became a dominant theme within the framework of revolutionary ideology. Camus continues: "With Napoleon and the Napoleonic philosopher Hegel, the period of efficacy begins. Before Napoleon, men had discovered space and the universe; with Napoleon, they discovered time and the future in terms of this world; and by this discovery the spirit of rebellion is going to be profoundly transformed." [38] However, Camus sees contemporary revolutionary ideology as self-defeating; tied to a total philosophical framework of conflict and absolute power:

> . . . the revolutionaries of the twentieth century have borrowed from Hegel the weapons with which they definitely destroyed the formal principles of virtue. All they have preserved is the vision of a history without any kind of transcendence, dedicated to perpetual strife and to the struggle of wills bent on seizing power. . . . The world today can no longer be anything other than a world of masters and slaves because contemporary ideologies, those that are changing the face of the earth, have learned from Hegel to conceive of history in terms of the dialectic of master and slave.[39]

For Camus, revolutionary movements tied to the ideological foundations laid down by Hegel and Marx will fail to improve the state of man because of their disregard for life, freedom, and individual integrity. One plausible reason for this conclusion lies in the fact that the ideology of revolutionary movements minimizes the role of the individual actor in determining social conditions and instead stresses societal dysfunctions and contradictions as the source of problems and offers collective solutions designed to achieve an "ideal" future state. Winston White, in Beyond Conformity, suggests that liberals and the Marxist Left see man as fundamentally good and maintain that all evil stems from the social

---

[37] Camus, op. cit., p. 134.
[38] Ibid., p. 134.
[39] Ibid., pp. 135–136.

structure.[40] For example, Marx and Engels, in discussing the "real basis of ideology," perceive class antagonisms and conflict as stemming from productive relationships based on a rural-urban division of labor.[41] Similarly, Bakunin, the Russian anarchist, saw the state and the social order as the cause of all crime and immorality. He wrote:

. . . every human individual, with no exception whatever, is but an involuntary product of natural and social environment. There are four basic causes of man's immorality: 1) Lack of rational hygiene and upbringing; 2) Inequality of economic and social conditions; 3) The ignorance of the masses flowing naturally from this situation; 4) And the unavoidable consequence of those conditions—slavery.[42]

As a consequence of this structural analysis of the source of dysfunction, coupled with the dialectical premise of conflict and a new world order, the revolutionary movement invariably finds itself in direct confrontation with the existing power structure. These features are illustrated in the following revolutionary document.

Excerpts from G. William Domhoff, "How to Commit Revolution in Corporate America" from the Peninsula Observer (Palo Alto, California, Spring 1968). Revised text of a speech given at the University of California at Santa Cruz on April 28, 1968. Reprinted by permission of William Domhoff.

ORDER OF PRIORITIES

There are three aspects, I think, to any good revolutionary program for corporate America. These aspects are closely intertwined, and all three must be developed alongside each other, but there is nonetheless a certain logic, a certain order of priorities, in the manner I present them.

First, you need a comprehensive overall analysis of the present-day American system. You've got to realize that the corporation capitalism of today is not the nineteenth century individual capitalism that conservatives yearn for. Nor is it the pluralistic paradise that liberals rave about

---

[40] Winston White, *Beyond Conformity* (Glencoe, Ill.: The Free Press, 1961), esp. pp. 20–24. As for resistance movements, White characterizes value-oriented "mobilizers" as placing the blame for problems and strains on individuals.
[41] Karl Marx and Frederick Engels, *The German Ideology* (New York: International Publishers, New World Paperbacks, 1963), pp. 43–69.
[42] Michael Bakunin, "Social and Economic Bases of Anarchism," in Irving Louis Horowitz, ed., *The Anarchists* (New York: Dell Publishing Co., 1964), p. 134. (Italicized in the original.)

and try to patch up. Nor is it the finance capitalism of the American Communists who are frozen in their analyses of another day.

Second, you need relatively detailed blueprints for a postindustrial America. You've got to show people concrete plans that improve their lot either spiritually or materially. There's no use scaring them with shouts of socialism, which used to be enough of a plan, however general, but which today only calls to mind images of Russia, deadening bureaucracy, and 1984.

And there's no use boring them with vague slogans about participation and vague abstractions about dehumanization. You've got to get down to where people live, and you've got to get them thinking in terms of a better America without the spectre of Russia, rightly or wrongly, driving any thought of risking social change out of their heads.

Third, and finally, you need a plan of attack, a program for taking power. For make no mistake about it—before most people get involved in revolutionary activity they take a mental look way down the road. Maybe not all the way down the road, but a long way down. They want to know what they are getting into, and what their chances are, and whether there is really anything positive in sight that is worth the gamble.

I suspect that most people just don't fit the formula that seems to be prevalent in America: get people involved in anything—rent strikes, antinuclear testing demonstrations, rat strikes, draft demonstrations, whatever, and gradually they will develop a revolutionary mentality. Ponder carefully about this activity for activity's sake. You need a plan of attack, not just some issues like peace or rats. And one thing more on this point: that plan has to come out of your analysis of the present socioeconomic system and out of your own life experience—that is, out of the American experience, and not out of the experiences of Russia, or China, or Cuba, all of which have been different from each other, and are different from the U.S.A.

The world moves, even in America, and as it moves new realities arise and old theories become irrelevant. New methods become necessary. If you expect to be listened to, you will have to look around you afresh and build your own plan, abandoning all the sacred texts on What Is To Be Done. . . .

FIRST REVOLUTIONARY ACT

This really brings you to your first revolutionary act. Research one thing and one thing only—the American power structure. Withdraw your libido from twelfth-century Antarctica, historical criticism of Viking poetry, and other such niceties, and get to where you are: here, America, the twentieth century.

Just turning the spotlight on the power elite is a revolutionary act, although only Act One. Ideas and analysis are powerful, and they shake people up. The problem of would-be American revolutionaries has not been an overemphasis on ideas, but the use of old ones, wrong ones, and transplanted ones. That is why C. Wright Mills grabbed American students and parts of American academia. He had new, relevant ideas and facts about the here and now—he exploded old clichés and slogans, and I think he created more radicals with his work than any hundred Oakland or Los Angeles policemen with their billy clubs.

A good analysis is essential in developing a program for taking power because it tells you what you can and cannot expect, what you can and cannot do, what you should and should not advocate. Let me give four examples:

1. Corporation capitalism, if it can continue to corporatize the "underdeveloped" world and displace small businessmen and realtors in the cities, may have a lot more room for reforms. In fact, if creature comfort is enough, it may come to satisfy most of its members. Be that as it may, and I doubt if it can solve its problems in a humanly tolerable way, the important point is that no American revolutionary should find himself shocked or irrelevant because the corporate rich agree to nationwide health insurance or guaranteed annual incomes, or pull out of one of their military adventures.

And don't get your hopes up for any imminent collapse. Better to be surprised by a sudden turn that hastens your time schedule than to be disappointed once again by the flexibility of the corporate rich. This means that you should rely on your own program, not depression or war, to challenge the system and to bring about change, and that you should have a flexible, hang-loose attitude toward the future. Predictions of the inevitability of anything, whether collapse or socialism, fall a little flat and leave us a little jaded after comparing earlier predictions with the experience of the twentieth century.

2. Corporation capitalism seems to be very much dependent on overseas sales and investments, probably much more so than it is on the military spending necessary to defend and extend the Free World empire. And even if some economists would dispute that, I think it is 100 per cent safe to say that most members of the corporate rich are convinced that this overseas empire is essential—and that is what affects their political and economic and military behavior. Thus, the corporate rich fear—indeed, have utter horror of—isolationism, and that suggests that you revolutionaries should agree with the conservatives about the need for isolationism.

3. The American corporate rich have at their command unprecedented, almost unbelievable firepower and snooping power. This makes it questionable whether or not a violent revolutionary movement has a chance of getting off the ground. It also makes it doubtful whether or not

a secret little Leninist-type party can remain secret and unpenetrated for long. In short a nonviolent and open party may be dictated to you as your only choice by the given fact of the corporate leaders' military and surveillance capability, just as a violent and closed party was dictated by the Russian situation.

4. The differences between present-day corporation capitalism and nineteenth century individual capitalism must be emphasized again and again if you are to reach those currently making up the New Right. Those people protest corporation capitalism and its need for big government and overseas spending in the name of small business, small government, competition, the marketplace—all those things destroyed or distorted by the corporate system.

You must agree with the New Right that these things have happened and then be able to explain to them how and why they have happened, not due to the communists or labor, or liberal professors, but due to the growing corporatization of the society and the needs of these corporations.

You can't give up on these New Rightists—they know that the Rockefellers, the J. J. McCloys, the Averell Harrimans, the Paul Hoffmans, the Adlai Stevensons, and the John B. Lindsays run American society. (Here I am just naming some of the relatively few multi-millionaire businessmen and corporation lawyers known to the American public.) And, like the New Left, the New Rightists don't like it.

It is your job to teach them that the new corporate system is the problem, not the motives and good faith of the corporate rich they call communists and dupes of liberal academics. . . .

PICTURE OF NEW SOCIETY

What could this post-industrial society look like? Naturally, I have a few suggestions, all tentative, and I will mention some of them. It is on this project that so many more people could become totally involved in the revolutionary process.

If it would be by and large intellectuals, academics, and students who would work on the analysis and critique of the growing corporation feudalism, it would be people from all walks of life who would be essential to this second necessity. You need men and women with years of experience—in farming, small business, teaching, city planning, recreation, medicine, and on and on—to start discussing and writing about ways to organize that part of society they know best for a post-industrial America.

You need to provide outlets via forums, discussions, papers, and magazines for the pent-up plans and ideals of literally millions of well-trained, experienced, frustrated Americans who see stupidity and greed all around them but can't do a thing about it.

You need to say, for example, "Look, Mr. and Mrs. City Planning Expert trapped in this deadly bureaucracy controlled by big businessmen, draw up a sensible plan for street development, or park development, in your town of 30,000 people." "Look, Mr. Blue Collar Worker, working for this big corporation, how should this particular plant be run in a sensible society?"

MANY MUST BE NEUTRALIZED

In addition, the neutralization of large masses should be one of the prime goals of a program to develop and present blueprints for a post-industrial America. To this end each person in America should receive a short, simple, one-page handbill especially relevant to his situation or occupation. It would begin, for example, "Policemen, standing here protecting us from Evil at this demonstration, Where Will You Be After The Revolution?"

And then, in a few short sentences you will tell this bewildered soul that there will still be a great need for policemen after the revolution, but that policemen will tend to do more of the things that they like to do—helping, assisting, guiding—rather than the things that get them a bad name—that is, faithfully carrying out the repressive dictates of their power elite masters.

You will tell him you know that some policemen are prejudiced or authoritarian, but you also know that is neither here nor there because orders to shoot or not to shoot come from officials higher up, who are intimately intertwined in the corporate system.

Similar handbills should be prepared for every person. . . .

TALK TO THE NEW RIGHT

. . . Perhaps most of all, there has to be a consideration of the role of Mr. John Bircher, Mr. Physician, Mr. Dentist, and others now on the New Right. These people are put off or ignored by increasing corporatization, and they have to be shown that their major values—individuality, freedom, local determination—are also the values of a post-industrial America.

This does not mean they will suddenly become revolutionaries, but it is important to start them wondering whether they would find things as bad in the new social system as they do in this system, which increasingly annoys them, exasperates them, and ignores them. They must be weaned from the handful of large corporations and multi-millionaires who use them for their own ends by talking competition while practicing monopoly, by screaming about taxes while paying very little, and by talking individuality while practicing collectivism.

What would a post-industrial America look like? First of all, it would be certain American institutions writ large—like the Berkeley food Co-op, which is locally controlled by consumers, like the Pasadena water and electric systems, which are publicly owned, like the Tennessee Valley Authority, which has allowed the beginnings of the sane, productive, and beautiful development of at least one river region in our country.

In simple terms, the system would start from local controls and work up, like it used to before all power and taxes were swept to the national level, mostly by war and the big corporations. And, as you can see, it would be a mixed system, sometimes with control by consumers, sometimes with control by local government, sometimes with control by regional authorities, and sometimes, as should be made clear in the handbill to certain small businessmen, with control in private hands.

For many retail franchises, for many novelty productions, and, I suspect, for many types of farms and farmers, depending on region, crop involved, and other considerations, private enterprise may be the best method of control.

MUST BE FLEXIBLE

. . . I have left the most obvious change for last. Of course the corporations would be socialized. Their profits would go to all people in lower prices (and thus higher real wages) and/or repair to local, state, and national treasuries in the amounts necessary to have a park on every corner (replacing one of the four gas stations), and medical, dental, educational, recreational, or arts facilities on the other corners (replacing the other three gas stations—there being no need for any but a few gas stations due to the ease of introducing electric cars when a few hundred thousand rich people are not in a position to interfere).

But how to man this huge corporate enterprise? First, with blue collar workers, who would be with you all the way in any showdown no matter how nice some members of the corporate rich have been to them lately. Second, with men from lower-level management positions who have long ago given up the rat race, wised up, and tacitly awaited our revolution.

Fantasy? Perhaps, but don't underestimate the cynicism at minor levels of the technostructure. I have spoken with and to these groups, and there is hope. They are not all taken in, any more than most Americans are fooled by the mass media about domestic matters. They are just trapped, with no place to go but out if they think too much or make a wave.

"Out" is easy enough if you're young and single, but it's a little sticky if you didn't wake up to the whole corporate absurdity until you were long out of college and had a wife and two kids.

Cultivate these well-educated men and women whose talents are wasted and ill-used. Remind them that the most revolutionary thing they can do—aside from feeding you information and money so you can further expose the system and aside from helping to plan the post-industrial society—is to be in a key position in the technostructure when the revolution comes. You may not win a large percentage of them, but then it wouldn't take many to help you through the transition.

END DUPLICATION

Then too, part of the corporate system would disappear—one computerized system of banking and insurance would eliminate the incredible duplication, paperwork, and nonsense now existent in those "highly profitable" but worthless areas of the corporate economy.

Corporate retails would be broken up and given to local consumer co-ops, or integrated into nationalized producer-retailer units in some cases. Corporate transports (air, rails, buses) would be given in different cases to state, local, and national government, as well as to, on occasion, the retailers or producers they primarily serve.

The public utilities, as earlier hinted, would finally be given to the public, mostly on the local and regional level, probably on the national level in the case of telephones.

The only real problem, I think, is manufacturing, where you have to hold the loyalty of technicians and workers to survive a transition. Blue collar control—syndicalism—may be the answer in some cases, regional or national government control in others. Here, obviously, is one of those questions that needs much study, with blue collar and white collar workers in the various industries being the key informants and idea men. . . .

Now to a program for taking the reins of government from the power elite in order to carry out the plan developed by revolutionary visionaries. It is on this point that we are likely to find the most disagreement, the most confusion, the most uncertainty, and the most fear.

But I think you do have something very important to go on—the ideas and experiences and successes of the Civil Rights and New Left and Hippie movements of the past several years. If they have not given you an analysis of corporate capitalism or a set of blueprints, which is their weakness, they have given you the incredibly precious gift of new forms of struggle and new methods of reaching people; and these gifts must be generalized, articulated, and more fully developed.

I have a general term, borrowed from a radical hippie, that I like to use because it so beautifully encompasses what these movements have given to you—psychic guerrilla warfare—the "psychic" part appealing to my psychologist instincts and summarizing all the hard-hitting nonviolent methods, the "guerrilla warfare" part hopefully giving to those who want to take to the hills some satisfaction, so that they will stick around and participate in the only type of guerrilla warfare likely to work in corporate America.

For make no mistake about it, psychic guerrilla warfare is a powerful weapon in a well-educated, sedate, highly industrialized country that has a tradition of liberal values and democratic political processes. . . .

Back to psychic guerrilla warfare. How do you direct this dynamite to its task of destroying the ideological cover of the corporate rich?

First, you start a new political party, a wide-open, locally-based political party dedicated to the development of blueprints for a post-industrial America and to the implementation of them through psychic guerrilla warfare. It should be a party open to anyone prepared to abandon all other political affiliations and beliefs—in other words, it would not be an Anti-This-Or-That coalition of liberal Democrats, Communists, Trotskyists, and Maoists.

In fact, ignore those groups. The best members will drop out and join yours. For the rest, they have no constituencies and would soon fall to fighting the Old Fights among themselves anyway—Communist and Anti-Communist, Pro-Soviet and Anti-Soviet, and On and On ad tedium.

No, you don't need that—it would destroy you like it destroyed them. Indeed, they need you, for if you got something going the party would be big enough for all of them to work in without seeing each other or having to defend the Old Faiths. . . .

WHO ARE CONSTITUENTS?

Now who does this party address itself to as its agitators and organizers drive around in open-air trucks, complete with folk rock bands, shouting out their message and distributing their handbills in every town, county fair, ghetto, and shopping center in the country? What is its potential constituency?

The answer is first of all a very general one, but this very generality frees American revolutionaries from trying to duplicate the past or fit into theoretical molds.

You should direct yourself to anyone disgusted with the present system and assume that your potential constituency is everyone not wrapped up in the power elite.

This even includes sons and daughters of the corporate rich who have seen enough and want out—and they've always been there in small numbers on the American Left and Right anyhow, so why pretend differently?

I suggest as follows: the initial base is, as C. Wright Mills said, radical intellectuals and students. The intellectuals have got to start talking like Gene Debs and Malcolm X. They have got to blaze out of the classroom and clinic like Mills and Benjamin Spock, carrying their revolutionary consultation services to every group in the country that will send them an airplane fare or bus ticket.

What with the protection of tenure and the right of academic freedom, and with lots of universities opening up in Canada, Australia, and New Zealand, professors are the least vulnerable group in American society. They ought to be ashamed of themselves for not raising a hundred times more ruckus than they are now.

These professors and their students also have to continue work on the analysis, and begin involving people in their local community to work on the blueprints. They should form small study-action groups in every university, college, and junior college town in the country.

YOUTH IS MOST VITAL

These small study-action groups have to prepare themselves for a psychic blitz of their most important constituency. That constituency is simply called youth—blue collar, white collar, white skin, black skin, who cares? They are pouring out of schools like crazy, affluence has made them somewhat independent and hang-loose, many of them don't communicate with their parents, and they're going to be a majority in a very few years. . . .

APPROACH THE NEW RIGHT

As I've implied throughout, an effort has to be made toward those on the Right. I'm under no illusions about the difficulties of this, but I insist that it is necessary to dismiss talk about racism and fascism on the Right: all white Americans are racists, and parts of the blue collar world are probably worse than the Right. As to fascism, if we get a European-style dictatorship in this country, it will probably be more like France anyway, and it will be instituted by the corporate rich presently in power in order to get around their difficulties with Congress and local governments.

So forget all this talk about fascism, which has scared American revolutionaries into the laps of the liberals almost as well as the cry of Communism has scared the Right into the arms of the corporate rich. Old Left and liberal talk about fascism amounts to their fear of angering the corporate masters to the point where they call on their supposed Right-wing shock troops.

See if you can make contact with those people on the New Right, who really have no place to go because there is no turning back now that the huge corporations have destroyed individual capitalism. Of course they don't share your program, but they do share your view of the power structure and your desire for more individuality and local autonomy.

In dealing with the New Right, it is essential to respect individuality and personality. Neither Left nor Right really does this despite their rhetoric. A revolution must transcend personality and respect individuality if it is to get to its task of reaching large masses of people. In fact, personal diversity will be an asset in getting the attention of all types of people. Different religions, different styles and different hair arrangements must be de-emphasized (not changed and consciously subordinated by self-analysis and devotion to common goals through the mechanism of the blueprints).

The enemy is corporation capitalism, not religion, personality structure, or type of oral indulgent—pot on the Left, alcohol on the Right—used to lessen anxiety and dispel depression.

LEAVE BLACKS ALONE

Why haven't I mentioned black people till now? Aren't they important? Am I just another Whitey who doesn't care about the black man? Not at all. I suggest that you do what the black man has told you to: let him do his own thing and you get to work building a party that can unite with him some day far off down the road after you've overcome your racism and he's made up his mind about where he's going and with whom. For now the black man is right—you've got nothing to tell him, and he's got to go it on his own in order to win his manhood. Nobody has ever been given anything worth having. Finally some black men are learning that freeing fact. . . .

BLUE COLLAR WORKERS

What about blue collar workers? First, create a party they have to react to. And don't waste time trying to control or shape labor unions, which are conservative bureaucratic institutions these days, rightfully looking out for the working man in day-to-day battles with the corporate leaders.

Confront these people at home, at school, and at play, and get them involved in the party and its activities. In short, don't get caught in Old Left fixations.

Now I know there are many thousands of dedicated and far-seeing blue collar workers who would be with you from the start, heart and soul, sweat and tears. But don't get the idea that any great percentage of organized labor will be willing to risk leaving the Democratic Party. Right now they have it relatively good—as long as they are working, or are insulated against automation, or have cost-of-living raises built into their contracts as checks against inflation. But no matter how nicely some of the corporate rich treat blue collar workers in wartime, don't worry because there is no question about where the blue collar masses would be in a showdown if you have done your homework carefully.

FORCE A CHOICE

Let's assume that the party is not snuffed out in its early stages and that it grows. Then the power elite is in a bind; they will have to compete with it, which means a move towards the Welfare State, or, failing that, they would have to repress it, which would be the great watershed for American liberals, liberalism, and democracy.

If you are nonviolent, open, of all religions, and not tied to a foreign power, they would be destroying America to move on you. Liberals would have no course but to join the fight on your side or admit that socioeconomic privileges are more basic than political institutions and values; some might even be annoyed enough to join you in air-conditioned, music-equipped prison cells that the corporate rich are likely to provide. More generally, at that point the masses of people in America would have to draw their own conclusions about what is to be done.

Your job is to force them to make that choice between democracy and corporate feudalism by taking the system on its promise and testing it to its limits. Either way, you win—a democratic, non-violent takeover or proof to all that when it gets down to the nitty-gritty, even in America, the only way to power is through the barrel of the gun. . . .

A number of important points about revolutionary movements are treated in this reading. In the first place, Domhoff makes it clear that the existence of a social issue (war, nuclear testing, slums, etc.) and the protest which it may engender (which we will analyze shortly as "expressive" activity) are not sufficient bases for revolution. The revolutionary must go beyond these issues and address himself to the nature of the unique power structure of his society which has brought these conditions into being. To the question "What is the locus of power in 'postindustrial' (or, perhaps more accurately, 'postcapitalist') America" Domhoff answers "Corporate capitalism, the increasing concentration of economic power in the hands of a relatively few corporations." [43] Second, he emphasizes that it is not enough simply to identify this locus of power—you must thoroughly understand its strengths and weaknesses to be able to combat it effectively. What should the revolutionary know about corporate capitalism?: (1) It is completely different from nineteenth-century capitalism (e.g., it is monopolistic rather than competitive, bureaucratic rather than individualistic, managed rather than characterized by free enterprise). (2) It has the resources and the flexibility for expedient reforms. (3) It is imperialistic, requiring continually expanding overseas markets. (4) It has unprecedented power to control or to crush opposition. Third, the program and plan of action of a movement must be logically extended from the analysis of how things are and how they came to be. Thus, the monopolistic and imperialistic trends of corporate capitalism must be reversed, but not to the extent of trying to reintroduce a now historically irrelevant laissez-faire capitalism. Domhoff's postindustrial America would be more isolationist economically, with the control and benefits of production passing largely into the hands of the consumer. Local determination, through consumer cooperatives and public ownership, would be greatly expanded. However, because of the flexibility and repressive ability of corporate capitalism, Domhoff cautions that these changes will take time, and must be wrought openly. Finally, if you are to be successful in recruiting a mass base for a movement, your appeals must relate the analysis and consequent plan of action to the existential condition of potential members. Thus, Domhoff appeals to students and intellectuals who already grasp the absurdity of corporate America; to members of the New Right, who yearn for individuality, freedom, and self-determination; to technicians and workers who suffer the conditions of alienating labor; and to young people whose education has left them ill-equipped to cope with the realities of corporate capitalism.

Of the types of social movements under discussion, revolutionary movements are the most nonlegitimate vis-à-vis the conscience collective. This has the effect of isolating revolutionaries from mass support and hence of denying them "pressure" types of tactics to bring about change. Frequently, therefore, revolutionaries are left with only one option in the realm of tactics: violence. Tocqueville, for one, saw violence as the primary characteristic of revolutionary movements.[44] Pettee also observes revolutionary movements in this context, stating that "widespread vio-

---

[43] For a more extensive discussion, see G. William Domhoff, *Who Rules America?* (New York: Prentice-Hall, 1967).
[44] Richter, *op. cit.*, p. 81.

lence, acute bitterness, brutality, and intense mass emotion" characterize revolution.[45]

Quite often, the ideology of revolutionary movements has stressed violent means. Marx, for one, saw "force as the midwife of social change." [46] Engels and Lenin perceived the state as the legitimated agent for the use of force. Since the state is subservient to the ruling class, the revolutionary proletariat must resort to counterforce to bring about a total change in power relationships.[47]

REGRESSIVE MOVEMENTS

Movements of the Right come about to counteract existing trends in society and to change the values and institutions of the system from their present (decadent) form to those of a historical or idealized past. Rightist movements such as the extreme Right in America and Italian Fascism are responses to changes in power relationships accompanying the social transition variously described as folk to urban, spiritual to secular, and Gemeinschaft to Gesellschaft, in which additional modes of social integration give way to new ones. Ideologically, this type of movement emphasizes individual weaknesses and "deviation" as the sources of social problems, and suggests as solutions individualism, charismatic leadership, and a return to past value systems. To the Rightist, the fact that social institutions do not function in an idealized way is not attributable to inherent weaknesses or contradictions in these institutions but rather to the weaknesses, fallibility, and evils of individual leaders. The contemporary American rightist's preoccupation with "international Communism" does not concern Communism as an emergent (and historically fluctuating) reality but rather focuses on Communism as a constant and immutable threat to the supremacy of individualism. Alan F. Westin, in discussing native American fundamentalists, describes the characteristics of rightists as follows:

However much factors like urbanization, the cold war, and status insecurities may have provided a new setting for native fundamentalists, a large and irreducible corps of such people has always existed in the United States. Unlike

---

[45] George Pettee, "Revolution—Typology and Process," in Freidrich, *Revolution, op. cit.*, p. 17.
[46] Karl Marx, quoted in H. Stuart Hughes, *Consciousness and Society* (New York: Vintage Books, 1958), p. 74.
[47] See Frederick Engels, *The Origin of the Family, Private Property and the State* (New York: International Publishers, 1933), and V. I. Lenin, *State and Revolution* (New York: International Publishers, 1932). Georges Sorel has a very illuminating discussion of the distinction between force and violence in "The Political General Strike," in *Reflection on Violence*, trans. T. E. Hulme and J. Roth (New York: Collier Books, 1951), esp. pp. 171–179.

American liberals and conservatives—who accept the political system, acknowledge the loyalty of their opponents, and employ the ordinary political techniques—the fundamentalists can be distinguished by five identifying characteristics:

(1) They assume that there are always solutions capable of producing international victories and of resolving our social problems; when such solutions are not found, they attribute the failure to conspiracies led by evil men and their dupes.

(2) They refuse to believe in the integrity and patriotism of those who lead the dominant social groups—the churches, the unions, the business community, and the like—and declare that the American Establishment has become part of the conspiracy.

(3) They reject the political system; they lash out at "politicians," the major parties, and the give and take of political compromise as a betrayal of the fundamental Truth and as a circus to divert the people.

(4) They reject those programs for dealing with social, economic, and international problems that liberals and conservatives agree upon as minimal foundations. In their place, the fundamentalists propose drastic panaceas requiring major social change.

(5) To break the net of conspiracy, they advocate "direct action," sometimes in the form of a new political party, but more often through secret organizations, push-button pressure campaigns, and front groups. Occasionally "direct action" will develop into hate-propaganda and calculated violence.[48]

Regressive movements, then, attempt to resist the present trends of change in a society (which are seen as leading away from "basic truths") and to introduce what may be called "inverse change." [49]

This characteristic of rightist ideology is illustrated in the following chapter from The Blue Book of The John Birch Society.

Robert Welch, The Blue Book of The John Birch Society, sixth printing, 1961, Section Six, "To Restore Responsibility," pp. 127–142. Reprinted by permission of the John Birch Society.

SECTION SIX: TO RESTORE RESPONSIBILITY

With that much explanation as background let's see what basic principle we can establish and what specific objective we can define, with regard

[48] Alan F. Westin, "The John Birch Society: 'Radical Right' and 'Extreme Left' in the Political Context of Post World War II—1962," in Daniel Bell, ed., The Radical Right (Garden City, N.Y.: Doubleday and Co., Inc., 1963), p. 203.
[49] In this sense, regressive movements are not unlike Blumer's "revivalistic" movements, which he describes as idealizing the past and which "venerate the ideal picture that they have and seek to mold contemporary life in terms of this ideal picture." See Blumer, op. cit., p. 220.

to the particular battle against collectivism, which would be sure to fit into and be encompassed by our general overall permanent purpose—although that total spiritual aspiration is as yet only foreshadowed. For thus making sharp and clear one part of our philosophy and program, where a concrete area of action is involved, will itself help to build a better understanding of the whole.

And it seems to me, gentlemen, that the whole essence of our purpose, and the guiding principle for our action, covering not only our fight *against* collectivism but our fight *for* our constructive replacement, can be summarized in the objective expressed by just five words: *Less government and more responsibility*. The principle is simple enough for all to understand. The direction signs leading to the goal expressed are clear enough for nobody to misjudge them. An honest adherence to that principle and those directions, against which to test either candidates or issues, will settle in the minds of our followers and ourselves almost all questions which may arise, concerning *either* candidates or issues, in the field of political effort. And yet it is broad enough, I believe, to be comprehensive with regard to all that we really desire to attain through political action.

Less government and more responsibility. I mean less government of every kind, federal, state, or municipal; and more true responsibility, not only on the part of individuals but on the part of such reduced governmental units as are necessarily permitted to exist. But of course I mean, primarily, less federal government, because that is where our greatest danger lies; and more individual responsibility, because that is our greatest need.

And now I want to give you some of the arguments and the reasoning by which we must try to inculcate this fundamental principle of less government and more responsibility into the minds of our contemporaries and successors. For we must try to make it a convincing political standard and an accepted goal on the part of not only our own dedicated followers, who go all the way with our principles and our ideals, of which this is only a segment. We must try to rally behind this concept thousands or possibly millions of anxious citizens who show a vital interest in their politically determined future, but are yet to be won to a dedication to ideals of more spiritual breadth.

So, again without your leave, I am going to utilize a few extracts from a talk I made a couple of years ago at a convocation of students and faculty of Dickinson College. I do so simply because, having put a lot of work into the preparation of that speech, I can cover the present ground more succinctly and quickly by quoting from it than in any other way. And this part is not long.

What we must start asking our fellow citizens everywhere to consider, as of overwhelming importance to the future of themselves and their families, is this: On the basis of all known past human experience, are there any general conclusions, with regard to the organization of society, which can be set forth with confidence? It seems to me clear that there certainly are.

1. First, government is necessary—some degree of government—in any civilized society. There are believers in the possibility and desirability of a governmentless anarchy, as a practicable form of human association. But the number of these advocates is comparatively very small, there is no evidence within human historical experience to support their thesis, and there is considerable evidence indicating otherwise.

2. Second, while government is necessary, it is basically a non-productive expense, an overhead cost supported by the productive economy. And like all overhead items, it always has a tendency to expand faster than the productive base which supports it.

3. Third, government is frequently evil. And we do not mean by this that they (governments) are merely dishonest. For all governments, with very rare exceptions indeed, are thoroughly dishonest. We made the statement in print, about two years ago, that there has never in the history of the world been a government (and this generalization includes our present one) that maintained honesty in the handling of a "managed" irredeemable currency. A few weeks later one of America's ablest and best-known economists quoted that statement with full approval.

But what we are talking about here is something far worse than dishonesty. In December, 1956, Professor Sorokin of Harvard—after quoting Lord Acton that great men, in the political arena, are almost always bad men—went on to reveal the results of his own survey of the criminality of rulers. This survey of the monarchs of various countries and the heads of various republics and democracies, in a selection large enough to constitute a very fair sample, revealed that there was an average of one murderer to every four of these rulers. "In other words," said Professor Sorokin, "the rulers of the states are the most criminal group in a respective population. With a limitation of their power their criminality tends to decrease; but it still remains exceptionally high in all nations."

An obvious reason for this is the greater temptation to criminality on the part of those who control or influence the police power of a nation, of which they would otherwise stand in more fear. Another is that ambitious men with criminal tendencies naturally gravitate into government because of this very prospect of doing, or helping to do, the policing over themselves. A third reason is that so many apologists can always be found, for criminal acts of government, on the grounds that such acts ultimately contribute to the public good and that therefore the criminal means are justified by the righteous ends. Kautilya wrote his *Arthashastra* in about 300 B.C. Machiavelli wrote his *Il Principe* in about 1500 A.D. And the arguments of both, that it is a virtue in a ruler to be unscrupulous for the good of his state, are heard in every age.

4. Fourth, government is always and inevitably an enemy of individual freedom. It seems rather strange that it was Woodrow Wilson, who more than any other one man started this nation on its present road towards totalitarianism, who also said that the history of human liberty is a history of the limitations of governmental power, not the increase of it. But Wilson could have boasted, as did Charles II of England, that he said only wise things even though he did only foolish ones. It is self-evident that government, by its very nature, *must* be an enemy of freedom, edging always towards a restriction of the individual's right and responsibilities.

5. Whatever must be done by government will always cost more than if it could be done by individuals or smaller groups. And the larger the government, the more disproportionate will be the cost. Letting a government do anything, therefore, which such individuals or smaller groups could properly do, is serious economic wastefulness. It is also contrary to the philosophy of the proper function of government that is derived from the whole body of past experiments.

6. Government, by its size, its momentum, and its authority, will not only perpetuate errors of doctrine or of policy, longer than they would otherwise retain acceptance, but it will multiply their effect on a geometric scale, as against the arithmetically cumulative effect of those errors if confined to individuals or smaller groups. The errors of tens of thousands of individuals, all thinking and probing in different directions and moved by different impulses, tend to cancel themselves out or to be softened by the attrition of doubt and disagreement. But let any one error become sanctified by government, and thus crystallized as truth, and little short of a revolution can discredit it or cause it to be discarded.

An easy illustration of this principle is the witchcraft terror in the early days of the colonial government of Massachusetts. If there had been no governmental power to give phantasmagoria the semblance of reality by official decree, the common sense of a majority of the citizens would have kept this manifestation of fanaticism from ever having such widespread support and cruel results. But once government had authoritatively said "This is truth," then the hitherto doubting citizen was willing to join others like himself in accepting it as truth. And we have at least a dozen idiocies, equally repugnant to man's common sense and sound experience, being perpetuated by our government in Washington today.

7. As any society becomes reasonably settled, and shakes down into a semi-permanent pattern of economic and political life, and as some degree of leisure on the part of its citizens becomes both possible and visible, the drive always begins to have government become the management of the social enterprise rather than merely its agent for certain clear purposes. Government is then increasingly allowed, invited, and even urged to do planning for and exercise control over, the total economy of the nation.

Next, it is pushed, and pushes itself, more and more into planning and control of the separate activities of the citizens and groups of citizens that make up the economic life of the nation. And in doing such planning and exercising such controls the government must assume more and more of the responsibility for the success of the economy and the welfare of its citizens.

Of course no government, short of being omniscient, can ever plan the specialized division of labor and the beneficial interchange of the various products of human effort, or can ever appraise the impact of changing circumstances and changing desires on the infinite ramifications of interrelated human activity, one half as well as the planning, appraisal, and resulting corrections will be accomplished by a completely free market if given the opportunity. For the free market *automatically* weighs, measures, and integrates into its decisions increments of needs, of difficulty, and of motivation, that are too small, too numerous, and too hidden for the planners ever to discover them. And the equations to be dealt with are too infinite to be resolved by any human brain or committee of human brains, even if all the variables and constants could be accurately set forth in such equations.

A government trying to step in and improve the workings of a free market is exactly like a man who takes a lighted lantern outdoors at noon of a bright June day to show you the sun. But a government's answer to any criticism as to the inadequacy of the lantern is always to bring more lanterns and then more lanterns—until eventually the smoke and glare of the lanterns so seriously interfere with and shut off the light of the sun that everybody actually has to work mainly by lanternlight.

It is interesting to note, too, that in any society the government, and its allies who want to use the lanterns, always claim the justification that the society's economy is more complex than those which have preceded it. They insist that therefore the lanterns of planning and control are necessary and helpful now, no matter how futile and harmful they have been shown to be in the past. Of course exactly the opposite is true. The more complex the economic life of a nation becomes; the more nearly infinite the shades and grades of impulse which determine the proper interchanges and relationships between its components become; then the more impossible and ridiculous is any undertaking to plan and control those relationships, and the more the automatic working of a completely free market is needed.

8. As a government increases in power, and as a means of increasing its power, it always has a tendency to squeeze out the middle class; to destroy or weaken the middle for the benefit of the top and the bottom. Even where there is no conscious alliance for this purpose, such as formed the basis for Bismarck's beginning of the socialization of Germany or Franklin Roosevelt's beginning of the socialization of America, the forces

to that end are always at work—as they have been in England for fifty years. In the nations that the gods would destroy they first make the middle class helpless, through insidious but irresistible government pressures.

9. The form of government is not nearly so important as its quality. Justice and a lack of arbitrariness, for instance, are two characteristics of a government that are most important to the welfare and happiness of a people. They are as likely to be found—or more accurately, as little likely to be found—under any one form of government as another. Rampant interference with personal lives is the most obnoxious characteristic of any government, and that is found just as readily under elected officials as under hereditary monarchs. In fact, as the Greeks pointed out, as has been well known to careful students of history ever since, and as the founding fathers of our own republic were well aware, when an elected government succeeds in attracting and maintaining an overwhelming majority behind it for any length of time, its mob instincts make it the most tyrannical of all forms of social organization.

Incidentally, a tragic result of the emphasis placed by historians and statesmen on the *form* of the American government has been the emulation by newly independent Asiatic nations of the wrong thing in our American system. Admiring the tremendous success of the United States, observing the unprecedented prosperity, freedom, and opportunities for happiness on the part of the people, looking up to the United States as the example to be followed, nation after nation in other parts of the world, but especially in Asia, has copied the American government for itself. Its budding political scientists have felt that this must be the key to national success and greatness—as it clearly would have been if they had copied the right thing, the very thing that made America great.

But what these new nations have taken for themselves are carbon copies of the American government *at the time* their own governments were being established. In far too many cases this has been since the New Deal had completely stultified the original virtues of the American Government. The Philippines, for instance, in 1948, took over every form of welfarism and every stifling regulation and suppression of private enterprise, and substitute therefor, which Roosevelt's newdealers had been able to impose on us even with a war to help them. The results were and still are pathetic, simply because they had been led to believe that it was the *form* of the American government which counted. But actually it had been *the small amount of government* in America throughout its centuries of mushrooming productivity, not the form of that government, which had been the vital factor of success. The Filipinos and others like them took over, instead, the excesses of government which were already in a fair way to start the decline of America itself.

10. Which brings us to the last, the most over-looked, and in my opinion the most important, of these basic generalizations concerning gov-

ernment. Thomas Jefferson expressed part of it in his famous dictum that the government is best which governs least. But Jefferson was thinking of the extent of a government's power more than of the extensiveness of the government itself. And our tenth point is that neither the form of government nor its quality is as important as its quantity. A thoroughly foul government, like that of Nero, which still did not reach its tentacles too far into the daily lives and doings of its subjects, was far better for the Roman Empire in the long run than the intentionally benevolent government of Diocletian or of Constantine, whose bureaucratic agents were everywhere.

Let's dramatize this fact—or opinion—by bringing it closer home. And your speaker would like to have it understood that he does not condone dishonesty in the slightest degree. Yet I had rather have for America, and I am convinced America would be better off with, a government of three hundred thousand officials and agents, every single one of them a thief, than a government of three million agents with every single one of them an honest, honorable, public servant. For the first group would only steal from the American economic and political system; the second group would be bound in time to destroy it. *The increasing quantity of government, in all nations, has constituted the greatest tragedy of the Twentieth Century.*

Let's spotlight just one particular result of this tragic development, which has occurred in connection with man's age-old worry—war. That result is the frequency, the length, the extensiveness, the horrible destructiveness, and the totality of impact on the population, of the wars of the Twentieth Century.

In the physical sciences we are accustomed to using combined measurements, such as foot-pounds, kilowatt-hours or man-days. Let's invent such a phrase for the measurement of war, and call it the day-number-horror unit. In the use of that three-way calculation we multiply the days of suffering by the number of people who suffer, by the depth of the suffering, to arrive at an appraisal. Then I believe you will find that pretty generally throughout history—despite other factors causing occasional exceptions—and very definitely throughout recent centuries, the day-number-horror measure of any war has been proportional to the *product* of the *quantities* of government in the nations involved at the time a war was fought.

Also, you will find that it is the huge quantity of government which, more than anything else, makes these tremendously destructive wars not only possible, but unavoidable. One illustration should make this statement too clear for argument. Do *you* want to fight the Russian people? Do you think the Russian *people* have the least desire to fight us? Do you think there would be the slightest chance of the American people and the Russian people fighting each other, with millions to be killed on both sides and great parts of both countries probably to be utterly destroyed, if there were only one-tenth as much government in each country as now exists? Stop and think about it for a minute.

It is not only that governments carry their peoples into horrible and utterly unnecessary wars, but it takes a very huge quantity of government to carry its people into the totalitarian struggle which war has now been made by this same quantity of government. Reduce all the governments of all the nations of the world to one-third of their present size—not one-third of their power, note, nor are we referring to their quality, but just to one-third of their bureaucratic numbers, their extensiveness, their meddling in the lives of their subjects—and you would immediately accomplish two things. You would reduce the likelihood of war between hostile nations to at most one-ninth of its present probability, and the destructiveness of any wars that did take place in the same proportion.

The greatest enemy of man is, and always has been, government. And the larger, the more extensive that government, the greater the enemy.

Now clearly the United States which, throughout its early centuries, was the greatest beneficiary from the scarcity of government that the world has ever known, should not only return to the right course for its own further growth in prosperity, freedom, and happiness, but should set an example again for the world. In fact, the word *americanist*, with a small *a*, should be made, and become understood, as the very antithesis of socialism, and communism, with a little *c*. For the *communist*—using the word now with a little *c* to denote a theoretician rather than a member of the conspiracy—the communist believes that a collectivist society should swallow up all individuals, make their lives and their energies completely subservient to the needs and the purposes of the collectivist state; and that any means are permissible to achieve this end. The true *americanist* believes that the individual should retain the freedom to make his own bargain with life, and the responsibility for the results of that bargain; and that means are as important as ends in the civilized social order which he desires. The same two words, with initial capitals, Communists and Americanists, should merely denote the aggressive fighters for these two mutually exclusive philosophies.

But Americanism, as either a phrase or a force on the contemporary world scene, has been eroded into something negative and defeatist. It has come to represent merely a delaying action against the victorious march of its enemy, collectivism. The air is full of clarion calls to Americans to organize, in order better to fight against socialism, communism, or some vanguard of their forces.

Twice each day the mail brings to my desk pleas for me to contribute money, or effort, or moral support, or all three, to some group which is battling to hold back some particular advance of collectivist storm troops. Even those organizations or activities which bear a positive label are motivated by negative thinking. An association *for* the Bricker Amendment is, in reality, an association *against* the intervention of international socalist forces in the control of our domestic lives.

Americanism has become primarily a denial of something else, rather than an assertion of itself. And there are many of us who think that this should be true no longer. We think that Americanism should again come to mean, and to be, a positive forward-looking philosophy; a design and example of social organization which boldly and confidently offers leadership along the one hard but sure road to a better world.

It is not just in the United States, of course, that all the aggressiveness is on the side of the socialist-communist allies. In the world-wide ideological struggle which divides mankind today, we conservatives fight always on the defensive. The very name by which we identify ourselves defines our objective. It is to conserve as much as we can, out of all we have inherited that is worth while, from the encroachments and destructiveness of this advancing collectivism. We build no more icons to freedom; we merely try to fend off the iconoclast.

Such has been the pattern during the whole first half of the twentieth century. From the bright plateaux of individual freedom and individual responsibility, which man had precariously attained, there has been a steady falling back towards the dark valleys of dependence and serfdom. But this ignominious retreat has been just as true of Americans, the heirs of a strong new society, as of the tired residual legatees of an old and enfeebled European civilization. During this long and forced retreat we have fought only a rearguard and sometimes delaying action. We have never been rallied to counterattack, to break through the enemy or rout him, and to climb again beyond our highest previous gains. And in the unending skirmishes, to hold as much as possible of the ground currently occupied, we have lost all sight of the higher tablelands of freedom which once were our recognized goals. I for one, and many others like me, are no longer willing to consider only when to retreat and how far. There is a braver and a wiser course.

If we heirs of all the ages are to find a turning point in this rapid and sometimes stampeding descent, in which we are abandoning instead of improving our inheritance; if the last half of the twentieth century is to see the curve that measures individual dignity turn upward; if the men who really wish to be free and self-reliant are to begin climbing back up the mountainside; then the goal must be known, and the purpose of aggressive offense must replace defensive defeatism as the banner under which we march. It is fatal to be merely against losing ground, for then there is no way to go but back. We have to be for something; we must know what that something is; and we must believe it is worth a fight to obtain. Reduced to its simplest and broadest terms, that something is less government and more responsibility. For both less government and more responsibility bring increasing opportunities for human happiness.

Due to the tremendous momentum given us by our hardworking, ambitious, and individualistic forefathers, our nation is still by far the most dynamic in the world in its productive processes, and in its influences on the whole world's standard of living. We must again become equally dynamic in our *spiritual* influence; in our positive leadership and example to provide a governmental environment in which individual man can make the most of his life in whatever way *he*—and not his government—wishes to use it.

There are many stages of welfarism, socialism, and collectivism in general, but communism is the ultimate state of them all, and they all lead inevitably in that direction. In this final stage, communism, you have a society in which class distinctions are greater than in any other, but where position in these classes is determined solely by demagogic political skill and ruthless cunning. You have a society in which all those traits which have helped to make man civilized, and which our multiple faiths have classified as virtues, are now discarded as vices—while exactly their opposites are glorified. And you have a society in which every *fault* of government that we have discussed above is held to be a *benefit* and a desirable part of the framework of life.

But there is an exactly opposite direction. It leads towards a society in which brotherhood and kindliness and tolerance and honesty and self-reliance and the integrity of the human personality are considered virtues; a society which venerates those traits exactly because they have helped the human animal to achieve some degree of humanitarian civilization, and are the common denominators of all our great religions. This direction leads toward a governmental environment for human life founded on the basis of long experience with government; on experience which shows government to be a necessary evil, but a continuous brake on all progress and the ultimate enemy of all freedom. It is the forward direction, the upward direction—and americanism, I hope, shall become its name.

There, gentlemen, is our argument, or that part of it which applies, as I think it should be used in the political field primarily for political purposes. To make it heard by, and really understood by, enough millions of Americans, is a colossal under-taking. But who says it cannot be done? For who has really tried? We have all been fiddling around with half way measures, with compromise measures, with delaying actions, instead of getting down to fundamental principles, standing on them with firmness, and remembering that future history is always determined by minorities who really know what they want. The whole newdeal march toward state socialism has been carried through and advanced to its present stage *by a determined minority*. We can bring about the necessary reversal of this trend if we, as a minority for what is right, stand as firm, work as hard, and give to the principles in which we believe the same dedication, as has the sophomoric minority of so-called liberals which brought us to our present crisis.

The question is not really whether we *can expunge* this disease of collectivism, and make America strong and healthy and a true example for all the world again, but whether we think it is worth the Herculean effort, the sacrifice and dedication, that would be required. I think it would, and I am hoping you think so too.

Regressive and revolutionary movements are similar to the extent that both desire total social change.[50] Both are nonlegitimate because they desire to redistribute power, removing it generally from most of those now holding it. In this connection, William Domhoff has observed: "Of course they [the New Right] don't share your [the New Left] program, but they do share your view of the power structure and your desire for more individuality and local autonomy." [51] Regarding the redistribution of power, regressive movements do have one advantage over revolutionary ones vis-à-vis the conscience collective. That is, regressive movements acknowledge a "legitimacy of tradition," whereby segments of the existing elite (e.g., the military) may retain power after corrupt or duped leaders have been deposed. On the other hand, a revolutionary movement desiring to give power to the "oppressed" will find little support from those now possessing it.

In the final analysis, the differences between revolutionary and regressive movements will not be found in the nature of the social problems they address, their membership, or their tactics. The main differences are those of ideological posture: an emphasis on "moral" versus "structural" analyses of the sources of dysfunction; the proposing of singular versus collective modes of action; a "tradition-oriented" versus a "futuristic" conception of utopia. These differences in ideology are illuminated in the following section from Winston White, where he discusses the divergent perceptions of the sources of strain by moralizers (regressive) and reformers (revolutionary).

[50] See Victor C. Ferkiss, "Populist Influences on American Fascism," *Western Political Quarterly*, 10 (June 1957): 350–373; Daniel Bell, "The Background of Marxian Socialism in the United States," in Donald Egbert and Stow Persons, eds., *Socialism in American Life*, vol. I (Princeton, N.J.: Princeton University Press, 1952), pp. 300–305; and Seymour Martin Lipset, *Political Man* (Garden City, N.Y.: Doubleday and Co., Inc., 1960), pp. 169–179.
[51] G. William Domhoff, "How To Commit Revolution in Corporate America," reprinted from the *Peninsula Observer* (Palo Alto, Calif.), Spring 1968. (Revised text of a speech given at the University of California at Santa Cruz on April 28, 1968.)

Excerpts from Winston White, Beyond Conformity (Glencoe: Free Press, 1961), pp. 20–23. Reprinted with permission of The Macmillan Company from Beyond Conformity by Winston White. © by The Free Press of Glencoe, Inc., 1961.

TWO APPROACHES TO CAUSE AND CURE

. . . We noted that ideology is one type of reaction to strain in the society. Strain was defined as the discrepancy between *what ought to be* and *what is*, between values and their implementation in society. Values are conceptions of the desirable. They formulate some notion of what ought to be. Social conditions present problems as to how the values can be implemented, problems for which the values by themselves supply specific solutions. Simply put, a value may tell you what ought to be done, but it doesn't tell you how to do it. Conditions in the society raise problems that go beyond simply attaining the desirable. The essential question is, "To what extent does a given social structure facilitate (or impede) the implementation of values?" The focus, then, of ideological issues lies in the relation between *values* and the *conditions of social structure*.

This relation provides an exceedingly useful dimension on which to classify ideologies. Ideologies, we have seen, are selective. In one way, they are selective by emphasizing only one side of the value-social structure relation (Geertz, 1957).

A value-oriented ideology asserts that strain is primarily the result of a weakening of the values of which the society is based. It recommends that these basic values be reasserted and appeals to "higher levels," such as "the American way of life," "the glory of France," "the Western heritage." It seeks to strengthen these values at the various structural levels so that they may be more effective guides in controlling social conditions, such as institutional arrangements. It emphasizes what are sometimes called "ideal factors"—values, morals, beliefs, and the like. Such an ideology tends to be *moralistic*, naïve about structural conditions (although this naïvete may have the unintended consequence of accepting them as they are), and vague about specific programs.

A social structure-oriented ideology sees strain as primarily the result of unsatisfactory social conditions. It recommends that these be *reformed (re-formed)*, and it appeals to the "hard realities" of the situation. It seeks to improve these conditions so that they may more effectively realize the values, which are *not* seen as problematical. It emphasizes what are called "real factors"—things like political and economic institutions, power and property. This type of ideology tends to be sophisticated about conditions (although this may backfire if it means pressing for too drastic, hence unacceptable change) and specific about programs.

This distinction between value-oriented and structure-oriented ideologies is useful in analyzing the intellectual case—where the consensus on symptoms and on evaluation of them is accompanied by differences in diagnoses on the causes of the symptoms and in recommendations of what is to be done. If we look at the issue as one of deficient individual freedom and development and excessive social pressure, we can discern two main streams: each one offers a different explanation of "whose fault it is."

One stream of thought is value-oriented and places the blame on individuals. It sees the present undesirable state of affairs as primarily due to their defection; individuals have become slack about living up to basic values, if not guilty of deserting them altogether. We need a reassertion of value-commitments by individuals. People are urged, for example, to reaffirm the (American) value of individualism and "not to conform," although what lines non-conformity should take are usually left unspecified; for, naturally, specification might hamper individual styles of non-conformity. It is left to the individual whether he should throw out his television set, grow a beard, or tell the boss off. Analysis in this case tends to follow a "humanistic" tone. For purposes of easier reference, I shall call those who share the value-oriented ideology *moralizers*.

The moralizers may or may not diagnose the structural conditions that have contributed to society's strain; but whatever the conditions are alleged to be, they are regarded as given—that is, not many structures can or should be changed. The emphasis here is on strengthening the underlying values that guide individual action within existing structures.

We may anticipate some conceptual difficulties at this point. Since various ideological statements use different terms, it is likely to be confusing when we try to compare and order them. The following discussion, however, may be more consistent than is apparent if it is kept in mind that values are conceptions of the desirable—the "oughts"—that in part determine the choices people make. Thus, terms like individualism, Protestant ethic, inner-direction, and the like express, among other things, criteria of what one ought to do.

The other stream of thought is social structure-oriented and places the blame for strain on social conditions. According to this version, the very structure of society itself prevents its members from developing their potentialities and from realizing the good life. Economic and political institutions, bureaucracy, and mass culture are such that no one could be expected to transcend their deadening clutch. What is needed is *structural reform*—the elimination of advertising or of middlebrow entertainment, of bureaucracy or of capitalism in general. This is necessary to release the potentialities of individuals, whose value commitments would have expressed themselves spontaneously had they not been corrupted by structural conditions. Analysis along these lines tends to follow a "sociological" tone. Those who share this point of view I shall refer to as *reformers.*

Reinhold Niebuhr, although talking in a slightly different context, has hit on the two types of emphasis discussed here:

The liberal world has always oscillated between the [structure-oriented] hope of creating perfect men by eliminating the social sources of evil and the [value-oriented] hope of so purifying human "reason" by educational technique [in this case, ideological exhortation] that all social institutions would gradually become the bearers of a universal human will, informed by a universal human mind.[52]

REFORM MOVEMENTS

Reform movements are directed at the alteration of a segment of the power distribution of a social system in order to achieve a specific goal. The most common goals of reform movements are to make an existing structure work more effectively, or to extend certain rights or privileges to given groups. Examples include the Populist, Suffragette, Anti-Saloon League, "Single Tax," and "Voting Rights" movements. Ideologically, reformists frequently borrow from either the left or the right, whichever persuasion suits their goals. For example, the labor movement borrowed heavily from the ideology of the Communists. Having accomplished its goals of industrial reform, the movement purged itself of all vestiges of Communism.[53]

Although reform movements follow patterns of development similar to regressive and revolutionary ones, they differ in that they are primarily "interest movements" designed specifically to aid their members. Their intent is only a modification of the power distribution. The labor movement, for example, did not wish to wrest factory control from corporations; it only desired that workers receive a larger share of the profits. Similarly, the Populists wished greater power for the farmer and the small rural merchant rather than the dissolution of capitalism. Only when it appeared to benefit labor or Populism did "radical" solutions such as the nationalization of railroads come to the fore.

Reform movements can be viewed as providing segmental solutions to the same strains which generate so-called extremist movements (left or right). They are directed at specific issues, and their membership will accept a good portion of the conscience collective and attempt to comple-

[52] Reinhold Niebuhr, *The Irony of American History* (New York: Charles Scribner's Sons, 1952), p. 68. [Editors' note.]
[53] See David Shannon, *The Decline of American Communism* (New York: Harcourt, Brace and Co., 1959), pp. 152–182.

ment or improve upon it. For example, the Townsend Movement of the 1930s appealed primarily to the elderly, who saw this plan as a remedy both to their own problems and to the entire Depression situation. Similarly, adherents of the Anti-Saloon League saw prohibition as a solution to their moral indignation over drink and as a solution to a myriad of other social ills, such as poverty and family strife, which existed during the so-called Progressive era.

In the following selection Grimes discusses the nature of reform movements and their relationship to the *conscience collective* in terms of the woman suffrage movement. His explicit thesis is that support for woman suffrage stemmed not so much from an ideal of equalitarianism but rather from a revival of the Puritan ethic.

Excerpts from Alan P. Grimes, The Puritan Ethic and Woman Suffrage *(New York: Oxford University Press, 1967) pp. 99–106, 118. Reprinted by permission of Alan P. Grimes and Oxford University Press.*

OUR COUNTRY

Liberty for *all* the people is coming out of the West.—Mabel Croft Deering.

For fourteen years following the triumphs of 1896 the woman suffrage movement in the states met only a dreary succession of defeats. Then, between 1910 and 1914, the golden age of statewide woman suffrage took place in the West, and only in the West. In 1910 Washington, in 1911 California, in 1912 Oregon, Arizona, and Kansas, in 1914 Nevada and Montana established woman suffrage. Thus, by 1914 Kansas, all the West Coast states and all the Rocky Mountain states except New Mexico had woman suffrage. How may we account for this regional pattern? Was it indeed a fact that by 1914 this vast western expanse manifested a high degree of equalitarianism?

If the lesson of Wyoming and Utah correctly portended the subsequent course of the woman suffrage movement, then we might have expected its growth to come in those areas in which there was significant political support for what we may call here the correlative values of woman suffrage, values which it was understood could be more securely achieved or preserved by bringing the support of women voters to the cause. Woman suffrage could be considered by those indifferent to its accomplishment as a goal in itself, as nevertheless an effective political instrument for achieving other, but related goals. It was the latter aspect of woman suffrage that gave it its especial significance in the West, where the social ethic of woman suffrage conveniently corresponded to the broader social ethic of progressivism itself. Woman suffrage was, like the direct primary, the direct election of the Senate, the initiative, the referendum, and the recall, not only a reform in itself but an instrument for further reform within the prevailing political conception of social goals.

We may consider, for example, the parallel instance of the adoption of the initiative, the referendum, and the recall (along with woman suffrage) in California in 1911. These measures of popular democracy drew support from many quarters, as in their enactment various groups saw the means of furthering their own particular goals. According to V. O. Key, Jr. and Winston W. Crouch in *The Initiative and Referendum in California*, the movement for direct legislation had the support of such diverse groups as labor and farmer organizations, some business and commercial groups, the prohibition forces, the Socialist party, and local reform leagues.[54] As part of the prohibitionists' strategy in support of direct democracy, one county superintendent of the Anti-Saloon League counseled: "Perhaps Anti-Saloon Leagues, as such, should not come out in the open but they should be in the ranks, urging all kindred organizations to take an official stand for the measure." [55] The major thrust of this movement for direct democracy in California was directed at the power of a corrupt political machine which was, in turn, the servant of the Southern Pacific Railroad. Yet it is revealing to see the interlocking relationships involved in the impetus toward reform. In May 1907, a committee of reform-minded editors and lawyers met in Los Angeles and drafted a three-point action program. "The policies decided upon at the first meeting were: (1) to break the political control of the Southern Pacific; (2) to secure gradually the adoption of certain legislation which was considered to be fundamental, namely (a) the direct primary and (b) the initiative, the referendum, and the recall; and (3) to secure woman suffrage." [56] In 1910 the Progressive forces put through the direct primary in California and elected Hiram Johnson governor. In a special election the following year, some 23 constitutional amendments were voted upon, with all but one passing. The direct-legislation amendment passed overwhelmingly, with 168,744 for, 52,093 against.[57] Woman suffrage, however, just squeaked by, with 125,037 for, 121,450 against.[58]

This association of the initiative, the referendum, and the recall with woman suffrage may be seen further when we note that of the eleven

---

[54] V. O. Key, Jr., and Winston W. Crouch, *The Initiative and Referendum in California* (Berkeley: University of California Press, 1939), p. 426.
[55] *Ibid.*, p. 427.
[56] *Ibid.*, p. 432.
[57] *Ibid.*, p. 440.
[58] Ida Husted Harper (ed.), *The History of Woman Suffrage* (National American Woman Suffrage Association, 1922), Vol. VI, p. 50.

states which had woman suffrage by the end of 1914, nine also had the initiative and referendum; while of the eleven states which had adopted the recall by this date, eight were also woman suffrage states.[59] The adoption of woman suffrage, however, generally ran behind that of direct legislation. For example, as early as 1902, Oregon adopted the initiative and referendum, yet woman suffrage was defeated there in 1900, 1906, and again in 1908, the year when the recall was adopted.

Clearly, the success of woman suffrage in the western states was due to its association in that region with the Progressive movement, which was bringing a new vitality to political reform forces during the years 1910–14. This made the woman suffrage movement a contributory part to a larger reform movement that was taking place in American politics. And it was this aspect of its relationship to the Progressive movement that made its associated goals significant. During the Progressive period the woman suffrage movement shared three social goals with the Progressives which made its own particular end, the enfranchisement of women, politically acceptable in the West. Goals is perhaps too limited a term to express the values, the status striving that permeate so much of the writing of woman suffrage advocates. Yet, recognizing the actual existence of some measure of imprecision, it nevertheless appears that the advocates of woman suffrage believed together with others in the Progressive movements in: the superiority of native-born, white Americans; the superiority of Protestant, indeed Puritan, morality; and the superiority of a kind of populism, of some degree of direct control over the state and city machines which, it was alleged, were dominated by the "interests." In this last point, there was, of course, a similarity to the Protestant Reformation itself with its intended search for a more direct relation between man and the Authority. Politically, this conjunction contributed to the overlap of the issues of woman suffrage with the direct primary, the initiative, the referendum, the recall, and the direct election of U.S. senators.

While woman suffrage resulted in a greater measure of equality in some sociopolitical relationships, it should not be overlooked that this benign result was often the by-product of a struggle for control by opposing forces committed to rather inequalitarian social goals. What may generally be defined as woman suffrage supporters consisted mostly of white, middle-class Protestants who were in the main native-born and who sought a purification, according to their lights, of the social and political

---

[59] For the initiative and referendum: South Dakota (1898), Utah (1900), Oregon (1902), Nevada (referendum 1904, initiative 1912), Montana (1906), Oklahoma (1907), Maine (1908), Missouri (1908), Michigan (1908), Arkansas (1910), Colorado (1910), California (1911), New Mexico (1911), Arizona (1911), Idaho (1912), Nebraska (1912), Ohio (1912), Washington (1912). For the recall: Oregon (1908), California (1911), Arizona (1912), Idaho (1912), Washington (1912), Colorado (1912), Nevada (1912), Michigan (1913), Louisiana (1914), North Dakota (1914), Kansas (1914). Harold V. Faulkner, *The Quest for Social Justice, 1898–1914* (New York: The Macmillan Company, 1931), pp. 85–86.

order. Ultimately, this purification would include the economic order as well, dealing with such issues as child labor, the working conditions of women in industry, and the range of economic opportunity for women. But initially, at least, these were subordinate issues, and the acknowledgments of support from trade unions, for example, in the official suffrage literature were so brief as to be nearly ungrateful when compared with the acknowledgments of support from the ministry, the womens' clubs, and the W.C.T.U. In this non-economic aspect the struggle for woman suffrage and its correlative values conforms to the pattern for the period which Richard Hofstadter has succinctly labeled "status politics." Many of those who led the Progressive movement toward reform "were Progressives not because of economic deprivations but primarily because they were victims of an upheaval in status that took place in the United States during the closing decades of the nineteenth and the early years of the twentieth century. Progressivism, in short, was to a very considerable extent led by men who suffered from the events of their time not through a shrinkage in their means but through the changed pattern in the distribution of deference and power." [60]

Among the most active supporters of woman suffrage were ministers of the various Protestant denominations, in particular the Methodists. Yet the clergy were, to turn again to Hofstadter, "probably the most conspicuous losers from the status revolution. . . . The increasingly vigorous interest in the social gospel, so clearly manifested by the clergy after 1890, was in many respects an attempt to restore through secular leadership some of the spiritual influence and authority and social prestige that clergymen had lost through the upheaval in the system of status and the secularization of society." [61] The truly remarkable economic and demographic changes that were transforming America, so largely due to the spread of communications and the increasing ease of transportation, were uprooting the old social system with its traditional lines of deference. As the early Protestant reformers sought to purify their religion by returning to primitive Christianity, so now did many of their descendants seek to purify America by curbing the new system of values if not reinstating the old. Woman suffrage could be seen as a device to achieve this end. The conspicuous evils of the present, now documented by the reporting of the muckrakers, could be contrasted with the purity of the past, and the purity possible in the future if men would choose wisely. George Mowry has observed: "This firm belief of the progressive in man's choice of ways helps to explain the evangelical character of the movement, the constant stress on 'the good man,' the 'moral position,' 'the right action.' Perhaps no other American political movement had such a righteous tone about it.

[60] Richard Hofstadter, *The Age of Reform* (New York: Random House, Inc., 1960), p. 135.
[61] *Ibid.*, pp. 150, 152.

It was, as Elmer Davis has said, a political 'carnival of purity.' "[62] The movement for woman suffrage was, to be sure, part of a movement for equal rights for women; but it would be a mistake to interpret the latter as simply making available to women the opportunities open to men. For, as Mowry noted,

> After seeing the manmade world at first-hand with its slums, dives, crooked politics, and almost ubiquitous double standards, many women naturally accepted the belief that their sex alone was the guardian of "the sacred vessels that held the ancient sanctities of life." . . . What they wanted was equality, but an equality based upon a standard of feminine virtue instead of masculine sin.[63]

There were many reasons for Americans to feel a sense of disenchantment, of resentment, of indignation about the established order in the opening decade of the twentieth century, for all that it was, in general, a time of economic prosperity. Various studies of the distribution of wealth at the time point to the conclusion that "fully eighty per cent of the people lived on the margin of existence while the wealth of the nation was owned by the remaining twenty per cent."[64] Yet even without any measurable degree of economic deprivation, there was a certain sense of disturbance that permeated much of the socially conscious literature of this era. Native-born Americans of every political outlook had a sharp sense of awareness that the older, traditional America was passing away, and that the newer America was not fulfilling the expectations of its founding fathers.

In part, this sense of resentment was a reaction to the conspicuous changes in America which had taken place after the Civil War. Industrialization, together with the extensive railroad system, had produced the sprawling metropolises which daily attracted young people from neighboring farms and from foreign lands. Urbanization made possible a new style of politics, as it made possible a new mode of life at every economic level, from the sordid slums of the tenement ghettos to the magnificent homes of the ostentatious rich. Both the splendor and the squalor were offensive to the middle class, which previously had not known either. An appeal for woman suffrage could be seen, in part, as an appeal for the standards of decency and righteousness that had prevailed at home; an appeal to the platitudes, the commonplaces, the little moral aphorisms which had been voiced in the kitchen or at the family table. In a sense, these provided the standard of justice for this secular reformation; these convictions of righteousness were, in a very basic sense, what the Progressive movement was all about.

[62] George E. Mowry, *The Era of Theodore Roosevelt* (New York: Harper & Row, Publishers, 1962), p. 51.
[63] *Ibid.*, pp. 35–36.
[64] Faulkner, *op. cit.*, p. 21.

In this sense of righteous indignation the woman suffragettes of the Progressive movement were reliving the response of their Populist predecessors who had first felt the radical change in style of life that had taken place in America. Theirs was not, it should be noted, the response of a dwindling and isolated minority crying out against oppression at the hands of a hostile and tyrannical majority. It was, rather, the response of a majority who, certain of their numerical strength and righteousness of cause, believed they were losing power to a highly organized minority because of the ignorance and apathy and falling from grace of their fellow man. Only with this conviction could they seek to restore majority rule as the guiding instrument in politics. Progressive rallies seemed to some observers akin to revival meetings, for they were filled with evangelical zeal. The common enemy, to both secular and devout, was the corrupt political machine, supported by big business, pandering to vice, and enlisting in its ranks the voting cadres of ignorant foreigners. Sodom and Gomorrah were seen again in San Francisco, Portland, and Seattle; and the visible hosts of the opposition were the newly arrived immigrants. "Anglo-Saxons, whether Populist or patrician," Hofstadter has noted, "found it difficult to accept other peoples on terms of equality or trust." . . .[65]

In sum, it may be said that the woman suffrage movement triumphed in the West during the Progressive era because it was aided by, even as it contributed to, the Progressive triumphs there. Had woman suffrage stood alone as an issue in itself doubtless it would have been defeated again as it had been in many of these states in the past. But as part of a broader movement which was seeking to arrogate political power to native-born white Americans, it was able to capitalize on the course of this general movement. Political equality for women in the western states can be seen, therefore, as a by-product of the western Puritan revival.

Before concluding this chapter, we should comment on a category of "quasi-movements" which is peripherally related to our criterion of social movements (viz., seeking to alter power relations). That is, although these movements may be responses to the existing distribution of power, they do not seek to alter it. These we shall term "expressive movements."

EXPRESSIVE MOVEMENTS

Expressive movements may be conceptualized as symbolic statements of dissent which are engendered by the existing structure of power but which are not in fact addressed to bringing about changes in power rela-

---

[65] Hofstadter, *op. cit.*, p. 83.

tionships. Inherent in the notion of such movements is the proposition that expressive actions are responses to a subjective sense of powerlessness or alienation.[66] For example, Lipton, in analyzing the "holy barbarians," noted that beatniks were disaffiliated from the political process since they felt there was little they could do to change the polity.[67] Levin makes similar conclusions about the nonvoter.[68]

The concept of expressive movements was first introduced into the literature by Herbert Blumer to identify movements which did not: ". . . seek to change the institutions of the social order or its objective character . . . however, in becoming crystallized [they] may have profound effects on the personalities of individuals and on the character of the social order." [69] Blumer goes on to identify religious and fashion movements as prime examples of this phenomenon. Horton and Hunt suggest that: "In the expressive movement the individual comes to terms with an unpleasant external reality by modifying his reactions to that reality, not by modifying the external reality itself." [70] They too see expressive movements as exemplified in millenarian religious movements, cults, and fashion trends.

The millenarian "cargo cult" provides a good example of the expressive movement. In the following reading, Peter Worsley discusses the relationship of the cargo cult to the existing social order, and the integrative effect the cult has on its members.

Excerpts from Peter Worsley, The Trumpet Shall Sound: A Study of "Cargo" Cults in Melanesia *(New York: Schocken Books, 1968), pp. 225–231. Reprinted by permission of Peter Worsley, Schocken Books, and Granada Publishing, Ltd.*

A RELIGION OF THE LOWER ORDERS

Certain obvious conclusions emerge from this brief comparative survey. Firstly, the activist millenarian movements—those which anticipate the coming of the millennium in the near future and which set about prepar-

[66] Cf. Melvin Seeman, "On the Meaning of Alienation," *American Sociological Review*, 24 (December 1959): 783–791. Seeman views this concept as being too frequently employed in explanations of the rise of social movements. For example, see Morton Grodzins, *The Loyal and the Disloyal: Social Boundaries of Patriotism and Treason* (Chicago: University of Chicago Press, 1956), pp. 133–143.
[67] Lawrence Lipton, *The Holy Barbarians* (New York: Julian Messner, Inc., 1949).
[68] Murray B. Levin, *The Alienated Voter: Politics in Boston* (New York: Holt, Rinehart and Winston, Inc., 1960), pp. 66–68.
[69] Blumer, *op. cit.*, p. 214.
[70] Horton and Hunt, *op. cit.*, p. 522. Italics in the original.

ing for this event—have found support at all levels of society at one time and another. But it is amongst people who feel themselves to be oppressed and who are longing for deliverance that they have been particularly welcomed: especially by the populations of colonial countries, by discontented peasants and by the jetsam of the towns and cities of feudal civilizations.

Expecting and hoping for, the millennium, people have destroyed their cattle, their crops, their means of livelihood. Southern Bantu died in their thousands in the nineteenth century through killing off their cattle and destroying their crops in response to a prophet's appeal; in this century, Eskimos in Greenland became so convinced of the imminence of the millennium that they stopped hunting and ate into their stores of food.

And in order to hasten their entry into the Promised Land, people have actually killed one another or committed suicide. In Crete, in the fifth century A.D., a band of Jews drowned themselves in the millenarian enthusiasm; in Baffin Land, in this century, Eskimos sacrificed two men to hasten the day; and a group of four hundred Guiana Indians massacred one another in order to be reborn in white skins.

Millenarian beliefs have recurred again and again throughout history despite failures, disappointments, and repression, precisely because they make such a strong appeal to the oppressed, the disinherited and the wretched. They therefore form an integral part of that stream of thought which refused to accept the rule of a superordinate class, or of a foreign power, or some combination of both, as in Taiping China. This anti-authoritarian attitude is expressed not only in the form of direct political resistance, but also through the rejection of the ideology of the ruling authority. The lower orders reject the dominant values, beliefs, philosophy, religion, etc., of those they are struggling against, as well as their material economic and political domination. It is therefore natural that millenarian doctrines often become openly revolutionary and lead to violent conflict between rulers and ruled. Because of this revolutionary potential millenarian movements are usually treated with the utmost suspicion by Church and State and have often been proscribed and persecuted. . . .

THE INTEGRATORY ROLE OF THE CULTS

The cults thus serve as an expression of reaction against what is felt as oppression by another class or nationality. But there are other important political characteristics shared by groups prone to millenarism, whatever their cultural differences.

The cults generally occur among people divided into small, separate, narrow and isolated social units: the village, the clan, the tribe, the people of a valley, etc. They occur, firstly, among people living in the so-called "stateless" societies, societies which have no overall unity, which lack centralized political institutions altogether. They have thus no suitable machinery through which they can act politically as a unified force when the occasion arises, except on a temporary, localized or *ad hoc* basis. They often have no chiefs, no courts of law other than the council of elders or of prominent or wealthy men, no police, no army and no administrative officials. In Melanesia, for example, centralized or even federal organs are often absent. Indeed, villages and clans speaking the same languages or dialects of one language and sharing a common culture get in a state of intermittent hostility with their neighbours, the very people with whom they trade and intermarry.

Such highly segmented societies are incapable of offering resistance to the incoming Europeans. When the need arises for large-scale joint action by members of these separate groups, now faced with the same common problems, they cannot act politically and militarily at all. Thus in Melanesia the discrete units were absorbed or defeated piecemeal by the colonial Powers in the nineteenth century.

The main effect of the millenarian cult is to overcome these divisions and to weld previously hostile and separate groups together into a new unity. The social necessity which produces this drive towards integration is the subjection of all the separate units to a common authority—the Europeans. Since the people have developed new common political interests where previously they had none, so they must create new political forms of organization to give expression to this new-found unity. It is precisely this integratory function which is served by the millenarian cult. It is therefore especially common in colonial countries in the early phases of the establishment of colonial regimes, particularly where the societies involved are without State machinery.

The second major type of society in which millenarian cults develop is the agrarian, and especially feudal, State. Such societies, of course, have indeed an elaborate formal hierarchical organization unlike stateless peoples, but the cults arise among the lower orders—peasants and urban plebeians—in opposition to the official regimes. These groups, like stateless Melanesians, lack any overall political organization. Their position has been well put in a famous passage by Marx:

The small-holding peasants form a vast mass, the members of which live in similar conditions but without entering into manifold relations with each other. Their mode of production isolates them from one another instead of bringing them into mutual intercourse. The isolation is increased by bad means of communication and by the poverty of the peasants. Their field of production, the small-holding, admits of no division of labour in its cultivation, no application of science, and therefore, no wealth of social relationships. Each individual peasant family is almost self-sufficient; it itself directly produces the major part of its consumption and thus acquires its means of life more through exchange with nature than in intercourse with society. A small-holding, a peasant and his family; alongside them another small-holding, another peasant and another family. A few score of these made up a village, and a few score of villages make up a Department. In this way, the great mass of the French nation is formed by simple additions of homologous magnitudes, much as potatoes in a sack form a sack of potatoes. In so far as millions of families live under economic conditions of existence that separate their mode of life, their interests and their culture from those of the other classes, and put them in hostile opposition to the latter, they form a class. In so far as there is merely a local interconnection among these small-holding peasants, and the identity of their interests begets no community, no national bond and no political organization among them, they do not form a class. They are consequently incapable of enforcing their class interest in their own name, whether through a parliament or through a convention. They cannot represent themselves, they must be represented, their representative must at the same time appear as their master, as an authority over them, as an unlimited governmental power that protects them against the other classes and sends them rain and sunshine from above. The political influence of the small-holding peasants, therefore, finds its final expression in the executive power subordinating society itself.[71]

The explanation of the "cult of the individual" in nineteenth-century France sheds a good deal of light on peasant society in other times and climes. Like people in stateless societies, peasants are divided into tight-knit discrete groups. They are associated in a hierarchical framework, but lack their own common political institutions. Due to the material conditions of their lives, they lack any organization which could give practical expression to their common interests, and they do not see their common interests except in times of social crisis.

When confronted with the necessity of taking concerted action, they are obliged to throw up a centralized political structure *a novo* just as much as any primitive society.

In the particular circumstances of nineteenth-century France, the peasants were thus likely, Marx suggested, to produce a Bonapartist cult, but as we have seen, under other social conditions they look for converance not to secular individuals but to supernatural powers. Secular Caesarism flourishes in advanced agrarian societies and under conditions of much greater cultural backwardness; peasants may equally look up to prophets who promise a mystical solution to their problems and fulfilment of their hopes. The millenarian cult is thus typical of early phases of peasant political organization.

There is a third type of social situation in which activist millenarian ideas are likely to flourish. This is when a society with differentiated po-

[71] From "The Eighteenth Brumaire of Louis Bonaparte," *Marx-Engels*, pp. 302–303.

litical institutions is fighting for its existence by quite secular military-political means, but is meeting with defeat after defeat. One may cite the case of the rise of the prophet Nongqause at a time when the Xhosa people were beginning to realize that they were losing the long drawn-out Kaffir Wars.

Again, when the political structure of a society is smashed by war or other means, or fails to answer the needs of a people who wish to carry on the struggle, then a prophetic, often millenarian, leadership is likely to emerge. Significantly, the Hau Hau movement among the Maori arose after the military defeat of the Maori Wars, when many tribes and many tribal leaders had ceased fighting and when others felt that resistance was hopeless. Renewal of the battle called for super-human and special measures in one last desperate attempt, and took the form of a religious appeal to join the divinely-inspired forces of liberation. There is more than a mere resemblance of names between the Hau Hau and the Mau Mau, for both arose when other political organizations had been broken, and both used extraordinary methods to revive the spirit of resistance and to weld the people together.

The millenarian movement thus brings together, for the first time, social units which have not only been separate from each other—though possessing some cultural links—but often even hostile, for the combination of hostility and cooperation between the very same groups is common. Other related types of religious organization have achieved this result, however, without being specifically millenarian. Professor Evans-Pritchard has shown how in Cyrenaica an Islam Order, the Sanusiya, succeeded in unifying the small, discrete Bedouin tribes, which feuded amongst themselves, into a solid resistance movement opposed to the Italians.

But the stimulus which drives a people to unite need not necessarily be something external to the society, such as conquest by foreigners. There are many instances of millenarian cults whose cutting edge has been directed not towards foreigners or conquerors but towards members of other classes within the same society. Internal and not merely external, antagonisms can equally produce millenarism. . . .

Thus, the expressive movement is largely one of dissent. As Herbert Marcuse suggests, given the "intolerance of tolerance" and the use of the "one-dimensional" lie, most current protest is fundamentally an exercise in symbolism rather than meaningful confrontation with the power structure.[72] However, with increasing technological and political sophistication and bureaucratization, expressive protests (such as peace marches against the Vietnam war and the Campaign for Nuclear Disarmament) may be-

[72] See Herbert Marcuse, *One Dimensional Man* (Boston: Beacon Press, 1964).

come more numerous. If such protest becomes ideological, the expressive movement may provide the organizational impetus for revolution.

SUMMARY

From a review of the literature, three distinguishing characteristics of social movements have been suggested: public definition and response, tactics, and type of social change advocated. However, all social movements are, to a greater or lesser degree, nonlegitimate vis-à-vis the conscience collective, and hence the range of tactics available to a movement is limited. Therefore we have selected the criterion of the type of change advocated in the distribution of power in society as the most viable element by which social movements may be distinguished one from the other. Bearing in mind the arbitrary nature of "ideal type" classification, we have discerned three major types of movements according to this criterion: (1) revolutionary, which seek to institute an idealized new set of power relationships; (2) regressive, which seek to reinstate an idealized past state of power distribution; and (3) reform, which seek limited modifications in the existing power arrangement. Revolutionary and regressive movements were respectively analyzed in terms of "left" and "right" political distinctions, and were found to be similar to the extent that both desire total changes in the power distribution of society. Neither can left and right be differentiated on the basis of the nature of the problems they address, their membership, or their tactics. The essential difference between left and right is that the former emphasizes structural sources of societal dysfunction and calls for collective solutions, whereas the latter stresses moral deviation as the source of problems and seeks to reorganize social power along more individualistic lines.

Additional nuances of ideology and the left-right distinction will be discussed in the final chapter. Prior to that, however, we shall consider, in the light of our "emergent reality" conceptualization, the career pattern and, more specifically, the truncation of social movements.

THE TRUNCATION OF SOCIAL MOVEMENTS

7

In chapter 4, we established the nature of social movements as ideological organizations addressing the power relationships of society. As such, social movements were viewed as nonlegitimate vis-à-vis the conscience collective. In chapter 5, the consequences of this nonlegitimacy for the fate of social movements as emergent realities were discussed, and it was pointed out that nonlegitimacy brings about both external and internal pressures on emergent movements. Once a movement has emerged, the activities of its members are of consequence to its career only inasmuch as they contribute to the ultimate demise of the movement. This demise is inevitable, for a movement ends either because its goals are not attained or, paradoxically, because they are. That is, if the goals of a social movement are so nonlegitimate that they cannot be realized, then the forces of social opposition will ultimately bring about either the dissolution of the movement or its transformation into a less societally threatening form. On the other hand, the success of a movement means that its goals then become a part of the status quo—in the dynamic of social evolution, this synthesis then becomes a new thesis, and the viability of the movement as an antithesis has come to an end.

We shall refer to the dissolution of a movement, or its transformation into another form, as a process of "truncation." This process is not specifically delimited by time, as the emaciated remains of many former social movements suggest. Nevertheless, specific historical occurrences may terminate the viability of a movement in the political arena. For example, the passage and later repeal of the Volstead Act rendered the prohibition movement socially insignificant despite its attempts to reappear and to reinstate its "dry" policies. After the point of social significance has been passed, an ideological organization may continue to exist in relation to some historically absolute "consciousness of dysfunction" defined by its membership. In cases where an organization continues to exist in spite of a lack of social significance, we have what can be termed a "post movement sect." Joseph Gusfield, in his analysis of the Woman's Christian Temperance Union (WCTU) several decades after the failure of the "great experiment" of prohibition, provides us with an example of such a development. Gusfield points out that, after the repeal of prohibition, the WCTU no longer represented the middle classes but instead developed a doctrine of moral indignation against upper-middle-class life. He concludes his study as follows:

Today the WCTU is an organization in retreat. Contrary to the expectations of theories of institutionalization, the movement has not acted to preserve organizational values at the expense of past doctrine. In adhering to less popular positions, it has played the role of the sect and widened the gap between WCTU membership and middle-class respectability. . . .

The moral indignation of the WCTU today is a very different approach to temperance and to the American scene from reformism and progressivism of the late nineteenth and early twentieth centuries. The plight of the "moralizer-in-retreat" is the plight of the once powerful but now rejected suitor. The symbols at his command no longer ring true in the halls where once they were heard with great respect. He cannot identify easily with those above him in status, because they now repudiate his morality. It is the sense of the historical shift, fully as much as the absolute clash in values, that has soured his reformism and generated his resentment.[1]

The longevity of a movement and the manner of its truncation are dependent upon the type of movement, its organizational and ideological structure, and the nature of the distribution of power in the society in which it has emerged. The latter variable is of considerable importance, since, as we have stressed in chapters 4 and 5, social movements must be regarded as essentially nonlegitimate ideological organizations which address the power relationships of society. In discussing the distribution of power in societies, the dichotomy frequently used in community power studies—the elitist versus the pluralist model—will be useful.[2] In the context of our discussion, the former refers to an absolute or near absolute exercise of power by an elite element in a social system, be it a company town or an entire nation state. Elitists exercise their control so as to prevent the alteration of the existing dominant-submissive relations of the social order. For example, the employing elite in a coal town may exercise its absolute power to raise the wages of miners or improve their working conditions,

[1] Joseph R. Gusfield, "Social Structure and Moral Reform: A Study of the Woman's Christian Temperance Union," *American Journal of Sociology*, 61 (November 1955): 232.
[2] For a review of the literature on community power studies, see John Walton, "Substance and Artifact: The Current Status of Research on Community Power Structure," *American Journal of Sociology*, 71 (January 1966): 430–438.

but the fundamental power distribution in the community will remain unchanged. In a pluralist society, on the other hand, power is distributed among a multiplicity of interest groups, political parties, and organizations which formulate policies and manipulate decision-making to the extent of their differential power.[3]

In chapter 6, we discussed types of social movements. The opportunity for these different types of movements to remain viable will vary according to the kind of social system in which they exist and function. In an elitist society, for example, revolutionary movements are subject to direct suppression by the government. The repression of the Russian narodniki (populists) by the Czarist police and the outlawing of opposition parties in Spain by the Falange are examples of this control. The existence of revolutionary groups in autocratic societies is not precluded, of course, but as movements they must wait to appear as immanently legitimate armed opposition, such as Castro's July 26 Movement in Cuba, in order to attain any measure of success. Reform movements fare almost as poorly as revolutionary ones in totalitarian states, as witness the purges of reform elements in the Soviet Union in 1936 and 1937, of moderates in numerous Latin American "banana republics," and of "revisionists" during the Chinese "cultural revolution."

In more democratic or pluralist societies, revolutionary movements are also subject to government control, but usually through less direct and total means than in elitist societies. These will be investigated presently. Reform movements fare somewhat better, and may become legitimated depending upon the strength of the organization and the types of goals and tactics stressed. For example, the industrial reform policies of the trade union movement in the United States became legitimated by the Wagner Act of 1936.

Given their opposition to ongoing social changes, regressive movements are customarily subject to social control in both elitist and pluralist societies except to the extent that they support the existing order against revolutionaries and reformers. The legitimacy of regressive movements is dependent upon a variety of sociohistorical factors. One such factor is the degree of power held by the ruling element in the society. For example, a recently enthroned revolutionary government attempting to institute new social changes will, in most cases, suppress any opposition to these programs of change. On the other hand, long-established dominant groups in a pluralist system may welcome regressive change, in which case they will either tolerate or openly support regressive movements. In the recent history of the United States, for example, regressive movements generally have been spared social sanctions. In fact, considerable support has been

---

[3] For a discussion of the notion of "countervailing power" see John Kenneth Galbraith, *American Capitalism: The Concept of Countervailing Power* (Boston: Houghton Mifflin and Company, 1952).

given to regressive organizations such as the American Liberty League and the John Birch Society by corporate business, one of the plurality of power holders in American society. Another factor affecting the legitimacy of a regressive movement is the extent of reaction it advocates. If the reactionary ideology of a movement advocates total alteration of existing power relationships, then the movement would certainly be viewed as nonlegitimate by those holding power. However, as the Nazi and Fascist movements illustrate, right wing movements rarely alienate all power holders in a society.

In sum, the viability of a social movement is predicated in large part upon the social milieu in which it exists, the type of ideology or world view which it embraces, and the extent to which the goals it advocates are realized. We shall now turn to a discussion of how these factors operate in specific modes of truncation.

MODES OF TRUNCATION

The truncation of social movements through external pressures can be conceptualized in terms of four types of social processes: co-optation, institutionalization, repression, and discreditation. Internally, movements are also threatened by institutionalization and by dissension over goals, tactics, and/or ideology.

Co-optation

Co-optation, as defined by Selznick, refers to a process of: ". . . absorbing new elements into the leadership or policy determining structure of an organization as a means of averting threats to its stability or existence." [4] This process occurs primarily in pluralistic types of societies, where competing political entities can appeal for public support and can pose a threat to the status quo. As Coser has pointed out, conflict can be costly.[5] Consequently, the dominant segment of such a society has considerable interest in establishing mechanisms which can silence discontent and lead to stability. As Roth states it: "A radical mass movement constitutes at least a potential source of instability, but if it can be legalized without sharing in governmental power it may contribute to the stability of the dominant system by leaving intact the latter's basic structure and develop-

[4] Philip Selznick, *TVA and the Grass Roots: A Study in the Sociology of Formal Organization* (Berkeley, Calif.: University of California Press, 1949), p. 13.
[5] See Lewis A. Coser, "The Termination of Conflict," *Journal of Conflict Resolution*, 5 (December 1961): 347–353.

ing vested interests in its own legal status." [6] In contrast, totalitarian societies do not ordinarily require such conciliatory gestures in order to maintain equilibrium in the face of dissent. Since the conscience collective of these societies generally legitimates the use of force and media censorship, dissent can be controlled through repression and discreditation. The freedom to use force is not total, however, since the excessive use of force may weaken the legitimacy of a government. For example, the Nazis did not choose to advertise the crimes perpetrated in their concentration camps.

Reform movements are most amenable to co-optation. This is due to their specific, rather than total, approach to change and to their acceptance of a portion of the conscience collective. Lewis Coser's discussion of the termination of conflict provides insight into the co-optative relationship between the leadership of a movement and the dominant power group. "In order to end a conflict the parties must agree upon rules and norms allowing them to assess their respective power position in the struggle. Their common interest leads them to accept rules which enhance their mutual dependence in the very pursuit of their antagonistic goals." [7] Applying this to the leadership of a movement, Coser continues:

The strike leader must know how to end a strike at the opportune moment, but his knowledge would serve him little if he did not also have the ability to communicate his knowledge to the led. This may often involve the highlighting for the rank and file of a partially attained victory in order to divert attention from a partially suffered defeat.

This is the stuff of which compromises are made. Often seen by the rank and file as a "betrayal" by the leader, they actually derive from the structural circumstances that the leaders' position allows them a view of the total situation which is denied to the led. Moreover, leadership roles require to so manage intragroup tensions as to keep the group united in adversity even though this might entail certain sacrifices insofar as the attainment of the group's goals are concerned.[8]

In conclusion: "Accommodation is facilitated if criteria are available which allow the contenders to gauge the situation. The change of attaining peace without victory depends on the possibility of achieving consensus as to relative strength and on the ability to make this new definition 'stick' within each camp." [9]

If a movement does not share a common interest with the dominant power holders of a society, it is not amenable to co-optation. For this rea-

---

[6] Guenther Roth, *The Social Democrats in Imperial Germany* (New Jersey: Bedminster Press, 1963), p. 8.
[7] Coser, *op. cit.*, p. 348.
[8] *Ibid.*, p. 352.
[9] *Ibid.*, pp. 352–353.

son, regressive and revolutionary movements are seldom truncated in this way. Revolutionary movements in particular adopt a radically critical stance toward existing political, economic, or other social institutions. The revolutionary "sense of reality" does not accept the validity of the status quo. Moreover, the prevailing conscience collective of the society, which reinforces existing power relationships, defines the revolutionary movement as nonlegitimate. These factors contribute to the movement's ideological and physical isolation. As a consequence, conflict between the movement and society tends to become an all-or-nothing "zero-sum" game. Under the circumstances, accommodation is not possible between the movement and the dominant social order. This position is cited by Georges Sorel, the French Syndicalist, as follows:

The Syndicalists solve this problem [of unifying the mass of sentiments manifested in the war against modern society] . . . by concentrating the whole of Socialism in the drama of the general strike; there is thus no longer any place for the reconciliation of contraries in the equivocations of the professors; everything is clearly mapped out, so that only one interpretation of Socialism is possible.[10]

However, under conditions of social disorganization, when the hegemony of the dominant power structure is beginning to break down, it is possible to find a revolutionary movement or its leadership being incorporated into the ruling element. This occurred in pre-Nazi Germany, when the Weimar Republic, in an attempt to avoid a total alteration in the distribution of political power, began co-opting the National Socialists. This process culminated in 1933 with the success of Franz von Papen's intrigue to have Hitler named chancellor. However, as the Nazis began to seize more and more power, the process of co-optation became one of institutionalization, and by 1939 the Thousand Year Reich was firmly established.

In sum, co-optation is a common means of neutralizing social movements in pluralist societies, where a certain legitimacy is given to political competition. It is most effective when applied to reform movements because they focus on a specific issue rather than on total change and because they adhere to at least a part of the status quo ideology. The fate of several American reform movements of the late nineteenth century was sealed through co-optation, for example, the Populist, Greenback, and Progressive movements. Populist collectivism foundered over the controversial "Plank 10" introduced by the American Federation of Labor. This proposal, which advocated collective ownership of all means of production and distribution, would have committed the Populists to a course of socialism. Under the conservative control of Clarence Darrow and Henry

[10] Georges Sorel, *Reflections on Violence* (Glencoe, Ill.: The Free Press, 1950), p. 140.

Lloyd, the Chicago convention of 1895 excluded the radical unionists and their programs and ensured control of the movement by middle class elements. As Destler states it:

> The leaders, platform, and candidates that found favor with the city convention all indicated how far toward the center the People's party in Chicago had moved from the radical, labor leadership of the previous November. Open championship of the "co-operative commonwealth" was hardly to be expected after "Plank 10" had been subordinated and the party's collectivism restricted to natural monopolies and a program of immediate reforms beneficial to the entire consuming public in the city.[11]

The type of movement leadership most prone to co-optation is exemplified by the bureaucrat in the following excerpt from Roche and Sachs, "The Bureaucrat and the Enthusiast." This article also provides considerable insight into the nature of ideologues and the ideological foundations of internal dissent in a movement.

Excerpts from John P. Roche and Stephen Sachs, "The Bureaucrat and the Enthusiast: An Exploration of the Leadership of Social Movements," Western Political Quarterly, 8 (June 1955), 249–252, 254–255. Reprinted by permission of John P. Roche, Stephen Sachs, and the Institute of Government, University of Utah.

. . . The examination of social movements which seek public support for their political, social, or religious objectives suggests that there is a tendency for two major leadership types to emerge. Their specific characteristics may vary greatly with the cultural context or with the type of goal toward which the organization is oriented, so that precise definition is elusive. Yet, granted this elusiveness, we feel that a meaningful typological distinction can be made, and we have designated the two leadership types the "bureaucrat" and the "enthusiast."[12] To forestall the criticism that we are indulging in psychological monism, we should state at the outset that one individual can, in varying social situations, display the characteristics of both, i.e., he can perhaps be a bureaucrat in his union and an

---

[11] Chester McArthur Destler, *American Radicalism, 1865–1901* (Chicago, Quadrangle Books, 1966), p. 241.
[12] Our "bureaucrat" is a first cousin of Max Weber's bureaucrat, sharing many of the latter's characteristics. Our "enthusiast" is on loan from theological studies where he has had a long and tumultuous career; *cf.* Mgr. Ronald Knox, *Enthusiasm* (London: Oxford University Press, 1950).

enthusiast in his religion. But in any one context, the pattern of behavior tends to remain constant and is thus subject to generalization.

The bureaucrat, as his name implies, is concerned primarily with the organizational facet of the social movement, with its stability, growth, and tactics. To put it another way, he concentrates on the organizational means by which the group implements and consolidates its principles. He will generally be either an officeholder in the organization or interested in holding office. While he may have strong ideological convictions, he will be preoccupied with the reconciliation of diverse elements in order to secure harmony within the organization and maximize its external appeal. He seeks communication, not excommunications.

In contrast, the enthusiast, seldom an officeholder,[13] and quite unhappy when in office, concerns himself primarily with what he deems to be the fundamental principles of the organization, the ideals and values which nourish the movement. No reconciler, he will concentrate on the advocacy of these principles at the risk of hard feelings of even of schism.[14] While the bureaucrat tends to regard the organization as an end in itself,[15] to the enthusiast it will always remain an imperfect vehicle for a

[13] The British Labour party's bureaucrats generally center in the party Executive and the Parliamentary Labour party, notably in the contingents supplied to each of these bodies by the trade-union movement. The enthusiasts formerly rallied around the standard of the affiliated Independent Labour party (ILP) and upon its disaffiliation migrated to the Socialist League. Since the latter was disbanded, there has been no nesting place organizationally, but functionally the enthusiasts can always be located in the Constituency Labour parties and can be spotted ideologically by their vigorous support for Aneurin Bevan. They constitute the readership of the journal *Tribune* and of the *New Statesman & Nation*, and are at present busy learning Chinese.

[14] For instance, Stafford Cripps' work for the constitution of a popular front with the Communists and other "anti-fascist" organizations which led in 1939 to his expulsion from the party. Cripps, of whom Churchill once observed: "There, but for the grace of God, goes God," never faltered for a second in his labors for this cause and, secure in his conviction that it was just, accepted expulsion as the stigma which proved it.

[15] The bureaucrat *par excellence* of the Labour party was Arthur Henderson, longtime party secretary and foreign minister in the 1929–1931 government. A good example of the bureaucratic preoccupation with organization and reconciliation was the preparation by Henderson of the 1918 party constitution, a masterpiece of organizational ingenuity; see G. D. H. Cole, *A History of the Labour Party* from 1914 (London: Routledge & Kegan Paul, 1948), pp. 44ff. Henderson was severely criticized for not leading opposition to Ramsay MacDonald during the 1929–1931 period, when it appeared to many that the Prime Minister was ignoring party policy, but to do so would have run contrary to Henderson's bureaucratic loyalty. As Cole puts it, Henderson "in that crisis . . . made . . . too many . . . concessions in the hope of holding the Party together." Cole, *ibid.*, p. 305. Henderson, of course, never dreamed that MacDonald would desert the party. Postgate's description of Henderson after that sad event is illuminating in this context: "Henderson seemed shrivelled and bowed, and his usually ruddy face was yellow. Disloyalty was a thing he could not understand. He had given his most unswerving support to the handsome, eloquent leader who had helped him build up the movement; he had never allowed himself to be influenced by the fact that he had not in his heart liked MacDonald and had more than once received discourtesy from him. Now that man has deserted the people in its greatest misery. He could not understand, though he would try to forgive; he looked like a man who

greater purpose. Whereas the bureaucrat is likely to equate "The Cause" with its organizational expression, the enthusiast, with his fondness for abstraction, identifies it with a corpus of principles.[16]

Several other typical characteristics emerge from this fundamental difference in outlook. Outstanding among them is the varying attitude towards compromise in policy matters. The bureaucrat approaches a policy question with a predisposition towards harmony; he is prepared to compromise in order to promote unity and cohesion within the organization and to broaden its external appeal. He considers policy, if not a mere expedient with which to build up organizational strength, no more than a flexible expression of intentions which can be modified as required by "practical" needs.[17] However, to the enthusiast policy is far more than a "political formula," far more than a sonorous exposition of attractive, organization-building slogans; on the contrary, he insists that policy must be the undiluted expression of first principles.[18] The bureaucrat specializes in studied ambiguity; the enthusiast, in credal precision. In short, while the former looks upon policy statements as something less than ex cathedra pronouncements of the whole "Truth," the latter views policy as the living Word and considers compromise as not only wrong, but also evil.[19]

The same approach to compromise is evident in attitudes towards membership: the bureaucrat is inclusionary, and holds a quantitative emphasis, while the enthusiast is exclusionary, desiring to limit the body

---

had been given a mortal wound." Raymond Postgate, *George Lansbury* (London: Longmans, Green & Co., 1951), pp. 271–272. Cole elsewhere notes Henderson's identification of the cause and the organization, *op. cit.*, p. 305.

[16] To understand this approach, a reading of the various studies by Archibald Fenner Brockway is invaluable. See his *Socialism over Sixty Years* (London: George Allen & Unwin, 1946); *Inside the Left* (London: The New Leader, 1942); and *Bermondsey Story* (London: George Allen & Unwin, 1949). Brockway was a paladin of enthusiasm and his various crusades, and those of the men he chronicles, against the party leadership make exciting reading. One is struck with the resemblance to *Pilgrim's Progress*, for he is transported to a world populated by moral "forms," and the perils of Socialist (the Christian of Brockway's epics) are frightful to behold.

[17] For an exhaustive treatment of this theme see Robert Michels, *Political Parties* (Glencoe, Ill.: The Free Press, 1949), and Gaetano Mosca, *The Ruling Class* (New York: McGraw-Hill Book Co., 1939). It is also discussed by Max Weber in his essay on "Bureaucracy" in H. H. Gerth & C. W. Mills, eds., *From Max Weber: Essays in Sociology* (New York: Oxford University Press, 1946).

[18] For example, George Lansbury's 1926 motion to "abolish the Navy by discharging 100,000 men," Postgate, *op. cit.*, pp. 236–237, as distinct from the regular Labour motions in favor of disarmament in the abstract. See also the ILP position on "the cruiser issue" in 1924, Brockway, *Inside the Left*, p. 156.

[19] The ILP split from the Labour party on precisely this point. The ILP Members of Parliament demanded the right of private judgment, asserting that an M.P. should vote on the merits of a proposal rather than under party instruction. The Labour party, operating on the maxim *ex nihilo nihil*, refused to permit this and the ILP disaffiliated. Brockway, *Inside the Left*, p. 215; Postgate, *op. cit.*, p. 278. The ILP saw the MacDonald defection as the logical conclusion of moderation: "Truly the policy of compromise has brought its reward." Brockway, *Socialism over Sixty Years*, p. 294.

of saints only to those full of grace.[20] That this problem of membership has plagued social movements from time immemorial hardly needs elaboration here; suffice it to say that the struggle between the inclusionists and the exclusionists, which inspired St. Augustine's polemics against the Donatists as it does those of the Bevanites against Attlee, is a contant feature in ideologically oriented groups.[21] In particular, it plagues political organizations, for the bureaucrat here is characterized by an acute hypersensitivity towards the marginal voter,[22] while the enthusiast, with full confidence in the truth of his convictions, operates on the principle that if the people refuse to share his vision, so much the worse for them. To the latter, defeat at the polls means nothing; a moral totalitarian, his slogan is "Damn the electorate! Full speed ahead!" [23]

It is perhaps, therefore, valid to suggest that the bureaucrat seeks to extend the area of compromise; the enthusiast, the area of principle.[24] Although we are not asserting that the bureaucrat always flees from principle, nor that the enthusiast is inevitably a moral totalitarian, there is in

[20] This is a function of the perfectionism of the enthusiast and is a common feature of all enthusiastic political, social, or religious movements. A man can not be saved by "good works," but only by true inspiration, which may or may not lead him to good works. The bureaucrat, essentially Niebuhrian in outlook, is prepared to settle for less on the assumption that while good works may be badly motivated, they are still preferable to bad works, however motivated.

[21] For a discussion of this aspect of the Donatist heresy, see Knox, *op. cit.*, chap. iv. Actually the Donatists were never officially ruled heretics, but they were treated as such by Augustine and his bureaucratic descendants.

[22] According to Cole, MacDonald objected to the ILP's "Socialism in Our Time" program because "it would only frighten the electorate and ensure a crushing Labour defeat." *Op. cit.*, p. 198. In contrast, the official 1929 program was, according to the same authority, "a moderate social reform programme, in which socialism found neither place nor mention. It was evidently drafted in contemplation of a result to the Election which, at best, might enable Labour to take minority office with a stronger backing than in 1924." *Ibid.*, p. 213. Following the 1931 defeat, Lansbury wrote Cripps that Henderson wanted "to trim our sails so as to catch the wind of disgust which will blow [MacDonald] and his friends out and that he is not anxious for us to be too definite about Socialist measures as our first objectives. Put them in our programme but be sure when we come to power we keep on the line of least resistance. . . ." Postgate, *op. cit.*, p. 280.

[23] For instance, in both 1924 and 1929, in each case when the Labour party became a minority government, the ILP sought to implement a radical program, knowing that it would bring defeat in Commons. Such a defeat, they urged, would put to the country in stark terms the issue of socialism versus capitalism, and would arouse the working class to full militancy in the class struggle. See Cole, *op. cit.*, pp. 157ff., 210ff., 218, 246, 281ff.; Postgate, *op. cit.*, pp. 225–226, 224; Philip Snowden, *An Autobiography* (London: Nicholson & Watson, 1934), II, 592ff.; Brockway, *Socialism over Sixty Years*, pp. 206ff., 214, 229ff., 253, 259ff.

[24] As, for instance, when Jowett and Wheatley, ministers in the 1924 government, refused to wear morning dress on a visit to the King; Brockway, *Socialism over Sixty Years, op. cit.*, pp. 208–210; or when Brockway himself, on principled grounds, refused to attend a party given by Lady Astor; *Inside the Left*, p. 201. Surely the high point of this symbolic rejection was achieved by Dr. Salter, a Republican, who kept his hat by his bed so he could quickly put it on when the chimes of a nearby church played "God Save the King" at seven in the morning. Brockway, *Bermondsey Story*, p. 14.

our view sufficient evidence to justify the establishment of these positions as typical.[25]

"Respectable, conventional, orthodox religion," wrote Emrys Hughes, an outstanding Labourite enthusiast, "is something very different from the living faith. And that is also true of politics." [26] Following this line of demarcation, the bureaucrat is the "respectable, conventional," and "orthodox" churchman. The organizational structure, from which he gets profound satisfaction, and with which he identifies himself, exists concretely—he need only look about him or open his desk drawer to appreciate its reality. His patient, untiring, and probably publicly unrecognized labor has gone into its creation, and the stable security that it offers acts as an antidote to his insecurity. Like the men and women who refused to leave slum hovels during intense wartime bombing because these were "home," the bureaucrat has a psychological commitment to the organization that far outweighs any economic attachments. Thus, it may be predicted that the bureaucrat will be reluctant to depart from habitual and tested practices which have fostered the past growth of the organization; he will assuredly take a dim view of experiments, although he will seldom oppose them frontally. He is the past master of the motion "To Table."

In part because he is tradition-oriented, and in part because of the psychological make-up of his opposition, the bureaucrat tends to be anti-intellectual. The proportion of intellectuals among enthusiasts is often quite high, although it must be added that in situations where organization and intellectualism have gone hand in hand, for example, in the Church of England, the enthusiasts may rally around anti-intellectualism and anti-rationalism of the crudest sort. But even given this qualification, the man who causes trouble in an organization must attempt a respectable intellectual case for his position—indeed, in the twentieth century we have seen the irony of intellectuals building an intellectual foundation for anti-intellectualism! [27]—and so the bureaucrat grows to look with suspicion on people who think too much, who are always popping up with new ideas. He is likewise suspicious of oratory and big meetings, where his hard-built discipline may tumble before the charismatic charm of an enthusiast-demagogue; his natural habitat is the committee room where even if a Messiah should reveal himself, he would not recruit more than half-a-dozen disciples. In short, the bureaucrat detests and fears unpre-

---

[25] That is to say, definable types. Obviously, a man may have a mixed personality, may be enthusiastic with respect to some things and passive about others. But this differentiation is not important for our purposes; we are solely concerned with the relationship of these types to the operation of social movements. How an individual integrates the different facets of his personality is a problem for the psychiatrist and psychoanalyst.
[26] Emrys Hughes, *Keir Hardie* (London: Lincolns-Prager, 1950), p. 5.
[27] Some of the German and Italian justifications for fascism, notably those of Schmitt and Gentile, fall into this category, as do certain contemporary French apologies for communism.

dictability and the flamboyance with which the unpredictable often gird themselves; the road to his affection and trust is through hard work, patiently and undramatically executed, and acceptance of hierarchical decision-making.[28]

Unlike the bureaucrat, the enthusiast has no tangible symbols to supply him with satisfaction and security; almost by definition, he must believe in the ultimate value of things unseen, and he is likely to scorn institutions as snares set to draw men from the paths of righteousness.[29] While the bureaucrat is an instinctive collectivist, holding as he does an almost Burkean view of the presumptive validity of tradition, the enthusiast is a militant individualist, prepared like Nietzsche's "Super Man" to achieve self-fulfillment at whatever cost to the social fabric. If the bureaucratic personality is dominated by caution and fear of the unorthodox, the enthusiast is a captive of *hubris*, of cosmic egotism, and of blindness to the fact that "Humanity" is not humanity. He lives in a world peopled by abstractions rather than by human beings, and it is quite possible for him to contemplate, in Koestler's phrase, "sacrificing one generation in the interest of the next." [30]

The ideals which the enthusiast seeks to realize, whether a glorious vision of heaven on earth, the resurrection of a romanticized past, or less ambitious versions of both, are hardly capable of attainment in this imperfect world; indeed, such is the nature of ideals. Yet, gripped by his Promethean quest, the enthusiast never ceases in his effort to storm heaven. Against the skeptical patience of the bureaucrat, he pits his passion and his chiliastic dedication; his is indeed a "living faith." [31]

[28] The respect for "channels" is very great in bureaucratic circles; indeed, one of the main complaints made against the enthusiast is his disregard for them, his willingness to "appeal to the movement" or to the "people" against unpleasant decisions instead of patiently appealing to the various hierarchical bodies in the apparatus, through "channels," for recourse. Much of Aneurin Bevan's unpopularity in the Labour party, notably among the trade-union potentates, is an outgrowth of his lack of respect for decisions collectively made, and his effrontery, as they see it, in appealing these to the wider constituency.
[29] This is particularly true of religious enthusiasts, who generally distinguish between true religion and the church much as Jesus contrasted Judaism with the religion of the Pharisees. See Knox, *op. cit., passim*, and for some rather unfriendly polemics in this vein, *The Journal of George Fox* (Everyman ed.; New York, E. P. Dutton & Co., 1924).
[30] Koestler used this figure of speech in an address in New York some years ago. We have not seen it used in any of his works.
[31] Eric Hoffer observes: "It is the true believer's ability to 'shut his eyes and stop his ears' to facts that do not deserve to be either seen or heard which is the source of his unequaled fortitude and constancy. He cannot be frightened by danger nor disheartened by obstacles nor baffled by contradictions because he denies their existence. Strength of faith, as Bergson pointed out, manifests itself not in moving mountains but in not seeing mountains to move. And it is the certitude of his infallible doctrine that renders the true believer impervious to the uncertainties, surprises and the unpleasant realities of the world around him." *The True Believer* (New York: Harper & Bros., 1951), pp. 78–79.

In many cases, co-optation will be a prelude to institutionalization, which we will consider next.

Institutionalization

The institutional stage, or "solidification" of a social movement, is the point at which movements must be "able to legalize or organize their power; they must become the in-group of the structure of political power." [32] This point essentially marks the termination of a social movement. In dialectical terms, this is a state of synthesis in which the movement loses its nonlegitimate character and becomes a part of the status quo social order.

Insofar as they achieve their goals, all social movements are prone to institutionalization, and this can occur in both pluralist and totalitarian societies. Perhaps the classic instance of institutionalization is when a revolutionary movement grasps control of power and begins to inaugurate its program of social change. The list of such institutionalizations includes the French Revolution, the Cuban Revolution, the Russian Revolution of 1917, the Chinese Revolution of 1949, and the FLN in Algeria, all of which faced regressive counterrevolutions after they became the dominant power bloc.

Since their goals enjoy a certain legitimacy within the conscience collective, reform movements are prone to institutionalization by having their goals adopted either by the society as a whole or by a legitimate political party. This attainment of its specific aim terminates the raison d'être of a reform movement. For example, the Abolitionist movement became nonexistent after the passage of its aims into law in the 1860s. However, the voluntary dissolution of a social movement after its aims have been achieved or have passed out of social significance is rare. The persistence of a movement under these conditions has already been discussed in relation to the WCTU, and will be referred to again in a later section.

In addition to institutionalization arising after the achievement of goals, reform movements are also prone to internal institutionalization, or bureaucratization. The bureaucratic aspects of leadership have been amply illustrated in Roche and Sachs' "The Bureaucrat and the Enthusiast," which was excerpted in the earlier discussion of co-optation. The leadership of regressive and, to a greater extent, revolutionary movements is seldom bureaucratized until the postmovement phase. As we have discussed earlier, movements which are in conflict with society are not prone to accommodation. Reform movements, on the other hand, are more tolerated by the conscience collective and often coexist with other interest

[32] Rex D. Hopper, "The Revolutionary Process: A Frame of Reference for the Study of Revolutionary Movements," *Social Forces*, 28 (March 1950): 277.

groups. *The bureaucratization which can result may be illustrated with reference to any number of movements.*

As Max Weber, Robert Michels, and C. Wright Mills have pointed out, the growth of an organization or movement is often accompanied by a process of bureaucratization which creates the structures of an institution.[33] Lipset, Trow, and Coleman, in their study of the International Typographical Union, have put it as follows: "Unions . . . tend to develop a bureaucratic structure, that is, a system of rational (predictable) organization which is hierarchically organized. Bureaucracy is inherent in the sheer problem of administration, in the requirement that unions be 'responsible' . . . in the need to parallel the structures of business and government. . . . "[34] Mills discusses industrial unionism in a similar vein: "Labor unions have become organizations that select and form leaders who, upon becoming successful, take their places alongside politicians in both major parties, among the national power elite."[35] Michels' classic study of the German Social Democrats traces the process by which the leadership of a political movement becomes institutionalized and wedded to the status quo.[36] Louis Lomax, in his study of black movements in the United States, points to the institutional character of the NAACP.[37] Because of its emphasis on the courts as a means to achieve civil rights rather than on more militant tactics, the NAACP has become a legitimate interest group with access to the White House. In Congress, it is treated as an institution representing the interests of the largest minority group in America. *In the following excerpts from S. M. Lipset's* Agrarian Socialism, *the process whereby the Cooperative Commonwealth Federation (CCF) of Canada graduated from a revolutionary socialist movement to an agrarian reform one as the prospect of political legitimatization became more imminent is discussed. As a footnote to Lipset's analysis, the institutionalization of this one-time agrarian movement was further underscored in 1961 when, as Canada's third-ranking political party, it changed its name to the New Democratic Party (NDP).*

[33] Max Weber, "Bureaucracy," in H. H. Gerth and C. Wright Mills, trans. and eds., *From Max Weber: Essays in Sociology* (New York: Oxford University Press, 1958), pp. 196–244; Robert Michels, *Political Parties* (Glencoe, Ill.: The Free Press, 1949); and C. Wright Mills, *The Power Elite* (New York: Oxford University Press, 1956).
[34] S. M. Lipset, Martin A. Trow, and James S. Coleman, *Union Democracy* (Glencoe, Ill.: The Free Press, 1956).
[35] C. Wright Mills, *The Power Elite, op. cit.*, p. 262. See also his *The New Men of Power* (New York: Harcourt Brace and Co., 1948).
[36] Robert Michels, *op. cit.* See particularly the section on "Democracy and the Iron Law of Oligarchy," pp. 393–409.
[37] Louis Lomax, *The Negro Revolt* (New York: Signet Books, 1962), pp. 112–132, 160–177.

Excerpts from Seymour Martin Lipset, Agrarian Socialism: The Cooperative Commonwealth Federation in Saskatchewan. A Study in Political Sociology (*Garden City, N.Y.: Doubleday and Company, 1968), Chapter 7, "Ideology and Program," pp. 160–164, 167–171, 173–175, 177–180, 182–185, 188–189, 191–193. Reprinted by permission of Seymour M. Lipset, Doubleday and Co., and the Regents of the University of California.*

The socialists in the farm movement and the urban Independent Labor Party were able to capture the ideological control of the new Farmer-Labor political movement as a result of the catastrophic depression and drought and the obvious inadequacy of the accepted rural institutions to cope with them. Economic conditions in 1931 and 1932 were desperate, and the militant agrarians of the U.F.C. were not in a mood to quibble over a program or a specific statement as being too radical. They were even willing to call the new party the "Socialist Party of Canada." The period up to the elections of 1934 and 1935 was distinctly a radical, agitational stage. The old socialists would brook little compromise and secured the acceptance of a program calling for a completely socialized society, including the ownership of land.

When campaigning for the new party in 1933–1934, however, the leaders soon found that to many people the word "socialism" had unfortunate connotations of atheism, confiscation of land, and dictatorship. Some of the agrarian CCF candidates realized that greater strength could be achieved for an independent farmers' party that opposed the eastern capitalists than for a socialist party. Even before the first election in 1934, party leaders began to omit all reference to socialism in their propaganda. Some rural leaders tried to discourage urban socialist speakers from mentioning socialism, Russia, and other tabooed topics when they visited rural areas. One very successful CCF candidate admonished such campaigners: "You can say anything you want about capitalism, the banks, and so forth. Be as radical as you want. But you can't speak here if you are going to talk about socialism. The farmers here hate the C.P.R. and the Grain Exchange and will fight like hell for the co-ops. . . . Socialism to them means Russia and antireligion. . . ."[38]

The electoral defeats of 1934 and 1935 and the rise of Social Credit as an opposition reform movement destroyed the confidence of many of the socialists in their program. Actually, the theoretical socialists in the top leadership of the provincial party now felt that they were wrong in attempting to force their program and terminology on the farmers. They

[38] Interview with a C.C.F. Leader.

accepted the arguments of agrarian leaders that converting farmers to complete socialism was a task of many decades and that a successful political movement must concentrate on immediate demands. . . .

The implications of the CCF's shift from being a socialist to a social reform party can be seen most directly in the crucial area of nationalization of industry. In Western democratic society, the foremost difference between socialist movements and progressive nonsocialist movements is their attitude toward changing the power structure of society by government ownership of industry. The original objective of the Saskatchewan CCF in the early 'thirties made it clear that the party believed in a completely socialized economy. "Objective: The social ownership of all resources and the machinery of wealth production to the end that we may establish a Co-operative Commonwealth in which the basic principle regulating production, distribution, and exchange will be the supplying of human needs instead of the making of profits. . . ." [39]

This forthright objective had been inserted in the program by the more socialist elements in the party; but this extreme statement on complete nationalization and the manner of compensation was not part of the traditional agrarian ideology favoring public ownership of only the more important industries, especially those that affected agriculture. Gradually, under the pressure of opposition criticism and electoral defeat, the socialists dropped the insistence on a totally socialized society. By the election year 1938, the CCF policy emphasized government planning more than ownership. It no longer directly attacked private ownership and profit, as the rewarding of the party objective indicates.

The purpose of the CCF is the establishment in Canada of a Cooperative Commonwealth in which the principle regulating production, distribution, and exchange will be the supplying of human needs.

To this end a CCF government in power in Saskatchewan would substitute social planning in the place of the ruthless competition now practiced under capitalism. . . . [40]

While modifying its goal of total socialization, the CCF has continued its emphasis on the extension of the social services rendered by the state, such as social security, health, and education. These services assume major importance in a province like Saskatchewan, where health and educational facilities tend to be poor because of the sparseness of the population. The farm movements of the province have always demanded more government aid for such services. All CCF literature and programs since the start of the party have urged government protection against illness, accident, old age, and unemployment, increased funds for education, and

---

[39] Saskatchewan Farmer-Labor Group (C.C.F.), *Handbook for Speakers* (Regina, 1933), p. 21.
[40] *Handbook to the Saskatchewan C.C.F. Platform and Policy* (Regina, 1933), p. 1.

socialized medicine. These social security aspects of the party's program gradually assumed greater importance in its propaganda as the stress on socialism declined, until today it is the most important part of the provincial program.

Both program and propaganda for social services have remained fairly constant. Party policy on education, however, changed drastically with the other shifts designed to accommodate to existing values. Many socialists in the party believed that the educational system was biased in favor of capitalist social and economic values. Under their influence, the party in its 1933–1934 program advocated not only increased expenditures for education but also basic changes in curriculum. "Education Program . . . (d) The teaching of the principles of cooperation. (e) The teaching of the origin of money and its function as a medium of exchange. (f) Elimination of all glorification of war, and to substitute calisthenic drill in place of cadet training. . . ." [41] . . . After the disastrous defeats of 1934 and 1935, the educational proposal was dropped. No mention of curriculum revision was made in the election programs of 1936 to 1938. The 1944 program suggested some general curriculum changes, but did not revert to the original platform. "Curriculum Revision: The CCF proposes to revise the school curriculum so that the material of school studies may prepare students adequately for intelligent participation in the life of their community and not, as now, inadequately for a University to which the majority will never go." [42]

The basic cultural conservatism of the Saskatchewan CCF, the fact that it was an outgrowth of significant permanent forces within western Canada rather than a new radical movement seeking to make far-reaching changes, can best be seen through analysis of the impact of religious beliefs on the party. Socialism has traditionally been identified as basically materialist and antireligious. Marx's classic statement, "Religion is the opiate of the people," has been reiterated by European socialist parties; for the tenser political situation in Europe showed the fundamental opposition of authoritarian religions and socialism more clearly than it has in Canada and the countries of the British Commonwealth. European socialism, accordingly, has been able to win its way in spite of its antireligious stand, because in many of these countries the church was identified in the minds of the lower economic groups with the upper class or with the state. In Germany the Lutheran Church was a state church; in Russia the same was true of the Greek Orthodox Church; in southern Europe the Roman Catholic Church possessed tremendous wealth and political power; in France anticlericalism was a deep and bitter heritage from the French Revolution which had fought the clergy as a part of the privileged class.

[41] Saskatchewan Farmer-Labor Group (C.C.F.), *Economic Policy* (Regina, 1933), p. 4.
[42] *Provincial Platform*, 1944.

The socialist and working-class movements of the self-governed countries of the British Commonwealth have, on the other hand, been unique in their ability to gain the support, or at least the real neutrality, of the churches toward their political efforts. This happened for three main reasons: (1) the Anglo-Saxon left-wing movements never accepted a Marxist theoretical approach to socialism with its initial antagonism to organized religion; (2) the strong nonconformist churches in the British countries were primarily poor men's churches, whose ministers often took part in the organization of workers' parties; and (3) the Catholic Church has been relatively weak in the British Commonwealth. . . .[43]

It is not surprising, therefore, that, like British socialism, the Saskatchewan CCF, from the time of its formation and right down to the present, has had a moralistic and religious emphasis. The CCF stresses its support of Christianity and the fact that many of its leaders are religious; and it makes political capital of the fact that some churches are anticapitalist. Since the CCF is dominated by those who think that socialism and Christianity are but secular and sacred versions of the same philosophy, the few in the party who hold Marxist materialist views have kept these in the background. The majority of the party agrees on the necessity of winning the religious people, and the British tradition has made it both easy and logical to abolish the antireligious connotation of socialism. . . .

Besides its socialist and social reform propaganda, the CCF concentrated on demonstrating that it was the only party that fought for the immediate economic interests of the people. To do so, it evolved a program supporting the economic demands of the three class groups to whom it directed its electoral appeal: farmers, urban workers, and small businessmen. The socialists drew up programs designed to convince each of these groups of their place in a completely socialized society. Such proposals were dropped after the election defeats. An analysis of the propaganda addressed to these groups is further confirmation of the thesis that the CCF grew culturally conservative as it moved toward power.

Historically, security of landownership is the farmer's deepest demand. The fact that he puts his own work into improving his land makes the tract on which his life depends more than a job. But single-crop farming makes the dependence of the Saskatchewan farmer on the price of wheat a more prominent factor in his political thinking than are prices in diversified farming areas: the whole life of the community depends perilously and visibly on a single price which the farmer is powerless to influence. This has meant that CCF ideology in Saskatchewan has to be based on two principles: long-run tenacity of landownership and the short-run, perennially fresh fighting issue of the price of "this year's" wheat.

[43] See Franz Lindner, *Sozialismus und Religion* (Leipzig: Tauchnitz, 1932), for a discussion of the British Labor Party's attitudes on religion.

The depression and drought of the 'thirties demonstrated to many farmers the comparative worthlessness of owning land if it would not produce an income. As tens of thousands of farm families were forced to leave the province or to trek to the northern bush frontier to earn a living, fear spread throughout the province. It is impossible to overemphasize the farmer's continuing fear of losing his entire means of livelihood. He was unable to pay the accumulated interest on his debts and taxes. The number of actual foreclosures and tax sales was, however, very small. The economic disaster was so overwhelming and universal that mortgage companies and banks could gain nothing by foreclosing, as a forced sale would bring little in return. The provincial government would have had to stop any mass wave of foreclosures, for no government could have remained in office if it permitted its citizens to lose all they had.

Debt-ridden farmers did not, however, stop to think logically. The threat of foreclosure was very real to each farmer who could not pay his debts. Between 1928 and 1932 the interest owed on debts in rural Saskatchewan rose from one-tenth to nearly three-quarters of the net cash operating income of the farmers. The threat to the farmers' ownership of land seemed to come from the mortgage companies. Many Saskatchewan farmers literally had "little to lose but their mortgages."

The militant agrarians' party, the CCF, concentrated on an effort to convince the farmers that it was the only party that could protect them—provincially, through government action to stop foreclosures, and federally, by government marketing of farm products, a guaranteed minimum price, and crop insurance. The CCF endeavored to identify the old parties with the banks, the Grain Exchange, the railroads, and eastern manufacturing interests. It contended that only a people's party, like the CCF, which was not dependent on campaign contributions from large corporations, could be expected to help the farmers. "He who pays the piper calls the tune" became the favorite propaganda attack on the old parties by the CCF. . . .

The socialists in the party succeeded, in the early period of the movement, in getting the farmers in the U.F.C. to accept the principle of nationalization of land. This proposal, however, was never suggested as a means of making farmers employees of the state or even members of cooperative farms. The CCF farmers accepted it as a means of guaranteeing permanent land tenure to working farmers. . . .

Though CCF leaders presented the program as one designed to protect the agrarian's control of his farm, the sheer suggestion of nationalization of land was the most controversial aspect of the program. The party leaders, therefore, dropped it in 1936, and concentrated on protection of the farmer's equity in his land. The CCF sought to appeal to the farmer in terms of his basic desire to become or to remain a property holder. Socialism for the farmer was henceforth to mean the protection of his property by control of the rest of the economy, and especially big business.

This goal was clearly stated in all party literature after 1936. "The CCF believes in the family farm as the basis of rural life. Living standards for farmers must rise with those in the rest of the community. . . ." [44]

The second element to which the CCF has appealed is the urban working class, 20 per cent of the population of the province if one includes all employees. The original (1932) name of the partner, Farmer-Labor Group, indicates the basic concept of the unity of the producing classes, farmers and workers, against their common economic enemies. Despite these gestures toward urban workers, however, the party was basically agrarian from the start. Success or failure for the new movement depended mainly on winning a majority in the rural districts. It is characteristic that the only appeal to workers in the first program of the provincial party for the 1934 campaign barely mentions labor in the course of a 1,500-word statement. "Social Legislation to secure to the worker and the farmer:— (a) An adequate income and leisure, with an effective voice in the management of his industry. (b) Freedom of speech and the right of assembly." [45] Specific labor planks such as an eight-hour day or a minimum wage were lacking. The speaker's handbooks and propaganda leaflets rarely mentioned labor, and then only incidentally. . . .

After its victories in the 1938 elections, the CCF began to gain working-class support. The leaders of the small trade-union movement in the province became interested in a party that professed to be more prolabor than the two old parties and now appeared to be capable of forming the next provincial government. As a result, the enlarged trade-union wing of the party drew up a complete labor program setting forth the traditional demands of organized labor, with the addition of certain social services. . . . It is significant to note that this [new program was] . . . basically a trade-union program, not a socialist one. There is no mention of the advantages to labor under socialized industry, nor of the possibilities of labor representation in the management of industry. Labor leaders, like the farmers, were primarily interested in the party as a means of advancing their own economic objectives.

Propaganda issued before the 1934 elections reemphasized state distribution and the employment of retailers as civil servants:

Business Men
You have always voted Grit and Tory
Because
You thought you were in business for Profits
You Never Made Any
The postmaster is sure of his income
Why not be sure of yours, under a planned economy,

---

[44] C.C.F. (Saskatchewan Section), *The Farmer and the C.C.F.* (Regina, n.d.), p. 3.
[45] C.C.F., *Provincial and Federal Program* (Saskatoon, 1933).

in which you will be guaranteed an income
as a distributor.
Vote CCF [46]

There were few small merchants in the new party, and there was no vocal opposition to the desire to eliminate their businesses. But in the 1934 and 1935 elections, merchants voted overwhelmingly against the CCF. Many constituencies were lost to the party because the old-party plurality in the small urban areas outweighed the CCF lead in the country. Moreover, Social Credit was able to secure the support of many businessmen who were attracted to its policy of increasing purchasing power by distributing money.

The Social Credit gains among small merchants and professional men showed that these people could be won away from the old parties. The CCF leaders, seeking votes, decided to attempt to win over small business to their own ranks. This necessarily involved the adoption of a policy designed to protect small business against the monopolies. The economic goal of the CCF, "Production for Use and Not for Profit," was changed by dropping out the last four words. George Williams, the provincial leader, clearly stated the reasons for the change: "The farmer and the small businessman in Saskatchewan have difficulty in understanding the CCF manifesto when they come to the section which sets out that production under socialistic policies can only be carried on when it is 'not for profit.' . . ." [47]

In spite of its programmatic appeals to small business, the CCF, after 1936, laid increasing stress on its identification with the cooperative movement. Organized by people active in the cooperatives, the party was able to capitalize on the previous acceptance by a large proportion of Saskatchewan farmers of non-profit enterprise as superior to private capitalism. The very name of the party, the Cooperative Commonwealth Federation, meant to many that it was the political arm of the cooperatives, an idea which the CCF did not try to dispel. . . .

Every election program of the CCF and most of the speeches by party leaders stressed this relationship between the CCF and the cooperatives. Anyone listening to CCF speeches or reading CCF literature by 1944 would think that he was asked to vote for the cooperatives' party, as an excerpt from an article in the *Commonwealth* makes clear.

This movement [the CCF], founded by the people has also grown by leaps and bounds, just as did the original cooperative movement, and it is now being viciously opposed by the same vested interests which oppose cooperation of any sort. The issue is, however, clear cut. The people are being asked to make their

[46] C.C.F. (Saskatchewan Section), election leaflet (Regina, 1935).
[47] Saskatchewan Liberal Party, *The C.C.F. Platform* (Regina, 1938), p. 3.

choice between cooperation and competition and the majority are choosing the former.

That which is founded on a just principle can not be stifled and so the cooperative movement—commercial and political—marches on.[48]

There can be little doubt that this propaganda has been effective in overcoming the prejudices against the CCF as a socialist party. Some CCF leaders publicly assert that they are cooperators and not socialists. In most places in the province there is a strong inter-relationship on the local level between CCF leaders and the cooperatives. The same men often lead both. . . .

When one considers the changes in CCF policy, together with the constant emphasis of the Saskatchewan CCF members of the House of Commons on raising the price of wheat, it becomes clear that the CCF has gradually changed, under external and internal pressure, from an agrarian socialist party to a liberal agrarian protest movement, following in the direct tradition of the Populists, the Non-Partisan League, and the Progressives. No single modification of party policy and emphasis was sufficient to change the character of the movement, but taken together they constitute a qualitative change. The socialists had won power, but the method and conditions under which they succeeded had in large measure adversely affected their socialism. . . .

Karl Mannheim has pointed out that a new doctrine can succeed only if it is based on attitudes already present in a society.

Only when the utopian conception . . . seizes upon currents already present in society and gives expression to them, when in this form it flows back into the outlook of the whole group, and is translated into action by it, only then can the existing order be challenged by the striving for another order of existence. Indeed, it may be stated further that it is a very essential feature of modern history that in the gradual organization for collective action social classes become effective in translating historical reality only when their aspirations are embodied in utopias appropriate to the changing situation.[49]

The CCF in Saskatchewan is a "class" party in the objective sense, since its program reflects the aspirations of a class created by constraining economic forces. As a result of the depression, it became the political voice of angry, exploited, rural Saskatchewan. Like the Russian Bolsheviks in 1917, the CCF adapted socialism to "currents already present" in agrarian society. This generalization still leaves the problem of deciding how far such present "currents" can be extended. There were plenty of currents in Saskatchewan that a socialist utopia could use—and the Social Credit movement shows how easy it is to hitch different utopias

[48] *Saskatchewan Commonwealth*, January 11, 1944, p. 4.
[49] Karl Mannheim, *Ideology and Utopia* (London: Routledge and Kegan Paul, Ltd., 1936), p. 187.

to existing needs. It is one thing, however, to attach the provocative title of "socialism" to a movement, and another to create the ideological structure capable of sustaining far-reaching social changes. It may be said of most political innovators not content with the role of a permanent minority that they err on the side of underplaying the potentialities of "currents already present." The problem of major social and political change balances between what one can surely get as a short-run objective and what one dares hope to gain by boldness. To choose the former, as democratic socialists traditionally have done, may mean to forego the possibilities of realizing the latter. . . .

While still in the early agitational state, . . . movements demanded total revolutionary change. But this stage could last only so long as the movements were illegal or comparatively small radical sects. Once a movement achieves legality and wins broad lower-class support, it finds that an ultrarevolutionary, antisocietal approach tends to repel groups who want a change but are not completely dissatisfied with the *status quo*. At this stage, radical parties must make a choice: either continue to try to win majority support for an all-out radical socialist program, without compromising the original revolutionary doctrine, or seek to win votes for a limited set of objectives by compromising and modifying the parts of the program that challenge the basic values of the more stable groups. . . .

The history of most leftist parties has been largely an evolution from the class-conscious internationalist Marxist position to an "opportunistic" national appeal in which large segments of the population are wooed with specific planks directed to their own interests. Socialist parties originally envisaged socialism as a society in which there would be some form of social ownership of all industry, business, and land. This concept has gradually been modified until today many socialist movements stand for national economic planning, state ownership of certain large-scale monopolies, private ownership of most of industry and the distribution system, and the maintenance and extension of family-owned farms.[50]

With this change in economic doctrine has come a shift in the cultural and philosophic phases of socialism. Antagonism to religion has died away, and efforts have been made to link socialism and religion. Opposition to patriotism and symbols of nationalism has also disappeared. Antagonism to the monarchy has died among the socialists of the British Commonwealth and Scandinavia and, until they consolidated power, among the Communists of Rumania. . . .

The social changes introduced by *democratic* radical movements appear to result more from objective pressures in the society for such

[50] See W. E. Walling, *Socialism As It Is* (New York: Macmillan Co., 1912), for a discussion of ideological shifts of socialist parties before the First World War. See also Franz Borkenau, *Socialism, National or International* (London: G. Routledge and Sons, Ltd., 1942).

changes than from a small doctrinaire minority converting the majority of the population. The stronger a radical social movement becomes in a democracy, the less radical it appears in terms of the general cultural values. As it captures society, society captures it. The amount of change that the movement introduces into the culture as a result of assuming power appears relatively slight compared to the original goals.

In sum, the demise of social movements through institutionalization occurs either because they develop, organizationally and ideologically, into an interest group; because their goals are made irrelevant through other social changes; or because they succeed in attaining their goals and become either a postmovement sect or the new status quo. In short, success, no matter how it may come about, sounds the death knell for social movements since their reason for being is no longer relevant or socially significant.

Repression

As we noted in chapter 5, temporary organized publics and social movements generally come to be viewed as nonlegitimate in terms of the conventional distribution of power in society. As a result, steps are often taken to forestall their development beyond the embryonic stage. This is not always the case, however, especially in pluralistic societies, where a certain amount of dissenting opinion is encouraged as healthy. As King suggests in Social Movements in the United States: "Unconcern is usually widespread when a movement is still at the innovation stage because so many people are unaware that it exists—or, having become aware of it, fail to see in the movement any meaning or significance for themselves. But mass apathy gradually gives way to a wide range of reaction: as the movement employs more aggressive tactics and the implication of proposals becomes more apparent, . . ." [51] *The reaction evoked by ideological movements is almost invariably negative—they are viewed as having carried dissent too far.* As Grodzins puts it: "In the political sphere, democratic society allows for easy protest. The existence of political parties channels discontents into socially approved forms . . . movements for world betterment challenge attention." [52] The repressive attention given to a social movement in pluralist societies depends upon the degree of threat that the movement is seen to pose to the conscience collective. This degree of threat is part of the social significance of a movement, which, as we pointed out in earlier chapters, varies accord-

[51] C. Wendell King, *Social Movements in the United States* (New York: Random House, 1956), p. 103.
[52] Morton Grodzins, *The Loyal and the Disloyal* (Chicago: University of Chicago Press, 1956), p. 32.

ing to historical circumstances. For example, the Communist Party of the United States (CPUSA) was relatively free to function, despite some public misgivings, for several decades prior to the advent of the so-called Cold War. After this, the CPUSA was publically condemned as a "threat" in terms of the "clear and present danger" of international Communism. Widespread repression of the CPUSA followed, including the passage of restrictive legislation such as the McCarran Act, government investigations (e.g., Senator McCarthy's Senate Committee on Government Operations and the House Committee on Un-American Activities), prosecution in the courts (e.g., the Smith Act Trials), and violent public reaction. As a result of the political climate, the CPUSA soon lost all semblance of a viable movement. In the following article, R. C. Myers illuminates the extent of overt public repression directed against the Communists in the late 1940s.

Robert C. Myers, "Anti-Communist Mob Action: A Case Study," Public Opinion Quarterly, 12 (Spring 1948), 57–67. Reprinted by permission of Robert C. Myers and Columbia University Press.

On Sunday evening, October 26, 1947, Gerhard Eisler, an acknowledged Communist of German nationality, was scheduled to address a public meeting under the auspices of the Communist Party of Mercer County, New Jersey, in a rented hall at Trenton. An attempt was made to open the meeting as scheduled, but the attempt was disrupted and eventually abandoned as a direct result of mob action. The incident provided an excellent opportunity for first-hand study of mob behavior, and it is believed that a fairly full, dispassionate account may add useful, contemporary material to the literature on this subject.

Some may accuse us of bias at the very outset because of the use of the term *mob*. (The local newspaper preferred in its early reports to call the assembled thousands of persons "a throng" and "an indignant crowd.") In the literature of social psychology and collective behavior, however, a mob is regarded as a specialized form of crowd, and there is little doubt that the collectivity in question fulfilled the definition.

PRELIMINARY REPORTS IN THE LOCAL PRESS

Several days before the scheduled meeting the City Commission of Trenton had adopted a resolution proposed by the Director of Public Safety that the management of the Contemporary Auditorium be requested to withdraw its permission for use of its auditorium for a meeting on the coming Sunday evening. The reason given for the resolution was that the meeting was being sponsored by the Communist Party of Mercer County (in which Trenton is situated) and that the chief speaker would be an alien Communist, Gerhard Eisler, who was currently at liberty pending an appeal from his conviction for contempt of the U.S. Congressional Committee on Un-American Activities.

Upon being apprised of the resolution, the management of the auditorium quickly acceded to the request and announced that it was cancelling its prior permission for use of the hall for this purpose. On the heels of this announcement, the Director of Public Safety, who is also a City Commissioner, and formerly held posts as mayor and as public prosecutor, let it be known that he had ordered the police to stand guard at the auditorium the coming Sunday evening and to "arrest anyone attempting to gain entrance there for purposes of a meeting."

During the week, the residents of Trenton had by press, radio, and rumor, been given brief blow-by-blow accounts of the attempts of the Communists to secure use of the Contemporary Auditorium for their meeting, and of the actions, taken or proposed, by the auditorium's management, the city commissioners, and the police to thwart these attempts. Then, on the Sunday morning of the meeting, the residents awoke to find these page one headlines in their only Sunday newspaper:

COURT ORDERS HALL OPENED TO EISLER; INJUNCTION ISSUED

Vice Chancellor Bigelow Opens Way For Red To Speak Here Tonight—Mayor, Other Officials Served—Vets To Stage Rally

Accompanying the two-column lead article which followed was a five by six photograph of the mayor being served with his copy of the restraining order by an attorney accompanied by a reporter. The photograph carried this legend:

With a look of scorn, Mayor Donal J. Connolly accepts from Solomon Golat a Chancery Court order restraining the City Commission, Police Department and the Contemporary from interfering with the Communist Party meeting at which Gerhard Eisler will speak tonight. John F. Norman, a *Daily Worker* reporter, stands at the right. Golat secured the injunction from Vice Chancellor John O. Bigelow on behalf of Manuel Cantor and the Communist Party of Mercer County.

The article explained that the Vice Chancellor in Newark had acted "after the Civil Rights Congress of New Jersey appealed to him to 'defend the civil rights of the Communist Party of Mercer County.'" It recounted the main events leading up to the securing of the injunction, and then quoted the mayor, upon receiving his copy, as saying, "It will be a pleasure to throw you and your kind out of City Hall any time." However, further on, the mayor was also quoted as saying, "The court has spoken and the law must be upheld. All the police facilities necessary to preserve good order will be available."

Other interesting information revealed by the article was the time (8 p.m.) and place of the scheduled Communist meeting, an announcement that the veterans would group on the State House steps (across the street from the Contemporary Auditorium) at 6:15 p.m. to "plan a program against Eisler and the supporters of his Communist philosophy," and a paragraph about Eisler having been "termed the No. 1 Communist of the country during his trial for refusal to testify before the House Committee on Un-American Activities." It also stated that Eisler had been convicted and sentenced to two years and a $1,000 fine.

Very few people work on Sunday in Trenton, and the story about the battle between the "Commies" on one side and the mayor, the police, and the "vets" on the other was the talk of the town. There was general agreement that "something ought to be done."

AGITATION

The Contemporary Auditorium is situated on State Street, the principal street of Trenton, across from the State Capitol and office buildings. A narrow alleyway from the street leads to the doors of the auditorium. On Sunday morning the auditorium's caretaker found a copy of the restraining order nailed to the door. In the afternoon the auditorium directors held a meeting, agreed to abide by the court order, and directed the caretaker to unlock the doors at 7:45 that evening.

Shortly before 6 p.m. groups of veterans, some wearing the distinctive campaign hats of their organizations, began arriving in front of the capitol buildings in response to calls from leaders of the Veterans' Alliance, representing eleven veterans' organizations in Trenton. Soon thereafter a relatively passive crowd of three or four hundred veterans had assembled, and was being addressed by seven leaders of the Alliance. This original crowd, or audience, of veterans included representatives of a colored American Legion post, Catholic War Veterans, Jewish War Veterans, and Disabled War Veterans, as well as other veterans' organizations. The leaders began to shout their directions and appeals, and their lecturings quickly assumed the character of harangues.

The gist of the leaders' appeals was that the Communists were standing on the Bill of Rights, but that the veterans would see to it that the rights of patriotic Americans were upheld and not jeopardized by the Communists.

The substance of the leaders' directions and calls for action was that an endless picket line was to be formed in front of the alleyway leading to the auditorium entrance. When the doors were opened, the veterans would thus be first to gain entrance and seize most of the seats in the hall for themselves. Thereafter, they were directed to boo and hiss everything that the Communist leader, Eisler, or his followers had to say. By this method, they reasoned, freedom of speech for both Communists and others would be upheld, but Communist doctrines would receive neither applause nor encouragement.

The harangues of the leaders, when referring to their own purposes, were interspersed with such symbolic references as: "The Constitution," "The Bill of Rights," "our way of life," "what we stand for," "Democracy," "what we fought for," "red-blooded Americans," and "The American Way." However, when the Communists and their purposes were being mentioned, the following symbolisms were most often heard: "Commies," "rats," "bastards," "sons of bitches," "Stalin-lovers," "dirt," and these were frequently modified by such words as "lousy" and "stinking." The only purposes ascribed to the Communists were to destroy the American way of life and turn the country over to Russia.

In effect, then, it was hammered home to the crowd over and over again that it was perfectly legal, correct, and necessary for "stinking lousy rats" to have freedom of speech, but that this right could be countered in "the American way" by giving full reign to the freedom of speech of "patriotic red-blooded Americans."

The original crowd of veterans was soon joined by 35 uniformed policemen under the direction of an acting captain of police and a deputy director of public safety. It was also augmented by the arrival of from three to four thousand residents of Trenton.

The auditorium doors were not opened until 8:30, so there was a period of two and one-half hours for crowd growth, pushing, shoving, muttering, yelling, swirling, packing and all the other stimuli which facilitate the transmutation of a passive crowd into an active mob.

By 8 p.m. the area between the capitol buildings and the auditorium was black with gesticulating, muttering humanity. About one out of ten were females, and, except for the very young and the aged, all age groups seemed to be fairly represented. Laughter and shouts of hilarity were not infrequent, a festive spirit of revelry quite often running through the thousands of persons as their emotions began to take over from their intellects. In the vortex of the mob were the several hundred original veterans milling about the entrance to the alleyway.

ACTION

Shortly before 8 o'clock a man and his wife from Newark wormed their way through the mob and presented themselves at the alleyway demanding admission to the auditorium.

"Who the hell do you think you are?" the man was asked.

He announced that he was a representative of the Civil Rights Congress of New Jersey.

"To hell with you," he was told. "You'll get in when we let you in."

At this point the local press of October 27 states that the man "was overheard to make a remark about 'So this is American liberty.' The word spread through the crowd and (they) were 'rushed' up State Street. They were 'rescued' by State House police and finally escorted to police headquarters."

This account, however, fails to do justice to the circumstances. Actually, as soon as the stranger said, "So this is American liberty," he was struck in the face and mouth, his glasses knocked off and broken, and he was punched and kicked at. The cry went up, "Hey, fellas, here's a coupla Commies, let's get 'em.", and everyone within reach struck out at the terrified couple. They were surrounded by a cordon of police which, with sheathed billie clubs and holstered sidearms, managed with difficulty to shove the couple through the mob to a parked patrol car and into it. But before the car could get underway the doors were jerked open, the man was pummeled some more, and the wife's clothing ripped and torn. The couple was taken to a nearby police station and placed in a detention room under what is sometimes known as "protective custody" while several hundred persons yelled and gesticulated outside the station. Soon, however, these hundreds rushed back to the main mob outside the auditorium, and the stranger and his wife were given police escort to their own car and advised to leave town.

The mob had struck first blood and howled for more.

Three men arrived surrounded by police. They made up the "welcoming committee" and were to sit on the platform and introduce Eisler. These three included the secretary of the Mercer County Communist Party, an executive committeeman of the Mercer County Communist Party, and a reporter from the New York *Daily Worker*, a Communist newspaper. They were herded by police through the mob and into the auditorium. During this procedure the jostling and shouting reached fever pitch, and frequent cries were heard such as: "Rats like you will burn in hell," "Where's the rope, boys?", "You bastards won't get out alive,"

"Lousy Commies." The county secretary, the one who had originally bearded the mayor and his commissioners in their council chambers, received the most specific abuse then and thereafter. Although two of the three Communists were of Jewish extraction, no racist appellations were shouted loud enough to be generally heard, but racist mutterings were apparent.

Tensions were built up for fifteen or twenty more minutes before the auditorium doors were finally opened. Two policemen were placed at the door where entrance tickets were sold at twenty-five cents apiece. Sixteen people are reported to have bought tickets before the shout went up, "Come on, boys, everybody in." The mob surged forward to the accompanying sound of breaking window glass and screams of semi-hysterical females. Side doors and windows were thrown open and the hall, arranged to seat but 375 persons, was quickly filled to overflowing. Persons seated on window ledges shouted word of what was transpiring inside to those left to mill about outside.

Pandemonium was general inside the hall. The three Communist committeemen sat at a table on the stage; a color-guard of veterans surrounded a large American flag planted in a standard nearby; twenty or more policemen ranged themselves between the stage and the riotous audience. The deputy director of public safety and the acting captain of police tried by sheer lung power alone (the hall had no public address system) to get some semblance of order, but to no avail. The principal speaker of the evening, Gerhard Eisler, did not appear, and it was later learned that the county secretary had managed to make a warning telephone call concerning the mob conditions that had arisen.

For over forty minutes various officials in the front of the auditorium, including the two police leaders and the leaders of the original veterans' groups, tried to get enough quiet so that the meeting at least could be opened officially, and thus the letter of the injunction obeyed. But each time any of the three acknowledged Communists on the stage arose to speak he was met with a crescendo of hoots, shouts, boos and stomping of feet. Some of the police-veteran pleas and shouted replies included the following:

Plea: "The police are here to do their duty. You can cooperate with them by sitting down and being quiet."
Answer: "We'll cooperate with the police, but not with those rats up there on the stage."
Plea: "The Director of Public Safety has ordered the police to protect these people's (i.e., the Communists') right to speak. Now, please won't you help them?"
Answer: "We'll help the cops leave the hall if that's what you mean."

Plea: "The police must stay here to maintain order. You, by your actions, are making it impossible for them to do so."

Answer: Cheers, whistles, stomping and handclapping. Yells of, "That's what we want to do, ain't it boys?"

Plea: "Men, this is no way to act. We have to obey the injunction. Now let these people on the stage talk. After all, they've rented this hall."

Answer: "Who's stopping them? Let them talk. We don't have to listen, do we?"

Plea: "These people can't talk with all this noise and disorder. Now let's be good Americans and hear what they've got to say."

Answer: "To hell with them. You listen to what the rats have got to say."

Plea: (A leader of one of the original veterans' groups) "Listen to me, fellows, I'm one of the men that started this thing. Now we didn't intend to deny anyone free speech, but simply to boo what these rats said *after* they said it. So let's be quiet for a minute, and let these rats talk."

Answer: "You're probably a damn Commie yourself. Why don't you get up there with them you goddamned Stalin-lover?" (At this sally the veteran leader blanched with the shock of the clear realization that a definite schism had taken place; that he and the other original leaders had lost all control, and that other and perhaps more sinister leaders had taken over.) [53]

Plea: "Men, that's certainly no way to talk to the commander of a respected (veteran's group) here in Trenton."

Answer: "Tell him to keep his mouth shut, then."

After every two or three pleas, hasty conferences took place between the police leaders and the three Communists on the stage. (There was no direct converse between the veteran leaders and the Communists.) It later was learned that the Communists were urging the police to call the whole thing off, but the police were insistent that attempts be continued to let the Communists be heard, if only for a very brief period, so that the police could report that the injunction had been obeyed. During these lulls the new mob leaders filled in by catcalls and by hurling taunts to the individuals on the stage, daring them to try to talk, and threatening them with the various forms of physical torture and bodily harm that were in store for them.

Plea: "Just let these men talk for one minute. Then we'll all go home."

Answer: "You go on home. Then we'll take care of those Commie bastards."

[53] LaPiere, in his *Collective Behavior*, and other social psychologists have pointed out that mob leadership is a profession fraught with danger and uncertainty. No mob leader can be assured that he will not fall victim to the mob which he has created, and the historical record is replete with cases where just this has occurred.

Plea: "Just ten seconds—."
Answer: "Hell, no. They'll have their ten seconds when we get hold of them."

During the forty minutes that this sort of thing had been going on there had been occasional attempts on the part of persons near the front to gain the stage. These had been gently pushed back by the police.

After the failure to gain even ten seconds of silence, the police and veteran leaders found themselves in agreement with the Communists that it would be impossible to comply with the injunction order. The press states that the reporter from the *Daily Worker* said, at this point, to the deputy director of public safety: "In the interest of their (the mob's) safety I give you permission to call off the meeting."

Plea: "The meeting's called off. Go on home."
Answer: "Come on, get the Commies to go first; we'll go after them."

The original group of veterans commenced singing "The Star Spangled Banner," and were joined in this by all in the hall, including those on the stage. Everybody stood and faced toward the flag during the singing.

Immediately upon conclusion of the national anthem cries arose: "Here they come, boys, get ready." and the mob parted down the middle of the auditorium, making a gauntlet from stage to entrance door. Individuals along the gauntlet's side spit upon their hands and rubbed them together. They made beckoning motions toward the stage, and shouted: "Come on you sons of bitches. We're ready for you."

Police on the stage stood in front and behind the three intended victims of the mob. It appeared as though an attempt would be made to run the mob's gauntlet. Suddenly the victims and their guardians turned on their heels and disappeared through a back exit of the stage.

For perhaps one or two seconds dead silence prevailed. Then, with a roar of rage, the mob surged up and over the stage, sweeping aside and, in one case, knocking to the floor the police left between mob and quarry. But the three Communists had escaped in a police car.

AFTERMATH

The next day the Trenton *Evening Times* printed an editorial pointing out that "there is no question that the democratic way was not upheld last night." The editorial commenced with this sentence: "Communism is hateful and despicable," and ended with the admonition: "Let us remember that our strength lies in the right of every man to believe, to read, to write and to speak as he chooses. That's the way to lick Communism."

Investigators found general approval of the fact that the Communists had been prevented from speaking. There was some mild disapproval of the mob activities, but the blame was most often placed upon the Chancery Court rather than elsewhere; the rationalization being: "The whole thing would never have happened if the judge had refused to issue that injunction."

Rationalizations regarding the failure to uphold the ideology of freedom of speech tended to fall into these two patterns:

"Freedom of speech can be carried too far. If you knew that a bunch of cut-throats were going to have a meeting to discuss how best to cut your throat, you'd do everything you could to stop the meeting wouldn't you? Well, this thing here last night was exactly the same thing."

"They got just what we'd get in Russia. There's no sense letting them get away with stuff here that we'd be shot for in Russia, is there?"

The New Jersey Communist Party issued a statement blaming the Trenton affair on the "Fascist-like hysteria whipped up by veteran leaders, the police, the mayor and the City Commission of Trenton, and by (the) Governor."

Five days after the mob action, a statement was issued by the Veterans Alliance disclaiming responsibility for the events that had occurred. Among the signatories were leaders of the original group who had agitated for picketing and booing. This statement observed that, "Members of the Alliance, who spoke and urged that the Communists be heard, did so to protect the right of free speech guaranteed to all in our United States Constitution," and, in reference to the mob leaders who had taken over from the veteran leaders, the statement charged that, "those self-styled Americans, who imitated Stalinite, hoodlum tactics, recreated by their perverted acts of violence methods despised by both veteran and non-veteran alike. Their type of demonstration is to be deplored and denounced."

Following this disavowal on the part of the veterans, the local press freely utilized the word "mob" instead of "indignant crowd" when referring to the activities of the previous Sunday evening.

Meanwhile, the full report of the President's Committee on Civil Rights had been made public. A quotation from the introduction to Section IV of this report was widely publicized. It said: "The pervasive gap between our aims and what we actually do is creating a kind of moral dry rot which eats away at the emotional and rational bases of democratic beliefs. There are times when the difference between what we preach about civil rights and what we practice is shockingly illustrated by individual outrages. There are times when the whole structure of our ideology is made ridiculous by individual instances. And there are certain continuing, quiet, omnipresent practices which do irreparable damage to our beliefs."

The events of October 26 were neither bizarre nor unique, but followed fairly closely the patterns of mob behavior which have been outlined by psychologists and sociologists. They cannot, however, be considered unimportant. Mounting international tensions, combined with the instability of certain social norms at home, provide a fertile soil for similar phenomena in other cities, and several such disturbances have occurred since the affair at Trenton. To those who would see the United States play a major role in the furtherance of civil liberties throughout the world, the understanding—and prevention—of mob action must present an objective of first rank.

The fate of the Black Muslims in America followed a similar path to that of the CPUSA. This organization existed for a decade prior to the civil rights disturbances of the late 1950s and early 1960s. Only then was it perceived as a threat and subjected to repression.

To summarize, the extent to which a social movement is subject to repression depends upon the advent of historical events which render the movement a threat to the status quo. History, then, can not only make a movement socially significant but can also accelerate negative responses to it. Outright repression of a social movement is most common in elitist social systems, where this technique is usually applied to the movement, particularly the leadership, in its early stages of development. In pluralist systems, repression is usually associated with conditions of political hysteria and temporary ascendancy of elitist elements. Repressive incidents like the Centralia massacre of members of the Industrial Workers of the World ("Wobblies") in 1919 and the assaults on demonstrators at the Democratic national convention in Chicago in 1968, although dramatic, are still rare in pluralist societies and hardly match the Stalinist purges in the Soviet Union during the late 1930s or the suppression of the Hungarian Revolution in 1956. A much more common mode of truncation in pluralist societies is through discreditation.

Discreditation

The techniques of discreditation most commonly employed by the holders of power in pluralist societies are: (1) public degradation and ridicule of a movement or its leadership; (2) denigration or amelioration of the problems leading to the consciousness of dysfunction which gives purpose to a movement. In recent decades the first technique, as applied by means of a controlled mass media, has been the most effective device for truncating social movements. Public degradation has altered the course of on-going movements such as the Universal Improvement Association (the Garvey Movement), the Townsend Movement, and the Industrial Workers of the World (IWW). Both Marcus Garvey and Dr. Townsend were publicly attacked by the mass media and accused of misappropriation of funds. The IWW, on the other hand, was vilified by charges of Communism and subversion. During World War I, the "Wobblies" were accused of treason for their refusal to support Wilson's "war to end all wars." During the Seattle strike of 1919, one editorial attacking the IWW was headed, "This is America not Russia." At the same time, according to Cook, "A cartoon entitled 'Not in a Thousand Years' showed the Red banner flying over the Stars and Stripes." [54] Ever since the Russian Revolution, "red baiting" has been a favorite tactic in America, and nearly every labor reform movement has at one time or another been subject to it.

A recent example of discreditation occurred in connection with the Vietnam Moratorium Day observed throughout North America on October 15, 1969. Four days later, at a Republican fund-raising dinner in New Orleans, Vice President Spiro Agnew spoke of the youthful Moratorium supporters in the following vein:

> Sometimes, it appears that we are reaching a period when our senses and our minds will no longer respond to moderate stimulation. We seem to be approaching an age of the gross. Persuasion through speeches and books is too often discarded for disruptive demonstrations aimed at bludgeoning the unconvinced into action.
>
> The young—and by this I don't mean by any stretch of the imagination all the young, but I'm talking about those who claim to speak for the young —at the zenith of physical power and sensitivity, overwhelm themselves with drugs and artificial stimulants. Subtlety is lost, and fine distinctions based on acute reasoning are carelessly ignored in a headlong jump to a predetermined conclusion. Life is visceral rather than intellectual, and the most visceral practitioners of life are those who characterize themselves as intellectuals.
>
> Truth to them is "revealed" rather than logically proved, and the principal infatuations of today revolve around the social sciences, those subjects which can accommodate any opinion and about which the most reckless conjecture cannot be discredited.
>
> Education is being redefined at the demand of the uneducated to suit the ideas of the uneducated. The student now goes to college to proclaim rather than to learn. The lessons of the past are ignored and obliterated in a contemporary antagonism known as the generation gap. A spirit of national masochism prevails, encouraged by an effete corps of impudent snobs who characterize themselves as intellectuals.[55]

---

[54] Fred J. Cook, *The F.B.I. Nobody Knows* (New York: The Macmillan Co., 1964), p. 82. See also R. K. Murray, *The Red Scare: A Study in National Hysteria* (Minneapolis: University of Minnesota Press, 1955).
[55] Excerpted from the text of an address at the Citizen's Testimonial Dinner, New Orleans, October 19, 1969.

Regressive movements have also been subject to some discreditation in the mass media, although attacks on the Right, as compared to those on the Left, are minimal. The San Francisco Chronicle, a liberal newspaper, in 1965 carried the following description of an official of the American Nazi Party: ". . . [he] is short with beady eyes that dart wildly as he talks. His voice is high pitched and he giggles almost constantly while conversing. His grammar is atrocious and his vocabulary limited—although from time to time he attempts to make use of pretentious words and phrases which often come out garbled." [56]

Reform movements are also prone to discreditation in the mass media, usually in the form of an "innocent dupe" or a "guilt by association" approach. During the 1950s, many liberal reform organizations such as the Americans for Democratic Action and the United World Federalists were compelled to devote a great deal of their time and literature to denials of un-Americanism and to avowals of anti-Communism so as to avoid association with the declining and discredited Left.

Mass media attempts to discredit social movements are not always effective, and may even result in reinforcing the consciousness of dysfunction and heightening the resolve of its members. For example, one study of the less-than-objective press and television coverage of the Berkeley Free Speech Movement concluded: ". . . associating a student movement with enemies of the state, lifted the movement into the area of violent attack—which it never was." [57]

Discreditation may also stem from a decline in the social significance of the issues which originally gave rise to a movement. A "movement without a cause" comes about either directly through the discreditation of its goals or programs or indirectly because a perceived remedy of the problem it addresses has taken place or because the movement's proposed solution is deemed untenable. The Single Tax Movement, Technocracy, and many organizations of the "Old Left" exemplify the latter process, while the Woman's Christian Temperance Union and the Townsend Movement have been victims of the discreditation of their goals or programs. These movements still maintain their shadow organization form, yet possess few of the characteristics of a dynamic social movement. This transformation of a movement because of the decline of the significance of the problem it addresses is illustrated in the following article on the remains of the Townsend Movement.

[56] Paul Avery, "Heil Hitler on Howard St.," *The San Francisco Chronicle*, January 25, 1965, p. 16.
[57] Colin Miller, "The Press and the Student Revolt, 1964," in Michael V. Miller and Susan Gilmore, eds., *Revolution at Berkeley* (New York: Dell Publishing Co., 1965), p. 348.

Sheldon L. Messinger, "Organizational Transformation: A Case Study of a Declining Social Movement," American Sociological Review, 20 (February 1955), 3–10. Reprinted by permission of Sheldon L. Messinger, Vice Chairman, Center for the Study of Law and Society, University of California, Berkeley, and the American Sociological Association.

It is generally recognized that the organized arms of value-oriented social movements [58] may remain intact long after the movements themselves have lost general impetus. While it is to be expected that these structures will adapt to their changed circumstances, little attention has as yet been given to either the process or product of this adaptation. This paper reports a study of certain organizational consequences of the decline of the Townsend Movements.

THE TOWNSEND MISSION AND THE END OF RECRUITMENT

While the old age pension movement seems to be gaining impetus in the United States, the Townsend Movement has all but vanished. To understand this seeming paradox it is necessary to examine the Townsend mission. This has been, and continues to be, not simply national pensions for the aged, but national pensions for the aged *as a mechanism for alleviating or preventing economic dislocation*. The mission is a blending of issues born of the 1930's, and the continued identification of Townsendites with it aids in understanding the movement's decline and the nature of its remaining structure.

Two sorts of data support this characterization of the Townsend mission, as well as the continued identification of the Organization with it.

First, the Townsend Plan,[59] major subject of most Townsend pronouncements, has maintained features directly linking pensions to economic reconstruction. Its provision requiring that the pension be spent

[58] "Value-oriented social movements" is a phrasing suggested to the writer by Ralph H. Turner. It refers to social movements fundamentally oriented toward rendering some change in the social structure and of sufficient force to develop organization.

[59] That version which received the widest publicity may be found in the pamphlet *Old Age Revolving Pensions, A National Plan . . . Proposed by Dr. F. E. Townsend* (Long Beach, California: Old Age Revolving Pensions, Ltd., 1934). For a more recent version see *Townsend National Weekly*, August 1, 1953. (These and other pamphlets, letters and newspapers cited here may be found in the Townsend Archives, Library, University of California, Los Angeles.)

within thirty days is intended to provide jobs by keeping money in circulation. Its stipulation that prospective recipients must cease work to become eligible is designed to combat "technological unemployment." [60] These are the key to Townsend claims that theirs is not "just another pension plan." Further, leaders justify changes in other features of the Plan as occasioned by the aim of economic reconstruction. For example, the famous "200 dollars a month," from the first a legislative impediment, was formally discarded in all forms in 1943. Informally it is still mentioned as "essential to the Plan" in the sense that at least this much is requisite to "keep the economy going." Other changeable features, justified in all their forms as necessary to economic reconstruction, include the means of financing and designation of those to receive the pension.

Second, the Organization aside from the Plan has continued to link the pension and depression issues. In 1936, a year after passage of national social security legislation, the Organization changed its name from "Old Age Revolving Pensions, Ltd." to "Townsend National Recovery Plan, Inc.," emphasizing that its mission was far from complete. Not until 1948 did the less anachronous "Townsend Plan, Inc." become the organizational style. The *Townsend National Weekly*, official newspaper of the Organization, has become since 1941 a veritable compendium of "signs" pointing to "impending" economic disaster. Throughout World War II and the post-war boom, Townsendites continued to circulate tracts stressing that their Organization aimed at "a program to bring about full industrial production for the Nation . . . [and] make jobs for the jobless." [61]

While such aims may again gain currency, it is suggested that under the changed conditions following the end of the depression the Townsend mission was deprived of relevance. Continued identification with this mission has constituted a serious block to Townsend membership maintenance and to the recruitment of new Townsendites. Combined with the short life-expectancies of old Townsendites, this has meant a rapid depletion of the Organization's ranks (see Table 1).[62] In this situation,

---

[60] See, e.g., *Do You Really Know the Townsend Plan?*, n.d.: a pamphlet published during World War II and still circulated.

[61] *Why I Am For the Townsend Plan* (Cleveland, Ohio: Townsend Press, n.d.).

[62] Since the age-sex composition of the Townsend membership is not available, it is not possible to gauge with any accuracy the loss of membership due to death and that due to dropping out. However, the large yearly membership declines following 1939 (when yearly figures first became available) indicate that major losses came from dropouts. See Abraham Holtzman, "The Townsend Movement: A Study in Old Age Pressure Politics," unpublished doctoral dissertation, Harvard University, Cambridge, Mass., 1952, p. 267, for yearly Townsend membership figures 1939–1951.

The long-run personnel problem is, of course, effective recruitment. The considered opinion of Townsend leaders and members is that remaining Townsendites are all "old-timers." In personal contacts with over one hundred California Townsendites, the

TABLE 1. NATIONAL AND CALIFORNIA TOWNSEND MEMBERSHIP DECLINE, 1936–1951 *

	National Membership	Per Cent Drop	California Membership	Per Cent Drop
1936	2,250,000		330,000	
1951	56,656	97.5	6,839	97.9

* Sources: National and California membership figures for 1936 from U.S. House of Representatives, Select Committee Investigating Old Age Pension Organizations pursuant to H. Res. 443, *Hearings*, 74th Cong., 2nd Sess., Washington, D.C.: 1936 (hereafter: *Hearings: H. Res.* 443), pp. 41–42, 208. National membership for 1951 from Holtzman, *loc. cit.* California membership figure for 1951 compiled from records in the Townsend Archives.

other "single-minded" old age groups, working to modify existing state aid legislation, have developed to absorb the membership which might earlier have gone to the Townsendites. It is in this context that the Townsend Organization has been transformed.

ORGANIZATIONAL TRANSFORMATION

The Tendency to Deflection. Townsend leaders have attempted to cope with the challenge to their social base. In the process, they have been constrained to direct action in ways deflecting the Organization from its central mission.

The first indication of this tendency came in early 1940 when California Townsendites were urged to aid in qualifying an initiative readjusting state aid legislation.[63] While the campaign was brief and the initiative was not qualified, the event is noteworthy since before this time national leaders had actively campaigned against any proposal at the state level.[64] Further, they had always carefully disassociated themselves from state

---

writer found no variation in this conjecture and met only one person who had joined the Organization since 1948. The growth of such structures as George McLain's California Institute of Social Welfare, since 1941 the major old age pressure group on the California scene, is an additional indication of what has happened to Townsend recruitment. Of McLain's 60–70,000 members in 1953, less than one per cent had ever belonged to the Townsend Organization. (According to a questionnaire administered by the Institute of Industrial Relations, University of California, Berkeley.)

[63] The text of the proposal is given in full in *Townsend National Weekly*, California Edition, April 13, 1940. Its major aim was to block state recovery measures directed at old age aid recipients. For evidence that the tendency to deflection, detailed here only for the California case, was general throughout the Organization see Holtzman, *op. cit.*, p. 512ff.

[64] See Holtzman, *op. cit.*, p. 510ff.

"aid" proposals. The "pension," on a national level and not involving indigence requirements, was the proper Townsend goal.

Leadership purposes in supporting this proposal are not far to seek. Urging his lieutenants to support the measure, the California leader said: "Even if we should fail [to qualify it], it is believed we can secure enough publicity and good will to justify the effort. We think we can enlist many to join our ranks as a result of this campaign." [65]

In 1943, California Townsendites entered a full-blown campaign for state old age pensions.[66] The nature of this measure permitted it to be presented by both national [67] and state leaders as a "first step" toward the national Townsend Plan. Thus, while only a state-wide proposal with a dollar demand geared to existing state aid legislation (60 dollars was asked), both the "compulsory spending" and "cease work" features of the national Plan were intact. Further, indigence requirements were absent, meaning effectively the end of a state "aid" program and the institution of "pensions" if the measure passed.[68]

The initiative was qualified and placed before the voters in November 1944. It was defeated by over a million votes.[69]

By 1947 membership was at a new low, recruitment at a dead halt, and George McLain's old age pressure-group successfully competing for the allegiance of the California aged. Aware of the challenge, the California leader proposed a new local effort to national headquarters by saying:

[Even] Dr. Townsend [who is generally opposed to local efforts] has consistently said that "we *must* put on an initiative in California . . . even if we know we will fail before we start. . . . [This] for the reason that GM [George McLain] has announced that he, too, is going to sponsor a constitutional amendment proposing practically the same objectives. . . . If we fail to present . . . [a local] program, it is only natural that a large number of our own members will be inclined to support him in his efforts. . . . Many people have

[65] Letter from John C. Cuneo, National Representative [for California], Townsend National Recovery Plan, Inc. (hereafter: TNRP, Inc.), to Members of the [California] State Advisory Board, Modesto, California: n.d. (mim.).
[66] The proposal may be found in State of California, Secretary of State, *Proposed Amendments to Constitution, General Election, 1944* (hereafter: Proposed Amendments: 1944) (Sacramento, California: State Printing Office, 1944), p. 11.
[67] Holtzman (*op. cit.*, p. 516) reports that national headquarters contributed over 69,000 dollars to the California campaign. Further, speakers were provided and the *Townsend National Weekly* covered the campaign in detail.
[68] In George McLain's opinion it also meant the end of grants-in-aid under Federal Social Security Legislation, as he took pains to point out in his "argument Against Initiative Proposition No. 11," *Proposed Amendments: 1944*, p. 12. He added: "The proposed law would pension rich and poor alike, thereby lessening the value of the dollar in the hands of the needy—an unjust and vicious proposal." Compare this with later Townsendite handling of McLain issues, below.
[69] State of California, Secretary of State, *Statement of Vote, General Election, 1944* (Sacramento: California State Printing Office, 1944), p. 29.

lost hope and interest in any national program becoming a reality in the near future.⁷⁰

By no stretch of the imagination could the new measure proposed by state leaders be identified as a "little Townsend Plan." ⁷¹ First, unlike the 1943–1944 proposal, it was specifically drawn within the framework of existing state legislation for old age assistance and indigence requirements were present.⁷² Second, both the all-important "compulsory spending" and "cease work" provisions of the Plan were absent. Townsend propaganda could no longer claim that their measure would effect any significant change in the economic structure.⁷³

National leaders at first opposed making a new localized proposal on the grounds that another defeat would do the Movement's national position no good.⁷⁴ In August 1947, conceding to California's pressures, they suggested that campaign funds should be raised *outside* the Organization.⁷⁵ As late as October 1947, in the midst of efforts to raise money in California for the promotion of the initiative, national leaders carried out two mass meetings in the state to collect funds for national headquarters over the unanswered objections of the California leader.⁷⁶

By June 1948 it was clear that Townsendites had not qualified their initiative, but that McLain had qualified his. State leaders remained as silent as possible in the face of this proposal with "practically the same objectives" and tried to refocus membership attention on national issues.⁷⁷

⁷⁰ Letter from John C. Cuneo, California State Organizer, TNRP, Inc. to Robert C. Townsend (son of Dr. F. E. Townsend and *de facto* head of the Organization), Treasurer, TNRP, Inc., Modesto, California: August 14, 1947.
⁷¹ The initiative, which may be found in the Townsend Archives, proposed raising state aid to 75 dollars per month, reduction of recipients' age to 60 years, and institution of a one per cent "gross income tax" to finance the measure.
⁷² It is clear from the *Minutes* of [the Townsend California] State Council Meeting at Los Angeles, California, July 26 to 27, 1947, p. 2, that California strategists felt a lesson of the 1943–1944 campaign to have been that the closer to existing legislation, the more chance of success.
⁷³ About this time, Townsend state leaders began to talk about instituting the "fundamental principles" of the Plan. This euphemism has since spread to the national level. In the 1947–1948 campaign the "gross income tax" was offered as "the fundamental principle."
⁷⁴ Letter from Robert C. Townsend, Treasurer, TNRP, Inc. to John C. Cuneo, California State Organizer, TNRP, Inc., Cleveland, Ohio: July 17, 1947.
⁷⁵ Letter from Robert C. Townsend, Treasurer, TNRP, Inc. to John C. Cuneo, California State Organizer, TNRP, Inc., Cleveland, Ohio: August 14, 1947.
⁷⁶ It should be noted that during the October national call the California leader advised members to raise money for *it* outside the Organization! See *California Club Bulletin*, Modesto, California: September 6, 1947.
⁷⁷ Of particular interest in this connection is the *California Club Bulletin*, Modesto, California: June 10, 1948, immediately following notification of the failure of the initiative to qualify for the ballot. State leaders also indirectly recommended a "no" vote on the McLain initiative through an issue-endorsing group of which they were members. See *News Letter* of the California Legislative Conference, San Francisco, California: n.d. Probably sent October 1948.

The passage of McLain's constitutional amendment at the polls was quickly followed by a move for repeal. When the repeal initiative qualified, California Townsend leaders faced a serious dilemma. They could not support repeal, for the advantages brought to the aged by McLain's amendment were patent—e.g., a raise in monthly grant, the end of "relative's responsibility." Nor could they fight repeal, lest an issue now entirely identified with McLain absorb all their membership's attention and funds. To meet the situation, California leaders tried to straddle the fence by proposing measures to the legislature to supplant McLain's.[78] National leadership, on the other hand, insisted that the Townsend Organization stay clear of the battle, on the belated grounds that it was for national, not state, pensions. In July 1949, with a repeal measure on the ballot, the California leader wrote the following to national headquarters:

We [California leaders] thought that [some anti-repeal statement] was necessary as many of our members are supporting McLain financially and attending his meetings, to do what they can to hold the gains they have received. . . . [Now, in view of your position] . . . it seems all we can do is drift; let McLain get the money and our members and let things take their course and keep trying to focus attention of the Washington, D.C. work.[79]

As late as 1953, the crisis continued. Too weak to promote state legislation directly, state leadership fluctuated between "preserving gains" made by others, "preventing setbacks," all within the framework of state aid legislation, and focusing attention on national issues. But now, for state leaders, the national issue, above all, is simply success. Late in 1952 the California leader wrote:

I realize that we have always felt that it was necessary to stick to our "full program," but if the Republicans will not now accept it "in full," it seems to me that we should try to take the lead with a bill *they will accept* and get something during the next session. . . . I feel that if we don't do something along this line, we can expect McLain to capitalize on the situation and we will lose more and more of our few supporters.[80]

---

[78] At least this was their declared intent; it is not clear whether action was taken. The California leader was driven to state his intentions by "the continued statements by Geo. H. McLain . . . inferring that Townsend Plan leaders and I in particular, are uniting with 'reactionary groups' to try to repeal [the McLain amendment] . . . THE TRUTH IS your leaders are on the job doing everything possible to see that the major gains made . . . ARE PRESERVED." *Intra-organizational Bulletin*, Modesto, California: January 22, 1949.

[79] Letter from John C. Cuneo, California State Organizer, Townsend Plan, Inc. (hereafter: TP, Inc.) to Robert C. Townsend, Treasurer, TP, Inc., Modesto, California: July 28, 1949.

[80] Letter from John C. Cuneo, California State Organizer, TP, Inc. to Robert C. Townsend, Treasurer, TP, Inc., Modesto, California: November 8, 1952.

What we have seen here is a tendency to deflection from central aims on the part of Townsend leaders. At the national level, this tendency has been largely checked through a clearer appreciation of the "drift of things" by national leaders themselves. For this drift could only eventuate in the break-up of the national Organization. At the state level, leaders have tended to exchange identity for security in their search for a viable mission. But here, the pressure from national leadership, plus the successful capturing of vital issues by competing groups,[81] have served to hold state leaders within the Organization and to the Townsend mission.

The Tendency to Salesmanship. Loss of mass support has brought increasing financial difficulty to the Townsend Organization.[82] Adaptation to this circumstance has transformed Townsend leader-follower relations in such a way as to make recruit interest in the Townsend mission increasingly problematical.

Aside from advertising in the *Townsend National Weekly*,[83] early Townsend income came largely from the small contributions of individual members. Propaganda materials were sold in large quantities, and royalties accrued from such items as Townsend auto-stickers, buttons, and license-plate holders. It is to be noted that all of these devices *assume commitment on the part of contributors* to the Townsend Organization and its mission.

By 1939, however, members were being urged to purchase consumable items bearing the Townsend name. This year saw a Townsend candy bar, then "Townsend Old Fashioned Horehound Drops." In 1940, a Townsend coffee was announced. A little later a "Townsend Club Toilet Soap" and a "Townsend Club Granulated Soap" appeared. In all of these enterprises the Organization merely lent its name; funds, if received, accrued from royalties. The change from auto-stickers, etc., was small but significant because purchases of these new items did not assume commitment to the Organization or its Plan. Townsendites were urged to ask for these items at their usual shopping places, thus, to encourage store owners to stock them. The Organization had yet to become a distributor itself. This was to come.[84]

[81] This should be taken to include the identification of the Townsend Organization with its traditional mission (*i.e.*, national pensions for economic reconstruction) by relevant publics. It is not a simple matter to escape an identity long and actively sought. Such escape is even more difficult when competing leaderships continually remind potential members of past failures.
[82] See Holtzman, *op. cit.*, pp. 313–318, 549–550, for 1934–1951 income figures.
[83] While income from this source was large in the early days of the Organization, it also seems that in those days this revenue went into pockets of Dr. Townsend and the "co-founder" of the Organization, Robert E. Clements. See *Hearings: H. Res. 443, passim.*, on this point. Such revenues are, of course, dependent on mass circulation, and presently the newspaper carries little advertising.
[84] Mention of these early items may be found in *California Club Bulletins* for 1939–1940. Apparently none were successful; they are gone without a trace in 1953.

Beginning in 1943, a series of health foods was offered to members. Of these, "Dr. Townsend's Vitamins and Minerals" soon became the major item. At first distributed only from national headquarters, by 1951 state offices had become distribution points, and Club members were selling pills on commission. In this year, the pills provided one-fifth of the total national income. Intra-organizational communications of all kinds reveal in this period a striking shift from programmatic matters to concern with promoting this product. Perhaps even more significant for the long run, advertising of the pills has come to leave the Organization and its Plan unmentioned. The most elaborate piece yet prepared (1953) is simply titled "Vitamins and Minerals by Francis E. Townsend, M.D." Its message is entirely one of "health" and "price." Headquarters for the pills is identified as "Dr. Townsend's Vitamins and Minerals" rather than the earlier "Townsend Plan, Inc." Besides this, national radio advertising has been considered, and discussions of this matter have placed promotion of the Plan aside.

This type of money-raising activity is to be clearly differentiated from that of earlier days. Townsend leaders have come to purvey items whose purchase assumes no commitment to the Townsend mission. The pills, especially, are amenable for presentation to others, *once to be seen as potential Townsendites*, without invoking any discussion of the Organization and its aims.

The transformation of leadership activities from the presentation of a program to the purveying of products can be traced in the present approach to recruitment as well. In May 1952, discussing a proposal to offer a 50 per cent commission to members who brought in new recruits, Dr. Townsend said: "We have innumerable people in our clubs who can be taught to sell. Let's push them into learning by making it necessary to do so if they wish to remain members of a club. After they have learned *what* to do, I believe they will continue to do—with a fifty per cent bait as inducement." [85]

In October of the same year, national headquarters distributed a "training manual" designed to "double the readership of *Townsend National Weekly* and the membership of each Townsend club." [86] The striking quality of this "manual" is that it makes clear that Townsend leaders *no longer even seek active support at large*. The issue has become simply support in itself. Members are told: "Many big business organizations give their salesmen sales manuals written from long experience in the technique of winning friends to a product. We've done the same for you. . . . Whether you're building a model boat or being a BUSY BEE,

---

[85] Letter from Dr. F. E. Townsend, President, TP, Inc. to Mildred Atwood, Secretary to John C. Cuneo, Los Angeles, California: May 19, 1952.
[86] *The Busy Bee Program*, n.p.: n.d. The "program" was part of a contest with prizes for those enlisting the most new members and readers.

tools and technique are the secret of success." [87] How to extract the "cost" in manageable installments is outlined; little is said about the urgency or value of the mission at hand. The total impression received is that the best salesman is he who receives money with the least pain to the customer. And this is no doubt correct. For Townsend leaders no longer seek "converts" so much as "customers."

The Tendency to "Pure" Recreation. Membership activity at the level of the Clubs [88] provides a final example of the transformation of the Townsend Organization.

Townsend Club "business meetings" are remarkably similar in both form and content. Similarity of form has been encouraged by the various *Townsend Club Manuals*, each containing a procedural outline, plus local leadership unpracticed in organizational ways. Whatever variation is found in content is largely accounted for by the make-up of the Club membership. Clubs with a preponderance of highly religious members substitute "sings" for card playing. Aside from formalities, Club meetings are given to discussions of plans for social activities such as are discussed below. The usual meeting is attended by less than fifteen persons, lasts a half an hour, and is adjourned. But no one leaves. More likely than not, five or ten more people enter. Card tables are set up, and what seems to the writer to be the "real" business of the evening begins: recreation. This latter may last for several hours.[89]

This pattern may even be formalized. Examination of Club minutes often revealed that at some time in the past a motion had carried to limit the "business meeting" to an hour or less. Not all members agree that this is the proper order of things. Almost every Club has its "vocal Townsendite," a member always ready to take the floor and present the Organizational mission. Precisely toward these members such motions had been directed. The "vocal Townsendite," once perhaps a Club president, had become an outcast in his own Club. If in any executive role, he can ordinarily be found on the membership committee—a position nobody seemed to want, for obvious reasons. And even there he may remain under fire: many members feel that the membership committees misrepresent Club aims by "selling the Plan too hard," *i.e.*, presenting its realization as imminent ("even now").

[87] *Ibid.*
[88] The Clubs, established early in the history of the Organization, have always played an important role for Townsend leaders as nuclei for education, recruitment, and fundraising. From 1100 Clubs in California in 1936, only 123 were left in 1952. They have shown a steady decrease in average membership, as well as numbers, since 1939 (the first year for which yearly records are available). E.g., in 1939 there were 91.3 members per California Club; in 1952, 45.0. (These figures are derived from records in the Townsend Archives.)
[89] At one large Los Angeles Club, far along in the transformation process described here, the meeting at 11 a.m. finds less than ten persons present. By 1 p.m., when card playing begins, there are ordinarily *over* 50 persons present. A check indicated that less than one-third of these had ever been members of the Townsend Organization.

Not only are membership social activities built right into Club meetings, but some Clubs have additional "pot-luck nights" or "weekly dances" specifically designed to attract non-members. These activities would seem to furnish ideal occasions for recruitment and the distribution of Townsend propaganda. The evidence in hand suggests that once they did, but no more. Several Club leaders informed the writer that propagandizing would only lower participation, thus reduce sorely needed funds. As public interest in the Plan has flagged, there has been a related change in the nature of Townsend social activities. They have become from the viewpoint of Townsend Club leaders purely fund-raising devices. In turn these activities have become, from the viewpoint of non-member participants, purely social.

The "vocal Townsendite" may object to this. In one Los Angeles Club a member insisted that the *Townsend National Weekly* be sold at social events and recruiting attempts be made. This same member, then Club president, was the occasion of so much dissension in Club ranks that he was not re-elected—which is unusual in Club histories. The next (and 1953) president, while mildly unhappy that many who attend Club social functions "don't know what we stand for," seems more distressed by any falling-off of attendance at these affairs. Further, he regards social groups (e.g., public park dance clubs) as his "most serious competition," not the McLain Organization.

This phenomenon is not far different from that of the Townsend pills. The object of these affairs, as with the pills, is to raise money. This is best done, now, on a "business" basis. The business at hand, in this instance is providing recreation. And to this business local Townsend leaders apply themselves.

SUMMARY AND CONCLUSIONS: THE PROCESS AND PRODUCT OF ADAPTATION TO DECLINE

In the ascendant phases, when social forces press for reconstruction and changes are still in the offing, the concern of leaders and members of social movements alike is with those things that must be done to translate discontent into effective and concerted action. An evident condition of this orientation is discontent itself. In turn, this discontent must be supplied or renewed by social forces which, it must be believed, can be ameliorated by banding together. These provide the dynamic of value-oriented social movements, as well as the characteristic missions with which their organized arms become identified.

When the movements themselves lose impetus through a shift in the co. stellation of social forces, their organized arms are deprived of conditions necessary to sustain them in their original form. But organizations are not necessarily dissolved by the abatement of the forces initially conjoining to produce them. They may gain a certain degree of autonomy from their bases and continue to exist. We will expect, however, that the abatement of the particular constellation of social forces giving rise to the movement will have important consequences for the remaining structure. The most general of these is, perhaps, increasing lack of public concern for the organizational mission. This is reflected in the ending of public discussion of the issues which the organization represents or, perhaps better put, with these issues in the frame of reference that they are placed by organizational representatives. Within the organization, the abatement of social forces spells dropping membership and, more serious in the long run, the end of effective recruitment. This latter may be reinforced by the development of alternative organizational structures competing for the same potential membership. The end of recruitment is quickly transformed into financial difficulty. Where the organization has been geared to financial support from its own adherents, this last consequence will be especially crucial.

The organized arms of declining social movements will tend to adapt to these changed conditions in characteristic ways. We can broadly describe this adaptation by asserting that the dominating orientation of leaders and members shifts *from the implementation of the values the organization is taken to represent* (by leaders, members, and public alike), *to maintaining the organizational structure as such*, even at the loss of the organization's central mission.[90] To this end, leaders will be constrained to direct action toward new issues or in new ways which will attenuate the organization's identification with the particular set of aims held to be central to it. In this process, the locus of issue-selection will tend to move outside the organization, to alternative leaderships who highlighted the growing irrelevance to most of the traditional central mission. Presumably, a new mission may be found.[91] Where this is not the case, leaders will be forced to search out new means of financing as the traditional mode of appeal and reap falls on fewer and deafer ears. In this process, members, and especially potential members, will cease to be regarded as "converts" and will come to be seen as "customers." Finally, membership activities, initiated in a context of declining public interest to support a faltering organization, will work to turn what were once the

[90] We do not mean to indicate that leaders do not at all times perform maintenance functions. The crucial issues are what they must do, under changed conditions, to accomplish this and the explicitness with which the function is carried out.

[91] This seems unlikely. It would seem to involve, as a minimum, a shift in the organization's core membership, highly identified with the central mission; as well as a shift in perspective that most leaderships seem unable to make. Further, the identification of the organization with its traditional mission by prospective members is almost assured by the actions of alternative leaders competing for this same social base.

incidental rewards of participation into its only meaning. This last, by altering the basis for whatever recruitment may take place, would seem to insure that the organization, if it continues to exist, will be changed from a value-implementing agency to a recreation facility. In sum, the organizational character will stand transformed.

In sum, discreditation, either of a movement itself or of the problem it addresses, is the most common process of truncation in pluralist societies and is facilitated by a mass media attuned to the values of the conscience collective. It does not incur the same liberal "backlash" that more overt repression does, yet it effectively minimizes the ability of a movement to effect changes in the distribution of power in the society.

DISSENSION

Not all the threats to the existence of a movement are external. We have already referred to the institutionalization of reform movements through bureaucratization. Internal problems of viability are also frequently related to ideology. As we have pointed out in earlier chapters, ideology is an essential element in the emergence and growth of a social movement, but it can also hamper the ability of a movement to sustain itself.[92] The concept of "radical opposition," which Wilson and Wilson use to refer to uncontrollable conflict within a social structure, can be used to characterize the internecine ideological warfare which has plagued many social movements, particularly revolutionary ones.[93] Perhaps the classic illustration of rigid ideological purity is found in the refusal of the German Communist Party to unite with the Social Democrats in opposing Hitler in 1932. A year later, leaders of both political groups were in concentration camps.

Personality disputes, which are usually related to ideological differences, can also hamper the effectiveness of a social movement. This often takes the form of questioning the legitimacy of leadership, citing personal ambition, or collusion with the status quo social system. Within the Negro movement, Black Power militants such as Eldridge Cleaver and Huey Newton have labeled leaders such as Roy Wilkins, Whitney Young, and Thurgood Marshall as "house niggers" because of their acceptance of the norms of the power holders of American society.

[92] See, for example, Egon Bittner, "Radicalism and the Organization of Radical Movements," *American Sociological Review*, 28 (December 1963): 928–940.
[93] Godfrey and Monica Wilson, *The Analysis of Social Change* (Cambridge: Cambridge University Press, 1945), esp. pp. 125–157.

The American Left of the 1920s and 1930s, especially those organizations adhering to Marxist-Leninist doctrines, provides an excellent illustration of the processes of internal dissension and fragmentation. The variables involved have been examined by Robert Alexander in his article on left wing splinter groups, which is excerpted below.

Excerpts from Robert J. Alexander, "Splinter Groups in American Radical Politics," Social Research, 20 (October 1953), 282–283, 306–310. Reprinted by permission of R. J. Alexander and the New School for Social Research.

One of the striking political developments in the United States during the last twelve years has been the almost complete disappearance of the Marxist and semi-Marxist radical movement. The Socialist Party has been reduced to an echo of its former self, continuing to exist largely on the prestige of its leader, Norman Thomas. The Communist Party has declined drastically since the end of World War II, when it reached the peak of its influence, and with only a few exceptions the numerous variants of the communist movement, which flourished particularly during the 1930's, have gone out of existence.

It would seem that the end of an era has been reached in the history of United States left-wing politics. The sharp reduction in the power of the left-wing political groups appears to indicate the end of attempts by radicals to build up ideological parties which would in time become as important in this country as the Socialist and Communist Parties are in Europe. This does not mean that Marxist or semi-Marxist radicalism is completely dead in the United States. Indeed, one of the surprising facts about the decline in the strength of the radical parties is that "socialists" now occupy more positions of importance in the labor movement, and in public life generally, than at almost any other time in this country's history.

The "splinter group" has almost always been a marked feature of the radical movement in the United States. The tendency among radicals to split on questions of doctrine and personality can be compared only to similar trends in the Protestant churches. Sometimes these divisions and subdivisions have produced a "lunatic fringe" which has kept apparently hopeless radical groups alive—groups distinguished from one another by nothing more relevant to the facts of life than was the mediaeval controversy about the number of angels who could stand on the head of a pin. But sometimes these splinter groups reflect tendencies that are characteristic of the radical movement as a whole. A study of the reasons why the various groups split off sheds light on the entire movement, and may help to explain why Marxist radicalism has never become a major force in United States politics. . . .

The history of splinter groups in the radical movement in the United States indicates some of the reasons why that movement never achieved major proportions, in spite of the fact that according to Marxist theory the United States, as the world's largest industrial nation, should have been the stronghold of a Marxist labor and political movement.

In the first place, these schisms reveal that personalities have played too great a role in the radical organizations. This is clearly illustrated by the case of Daniel De Leon, whose personality was the chief cause of the 1899 split in the Socialist Labor Party. Similarly, the various divisions in the communist movement were struggles for power among individual leaders at least as often as they were quarrels over political issues.

Of course this "personalist" tendency—which runs counter to Marxist theories concerning the role of impersonal economic forces in dominating historical events—is intensified by the aura of orthodoxy which hangs over the whole movement. Since all these parties and groups have been organizations with hard-and-fast doctrines and rules of procedure, each successive leader has tended to wrap the cloak of orthodoxy around himself and to assume a position as the one true interpreter of the "true" doctrine, be it that of Marx, Lenin, Stalin, Trotsky, or Daniel De Leon.

Furthermore, the doctrinaire nature of the Marxist and semi-Marxist political groups has been a severe drawback to them in making headway in the political atmosphere of the United States. Even the most liberal of these radical groups has had a comparatively rigid body of party doctrine and a comparatively narrow concept of party discipline; the Socialist Party has been about as tolerant as any of these groups, yet it has not been unusual for the party to bring members "up on charges" for violation of doctrine or discipline. In the Socialist Labor Party, and in the various offshoots of the communist movement, doctrinal orthodoxy and political discipline have been far more rigid.

Such ideas are alien to the American tradition. Almost since political parties first evolved in the United States, ideas of party orthodoxy have been notoriously lax. There is little or no Democratic or Republican "orthodoxy" on anything. There are almost as many "factions" in each party as there are members. It has been possible, for example, for the economically liberal, politically reactionary, white-supremacist Southern Democrats to live within the same political walls as the economically socialist, politically liberal, racially mixed Democrats of the North, just as it has been possible for the predominantly rural, isolationist, and extremely conservative "Chicago Tribune Republicans" of the Middle West to live in the same party as the urban, internationalist, New Deal Republicans of the Northeast and Northwest.

Party discipline, too, is almost unheard of. Coolidge attempted for a while to oust the Republicans who supported Robert M. La Follette in 1924, but not to much avail. More recently, Truman tried to discipline the Dixiecrats, but that attempt also seems to have come to nothing. Even such major upheavals as the 1912 Bull Moose revolt have cracked party walls only slightly and for only a short time.

This is not to say that disregard for party orthodoxy and discipline is necessarily desirable. It is merely to point out that this disregard is traditional in United States politics, and that by running counter to the tradition the radical parties naturally found themselves facing difficulties that might not confront a more loosely disciplined, less rigidly oriented movement.

The doctrinaire nature of the radical parties has also tended to make them ingrown, more interested in hammering out fine points of doctrine than in going out and winning the majority of the American people. This was strikingly shown by the Lovestoneite and Trotskyite communist Oppositions in the late twenties and early thirties, which were avowed "Oppositions" to the official Communist Party, concerned first of all with persuading that party to mend its ways. The same objective was noteworthy in the Socialist Party in the 1930's, when each of the numerous party factions had its own version of what the orthodox position of the party should be, and each tended to regard a different Marxist theoretician—Lenin, Kautsky, Rosa Luxemburg, even Morris Hillquit—as the fount of wisdom.

Finally, it is obvious from a study of these splinter groups that the radical parties have been unduly concerned with events in other countries. In part, of course, this was because immigrants have played such an important role in the radical movement. Perhaps only the Socialist Party before World War I really came to grips with American problems in a way that aroused wide support from the rank and file; and it may be significant that this was the only period when there seemed to be a real possibility that the Marxists might become a major factor in United States politics.

To be sure, the cry that a party must be "Americanized" has recurred over and over again. It was raised by Victoria Woodhull and Tennessee Claflin among the adherents of the First International in the 1870's. The Rosenberg faction of the Socialist Labor Party sounded the same note in 1889. The issue was important at the time of the communist split in 1919, when the English-speaking sympathizers with the Comintern formed a rival party to that of the foreign-language federations; and again at the time of the socialist break in the 1930's, when one of the Militant slogans was that the party must be "Americanized."

Yet in spite of this periodic emphasis on "Americanization," the radical movement has remained fundamentally oriented toward European questions and developments rather than American ones. As far back as the 1880's the Socialist Labor Party was split wide open by the struggle between the followers of Karl Marx and those of Michael Bakunin over issues that had little to do with events in the United States. The 1919 break in the socialist ranks which resulted in the formation of the Communist Party had its origins almost entirely in the Russian Revolution; in creating the Communist Party the dissidents were responding to Lenin's appeal that a new International be formed, associated with and led by the Russian Bolshevik Party. Each subsequent split among the communists themselves was caused mainly by events in Russia: the Russian influence in the Trotskyite scission of the late 1920's is obvious, for example, and the Lovestoneite break was associated with the expulsion of the Bukharin group in the Soviet Union and the Thalheimer element of the German Communist Party. The Trotskyite wanderings in and out of the Socialist Party in 1936–1937 were in direct obedience to orders from Trotsky, and repeated manoeuvres that had first been planned and executed in Czechoslovakia and France.

Similarly, the divisions in the Socialist Party in the 1930's represented the reaction of its members to events in Germany, France, and the Soviet Union rather than to developments in this country. The attention of the Old Guard and the Militants alike was centered on the success or failure of the Soviet experiment, on the advisability or inadvisability of a Popular Front, as in France, and on the failure of the socialists to defeat Hitler in Germany. By contrast, the New Deal was not a major issue when the Old Guard left the party in 1937 to form the Social Democratic Federation— although after the split had occurred the socialists and the social democrats did take different stands on the Roosevelt administration. Two years later the "silent split" in the Socialist Party (which resulted in the formation of the Union for Democratic Action) was caused by the party's attitude toward foreign affairs and World War II.

To sum up, the history of splinter groups in the American radical movement points to a variety of reasons why Marxism has so far failed to become a major force in United States politics. The most important reasons have been the tendency toward "personalism" in the radical groups; their narrow concepts of orthodoxy and party discipline, in contrast to the general indifference of the major political parties to these matters; their tendency to quarrel among themselves over points of doctrine; and their excessive concentration on events abroad rather than on problems that are vital to the welfare of the United States.

Observers of the contemporary New Left have noted similar ideological and tactical disputes. For the most part, these revolve around the notions of "oppositionism" versus "permeationism" reminiscent of the Lenin-Kautsky debates of the early 1900s.[94]

Internal dissension downgrades the viability of a movement, since any semblance of cohesion is lost. The lack of cohesion and solidarity makes it difficult for a social movement to act in a concerted way toward social change. For example, the ideological and membership heterogeneity of the Knights of Labor hampered the ability of this early labor movement to attain its objectives. Moreover, under certain conditions of internal dissension, members will begin to withdraw, thus contributing to the disintegration of the movement.[95]

Even if one faction in an internecine dispute emerges victorious, the quest for ideological purity does not end. In fact, the very need to construct a new ideological base usually results in renewed conflict, to the further isolation and discredit of the movement. Ultimately, what was once a movement may degenerate into a sect. Shannon, in his discussion of the decline of the Socialist Party in America, writes that a social movement:

. . . may be able to contain within it people and groups with . . . divergent points of view; a political sect cannot, for a sect by its very nature demands doctrinal unity and purity. The [Socialist] convention of 1937 made an effort to put an end to the factional fighting, but in the very discussion of party factions the passions of factionalism became hotter. After long argument the convention voted to suppress factionalism by demanding the discontinuance of all factional publications . . . and the establishment of an official party publication to be governed by a board representing all points of view. . . .

The Trotskyites, the most zealous seekers of doctrinal purity of any revolutionary groups, would not obey the injunction of the convention. Believing, like the Puritan hierarchy of seventeenth century New England, that they and only they had a grip on truth, they held that to compromise their position would be to compromise with evil.[96]

The end result of the 1937 convention was that the Socialist Party lost any chance it may have had for social significance, and the Trotskyists became an isolated sect. Thus, ideological purity, as much as any other factor, isolates the adherents of a social movement from the mainstream of any social system.

One of the commonest sources of dissension, particularly in revolutionary movements, comes from the unintended consequences of tactical actions. That is, every action to attain the goals of the movement will be

[94] Bayard Rustin, "From Protest to Politics: The Future of the Civil Rights Movement," *Commentary*, 39 (February 1965): 25–31.
[95] Robert Frank Weiss, "Defection from Social Movements and Subsequent Recruitment to New Movements," *Sociometry*, 26 (March 1963): 1–20.
[96] David Shannon, *The Socialist Party of America* (Chicago: Quadrangle Books, 1967), p. 253.

met with a reaction or response from the status quo holders of power. Part of the strategy for the movement must therefore be to anticipate these responses and to develop a program for handling them. However, since the opponents of the movement are human, and therefore not completely predictable, many of their reactions will be unforeseen. Internal dissension arises from competing interpretations of the course of action dictated by the movement's ideology. In short, dissension arises because the revolutionary must apply his ideology on the run.

Ideological movements having as their goals total and permanent changes in power relationships are bound to fail, precisely because they are attempts to achieve utopia by means of a dialectical methodology. This contradiction is succinctly posed by Dahrendorf:

All utopias from Plato's Republic to George Orwell's brave new world of 1984 have had one element of construction in common: they are all societies from which change is absent. Whether conceived as a final state and climax of historical development, as an intellectual's nightmare, or as a romantic dream, the social fabric of utopias does not, and perhaps cannot recognize the unending flow of the historical process.[97]

If such total movements are not truncated by repression, co-optation, or discreditation, they then face an ignominious demise as postmovement sects without social significance. If, on the other hand, these movements succeed in their goals, their failure is equally assured—they become institutionalized as the new status quo. A recognition of historical process implies one sure lesson: a commitment to viable change requires a commitment to a state of permanent revolution. Such a commitment may form the basis of the increasingly existential nature of today's Left—a possibility which we will investigate in the next chapter.

[97] Ralf Dahrendorf, "Out of Utopia: Toward a Reorientation of Sociological Analysis," *American Journal of Sociology*, 64 (September 1958): 115.

THE "END OF IDEOLOGY" AND CONTEMPORARY SOCIAL MOVEMENTS

Throughout our analysis, we have continually referred to the role of ideology in the emergence, growth, and decline of social movements. We have also stressed the part ideology plays in defining the character, goals, and tactics of a social movement. In particular, we have emphasized the relationship between social structure, history, and conflicting ideologies in determining what kinds of movements will emerge at various junctures in time. It would therefore seem appropriate to close our analysis with some speculations about the ideological aspects of contemporary social movements.

The concept of ideology has been used extensively, if not consistently, in social and philosophical writings. Antoine Destutt de Tracy, the French philosopher, coined the term at the turn of the nineteenth century to refer to his theory of human thought processes, which emphasized the physiological character of sensations. During the turbulent Napoleonic era, ideology came to mean any republican or revolutionary political belief hostile to Napoleon or to the status quo.[1] Since the writings of Marx and Mannheim, ideology has come to be viewed either as the prevailing mode of thought (the conscience collective) in a given socioeconomic system or as the "brave new world" of radicals and revolutionaries. Marx saw the dominant ideas of the ruling classes, which upheld an inequitable division of labor in society, as generating "false class consciousness." In accepting this false ideology, people accepted the existing order. Therefore, those wishing to change the social order must liberate themselves from the ideology of the owners of the means of production. This liberated perspective Mannheim defined as "utopian"—an orientation "which transcends reality and which at the same time breaks the bonds of the existing order. . . ."[2]

[1] Henry D. Aiken, *The Age of Ideology* (New York: Mentor Books, 1956), pp. 16–17.
[2] Karl Mannheim, *Ideology and Utopia* (New York: Harcourt, Brace and World, Inc., 1961).

Marxist revolutionaries, particularly Lenin, viewed correct ideology as essential to social change: the Communist vanguard must possess "political consciousness" and, most importantly, must communicate it to the masses through propaganda and agitation.

Most social scientists concerned with the problems and processes of sociopolitical change have come to see ideology as necessary for the founding and maintenance of a social movement. David Apter, for example, describes ideology as essential for binding a movement or community together and for organizing the role personalities of adherents.[3] Nevertheless, in recent years the role, and indeed the existence, of ideology in the second half of the twentieth century has been called into question. One of the prime movers in this reassessment has been Daniel Bell. Let us examine the controversy that has arisen over his analysis.

Bell, in his oft-quoted paper on the end of ideology, posited that ideology—once a road to action—has come to a dead end. He contends that passion once gave ideology its force but that this fervor has now been dissipated by a number of sociohistorical events, such as the discreditation of Marxism and the rise of mass culture. Moreover, Bell continues, the social problems of today cannot be solved in terms of the grandiose cosmic schemes of the past, which now seem shop-worn.

Daniel Bell, The End of Ideology: On the Exhaustion of Political Ideas in the Fifties, *new, revised edition* (*New York: Collier Books, 1961*), "The End of Ideology in the West: An Epilogue," *pp. 393–407. Reprinted by permission of Daniel Bell and The Free Press.*

There have been few periods in history when man felt his world to be durable, suspended surely, as in Christian allegory, between chaos and heaven. In an Egyptian papyrus of more than four thousand years ago, one finds: ". . . impudence is rife . . . the country is spinning round and round like a potter's wheel . . . the masses are like timid sheep without a shepherd . . . one who yesterday was indigent is now wealthy and the sometime rich overwhelm him with adulation." The Hellenistic period as described by Gilbert Murray was one of a "failure of nerve"; there was "the rise of pessimism, a loss of self-confidence, of hope in this life and of faith in normal human effort." And the old scoundrel Talleyrand claimed

---

[3] David Apter, ed., *Ideology and Discontent* (New York: Free Press, 1964), pp. 18–26. See also Erik H. Erikson, *Young Man Luther: A Study in Psychoanalysis and History* (New York: W. W. Norton and Co., 1958).

that only those who lived before 1789 could have tasted life in all its sweetness.⁴

This age, too, can add appropriate citations—made all the more wry and bitter by the long period of bright hope that preceded it—for the two decades between 1930 and 1950 have an intensity peculiar in written history: world-wide economic depression and sharp class struggles; the rise of fascism and racial imperialism in a country that had stood at an advanced stage of human culture; the tragic self-immolation of a revolutionary generation that had proclaimed the finer ideals of man; destructive war of a breadth and scale hitherto unknown; the bureaucratized murder of millions in concentration camps and death chambers.

For the radical intellectual who had articulated the revolutionary impulses of the past century and a half, all this has meant an end to chiliastic hopes, to millenarianism, to apocalyptic thinking—and to ideology. For ideology, which once was a road to action, has come to be a dead end.

Whatever its origins among the French *philosophes,* ideology as a way of translating ideas into action was given its sharpest phrasing by the left Hegelians, by Feuerbach and by Marx. For them, the function of philosophy was to be critical, to rid the present of the past. ("The tradition of all the dead generations weighs like a nightmare on the brain of the living," wrote Marx.) Feuerbach, the most radical of all the left Hegelians, called himself Luther II. Man would be free, he said, if we could demythologize religion. This history of all thought was a history of progressive disenchantment, and if finally, in Christianity, God had been transformed from a parochial deity to a universal abstraction, the function of criticism—using the radical tool of alienation, or self-estrangement—was to replace theology by anthropology, to substitute Man for God. Philosophy was to be directed at life, man was to be liberated from the "spector of abstractions" and extricated from the bind of the supernatural. Religion was capable only of creating "false consciousness." Philosophy would reveal "true consciousness." And by placing Man, rather than God, at the center of consciousness, Feuerbach sought to bring the "infinite into the finite." ⁵

If Feuerbach "descended into the world," Marx sought to transform it. And where Feuerbach proclaimed anthropology, Marx, reclaiming a root

---

⁴ Karl Jaspers has assembled a fascinating collection of laments by philosophers of each age who see their own time as crisis and the past as a golden age. These—and the quotations from the Egyptian papyri as well as the remark of Talleyrand—can be found in his *Man in the Modern Age* (rev. ed.) (London, 1951), Chapter II. The quotation from Gilbert Murray is from *Five States of Greek Religion* (2d ed.) (New York, 1930), Chapter IV.

⁵ The citation from Marx from the celebrated opening passages of *The Eighteenth Brumaire of Louis Napoleon* has a general discussion of alienation, but I have followed here with profit the discussion by Hans Speier in his *Social Order and the Risks of War* (New York, 1952), Chapter XI.

insight of Hegel, emphasized History and historical contexts. The world was not generic Man, but men; and of men, classes of men. Men differed because of their class position. And truths were class truths. All truths, thus, were masks, or partial truths, but the real truth was the revolutionary truth. And this real truth was rational.

Thus a dynamic was introduced into the analysis of ideology, and into the creation of a new ideology. By demythologizing religion, one recovered (from God and sin) to potential in man. By the unfolding of history, rationality was revealed. In the struggle of classes, true consciousness, rather than false consciousness, could be achieved. But if truth lay in action, one must act. The left Hegelians, said Marx, were only *litterateurs*. (For them a magazine was "practice.") For Marx, the only real action was in politics. But action, revolutionary action as Marx conceived it, was not mere social change. It was, in its new vision, a new ideology.

The analysis of ideology belongs properly in the discussion of the intelligentsia. One can say that what the priest is to religion, the intellectual is to ideology. This in itself gives us a clue to the dimensions of the word and the reason for its multivariate functions. The word *ideology* was coined by the French philosopher Destutt de Tracy, at the end of the 18th century. Together with other Enlightenment philosophers, notably such materialists as Helvetius and Holbach, de Tracy was trying to define a way of discovering "truth" other than through faith and authority, the traditional methods encouraged by Church and State. And, equally, under the influence of Francis Bacon, these men were seeking some way to eliminate the accidents of bias, the distortions of prejudice, the idiosyncracies of upbringing, the interventions of self-interest, or the simple will to believe, all of which, like shadows in Plato's cave, created illusions of truth.[6] Their aim was to "purify" ideas in order to achieve "objective" truth and "correct" thought. Some of them, Helvetius, for example, believed that one had to go back to the origin and development of ideas in order to see how distortions entered. De Tracy believed that one "purified" ideas by reducing them to sense perceptions—a belated French variant of British empiricism with a barely concealed anti-religious bias—and this new science of ideas he called "ideology."

The negative connotations of the term arose with Napoleon. Having

[6] Francis Bacon in the *Novum Organum* sought to release Reason from the "imperfections of the mind" by positing different kinds of distortion. These he called *The Idols of the Tribe; The Idols of the Cave* ("everyone . . . has a case or den of his own, which refracts and discolors the light of nature; owing . . . to his education and conversation with others; or to the reading of books, and the authority of those he esteems and admires . . ."); *The Idols of the Market-Place;* and *The Idols of the Theatre* ("because in my judgment all the received systems [of philosophy] are but so many stage-plays representing worlds of their own creation after an unreal and scenic fashion"). For a discussion of the history of the idea of bias in the social sciences in relation to ideology, see Reinhard Bendix's *Social Science and the Distrust of Reason* (University of California Press, 1951).

consolidated his power, he forbade the teaching of moral and political science at the Institut National and denounced the "ideologues" as irresponsible speculators who were subverting morality and patriotism. As a republican, Napoleon had been sympathetic to the ideas of the philosophers; as Emperor, he recognized the importance of religious orthodoxy for the maintenance of the State.

But it was with Marx that the word "ideology" went through some curiously different transmutations. For Marx, as in his work *The German Ideology*, ideology was linked to philosophical idealism, or the conception that ideas are autonomous, and that ideas, independently, have the power to reveal truth and consciousness. For Marx, as a materialist, this was false since "existence determined consciousness" rather than vice versa; any attempt to draw a picture of reality from ideas alone could produce only "false consciousness." Thus, for example, in following Feuerbach—from whom Marx drew most of his analysis of ideology and alienation—he considered religion to be a false consciousness: Gods are the creation of men's minds and they only appear to exist independently and determine man's fate; religion therefore is an ideology.

But Marx went one step further. Ideologies, he said, are not only false ideas, but they mask particular interests. Ideologies claim to be true, but reflect the needs of specific groups. In his early essays on *The Jewish Question*, one of the few places where he dealt specifically with the philosophical problems of State and Society, Marx sharply attacked the concept of "natural rights" as it appeared in the French Revolution's Declaration of the Rights of Man, and as these rights were specified in the State constitutions of Pennsylvania and New Hampshire. The presumption of "natural rights"—the freedom to worship or the freedom to own property—was that they were "absolute" or "transcendent" rights; for Marx, they were only "bourgeois rights," historically achieved, which made false claim to universal validity. The function of the State, Marx pointed out, was to create some basis for the "general will." In the "civil society" which the bourgeoisie had created, the State presumably was to be negative or neutral. Each man would pursue his own self-interest, and a social harmony would prevail. But in fact, he argued, the State was used to enforce the rights of particular groups. Thus the claim of "natural rights" simply masked the demand of the bourgeoisie to be able to use property to their own advantage. Marx believed that the individualism of "natural rights" was a false individualism, since man could only "realize" himself in community, and that true freedom was not freedom *of* property or freedom *of* religion, but freedom *from* property and freedom *from* religion—in short, from ideology. The attempt, therefore, to claim universal validity for what was in fact a class interest, was ideology.

Marx differed from Bentham, and other utilitarians, in recognizing that individuals were not always motivated by direct self-interest. (This was "vulgar hedonism.") Ideology, he said, was a meaningful force. "One must not form the narrow-minded idea," he wrote in *The Eighteenth Brumaire*, "that the petty-bourgeoisie wants on principle to enforce an egoistic class interest. It believes, rather, that the *special* conditions of its emancipation are the *general* conditions through which alone modern society can be saved and the class struggle avoided." The "unmasking" of ideology, thus, is to reveal the "objective" interest behind the idea, and to see what function the ideology serves.[7]

The implications of all this are quite direct. For one, a rationalistic analysis of politics alone is inadequate. What people say they believe cannot always be taken at face value, and one must search for the structure of interests beneath the ideas; one looks not at the *content* of ideas, but their *function*. A second, more radical conclusion is that if ideas mask material interests, then the "test of truth" doctrine is to see what class interests it serves. In short, truth is "class truth." Thus, there is no objective philosophy, but only "bourgeois philosophy" and "proletarian philosophy"; no objective sociology but only "bourgeois sociology" and "proletarian sociology." But Marxism is not simply a relativistic doctrine: there is an "objective" ordering of the social universe, which is revealed through "history." History, for Marx as for Hegel, is a progressive unfolding reason, in which society, through man's conquest of nature and the destruction of all mythologies and superstitions, moves on to "higher stages." The "truth" of doctrine, therefore, is to be determined by its "closeness of fit" to the development of history; and in practice, it has meant that "truth" was determined by whether or not it contributed to the advancement of revolution.

There are many difficulties to the theory of the "social determination of ideas." One is the role of science. Marx did not speak of the natural sciences as ideologies. Yet a number of Marxists, particularly in the Soviet Union in the 1930's, did claim that there was a "bourgeois science" and a "bourgeois physics" and a "proletarian science" and a "proletarian physics." Thus, the relativity theories of Albert Einstein were attacked as "idealistic." And while today in the Soviet Union, there is hardly any talk of "bourgeois physics," the theories of Sigmund Freud are officially condemned as "idealistic." Yet if science is not class-bound, is this equally true of the social sciences? The question of the autonomy of science is one that has never been satisfactorily resolved in Marxian thought.

A second difficulty is the deterministic presumption that there is a *one-to-one* correspondence between a set of ideas and some "class" purpose. Yet this is rarely the case. Empiricism is usually associated with

[7] To this extent, the "unmasking of ideology" is somewhat akin to the theory of "rationalization" in the Freudian system. A rationalization hides an underlying motive. This does not mean it is necessarily false. In fact to function effectively, a rationalization has to have some "close fit" with reality. Yet an ulterior or underlying motive exists as well, and analysis seeks to point this out.

liberal inquiry. Yet David Hume, the most "radical" empiricist, was a Tory, and Edmund Burke, who had argued the most vigorously against rationalist efforts to blueprint a new society, was conservative. Hobbes, one of the most profound of materialists, was a royalist, and T. H. Green, one of the leaders of the idealist revival in Great Britain, a liberal.

And the third difficulty is the definition of class. For Marx (though class was never rigorously defined in his work) the key social divisions in society arose out of the distribution of property. Yet in a politico-technological world, property has increasingly lost its force as a determinant of power, and sometimes, even, of wealth. In almost all modern societies, technical skill becomes more important than inheritance as a determinant of occupation, and political power takes precedence over economic. What then is the meaning of class?

And yet, one cannot wholly discount the force of the proposition that "styles of thought" are related to historic class groups and their interests, or that ideas emerge as a consequence of the different world-views, or perspectives, of different groups in the society. The problem is how to specify the relationships between the existential base and the "mental production." Max Weber, the sociologist, argued, for example, that there is an "elective affinity" between ideas and interests. The social origin of an idea, or of a theorist, or a revolutionist, is less relevant than the fact that certain ideas become "selected out," so to speak, by social groups that find them congenial and thus espouse them. This was the basis for the theory of the "Protestant Ethic," in which he argued that certain features of Calvinistic thought, and the kind of personality that such a doctrine sanctioned, became necessary, and causal, in the development of capitalism, despite the other-worldly foundation of these ideas. Karl Mannheim, another sociologist, sought to divide social thought into two fundamental styles, which he called "ideological" and "utopian." He accepted the proposition, derived from Marx, that ideas are "time-bound," but insisted that Marx's ideas, as those of all socialists, came within the same stricture. Since all ideas serve interests, those which defended the existing order he called "utopian." But was all effort, then, at objective truth hopeless? Was Bacon's quest therefore a mirage? Mannheim felt that one social group could be relatively objective—the intellectuals. Since the intelligentsia were a "floating stratum" in society, and therefore were less bound than other class groups, they could achieve multi-perspectives that transcended the parochial limits of the other social groups.

In the development of the social sciences, the problem raised by Bacon, de Tracy, Marx and others—the clarification of the role of ideas in "social change"—has become part of a technical field known as the "sociology of knowledge." (For a clear discussion of these issues, see the chapter by Robert K. Merton in his *Social Theory and Social Structure*.) But in popular usage the word *ideology* remains as a vague term where it seems to denote a world-view of belief-system or creeds held by a social group about the social arrangements in society, which is morally justified as being right. People then talk of the "ideology of the small businessman," or of liberalism, or fascism, as an "ideology." Or some writer will talk of "the dream-world of ideology (in which) Americans see their country as a place where every child is born to 'equality of opportunity,' where every man is essentially as good as every other man if not better." In this sense, ideology connotes a "myth" rather than just a set of values.

Clearly, such usages, by mixing together many things, create only confusion. Some distinctions, therefore, are in order.

We can, perhaps, borrow a distinction from Mannheim, and distinguish between what he called "the *particular* conception of ideology," and "the *total* conception of ideology." In the first sense, we can say that individuals who profess certain values do have interests as well, and we can better understand the meaning of these values or beliefs, or the reasons why they come forth where they have, by linking them up with the interests they have—though the interests may not always be economic; they may be status interests (such as an ethnic group that wants higher standing or social approval in a society), political interests, such as representation, and the like. It is in this sense that we can talk of the *ideology* of business, or of labor, or the like. (When Charles E. Wilson, the Secretary of Defense in the Eisenhower Administration and one-time president of General Motors, said "What is good for the United States is good for General Motors, and vice-versa," he was expressing ideology—i.e., the view that economic policy should be geared to the needs of the business community, since the welfare of the country depended on the health of business.) A *total* ideology is an all-inclusive system of comprehensive reality, it is a set of beliefs, infused with passion, and seeks to transform the whole of a way of life. This commitment to ideology—the yearning for a "cause," or the satisfaction of deep moral feeling—is *not* necessarily the reflection of interests in the shape of ideas. Ideology, in this sense, and in the sense that we use it here, is a secular religion.

Ideology is the conversion of ideas into social levers. Without irony, Max Lerner once entitled a book "Ideas Are Weapons." This is the language of ideology. It is more. It is the commitment to the consequences of ideas. When Vissarion Belinsky, the father of Russian criticism, first read Hegel and became convinced of the philosophical correctness of the formula "what is, what ought to be," he became a supporter of the Russian autocracy. But when it was shown to him that Hegel's thought contained the contrary tendency, that dialectically the "is" evolves into a different form, he became a revolutionary overnight. "Belinsky's conversion," comments Rufus W. Mathewson, Jr., "illustrates an attitude toward ideas which is both passionate and myopic, which responds to them on the basis of their immediate relevances alone, and inevitably reduced them to tools." [8]

What gives ideology its force is its passion. Abstract philosophical inquiry has always sought to eliminate passion, and the person, to rationalize all ideas. For the ideologue, truth arises in action, and meaning is given to experience by the "transforming moment." He comes alive not in contemplation, but in "the deed." One might say, in fact, that the most important, latent, function of ideology is to tap emotion. Other than religion (and war and nationalism), there have been few forms of channelizing emotional energy. Religion symbolized, drained away, dispersed emotional energy from the world onto the litany, the liturgy, the sacraments, the edifices, the arts. Ideology fuses these energies and channels them into politics.

But religion, at its most effective, was more. It was a way for people to cope with the problem of death. The fear of death—forceful and inevitable—and more, the fear of violent death, shatters the flittering, imposing, momentary dream of man's power. The fear of death, as Hobbes pointed out, is the source of conscience; the effort to avoid violent death is the source of law. When it was possible to believe, really believe, in heaven and hell, then some of the fear of death could be tempered or controlled; without such belief, there is only the total annihilation of the self.[9]

It may well be that with the decline in religious *faith* in the last century and more, this fear of death as total annihilation, unconsciously expressed, has probably increased. One may hypothesize, in fact, that this is a cause of the breakthrough of the irrational, which is such a marked feature of the changed moral temper of our time. Fanaticism, violence, and cruelty are not, of course, unique in human history. But there was a time when such frenzies and mass emotions could be displaced, symbolized, drained away, and dispersed through religious devotion and practice. Now there is only this life, and the assertion of self becomes possible—for some even necessary—in the domination over others.[10] One can challenge death by emphasizing the omnipotence of a movement (as in the "inevitable" victory of communism), or overcome death (as did the

[8] Rufus W. Mathewson, Jr., *The Positive Hero in Russian Literature* (New York, 1958), p. 6.
[9] See Leo Strauss, *The Political Philosophy of Hobbes* (Chicago, 1952), pp. 14–29.
[10] The Marquis de Sade, who, more than any man, explored the limits of self-assertion, once wrote: "There is not a single man who doesn't want to be a despot when he is excited . . . he would like to be alone in the world . . . any sort of equality would destroy the despotism he enjoys then." De Sade proposed, therefore, to canalize these impulses into sexual activity by opening universal brothels which could serve to drain away these emotions. De Sade, it should be pointed out, was a bitter enemy of religion, but he understood well the latent function of religion in mobilizing emotions.

"immortality of Captain Ahab) by bending others to one's will. Both paths are taken, but politics, because it can institutionalize power, in the way that religion once did, becomes the ready avenue for domination. The modern effort to transform the world chiefly or solely through politics (as contrasted with the religious transformation of the self) has meant that all other institutional ways of mobilizing emotional energy would necessarily atrophy. In effect, sect and church become party and social movement.

A social movement can rouse people when it can do three things: simplify ideas, establish a claim to truth, and, in the union of the two, demand a commitment to action. Thus, not only does ideology transform ideas, it transforms people as well. The nineteenth-century ideologies, by emphasizing inevitability and by infusing passion into their followers, could compete with religion. By identifying inevitability with progress, they linked up with the positive values of science. But more important, these ideologies were linked, too, with the rising class of intellectuals which was seeking to assert a place in society.

The differences between the intellectual and the scholar, without being invidious, are important to understand. The scholar has a bounded field of knowledge, a tradition, and seeks to find his place in it, adding to the accumulated, tested knowledge of the past as to a mosaic. The scholar, qua scholar, is less involved with his "self." The intellectual begins with *his* experience, *his* individual perceptions of the world, *his* privileges and deprivations, and judges the world by these sensibilities. Since his own status is of high value, his judgments of the society reflect the treatment accorded him. In a business civilization, the intellectual felt that the wrong values were being honored, and rejected the society. Thus there was a "built-in" compulsion for the free-floating intellectual to become political. The ideologies, therefore, which emerged from the nineteenth century had the force of the intellectuals behind them. They embarked upon what William James called "the faith ladder," which in its vision of the future cannot distinguish possibilities from probabilities, and converts the latter into certainties.

Today, these ideologies are exhausted. The events behind this important sociological change are complex and varied. Such calamities as the Moscow Trials, the Nazi-Soviet pact, the concentration camps, the suppression of the Hungarian workers, form one chain; such social changes as the modification of capitalism, the rise of the Welfare State, another. In philosophy, one can trace the decline of simplistic, rationalistic beliefs and the emergence of new stoic-theological images of man, e.g. Freud, Tillich, Jaspers, etc. This is not to say that such ideologies as communism in France and Italy do not have a political weight, or a driving momentum from other sources. But out of all this history, one simple fact emerges: for the radical intelligentsia, the old ideologies have lost their "truth" and their power to persuade.

Few serious minds believe any longer that one can set down "blueprints" and through "social engineering" bring about a new utopia of social harmony. At the same time, the older "counter-beliefs" have lost their intellectual force as well. Few "classic" liberals insist that the State should play no role in the economy, and few serious conservatives, at least in England and on the Continent, believe that the Welfare State is "the road to serfdom." In the Western world, therefore, there is today a rough consensus among intellectuals on political issues: the acceptance of a Welfare State; the desirability of decentralized power; a system of mixed economy and of political pluralism. In that sense, too, the ideological age has ended.

And yet, the extraordinary fact is that while the old nineteenth-century ideologies and intellectual debates have become exhausted, the rising states of Asia and Africa are fashioning new ideologies with a different appeal for their own people. These are the ideologies of industrialization, modernization, Pan-Arabism, color, and nationalism. In the distinctive difference between the two kinds of ideologies lie the great political and social problems of the second half of the twentieth century. The ideologies of the nineteenth century were universalistic, humanistic, and fashioned by intellectuals. The mass ideologies of Asia and Africa are parochial, instrumental, and created by political leaders. The driving forces of the old ideologies were social equality and, in the largest sense, freedom. The impulsions of the new ideologies are economic development and national power.

And in this appeal, Russia and China have become models. The fascination these countries exert is no longer the old idea of the free society, but the new one of economic growth. And if this involves the wholesale coercion of the population and the rise of new elites to drive the people, the new repressions are justified on the ground that without such coercions economic advance cannot take place rapidly enough. And even for some of the liberals of the West, "economic development" has become a new ideology that washes away the memory of old disillusionments.

It is hard to quarrel with an appeal for rapid economic growth and modernization, and few can dispute the goal, as few could ever dispute an appeal for equality and freedom. But in this powerful surge—and its swiftness is amazing—any movement that instates such goals risks the sacrifice of the present generation for a future that may see only a new exploitation by a new elite. For the newly-risen countries, the debate is not over the merits of Communism—the content of that doctrine has long been forgotten by friends and foes alike. The question is an older one: whether new societies can grow by building democratic institutions and allowing people to make choices—and sacrifices—voluntarily, or whether the new elites, heady with power, will impose totalitarian means to transform their countries. Certainly in these traditional and old colonial societies where the masses are apathetic and easily manipulated, the answer lies with the intellectual classes and their conceptions of the future.

Thus one finds, at the end of the fifties, a disconcerting caesura. In the West, among the intellectuals, the old passions are spent. The new generation, with no meaningful memory of these old debates, and no secure tradition to build upon, finds itself seeking new purposes within a framework of political society that has rejected, intellectually speaking, the old apocalyptic and chiliastic visions. In the search for a "cause," there is a deep, desperate, almost pathetic anger. The theme runs through a remarkable book, *Convictions*, by a dozen of the sharpest young Left Wing intellectuals in Britain. They cannot define the content of the "cause" they seek, but the yearning is clear. In the U.S. too there is a restless search for a new intellectual radicalism. Richard Chase, in his thoughtful assessment of American society, *The Democratic Vista*, insists that the greatness of nineteenth-century America for the rest of the world consisted in its radical vision of man (such a vision as Whitman's), and calls for a new radical criticism today. But the problem is that the old politico-economic radicalism (pre-occupied with such matters as the socialization of industry) has lost its meaning, while the stultifying aspects of contemporary culture (e.g., television) cannot be redressed in political terms. At the same time, American culture has almost completely accepted the avant-garde, particularly in art, and the older academic styles have been driven out completely. The irony, further, for those who seek "causes" is that the workers, whose grievances were once the driving energy for social change, are more satisfied with the society than the intellectuals. The workers have not achieved utopia, but their expectations were less than those of the intellectuals, and the gains correspondingly larger.

The young intellectual is unhappy because the "middle way" is for the middle-aged, not for him; it is without passion and is deadening.[11] Ideology, which by its nature is an all-or-none affair, and temperamentally the thing he wants, is intellectually devitalized, and few issues can be formulated any more, intellectually, in ideological terms. The emotional energies—and needs—exist, and the question of how one mobilizes these energies is a difficult one. Politics offers little excitement. Some of the younger intellectuals have found an outlet in science or university pur-

---

[11] Raymond Aron, *The Opium of the Intellectuals* (New York, 1958); Edward Shils, "Ideology and Civility," *Sewanee Review*, Vol. LXVI, No. 3, Summer 1958, and "The Intellectuals and the Powers," in *Comparative Studies in Society and History*, Vol. I, No. 1, October, 1958.

suits, but often at the expense of narrowing their talents into mere technique; others have sought self-expression in the arts, but in the wasteland the lack of content has meant, too, the lack of the necessary tension that creates new forms and styles.

Whether the intellectuals in the West can find passions outside of politics is moot. Unfortunately, social reform does not have any unifying appeal, nor does it give a younger generation the outlet for "self-expression" and "self-definition" that it wants. The trajectory of enthusiasm has curved East, where, in the new ecstasies for economic utopia, the "future" is all that counts.

The end of ideology is not—should not be—the end of utopia as well. If anything, one can begin anew the discussion of utopia only by being aware of the trap of ideology. The point is that ideologists are "terrible simplifiers." Ideology makes it unnecessary for people to confront individual merits. One simply turns to the ideological vending machine, and out comes the prepared formulae. And when these beliefs are suffused by apocalyptic fervor, ideas become weapons, and with dreadful results.

There is now, more than ever, some need for utopia, in the sense that men need—as they have always needed—some vision of their potential, some manner of fusing passion with intelligence. Yet the ladder to the City of Heaven can no longer be a "faith ladder," but an empirical one: a utopia has to specify *where* one wants to go, *how* to get there, the costs of the enterprise, and some realization of, and justification for the determination of *who* is to pay.

The end of ideology closes the book intellectually speaking, on an era, the one of easy "left" formulae for social change. But to close the book is not to turn one's back upon it. This is all the more important now when a "new Left," with few memories of the past, is emerging. This "new Left" has passion and energy, but little definition of the future. Its outriders exult that it is "on the move." But where it is going, what it means by Socialism, how to guard against bureaucratization, what one means by democratic planning or workers' control—any of the questions that require hard thought, are only answered by bravura phrases.

It is in attitudes towards Cuba and the new States in Africa that the meaning of intellectual maturity, and of the end of ideology, will be tested. For among the "new Left," there is an alarming readiness to create a *tabula rasa*, to accept the word "Revolution" as an absolution for outrages, to justify the suppression of civil rights and opposition—in short, to erase the lessons of the last forty years with an emotional alacrity that is astounding. The fact that many of these emerging social movements are justified in their demands for freedom, for the right to control their own political and economic destinies, does not mean they have a right to a blank check for everything they choose to do in the name of their emancipation. Nor does the fact that such movements take power in the name of freedom guarantee that they will not turn out to be as imperialist, as grandeur-concerned (in the name of Pan-Africanism or some other ideology), as demanding their turn on the stage of History, as the States they have displaced.

If the end of ideology has any meaning, it is to ask for the end of rhetoric, and rhetoricians, of "revolution," of the day when young French anarchist Vaillant tossed a bomb into the Chamber of Deputies, and the literary critic Laurent Tailhade declared in his defense: "What do a few human lives matter; it was a *beau geste*." (A *beau geste* that ended, one might say, in a mirthless jest: two years later, Tailhade lost an eye when a bomb was thrown into a restaurant.) Today, in Cuba, as George Sherman, reporting for the *London Observer* summed it up: "The Revolution is law today although nobody has said clearly what that law is. You are expected to be simply for or against it and judge and be judged accordingly. Hatred and intolerance are wiping out whatever middle ground may have existed."

The problems which confront us at home and in the world are resistant to the old terms of ideological debate between "left" and "right," and if "ideology" by now, and with good reason, is an irretrievably fallen word, it is not necessary that "utopia" suffer the same fate. But it will if those who now call loudest for new utopias begin to justify degrading *means* in the name of some Utopian or revolutionary *end*, and forget the simple lessons that if the old debates are meaningless some old verities are not—the verities of free speech, free press, the right of opposition and of free inquiry.

And if the intellectual history of the past hundred years has any meaning—and lesson—it is to reassert Jefferson's wisdom (aimed at removing the dead hand of the past, but which can serve as a warning against the heavy hand of the future as well), that "the present belongs to the living." This is the wisdom that revolutionists, old and new, who are sensitive to the fate of their fellow men, rediscover in every generation. "I will never believe," says a protagonist in a poignant dialogue written by the gallant Polish philosopher Leszek Kolakowski, "that the moral and intellectual life of mankind follows the law of economics, that is by saying today we can have more tomorrow; that we should use lives now so that truth will triumph or that we should profit by crime to pave the way for nobility."

And these words, written during the Polish "thaw," when the intellectuals had asserted, from their experience with the "future," the claims of humanism, echo the protest of the Russian writer Alexander Herzen, who, in a dialogue a hundred years ago, reproached an earlier revolutionist who would sacrifice the present mankind for a promised tomorrow: "Do you truly wish to condemn all human beings alive today to the sad role of Caryatids . . . supporting a floor for others some day to dance on? . . . This alone should serve as a warning to people: an end that is infinitely remote is not an end, but if you like, a trap; an end must be nearer—it ought to be, at the very least, the labourer's wage or pleasure in the work done. Each age, each generation, each life has its own fullness. . . ." [12]

This epitaph for ideology and rhetoric provoked a considerable number of counterarguments. Henry David Aiken, for one, strongly objected to Bell's seeming idealization of pluralism and pragmatism. He argues that moral discourse and idealism are rooted in American society and are not to be dismissed as mere rhetoric. Aiken's arguments, and his appeal for the "eloquence" of ideology, are summed up in the following quote:

In asking for an end to rhetoric, what Bell appears to be calling for is, among other things, an end to moral discourse and a beginning of consistent "pragmatic discourse" in every sphere of political life. What does this mean? So far as I can make out, it means an end to judgment and to principle, to praise and to blame, in the political domain and a beginning of plain, unvarnished "politicking" in the name of our "realistic" national, social, or individual "interests." It means, in effect, that in political discourse two and only two forms of expression are to be regarded as legitimate: (a) realistic, verifiable statements of fact; and (b) bald, undisguised expressions of first-

[12] To see history as changes in sensibilities and style or, more, how different classes or people mobilized their emotional energies and adopted different moral postures is relatively novel; yet the history of moral temper is, I feel, one of the most important ways of understanding social change, and particularly the irrational forces at work in men. The great model for a cultural period is J. H. Huizinga's *The Waning of the Middle Ages*, with its discussion of changing attitudes toward death, cruelty, and love. Lucien Febvre, the great French historian, long ago urged the writing of history in terms of different sensibilities, and his study of Rabelais and the problem of covert belief (*Le probleme de l'incroyance du XVIeme siecle*) is one of the great landmarks of this approach. Most historians of social movements have been excessively "intellectualistic" in that the emphasis has been on doctrine or on organizational technique, and less on emotional styles. Nathan Leites' *A Study of Bolshevism* may be more important, ultimately, for its treatment of the changing moral temper of the Russian intelligentsia than for the formal study of Bolshevik behavior. Arthur Koestler's novels and autobiography are a brilliant mirror of the changes in belief of the European intellectual. Herbert Leuthy's study of the playwright Bert Brecht (*Encounter*, July 1956) is a jewel in its subtle analysis of the changes in moral judgment created by the acceptance of the image of "the Bolshevik." The career of Georg Lukas, the Hungarian Marxist, is instructive regarding an intellectual who has accepted the soldierly discipline of the Communist ethic; other than some penetrating but brief remarks by Franz Borkenau (see his *World Communism* [New York, 1959], pp. 172–175), and the articles by Morris Watnick (*Soviet Survey* [London, 1958], Nos. 23–25), very little has been written about this extraordinary man. Ignazio Silone's "The Choice of Comrades" (reprinted in *Voices of Dissent* [New York, 1959]) is a sensitive reflection of the positive experiences of radicalism. An interesting history of the millenarian and chiliastic movements is Norman Cohn's *The Pursuit of the Millenium*. From a Catholic viewpoint, Father Ronald Knox's study *Enthusiasm*, deals with the "ecstatic" movements in Christian history.

personal (singular or plural) interest. . . . What is wrong with moral, as distinct from "pragmatic," discourse? It is not to be doubted that moral discourse is more eloquent and more incitive, and in this sense more rhetorical, than the "pragmatic" forms of speech which Bell prefers. But what is wrong with eloquence per se? No doubt it should not be used to cloud an issue, to obscure relevant facts, or to promote unreason. But this is no more a necessary consequence of moral discourse than of any other form of eloquence. Without eloquence, especially in times of crises, few great political movements would succeed. In fact, eloquence, including the eloquence of moral judgment, is native to the language of politics, and particularly so, as Bell himself admits, in democratic societies where persuasion of the great masses is a condition of success. Thus to put an end to eloquence would be to put an end, not only to "moralism" (which is usually nothing more than the morality of those with whom we disagree) and to "ideology," but also to any form of politics in which great issues are stated or argued in terms of human rights and responsibilities and in which it is essential to gain the approval of the people, or their representatives, before any fundamental change in governmental policy is made.[13]

Several months after this initial assault on the anti-ideologists, Aiken and Bell crossed swords in the pages of Commentary.[14] The following selected quotes illustrate the viewpoint of each author on the subject of ideology and social change. First, let us examine the position taken by each on the nature of desirable social changes:

Bell:

To my mind, the fundamental structure is the democratic process, and this I do not want to change. To speak further for myself, since the question of political identification is at issue, I am a democratic socialist, and have been for almost all of my politically conscious years. As such I wish to see a change in the fundamental structures of our economic life. I deplore the social and economic power of the corporation. I detest the cult of *efficiency* which sacrifices the worker to the norms of productivity. I favor national planning in the economy. I want to see more public enterprise. And I want

Aiken:

. . . Mr. Bell's "socialism," the wishful and wistful sincerity of which we need not question, is, in Marx's sense, entirely utopian, and hence practically and functionally meaningless. Mr. Bell often has written perceptively and relevantly about sources of alienation among American workers. But what has he to offer, as a socialist, *toward its drastic alleviation?* I submit: nothing, or next to nothing. Here is precisely the sort of ideological schizophrenia which, in part, my essay was designed to expose [p. 74].

I believe in the necessity of constant, incessant pressure from the

[13] Henry David Aiken, "The Revolt Against Ideology," *Commentary*, 37 (April 1964): 36.
[14] Daniel Bell, Henry David Aiken, "Ideology—A Debate," *Commentary*, 38 (October 1964): 69–76. Relevant page numbers are indicated.

Bell:

to introduce other criteria than those of the market or the private profit motive as means of allocating resources in the society. I have guiding general principles, rooted in conceptions about the nature of work and community, which shape these views [p. 71].

Aiken:

Left upon the Establishment and the status quo in order to rectify grave social wrongs: injustices, inequalities, and other miseries that are removable through collective social action. I believe, furthermore, in a neverending "resistance" and spiritual rebelliousness [p. 75].

Next, consider the methodology proposed by each:

Bell:

. . . the theme of the "end of ideology" has become a call for an end to apocalyptic beliefs that refuse to specify the costs and consequences of the changes they envision. The "end-of-ideology" school (if a school it is) is skeptical of rationalistic schemes that assume they can blueprint the entire life of a society; it argues that the existing political tags "conservative" and "liberal" have lost their intellectual clarity; it is critical of existing institutions, but it does not accept the assumption that social change is necessarily an improvement. In short, it is pragmatic in the triple sense in which Dewey used the term: it defines the consequence of an action as a constitutive element of the truth of a proposition; it assumes the inextricable relation of ends and means; and it believes that values, like any empirical proposition, can be tested on the basis of their claims [p. 70].

Aiken:

. . . for Mr. Bell it appears that problems of politics generally are to be viewed, first, as problems of calculation and, secondly, as problems of adjustment (or compromise). For me, they involve much more, as is evident in my views about the role of rhetoric in political thought and discourse. To my mind, therefore, the end of ideology is, in a sense, almost tantamount to the end of politics itself. Beneath all, the anti-ideologists are men of doubt; their temperament, in the language of William James, is that of the "tough-minded.". . . Thought, analysis, inquiry—and the itch of doubt which animates inquiry—are of course indispensable conditions of rational life. But aspiration, passion, hope, volition, and choice also belong inalienably to the life of the mind and the spirit. . . . We must not allow ourselves to be paralyzed by thought; rather we must use it. We must not let it divert us from the necessity of action [p. 76].

Finally, the foundation of Bell's end-of-ideology thinking, and Aiken's critique of it, are expressed as follows:

Bell:

The intention, then, of the "revolt against ideology" is not to make one insensitive to injustice or to the need

Aiken:

Mr. Bell's own variations on a theme by Marx are, from my point of view, conceptually and historically regres-

Bell:

for a transcendent moral vision. It is, rather, to make one wary of the easy solution. . . . The thinking connected with the "end of ideology" is not directed against Marxism or any other radical creed; nor does it involve a quarrel with utopianism and its visions. What it does is give us a perspective on modern history which emphasizes that the achievement of freedom and the defense of the individual constitute a permanent revolution; and it tells us that this revolution resists any final definition. It is for the sake of individual freedom that the claims of doubt must always take precedence over the claims of faith, and that the commitment to action must proceed from the ethic of responsibility [p. 73].

Aiken:

sive, polemically misleading, and ultimately (when taken seriously) debilitating so far as the causes of the alienated, the disenfranchised, and the disinherited are concerned. . . . The anti-ideologists . . . are in effect merely quasi-Marxian conservatives who have done little or nothing to advance the master's theory of ideology, but on the contrary have merely applied his ideas rather mechanically and obviously to Communism itself in defense of the primary political and social status quo in the "free world." My contention was—and is— that the anti-ideologists leave us at once morally, intellectually, and, if I may say so, metaphysically helpless . . . [p. 74].

In the same year that Bell published The End of Ideology, S. M. Lipset brought together a number of his earlier essays in the format of Political Man.[15] Lipset also hails the end of ideology, and introduces the liberal welfare state as the "good society." Rousseas and Farganis, sharing in part Aiken's opposition to the compromise inherent in pluralistic politics, attempt, in the following article, to refute the end-of-ideology assumption that American democracy has ameliorated all the major structural contradictions and social problems of industrial society.

Excerpts from Stephen W. Rousseas and James Farganis, "American Politics and the End of Ideology," British Journal of Sociology, 14 (December 1963), 347–389. Reprinted by permission of S. W. Rousseas and Routledge and Kegan Paul Ltd.

In a loose collection of essays written over a ten-year period, Daniel Bell [16] hails the end of ideology. In a similar potpourri of previously published essays, Seymour Martin Lipset [17] joins Bell in the apotheosis of a non-

[15] S. M. Lipset, *Political Man* (Garden City, N.Y.: Doubleday and Co., 1960).
[16] *The End of Ideology: On the Exhaustion of Political Ideas in the Fifties* (New York: Rev. Ed., 1961).
[17] *Political Man* (New York, 1960).

committed scientism, or what amounts to a pragmatism leached of all its passion for meaningful social reform. This growing litany in the United States, on the European Continent, and in England, in praise of the *status quo* continues to remain, in its own image, inherently liberal. It is convinced that democracy today has solved all the major problems of industrial society, and that those which do remain are of a second-order magnitude involving merely technical adjustments within a now prevailing *consensus gentium*. If modern liberalism has thus been recast into a less critical mold, it is because of its conviction that modern democracy is the good society. Lipset makes this very clear in the epilogue to his book. "Democracy," he writes, "is not only or even primarily a means through which different groups can attain their ends or seek the good society; *it is the good society itself in operation.*" [18]

More explicitly, we are told by Lipset that within the Western democracies "serious intellectual conflicts among groups representing different values have declined sharply"; that "the ideological issues dividing left and right [have] been reduced to a little more or a little less government ownership and economic planning"; and that it really makes little difference "which political party controls the domestic policies of individual nations." All this, according to Lipset, "reflects the fact that the fundamental political problems of the industrial revolution have been solved: the workers have achieved industrial and political citizenship; the conservatives have accepted the welfare state; and the democratic left has recognized that an increase in over-all state power carried with it more dangers to freedom than solutions for economic problems." [19]

[18] *Ibid.*, p. 403, italics supplied. In response to criticisms of *Political Man*, Lipset has somewhat modified this statement and has sought to restate his liberalism ("My View From Our Left," *Columbia University Forum*, Fall 1962). "Democracy," now, "is not simply a means to the end of the good society, it is itself the only society in which social tendencies which press man to exploit man may be restrained." This rather negative approach to democracy and the good society is further confirmed by his statement that his espousal of democracy "rests on the assumption that only a politically democratic society can reduce the pressures—endemic in social systems—to increase the punitive and discriminatory effects of stratification." For it is the democratic freedom of the underprivileged classes to organize which gives rise to an effective and levelling "counter-power" operating within the rules-of-the-game of institutionalized conflict. The similarity of this to John K. Galbraith's theory of "countervailing power" is obvious, and is subject to the same limitations. Lipset's ideal is the non-ideological welfare state toward which, he believes, the United States is moving.

[19] *Political Man*, pp. 403–406. In addition Lipset cites, with apparent approval, a comment made to him by the editor of a leading Swedish newspaper: "Politics is now boring. The only issues are whether the metal workers should get a nickel more an hour, the price of milk should be raised, or old-age pensions extended." Similarly in Bell we have: "In the Western world . . . there is today a rough consensus among intellectuals on political issues: the acceptance of the Welfare State; the desirability of decentralized power; a system of mixed economy and of political pluralism. . . . [And] the workers whose grievances were once the driving energy for social change, are more satisfied with the society than the intellectuals" (pp. 397–399).

For other views reflecting the end of ideology the following recent works should be consulted: John Strachey, *Contemporary Capitalism* (New York, 1956); C. A. R.

In this milieu intellectuals functioning as critics of society have become disaffected, according to Lipset, because "domestic politics, even liberal or socialist politics, can no longer serve as the arena for serious criticism from the left." [20] Disorganized, at a loss for a cause, and unable to fulfill their self-image, the liberal intellectuals "have turned from a basic concern with political and economic systems to criticism of other sections of the basic culture of society, particularly of elements which cannot be dealt with politically." [21] Or, in Bell: "Some of the younger intellectuals have found an outlet in science or university pursuits, but often at the expense of narrowing their talent into mere technique." [22]

The full import of the Bell and Lipset thesis can be derived principally from Bell's misinterpretation of Max Weber: a misinterpretation which leads him to consider Machiavelli and Weber in the same light, and to quote them at the head of the two key chapters of his study.[23] In keeping with his own interpretation of Weber, Bell distinguishes between the normative "ought" and the empirical "is" of politics and the "ineluctable tension" between the two. Ethics is concerned with justice, whereas concrete politics involves "a power struggle between organized groups to determine the allocation of privilege." [24] Concrete politics, in other words, is not concerned with the realization of an ideal, but, following Lord Acton, with the reaping of particular advantages within the limits of a given ethic—an ethic which sets out clearly the rules of the game governing the political jockeying for position and privilege. Thus, modern, mature democracies representing the end of ideology have, in effect, separated ethics from politics; and ideology, in so far as it continues to exist as a force in modern society, is nothing more than a cynical propaganda cover for the specific self-interest of competing groups. Modern politics, therefore, becomes amenable to analysis in terms of the mixed strategies of

---

Grossland, *The Future of Socialism* (New York, 1957); John K. Galbraith, *American Capitalism* (Boston, Rev. Ed., 1956), and *The Affluent Society* (Boston, 1958); Henry Wallich, *The Cost of Freedom* (New York, 1960); and the debate going on in England between the neo-revisionists and the fundamentalists in the pages of *Encounter*, *New Left Review*, and the *New Statesman*, particularly during 1960–1961. Limitations of space preclude any examination of these various approaches. With the exception of the English "fundamentalists," they all reflect the view, in greater or lesser degree, that the major problems of industrial society have been solved and that the remaining problems are basically technical and easily within our grasp. Perhaps the most unabashed statement of this position is to be found in Arthur Schlesinger, Jr., "Where Does the Liberal Go From Here?" *New York Times Magazine*, August 4, 1957.
[20] *Political Man*, p. 408.
[21] *Ibid.*, p. 409.
[22] *The End of Ideology*, p. 399.
[23] *Ibid.*, Chap. 12, and "The End of Ideology in the West: An Epilogue." The quotations used by Bell are: "He who seeks the salvation of souls, his own as well as others, should not seek it along the avenue of politics" (Weber); and "Men commit the error of not knowing when to limit their hopes" (Machiavelli).
[24] *Ibid.*, p. 279.

game theory (though neither Bell nor Lipset, surprisingly, have done so). The game is to be played, however, according to the generally accepted constitutional limits of a Weberian "ethic of responsibility." It implies, above all, the flat rejection of the radical commitment required by an "ethic of conscience" which "creates 'true believers' who burn with pure, unquenchable flame and can accept no compromise with faith." The ethic of responsibility is, in sum, "the pragmatic view which seeks reconciliation as its goal." [25] Modern liberals, willing as they are to accept their progress piecemeal and within the rules of the game are, therefore, to be distinguished from genuine ideologues who are seemingly unaware that the good society has already been achieved.

The basic distinction between the modern liberal and the ideologue revolves around the notion of commitment. If the ideologue, in Bell's terms, is committed to the consequences of ideas and is governed by passion, then, in contradistinction, the non-ideological liberal is uncommitted and free of any chiliastic vision of the transforming moment. The ideologue seeks political success, according to Bell, by organizing and arousing the masses into a social movement, and the function of ideology, therefore, is to fuse the energies of the great unwashed and ignite their passions into a mighty river of fire. But in order to do so, ideology must "simplify ideas, establish a claim to truth, and, in the union of the two, demand a commitment to action." [26]

The end of ideology is therefore linked to its inability nowadays to arouse the masses. And this inability, as we have seen, is the direct consequence of modern society's having solved the basic problems of industrial society. In this kind of society there is no room for ideologues who, standing on the upper rungs of the faith ladder, have become politically destabilizing factors. They are, if anything, a direct threat to the continuation of the good society. The modern politician *qua* politician is the man who understands how to manipulate and how to operate in a Machiavellian world which divorces ethics from politics. Modern democracy becomes, in this view, transformed into a system of technique *sans telos*. And democratic politics is reduced to a constellation of self-seeking pressure groups peaceably engaged in a power struggle to determine the allocation of privilege and particular advantage. Compromise and evolution are to be the means for achieving, in the context of this struggle, the few second-order social goals which continue to remain in an otherwise near perfect society. It is in this limited sense that the end of ideology clings desperately to its self-imposed label of enlightened, non-ideological, non-committed liberalism. And the *status quo* it defends in the name of democracy is a fundamental one—the already achieved good society.

All this, by Bell, is carefully nailed onto Max Weber's door. Had Bell,

[25] *Ibid.*, pp. 279–280.
[26] *Ibid.*, p. 396.

instead, opened the door and looked inside, he would have found that Weber's primary concern was the fusion of the "ethic of responsibility" and "the ethic of absolute ends." Contrary to Bell's facile interpretation, Weber was in no sense advocating a politics without passion. Passion without responsibility and politics without commitment were equally unacceptable to Weber. "Passion," "a feeling of responsibility," and a "sense of proportion" were for Weber the three pre-eminent qualities which were decisive for the politician. For Weber, the problem was the forging of "a warm passion and a cool sense of proportion . . . in one and the same soul." [27] In so far as the politician plays the game of politics without any sense of purpose, his actions are without meaning. In Weber's words, "The mere 'power politician' may get strong effects, but actually his work leads nowhere and is senseless."

In Weber, the "ethic of responsibility" and the "ethic of ultimate ends" were not to be regarded, as Bell seems to have done, as absolute contrasts. They were, instead, to be thought of as supplements reinforcing each other within the mind of the true politician, who was to act as the agent of social progress. In failing to take into account the consequences of his actions, and in refusing to admit the condition of human frailty, the chiliast was irresponsible and ineffective. But equally vacuous, in Weber's opinion, was the politician who sought to enhance his own power without any vision in mind. "Certainly all historical experience," wrote Weber, "confirms the truth—that man would not have attained the possible unless time and again he had reached out for the impossible."

Despite Bell's misinterpretation of Weber, there can be little doubt that his arguments and those of Lipset on the decline, if not the end, of ideology as an operative force in the Western world are based largely on fact. But whether or not this represents a desirable state of affairs is quite another matter. The favorable interpretation given to this development by Bell and Lipset has been generally accepted, if not applauded, by most observers. Yet, there seems to be a great deal of potential confusion over the meaning of "ideology" and "ideological thought" if care is not taken to use these terms consistently. The most exhaustive analysis of the concept appears in Karl Mannheim's well-known *Ideology and Utopia*.[28] In Mannheim, ideology is taken to mean the ideas and thought-patterns of the interest-bound ruling groups which explain, justify, and rationalize the *status quo*, while utopia is the intellectual stimulus provided by the oppressed groups who challenge the established order and seek to transform it into the good society. When Bell and Lipset speak of the "end of ideology," what they mean is the "end of utopian thought," for they are

[27] For Weber's position and the quotations used, see Hans H. Gerth and C. Wright Mills (eds.), *From Max Weber* (New York, 1946), pp. 115–116, 127–128.
[28] *Ideology and Utopia* (New York, 1955).

both clearly referring to the decline of socialist or Marxian ideas within the context of an affluent Western society. Lipset, however, pushes his argument further (and more explicitly than Bell) when he declares, contrary to the judgment of the most profound minds of Western political thought, that democracy "is the good society itself in operation." The classical distinction between "nature" and "convention" is thus obliterated, and the traditional role of the intellectual as social critic is no longer logically possible. For if "what ought to be" already is, then the intellectual has no other function than to describe and to celebrate the arrival of a Lipsetian utopia. Yet much of the intellectual output of today in film, on the stage, and in art reveals a profound discontent with things as they are. Lipset and Bell recognize this intellectual alienation but conclude that it is not political. It is only by narrowly defining politics as concerned with "voting behavior" or with "welfare measures" that they can come to such a conclusion. But if the traditional idea of political philosophy is maintained, there is yet some small contribution that intellectuals can make, which will be something other than a justification, tacit or overt, for whatever is.

"Liberals such as Lipset," writes one political scientist, "are proud of the progress which has been made in the Western world, but it is curious that they never acknowledge the fact that we have gotten as far as we have precisely because of the ideologies which stirred men to action." And if the end of ideology is, in fact, the case, "then we have the best explanation of why we in the West are standing still." [29]

But the most bitterly forceful comments have come from another source. C. Wright Mills and Bell and Lipset have been each other's severest critics,[30] and Mills, defining the end of ideology as "an intellectual celebration of apathy" which has collapsed reasoning into reasonableness, attacks the emphasis of Bell and Lipset on strictly factual analysis: "The disclosure of fact . . . is the rule. The facts are duly weighed, carefully

---

[29] Andrew Hacker, in an otherwise favorable review of Lipset's book (*Commentary*, June 1961). A further criticism made by Hacker concerns the limitations of a purely empirical approach to the problems of modern society. If the myths of the left-wing ideology have in fact declined, this does not necessarily imply that we have matured, politically, in the sense of being willing not only to face, but to live with the facts. In the words of Hacker: "Lipset hopes to supplant myth with fact. Empiricism, like it or not, forces one to concentrate on things as they are or as they have been. A description of how things *might be* were we to embark on changing the social order is bound to be speculative, not factual. . . . The visions of ideologues, then, coupled with their mythologies about the world of reality, should be evaluated not on empirical but on strategic grounds."
[30] For an incredibly nasty reference to the late C. Wright Mills, see Seymour M. Lipset and Neil Smelser, "Change and Controversy in Recent American Sociology," *British Journal of Sociology*, March 1961, reprinted by the Institute of Industrial Relations, Reprint No. 164, Berkeley, 1961, pp. 50–51.

balanced, always hedged. Their power to outrage, their power truly to enlighten in a political way, their power to aid decision, even their power to clarify some situation—all that is blunted and destroyed." [31]

Facts, of course, do not in themselves have the power to outrage, enlighten, or clarify. And perhaps, for this reason, Mills' argument is in need of some elaboration. An empiricist, devoid of any "passion," is no more capable of describing the world as it is than is an ideologue who views the world around him solely through the lens of his ideological *Weltanschauung*. The hope, or the belief, that the end of the ideological cast of mind will permit us to view the world uncolored by value judgments is nothing but the delusion of an unsophisticated positivism; which is, in essence, a flight from moral responsibility. For facts are themselves the product of viewing "reality" through theoretical preconceptions which, in turn, are conditioned by the problems confronting us. And the theoretical precepts which determine the relevant facts of a particular view of "reality" are not themselves entirely value free. Social theories, in short, are the result of our concern with specific problems. And social problems are concerned with ethical goals. Social theorists, furthermore, differ in their value judgments and thus differ in their theoretical constructions of "reality." They differ, that is, in the problems they see, or, what amounts to the same thing, they see a given problem in different ways. Consequently, they differ as to the facts relevant to a given problem. There is, in other words, a selectivity of facts in the analysis of social problems. Some facts included in one approach are excluded in another; and even those held in common may, and usually do, differ in the weight given to them and in their theoretical and causal interrelations.

All this raises the following possibilities: that the theory of verification in the social sciences is of a different order from that found in the other sciences; that the moral preconceptions of social theorists unavoidably determine the shape of their theories, the classification systems they employ, and their concepts and hypotheses; and that objective criteria of relevance for the evaluation of competing constructions of social reality, therefore, may not exist. Perhaps the best we can hope for is some form of objective relativism. But however that may be, it is clear that those who would suggest that sociological analysis is a pure science objectively concerned with pure "facts" are indulging in an ideological positivism uniquely their own; a *wertlos* [32] positivism which amounts to nothing more than an unthinking apologia for whatever is. And their value judgments, because of their implicit subconsciousness, are all the more inflexible and rigid. Their pronouncements, moreover, do not admit of com-

[31] "Letters to the New Left," *New Left Review*, Sept.–Oct. 1960.
[32] Max Weber distinguishes between science as being *wertfrei* and *wertlos*. *Wertfrei* is defined as being free from prevailing passion and prejudice; free, that is, to create its own values. *Wertlos*, on the other hand, is applied to the falsely objective or "scientistic" approach to social problems.

promise and take on an *ex cathedra* quality found only in those who believe they have somehow secured *the* truth—or *the* good society.

Along these lines, C. Wright Mills would agree that the end of ideology makes a fetish of empiricism and entails an ideology of its own—an ideology of political complacency for the justification of things as they are, and the celebration of modern society as a going concern. Utopian thought, or left-wing criticism, according to Mills, is concerned with a "structural criticism" of the institutions of society and with the formulation of programs for reform and fundamental change. It need not entail an apocalyptic or dogmatic vision. The choice is not between the wild-eyed fanatic and the cool, uncommitted pragmatist who is willing to take his progress piecemeal, if at all. Ideology need not be, as Bell tends to, equated with chiliastic fanaticism. Its major function is to apply intelligence—the fusion of passion and critical reason—to the problems of the modern world. And intelligence can never lie down with itself in a passionate embrace of self-love. It must be concerned with the human condition and its betterment in an always imperfect world. Its justification for being is, in a word, progress.

Whether or not it is true that progress in the past has been exclusively the result of ideological conflict, it is nevertheless true that progress, as distinct from mere change, can be defined meaningfully only in terms of some "vision." For progress, as Santayana has observed, "is relative to an ideal which reflection creates." And it is here that, perhaps, the most serious criticism of the end of ideology can be made.

The modern politician is viewed, appreciatively by Bell and Lipset, as a non-committed individual drenched in the art of compromise. The ideologue, on the other hand, is committed to some pattern of institutional change which, in terms of his values, becomes transformed into social progress. It is irrelevant whether one agrees with the vision of a particular ideology. The important point is that freedom, in the philosophical sense, and a social commitment which transcends the *status quo* are interrelated and interdependent.

Rejecting the notion of man tied to a merciless fate which robs him of his future, we are left to regard him free and immersed in the process of becoming. Man is, in other words, a potential, and his willingness or ability to seize life by the throat, as it were, and force it to serve his needs, is a measure of his freedom. Freedom, in short, excludes a complacency which rests on past or present achievements, or which nurtures the illusion of having already achieved the best of all possible worlds where progress, in any meaningful sense is, by definition, no longer possible. If man, living as he does in a grossly imperfect world, is not uniquely determined by his past and is nothing but a potential in terms of his impending future, then the act of commitment is a prior requirement for the realization of his freedom and thus his future. And if modern democracy is predicated on the end of ideology, that is, on the end of commitment, then it negates itself and becomes the very denial of freedom. If it has any commitment at all, it is the false commitment to itself—to the narcissistic approval of itself as it is in all its sparkling perfection—with the net result that it has retreated from the problems of the world about it, spending its time, as it does, idly admiring its reflection in the looking glass, and only now and then showing some concern over the occasional pimple which erupts to mar its beauty temporarily.

Another objection to the end of ideology lies in its inability to make the fundamental distinction between what it considers to be the good society and a social theory which has become obsolete as a result of the changing values and problems of succeeding generations. Confusing the two and still obsessed and blinded by the liberal orientation of the 1930's, it looks at the current situation and proudly declares that the problems of the Great Depression have been, by and large, satisfactorily resolved.

Bell's book was accurately subtitled "On the Exhaustion of Political Ideas in the Fifties." Indeed, we have been, and continue to be, faced with a bankruptcy of political ideas at a time when certain critical developments have been taking place in the United States—developments for which the end of ideology is in large measure responsible. On the international front there is the tendency to apply a splintering empiricism to our international problems, and on the domestic front there is our inability to cope with, let alone admit, the economic malaise that has seized the American economy since the end of the Korean war.

Concerning international matters, Hans J. Morgenthau writes of our "surrendering piecemeal to the facts of foreign policy . . . of thinking and acting as though there were nothing else to foreign policy but this [or that] particular set of empirical facts" concerning this or that foreign policy problem.[33] The latter-day pragmatists, in Morgenthau's opinion, are basically anti-theoretical, anti-utopian empiricists who pride themselves on having "no illusions about the facts as they are nor any grand design for changing them." Indeed, their crowning achievement, in their own view, is their "courage to look the facts in the face and . . . deal with each issue on its own terms." Underlying their entire approach is their profound belief that "the problems of the social world [will] yield to a series of piecemeal empirical attacks, unencumbered by preconceived notions and comprehensive planning." As a result our foreign policy lacks an overall cohesiveness and has degenerated into a series of unrelated operations not always consistent with each other, and often far removed from the realities of the situation which the facts, of their own accord, are supposed to make clear. Thus, according to Morgenthau, in trying to escape the Scylla of utopianism we are foundering on the Charybdis of empiricism. In the name of "facts" we are reduced to approaching the

[33] "The Perils of Political Empiricism," *Commentary*, July 1962.

major problems of our existence as though they were mere matters of technical manipulation. What is obviously needed is an ideology to interpret the "facts" of a social situation and to suggest meaningful solutions in terms of a particular reading of these self-same "facts." [34]

In a similar vein, other end-of-ideology advocates deny that there is anything substantively wrong with the American economy. It is their unwillingness to engage in any form of structural criticism, and their tendency to look upon those who do as vestigial appendages of modern democratic society that compels them to regard the existing tools as adequate for the correction of what they consider to be a temporary and fleeting imbalance. They deny the necessity for any structural reorganization of society and insist that it is all a matter of mere technical adjustment within the existing canons of responsibility. . . .

It is time that the graduate departments of our major universities became more than just places where competent technicians are trained. Rather than making what Mills called "structural criticism" their business, they have enthroned a false scientism, made a fetish of an objectivity which, of necessity, must also be false, and have in the process become centres for radiating the end-of-ideology approach to social problems. In essence, they have become the great defenders of the American Establishment.

Though the intellectuals in our universities have rationalized and made the end of ideology respectable, they have done so *ex post facto*; they were preceded by the politicians who, without being conscious that their actions had a name, practiced it nevertheless. The politicians have long become, to use Max Weber's terminology, scientists without vision and sensualists without heart, but at least they have had the saving grace, unlike the intellectuals, of not rationalizing their intellectual bankruptcy into the good society.

It has been agreed that Bell's and Lipset's account of the end of ideology in the West is, in large part, accurate. There is, nevertheless, a judgment to be made apart from the accuracy of their account. Bell and Lipset regard the end of ideology as good. Our point here is that it must be judged contextually, and that under the present conditions it borders on the disastrous. This can be illustrated by comparing the two supreme

---

[34] Hans Morgenthau denies the existence of unalloyed facts as follows: "Facts have no social meaning in themselves. It is the significance we attribute to certain facts of our sensory experience—in terms of our hopes and fears, our memories, inventions, and expectations—that creates them as social facts. The social world itself, then, is but an artifact of man's mind, the reflection of his thoughts and the creation of his actions. Every social act (and even our awareness of empirical data as social facts) presupposes a theory of society, however acknowledged, inchoate, and fragmentary. It is not given to us to choose between a social philosophy consistent with itself and founded on experience which can serve as a guide to understanding and an instrument for successful actions, and an implicit and untested philosophy which is likely to blur understanding and mislead action."

technicians of American politics—Franklin D. Roosevelt and John F. Kennedy.

Early in his campaign of 1960 Kennedy assumed the mantle, sceptre, and orb of Franklin Delano Roosevelt. He presented himself to the electorate in Roosevelt's image and proclaimed the New Frontier. Sounding very much like a committed ideologue with a vision, he vowed to get America moving again. That the New Frontier, unlike the New Deal, bogged down in a series of debilitating political compromises in no way destroys the basic validity of President Kennedy's self-identification with Roosevelt. Both are supreme examples of the non-committed, non-ideological politician acting strictly out of political expediency. Both placed the highest value on political success at the polls and regarded such success as the *sine qua non* of their existence. And neither had any fixed, or well-defined vision of the good society. Any social interests they upheld were not so much out of conviction as out of their inherent political value at the polls. Yet, though they are similar in all these and other respects, the consequences of their common and purely political approach to politics are not the same. The 1960's are, obviously, not the 1930's. And it is in the context of each of these two periods of crisis that the end of ideology common to both Roosevelt and Kennedy must be judged.

The crisis of the 1930's gave rise, through the New Dealers, to a new wave of hope, and to the conviction that by social engineering, things could be put aright. The flood of social legislation in the early days of the New Deal was an extraordinary attempt to bring about the needed institutional changes. This passion for pragmatic social experimentation was deeply rooted in the belief that human nature was highly, if not infinitely plastic. It was, in other words, basically optimistic and full of hope in a time of crisis. It was an age of critical thought, of regeneration, of faith in man's power to change the institutional complex within which he lived. It engaged, unstintingly, in a fundamental criticism of man and the institutional melange within which he had entrapped himself. Society, in short, was to be reconstructed in the image and in the interests of the so-called common man. But there was no overall blueprint. It was an empirical approach to democracy.

If there was no ideological cohesion, there was at least general agreement that something had to be done and a clear understanding of the problem in personal terms. The ugly tear in the social fabric of a once prosperous society was readily understood by the man in the street. It was a part of his everyday experience and affected or was a direct and frightening threat to his continued well-being. And it was on this stage that the end of ideology entered in the form of President Roosevelt.

Being a non-ideologue, Roosevelt responded to the political pressures of his time. This supreme politician could wet his finger and hold it up to the prevailing winds. When he found the winds blowing steadily, in gale force, in one particular direction, it was not difficult for him to determine the conditions of political success and thus to bring an enormous pressure to bear on the Congress in support of his program. The political coloration and social innovations of the New Deal were largely the result of political expediency in a country where political success counts for all. The tune of the New Deal was played by ear, and the end of ideology in the guise of a charismatic president served to make the vast power of the presidency responsive to the public will.

The current crisis is not immediately understandable in direct, personal terms by the ubiquitous man-in-the-street. The threat of nuclear annihilation numbs his sense of credulity and is so vast as to be beyond his conceptual capacity. The problem of disarmament is also much too complicated to be fully comprehended by him, except in the perversely myopic sense of realizing that his economic welfare is somehow tied to the continuance of the arms race. Despite the poor performance of the economy since 1953 and the growth of unemployment, the affluent society continues to maintain its image unimpaired. There are no breadlines, as in the 1930's, and the economic problem has not yet pierced the individual's consciousness, since, for most people, it is not yet a direct threat. And if one major aspect of the economic problem is the long-run power threat implied by the disparate rates of economic growth between the United States and the Soviet Union, then surely this is the most remote of his immediate concerns. Furthermore, foreign policy has become so caught up in the ideology of the Cold War that the common man can only react to it emotionally, and unthinkingly approve the vast expenditures needed for a senseless and suicidal arms race. In short, the problems of the 1960's are much too abstract for the limited social vision of the common man.

It is in this totally different context that a non-ideological man like President Kennedy had to operate. It is not the kind of crisis which confronts the individual with understandable, let alone meaningful, problems to which he can respond politically. So when President Kennedy wet his finger and held it up to the political winds, he found them blowing simultaneously in all directions. As a non-ideologue he had no commitment, with the result that he was found standing squarely in the center, surrounded on all sides by advisers who were similarly uncommitted. Democratic politics has thus degenerated into a conforming consensus around the middle. This does not mean, of course, that nothing at all was done. In both foreign and domestic policy the President moved first in one direction, felt the situation out and then, according to his political sensibilities, moved in another. He excelled in practicing a pragmatism that has become wishy-washy; an "ideology of caginess" that became internally inconsistent and directionless. There was no coherence; no well-thought-out sense of purpose in foreign policy, as Hans Morgenthau has pointed out, and this was even more obvious with respect to domestic policy.

Above all, and unlike the 1930's, there was no general consensus in the body politic to which the President could respond, out of sheer political expediency, in a clear and consistent manner. In short, there was no limiting frame of reference within which to innovate, and, lacking one of his own, he floundered, compromised, and tried to be all things to all men. Leadership in these circumstances requires vision as well as technique. President Kennedy failed to provide the needed leadership precisely because he had no clear picture of what ought to be done. Indeed, like Lipset, he rationalized the emptiness of modern society and declared that it is the good society and that all the problems which do remain are purely technical.

Two talks by the late President more than amply demonstrate just how deeply "committed" he was to the Bell and Lipset thesis. In his remarks before the Economic Conference held in Washington on May 21, 1962, the President distinguished between myth and reality in these words:

I would like also to say a word about the difference between myth and reality. Most of us are conditioned for many years to have a political viewpoint, Republican or Democrat—liberal, conservative, moderate. The fact of the matter is that most of the problems, or at least many of them that we now face, are technical problems, are administrative problems. They are very sophisticated judgments which do not lend themselves to the great sort of "passionate movements" which have stirred this country so often in the past. Now they deal with questions which are beyond the comprehension of most men.

A month later, at his 1962 commencement address at Yale University, Kennedy further elaborated on this theme.

Today . . . the central domestic problems of our time are more subtle and less simple. They do not relate to basic clashes of philosophy and ideology, but to ways and means of reaching common goals—to research for sophisticated solutions to complex and obstinate issues.

What is at stake in our economic decisions today is not some grand warfare of rival ideologies which will sweep the country with passion but the practical management of a modern economy. What we need are not labels and clichés but more basic discussion of the sophisticated and technical questions involved in keeping a great economic machinery moving ahead. . . . Political labels and ideological approaches are irrelevant to the solutions.

. . . The problems of . . . the Sixties as opposed to the kinds of problems we faced in the Thirties demand subtle challenges for which technical answers—not political answers—must be provided.

Thus, the art of compromise and technical manipulation is all that remains. The problems usually associated with an ethic of conscience are no longer with us. The faith ladder has been stripped of its rungs, and we are all standing on the hard ground of objective fact.

Bell and Lipset are of one mind. Whereas the old ideologies of the West have become exhausted by the march of Western progress, new ideologies have arisen in Asia and Africa—the ideologies, according to Bell, of industrialization, modernization, Pan-Arabism, color, and nationalism. The new ideologies, unlike the old, are not being fashioned by intellectuals along universal or humanistic lines. Rather, they are instrumentally parochial and employed by political leaders who have created them for purposes of rapid development and national power. And the disoriented Western liberals have desperately embraced the new ideology of economic development to "wash away the memory of old disillusionments." [35] In this sense, Lipset believes there is "still a real need for political analysis, ideology, and controversy, within the world community, if not within the Western democracies," and the Western ideologue, stripped of issues, must now focus his attention on this new area. Though ideology and passion are no longer necessary in the affluent democracies of the West, they are very much needed in the less affluent countries of the world. In the underdeveloped countries, we should encourage the radical and socialist politicians because, according to Lipset, "only parties which promise to improve the situation of the masses through widespread reform . . . can hope to compete with the communists." [36] Therefore, the disaffected liberals of the West, the unreconstructed intellectuals, the trade union leaders (at least those who are still liberal), and the socialists have a positive role to play—abroad; where their "irresponsible and demagogic" visions and their psychological or pathological need to criticize can be put to good use in developing free political and economic institutions.

In time, if we are successful, the underdeveloped countries will become developed and as they, too, solve all their pressing political, social, and economic problems, ideologies will wither on the vines. Then peace will break out in an enlarged West and international relations and disputes will, like purely internal problems, be governed by an international ethic of responsibility. The Soviet Union, in the process, will, like some execrable disease, have been effectively quarantined and left to dissolve in its own juices. Or, if the rapid industrialization of the Soviet Union were also to result in a decline of dogma, there would then be an end to ideology throughout the world, and peace, in the absence of commitment, would descend like a dove which would forever roost in the parliaments of man.

Lipset and Bell are, in effect, arguing that the nations of the world are all racing toward a static state of equilibrium; only some countries have had a head start. A few have already achieved the good society. Others are fast approaching it. And still others, the underdeveloped countries, have only just begun their ascent. In time, all will have arrived, but

[35] *The End of Ideology*, pp. 397–8.
[36] *Political Man*, p. 416.

until such time it will be the responsibility of those already at the pinnacle to reach down and help the others up. In all this, it would seem, dynamic change is a transitory phenomenon, and all of human history, in all its turmoil and in all its travail, has been moving, inexorably, toward this supreme goal of universal peace. At bottom, what Bell and Lipset are giving us is a philosophy of history—if not of the past, then certainly of the future.

The argument is incredible. Indeed, it is more than that. It is the Marxian dialectic brought to a halt in the final synthesis of the modern, non-ideological, democratic welfare state shimmering in the radiance of a non-committed scientism. It has, furthermore, one element in common with most other philosophies of history—it celebrates the present. The present becomes the touchstone for measuring the past and the future. Bell and Lipset have stood Hegel on his head once more. Instead of the better being the critic of the good, the good, in Bell and Lipset, insures that the better will not come into existence.[37]

The end of ideology of Bell and Lipset is nothing more than the ideology of the *status quo*. It can be so described in the sense that if the good society has already been achieved, then, by definition, the need for structural criticism no longer exists. And American political thought, in so far as it shares the convictions of Bell and Lipset, is fast approaching the end of its ideological line. The danger is that this end-of-ideology approach to social problems will promote an ideological brittleness and intransigence which will effectively rule out any criticism of any of the basic presuppositions concerning the righteousness of its cause. For the worship of "scientism" tends to convert "facts" into revealed truths which, by their nature, brook no challenge and refuse to be negotiated.

As for the underdeveloped countries, the ideology of the *status quo* in this country, despite the admirable exhortations of Bell and Lipset, has consistently supported reactionary regimes in these underdeveloped areas and has resisted, or sought to modify in most cases, the pressures for fundamental change. The ideology of the East, on the other hand, poses with some measure of success as the champion of downtrodden peoples and as the vehicle of change. In this sense it has shown itself to be more viable and more willing to adapt itself to the pragmatics of the situation. At any rate it does not present itself in the ludicrous light of proposing to export its unwanted and socially useless ideologues to the underdeveloped countries.

As an epilogue to Bell, if it is true, as he argues, that the New Left in Britain "has passion but little definition of the future," it is also true that in the liberalism of the United States even the passion has been

[37] On this, see Irving Louis Horowitz, "Another View from Our Left," *New Politics*, Winter 1963; and the discussion on Horowitz' critique, "Two Views from the Left," Joseph Clark and Elwin Powell, *New Politics*, Spring 1963.

leached out. Liberalism in this country is dead and the end of ideology is its legacy.

As we have seen, there is a great deal of controversy centering around many of the assumptions underlying the end-of-ideology hypothesis. Nevertheless, Bell's and Lipset's essential theme that traditional Marxist movements in America have failed is irrefutable.[38] The Communist Party of the United States, after reaching its zenith in the late 1930s, had deteriorated into an insignificant ideological sect by the mid-1950s. By blinding party members to social reality, ideology played a significant role in the decline of the American Communist movement. Regarding ideologies of total change, Max Weber noted: "The believer in an ethic of ultimate ends feels "responsible" only for seeing to it that the flame of pure intentions is not quenched: For example, the flame of protesting against the injustice of the social order." [39] Within a social movement, this "flame of pure intentions," or radical consciousness, serves a cohesive function. That is, it defines directions for social change and helps members to reinforce each other's belief systems. However, if a social movement desires to achieve its goals it must appeal to those outside the movement, especially in a pluralistic society. In other words, a social movement must have at least tacit external support to achieve its aims. A social movement exhibiting a radical consciousness antithetical to the common-sense world will have little chance to achieve its objectives. For example, one of the authors, in an examination of the propaganda songs of the American Communist Party, found that the world view of Communists and "fellow travelers" guided the movement on a false course in its attempt to mobilize the urban masses.[40] Southern ballads addressed to Benny Goodman enthusiasts failed dismally. Jeans and work-shirted singers did not convert unionists dressed in their Sunday best at weekend CIO picnics. Lyrics stating that President Franklin Roosevelt was a mass murderer did little to enhance the ability of the Almanac Singers to communicate with the masses. Folk-styled propaganda songs did not create class consciousness among urban workers, most of whom were committed to "swing and sway." Yet the ideology of the Stalinists and their supporters dictated these

[38] Daniel Bell, "The Background and Development of Marxian Socialism in the United States," in Donald Egbert and Stow Persons, eds., *Socialism and American Life*, vol. 1 (Princeton, N.J.: Princeton University Press, 1952), pp. 215–405; and S. M. Lipset, *Political Man, ibid.*, pp. 403–417.
[39] Max Weber, "Politics as a Vocation," in Hans Gerth and C. Wright Mills, eds., *From Max Weber: Essays in Sociology* (New York: Oxford University Press, 1946), p. 121.
[40] R. Serge Denisoff, *Folk Consciousness: People's Music and American Communism* (unpublished Ph.D. thesis) (Department of Sociology, Simon Fraser University, 1968).

approaches in opposition to the more conventional musical wisdoms of the times. In short, the ideology of the Communists segregated them from the very people they were trying to organize and thwarted the goals their songs espoused.

Thus, while a rigid ideological purity may promote the cohesiveness of a movement by reinforcing a particular set of goals, it can simultaneously hamper the movement's tactical effectiveness by limiting the range of means available to those having an ideological imprimatur. In his Revolution in the Revolution? the Marxian theoretician Regis Debray discusses the tactical dangers inherent in a doctrinaire transplanting of revolutionary theory and credits the success of Castro's Cuban Revolution to its freedom from imported political conceptions: "One may well consider it a stroke of good luck that Fidel had not read the military writings of Mao Tse-tung before disembarking on the coast of Oriente: he could thus invent, on the spot and out of his own experience, principles of a military doctrine in conformity with the terrain." [41] Concerning the ideologue's theoretical or intellectual approach to revolution, Debray writes: ". . . the intellectual will try to grasp the present through pre-conceived ideological constructs and live it through books. He will be less able than others to invent, improvise, make do with available resources, decide instantly on bold moves when he is in a tight spot. Thinking that he already knows, he will learn more slowly, display less flexibility." [42]

As we have noted elsewhere, historical change also serves to invalidate the ideology of a social movement. The Socialist Party of the United States is a case in point. During the first two decades of the twentieth century, the party gained increasing support on its planks of woman suffrage, old-age pensions, unemployment, accident and health insurance, labor reforms, and public ownership of utilities. During the Depression years, many of the changes sought by the Socialists, particularly in the area of labor-management relations, were embodied in Roosevelt's New Deal legislation. The elections of 1948 mark the last major attempt of the Socialists to gain political recognition and power. This was the year that the defecting left wing of the Democratic Party formed the Progressive Party and nominated Henry Wallace for the presidency. It was also the last year that Norman Thomas, six-time candidate for the Socialist Party, ran for this office. In announcing his retirement from future presidential races, Thomas observed that most of the reforms the Socialists had been fighting for had come into being.

Thus, it would seem that traditional Marxist movements—both Communist and Socialist—had become ideologically passé, at least in North America, by the early 1950s. However, does the decline of Marxist move-

[41] Regis Debray, *Revolution in the Revolution?* (New York: Grove Press, Inc., 1967), p. 20.
[42] *Ibid.*, p. 21.

ments mean the end of ideology per se, or just the end of one ideological school? We shall argue, in what follows, that the "end of ideology" indeed signifies the end of a Hegelian world view based on the notion of progress and that contemporary movements, both right and left, are predicated on a more apocalyptic twentieth-century world view.

THE END OF PROGRESS

It must be borne in mind that, although Marx accurately perceived the contradictions inherent in the division of labor in nineteenth-century Europe, his perception of the road to a utopian Socialist state was based on the productive capacity inherent in the Industrial Revolution. In this respect, Marx's orientation to the idea of progress was that of the positivist school of philosophy. As Georg Iggers has pointed out in "The Idea of Progress," this dominant ideology of the nineteenth century embodied an unquestioned faith in scientific, technical, intellectual, and political progress:

Scientific inquiry [for the positivists] would inevitably reveal the lawfulness of the universe and social science the lawfulness of society. For Pierre Proudhon, Condorcet, Comte, Marx, Mill, and Spencer, there was such a thing as a scientific or rational society. For most of these thinkers, the steady advance of the sciences became identical with the progress of society. . . . For them the scientific study of society aimed at the discovery of general laws governing social movements, and these general laws were formulated as laws of social progress. History was seen as a movement toward a normative society.[43]

However, this faith in progress began to break down at the turn of the twentieth century. Within a period of less than sixty years, two world wars, a major economic depression, the thermonuclear age, imminent environmental collapse, the population explosion, and the increasing destitution of over half the world's population have almost completely destroyed any illusions about progress. On the political scene, a number of developments have contributed to the decline of a radical intellectual tradition based on the idea of progress.

1. The ideals of liberalism, on which Western intellectual and political thought is predicated, have become divorced from the realities of modern social structure. Liberal ideals, although relevant to the conditions of at least the eighteenth and early nineteenth centuries, were anchored in several assumptions about the nature of society that are not applicable today. C. Wright Mills, in his essay "Liberal Values in the Modern

[43] Georg G. Iggers, "The Idea of Progress: A Critical Reassessment," *American Historical Review*, 71 (October 1965): 3–4.

World," discusses these assumptions, which we have paraphrased as follows: [44]

(a) Liberalism assumes that both freedom and security flourish in a world of small entrepreneurs. However, in the twentieth century, ownership of property has become enormously concentrated and an increasing number of citizens have no expectation of ownership.

(b) Liberal ideas of the "general will" and "public opinion" have assumed the predominance of rural or small-scale communities. However, we no longer live in this sort of small-scale world—70 percent of North Americans live in large urban centers.

(c) Classical liberalism stresses the autonomy of different institutional orders. On the other hand, a reality of the modern planned and rationalized state is the fusion of several institutional orders (the economic, political, military, educational, etc.).

(d) An important assumption of liberal thought is that rationality, the basis of judgment and decision-making, resides in the individual. However, the exercise of decision-making rationality has shifted away from the individual and is now held by large corporate and government institutions. Consequently, the individual has little basis on which to exercise reason.

(e) Related to the exercise of substantive rationality by the individual is a belief in the explicitness of authority. That is, man must know who exercises power so that he has a basis for deciding whether to obey it or challenge it. Today, however, it is difficult to locate the specific holders of power in society—they are hidden behind increasingly large bureaucracies.

2. A number of conditions related to the development of mass society have altered the context in which radical political opposition can be expressed. This theme is developed by Haber in "The End of Ideology as Ideology." Again, we paraphrase his discussion: [45]

(a) Radical opposition is not possible either within or outside the existing two-party system in America.

(b) Revolutionary opposition is not possible where a state controls highly sophisticated and efficient means of violence.

(c) In modern society, the public is excluded from political responsibility. Information and alternatives of choice are often not made available to the public. The distribution of information is controlled by the mass media. Decisions are not made publicly, nor are decision-makers held publicly accountable.

(d) The state, through its control of social resources, can ameliorate

[44] C. Wright Mills, "Liberal Values in the Modern World," in Irving Louis Horowitz, ed., *Power, Politics and People: The Collected Essays of C. Wright Mills* (New York: Ballantine Books, 1963), pp. 187–195. Paraphrased at pp. 191–194.
[45] R. Alan Haber, "The End of Ideology as Ideology," *Our Generation*, 4 (November 1966): 51–68. Paraphrased at pp. 56–57. See also the full text of this reading on pp. 458–475.

grievances which could be used as a basis of political opposition. In this sense, conflict, which is endemic to society, is managed. For example, the government can institute and accomplish short-run goals to "cool off" any dissidence in the areas of civil rights, poverty, unemployment, etc.

(e) Fear of "international Communism" is used to discredit actions based on a criticism of the domestic system. "Anti-Communism" is not only a rallying cry for social integration but also a convenient charge by which to undermine any social criticism. The repression of dissent by playing on fears of Communism did not end with the death of Senator McCarthy.

3. With the exception of minor recessions in 1953–1954 and 1957–1958, the decade of the 1950s was one of prosperity, and economic goals became paramount in American society. After World War II, increased purchasing power plus a shortage of consumer goods led to a threat of inflation. In the late 1940s and early 1950s public spending, particularly in military expenditures, was cut back and the production of consumer goods was encouraged. Unemployment was generally low and a vast new army of white collar workers came into being—the middle class, nonunionized, apolitical "organization man." Americans never had it so good, and unparalleled affluence was not a breeding ground for radical discontent and criticism.

4. The various reversals of Soviet policy in the early days of World War II (for example, the Russian-German Nonaggression Pact and the invasion of Poland), the excesses of the Stalinist era, the ruthlessness during the Chinese Revolution, and the invasions of Hungary and Czechoslovakia, disillusioned many American left wing radicals with the Communist model. American radicals found that Communism could be just as repressive of and antagonistic to basic human values as fascism or imperialism.

5. With the beginning of the Cold War, the realization came to Americans that the United States had assumed the responsibility of being the world's "top nation." The resources of the nation and its cultural rhetoric thus became concerned with such matters as "police action," "balance of power," "making the world safe for democracy," "peace keeping," and a host of other stabilizing and conservative goals. Radical dissent in the United States reached its lowest point during the Korean War and its aftermath of military defeat.

Concomitant with this decline in radical social thought there arose the end-of-ideology intellectual thesis, which held that contemporary liberal democracy marked the penultimate stage in social progress. All that remained to achieve utopia, according to this thesis, was to apply the principles of liberal democracy to the solution of critical social problems. This ideological content of the end-of-ideology thesis is labeled "reformist" by R. Alan Haber in the following article.

R. Alan Haber, "The End of Ideology as Ideology," Our Generation, 4 (November 1966), 51–68. Reprinted by permission of R. Alan Haber and Our Generation.

INTRODUCTION

Since the mid-1930's, a sociological literature has developed analyzing or forecasting "the end of ideology" in the West. Major statements of this theory have been: Daniel Bell, *The End of Ideology*; Seymour Lipset, *Political Man*; and Edward Shils, "Ideology and Civility: on the Politics of the Intellectual."

While some left wing intellectuals have taken issue with the theory, in general, its pronouncement was welcomed as an important air-clearing statement of the self-evident.

The "end of ideology" theory states that political theory and practice which aims at radical social transformation has ended, at least in the West. The reasons for this are: first, the disillusionment of the last 40 years with mass movements, with revolution and with the socialist-classless utopia projected by Marxism. Second, Marxism-Leninism, which has been the main carrier of ideology, has been discredited as an intellectual-political system. Third, the class conflicts and system-wide problems which give rise to ideology have generally been solved, so no longer is there an objective base for such a social analysis. Further, the problems which are pressing for the society are of high complexity, do not have clear solutions, and political methods don't appear the most fruitful means of treatment. Finally, the social and economic theories, on which ideology has been based, have been disproved or brought into serious question, so the intellectual underpinnings for ideological politics is removed.

In addition, to this contention about reality, the "end of ideology" theorists make a value assertion. They see the end of ideology as a desirable development. In its place they describe a different kind of politics—the politics of "civility," or as it will be called in this paper, reformism.

There are several key problems in analyzing this theory:

1. "Ideology" has passed through many meanings. The theorists use it vaguely. Can the concept be given a rigorous definition?

2. There is an empirical problem of verification. Has "it" ended? And, if so, are the causes those suggested by the theorists?

3. The theory is both descriptive and evaluative. It describes a change and holds that the change is *good*. Does the value judgment influence the empirical analysis?

This paper will attempt to give a precise statement of the theory and to subject it to critical analysis. It will give particular attention to the social conditions alleged to underlie the end of ideology, as contrasted with those leading to ideology.

WHAT IS MEANT BY THE "END OF IDEOLOGY"?

The writers give numerous examples of ideology. They include older views like Nazism, McCarthyism, Bolshevism, and contemporary passions like nationalism, Pan-Africanism and economic development. However, they are quite imprecise in defining ideology, in specifying the applicability of the theory, or in making clear the key variables responsible for the change they describe.

For instance, they attribute a number of characteristics to ideology: the discontinuity of good and evil, the secularization of religious fervor, the ease with which rhetoric replaces reason, passion substitutes for analysis, and double standards and distortion displace objective criteria of evaluation. But they do not include in their theory status quo ideology like the American Way of Life and Anti-Communism, even though these exhibit many of the same characteristics.

Also, they disclaim the applicability of the theory to the newly developed countries—where it is acknowledged, and lamented, that ideology *is* the basis of politics. However, they fail to specify the institutional or other characteristics which differentiate the "West" from the non-West for the purpose of indicating the decline or ascendance of ideology.

They do not analyze the radical right in America as a mass political movement having ideological bases, nor do they deal with the scope, social basis and ideological character of the "New Conservatism" such as represented by the *National Review*, the Chicago economists and related intellectual centers. Nor do they deal with the neo-fascistic movements in Western Europe and Japan. Often they seem to equate ideology with Marxism, and hence with a materialist analysis of society, a social dynamic built on class struggle, and a dialectic of history leading inevitably, though convulsively, to the "good society." Yet they do not identify the critical conditions which lead to the decline of the left while invigorating the right.

Several points can give specification of the object of their analysis:

First, the "end of ideology" is meant to be historically specific. It refers to the end since the last war of a kind of *idea system* held by intellectuals. It does not mean a rejection of the intellectual theory that ideas are socially determined or that they mask and rationalize economic or social relations.

Second, the theory concerns what Mannheim would call *utopian* thinking—ideas which transcend reality and themselves enter the dialectic as instruments of change. It is not referring to the relatively stable set of ideas with which a society justifies and mythologizes itself.

Third, the theory is almost wholly concerned with *"left"* ideology, that is, with utopian ideas oriented around equalitarian, democratic values, and critical of the existing order.

Fourth, their use of ideology refers to politics, the set of ideas underlying a political movement which seeks radical social transformation. The "end of ideology" theory is really an "end of ideological politics" theory.

IDEOLOGY AND IDEOLOGICAL POLITICS

The writers identify a number of values and attitudes alleged to define ideology. They stress its projection of a utopia, qualitatively different from present society, its belief in revolution or apocalyptic change, its willingness to sacrifice the present for the future, its rejection of the existing institutions of change and above all, its passionate, irrational and millenarian conviction in the truth and ultimate triumph of its position.

This description fundamentally confuses the problem. In the first place, it is highly value laden, reflecting the anti-ideology position of the theorists. A theorist's values should be clear in his writings, and research should have explicit policy motivation. But clarity of values does not excuse the requirement of scholarly rigor in defining independent and dependent variables.

More importantly, the theory fails to differentiate ideology—the set of ideas underlying a political movement—from the emotional bonds which fire and sustain the movement on a mass basis. The neglect of this crucial distinction derives from the failure to distinguish ideology from ideological politics.

Such a distinction is important. Ideology is an intellectual production describing the society. In understanding ideology, the social position of the intellectual is crucial. Politics is an attempt to influence the allocation of rewards in the society. In understanding politics, the institutional context of the political action is crucial.

Ideology as an intellectual production has several elements: 1.) a set of moral values, taken as absolute, 2.) an outline of the "good society" in which those values would be realized, 3.) a systematic criticism (or, in the case of status quo ideology, affirmation) of the present social arrangements and an analysis of their dynamics, 4.) a strategic plan of getting from the present to the future (or, in the case of status quo ideology, how continued progress is built into the existing system).

For ideology to be linked to a political movement and for that movement to develop a mass following certain requisites must be met: 1.) the ideas must be easily communicated which usually involves their simplification and sloganization, 2.) they must establish a claim to truth, and 3.) they must demand a commitment to action.

In this process the ideology as an intellectual production is altered. A basis of authority—divine, institutional or charismatic—is invoked to establish and maintain the claim to truth and the focus of the idea system is shifted to intermediate goals and instrumental actions.

Appeal may be pointed to the direct psychological experience of prospective recruits with society, rather than to the theoretical abstractions of that experience. The "passions of the mass" are attached to the movement by having it serve each individual as a vehicle for his own self-realization and as a release for his particular frustrations, aggressions and fears. The individual becomes psychologically dependent on the movement and sees society through its medium. Thus, many of the bonds on which the solidarity of the political movement is built may be quite irrelevant (and even contrary to) the ideals in the ideology behind that movement. As a consequence there is a wide range of both intellectual and psychological commitment to the movement.

The goal in this process for a left or opposition movement is to create a language and a common frame of reference which, on the one hand, separates the adherents of the movement from the dominant or status quo ideology of the society, and on the other, breaks the hold of that ideology on their thinking and unifies them behind a program of political opposition, leading ultimately to the overthrow of the dominant ideology and the interests it represents.

There is an implicit rejection of the socially sanctioned institutions of change, holding that they function to maintain social equilibrium within the fixed assumptions and power relations of the status quo.

An opposition movement based on ideology, however, need not be doctrinaire, it need not be demogogic; it need not be dehumanizing of either its members or its antagonists. It need not advocate violent revolution or sacrificing of the present for the future. Such conditions are historically specific, depending on the values of the movement, its leadership, the nature of the conflict it engages and the social experience of its adherents. For instance, none of these attributes apply to the non-violent civil rights movements in the United States, yet they possess in varying degrees all the defining features of ideology and ideological politics.

Further, millenarian or chiliastic expectations are associated not with ideological movements in general, but with movements involving groups from the lowest social stratum whose possibilities for mobility within the existing system are substantially blocked. And when these tendencies exist, as they do in parts of the Negro movement, they are not necessarily associated with the doctrinaire and dehumanizing qualities which the "end of ideology" theorists ascribe to all ideology.

THE "END OF IDEOLOGY" HYPOTHESIS

In its most limited form, the theory states that the mass socialist movements of the 1930's have declined and that the vulgar Marxism which provided a base for those movements has been abandoned.

This is obvious, and hardly profound. One would expect political opposition to alter its form and its analysis on the basis of its own experience (and failures) and in response to the massive changes in the society as a whole. Even so, organizational remnants of the Old Left continue to exist and to recruit new members. Furthermore, the hypothesis begs the question of how *mass* any of these old ideological movements were, even at their height.

However, the "end of ideology" theorists are making more general and serious assertions. They are saying: 1. Radical movements of all sorts have ceased to exist in the West, and 2. The ideas which intellectuals contribute to political movements have changed in quality. They are no longer ideological.

Both these hypotheses have an obvious range of truth; but also both have evident exceptions. The Communist Party has a mass base in Italy and France. The left wing of the Social Democratic Party is vigorous, if suppressed, in Germany and is even ascendant in England. In America, the civil rights and peace movements, while not having explicit political structure, do have radical ideological currents.

And an intellectual community, loosely known in the United States, Canada and Europe as the "New Left," is clearly ideological in its orientation. Outside of the United States materialism and various forms of economic determinism remain legitimate intellectual positions. The existence of exceptions suggests the hypotheses need closer examination.

WHAT HAS HAPPENED TO LEFT POLITICAL MOVEMENTS?

The lack of oppositional political movements from the left is attributed to the ending of class conflict and the decline of the objective deprivations on which class conflict was based. It is undoubtedly correct that welfare capitalism has remedied many of the injustices of its laissez-faire predecessor. But it is highly oversimplified to see the decline of political opposition solely in these terms.

Conflicts can decrease because there is increased harmony and real consensus among the various interests in the society. And it can decrease because it is suppressed, overtly through coercion and intimidation, or covertly through manipulation, the building of false consciousness and the structuring of the institutions and processes which are necessary for "conflict resolution." The "end of ideology" theorists put great emphasis on the decrease in conflict because of consensus; they virtually ignore the more *important suppression* of conflict.

There have been a number of major developments, particularly in the United States, but having their parallels in the West generally, which have substantially altered the *context* in which political opposition can be expressed.

1. *Radical opposition is not possible within the political system.* An opposition (third) party cannot operate in the United States because of election laws, lack of money and organizational resources necessary to operate in each state, anti-subversion laws, issue raiding by the major parties, etc. And a radical faction cannot function within the two major parties, not only because they represent converging economic and social interests, but also because they are personality rather than issue-oriented and there are no continuing deliberative bodies in which a factional (minority) caucus could operate. Consequently, it is not possible to organize and maintain a formal political constituency committed to a radical program.

2. *Revolutionary opposition has ceased to be possible.* The means of violence have reached a degree of sophistication and efficiency that their control by the state cannot be broken or challenged by extra-legal, private groups. To overthrow the government is no longer a realistic strategic goal; change must be in the context of an "evolutionary" process.

3. *The public is excluded from political responsibility.* A process of "concurrent consensus" maintains harmony among representatives of competing interests. This consensus is not necessarily static—but the decisions which lead to change are not made publicly nor publicly accountable. The information and alternatives of choice made directly available to the people are sharply limited. The press and mass media are virtually closed. An opposition must orient to the managerial elites rather than to constituents of those elites who have any functioning democratic control. Consequently, opposition organization is forced into an elite pattern and its primary strategic problem is gaining access to and influence in centers of power, rather than building a base of independent power through mass organization.

4. *Conflict is managed.* The state or the dominant institutions sharing in the status quo consensus have sufficient control of social resources to ameliorate any grievance which is used as a basis of generalized political opposition. The mechanism of "reform" is sensitive to the magnitude of the pressure for change. It operates to satisfy those whose psychological and intellectual commitment to the generalized movement is weakest. It thereby serves to divide the radical organization on short run goals and to undermine the mass base of its leaders. The existence of a plurality of "intermediate groups" serves further as a cushion to absorb disruptive conflict,

to divide its focus, and to siphon off the loyalties of dissidents by a variety of material and non-material enticements.

5. *The "foreign threat" is used to discredit any action which rests on generalized criticism of the domestic system.* "Anti-communism" is a basis to provide system integration as well as to specifically undermine any conceptual formulation which has Marxist or "pro-communist" implications. The post war "red-purges" in the trade unions, in universities, in journalism and entertainment, in politics, the professions and liberal voluntary organizations were the specific historical means by which dissent from the left was isolated, destroyed or forced to conform to a non-ideological mold within the great American consensus.

These five aspects of the contemporary political system seem decisive in undercutting the generalization of social conflict and the limitation of mass political activity. Changes in the institutional context of politics have combined with direct and sustained attack on the individuals and organizations which were the vehicles of radical dissent. This suggests an end to politics, not an end to ideology.

The decisive factor in the decline of ideological politics is the end of a revolutionary alternate. Revolution has consistently been the basic framework of radical ideology. This is for good reason.

The defining characteristics of any social system is not the distribution of rewards—material, status, safety, etc.—but the *process* by which they are allocated. The "power structure" is not defined by its share of the wealth, but by the means through which it controls the allocation of wealth. (Of course, it also gets the lion's share.)

It is able to incorporate potentially disruptive movements by reallocating resources, thus meeting material, immediate demands.

As already described, any political opposition movement consists of two (not discontinuous) types: 1) people with an integrated critique of society, ideologues committed to opposition of basic structural characteristics of the going social order, and 2) people with an immediate discontent who join and support the movement because it promises to relieve their grievances.

The second group is the larger, but in terms of radical goals it is politically impotent. If it becomes politically dangerous because a radical leadership gives it certain organization and articulated objectives, then it can be separated from the leadership (or the leadership bought off to forestall such separation) by the offer of concessions. These "reforms" meet immediate demands and they establish a constitutional (i.e., controlled) process of working for continued change.

The "power structure" thus neutralizes the radical potential of a movement through its control of the allocation decisions. This means 1) that the constituents of the opposition movement become beholden to established power interests for progress achieved, and 2) that the opposition leadership is pressured by the constituent to seek further benefits or concessions from the "power structure," that is to seek influence in the allocation process and consequently not to threaten the interests of any group presently dominant in that process.

The power structure has the advantage, because they have power: they are able to *deliver*. Leaders of the opposition are able only to motivate demands and promise rewards. A concession by the system solidifies an individual's commitment to the system. It weakens the vital "separating function" of radical ideology.

Radicals have recognized this situation. In its ideological formulation, they hold that the economic-political system functions as an integrated whole. Adjustments or reforms cannot fundamentally reorient it to public, democratic values and away from exploitative, manipulative and anti-democratic ones. The magnitude of change does not determine its political quality. There can be tremendous changes in Gross National Product, standard of living, education, leisure, health, all without altering the exploitative character of the system. There may be incremental improvements in living standards, care of marginal people, security, social justice and equality before the law, etc., without there being any alteration in the political control of the society or change in the goals to which social resources are directed, or without there being any improvement in the non-material aspects of social existence.

In its political formulation, the revolutionary objective has generally been the response to this situation. This means the opposition seeks power rather than influence. Its goal is to replace the existing power structure: to overthrow it by killing or jailing its personnel, and by seizing the vital means of its functioning—the communication media, the police power and the legislative authority. This means that they can organize on the basis of and build primary commitment to the utopia consequent on the social restructuring to be accomplished by the revolution. The promise of the utopia cannot be delivered, or even seriously challenged by the existing system. So there is no danger of the revolutionary organization being driven by minor reforms or concessions.

This revolutionary objective has *not* been adopted in the United States. The *political reasons* for this, as already noted, are that the established system is too decentralized, has too strong a control of the means of violence and facilities of organization for revolution either to be organized or to succeed. But there are also *ideological reasons* based on the political experience of this century: a revolutionary leadership won't give up elite power any more than the previous elite would. *If the central issue of the "revolution" is more democratic control, as it is for the contemporary radicals, then anti-democratic organization can hardly insure it.*

Furthermore, the idea of non-violence develops tremendous moral force for people horrified by the wars of our century and seeking freedom from the oppression of state or private power.

The non-violent strategy involves several untested, and even unlikely assumptions:

1. That the political process is sufficiently disjunctive from the economic so that the former can be used to gain control of and to change the latter; i.e., it is possible to gain political power without having economic power.

2. That the economic system can be attacked directly and in a way to highlight those points at which constitutionally superior political power must intervene.

3. That change can be made and sustained in terms of new values in small sections of social relations, while most relations are left intact and still reflect old values.

4. That successive demands for change in the allocation of resources can reach a point beyond which the system cannot adjust—that there are structural limitations on the ability of the system to satisfy the kind of immediate demands on which disadvantaged people can be organized—and when pushed to those limits, the system, itself will be open to fundamental change.

5. That people can be organized in terms of a common interest beyond immediate gain, that they can see the enemy as those who profit from the status quo and not those who are in the same exploited position as themselves within the system, competing for its scarce resources: that reason can prevail over immediate perceived necessity.

Within a revolutionary strategy, none of these assumptions are necessary. But now, a political movement must build in terms of *all* of them. The ground is uncharted; since the organizational experience of previous movements has generally been within the revolutionary framework, it is not now directly applicable. If any of these assumptions prove false, that is, fail in practice, then the possibility for radical change in the organization and allocation of resources is highly unlikely.

HAS IDEOLOGY ENDED?

The existence of a "new left" struggling with the intellectual and organizational problems of a non-revolutionary radicalism indicates that ideology has not ended. That it has changed, and must necessarily have changed, should be obvious from what has already been said about the altered conditions in which ideology is transformed into political action. The major changes are:

1. *Values:* No longer is there a complete rejection of the system. Many of the equalitarian values mythologized (but barely realized) by contemporary society are embraced by new left intellectuals. The points of attack are more the processes by which minority economic interests dominate formally democratic institutions and misallocate public resources for selfish ends.

2. *Utopia:* The oppositional emphasis is modified by a much greater uncertainty about the institutional structure of the good society. Concrete slogans such as nationalization, workers' control, state planning and socialism are replaced by more complicated and speculative formulations of the market economy, decentralized planning and participatory democracy. The experiences and failures of the "socialist" countries have not yet been incorporated in a new utopian synthesis.

3 *Critique:* The aspects of contemporary society that are criticized include more than economic and political components. Increasing concern is given, for instance, to cultural and educational problems. How to extend the freeing potentiality of material abundance to the masses without losing the quality of high culture developed in the context of aristocratic or bohemian leisure.

4. *Strategy:* As noted, revolution and the crude marxian dynamics of the class struggle are rejected or highly modified as a basis of historical analysis and as political strategy.

In spite of these changes in content and emphasis, the thinking of the "new left" retains a basic ideological character. It begins from moral values which are held as absolute. It develops an image of utopia and a systematic critique of the present. While it doesn't see change as apocalyptic, it does hold a fundamental discontinuity: the good society will look and function very differently from this one.

The necessary conditions for ideological thinking must be analyzed in order to understand this change. By hypothesis these conditions are:

1. an independent intellectual class or group
2. the existence of real conflict
3. the existence of institutions which can develop and carry ideology
4. a language in which it can formulate its critique
5. the possibility of change.

That these conditions exist much less now than earlier in this century or in the 19th century suggests that ideological thinking should be decreased in amount and ideologists should be a rarer breed of intellectual. The way in which these conditions are realized, to the extent they are, suggests some of the particular aspects of contemporary ideology.

1. *An independent intellectual class.* If the intellectual is beholden to the system, he cannot separate himself from its values and assumptions, and hence, cannot create or embrace a total analysis of it. In part or

whole he is committed to the ideology of the system, since his socially supported roles and rewards are rationalized and given importance in terms of that ideology.

The intellectual is not now independent. No longer is he denied status or material rewards; no longer is he limited in his location to the relatively segregated academic communities. He is employed as a consulting technician (where other people set the policy goals) by all the mainstream institutions—corporations, unions, government, professional societies, foundations, churches, etc. He can get research money for work that is rationalized in terms of general social benefit. He can publish, and indeed, his advancement is largely conditional on publication that meets the scrutiny (i.e., conforms to the broad value framework) of his colleagues. The academic community is actively hostile to ideological formulations. In all these things, his advancement draws him into the thinking and values of the society. Whereas, intellectual independence requires either being cut off from or consciously rejecting the sanctioned or available social rewards.

Furthermore, ideological thinking is wholistic. To the degree that numerous opportunities and alternatives exist within the system, as they do for contemporary intellectuals, the approach to planning and conceptualization is more likely to be piecemeal than organic. This is reinforced by increasing professional specialization.

2. *The existence of real conflict.* Ideology is formulated in terms of conflicts of interest, the blocking of values by the holders of power. When conflict does not exist, or when contending interests are not directly laid bare, then there is no existential basis for ideology.

There is now very little visible conflict, except in the area of Negro rights. A plurality of government and voluntary institutions create bureaucratic channels of remedy which segregate issues. The most exploited groups are without the political facilities of self expression. The ethic of service seeks to aid the welfare of the oppressed without providing trust or building their sovereignty. Lingering Social Darwinism combines with the conservative ethic of individual initiative to undermine the psychological basis of an assertion by the oppressed of a claim against society.

Expressed conflict is channeled into forms which obscure the underlying causes of the conflict and the real centers of power which govern the reward allocation and are responsible for the oppression complained of. Intermediate institutions are made visible and become targets of attack, while masking the decisive economic interests responsible both for the oppression and the maintenance of the intermediate buffer.

Not only is conflict suppressed, atomized and misdirected; but intellectuals are isolated from the places of conflict and its passion. The university is the place where the intellectual has the greatest freedom (compared with technical and consulting roles in government and other organizations) but it is an isolated institution providing a self-contained, highly artificial and modulated environment.

Furthermore, not only is freedom bought at the price of isolation, but it is anesthetized by a "professional standard" which prescribes that things be studied without reference to the observer's values—lest biasing commitment becloud "objectivity."

3. *The existence of institutions which can develop and carry the ideology.* An essential aspect of ideology is strategic. There must be the interplay between the experience of political action and the intellectual formulation. The action component of an ideological development must have organization form; it must be able to communicate and to organize people.

No institutions exist on a national scale which are sufficiently independent to be a vehicle for ideology. The labor unions to which leftists have traditionally looked, are legally, intellectually and psychologically part of the system. Many universities are semi-independent, but as noted, the university is isolated from community power structure. In some areas, the church has the requisite independence, but it directs emotional energy to religious rather than political goals. There is no mass distribution opposition newspaper or opposition political party. The monopolization of financial and organizational resources by the status quo—supported by the direct coercive power of the state—prevents the creation of such an independent vehicle of mass communication and action.

4. *A language in which its critique can be formulated.* The main currents of left ideology have been broken by the discrediting of the Soviet translation of marxist ideology and by the attack of social science methods and values. The old utopia has been shattered and not yet rebuilt.

The system has monopolized much of the language. Freedom, democracy, social justice, equality, and individualism are values which exist in the traditions of the society and are used to rationalize the institutions. It is difficult to use them also as points of appeal against the traditions.

5. *The possibility of change.* Another condition for ideology is a possibility of success. If intellectuals see no chance to alter the present they will retreat to apathy, privatism and cynicism and express their political energy within the established institutions for piecemeal reform. Passion will attach only to a cause that is real.

The degree to which these conditions do not now exist explains some of the features of contemporary ideological thinking.

1. The people who are doing it are often young. They are independent because they have yet to undertake family and social commitments. They are dissociated from the main academic currents of their discipline and they associate themselves with independent publications, institutes or organizations.

2. They are likely to have some involvement in a non-traditional

sort of political action. Where direct conflict does exist there is likely to be a greater degree of ideological thinking.

3. The lack of avowed institutions leads to a preoccupation with questions of "agents of social change." The labor movement, the universities, the civil rights movement, the Democratic Party, a third party are all exhaustively evaluated as to whether they can carry ideology and an ideological movement.

4. The monopolization of language has led to an elaborate rhetoric of participatory democracy, a shying from the traditional language of marxism and socialism, and an overworking of some of the less tarnished ideas like alienations.

5. The realistic doubt that anything is possible leads to a pre-occupation with strategy. Debates abound on realignment versus a labor party, university reform, violence versus non-violence.

THE "END OF IDEOLOGY" AS IDEOLOGY

A substantial number of those left intellectuals who, 20 or 30 years ago, were ideologists have since changed their position. They now represent a mode of political thought which might be called "reformist." In this group would fall the "end of ideology" theorists.

The "end of ideology" theorists present a fairly consistent set of values, which might be called "transitional values," in terms of which they justify a rejection of ideology as a basis for politics.

1. History is unknowable. The persecutions, manipulation and suffering of people in the present cannot be morally justified as necessary conditions in the building of a future utopia.

2. The evils of the present are not so bad as the evils *inherent* in revolutionary or disruptive change.

3. The dangers inherent in mass action are greater than the evils of injustice more slowly ameliorated through parliamentary process.

4. No class or elite, once it gains privilege, will voluntarily give it up, hence no political strategy can "level" a present elite which is to serve as the vehicle for equalitarian transformation.

5. The values of free expression, association, and political organization are fundamental, both in the present and in any future. There is no conceivable ground on which they can be abrogated.

These values held in conjunction, fairly well commit one's political energies to working within the system. Ideology is certainly a dangerous business and its end is much to be desired. The crucial elements however are Number 2 and Number 3. The others, particularly the civil liberties emphasis, are all compatible with an ideological approach to politics (though they are certainly not characteristic of all ideologies). Numbers 2 and 3, however, disallow or at least treat with great suspicion, the value of social dislocation and of change which is not mediated through established parliamentary institutions. They are values which essentially ratify the present social order.

The origin of these values, according to the "end of ideology" theorists, is in the reflection on the horrors of Nazism, the atrocities and failures of Communists and the shattered hopes of the democratic left in the face of mass psychology and totalitarian attack.

It should be granted that catastrophic events can have a permanent effect on the ideas of a generation—independent of any shift in the social or economic position of the people involved. However, the reformist position reflects a fundamentally different perspective on the society, and, by hypothesis, a fundamentally altered social location of the reformist intellectual.

The essential points of the reformist position are:

1. A positive commitment to the values of the present, historically specific system of Welfare Capitalism. The system embraces his values —democracy, equality, and individual freedom. And the system is highly successful.

He celebrates the high level of material abundance, the progressive lessening of inequality and the progressive remedying of specific deprivations. He notes the wide degree of personal freedom from arbitrary authority: for production workers, guaranteed by trade unions; for the white collar worker, afforded by the impersonalization of bureaucratic roles; for the political dissenter, guaranteed by civil liberties. He sees remarkable advance in education, science and culture. And most important, he sees the general acceptance of welfare goals by all interests in the society and thereby the assurance of continued progress.

His perspective is on how far we have come. He has participated in the struggles for change and identifies himself with their successes. What was sound in the old ideologies has been realized, and what was unsound has been disproved and properly rejected.

He believes that the good society is defined by the *process* through which conflict is mediated and progress achieved, rather than by a new *structural* ordering of power, social relations and resources. American democracy, of course, reflects (or closely approximates) that ideal process.

2. A belief that no issues of generalized conflict exist. There are limited situations of conflict—like the race issue, or poverty or unemployment—but these are essentially discontinuous and the product of specialized anomalous conditions. They can be dealt with in isolation; they do not derive from fundamental contradictions or weakness in the system. Mechanisms within the system are fully adequate for their solution—such

as constitutional legislation, public education, welfare programs, increased production, etc. There is no need to see solutions in the perspective of (or conditional on) total social reorganization.

3. The problems that do exist—like those of mass culture and mass education—are too complex to be conceptualized in solely political terms. And the value questions, as to what is desirable, are too indeterminant to allow coherent political solution. Issues must be dealt with in a pragmatic piecemeal way. Action should follow only when the goal is precise and its consequences understood and desirable. The interplay of differing interests and perspectives *over time*, within a libertarian constitutional framework, will yield the *best* solution, with the least danger of grave error.

4. The interests of all groups is to mediate and compose these conflicting interests. No group can be deprived of its rights or subjected to arbitrary authority in the name of some abstract value. Constitutional process is the only guarantee against the abuse of authority or extra-legal power. The side of justice is never so clean as to warrant an abridgement of the formal processes by which justice is publicly determined—for in that process the interests of all are assured a fair hearing and equitable treatment. This is essentially a position of moral relativism—that each group whatever its objective position contributes to the common good and that every group is important in making up the composite.

5. The realities of world politics do not permit ideological non-alignment. Whatever one's views on domestic politics, the issues of the international scene must take precedence. It is necessary to oppose Communist expansion and to provide democratic influence in the "third world" and in non-Communist revolutions. This requires an orientation to and support of national authority internationally.

These values—the acceptance of the present, discontinuity of conflict, complexity of issues, legitimacy of all interests and separation of domestic and international issues are exactly opposite of the values inherent in ideology. They suggest a number of hypotheses about social position of those intellectuals who hold them. Again, exactly contrary hypotheses would be suggested for ideologists.

1. They do not have an independent perspective on the social system. They have a wide variety of alternatives and possibilities within the system.

2. Conflict is not salient to them, in terms either of being involved in social conflict, or of perceiving their own interests as directly at stake, or of a high identification and involvement with groups whose interests are so at stake.

3. Their approach to problems is in terms of specialization: formal criteria of method and validity, and scientific "objectivity," rather than speculation and wholistic or value-oriented analysis.

4. They are defensive of their status, every action must be defensive in the face of expected criticism.

5. They have experience with and are in relations of interdependency with a wide variety of groups in society.

6. They identify with national authority as an object of loyalty and patriotism.

A good deal of ideological thinking would come from youth and particularly students for several reasons. They have little established connection with the reward system of the society. They are often subsidized and enjoy a variety of immunities from social demands and obligations. Potentially, they have greater "independence" than any other group.

Their lack of responsibilities gives them greater possibility of geographical mobility and hence direct access to conflict situations. Their own incomplete socialization can give increased emotional saliency to conflict by transference of psychological and familial tensions.

They lack specialized skills and attachment to a professional discipline, so reflection on social issues is much more apt to take a wholistic form. And as students they are exposed to a variety of ideological and political positions as objects of study and as adjuncts to non-academic (extra-curricular) activities.

They have experienced little vertical mobility and have no recognized social status. Rather than being defensive, they are more apt to be assertive in an effort to define their own identity in the society.

CONCLUSION

One of the major problems in the sociology of knowledge is to demonstrate the linkage between "mental productions" and the existent base. The foregoing analysis of the "end of ideology" thesis has been developed with the view of providing the opportunity for an empirical test of some of these relationships.

The analysis has:

1. distinguished two types of political thinking, ideological and reformist, each characterized by a set of specific and mutually exclusive attributes;

2. hypothesized a number of social conditions necessary for ideological thinking;

3. hypothesized a number of values (called transitional values) held characteristically by those intellectuals who in the course of their lives have shifted from ideological to reformist thinking;

4. developed a number of hypotheses designed to differentiate ideological from reformist intellectuals on such dimensions as social position,

past experience, status, self-image, approach to work, and attitude to national authority.

It should be possible to test the relationships suggested in these hypotheses. A sample of intellectuals would be divided on the basis of ideological versus reformist (as determined by questionnaire, interview or content analysis of their writing). Correlations would then be sought with the social conditions.

The outcome of such an empirical study would, I believe, confirm that the "end of ideology" is a status quo ideological formulation designed to rationalize the incorporation of intellectuals into the American way of Life.

A POLICY POST SCRIPT

This paper has indicated the difficulty of maintaining an ideological movement within the political context of contemporary Western-American society.

The reasons for the "End of Ideology" given by Bell, Lipset, Shils, and others are reasons derived from their own transitional values away from left ideology. These values are false.

1. The major problems haven't been solved: poverty, exploitation, giving meaning to work and work to people, war, and enough others that it's amazing that the contrary position could for a moment be given credence.

2. The existing mechanisms of social "adjustment" do not guarantee and do not offer great promise for future solution to these problems: full employment achieved through private growth in a context of increasing automation; peace through a foreign policy serving military and business interests; equality and welfare through a political system dominated by minority economic groups, etc.

3. Freedom is not assured by social manipulation which restricts the range within which people desire to exercise their freedom.

4. Democracy is not assured by the manipulation restriction of the range of choice so that the interests of the elites are never threatened by the sovereignty of the people.

Radical ideology is very much needed: not only because American democracy is *not* the good society in operation, but because the problems facing the society cannot be solved within the now ascendent intellectual and political framework.

The requirements for an ideological movement must be:

First, creation of a community of social reference by which intellectuals can maintain "independence" from the system.

Second, the development of radical ideology itself to heighten the areas of conflict between intellectuals and their professional disciplines, so that independence is maintained.

Third, the systematic development and testing of the several assumptions on which the viability of non-revolutionary radicalism depends.

This last point requires particularly the *development of theory* on those aspects of the economic system which are critical in maintaining minority economic control, and *then* experimentation with forms of action which focus discontent on those areas with the aim of invoking formal political—democratic—control of those areas (assumption 2).

Further, it requires the development of an *image of utopia*, keyed to a sufficiently wide range of human needs and felt problems, that movement can sustain itself beyond its immediate tactical objectives (assumption 5).

These tasks are difficult. They demand a great deal from the few and young intellectuals who now devote themselves to ideological politics: discipline in pursuing the problems that are important, rather than opportunism in following the currents of reformist discontent; patience in developing goals and strategy rather than haste to reenact the frustration of mass organization where the mass is politically impotent; introspection in examining their own role in society, rather than enthusiasm which leads to submerging personal identity within a collective enterprise; and not the least is courage to stand as opponents within their disciplines and professions against those once-leftists who proclaim the End of Ideology as either necessary or desirable.

The historical conditions which marked the mid-century decline in revolutionary ideology in North America provided a breeding ground for more than the reform ideology discussed by Haber. They also set the stage for the emergence of a significant regressive movement in the political arena—the extreme Right.

THE IDEOLOGY OF THE EXTREME RIGHT

During the late 1940s and early 1950s, the extreme Right arose Phoenix-like out of the ashes of the second World War. The first contemporary appearance of this phenomenon dates at least from January 3, 1945. On this, the opening day of the Seventy-Ninth Congress, the dormant Dies' Special House Committee for the Investigation of Un-American

Activities was changed, through the passing of an amendment introduced by representative John Rankin, into a permanent committee—the House Committee on Un-American Activities. Three months later, on April 12, 1945, the New Deal passed into history with the death of Franklin Delano Roosevelt.

During the following years, the extreme Right gained further momentum, both publicly and privately. Publicly, the investigative process became further diversified with the formation, in 1946, of the Senate Permanent Subcommittee on Investigations of the Committee on Government Operations. Privately, one of the first voluntary association groups of the extreme Right, America's Future Incorporated, was founded in New Rochelle, New York. The House Committee on Un-American Activities was active in 1947 with the "Hollywood investigations" and again in 1948 with the Elizabeth Bentley and Whittaker Chambers hearings. Their testimony gave rise, during 1948 and 1949, to the perjury trials of Alger Hiss and William Remington.

On the international scene, American faith in China as a great power and friend was destroyed by the defeat of Chiang Kai-shek's Nationalist armies by the Communists in 1949. This was also the year that the Soviet Union exploded its first atomic bomb, several years ahead of the date estimated by American scientists. As was revealed later, Soviet technology had received assistance from the West in the person of Dr. Klaus Fuchs.

There can be no doubt that the events of 1945 to 1950 helped to establish a climate that made many millions of Americans receptive to McCarthy and McCarthyism. In February, 1950, when he made his startling allegation about Communists in the State Department to a Women's Republican Club in Wheeling, West Virginia, the Senator from Wisconsin was still a "free lance" investigator. Undoubtedly, the tensions created by the Korean War, entered into by the United States in the summer of 1950, helped to sustain the wave of hysteria on which he rode until the abrupt end of his political career in 1954. Although over-shadowed by McCarthyism at the time, the year 1950 also marks the inception of the McCarran Senate Subcommittee on Internal Security. In 1953, McCarthy attained full investigative powers with his appointment as chairman of the Senate Committee on Government Operations and of its Permanent Subcommittee on Investigations. Paradoxically, this year also marks the beginning of the end for McCarthy, for it was then that he began the investigations that were to terminate in the disastrous Army-McCarthy hearings.

With the end of McCarthyism per se in the mid-fifties, many observers heralded a return to normalcy in American society. The tension created by the Korean War had been dispelled, Joseph Stalin was dead, and it appeared that a better understanding between the East and the West was in the offing. The first Republican government in twenty years appeared to have survived its initial difficulties. This was the occasion for many analysts to sit back and view the American right wing in retrospect.

The right wing, however, was not dead. Quietly, it was growing and spreading, and new groups of supporters for extreme Right doctrine were forming throughout the country. What has turned out to be one of the most sensational of these new groups—the John Birch Society—was organized by Robert Welch in Indianapolis on December 8 and 9, 1958. The society achieved notoriety early in 1961 when the contents of a "personal letter" of Welch's entitled "The Politician" became publicly known. In this manuscript, Welch accused some of the nation's leading figures of being either Communist agents, supporters, or sympathizers. Among those accused were General George Marshall, President Eisenhower, Milton Eisenhower, Chief Justice Earl Warren, late Secretary of State John Foster Dulles, and Alan Dulles, former head of the Central Intelligence Agency. Following up the initial storm of controversy which disclosure of this document created, Welch himself, in April, 1961, publicly urged a congressional investigation of the John Birch Society—a move no doubt intended to silence a growing opposition to that organization. In May of the same year Welch appeared on the television program "Meet the Press"—rare exception to his no-interview policy. Meanwhile, the calls for congressional investigation of the John Birch Society from other quarters were helping to ensure that organization a recognition not afforded to any group since the era of McCarthyism.

The political crises of the sixties, both domestic and foreign, have contributed immeasurably to the crystallization of an ideology for the American Right. These issues included the installation of a Communist regime in Cuba and the abortive Bay of Pigs invasion, the Vietnam War and its attendant antiwar and draft resistance movements, and the culmination of the civil rights movement in Black Power.

It would be a mistake to view the extreme Right simply as a resistance to social change or as a search for the idealized values of the past. Although these elements are incorporated into the ultraconservative ideology, extreme right movements do have a definite utopian blueprint for the future. In their study of the Young Americans for Freedom (YAF) and other student political activists, Westby and Braungart characterize the ideology of this element of the extreme Right as a "conversionist utopian mentality." This ideological framework is described by them as follows:

(1) The direction or route of change, following general conservative theory, is a return to a former state of affairs idealized as a perfect or near-perfect condition. In the case of YAF youth, of course, this condition is allegedly found in pre-20th century times and involves myths of free enterprise and the self-reliant, risk-taking individualist making it on his own. . . .

(2) The dynamics of change involve a sudden shift rather than a gradual

movement or process. . . . Since contemporary society is in fact moving away from professed conservative principles and is perceived as such by the vast majority of YAF, it would make little sense to espouse gradualism.

(3) Conversion is effected through the medium of a hero, the archetype of conservative ideals, who becomes the focus of collective identification of the people. YAF expectations of conservative rebirth are strongly linked to the role of the leader-hero. Images of Goldwater or more currently Reagan, smashing the opposition (whether Democrats or liberal Republicans) function as catalytic agents essential to the conversion process. . . .

(4) The conversionist shift is a total one, involving a complete societal transformation and embracing all conservative principles. Piece-meal efforts and partial reforms are out. Social Security will not be modified but abolished. Federal regulatory agencies will not be considered individually and adjustments made, but will be collectively eliminated. Total conversion implies, in addition, the removal of conflict and organized dissent from society, for if everyone is converted to internally consistent sets of ideals conflict is automatically eliminated.

(5) The conservative principles instituted through conversion are more important as abstractions and for what they stand against and replace than for their detailed substantive content. A society converted back to conservatism is good as a totality not because this, that or the other change has presumed or observable effects, but because the society in toto embodied conservative truth and stands in the stead of the horror it replaced.

(6) Finally, conversion results in a return to a higher place among nations whereby prestige is restored, and lost honor recovered. The conversion process is seen either as restoring status, or . . . as providing the condition under which status can be regained. Usually, this is linked to and articulated through themes of militancy.[46]

Many observers have suggested that the ideology of the extreme Right is based on military anti-Communism. However, this oversimplifies the case far too much, since anti-Communism is not exclusive to the extreme Right. For example, the escalation of the Vietnam war was, in large part, a move intended to contain Communism in Southeast Asia. Thus, anti-Communism becomes part of the de facto policy of the United States government. Moreover, much of the periodic liberation ideology of Eastern Europe has been anti-Communist, or at least in opposition to the repressive and bureaucratic excesses of Soviet Communism. Finally, anti-Communism has deep historical roots in American society and has long been the refuge of the superpatriot. The most common discreditation tactic of the extreme Right is to label as Communists those under attack. Therefore, anti-Communism in this context may simply be an exaggerated affirmation of "pro-Americanism."

[46] David L. Westby and Richard G. Braungart, "Utopian Mentality and Conservatism: The Case of the Young Americans for Freedom," paper presented at the annual meetings of the American Sociological Association, San Francisco, California, August 30, 1967, pp. 33–35.

What underlies the extreme Rightist's opposition to Communism is his ideological aversion to collectivism: in this light, Communism must be viewed as the ultimate manifestation of a collectivism which threatens the very existence of man as an individual.

When the extreme Rightist looks around him, he sees the values of individualism being threatened by "creeping collectivism." He decries the increasing government role in control and regulation of the economy, public welfare and assistance programs which permit men to consume without producing, infringement upon states' rights by the federal government, the collectivism incarnate of the United Nations, and, worst of all, the threat to individualism posed by Socialism and Communism throughout the world.

Although the right wing extremist may be affected by the depersonalization, bureaucratization, and complexity of modern social institutions, he does not rely on structural analysis to explain why these conditions have come about. Instead, he places the blame for his existential state on individual weakness on the part of both the corrupt leaders who have brought the people into the valley of the shadow of collectivism and those who would be seduced into giving up their birth right of individual freedom of action.

The Rightist alternative to collectivism similarly focuses on individual action. If it is from the weakness of men that social problems arise, then it will be through the righteousness of men that the conservative utopia will come to pass. Righteousness, as it appears in the radically conservative press, refers to a return to the primacy of traditional norms and values. Slogans emphasizing a return to "law and order," "old-time religion," and "market-place economy" are illustrative. In sum, the utopian ideology of the extreme Right can be seen as millenarian, advocating the supremacy of the individual in opposition to the collectivism inherent in contemporary government, corporate life, foreign affairs, and social values. Disillusioned by the existing political system, the extreme Right places its hopes for the future on a policy of unilateral action designed to bring about desired changes in the political system. It is in this sense that the extreme Right may be regarded as a political ideology: it embodies a set of absolute and idealized values, a critique of existing social arrangements which subvert these values, a conception of an ideal society in which these values would be realized, and a strategy for getting from here to there.

The rhetoric and policy of the extreme Right prove that radical consciousness, ideology, and a utopian blueprint for the future are not dead. This emergence of rightist ideology would suggest that a reassessment of the end-of-ideology argument is warranted. Given the confluence of particular historical factors in the 1950s, it is not surprising that many authors, like Bell and Lipset, should herald an end of radical thought in America. The conditions of the 1940s and 1950s had not created contemporary counterparts of the critics and ideologues of the 1920s and 1930s, men like Sinclair Lewis, Ernest Hemingway, D. H. Lawrence, Eugene Debs, and Norman Thomas. The young people of the 1950s, born in a Depression and socialized by a world war, have been aptly named the "silent generation." Born hungry, nurtured on the hope of a brave new world, and seduced by inflationary affluence, these people epitomized Whyte's "organization men." Eager to escape the economic, social, and political insecurities that were their legacy, they joined the rapidly expanding ranks of the white collar class, their aspirations centering around a split-level in the suburbs, a station wagon, and two and a half children. The only voice of protest during the 1950s was that of withdrawal—the apolitical "beatniks" —which offered no threat to the status quo. Young people of the 1960s, however, not having had to face the same insecurities as their predecessors, have tended to react ideologically to what they see as the false values, materialism, pretentiousness, and hypocrisy of their society. Thus, the very same social, economic, and political conditions of the second half of the twentieth century, which nurtured an apparent end of ideology and a resurgence of conservatism, even ultraconservatism, have given rise to a new genre of left wing ideology in North American politics. At the same time Bell and Lipset were publishing their end-of-ideology analyses, their arguments for the currency of pluralism and pragmatism in the political arena were being refuted by an emerging entity variously labeled "the New Left," "the New Fraternity," "the Student Left," "Campus Protesters," or "the Movement."

THE IDEOLOGY OF THE NEW LEFT

Radical politics of the 1960s is primarily expressed through what has been called the New Left. This movement has been based largely on a membership consisting of rural and urban poor (mainly Negroes), students, and older middle class radicals. As Newfield points out, the New Left must be regarded as a unique product of modern political and social conditions:

The New Radicalism is authentically new in its vague weaving together of anarchist, existential, transcendental, Populist, socialist, and bohemian strands of thought. It is not the logical outgrowth of the older radical tradition in the West. It is not built upon the same discontents as the Old Left—the depression and the threat of fascism—but upon newer discontents like powerlessness, moral disaffection, the purposelessness of middle-class life—all of which are the special products of an abundant, technocratic urban culture.[47]

[47] Jack Newfield, A Prophetic Minority (Toronto: New American Library of Canada, 1966), p. 132.

The social issues which have concerned the New Left are poverty, war, and civil rights. In the United States, the most significant event in shaping the ideology of these new politics was the 1954 Supreme Court ruling on school desegregation. From this initial focus on the educational rights of Negroes, attention spread to other civil rights and political concerns: "sit-ins" (desegregation of lunch counters, 1960); the "freedom rides" (integration in interstate commerce, 1961); voter registration drives in the Southern states, 1961 and following; the formation of the Mississippi Freedom Democratic Party, 1964. The political consciousness of the new radicals was also developing during the early 1960s, as shown by the formation of Students for a Democratic Society, 1961; picketing of the House Committee on Un-American Activities hearings in San Francisco, 1960; and the Berkeley Free Speech Movement, 1964. Concern over the issue of war is reflected in the campaign for nuclear disarmament, Vietnam war protests, and draft resistance. Increasingly since the mid-1960s, student elements of the New Left concentrated on university reform.

It has been difficult, however, to regard the New Left as a unified political entity. As late as 1969, one observer saw the "new radicals" as consisting of three distinct groups:

1. Pragmatic protesters who are dissatisfied with the political, economic or academic structure and who want reforms without total upheaval of the existing system.
2. Existential protesters who are alienated from the status quo but undecided as to whether its change requires violent destruction.
3. Revolutionary protesters, militants who believe that American society is so corrupted by its military-industrial governing class and by its imperialist foreign policy that only a revolution can result in meaningful change.[48]

The vanguard of this New Left movement has been students, not workers. Since World War II, North American society has undergone a number of fundamental changes. One of these was the increasing consolidation of "big labor" as a powerful economic and political force. The "house of labor" became, in a sense, a silent partner in the military-industrial complex as the revolutionary fervor of prewar labor was bought off. Another significant change was the growth of a college-trained technostructure. If, as Marx argues, the capitalist system carries within itself the seeds of its own destruction, then surely these seeds have been nurtured in the bourgeois educational system, particularly in its institutions of higher learning. By the end of the 1960s, approximately forty percent of the college-age population of the United States was enrolled in colleges and universities; the proportion in Canada was about half that. Young people came to universities for three major reasons: (1) The technological up-

[48] Milorad M. Drachkovitch, quoted in Daryl Mebke, "Momentum of New Left Seen Running Down," *Los Angeles Times*, April 6, 1969, Section F, p. 7.

grading of labor demanded increasingly higher educational qualifications. (2) Concomitant with this was a decline in the absolute size of the labor force—colleges and universities thus served to keep young people out of the labor market. (3) In the United States, Selective Service deferments encouraged young people to continue their education. Ironically, one of the effects of the deferment system was to drive war objectors onto the campuses.

In terms of social class background, college students have come from relatively well-to-do, middle class families. Within these families, three important aspects of socialization have taken place. First, middle class youth has come to accept affluence, and the material objects it brings, as given. These young people have not experienced the struggle for material existence which their parents underwent and which, within their families, motivated the older generation to struggle for the material symbols of status. As a corollary to this devaluation of materialism, there has been a tendency for middle class youth to reject those values and behaviors of their class which are consistent with, and reinforce, the materialist ethic. Thus, radical middle class youth has rejected the principle of "deferred gratification": an increasing number of young people have turned their eyes from the future to the existential present. Moreover, one of the central aspects of the value system of young people has been a rejection of the hypocrisy essential to the effective operation of the business world. When the organization men complained, during the fifties, that the business world was a "rat race," young people listened, believed, and came to regard the rat race as nothing more than a race for rats.

Although socialization into this perspective was largely unintentional, middle class society has contributed to the ideology of the New Left through intentional socialization. Among those values which middle class parents have consciously transmitted to their children are: intellectualism and a high premium on education, which has been instrumental in leading young people to a search for truth and a critical evaluation of their society; individualism, which young people, in accepting for themselves, have come to regard as a right for others; tolerance of other persons and ideas; and the principles of freedom, justice, and equality, which young people regard as viable principles and not just musty rhetoric.

Motivated by a number of factors, not the least of which has been a strong commitment to education in Western society since the mid-1950s, an increasing number of young people have been moving into a university environment at an age where they are approaching physical, emotional, and intellectual maturity. In a university environment, they are expected, even encouraged, to reflect on their state of existence and to acquire and test new social and political ideas. From among these students, a small but growing number of activists have emerged, described by Hayden as follows:

A student movement. If poor people are in The Movement because they have nothing to gain in the status system, students are in it because, in a sense, they have gained too much. Most of the active student radicals today come from middle to upper-middle-class professional homes. They were born with status and affluence as facts of life, not goals to be striven for. In their upbringing, their parents stressed the right of children to question and make judgments, producing perhaps the first generation of young people both *affluent* and *independent of mind*. And then these students so often encountered social institutions that denied them their independence and betrayed the democratic ideals they were taught. They saw that men of learning were careerists; that school administrators and ministers almost never discussed the realities the students lived with; that even their parents were not true to the ideals they taught the young.

It was against this background of tension that young people became concerned in the early sixties about war, racism, and inequality. By now the empty nature of existing vocational alternatives has pushed several hundreds of these students into community organizing. Working in poor communities is a concrete task in which the split between job and values can be healed. It is also a position from which to expose the whole structure of pretense, status, and glitter that masks the country's real human problems. And, finally, it is a way to find people who want to change the country, and possibly can do so.[49]

Although campus activists have constituted a minority of students—probably no more than five percent at any time through the 1960s—it would be a mistake to view this element as a "lunatic fringe." As Duberman points out, activists tend to be measurably different from other students:

The activists score consistently higher on a wide variety of personality tests, including theoretical skills, aesthetic sensitivity, degree of psychological autonomy, and social maturity. They are also the better students, with significantly higher grade-point averages than the nonactivists. In trying to account for the recent emergence of student activism, Sanford points to various changes since the 1930's in family life and child training. But he feels that student activism is primarily a response to social conditions both within the university and in the world at large.[50]

Certainly the structural fact of certain kinds of people coming together on university campuses has been important for the development of the new radicalism, yet equally important was the students' awareness of and response to external historical events. The most significant of these

[49] Tom Hayden, "The Politics of 'The Movement,'" in Irving Howe, ed., *The Radical Papers* (Garden City, N.Y.: Doubleday Anchor Books), pp. 374–375.
[50] Martin Duberman, "On Misunderstanding Student Rebels," *Atlantic Monthly*, 222 (November 1968): 66.

were the political revolutions in China, Cuba, and Vietnam, counterrevolutions such as those in Hungary and Czechoslovakia, and the American intervention in the Dominican Republic and the Bay of Pigs episode. Regarding the latter event, Dale Johnson provides an illuminating comment on the effect this had on student radicalism:

> Postscript: The American intervention in Cuba, undertaken after this communication was in print, has had a tremendous impact on both the size of the student movement and its ideology, at least in the Bay Area. Many student "hangers-on" and potential rebels have been activated by the gross nature of the irrationality in high places. Most important, however, is the fact that U.S. imperialistic ventures have served to radicalize the dissenters. For example: (a) the concept of demonstration has been altered to include "dramatic non-violent acts of civil disobedience"; (b) new and truly radical students have gained leadership positions and the old activists have moved left along with their student base of support.[51]

In many respects, it has been difficult to specify the ideological nature of the New Left. The initial consciousness of dysfunction of the radicals concerned the social issues of poverty, war, and civil rights. Thus, the New Left, at least in its formative years in the early 1960s, was basically reformist—a politics of morality. At this stage, the movement lacked a utopian plan for the future but was concerned instead with existential "engagement." As one observer wrote in 1962: "The truth is that man cannot live for himself alone, that sooner or later the emptiness of such life overcomes him and he seeks involvement with others. The community of men and their history has the power to complete us in a way which we never would be otherwise completed. It involves us in a way in which we cannot escape being involved." [52] Concerning student activism, another author wrote: "The new student radicalism is so fundamentally at odds with our conventional political categories because it is, above all, an existentialist revolt . . . the students are in rebellion, not so much because things are bad for them, or for others, but because things are what they are for them and for others." [53] The vague and undefined program of the New Left in the midsixties has been aptly described by Michael Munk:

> Where the new left becomes vaguest in its vision is the translation of the power of radical constituencies into social change. One tendency agrees with the necessity of the radical constituency entering into coalitions with reformists social movements—but only after it has developed sufficient political strength

[51] Dale L. Johnson, "On the Ideology of the Campus Revolution," *Studies on the Left*, 2, no. 1 (1961): 75.
[52] David Horowitz, *The Student* (New York: Ballantine Books, 1961), p. 17.
[53] Irving Kristol, "What's Bugging the Students," *Atlantic Monthly*, 216 (November 1965): 109.

to do so on its own terms. On the other hand, the concepts of "counter-community" sometimes imply rejection of electoral and party politics on the basis of anarchistic and ideological principles. Some within the SDS and SNCC ask: Do not electoral politics include the worst features of manipulative organization, and are they not decadent forms of social change relevant only to the manipulative system? The question implies the search for new forms of political organization and action.

The ideological New Left is in fact characterized by its tendency to ask questions, rather than provide answers. It includes far more young people who are engaged in searching than in preaching and thus far its loosely organized and decentralized structure, together with militant opposition to red baiting and exclusion, has been one of SDS's and SNCC's most widely praised characteristics. But the time is fast approaching when the accumulation of more than a year's experience in the slums and rural areas will demand systematic re-evaluation, with rejection of concepts proved unworkable, and experimentation with new ones.[54]

Yet the New Left has exhibited a revolutionary potential in its opposition to the structure of power in society. Radical protest has been generally addressed to locating and pressuring the "power elite." This we elaborated in chapter 6 with the discussion of G. William Domhoff's "How to Commit Revolution in Corporate America." Jack Minnis' SDS pamphlet, widely circulated during the 1960s, concluded: "Informing the people about the nature of power in the community strikes a very real blow at the power structure, mobilizing the people to united action toward specific objectives will unstructure the power structure."[55] Other observers have suggested:

What began perhaps as a rebellion against affluence and liberal hypocrisy grew in a few years into a radical activism that protested injustice at the very core of the society. But when even this was tolerated by the structures that were under attack, some of the young radicals began to think about something beyond rebellion or radical protest. The Movement now is struggling to develop an ideology that will guide them toward building an organization that can compete for political power.[56]

The initial reform orientation of the New Left was reflected in its early tactics of "participatory democracy" and "parallel structures." These are described in the following excerpts from a paper by Peter Lewis.

[54] Michael Munk, *The New Left* (New York: National Guardian Pamphlet, 1965), p. 7.
[55] Jack Minnis, *The Care and Feeding of Power Structures* (Chicago: SDS Pamphlet, n.d.), p. 7.
[56] Paul Jacobs and Saul Landau, *The New Radicals* (New York: Vintage Books, 1966), p. 14.

Excerpts from R. Peter Lewis, "The New Left: A Political Movement?" (unpublished paper, San Francisco State College, 1966), pp. 31–38. Reprinted by permission of R. Peter Lewis.

SPECIFIC TACTICS AND IDEOLOGICAL EMERGENCE: PARTICIPATORY DEMOCRACY

The primary specific tactic of these "grass-roots" organizational drives seems to be to get *everyone* in the community *committed*, by becoming personally involved and responsible to the organization.[57] (The organization itself is *initially* formed around issues that *directly* affect the people's lives—but these are only the catalysts, remember.) All functional positions are filled by the local people and necessary *skills* are learned by painful trial-and-error. Even the minutest mundane *decisions* are collectively arrived at by endless discussion and debate until near-consensus is achieved. This approach is known as *"participatory* democracy," and it has several other crucial ramifications.[58]

In conjunction with this approach, scrupulous care is taken to find and cultivate *indigenous "leadership." However,* leadership as a phenomenon cannot arise, because these positions (as well as all others) must be constantly *rotated.* The first reason for this approach is the philosophical commitment to Jeffersonian democratic forms, and in some ways it contains elements of the old anarcho-syndicalism implied above. Second is the oft-confirmed "iron law of oligarchy," supplemented by modern-day "power of incumbence"; wherein static forms of power build upon and perpetuate themselves, and further "vested interests" develop around them. In addition, there are several more pragmatic reasons for this approach to leadership and power in the New Left. Experience with leaders who have been bought-off or "co-opted" by "the establishment,"[59] and with others who have been "forced" to "compromise," or who have been politically sidetracked, has been taken very seriously.

Then, there is also the practical need not to depend too heavily on one leader, because of the above reasons, and because he is very likely

[57] Blumer makes the point that the employment of *tactics* marks the fifth and climactic stage of the development of a specific social movement. They serve to gain and hold adherents and to reach objectives; "Collective Behavior," in *Principles of Sociology,* Logan Wilson & Wm. Kolb (eds.) (N.Y.: Harcourt, Brace & Co., c. 1949), p. 211. This discussion is consonant with that interpretation.

[58] See Staughton Lynd, *The New Radicals and "Participatory Democracy,"* S.D.S. Pamphlet, 1965. *Passim.*

[59] The case of James Farmer, former director of C.O.R.E., who is now making a large salary from the Federal Office of Economic Opportunity, is still a point of much disgust in the New Left.

to be jailed or murdered (the case of Medgar Evers is only one of many such). And finally, particularly in organizations which attempt to build and satisfy all their needs *outside* of all other institutions, there is the need for "collective leadership"—not only to meet the *various* needs of the organization, but to be able to flexibly confront the rapidly-changing contingencies of dynamic growth and experimentation.[60]

What this approach obviously indicates is that the existence and role of "charismatic leaders" are rejected by the New Left. Thus, *by traditional criteria*, the New Left cannot (by its own basic tenet) be analyzed as a "*political* movement." Perhaps, then, sociologists and political theorists must review their "inductive-analytical" approaches.[61]

The role of "*community organizer*," therefore, is quite peculiarly *behind the scenes*. He is to come into the community, become known to the people and their habits—on their own level, attempt to *not* let his presence and his new ideas become an insult to the people, subtly implant ideas and tactics, and advise and inspire confidence in those "indigenous leaders" and organizational participants. Above all, "the organizer's first job is to organize, not to right wrongs, not to avenge justice, not to win the battle for freedom. These are the tasks of the people who will accomplish them through the organization if it ever gets built."[62] For the most part, he sits quietly in the last row. When he finally leaves, he should be un-thanked, un-appreciated—obviously, this type of organizing takes a great deal of patience and dedication.[63]

These community organizers fit rather closely Blumer's description of the "second type of *agitator*." He is calm, quiet and dignified—but caustic and incisive; he leads people to become aware of their situations, to raise questions, to form inclinations and hopes. But in order to "stir up" people and to start them moving in new directions, he must be aware of *their* thoughts, interests, and values.[64] Similarly, Abel sees these individuals as the "dynamic elements" who initiate and ensure the growth and direction of the movement.[65]

It is interesting to note that although "efficiency" may be sacrificed, everyone who is affected does participate, on all levels—and no one gets dragooned. Aside from the previously discussed differences in the basic

---

[60] For a rather thorough discussion of these New Left rationales, see Nicholas Von Hoffman, *Finding and Making Leaders*, S.D.S. Bulletin, 1965, particularly pp. 13–14.
[61] See Abel, "The Pattern of a Successful Political Movement," in *Sociological Analysis*, Logan Wilson & Wm. Kolb (eds.) (N.Y.: Harcourt, Brace & Co., c. 1949), p. 30. However, more recent theorists do not rely so heavily on the need for charismatic leaders, as such; see Blumer, *op. cit.* pp. 203–205.
[62] From: Von Hoffman, *op. cit.*, p. 8 (and see *passim*).
[63] Presumably, one such organizer in the Mississippi Freedom Democratic Party is Stokely Carmichael. See a rare interview; *It's Very Simple; We Intend to Take Over Lowndes County*.
[64] Blumer, *op. cit.*, pp. 204–205.
[65] Abel, *op. cit.*, p. 830.

issues-orientation, and theologies, and aside from mutual suspicion of "sell-outism" and "Uncle Tomism" on one side, and "Communist-inspired" on the other, the above may shed further light on the increasing distance between the New Left and the older civil-rights groups and community-organizers. When Martin Luther King, Bayard Rustin, Saul Alinsky (or even Robert Pickus, on the "peace front") came into a community in which slow, painful grass-roots participatory and separatist organizing has been going on, they are more and more resented. By coming in with a well-trained army of "bureaucrats" (middle-class Northern Negroes and white college students), and efficiently taking over all the chores from the little people who were just getting involved but still groping for basic skills, the latter tend to withdraw again. They watch the community (e.g. Selma) come into the international spotlight with the presence of the great charismatic leader. Then perhaps something big is accomplished (e.g., a new voting rights bill is passed).[66] Just as suddenly the great leader moves on to the next confrontation, and the little people wait for the promised changes—which do not occur. A great weight of court costs, and bitterness on the part of the local whites *may* ensue.

During this experience the incipient indigenous organization has fallen apart, and later it is totally demoralized. However, it may take such a lesson to "radicalize" the people, by convincing them that their answer lies in their first attempts—and perhaps they will begin to re-organize—this time convinced that the ultimate answers are *not* in this form of "coalitionism" or in any form of "permeationism." [67]

UNCLEAR IDEOLOGY: PARALLEL STRUCTURES

What does all of the foregoing add up to in terms of the radical organizations' relationships to the larger society and its various institutions? It will be recalled that the New Left is, on the one hand, convinced of the inability to truly permeate these social structures (at least with black skins and moral demands). On the other hand, it is by the very definition of a New Left that, even if the "Establishment" institutions were truly permeable and flexible, they are so structurally damnable that it is *undesirable* to attempt to join or even to reform them.

Therefore, the first objective and main goal of organization-building is to build *outside* of the social institutions insofar as possible. "Parallel-

---

[66] In reference to Saul Alinsky's methods *vis à vis* this "demoralization," see Danny Strechter, *Reveille for Reformers: Report from Syracuse; Studies on the Left*, Vol. 5, No. 4, Fall 1965, pp. 86–87. Lynd also writes of Rev. King's legacy of disillusion in Selma; *op. cit.*, pp. 3–4.

[67] Hal Draper, *Berkeley: The New Student Revolt* (N.Y.: Grove Press, c. 1965), pp. 12–15, discusses these points—which necessarily lead to a consideration of building *outside* of the social structures; "counter-communities."

structures" fulfill only to a minor extent the negative purpose of withdrawal and protest and obstructionism—this is the "anti-establishment" side of the venture. "For the moment, participatory democracy cherishes the practice of parallelism as a way of saying 'No' to organized America, and of initiating the unorganized into the experience of self-government." [68]

On the positive side, *"counter-communities"* have several levels of purpose; and are the natural extensions of participatory democracy and the main thrusts of New Left organizing.[69] They also hold the key to the ideological reality of the New Left—and at the same time are the foci of its most serious controversy: coalitionism/permeationism *versus* separatism/left-opposition.

On the mundane level, counter-communities such as Freedom Schools, ghetto neighborhood unions, food and department store cooperatives, day-care centers, and parallel anti-poverty agencies, provide (at least temporarily) those services—particularly employment—which are unavailable from other sources. And they provide them *by the same people who benefit*—on their own terms and with the quality desired. There is even a leather processing factory in Tennessee, and numerous co-op farms throughout the South.[70]

On another level, the counter-communities begin to resemble other forms of Utopian Communities. Within the community can be established the style of life which is desired—"the very existence of the parallel institution is felt to be a healthier and more genuine experience than any available alternative." [71] Inasmuch as all functions and decisions are carried out by the people, this may be their first real experience in self-government and self-sufficiency.

Also, a real sense of community, and "brotherhood" can be established in these counter-communities. There is much talk in the literature about *feelings* of mutual trust and true cooperation through interparticipation, of openness and *honesty* through the need to carry grievances directly to those concerned rather than to a third party. Finally, the undesirable social/psychological effects resulting from overspecialization and the extreme division of labor can be meliorated by the greater interchangeability of organizational roles. In short, the type of "spiritual" life which institutional America *cannot* offer is to be found in these counter-communities.[72]

Obviously, these efforts to exist outside of all other, social structures are perceived to be necessarily long-term, sometimes painful, and beset

[68] Lynd, *op. cit.*, p. 5.
[69] See Munk, *The New Left*, A National Guardian Pamphlet (New York, 1966), p. 13.
[70] Lynd, *op. cit.*, p. 5.
[71] *Ibid.*
[72] See especially, *ibid.*, pp. 7–8.

with failures and setbacks. However, the process allows for *experimentation* along the lines that the participants desire and find feasible. During the *process*, moreover, strong in-group identifications develop, and an eventual "consciousness of kind" may result among members of such counter-communities throughout the country.

Nevertheless, these attempts are under constant re-evaluation and even strong criticism—particularly from the Old Left elements. They are criticized for their failure to have complete and detailed plans, i.e. for the lack of a "precise" ideology (this missed the point, however, for the *rejection* of any "precise" formula is a basic tenet of the New Left). They are also criticized for the lack of political, and especially economic, realism—it is *impossible* to exist without *some* intercourse with capitalistic and official institutions (this latter is especially so if they do not have the *power* to resist official controls of various types). Finally, the notion of community in this sense precludes incorporation or coalition with other population sectors and—as the following discussion indicates—the question of *building effective* power is not squarely met.[73]

One *might*, instead, describe the whole vision and venture as a vague form of *Utopian* humanistic-cooperative-socialism (with strong overtones of anarcho-syndicalism). This could be a critique of a "utopian state of mind," which is "incongruous with the state of 'reality' within which it occurs."[74]

In a different manner, what is now known of the New Left counter-communities is precisely described by Smelser as a "value-oriented social movement." This includes nativistic, nationalistic, Utopian and millenarian movements, as well as political and religious revolutions: the New Left does indeed infuse at least elements of all these types. According to Smelser, a value-oriented social movement is: "a collective attempt to restore, protect, modify or create *values* in the name of a generalized belief. Such a belief necessarily involves *all* of the 'components of action'; that is, it envisions a re-constitution of values, a re-definition of norms, a re-organization of the motivation of individuals, and a re-definition of structural facilities."[75]

By Abel's analysis of an "adequate ideology," the New Left counter-community tactic and goal fulfills all but one requirement: (a) It appeals to some ideal (e.g. freedom, honesty, sharing); (b) it is expressed in terms of current catch-phrases (i.e. propaganda devices) (e.g. "freedom now!", "we shall overcome!", "burn, baby burn!"); (c) it links up issues with

---

[73] For a short discussion of these criticisms, particularly in reference to the total exclusion of the organized labor, see Proctor, "The New Left," *Political Affairs*, Vol. LXIV, No. 12, December 1965, pp. 34–36. Genovese, "Genovese Looks at American Left—New and Old," *National Guardian*, Vol. 18, No. 20, February 19, 1966, p. 6, makes the same critiques.
[74] From Karl Mannheim, *Ideology and Utopia*, New York: Harcourt Brace & Co., 1936, p. 192 and on.
[75] From Smelser, *Theory of Collective Behavior* (New York: Free Press, 1962), pp. 313–314.

goals (see above analyses); (d) *but*, it does *not* have a *charismatic leader* (it now rejects them, by basic tenet). Perhaps Abel had in mind more *specifically* "political movements"; but, on the other hand, the writer would suggest revising the theory in light of all of the above.[76]

Finally, it should be instructive to examine some of Blumer's notions re the above . . . The New Left and counter-communities seem to fulfill stages: 1) the development of *Espirit de Corps* (including in-group-out-group relations and ceremonial behavior); 2) the development of groups morale (although it lacks a "sacred literature"); 3) the development of group ideology; and 4) it fulfills the role of tactics (as discussed, above)—of the development of specific *social* movements. In fact, they "can be viewed as societies in *miniature*, and as such, represent the building up of organized and formalized collective behavior out of what was originally amorphous and undefined. In their growth a social organization is developed, new values are formed, and new personalities are developed."

It is yet too early to ascertain if the counter-communities will "*leave behind* an institutional structure and a body of functionaries, new objects and views, and a new set of self-conceptions." [77]

By the end of the 1960s, however, particularly as the New Left became increasingly frustrated in creating viable counterstructures, there was evidence that the movement was becoming more revolutionary. In addition to maintaining an analysis of the contradictions in existing structures, radical theorists began to revise the idea of revolution for application to advanced industrial settings. This is clearly evident in the writings of Herbert Marcuse, who has become a leading mentor of the New Left. In 1968, Marcuse argued that changes in the framework of Marxian theory were necessary to incorporate the fact that the social basis for potential revolution had expanded from a national to a global one: [78]

In reality, the global situation militates against a mechanistic division into the Third World and the others. Rather we are confronted with a tripartite division of historical forces which cut across the division into the First, Second, and Third World. The contest between capitalism and socialism divides the Third World too and, as a new historical force, there appears what may be called (and what is thus called by the New Left) an alternative to the capitalist as well as to the established socialist societies, namely, the struggle for a different way of socialist construction, a construction "from below," but from a "new below" not integrated into the value system of the old societies—a socialism of cooperation and solidarity, where men and women determine collectively

---

[76] Taken from Abel, *op. cit.*, pp. 829–830.
[77] Blumer, *op. cit.*, pp. 205–211, and 214.
[78] Herbert Marcuse, "Re-examination of the Concept of Revolution," *Diogenes*, 64 (Winter 1968): 17–26.

their needs and goals, their priorities, and the method and pace of "modernization." [79]

Marcuse points out that the new potential for revolution is carried not in the proletarian majority of societies but rather in two different, and often opposing, groups: the ghetto population and the middle-class intelligentsia, particularly students. The common denominator of rebellion expressed by these two groups is described by Marcuse as follows:

Common to these different and even conflicting groups is the total character of the refusal and rebellion:
    1) Insistence on a break with the continuity of domination and exploitation—no matter in what name, insistence not only on new institutions but on self-determination.
    2) Distrust of all ideologies, including socialism made into an ideology.
    3) Rejection of the pseudo-democratic process sustaining the dominion of corporate capitalism.[80]

The new contradictions in advanced capitalist societies do not center around alienated labor but rather reflect the tensions "between vast social wealth and its wasteful and destructive use, between the potential of freedom and the actuality of repression, between the possible abolition of alienated labor and the capitalist need to sustain it. . . ." [81] Marcuse summarizes this new historical development as follows:

Conclusion: the Marxian concept of a revolution carried by the majority of the exploited masses, culminating in the "seizure of power" and in the setting up of a proletarian dictatorship which initiates socialization, is "overtaken" by the historical development: it pertains to a stage of capitalist productivity and organization which has been overtaken; it does not project the higher stage of capitalist productivity, including the productivity of destruction, and the terrifying concentration of the instruments of annihilation and of indoctrination in the hands of the powers that be.[82]

This, then, is the nature of the New Left as an emergent reality at the opening of the 1970s: existential in its world view, Marxian in its analysis and methodology, global in its perspective, coalitional in its class base.

CONCLUSION

Bearing in mind the framework of analysis developed in the preceding chapters, what generalizations may be made about the potential for ideo-

[79] *Ibid.*, p. 20.
[80] *Ibid.*, p. 21.
[81] *Ibid.*, p. 23.
[82] *Ibid.*, p. 21.

logical movements in advanced capitalist societies such as the United States and Canada? What structural conditions seem likely to give rise to a consciousness of dysfunction concerning the distribution of power in society, and what social groups are prone to a sense of powerlessness in the face of these conditions? Let us first consider the potential for the development of revolutionary movements.

To begin with, it is evident that the nature of productive relationships has been undergoing a qualitative change in our postcapitalist economy. With the increasing necessity for a managed economy, the contradictions which Marx saw between ownership and wage labor are being reduced.[83] However, the integration of labor into the existing economic structure serves only to heighten the sense of frustration of those who are excluded from both the production and the consumption of material goods. Thus, while labor moves closer to the middle of the political spectrum, the underemployed classes are becoming increasingly conscious of their disadvantaged position. Who are the underemployed? Here we must include, at least in North America: (1) young people, who, as students, are more and more constrained to defer their roles as producers and consumers for up to a third of their lives, being either undertrained (not yet qualified) or overtrained (too qualified) for most employment; (2) women, who, because of sexual discrimination and the male closed shop in many trades and professions, are either barred from the labor market, relegated to menial occupations, or paid inferior wages for equal work with men; (3) blacks and native Indians, who, because of racial discrimination and attendant low levels of education and training, have little hope of ever being absorbed into a saturated labor market.[84] Under depressed economic conditions (which, at this writing, seem to be upon us), the disadvantaged situation of the underemployed will become exacerbated, and their consciousness of dysfunction will become more acute.

Another factor which is likely to influence the development of ideological movements, particularly in North America, is the capability or willingness of the existing power structure to address the social problems which are creating a consciousness of dysfunction for increasingly large numbers of people. Here we refer not only to obvious problems such as the Vietnam war, environmental pollution, and the like but also to more specific problems which affect selected elements of the population. These include technological changes which exclude the poorly trained or educated from employment and the policy of repression and intimidation directed toward youthful protest.

[83] For an enlightening analysis of the new relationships emerging in advanced capitalist society, see John Kenneth Galbraith, *The New Industrial State* (Boston: Houghton Mifflin Co., 1967).

[84] After careful consideration, we have excluded blacks from analysis under a revolutionary framework in this chapter, since the black power movement marks only a very recent shift away from a reformist ideology (civil rights, "freedom now") to a revolutionary one advocating structural changes in the power system.

A third condition which will undoubtedly have a bearing on future social movements, especially to the extent that they involve young people, is a demographic one. The high birth-rate years of the late 1940s and early 1950s, following as they did the low birth-rate years of the 1930s, are causing a shift in the population pyramid of North America so that, by the early 1970s, about half the population will be under twenty-five.[85] If indeed much of the conflict in our society is intergenerational, such shifts in the population may well be followed by shifts in the power structure. In addition, we must also consider that the present rate of world population growth will likely exacerbate social problems throughout the world.[86]

Given the foregoing conditions, there is considerable potential for movements carried forward by young people in the present decade. Not only is youth directly affected by the conditions we have discussed but young people are also becoming increasingly incensed by the social problems created by corporate capitalism throughout the world. Not all youthful response will take the form of revolutionary movements, however, and we may anticipate, in North America at least, an increase in reformist and expressive movements. Moreover, we must not discount the very considerable ability of the power structure to neutralize or repress dissent. The possible introduction of a guaranteed annual income and continued action through the courts against young people and blacks, as well as more overt repression by the state, are likely historical events which will influence the future course of movement activity.

Thus far, we have been discussing structural conditions likely to lead to revolutionary or reform movements. The potential for regressive movements will also increase under these circumstances. In the first place, the ideologically conservative small businessman and independent professional suffer direct economic and status disadvantages under corporate capitalism. Second, any inability or unwillingness on the part of the existing power system to find solutions to ongoing social problems tends to heighten the conviction of the right that this system is corrupt and ineffectual. Moreover, the power structure, throughout the decade of the sixties, has been somewhat less than effective in repressing dissent from the left. This is interpreted by the right as further evidence of the weakness of those in command.

At this juncture in history, the established power system is under increasing attack from both the left and the right. If the power structure moves to crush opposition from the left, this may increase radical con-

[85] As of this writing the median age in the United States is approximately 27, and in Canada approximately 25. See (1) *The World Almanac and Book of Facts 1969* (New York: Doubleday and Co., Inc., 1968), p. 596; (2) *Canada Year Book 1968* (Ottawa: Queen's Printer, 1968), p. 206.
[86] For a good discussion of the implications of present world population growth, see Larry K. Y. Ng, ed., *The Population Crisis: Implications and Plans for Action* (Bloomington, Ind.: Indiana University Press, 1965).

sciousness in the society, and parts of the liberal middle may move left. At the same time, such an action will tend to legitimate a more regressive conscience collective in the society as a whole. Moreover, the machinery of the state is certainly powerful enough to repress revolutionary social movements at least temporarily. If, on the other hand, the power structure does not move against the left, this may increase the consciousness of dysfunction of the right and recruit members to it from the middle. Since, as we have said, the ideology of the right is closer to the status quo than is the ideology of the left, there could be a significant shift to right wing support under these circumstances.

At this juncture in history—given the confluence of social conditions we have described—there seems considerable potential for an increasing polarization of political thought and action in advanced capitalist societies. We must also consider the fact that the power structures of these societies, particularly in the United States, must deal not only with domestic problems but also with movements for national liberation in the underdeveloped nations—nations on which the technology of advanced capitalism is vitally dependent for raw materials. At the risk of being caught in a self-falsifying assertion, we may predict that these pressures may well lead to an increasingly conservative conscience collective in the near future. However, we do not foresee the advent of mass movements, either of the left or the right, during the coming years. Aside from the fact that such movements are historically rare, it would take rather severe social crises to galvanize the apathetic middle—Nixon's "silent majority"—into revolutionary or even regressive action. What is most likely is increasing support for reform movements—which do not severely challenge the existing distribution of power—from the middle. In any case, we are convinced that the dominant ideology of the middle—the status quo perception of an end of ideology—is becoming increasingly irrelevant to the historical conditions of today. Consider the following ideological statements.

From the middle: "A basic premise of this book is that democracy is not only or even primarily a means through which different groups can attain their ends or seek the good society; it is the good society itself in operation." [87]

From the left: ". . . The Movement is a community of insurgents sharing the same radical values and identity, seeking an independent base of power wherever they are. It aims at a transformation of society led by the most excluded and 'unqualified' people. Primarily this means building institutions outside the established order which seek to become the genuine institutions of the total society." [88]

From the right: "Our leading classes, for more than a century, have been more self-indulgent than they ought, though scarcely so profligate as Veblen

[87] Seymour Martin Lipset, *Political Man*, op. cit., p. 403.
[88] Tom Hayden, "The Politics of 'The Movement,'" op. cit., p. 376.

thought they were. In this present iron hour, the leisure class, so far as it still survives, has very great duties and very small regards. But some classes, like some men, are ennobled by adversity; and if the men who still retain a degree of moral and political ascendancy over the masses have in them the courage to make the endeavor, it is not yet too late to preserve to posterity the unbought grace of life, and to keep at bay the squalid oligarchs who detest the world of silence and of freedom." [89]

Internal and external pressures for a qualitative change in the distribution of power in industrial societies are immanent. How the presiding ideologues of the middle will respond to the pressures for change from other quarters will determine the future of modern industrial capitalism as a form of social order.

[89] Russell Kirk, *A Program for Conservatives* (Chicago: Henry Regnery Co., 1954), p. 139.

A SELECTED BIBLIOGRAPHY OF POLITICAL AND RADICAL SOCIAL MOVEMENTS

Aaron, D.
 1965 Writers on the Left. New York: Avon Library.
Abcarian, G., and S. M. Stanage
 1965 "Alienation and the Radical Right." Journal of Politics 27: 776–796.
Abel, T.
 1937 "The pattern of a successful political movement." American Sociological Review 2:347–352.
Adamic, L.
 1934 Dynamite: The Story of Class Violence in America. New York: Viking.
Adams, B.
 1913 The Theory of Social Revolutions. New York: Macmillan Co.
Adorno, T. W., et al.
 1950 The Authoritarian Personality. New York: Harper and Bros.
Aiken, H. D.
 1964 "The revolt against ideology." Commentary 37:29–37.
Alexander, R. J.
 1953 "Splinter groups in American radical politics." Social Research 20:282–310.
Alinsky, S.
 1949 John L. Lewis: An Unauthorized Biography. New York: Putnam's.
 1946 Reveille for Radicals. Chicago: University of Chicago Press.

Allen, W. S.
 1967 The Nazi Seizure of Power: The Experience of a Single German Town, 1930–1935. Chicago: Quadrangle Books.
Allport, G. W.
 1929 "The composition of political attitudes." American Journal of Sociology 35:220–238.
Almond, G.
 1954 Appeals of Communism. Princeton, N.J.: Princeton University Press.
Ambler, J. S.
 1968 Soldiers against the State: The French Army in Politics. Garden City: Doubleday.
Amis, K.
 1957 Socialism and the Intellectuals. London: The Fabian Society.
Anderson, E.
 1945 Hammer or Anvil: The Story of the German Working-Class Movement. London: Victor Gollancz.
Anderson, N.
 1942 Desert Saints. Chicago: University of Chicago Press.
Apter, D. E. (ed.)
 1964 Ideology and Discontent. New York: Free Press.
Aptheker, H.
 1939 Negro Slave Revolts in the U.S.: 1526–1860. New York: International Publishers.

Arendt, H.
1953 "Ideology and terror: a novel form of government." Review of Politics 15:303–327.
1951 The Origins of Totalitarianism. New York: Harcourt Brace.
Arkwright, F.
1933 The ABC of Technocracy. New York: Harper and Brothers.
Armstrong, R.
1965 "The explosive revival of the Far Left." Saturday Evening Post 238:27–39.
Auerbach, M.
1959 Conservative Illusion. New York: Columbia University Press.
Axelrod, M.
1956 "Urban structure and social participation." American Sociological Review 21:13–18.
Babcock, J. O.
1934 "The farm revolt in Iowa." Social Forces 12:369–373.
Ball, D. W.
1964 "Covert political rebellion as ressentiment." Social Forces 43:93–101.
Ball, W. M.
1952 Nationalism and Communism in East Asia. Melbourne: Melbourne University Press.
Banerjee, D. N.
1952 "Political ideologies and political behavior." Modern Review XCII (6):444–450.
Banks, J. A., and Olive Banks
1964 "Feminism and social change—a case study of a social movement." Pp. 547–566 in G. K. Zollschan and W. Hirsch (eds.), Explorations in Social Change. Boston: Houghton Mifflin Co.
Barber, B.
1941 "Acculturation and messianic movements." American Sociological Review 6:663–669.
Barnes, S. H.
1966 "Ideology and the organization of conflict: on the relationship between political thought and behavior." Journal of Politics 28:513–530.

Bax, E. G.
1903 Rise and Fall of the Anabaptists. London: Swan Sonnenschein and Co.
Beals, C.
1960 Brass-Knuckle Crusade: The Great Know Nothing Conspiracy: 1820–1860. New York: Hastings House.
Beard, M. R.
1939 American Labor Movement: A Short History. New York: Macmillan.
Beck, C.
1959 Contempt of Congress: A Study of the Prosecutions Initiated by the Committee on Un-American Activities, 1945–1957. New Orleans: Phanser Press.
Becker, H.
1946 German Youth: Bond or Free. New York: Oxford University Press.
Bell, D. (ed.)
1964 The Radical Right. Garden City, N.Y.: Anchor Books.
Bell, D.
1960 The End of Ideology. New York: Free Press.
Bennett, L., Jr.
1968 Pioneers in Protest. Chicago: Johnson Publishing Company.
Bernstein, I.
1960 The Lean Years: A History of the American Worker, 1920–1933. Boston: Houghton Mifflin.
Bimba, A.
1927 The History of the American Working Class. New York: International Publishers.
1932 The Molly Maguires. New York: International Publishers.
Binkley, R. C.
1934 "An anatomy of revolution." The Virginia Quarterly Review 10:502–514.
Bloor, E.R.
1940 We Are Many. New York: International Publishers.
Bohn, F.
1925 "The Ku Klux Klan interpreted." American Journal of Sociology 30:385–407.

Borgese, G. A.
  1937 Goliath: The March of Fascism. New York: Viking Press.
Borkenau, F.
  1939 World Communism: A History of the Communist International. New York: W. W. Norton.
Bottomore, T. B.
  1968 Critics of Society: Radical Thought in North America. New York: Pantheon Books.
  1956 Some reflections on the sociology of knowledge." British Journal of Sociology VII:52–58.
Boyer, R. O., and H. M. Morais.
  1955 Labor's Untold Story. New York: Cameron.
Braden, C. S.
  1956 These Also Believe: A Study of Modern American Cults and Minority Religious Movements. New York: Macmillan.
Brandmeyer, G. A., and R. S. Denisoff.
  1969 "Status politics: an appraisal of the application of a concept. Pacific Sociological Review 12:5–11.
Breslow, P.
  1965 "New Left in America." Twentieth Century 174:40–44.
Brewer, E. D. C.
  1951–1952 "Sect and church in Methodism." Social Forces 30:400–408.
Brinton, C.
  1934 A Decade of Revolution: 1789–1799. New York: Harper and Brothers.
  1958 The Anatomy of Revolution. New York: Vintage Books.
Brissenden, P. F.
  1920 The I.W.W.: A Study of American Syndicalism. New York: Columbia University Press.
Brock, C.
  1962 Americans for Democratic Action. Washington: Public Affairs Press.
Brooks, J. G.
  1913 American Syndicalism: The I.W.W. New York: Macmillan.
Browder, E.
  1935 Communism in the United States. New York: International Publishers.
  1938 The People's Front. New York: International Publishers.
Brumberg, A.
  1953 "Soviet campaign against survivals of capitalism." Russian Review XII:65–78.
Buck, S. J.
  1920 The Agrarian Crusade: A Chronicle of the Farmer in Politics. New Haven, Conn.: Yale University Press.
Buck, T.
  1967 Canada and the Russian Revolution. Toronto: Progress Books.
Bukharin, N.
  1925 Historical Materialism: A System of Sociology. New York: International Publishers.
Bullock, A.
  1958 Hitler: A Study of Tyranny. New York: Bantam Books.
Burden, H. T.
  1967 The Nuremberg Party Rallies: 1923–1939. New York: Frederick Praeger.
Burgess, J. S.
  1943–1944 "The study of modern social movements as a means for clarifying the process of social action." Social Forces 22:271–275.
Burlingame, R.
  1962 Sixth Column. New York: Lippincott.
Burns, E. M.
  1960 Ideas in Conflict: The Political Theories of the Contemporary World. New York: W. W. Norton.
Cameron, W. B.
  1969 Modern Social Movements. New York: Random House.
Camus, A.
  1956 The Rebel. New York: Vintage Books.
Cannon, J. P.
  1944 The History of American Trotskyism. New York: Pioneer Publishers.
Cantril, H.
  1941 Psychology of Social Movements. New York: Wiley and Sons.

Carlson, J. R.
1946 The Plotters. New York: E. P. Dutton.
Carr, R. K.
1952 The House Committee on Un-American Activities: 1945–1950. Ithaca, N.Y.: Cornell University Press.
Carter, H., III.
1959 The South Strikes Back. New York: Doubleday.
Cash, W. J.
1954 The Mind of the South. Garden City, N.Y.: Doubleday Anchor.
Cassinelli, C. W.
1960 "Totalitarianism, ideology and propaganda." Journal of Politics XXII:68–95.
Caute, David.
1966 The Left in Europe Since 1789. New York: McGraw Hill.
Cayton, H. R., and G. S. Mitchell.
1939 Black Workers and the New Unions. Chapel Hill, N.C.: University of North Carolina Press.
Chalmers, D. M.
1968 Hooded Americanism: The History of the Ku Klux Klan. Chicago: Quadrangle Books.
Chamberlain, J.
1932 Farewell to Reform. New York: John Day Co.
Chaplin, R.
1948 Wobbly. Chicago: University of Chicago Press.
Chapman, P. C.
1960 "New conservatism: cultural criticism versus political philosophy." Political Science Quarterly 75: 17–34.
Churney, G.
1969 A Long Journey. Chicago: Quadrangle Books.
Chase, S.
1933 Technocracy: An Interpretation. New York: John Day.
Christie, R., and M. Jahoda (eds.).
1954 Studies in the Scope and Method of the "Authoritarian Personality." Glencoe, Ill.: Free Press.
Cleveland, C. C.
1916 The Great Revival in the West, 1797–1805. Chicago: University of Chicago Press.
Cobban, A.
1951 "An age of revolutionary wars: a historical parallel." Review of Politics 13:131–141.
Cohen, A. A.
1956 "Religion as a secular ideology." Partisan Review XXIII:495–505.
Cohen, M., and D. Hale (eds.).
1966 The New Student Left. New York: Beacon Press.
Cohen, S.
1957 "Conservatism, radicalism, and unionism." American Journal of Economics and Sociology 16: 127–143.
Cohn, N.
1962 The Pursuit of the Millenium. London: Mercury Books.
Cole, G. D. H. A.
1948 A History of the Labour Party from 1914. London: Routledge and Kegan Paul.
Cole, W.S.
1953 America First: The Battle Against Intervention 1940–1941. Madison, Wis.: University of Wisconsin Press.
Coleman, M.
1943 Men and Coal. New York: Farrar and Rinehart.
Colgrove, K. W., and H. Bartlett.
1961 Menace of Communism. New York: Van Nostrand.
Colton, E.
1935 Four Patterns of Revolution. New York: Association Press.
Commons, J. R., et al.
1918–1940 History of Labour in the United States. 4 vols. New York: Macmillan.
Conkin, P. K.
1964 Two Paths to Utopia. Lincoln, Neb.: University of Nebraska Press.
Cook, F. J.
1964 The FBI Nobody Knows. New York: Macmillan.
1962 The Warfare State. New York: Macmillan.
Cooke, A.
1952 A Generation on Trial: U.S.A.

v. Alger Hiss. New York: Alfred Knopf.
Cox, O. C.
1948 Caste, Class and Race. New York: Doubleday.
Crampton, J. A.
1965 The National Farmers Union. Lincoln, Neb.: University of Nebraska Press.
Crespi, I.
1965 "Structural basis for rightwing conservatism: the Goldwater case." Public Opinion Quarterly 29:523–543.
Cronon, E. D.
1955 Black Moses. Madison, Wis.: University of Wisconsin Press.
Crook, W. H.
1960 Communism and the General Strike. Hamden, Conn.: Shoe String Press.
Crossman, R. (ed.).
1949 The God That Failed. New York: Harper and Bros.
Daniels, R. F.
1951 "The Kronstadt Revolt of 1921: a study in the dynamics of revolution." American Slavic and East European Review 10:241–254.
Daugherty, C. R.
1941 Labor Problems in American Industry. Boston: Houghton Mifflin.
David, H.
1936 The History of the Haymarket Affair. New York: Farrar and Rinehart.
Davies, J. C.
1959 "Note on political motivation." Western Political Quarterly 12:410–416.
1962 "Toward a theory of revolution." American Sociological Review 27:3–16.
Davis, A. F.
1967 Spearheads for Reform. New York: Oxford University Press.
Davis, J.
1930 Contemporary Social Movements. New York: Appleton-Century.

Debray, R.
1967 Revolution in the Revolution? New York: Grove Press.
Delaney, R. F.
1967 Literature of Communism in America: A Selected Reference Guide. Washington, D.C.: Catholic University of America Press.
DeMan, H.
1927 Psychology of Socialism. New York: Henry Holt and Co.
Denisoff, R. S.
1969 "The proletarian renascence: the folkness of the ideological folk." Journal of American Folklore 82:51–65.
1968 "Protest movements: class consciousness and the propaganda song." Sociological Quarterly 9:228–247.
Derry, J. W.
1967 The Radical Tradition. New York: St. Martin's Press.
Desmond, H. J.
1912 The A.P.A. Movement. Washington: New Century Press.
1904 The Know-Nothing Party. Washington: New Century Press.
Destler, C. M.
1966 American Radicalism, 1865–1901. Chicago: Quadrangle Books.
Dewees, F. P.
1877 The Molly Maguires. New York: Lippincott.
Diamond, S.
1936 "A study of the influence of political radicalism on personality development." Archives of Psychology 203:53.
Dies, M.
1940 The Trojan Horse in America. New York: Dodd Mead and Company.
Dohrman, H. T.
1958 California Cult: The Story of "Mankind United." Boston: Beacon Press.
Draper, H.
1965 Berkeley: The New Student Revolt. New York: Grove Press.

Draper, T.
1957 The Roots of American Communism. New York: Viking Press.

Dreiser, T.
1932 Harlan Miners Speak. New York: Harcourt Brace.

Dumond, D. L.
1961 Anti-Slavery: The Crusade for Freedom in America. Ann Arbor, Mich.: University of Michigan Press.

Dunson, J.
1965 Freedom in the Air. New York: International Publishers.

Ebenstein, W.
1954 Today's Isms. New York: Prentice-Hall.

Edwards, L. P.
1927 The Natural History of Revolution. Chicago: University of Chicago Press.

Egbert, D. D., and S. Persons (eds.).
1952 Socialism and American Life. 2 vols. Princeton, N.J.: Princeton University Press.

Ellwood, C. A.
1905–1906 "A psychological theory of revolutions." American Journal of Sociology 11:49–59.

Elsner, H.
1967 The Technocrats: Prophets of Automation. Syracuse, N.Y.: Syracuse University Press.

Erbe, W.
1964 "Social involvement and political activity: a republication and elaboration." American Sociological Review 29:198–215.

Ernst, M., and D. Loth.
1962 Report on the American Communist. New York: Capricorn Books.

Essien-Udom, E. U.
1965 Black Nationalism. New York: Dell Books.

Farmer, H.
1930 "The economic background of Southern Populism." South Atlantic Quarterly 29:77–91.

Fast, H.
1951 Peekskill USA. New York: Civil Rights Congress.

Feiling, K.
1953 "Principles of conservatism." Political Quarterly 24:129–38.

Ferkiss, V. C.
1962 "Political and intellectual origins of American radicalism, Right and Left." The Annals 344:1–12.
1961 "Populism: myth reality, current danger." Western Political Quarterly 14:737–740.
1957 "Populist influences on American Fascism." Western Political Quarterly 10:350–373.

Festinger, Leon, et al.
1956 When Prophecy Fails. Minneapolis: University of Minnesota Press.

Feuer, L. S.
1958 "The sociology of philosophic ideas." Pacific Sociological Review I:77–80.

Fiedler, L.
1955 "The middle against both ends." Encounter 5:16–23.

Filler, L.
1960 Crusade Against Slavery 1830–1860. New York: Harper and Brothers.

Fine, N.
1928 Labor and Farmer Parties in the United States, 1828–1928. New York: Rand Book Store.

Finer, H.
1935 Mussolini's Italy. London: Victor Gollancz, Ltd.

Finn, J.
1968 Protest: Pacifism and Politics. New York: Random House.

Fleischman, H.
1964 Norman Thomas. New York: W. W. Norton.

Flemming, H. C.
1956 "Resistance movements and racial desegregation." Annals 304:44–52.

Florinsky, M. T.
1931 The End of the Russian Empire. New Haven, Conn.: Yale University Press.

Foner, P. S.
1967 The Bolshevik Revolution: Its Impact on American Radicals, Liberals and Labor. New York: International Publishers.

1947–1966 History of the Labor Movement in the United States. 4 vols. New York: International Publishers.

Forster, A., and Epstein, B. R.
1952 Troublemakers. New York: Doubleday.

Foster, W. Z.
1937 From Bryan to Stalin. New York: International Publishers.
1952 History of the Communist Party of the United States. New York: International Publishers.

Fountain, C. W.
1949 Union Guy. New York: Viking Press.

Frazier, E. F.
1926 "The Garvey Movement." Opportunity 4:346–348.

Freud, S.
1962 Civilization and Its Discontents (trans. J. Strachey). New York: Norton and Co.

Friedrich, C. I. (ed.).
1966 Revolution. New York: Atherton Press.

Fromm, E.
1941 Escape from Freedom. New York: Farrar and Rinehart.

Fruchter, N., and T. Hayden, S.S.
1966 "New radicalism: round IV." Partisan Review 33:34–60.

Fulford, R.
1957 Votes for Women: The Story of a Struggle. London: Faber and Faber.

Galenson, W. (ed.).
1952 Comparative Labor Movements. New York: Prentice-Hall.

Gambs, J. S.
1932 The Decline of the I.W.W. New York: Columbia University Press.

Garfinkel, H.
1959 When Negroes March. Glencoe, Ill.: Free Press.

Gates, J.
1958 The Story of an American Communist. New York: Thomas Nelson and Sons.

Gay, P.
1952 The Dilemma of Democratic Socialism. New York: Columbia University Press.

George, C. H. (ed.)
1962 Revolution: Five Centuries of Europe in Conflict. New York: Dell Books.

Gerth, H.
1940 "The Nazi Party: its leadership and composition." American Journal of Sociology 45:517–541.

Gilbert, G. M.
1950 The Psychology of Dictatorship. New York: Ronald Press.

Gillespie, J.
1960 Algeria: Rebellion and Revolution. New York: Frederick A. Praeger.

Gillin, J. L.
1910 "A contribution to the sociology of sects." American Journal of Sociology 16:236–252.

Ginzburg, R.
1962 100 Years of Lynching. New York: Lancer.

Glantz, O.
1958 "Class consciousness and political solidarity." American Sociological Review 23:375–383.

Glazer, N.
1961 The Social Basis of American Communism. New York: Harcourt, Brace, and World.

Goldberg, Harvey.
1957 American Radicalism: Some Problems and Personalities. New York: Monthly Review Press.

Goldman, E. F.
1952 Rendevous with Destiny. New York: A. A. Knopf.

Gordon, A. I.
1967 The Nature of Conversion. Boston: Beacon Press.

Gottschalk, L.
1944 "Causes of revolution." American Journal of Sociology 50: 1–8.

Grant, J. (ed.)
1968 Black Protest: History, Documents, and Analyses 1619 to the Present. Greenwich, Conn.: Fawcett Publications.

Green, T. H.
1949 American Social Reform Move-

Greenway, J.
1953 American Folksongs of Protest. Philadelphia: University of Pennsylvania Press.

Greer, T. H.
1949 American Social Reform Movements: Their Pattern Since 1865. New York: Prentice-Hall.

Griswold, A. W.
1934 "New thought: a cult of success." American Journal of Sociology 40:309–318.

Grodzins, M.
1956 The Loyal and the Disloyal. Chicago: University of Chicago Press.

Gross, F.
1958 The Seizure of Political Power in a Century of Revolutions. New York: Philosophical Library.

Grove, G.
1961 Inside the John Birch Society. Greenwich, Conn.: Fawcett.

Guevara, C.
1968 The Diary of Che Guevara. New York: Bantam Books.

Gusfield, J. R.
1955 "Field work reciprocities in studying a social movement." Human Organization 14:28–33.
1962 "Mass society and extremist politics." American Sociological Review 27:17–30.
1963 Symbolic Crusade. Urbana, Ill.: University of Illinois Press.

Guttman, A.
1965 "Political ideals and the military ethic." American Scholar 34: 221–237.

Hale, W. H.
1947 The March of Freedom. New York: Harper.

Handlin, O.
1951 "How U.S. anti-Semitism really began." Commentary 11:541–548.

Hansberry, L.
1964 The Movement. New York: Simon and Schuster.

Harris, H.
1940 Labor's Civil War. New York: A. A. Knopf.

Harrison, G. A.
1954 Road to the Right: The Tradition and Hope of American Conservatism. New York: Morrow.

Haynes, F. E.
1916 Third Party Movements Since the Civil War with Special Reference to Iowa. Iowa City, Iowa: State Historical Society.

Haynes, G. H.
1897–1898 "The causes of Know-Nothing success in Massachusetts." American Historical Review 3:67–82.

Haywood, W.
1929 Bill Haywood's Book. New York: International Publishers.

Heberle, R.
1949 From Democracy to Nazism. Baton Rouge: Louisiana State University Press.
1949 "Observations on the sociology of social movements." American Sociological Review 14:346–357.
1951 Social Movements. New York: Appleton-Century-Crofts.

Heiden, K.
1944 Der Fuehrer Hitler's Rise to Power. Boston: Houghton Mifflin.
1935 A History of National Socialism. New York: A. A. Knopf.

Hentoff, N.
1963 Peace Agitator: The Story of A. J. Muste. New York: Macmillan.

Hentoff, N., and M. Harrington.
1965 "Is there a new radicalism?" Partisan Review 32:183–205.

Herzog, E. G.
1949 "Patterns of controversy." Public Opinion Quarterly 13:39–52.

Hetzler, S. A.
1954 "Social mobility and radicalism-Conservatism." Social Forces 33: 161–166.

Hicks, J. D.
1931 The Populist Revolt: A History of the Farmers Alliance. Minneapolis: University of Minnesota Press.

Hillquit, M.
   1903   History of Socialism in the United States. New York: Funk and Wagnalls Co.

Himelstein, M.
   1963   Drama Was a Weapon. N.J.: Rutgers University Press.

Hinds, W. A.
   1878   American Communities. Oneida, N.Y.: Office of the American Socialist.

Hobsbawm, E. J.
   1959   Primitive Rebels: Studies in Archaic Forms of Social Movement in the 19th and 20th Centuries. Manchester, Eng.: Manchester University Press.

Hoffer, E.
   1958   The True Believer. New York: Mentor Books.

Hofstadter, R.
   1955   The Age of Reform. New York: Vintage Books.
   1963   Anti-Intellectualism in American Life. New York: A. A. Knopf.
   1963   The Progressive Movement 1900–1915. Englewood Cliffs, N.J.: Prentice-Hall.

Holbo, P. S.
   1961   "Wheat or what? Populism and American Fascism." Western Political Quarterly 14:727–736.

Hooper, R.
   1959   "The revolutionary process." Social Forces 28: 270–279.

Hoover, J. E.
   1958   Masters of Deceit. New York: Henry Holt.

Hopkins, C. H.
   1940   The Rise of Social Gospel in American Protestantism 1865–1915. New Haven, Conn.: Yale University Press.

Horn, S. F.
   1939   Invisible Empire: The Story of the Ku Klux Klan 1866–1871. Boston: Houghton Mifflin.

Horowitz, D.
   1962   Student. New York: Ballantine Books.

Horowitz, I. L. (ed.)
   1964   The Anarchists. New York: Dell Books.

Horowitz, I. L.
   1968   Radicalism and the Revolt Against Reason: The Social Theories of Georges Sorel. Carbondale, Ill.: Southern Illinois University Press.

Howe, I.
   1965   New Styles in Leftism. New York: Dissent Publishers Pamphlet.
   1966   Steady Work. New York: Harcourt, Brace.

Howe, I., and L. Coser.
   1957   The American Communist Party: A Critical History. Boston: Beacon Press.

Howe, I., and B. J. Widick.
   1949   The UAW and Walter Reuther. New York: Random House.

Howe, I. (ed.)
   1966   The Radical Papers, New York: Doubleday Books.

Howe, I., and S. Rousseau.
   1965   "New radicalism: round II." Partisan Review 32:341–347.

Hughes, H. S.
   1968   The Obstructed Years: French Social Thought in the Years of Desperation 1930–1960. New York: Harper and Row.

Hughes, L.
   1962   Fight For Freedom: The Story of the NAACP. New York: Norton.

Hunter, R.
   1940   Revolution: Why, How, When? New York: Harper and Brothers.

Huntington, S. P.
   1957   "Conservatism as an ideology." American Political Science Review LI:454–473.

Hyndman, H. M.
   1921   The Evolution of Revolution. New York: Boni and Liveright.

Ignotus, P.
   1959   "Left and Right." Twentieth Century 165:5–12.

Jacobs, P.
   1965   Is Curly Jewish: A Political Self Portrait. New York: Atheneum.

Jacobs, P., and S. Landau.
   1966   The New Radicals. New York: Vintage Books.

Johnson, C.
1943 Patterns of Negro Segregation. New York: Harper.
Jones, E.
1921 "Evolution and revolution." International Journal of Psychoanalysis 22:193–208.
Kampelman, M.
1957 The Communist Party Versus the CIO. New York: Praeger.
Kaufman, A.
1966 The Radical Liberal: New Man in American Politics. New York: Atherton Press.
Keller, T.
1967 "A new vocabulary for the New Left." Journal of Contemporary Revolution 1:10–31.
Kessel, J. H.
1968 The Goldwater Coalition Republican Strategies in 1964. Indianapolis: Bobbs-Merrill Co.
Kile, O. M.
1921 The Farm Bureau Movement. New York: Macmillan.
Killian, L. M.
1959 "The purge of an agitator." Social Problems 7:152–156.
1964 "Social movements." Pp. 426–455 in Robert E. L. Faris (ed.), Handbook of Modern Sociology. Chicago: Rand McNally.
King, C. W.
1956 Social Movements in the United States. New York: Random House.
Kipnis, I.
1952 The American Socialist Movement 1877–1912. New York: Columbia University Press.
Kirshen, H. B.
1960 "The ideology of American labor." Politico XXV:581–595.
Kitagawa, D.
1967 Issei and Nisei: The Internment Years. New York: The Seabury Press.
Kling, M.
1962 "Cuba: a case study of a successful attempt to seize political panels by the application of unconventional warfare." AAAPSS 341: 42–52.
Kornbluh, J. (ed.)
1964 Rebel Voices: An I.W.W. Anthology. Ann Arbor, Mich.: University of Michigan Press.
Kornhauser, W.
1959 The Politics of Mass Society. New York: Free Press.
Kraditor, A. S. (ed.)
1968 Up From the Pedestal: Selected Writings in the History of American Feminism. Chicago: Quadrangle Books.
Krimerman, L. I., and L. Perry (eds.)
1966 Patterns of Anarchy. Garden City, N.Y.: Doubleday.
Kristol, I.
1952 "Civil liberties, 1952—a study in confusion; do we defend our rights by protecting communists?" Commentary 13:288–236. 236.
Krout, J. A.
1925 The Origins of Prohibition. New York: A. A. Knopf.
Krout, M., and R. Stagner.
1939 "Personality development in radicals: a comparative study." Sociometry 2:31–46.
Krugman, H. E.
1952 "The appeal of Communism to American middle class intellectuals and trade unionists." Public Opinion Quarterly XVI:331–355.
Ladd, E. C., Jr.
1966 "Radical Right: the white-collar extremists." South Atlantic Quarterly 65:314–324.
Laidler, H. W.
1927 A History of Socialist Thought. New York: Thomas Y. Crowell.
1944 Socio-Economic Movements. New York: Thomas Y. Crowell.
Lane, R. E.
1966 "Decline of politics and ideology in a knowledgeable society." American Sociological Review 31:649–662.
Lang, K., and G. E. Lang.
1961 Collective Dynamics. New York: Thomas Y. Crowell.
LaPalombara, J.
1966 "Decline of ideology: a dissent

and an interpretation" (with reply by S. M. Lipset, and rejoinder). American Political Science Review 60:5–18, 110–111.

Lasch, C.
1965 The New Radicalism in America, 1889–1963: The Intellectual as a Social Type. New York: A. A. Knopf.

Lasswell, H. D.
1941 "The garrison state." American Journal of Sociology 46:455–468.
1952 "The political role of ideologies." Paper presented at the Hague Congress of the International Association of Political Science, September 8–12.
1933 "The psychology of Hitlerism." Political Quarterly 4:373–384.

Lasswell, H., and D. Blumenstock.
1939 World Revolutionary Propaganda. New York: A. A. Knopf.

LeBon, G.
1947 The Crowd. London: Ernest Bonn Ltd.

Lederer, E.
1940 State of the Masses. New York: W. W. Norton.

Lee, A. M.
1944 "Techniques of social reform: an analysis of the new prohibition drive." American Sociological Review 9:65–77.
1943 Race Riot. New York: Dryden Press.

Leggett, J. C.
1963 "Working-class consciousness, race and political choice." American Journal of Sociology 69:171–176

Lemmon, S. M.
1951–1952 "The ideology of the 'Dixiecrat' movement." Social Forces 30:162–171.

Lenin, V. I.
1929 Collected Works. New York: International Publishers. Vol. 4.

Lens, S.
1949 Left, Right and Center. New York: Regency Press.
1964 The Futile Crusade. Chicago: Quadrangle Books.
1966 Radicalism in America. New York: T. Y. Crowell.

Lerner, D.
1951 The Nazi Elite. Stanford, Calif.: Stanford University Press.

Lerner, D., et al.
1951–1952 "Comparative analysis of political ideology: a preliminary statement." Public Opinion Quarterly XV:715–733.

Lewin, J.
1968 The Struggle for Racial Equality. New York: Humanities Press.

Lewy, G.
1964 The Catholic Church and Nazi Germany. New York: McGraw Hill.

Lichtheim, G.
1969 The Origins of Socialism. New York: Frederick Praeger.
1963 "Power and ideology." Partisan Review 30:241–255.

Lincoln, C. E.
1961 The Black Muslims in America. Boston: Beacon Press.

Lincoln, J. H.
1968 The Anatomy of a Riot: A Detroit Judge's Report. New York: McGraw Hill.

Lindner, R.
1952 Prescription for Rebellion. New York: Holt, Rinehart and Winston.

Lipset, S. M.
1968 Revolution and Counterrevolution: Change and Persistence in Social Structures. New York: Basic Books.
1950 Agrarian Socialism: The Cooperative Commonwealth Federation in Saskatchewan. Berkeley, Calif.: University of California Press.
1963 Political Man (rev. ed.). Garden City, N.Y.: Anchor Books.

Lipset, S. M., and S. Wolin (eds.).
1965 The Berkeley Student Revolt. Garden City, N.Y.: Doubleday.

Lipsitz, L.
1964 "Work life and political attitudes." American Political Science Review 58:951–965.

Lipton, L.
1959 The Holy Barbarians, New York: Julian Messner.

Lofland, J., and R. Stark.
 1965 "Becoming a world saver: a theory of conversion to a deviant perspective." American Sociological Review 30:862–874.
Lomas, C. W.
 1968 The Agitator in American Society. Englewood Cliffs, N.J.: Prentice-Hall.
Loomis, C. P. and A. Beagle.
 1946 "The spread of German Nazism in rural areas." American Sociological Review 11:724–734.
Lorwin, V.
 1954 The French Labor Movement. Cambridge, Mass.: Harvard University Press.
Loucks, E. H.
 1936 The Ku Klux Klan in Pennsylvania. Harrisburg, Pa.: Telegraph Press.
Lowenthal, L., and N. Guterman.
 1949 Prophets of Deceit. New York: Harper and Bros.
Luethy, H.
 1956 "Poujade: Hitler or Pierrot?" Commentary XXI:301–310.
Lyons, E.
 1941 The Red Decade: The Stalinist Penetration of America. New York: Bobbs-Merrill.
MacDougall, C. D.
 1965 Gideon's Army v. I–III. New York: Marzani and Munsell.
MacKinnon, W. J., and R. Centers.
 1956 "Authoritarianism and urban stratification." The American Journal of Sociology LXI:610–620.
MacRae, D. G.
 1958 "Class relationships and ideology." Sociological Review 6:261–272.
Madison, C. A.
 1947 Critics and Crusaders, A Century of American Protest. New York: Holt.
Maier, N.
 1942 "The role of frustration in social movements." Psychological Review 49:586–599.
Malcolm X.
 1966 The Autobiography of Malcolm X. New York: Merit Publishers.
Mannheim, K.
 1936 Ideology and Utopia: An Introduction to the Sociology of Knowledge. New York: Harcourt Brace.
Martin, E. W.
 1961 "Radicalism and culture." Contemporary Review 200:407–410.
Moore, B., Jr.
 1962 "Notes on the process of acquiring power." Pp. 1–29 in Political Power and Social Theory. New York: Harper Torch Books.
Morris, J. O.
 1958 Conflict Within the AFL: A Study of Craft Versus Industrial Unionism 1901–1938. Ithaca, N.Y.: Cornell University Press.
Munk, M.
 1965 The New Left. New York: National Guardian Pamphlet.
Murray, M.
 1955 The Red Scare: A Study in National Hysteria. Minneapolis: University of Minnesota Press.
Myers, G.
 1960 History of Bigotry in the U.S. New York: Capricorn.
Nelson, S.
 1953 The Volunteers. New York: Masses and Mainstream.
Neumann, F.
 1944 Behemoth: The Structure and Practice of National Socialism, 1933–1944. New York: Oxford University Press.
Neumann, S.
 1942 Permanent Revolution. New York: Harper and Bros.
 1949 "The structure and strategy of revolution: 1848 and 1948." Journal of Politics 11:532–544.
Newfield, J.
 1966 A Prophetic Minority. New York: New American Library.
New Republic (the eds.).
 1965 Thoughts of the Young Radicals. Washington, D.C.: The New Public Publishing Co.

Noebel, D.
   1966   Rhythm, Riots, and Revolution. Tulsa, Okla.: Christian Crusade Publications.

Nomad, M.
   1932   Rebels and Renegades. New York: Macmillan Co.

Noyes, J. H.
   1961   History of American Socialisms. New York: Hilary House Publishers, Ltd.

O'Connor, H.
   1964   Revolution in Seattle. New York: Monthly Review Press.

Odegard, P. H.
   1928   Pressure Politics: The Anti-Saloon League. New York: Columbia University Press.

Ogden, A.
   1945   The Dies Committee: A Study of the Special House Committee for Investigation of Un-American Activities: 1938–1944. Washington, D.C.: Catholic University of America Press.

O'Neill, W. (ed.).
   1967   Echoes of Revolt: The Masses 1911–1917. New York: Quadrangle Books.

Ortega y Gasset, J.
   1932   The Revolt of the Masses. New York: W. W. Norton.

Overstreet, H. A., and B. Overstreet.
   1958   What We Must Know About Communism. New York: Norton.

Parkin, F.
   1968   Middle Class Radicalism. New York: Frederick Praeger.

Parsons, T.
   1942   "Some sociological aspects of the Fascist movement." Social Forces XXI:138–147.

Paulson, R. E.
   1968   Radicalism and Reform: The Vrooman Family and American Social Thought, 1837–1937. Lexington, Ky.: University of Kentucky Press.

Pauschning, H.
   1939   The Revolution of Nihilism. New York: Alliance Book Corp.

Payne, T., and C. M. White.
   1962   "Renaissance of the Radical Right. Western Political Quarterly 15:20–22.

Peck, J.
   1962   Freedom Rider. New York: Simon and Schuster.

Perlman, S.
   1937   A History of Trade Unionism in the United States. New York: Macmillan.

Peterson, E.
   1954   Hjalman Schacht: For and Against Hitler: A Politico-Economic Study of Germany, 1923–1949. Boston: Christopher Publishing House.

Petras, J., and M. Zeitlin (eds.).
   1968   Latin America, Reform or Revolution. Greenwich, Conn.: Fawcett Publications.

Pettee, G. S.
   1938   The Process of Revolution. New York: Harper.

Peyre, H.
   1949   "The influence of eighteenth century ideas on the French Revolution" (trans. Arthur L. Kurth). Journal of the History of Ideas 10:63–87.

Plamenatz, J.
   1951   "The Communist ideology." Political Quarterly XXII:16–26.

Pole, J. R.
   1962   "Forward from McCarthyism: the Radical Right and the conservative norm." Political Quarterly 33:196–207.

Polsky, N.
   1966   The New Student Left. Chicago: Aldine.
   1960   "Towards an explanation of McCarthyism." Political Studies 8:250–271.

Pope, L.
   1958   Millhands and Preachers: A Study of Gastonia. New Haven, Conn.: Yale University Press.

Postgate, R. W.
   1920   Revolution from 1789 to 1906. London: Richards.

Powledge, F.
   1967   Black Power, White Resistance:

Notes on the New Civil War. Cleveland: World Publishing.

Pye, L. W.
1961 "Personal identity and political ideology." Behavioral Science VI:205–221.

Qualtar, T.
1962 Propaganda and Psychological Warfare. New York: Random House.

Quint, H. H.
1953 The Forging of American Socialism. Charleston, S.C.: University of South Carolina Press.

Rattner, F.
1967 Reform in America. Chicago: Scott, Foresman and Co.

Record, C. W.
1947 The Negro and the Communist Party. Chapel Hill, N.C.: University of North Carolina Press.

Reddich, L. D.
1959 Crusader Without Violence. New York: Harper.

Reed, J.
n.d. Ten Days That Shook the World. New York: International Publishers.

Reeve, S. A.
1933 The Natural Laws of Social Convulsion. New York: E. P. Dutton and Co.

Renshaw, P.
1967 The Wobblies. New York: Anchor Books.

Rhynd, R.
1962 "Patterns of subversion by violence." AAAPSS 34:65–73.

Riezler, K.
1943 "On the psychology of modern revolution." Social Research 10: 320–336.

Rinaldo, J.
1921 Psychoanalysis of the Reformer. New York: Lee Publishing Co.

Robertson, P.
1960 Revolutions of 1848: A Social History. New York: Harper and Brothers.

Roche, J. P., and S. Sachs.
1955 "The bureaucrat and the enthusiast: an exploration of the leadership of social movements." Western Political Quarterly 8: 248–261.

Rochester, A.
1943 The Populist Movement in the United States. New York: International Publishers.

Rogin, M.
1966 "Wallace and the middle class: the white backlash." Public Opinion Quarterly 30:98–108.

Rogin, P. R.
1967 The Intellectuals and McCarthy: The Radical Specter. Cambridge, Mass.: Massachusetts Institute of Technology Press.

Rolfe, E.
1939 The Lincoln Battalion. New York: Random House.

Rose, A. M.
1968 Libel and Academic Freedom: A Lawsuit Against Political Extremists. Minneapolis: University of Minnesota Press.
1952 Union Solidarity: The Internal Cohesion of a Labor Union. Minneapolis: University of Minneapolis Press.

Rossi, A.
1949 A Communist Party in Action. New Haven, Conn.: Yale University Press.
1938 The Rise of Italian Fascism, 1918–1922. London: Methuen and Co.

Rossiter, C. L.
1955 Conservatism in America. New York: A. A. Knopf.
1952 "Two conservatisms." South Atlantic Quarterly 51:64–69.

Rousseau, S. W., and J. Farganis.
1963 "American politics and the end of ideology." British Journal of Sociology 14:347–362.

Rude, G.
1959 The Crowd in the French Revolution. New York: Oxford University Press.
1964 The Crowd in History. New York: John Wiley.

Rush, G. B.
1967 "Status consistency and right-wing extremism." American Sociological Review 32:86–92.

1963 "Toward a definition of the Extreme Right." Pacific Sociological Review 6:64–73.
Salvemini, G.
1927 The Fascist Dictatorship in Italy. New York: Henry Holt.
Saposs, D. J.
1954 "Current trade-union movements of Western Europe." Social Research XXI: 297–313.
Schiff, L. F.
1964 "Obedient rebels: a study of college conversions to conservatism." Journal of Social Issues 20:74–95.
Schlesinger, A. M.
1950 The American as Reformer. Cambridge, Mass.: Harvard University Press.
Schlesinger, A., Jr.
1957 Crisis of the Old Order. Boston: Houghton Mifflin.
Schmidt, K. M.
1960 Henry A. Wallace: Quixotic Crusade. Syracuse, N.Y.: Syracuse University Press.
Schneider, D. M.
1928 The Workers' (Communist) Party and American Trade Unions. Baltimore: Johns Hopkins Press.
Schorske, C. E.
1955 German Social Democracy 1905–1917, The Development of the Great Schism. Cambridge, Mass.: Harvard University Press.
Schumpeter, J.
1947 Capitalism, Socialism, and Democracy. New York: Harper and Bros.
Selznick, P.
1952 The Organizational Weapon. New York: McGraw-Hill.
Shannon, D. A.
1959 The Decline of American Communism. New York: Harcourt, Brace, and Co.
1955 The Socialist Party of America. New York: Macmillan Co.
Shils, E. A.
1956 The Torment of Secrecy. Glencoe, Ill.: The Free Press.
1958 "Ideology and civility: on the politics of the intellectual." Sewanee Review LXVI:450–480.
1954 "Populism and the rule of law." University of Chicago Law School Conference on Jurisprudence and Politics, pp. 91–107.
Shirer, W. L.
1960 The Rise and Fall of the Third Reich. New York: Simon and Schuster.
Simon, R. J. (ed.).
1967 As We Saw the Thirties, Essays on Social and Political Movements of a Decade. Urbana, Ill.: University of Illinois Press.
Sinclair, T.
1938 "The Nazi Party rally at Nuremberg." Public Opinion Quarterly 2:570–583.
Smelser, N.
1963 The Theory of Collective Behavior. New York: Free Press.
Sorel, G.
1950 Reflections on Violence. Glencoe, Ill.: The Free Press.
Sorokin, P. A.
1947 Society, Culture, and Personality. New York: Harper.
1925 Sociology of Revolution. Philadelphia: J. B. Lippincott.
Stephens, H. M.
1886 A History of the French Revolution. New York: Charles Scribner's Sons.
Stewart, D. K., and G. C. Smith.
1964 "Celebrity structure of the Far Right." Western Political Quarterly 17:349–355.
Stouffer, S. A.
1955 Communism, Conformity, and Civil Liberties. Garden City, N.Y.: Doubleday.
Strachey, R.
1928 The Cause: A Short History of The Women's Movement in Britain. London: Bell and Sons.
1938 Struggle: The Stirring Story of Woman's Advance in England. New York: Duffield (U.S. edition).
Suziki, H.
1957 "Conception of ideology and

utopia." Japanese Sociological Review VII(1):50–54.

Swift, L.
1900 Brook Farm: Its Members, Scholars and Visitors. New York: Macmillan.

Symes, L., and T. Clement.
1934 Rebel America: The Story of Social Revolt in the United States. New York: Harper.

Tager, J.
1968 The Intellectual as Urban Reformer. Cleveland: Western Reserve University Press.

Talmon, J. L.
1952 The Rise of Totalitarian Democracy. Boston: Beacon Press.

Tarrow, S. G.
1967 Peasant Communism in Southern Italy. New Haven, Conn.: Yale University Press.

Taylor, C. C.
1952 The Farmer's Movement. New York: American Book Co.
1936 The Theory of the Proletarian Revolution. New York: International Publishers.

Thomas, D. J.
1966 "Ideology—death or transfiguration?" Harvard Review 4:88–95.

Thompson, F.
1955 The I.W.W.: Its First Fifty Years. Chicago: I.W.W.

Tippett, T.
1931 When Southern Labor Stirs. New York: Jonathan Cape and Harrison Smith.

Toch, H.
1965 The Social Psychology of Social Movements. Indianapolis: Bobbs-Merrill.
1955 "Crisis situations and ideological revaluation." Public Opinion Quarterly 19:53–67.

Trotsky, L.
1932 The History of the Russian Revolution. New York: Simon and Schuster.

Trow, M.
1958 "Small businessmen, political tolerance, and support for McCarthy." The American Journal of Sociology LXIV:270–281.

Tufts, J. H.
1936 "Liberal movements in the United States—their methods and aims." International Journal of Ethics 46:253–275.

Turner, R., and L. Killian.
1957 Collective Behavior. Englewood Cliffs, N.J.: Prentice-Hall.

Ulam, A. B.
1960 The Unfinished Revolution: An Essay on the Sources of Influence of Marxism and Communism. New York: Random House.

Viereck, P.
1956 Conservatism From John Adams to Churchill. New York: D. Van Nostrand.

Von Stein, L.
1964 The History of the Social Movement in France, 1789–1850 (trans. K. Mengelberg). Totowa, N.J.: Bedminster Press.

Wagner, D. O.
1934 Social Reformers. New York: Macmillan Co.

Ware, N. J.
1929 The Labor Movement in the United States 1860–1895. New York: D. Appleton and Co.

Warren, F. A.
1966 Liberals and Communism: "The Red Decade" Revisited. Bloomington, Ind.: Indiana University Press.

Waskow, A. I.
1966 From Race Riot to Sit-In, 1919 and the 1960's. Garden City, N.Y.: Doubleday.

Weinstein, J.
1966 "Radicalism in the midst of normalcy." Journal of American History 52:773–790.

Westin, A. F.
1952 "Our freedom—and the rights of Communists; a reply to Irving." Commentary 14:33–40.

White, Morton.
1957 Social Thought in America: The Revolt Against Formalism (rev. ed.). Boston, Beacon Press.

Wiebe, R. H.
 1968 Businessmen and Reform: A Study of the Progressive Movement. Chicago: Quadrangle Books.
Wilensky, H. L.
 1956 Intellectuals in Labor Unions: Organizational Pressures on Professional Roles. New York: Free Press.
Williams, R. F.
 1962 Negroes With Guns. New York: Marzani and Munsell.
Wilson, B. R. (ed.).
 1968 Patterns of Sectarianism: Organization and Ideology in Social and Religious Movements. London: Heinemann Educational Books.
Wilson, E.
 1964 "Frank Keeney's coal diggers." Pp. 310–327 in E. Wilson's The American Earthquake. Garden City, N.Y.: Anchor Books.
Wilson, F. G.
 1960 "Anatomy of conservatives." Ethics 70:165–181.
Winter, G.
 1959 "Conception of ideology in the theory of action." Journal of Religion XXXIX:43–49.
Witridge, A.
 1948 "1848: the year of revolution." Foreign Affairs 26:264–275.
Wittenmyer, A.
 1878 History of the Women's Temperance Crusade. New York: J. H. Earle Co.
Wolf, H. C.
 1952 On Freedom's Altar: The Martyr Complex in the Abolition Movement. Madison, Wis.: University of Wisconsin Press.
Wolfe, B. D.
 1948 Three Who Made a Revolution. New York: Dial Press.
Woodcock, G.
 1962 Anarchism: A History of Libertarian Ideas and Movements. New York: World Publishing Co.

Woodcock, G., and I. Avakumovic.
 1968 The Doukhobors. New York: Oxford University Press.
Worth, S.
 1956 "Some observations on the pragmatism of the Left and the Right." Southwestern Social Science Quarterly 37:143–156.
Wright, E.
 1956 "Radicals of the Right." Political Quarterly 27: 366–377.
Wright, G.
 1953 "Agrarian syndicalism in postwar France." American Political Science Review XLVII:402–416.
Yoder, D.
 1926–1927 "Current definitions of revolution." American Journal of Sociology 32:433–441.
Young, A. N.
 1916 The Single Tax Movement in the United States. Princeton, N.J.: Princeton University Press.
Young, W. J.
 1961 Visible Witness: A Testimony for Radical Peace Action. Wallingford, Pa.: Pendle Hill Pamphlets.
Zakuta, L.
 1958 "Membership in a becalmed protest movement." Canadian Journal of Economics and Political Science 24:190–202.
Zald, Mayer N., and Roberta Ash.
 1966 "Social movement organizations: growth, decay and change." Social Forces 44 (March):327–341.
Zeitlin, M.
 1968 Ideology and the Development of Sociological Theory. Englewood Cliffs, N.J.: Prentice-Hall.
 1967 Revolutionary Politics and the Cuban Working Class. Princeton, N.J.: Princeton University Press.
 1958 The Decemberists. New York: International Universities Press.
Zinn, H.
 1968 Disobedience and Democracy. New York: Random House.
 1964 The New Abolitionists. Boston: Beacon Press.

INDEX

Abel, Theodore, 1, 103, 140n, 181n, 256n, 279–85, 487, 490–91
Adams, Stuart, 75n
Adorno, Theodore W., 19, 144, 151, 155, 156, 157, 182, 286
Aiken, Henry D., 421n, 435–38
Allport, Gordon, 94
Almond, Gabriel A., 302n, 313
Apter, David, 422
Aptheker, Herbert, 14, 20n
Arendt, Hannah, 39–40, 42, 88, 100
Aron, Raymond, 432n
Avery, Paul, 402n

Bacon, Francis, 424, 427
Bakunin, Mikhail, 39, 325, 327, 418
Barnes, Harry Elmer, 12n
Barton, Allen H., 61n
Bates, Frederick L., 79n
Bay, Christian, 140, 151–56
Becker, Howard, 19, 140
Beenion, L. L., 277n
Belinsky, Vissarion, 428–29
Bell, Daniel, 89, 123, 169n, 316n, 340n, 350n, 422–35, 435–39, 440–44, 445, 446, 447–48, 450, 451–53, 458, 479
Bendix, Reinhard, 77n, 86n, 289n, 319, 424n
Bennet, John W., 159
Benoit-Smullyan, Emile, 75n, 76, 77, 79n

Bensman, Joseph, 98n
Bentham, Jeremy, 169n, 425
Berger, Peter L., 185n
Bierstedt, Robert, 237n
Bittner, Egon, 285, 286–89, 414n
Bloombaum, Milton, 79
Bloor, Ella Reeve, 20n
Blumenstock, Dorothy, 160n
Blumer, Herbert, 181n, 182, 258, 320, 321, 323, 340n, 360, 486n, 487, 491
Bochenski, Joseph M., 289n
Bone, Hugh, 178n
Borkenau, Franz, 389n, 435n
Bottomore, T. B., 13
Brand, Oscar, 31, 33n, 34n
Brandmeyer, Gerard A., 78, 90–98
Braungart, Richard, 477–78
Briggs, Asa, 267
Brinton, Crane, 99, 322n
Brockway, Archibald Fenner, 375n, 376n
Broom, Leonard, 2, 180n
Brown, Roger W., 181n
Broyles, J. Allen, 313n
Bruner, Jerome S., 150, 156
Brzezinski, Zbigniew, 289n
Bukharin, Nikolai N., 13n, 16–19, 21, 63–71
Bunzel, John R., 89n
Burgess, J. Stewart, 4–12, 181n
Burke, Edmund, 38, 39, 169n, 427

Cameron, William Bruce, 139n
Camus, Albert, 153, 154, 155, 321, 322, 325, 326
Cantril, Hadley, 9–10, 88, 100, 137, 157
Carlyle, Thomas, 193
Carr, Edward, 104
Cassinelli, C. W., 289n
Castro, Fidel, 218–36
Centers, Richard, 74, 159
Chambliss, William J., 78
Chase, Richard, 432
Christie, Richard, 159, 286n
Clark, Joseph, 452n
Cohen, Morris R., 165n
Cohn, Norman, 435n
Coleman, James C., 3
Coleman, James S., 380
Comte, Auguste, 12, 38, 59, 169
Cook, Fred J., 401n
Cook, Peggy, 159
Corey, Lewis, 88n, 89, 323
Coser, Lewis, 119, 160, 194, 316n, 370, 371
Crouch, Winston W., 355

Dahl, Robert, 48
Dahrendorff, Ralf, 21, 50n, 420
Davies, Alan F., 154n, 155
Davies, James C., 99, 270n
Davis, Allison, 159
Davis, Elmer, 358
Davis, Jerome, 280
Davis, Kingsley, 13
Davis, Michael, 7, 8
Debray, Regis, 215–16, 218, 219, 224, 225, 226, 229, 233, 237, 454
Denisoff, R. Serge, 28–34, 90–98, 453n
Destler, Chester M., 373
Dewey, John, 189, 437
Dickenson, R. L., 8
Dohrman, H. T., 158n
Domhoff, G. William, 327–38, 350, 485
Dorson, Richard, 32n
Drachkovitch, Milorad M., 481n

Draper, Hal, 488n
Draper, Theodore, 205
Drath, Martin, 290n
Duberman, Martin, 483
Dunson, Josh, 29, 31
Durkheim, Emile, 12n, 13, 37, 38–39, 54–61, 62, 99, 169n, 185, 186, 189, 295–96, 297

Edelman, Murray, 49
Edwards, Allen L., 3, 122
Elliot, Mabel, 20
Ellsworth, Ralph E., 165
Engels, Friedrich, 20, 65, 193, 327, 339
Erikson, Erik H., 154–55n, 422n
Ernst, Morris L., 19

Faris, Robert E. L., 19–20, 181n, 321, 323n, 324
Febvre, Lucien, 435n
Ferkiss, Victor C., 350n
Festinger, Leon, 313
Feuer, Lewis, 52n
Fishman, Jacob R., 138
Flacks, Richard, 146, 153
Foster, William Z., 315n
Frenkel-Brunswick, E., 155, 286n
Freud, Sigmund, 121–22, 123, 139, 140, 156, 159, 426, 430
Friedrich, Carl J., 289n
Fromm, Erich, 12n, 39–40, 43n, 88, 122
Furfey, Paul, 14n

Galbraith, John Kenneth, 369n, 439n, 493n
Gambs, John S., 158n
Gans, Herbert J., 82n
Gass, Oscar, 52
Geertz, Clifford, 351
George, Alexander, 154n, 155
George, Juliette, 154n, 155
Gerth, Hans H., 75n, 90n, 92n, 121, 442n
Girvetz, Harry K., 166n, 167n, 170
Glazer, Nathan, 89n

Goffman, Irwin W., 76n, 77
Goldberg, Harvey, 118
Goode, William J., 15n
Gouldner, Alvin, 14–15, 59n
Green, Archie, 34
Greenstein, Fred J., 154n, 155
Greenway, John, 28n, 29–30, 120
Greer, Thomas H., 264n
Grodzins, Morton, 53, 54n, 360n, 390
Grove, Gene, 315n
Guevara, Che, 195–204, 215, 216, 219, 223, 225, 233–34
Gusfield, Joseph R., 21–27, 40–52, 91, 93, 94, 96–97, 98, 103, 368
Guterman, Norbert, 95

Haber, R. Alan, 456n, 457, 458–75
Hacker, Andrew, 443n
Hagan, Roger, 89n
Hagstrom, Warren O., 146–47, 156
Hamilton, Alexander, 44
Harbison, E. Harris, 204
Harrington, Michael, 100
Harris, Sarah M., 165
Hatt, Paul K., 15n
Havighurst, Robert J., 159
Hayden, Tom, 482–83, 495n
Heberle, Rudolph, 122, 140, 160, 178n, 181n
Hegel, Georg, 37, 52, 325–26, 423, 424, 428, 452
Heist, Paul, 148, 155
Herzen, Alexander, 434–35
Hicks, John D., 118–19
Hobbes, Thomas, 39, 169n, 427, 428
Hochschild, Adam, 53n
Hoffer, Eric, 151, 155, 156–57, 158, 179, 378n
Hofstadter, Richard, 48n, 84, 89, 91, 92–94, 95, 96, 97n, 98n, 103, 123, 140, 178, 239, 357, 359
Hoggart, Richard, 99n
Holtzman, Abraham, 404n, 405n, 406n, 409n
Homan, George C., 80–81n
Hopper, Rex D., 256n, 258, 379n

Horowitz, David, 53, 484n
Horowitz, Irving Louis, 14n, 214–37, 327n, 452n
Horton, Paul B., 177, 178, 179, 319, 320n, 321, 324n, 360
Hoselitz, Bert F., 104
Howe, Irving, 119, 160, 194, 316n
Hughes, H. Stuart, 339n
Huizinga, J. H., 435n
Hume, David, 169n, 427
Hunt, Chester L., 177, 178, 179, 319, 320n, 321, 323, 324n, 360
Hyman, Martin D., 78, 89

Iggers, Georg G., 104, 455
Inkeles, Alex, 289n

Jackson, Maurice, 119, 182, 255–66
Jacobs, Paul, 297–98, 485n
Jahoda, Marie, 286n
James, Thelma, 32n
Jaspers, Karl, 423n, 430
Jenness, Doug, 247
Johnson, Chalmers, 190
Johnson, Dale, 484
Josephson, Eric, 99
Josephson, Mary, 99
Joynt, Carey B., 104n
Jung, Carl G., 3

Kallen, Horace M., 287n
Kaplan, Samuel, 160, 238n
Katz, Daniel, 150–51, 155, 156
Keller, Theodore, 270n
Kelly, K. Dennis, 78
Kenkel, William, 77, 78
Key, V. O., 44n, 355
Killian, Lewis, 136, 137, 139n, 164, 178, 179n, 181n, 256n, 320, 323n
King, C. Wendell, 258, 390
King, William Bruce, 181n, 182
Kirk, Russell, 496n
Knox, Ronald A., 288n, 291n, 293n, 373n, 376n, 378n, 435n
Koestler, Arthur, 378, 435n
Kolakowski, Leszek, 434
Kolb, William, 2

Kornhauser, William, 39–40, 41n, 43n, 46–47, 62, 89n, 159n, 178–79, 299–313
Kramer, Judith R., 82n
Kristol, Irving, 484n
Krout, Maurice, 136–37
Kuhn, Thomas S., 189–90

Labenz, Leopold, 15n
Landau, Saul, 485n
Lane, Robert E., 154n, 155, 182
LaPalombara, Joseph, 49
LaPiere, Richard T., 397n
Lasswell, Harold D., 122–23, 160, 161
Lazarsfeld, Paul F., 61n
Leites, Nathan, 45n, 435n
Lemert, Edwin E., 285
Lenin, V. I., 71–74, 193–94, 204–5, 215, 217, 219, 316, 339, 415, 418, 422, 458
Lens, Sidney, 194, 268n
Lenski, Gerhard E., 75n, 77, 78
Lerner, Max, 428
Leuthy, Herbert, 435n
Levetman, Seymour, 82n
Levin, Murray B., 53, 159n, 360
Levinson, D. J., 155, 286n
Lewis, R. Peter, 485, 486–91
Lindner, Franz, 384n
Lindner, Robert, 139, 145, 146
Linz, Juan, 61n
Lipset, Seymour M., 13, 21n, 46n, 48n, 49–50, 52n, 53n, 54, 61, 62, 77n, 85–86, 88, 91–92, 94, 95–96, 98, 100, 103, 123, 156, 159, 164n, 238n, 286, 289, 291n, 350n, 380, 381–90, 438–40, 441, 442–44, 445, 447–48, 450, 451–52, 453, 458, 479, 495n
Lipton, Lawrence, 360
Lockwood, Leen, 85n, 226, 227, 237
Lofland, John, 123
Lomax, Louis, 380
Loth, David, 19
Lowe, Adolf, 52n
Lowenthal, Leo, 95
Lundberg, George, 15–16

Lynd, Robert, 13–14
Lynd, Staughton, 486n, 488n, 489n

McClosky, Herbert, 145–46, 151–52, 156
McCormack, Thelma, 139n, 140
Mack, Raymond, 46n
McKinnon, William, 159
Madison, James, 44
Maier, Norman R., 122
Malewska, Hannah E., 153, 154n, 156
Mannheim, Karl, 34, 40, 47, 50, 182, 189, 296, 388, 421, 427, 428, 442, 459–60, 490n
Mao Tse-tung, 232
Marcuse, Herbert, 12, 364, 491–92
Marx, Karl, 12, 20, 37, 39, 52–53, 54–61, 63, 70, 71, 72–73, 74, 75, 77, 100, 160, 174, 186–87, 189, 193, 215, 217, 219, 236, 270–71, 276–77, 291n, 316, 323, 325, 326, 327, 339, 362–63, 415–16, 417, 418, 421, 423–24, 425–26, 427, 436, 438, 453, 455, 458, 481, 491, 492, 493
Mathewson, Jr., Rufus W., 428–29
Matusow, Harvey, 298n
Mead, Margaret, 89n
Mebke, Daryl, 481n
Merrill, Francisco, 20
Merton, Robert K., 13, 19, 427
Michels, Robert, 375n, 380
Mill, John Stuart, 39
Miller, Colin, 402n
Miller, Daniel, 156n
Mills, C. Wright, 12, 14, 21, 41n, 49n, 50n, 63, 75n, 91n, 92n, 100, 121, 140, 271n, 329, 335, 380, 442n, 443–44, 445, 447, 455–56
Milosz, Czeslaw, 289n
Minnis, Jack, 485
Moore, Wilbert, 13
Morgan, H. Wayne, 120
Morgenthau, Hans J., 446–47, 449
Mosca, Gaetano, 375n
Mowry, George E., 357–58
Munk, Michael, 484–85, 489n

Murphy, Gardner, 151, 156
Murray, Gilbert, 422, 423n
Murray, Robert K., 401n
Myrdal, Gunnar, 13

Nagel, Ernest, 165n
Naylor, Robert W., 152, 156
Nenmeye, Gerhard, 289n
Nettler, Gwynn, 52n
Neumann, Franz, 48n
Neumann, Sigmund, 321
Newcomb, Theodore M., 142, 156
Newfield, Jack, 480
Nicolaus, Martin, 101n
Niebuhr, Reinhold, 353
Nisbet, Robert, 40
Noyes, John H., 205

Orrmont, Arthur, 158n

Pareto, Vilfredo, 289–90
Parsons, Talcott, 13, 57–58, 169n, 185, 271–79, 286n, 292n, 293
Pellegrin, Roland J., 79n
Perlman, Selig, 20, 51n
Pettee, George, 338–39
Pogosyan, Ervand, 140n
Polsby, Nelson W., 98
Powell, Elwin, 452n
Priestley, J. B., 10
Proudhon, Pierre J., 39, 325

Ranney, Austin, 178n
Record, Wilson, 20n
Reissman, Leonard, 159
Rescher, Nicholas, 104n
Richmond, Patricia, 154n, 155
Richter, Melvin, 321n, 338
Riesman, David, 41n, 49, 89, 154n, 156, 169n
Rinaldo, Joel, 122–23
Ringer, Benjamin, 62n, 77
Rochester, Anna, 20n
Rogow, Arnold A., 154n, 156
Rohter, Ira S., 123–36
Rokeach, Milton, 45n, 144–45, 151, 154n, 156

Roth, Guenther, 268n, 370–71
Rush, B. B., 136n
Rush, Gary B., 77–78, 163–72
Russell, Bertrand, 267
Rustin, Bayard, 419n

Saint-Simon, Henri, 12, 325
Sanford, Nevitt R., 155, 286n, 483
Santayana, George, 445
Sarnoff, Irving, 151, 156
Schiff, Lawrence, 100, 138
Schlesinger, Arthur M., 316
Schumpter, Joseph A., 20n
Seabury, Paul, 53n, 54n
Seeman, Melvin, 52n, 360n
Selvin, Hanan C., 156
Selznick, Philip, 2, 20n, 40, 43, 180n, 195, 293n, 313, 370
Shannon, David, 105, 118, 120, 353n, 419
Sherman, George, 434
Shils, Edward A., 41n, 45, 52n, 156, 432n, 458
Silber, Irwin, 31
Sills, David, 62n, 77
Simmel, Georg, 24, 38
Smelser, Neil J., 37n, 123, 182, 320, 321, 323, 324, 443n, 490
Smith, M. Brewster, 150, 154n, 156
Sokol, Robert, 78, 83–84
Solomon, Fredric, 138
Somers, Robert H., 147–48, 149, 156
Sorel, Georges, 339n, 372
Sorokin, Pitirim, 76–77
Speier, Hans, 423n
Spencer, Herbert, 58, 169n
Stagner, Ross, 136–37
Stalin, Joseph, 173, 204, 285, 297
Stark, Rodney, 123
Stark, Werner, 50n
Stedman, Murray, 49n
Stedman, Susan, 49n
Stegner, Page, 31n
Stein, Lorenz von, 38
Stekert, Ellen, 30n, 31, 32, 33n
Stouffer, Samuel A., 46n, 143–44, 156
Strachey, John, 439n
Strauss, Leo, 429n

Strechter, Danny, 488n
Swados, Harvey, 62n
Swanson, Guy, 156n

Thomas, W. I., 170n, 277
Tillich, Paul, 430
Toch, Hans, 3, 137, 138, 157–58, 179–80, 181n, 182
Tocqueville, Alexis de, 321, 338
Tonnies, Ferdinand, 38, 282n
Tracy, Destutt de, 424, 427
Treuhaft, Jessica Mitford, 269
Trow, Martin, 51, 89, 90n, 92, 98, 380
Truman, David, 44n
Tumin, Melvin, 159
Turner, Ralph H., 136, 137, 139n, 164, 178, 179n, 181n, 256n, 320, 323n, 403n

Vidich, Arthur, 98n
Von Hoffman, Nicholas, 487n

Waller, Willard, 159
Walling, W. E., 389n
Walton, John, 368n
Warner, W. Lloyd, 87
Watnick, Morris, 435n
Watts, William, 148–50, 156
Webb, Beatrice, 51n

Webb, Sidney, 51n
Weber, Max, 13, 35, 37, 38, 75, 76, 89, 90–91, 92, 100, 170, 182, 183, 193, 277–78, 283, 288–89, 290, 291, 293n, 294, 319, 373n, 375n, 380, 427, 440, 441–42, 444n, 447, 453
Weinstein, James, 120
Weiss, Robert Frank, 419n
Werkmeister, W. H., 14n
Westby, David, 477–78
Westin, Alan F., 339–40
White, Robert W., 150, 156
White, Winston, 326–27, 350, 351–53
Whittaker, David, 148–50, 156
Wigforss, Ernst, 85n
Wilson, Edmund, 187–88
Wilson, Godfrey, 414n
Wilson, Logan, 2
Wilson, Monica, 414n
Wirth, Louis, 321, 323
Wolff, Kurt A., 60n
Wolin, Sheldon S., 156, 238n

Young, Milton, 52n
Young, William H., 178n

Zeitlin, Maurice, 237
Znaniecki, Florian, 280n